SO-BFA-517

...aloging in Publication Data

...e and administration.

...ment and organization. I. Sergio-

....2   79-20138

Printed in the United States of America

10   9   8   7   6   5   4   3   2   1

Editorial/Production Supervision by
Barbara Kelly
Cover design by *Miriam Recino*
Manufacturing Buyer: *John Hall*
PRENTICE-HALL INTERNATIONAL, INC., *London*
PRENTICE-HALL OF AUSTRALIA PTY. LIMITED, *Sydney*
PRENTICE-HALL OF CANADA, LTD., *Toronto*
PRENTICE-HALL OF INDIA PRIVATE LIMITED, *New Delhi*
PRENTICE-HALL OF JAPAN, INC., *Tokyo*
PRENTICE-HALL OF SOUTHEAST ASIA PTE. LTD., *Singapore*
WHITEHALL BOOKS LIMITED, *Wellington, New Zealand*

Edu Gove and Adminis

Thomas J. Sergiovanni
Martin Burlingame
Fred D. Coombs
Paul W. Thurston

all University of Illinois, Urbana

Prentice-Hall, Inc., Englewood Cliffs, New Jersey 07632

Library of Congress Ca

Main entry under title:

Educational governanc

Includes index.
1. School manage
vanni, Thomas J.   37
LB2805.I47
ISBN 0-13-236653-

CONTENTS

II
INTRODUCTION TO GOVERNANCE
IN EDUCATION

99

4 THE SCHOOL AS A POLITICAL
ORGANIZATION 101

5 POLICY-MAKING IN THE LOCAL SCHOOL
DISTRICT 127

III
THE CONTEXT OF WORK
IN ADMINISTRATION   253

10   ADMINISTRATIVE TASKS   255

11   ADMINISTRATIVE ROLES   284

IV
DECIDING ON AN ADMINISTRATIVE CAREER 373

15 PERSONAL GOALS, TRAITS, AND THE EDUCATIONAL-ADMINISTRATION CAREER 375

CONTENTS

II
INTRODUCTION TO GOVERNANCE
IN EDUCATION

99

4   THE SCHOOL AS A POLITICAL
ORGANIZATION   101

5   POLICY-MAKING IN THE LOCAL SCHOOL
DISTRICT   127

CONTRIBUTING
AUTHORS

THOMAS J. SERGIOVANNI is Professor of Educational Administration and Supervision; and Chairperson, Department of Administration, Higher and Continuing Education, University of Illinois, Urbana-Champaign. He received the Ed.D. in educational administration from the University of Rochester. A former editor of *Educational Administration Quarterly,* Dr. Sergiovanni has published widely in his field and is presently associated with the Advanced Executive Development Program at the University of Illinois.

MARTIN BURLINGAME is Professor of Educational Administration and a Research Associate in the Office for the Analysis of State Educational Systems at the University of Illinois, Urbana-Champaign. A Ph.D. graduate from the University of Chicago, Dr. Burlingame was formally a Senior Associate in the National Institute for Education. He presently is editor of the *Educational Researcher.*

FRED D. COOMBS is Associate Professor of Educational Policy Studies, and Director of the Office for the Analysis of State Educational Systems, University of Illinois, Urbana-Champaign. A Ph.D. graduate in political science from the University of Illinois, he was Assistant Professor of Political Science at the University of Illinois before joining the Educational-Policy Studies faculty. He has published widely in the areas of public participation in educational policy, comparative educational policy making, and the politics of education.

PAUL W. THURSTON is Assistant Professor of Educational Administration and Research Associate in the Office for the Analysis of State Educational Systems at the University of Illinois, Urbana-Champaign. He received the J.D. degree and Ph.D. degree in educational administration from the University of Iowa. Dr. Thurston has broad interests in the law as it relates to educational policy making and to administrative roles and responsibilities.

PREFACE

This is a book intended to introduce readers to administration and governance in education. Three audiences for the book are envisioned. One audience is teachers and others who aspire to be educational administrators and supervisors. For them the book will provide an overview of the field and a preview of more specialized courses and experiences they are likely to encounter in later professional study. In addition, the book is designed to help this audience assess the suitability of their own capabilities, dispositions, and interests as they consider a career in educational administration. Part IV, "Deciding on an Administrative Career," is designed particularly for this purpose.

Other audiences include teachers and teacher-organization leaders, and nonprofessionals such as citizens and citizen-board members who desire to be better informed about the nature and structure of administration and governance in education.

This book is introductory in the sense that prior knowledge of administration and governance in education is not assumed of readers. Further, no attempt is made to treat topics and issues exhaustively or to survey all topics which might be considered as part of the field. Traditionally, introductory books in educational administration have tended to be encyclopedic, as authors have attempted to prepare compendiums of knowledge in the field. Books of this type were perhaps feasible even a short time ago, but today schools and particularly school settings are too complex for such exhaustive examination in one book. We are therefore selective in what is covered, hoping to provide readers with a manageable introduction and an informative forward for further study.

Both administration and governance are themes of this book. One cannot view the issues of educational administration separate from those of educational governance, and an introduction to administration without strong attention to governance in education paints too simple a portrait of the field. Educational administration is concerned with the process of administering, the execution of public affairs in educational organizations, the performance of executive functions, the guiding, controlling, and directing of educational organizations, and the judicious use of means to accomplish educational ends. Educational governance is concerned with the political function of policy making in education; the organization and machinery through which political units such as federal agencies, state departments, and local school districts exercise authority and perform functions; and the complex political institutions, laws, and customs that comprise the setting for the performance of administrative functions and responsibilities. Long gone are the days when educational administrators could function as independent entrepreneurs of autonomous school districts.

Part I of the book introduces readers to educational administration as a profession and as a field of study. The purposes of this section are to provide readers with perspectives of how the field has emerged and of the condition of its professional and intellectual roots. This appraisal is of necessity critical, for as a relatively young field, educational administration is characterized by progress and promise, and by problems and dim prospects. Contingency theory is also discussed as an integrating framework for resolving the array of contradictory findings in the literature and contradictory prescriptions for practice which plague the field of educational administration.

Important to Part I, and indeed to this entire book, is the assumption that though educational administrators must of necessity assume managerial and political roles, they are first and foremost educators. Thus educational leadership and statespersonship roles require highest priority.

Part II introduces readers to governance structure and issues in education. In addition to describing the legal structure of education, this section includes discussions of policy making in local school districts, state and federal influences on education, the law and its effect on broad policy making and on the administration of local school districts, and the financial structure and condition of education. Part II also includes a discussion of schools as political organizations. This perspective is contrasted with the more traditional bureaucratic and professional views of schools.

Part III introduces readers to the substantive aspects of administration in education. Using decision making as an example, emphasis is given to understanding what administrative theory is and how it can be used to gain insights about administrative practice. Greater emphasis, however, is given to how educational administrators actually spend their time on tasks they actually accomplish. This descriptive analysis is examined in light of prescriptions found in the literature for educational, organizational, administrative, and supervisory leadership. These analyses should help readers determine "the way it is" and contrast this with best thinking on "how it should be." The array of administrative tasks and roles in schools are selectively analyzed in Part III. Such tasks as school-community relations, pupil personnel, curriculum administration, staff personnel, facilities, business management, staff development, and evaluation are included. The roles of superintendent, central-office staff, and principal are discussed and contrasted by examining such integrating mechanisms as role expectations, job objectives and descriptions, and team administration.

Part IV, especially designed for those considering educational administration as a possible career choice, includes a treatment of career planning and an exploration which actually takes the reader through a career-planning exercise. This exercise is intended to help readers identify their own professional and personal goals, to help examine these goals first for internal conflict and again against the demands of the job of administration in education.

A book such as this requires a collaborative effort over a period of time, and this requirement was well suited to our interests, workstyles, and place of employment. Within the writing team, we were privileged to share in the insights of others as plans for the book developed and individual chapters were prepared. In this sense, the book is a result of a team effort. Individual authors did, however, assume general responsibility for certain parts of the book as follows: TJS, Chapters 1, 2, 12, 13, and 15; MB, Chapters 3, 10, 11 and 14; FDC, Chapters 4, 5, and 6; and PWT, Chapters 7, 8, and 9.

In some respects we are at a crossroads in the administration and governance of education. Education is now considered by many as a declining industry plagued by failure to meet social expectations, by declining enrollments of students with subsequent declines in financial support, by concern in the eyes of the public as to the productive value of schools given dollars spent, and by lowering of esteem in the eyes of many for careers in education and educational administration. Certainly teacher militancy has ended once and forever the hallowed im-

ages of teaching as a missionary profession. And true indeed is the
skepticism of many as to the value of benefits obtained from schools,
given costs, after having experienced a period of unprecedented promises and short deliveries. Hard felt too are the results of declining
enrollments as expressed in curtailing educational programs, closing
facilities, centralizing services, and reducing teaching staffs. In many
respects, these are hardly bright times for one to be considering a
career in educational administration. But out of these difficulties have
come new understandings of educational administration—most noteworthy, understandings about its political nature and its interdependence with a variety of external forces, many of which are beyond the
control of the local school administrator. The need for more administrators is not great, but the need for new administrators is pressing—
men and women who understand the complexities of modern administration and who can cope with its new dimensions. This book is intended to be a first step in that direction.

PART I

Introduction to Educational Administration

1

EDUCATIONAL ADMINISTRATION: AN OVERVIEW

Administrators—who are they? What are their responsibilities? How do they obtain and exercise administrative prerogatives? How can their authority be checked? Are they really necessary? Parents and teachers often ask such questions, and occasionally some of the questions are asked with a tone of skepticism. But few would deny that ours is an organized society—complex but awesome in its ability to tackle the most difficult problems, to set the highest goals, and to accept challenges of marshaling its vast resources on behalf of these goals. In Tead's classic treatment of the art of administration, he invites readers to journey with him on a mythical voyage to grasp the complexity of organizational and administrative arrangements in our society.

Fly over New York City imaginatively in an airplane, and remove the roofs from successive buildings in your mind's eye. What do you see? You see people, tens of thousands of them, at work. You see top executives in quiet offices thinking, planning, conferring, issuing orders which affect people in distant localities where their companies have plants. You see boards of directors hearing reports and adopting policies which may mean more or less employment in Akron, Detroit, Pittsburgh. You see department store heads in conference with merchandise managers. you see office managers in insurance companies, banks, investment houses, wholesaling firms, facilitating the labors of many. You see huge hospitals in which doctors, nurses, and auxiliary

3

staffs are working to restore health. You see universities, colleges, and schools in which administrators and teachers are providing education. You see governmental bureaus—Federal, state and municipal—in all of which some phase of the public welfare is being served.

Everywhere there are people managing and there are people being managed. This is taking place in organizations, large or small, and for all kinds of purposes.[1]

The governance and administration of education is a good example of the nature and importance of administrative activity in our society. The educational establishment ranks among the largest of public and private enterprises. Over two million teachers and sixty million students in thousands of schools throughout the nation function daily. Fifty state departments of education, several departments of our federal government, as well as dozens of private and semiprivate organizations assume responsibility for the analysis and development of broad policy to guide this vast enterprise. Tens of thousands of school boards and tens of thousands of administrators function as well in the development and administration of policies which govern the day-by-day operation of schools. This nation has set as its goal the mass education of its youth through the high school and in some communities through the community college level. No other country comes close to so fully educating its young people. Providing for the social mobility of young people beyond the socioeconomic status of their parents two times greater than any other society, and the mass education of extremely diverse groups for citizenship and productive work, are two accomplishments cited by Ralph W. Tyler in his analysis of school accomplishments these past 200 years.[2]

Much more needs to be done, and indeed some would say that we have just begun the task of providing the highest quality education for our society. Past accomplishments and future success have relied and still continue to rely in a large part on the quality of educational leadership and statespersonship available to local schools. Educational administration and supervision at all levels, from superintendent to chairperson, assume key roles in the process of building quality education. That administrators are often limited and constrained by forces beyond their reach does not distract from the significance of their roles. No one would deny the importance of enacting sound public policy on education at the state and federal levels, but sound policy in itself is

[1]Tead Ordway, *The Art of Administration* (New York: McGraw-Hill, 1951), p. 1.
[2]M. Frances Klein, "Tyler and Goodlad Speak On American Education: A Critique," *Educational Leadership*, Vol. 33, no. 8 (1976) 565.

not the answer to school problems and issues. One cannot legislate or mandate superior teaching, humane learning, and other aspects of quality education. These result from the efforts of competent and committed professionals who work with youngsters day by day, the commitment and support a school enjoys from its community, and organizational and other logistical support provided to the school— characteristics which are the domains of educational leadership, statespersonship, and administration.

The journey to an administrative position in education is an important one, and once accomplished, can result in a professionally significant and personally rewarding career. This book is intended, in part, to help some who are considering becoming educational administrators to decide whether such a choice is suitable. Others may wish to gain insight into the nature and functioning of educational governance and adminstration for reasons other than career choice. In either event, our overview will be forthright, for we examine problems and prospects which characterize the field and provide descriptions and analyses which reflect what is and what ought to be the state of educational administration both as fields of academic study and of professional practice.

ADMINISTRATION DEFINED

Administration is generally defined as the process of working with and through others to efficiently accomplish organizational goals. There is a performance quality to most definitions of administration, and since resources are always limited and decisions must be made as to how best to allocate these resources, efficiency becomes an additional quality. Administrators are responsible for efficiently accomplishing certain objectives, and administration is viewed as the art and science of "getting things efficiently done."

Some theorists, most notably Chester Barnard,[3] Herbert Simon,[4] and Dan Griffiths,[5] define administration with a shift in emphasis from "doing" to "deciding." For them, administration is the art and science of decision making, and it is this task, they would argue, which pervades the entire administrative organization. Decision making is con-

[3]Chester I. Barnard, *The Function of the Executive* (Cambridge: Harvard University Press, 1938).

[4]Herbert A. Simon, *Adminstrative Behavior—A Study of Decision-Making Processes in Administrative Orgainzations* (New York: Free Press, 1945).

[5]Daniel E. Griffiths, *Administrative Theory* (New York: Appleton-Century-Crofts, 1959).

sidered sufficiently important by authorities to warrant separate and detailed treatment by us in Chapter 14.

Typically, a distinction is made between administration and leadership. The school principal, for example, is responsible for a number of teachers and other employees, each with specific tasks to do. The principal's job is to coordinate, direct, and support the work of others by defining objectives, evaluating performance, providing organizational resources, building a supportive psychological climate, running interference with parents, planning, scheduling, bookkeeping, resolving teacher conflicts, defusing student insurrections, placating the central office, and otherwise helping to make things go. Hemphill[6] and Lipham,[7] among others, would consider these administrative rather than leadership activities. Administration, according to this view, refers to the normal behaviors associated with one's job. To them, the differences between the two can be seen in the behavior of leaders who initiate new structures, procedures, and goals. Leadership, they would suggest, emphasizes newness and change.

Abraham Zaleznick, for example, describes leaders as follows:

> They are active instead of reactive, shaping ideas instead of responding to them. Leaders adopt a personal and active attitude toward goals. The influence a leader exerts in altering moods, evoking images and expectations, and in establishing specific desires and objectives determines the direction a business takes. The net result of this influence is to change the way people think about what is desirable, possible, and necessary.[8]

Though this distinction between administration and leadership has become widely accepted in the literature and has a number of advantages, particularly to researchers seeking to understand more fully administrative behavior, on balance, negative consequences seem to dominate. Administration has come to be seen as a less essential, lower-status activity, while leadership is viewed as superior. Further, the glamour of the leadership concept has resulted in its receiving far more attention in the prescriptive literature (literature which tells administrators how they ought to behave), as compared to administrative be-

[6]James K. Hemphill, "Adminstration as Problem Solving," in Andrew Halpin, ed., *Administrative Theory in Education* (Chicago: Midwest Administration Center, University of Chicago, 1958) p. 98.

[7]James Lipham, "Leadership and Administration," in National Society for the Study of Education, *Behavioral Science and Educational Administration*, 1964 Yearbook, pp. 119–141.

[8]Abraham Zaleznick, "Managers and Leaders: Are They Different?" *Harvard Business Review*, Vol. 55, No. 3 (1977) p. 71. See also, Robert J. Starrett, "Contemporary Talk on Leadership: Too Many Kings in the Parade?" *Notre Dame Journal of Education*, Vol. 4, No. 1 (1973) 5–15.

havior, than is warranted. Indeed, administration is viewed as the straw concept as writers glamorize leadership. One result is a prescriptive literature that is out of kilter with reality. This literature encourages unreasonable expectations for change for administrators, causes feelings of inferiority, anxiety, and guilt among them, and provides the public with unrealistic images of what administrators can actually do. Chapter 12 provides a detailed description of the actual work of educational administrators.

Leadership and administration are operationally so interrelated that, practically speaking, both behavior modes should be considered as necessary and important variations in administrative style. The choice is not either leadership or administration, but a better balance between the two and a more realistic view of the possibilities for each. Excluded from this discussion are issues of education and the importance of educational leadership. Later in this chapter we examine leadership qualities, missions, and roles in *education* as a set of concepts distinct from leadership and adminstration in general.

In business and other settings, the terms *management* and *management behavior* are used to refer to administration and sometimes to both administration and leadership. As the footnotes to this book suggest, much of the management literature is appropriate to educational adminstration, but the term has not "caught on"; indeed, when used at all, the term is often used in a derogatory sense. Popular articles, for example, often ask the question, "Should a principal be a manager or an educational leader?" implying that the first choice is demeaning. Perhaps one reason for the unpopularity of the term management is an attempt to keep the administration of schools separate from that of business and industrial organizations. Differences between private management and public administration are indeed significant, as will be discussed. In the sections which immediately follow, critical responsibilities of administrators, generally accepted administrative processes, and necessary administrative skills are reviewed in an attempt to provide a basic overview, definition, statement of purpose, and conception of educational administration. Later we speak more specifically to the educational administrator's responsibilities for providing educational leadership to his or her school community.

CRITICAL RESPONSIBILITIES
OF ADMINISTRATORS

All organizations, schools included, seem to manifest certain similar kinds of activities. Argyris refers to these as organizational-core activities or, more simply, core activities. The core activities are *achiev-*

ing objectives, maintaining the organizational system, and *adapting to forces in the organization's external environment.*[9] Each of the core activities comprises a set of organizational imperatives for the school, to which administrators and school boards must attend. To these three can be added an additional imperative particularly suited to the school —*maintaining cultural patterns.*[10] As core activities, the four can be seen as composed of many subactivities, and these in turn result in behaviors called administrative functions. Function might include, for example, planning, organizing, controlling, coordinating, teaching, communicating, and evaluating. Functions are directed toward particular intended consequences. The consequences, in turn, are defined by the core activities of achieving goals, internal maintenance, external adaptation, and maintaining cultural patterns.[11] The core activities are imperatives because a neglect of any can threaten the survival of the school. Schools must experience certain levels of success in achieving goals, in maintaining themselves internally, in adapting to their external environment, and in maintaining their cultural patterns. Let us consider each of the core activities in more detail.

Maintaining the school's *cultural pattern* is concerned with the protecting and nurturing of school and community traditions and cultural norms. School administrators and school board members typically are sensitive to the salient motivational and cultural patterns which exist in the community over time, and these patterns are an important part of the school's official and hidden curricula. School traditions emerge, images are fabricated and nurtured, and accepted ways of operating become established in a system of written and unwritten norms which provide a given school or school community with a distinct personality. Graduation ceremonies, football games, Christmas programs, newsletters, and public-relations programs are some of the more visible ways of fabricating and maintaining cultural pattern images, as are student-conduct codes, policy handbooks, and other attempts to publicly control the behavior of students. Often the symbols of cultural-pattern maintenance are more important than actual conditions. Some schools are known for their athletic prowess, others foster an elite academy image, and still others are thought of as well-rounded traditional schools where the ideal student is viewed as having a "B" average, being a cheerleader or athlete, active on the yearbook, a junior

[9]Chris Argyris, *Integrating the Individual and the Organization* (New York: John Wiley, 1964) p. 315.

[10]See for example, Talcott Parsons, *Structure and Process in Modern Society* (Glencoe, IL: Free Press, 1960), and *Toward a General Theory of Social Action* (Cambridge: Harvard University Press, 1951). See also R. Jean Hills, *Toward a Science of Organization* (Eugene, Oregon: Center for the Advanced Study of Educational Administration, 1968).

[11]Argyris, *Integrating the Individual*.

prom king or queen, and one who will attend the local state university. Some of the most critical times for school administrators occur when cultural-pattern demands are in transition, often as a result of population shifts, desegregation mandates, or other abruptions in the normative character of the school community.

Goal Attainment suggests administrative and school board responsibilities which are direct and well understood; defining objectives and mobilizing resources to attain them. Because of its visibility, goal attainment becomes the *public* agenda for recruiting and evaluating administrators and board members, though in reality, judgments of ineffectiveness result most frequently from deficiencies in *other* responsibility areas, such as maintaining the school's cultural pattern.

Peshkin's account of the hiring of a new school superintendent in Mansfield[12] illustrates the public acknowledgment of goal-attainment criteria by the school board, but the actual concern is for maintaining the school-community cultural pattern in making the hiring decison. Consider, for example, the following excerpts from school-board member discussions in Mansfield following interviews of several candidates.

Should we talk about Hagedorn to see why we don't want him?

Yes, let's get the feeling of the board on him. I believe we have better men. Not quality wise, though. He could handle the job and the P.R. (Public Relations). I don't think he's the type we're looking for.

I hate to say it, but his physical appearance is against him. You need to call a spade a spade.

He's not stable like some of the others.

I'm afraid he'd be the brunt of behind-the-back jokes.

He's carrying far too much weight. That's a strain on the heart.

He was tired. A man that size gets physically tired. We shouldn't kid ourselves. Image is very important. That size is against him.

The next one is Dargan.

I was impressed, but I feel he is too big for our town and school. His ideas are for the city, for bigger schools. We're not ready for all that.

I felt he would probably be anxious to start a lot of things I don't know if we're ready for. He's definitely for a nongraded system. He said he'd start slow, but he wanted it pretty bad. Knocking down walls scares you just a bit.

I was impressed, but then we had more fellows in. We learned more about this nongraded idea. He would be a pusher, I'm sure.

[12]Mansfield is the name Peshkin gives to a small rural area community in the Midwest as part of his extensive case study. Alan Peshkin, "Whom Shall the Schools Serve? Some Dilemmas of Local Control in a Rural School District," *Curriculum Inquiry*, Vol. 6, No. 3 (1977) 181–204.

He had too many ideas to start off with. You need to see what a school has before jumping in.

I thought he might be a little slow with discipline problems.

I saw dollar signs clicking around in my head when he talked. He may be too intelligent for this community. He may talk over the heads of the community.

Another thing. He was emphatic about four weeks vacation.

Salary-wise he asked for the most.

Well, this Dargan, he said he wanted to come to a small community. I think he may want to bring too many ideas from the city with him. He may be more than we want.

What did you like about Morgan? These next three are a hard pick.

He gave a nice impression here, I believe, of getting along with the public and the kids. This impressed me more than anything.

To me he talked generalities.

He had a tremendous speaking voice. He's young.

His voice got very nasal at the end when he got relaxed.

He wouldn't stay.

I believe he'd be a forceful individual.

Take this other man, Rogers. I had a feeling about him. He said, 'If you hired me and I accepted it.' I don't think he's too anxious for the job.

I can see why he was offered a job selling real estate. He's got the voice. He'd have your name on the line. I'm inclined to believe he'd talk himself out of most situations. Getting down to brass tacks, he spoke in generalities. He admitted he didn't know too much about new things in education. We need more specific answers.

More or less, this leaves us with Vitano.

He's the man to put on top.

I'd hate to pick any of the top three over the others.

Both Vitano and Rogers said that they have no hours. They work by the job. Vitano worked his way through college.

He was on ground floor as far as salary goes.

And he's country.[13]

Though the board had established public selection criteria around the theme of goal attainment, it's actual criteria revolved around the cultural-pattern theme. As Peshkin notes, "Perhaps it should have been self-evident that no one could be chosen Superintendent of Schools in Mansfield who did not appear 'country,' the board's short-

[13]*Ibid*., pp. 187–188.

hand term to describe a person who would be suitable for their rural dominated, traditionally oriented school."[14]

A third area of critical responsibility for school administration reflects the need for schools and communities to *adapt* to their *external environments*. Communities change and schools change with them. The advance of technology and the evolution of political processes place enormous pressures on schools. Coping with environmental demands for change as a result of declining enrollments, for example, has required substantial changes in finance formulas, personnel policies, organizational structures, facility usages, school boundary lines, teacher-association–board contracts, and educational-program designs. The challenge for school administrators and boards is adapting externally in a fashion which preserves some sense of internal identity, continuity, and balance. A growing literature deals with adaptation problems of schools from the perspectives of politics and public policy, the sociology and politics of innovation, and the socio-psychology of change.

The fourth critical responsibility area has to do with meeting the schools' need for *internal maintenance*. Structurally, internal maintenance requires the coordination and unification of units, departments, and schools into a single entity. Psychologically, internal maintenance refers to the building of a sense of identity and loyalty to the school among teachers and students and providing them with a sense of satisfaction and well-being in return. Some theorists have defined administrative effectiveness around the internal-maintenance theme by suggesting that effectiveness is the integration of individual and organizational needs; indeed, this social-systems theme dominated the literature of educational administration during the 1950s and 1960s.[15]

Different schools and school districts can be expected to emphasize different patterns of core activities in response to their unique situational characteristics, but all four must be provided for to some degree by all schools and school districts. The problem becomes more complex with the realization that too much emphasis in one area often can jeopardize the other areas. For example, an overemphasis on internal maintenance may actually jeopardize goal attainment, and an overemphasis on external adaption can often upset the maintenance of cultural patterns. In the first instance, consider a school which agrees to

[14]*Ibid.*, p. 188.

[15]See for example, J. W. Getzels, "Administration as a Social Process," in Andrew Halpin, ed., *Administrative Theory in Education*, pp. 150–165. See also J.W. Getzels, James M. Lipham, and Ronald F. Campbell, *Educational Administration as a Social Process*, (New York: Harper & Row, 1968).

a policy of teacher supervision and evaluation which emphasizes the development of good human relationships and high morale (internal maintenance) at the expense of providing teachers with sufficient responsibility, evaluative feedback, and other performance incentives (goal attainment). A "happy teacher" emphasis does not in itself ensure high-quality teacher performance. In the second instance, consider a school which responds to its perception of societal needs by implementing an educational program characterized by individualized instruction and an abundance of student alternatives (external adaption), but in so doing, projects an image of permissiveness and anarchy to a community with a more traditional conception of schooling (maintaining community cultural patterns). Here, adapting to the perceived needs of society in general is at odds with the prevailing value system of the local community. As even a brief study of educational administration will reveal, progress is slow and incremental; administrative activity takes place within time constraints. Typically, administrators are not able to wait until everything is perfect before making or implementing decisions. Compromises are more the rule. Satisfactory solutions which are agreeable under current circumstances are accepted in favor of better or ideal solutions which presently are not possible. Each of the core activities which comprise critical administrative responsibilities are, therefore, better seen as having qualities of elasticity which enable stretching and contracting. By capitalizing on this elastic quality, administrators seek to balance one critical responsibility area against another without forcing one or neglecting another to the point where survival of the school is endangered.

CRITICAL ADMINISTRATIVE PROCESSES

We have defined administration broadly as the process of working with and through others to efficiently accomplish organizational goals. This definition was supplemented by identifying four broad areas of administrative responsibility: maintaining the school's cultural pattern, goal attainment, internal maintenance, and external adoption. Administration can also be defined as a process of functions. *Planning*, *organizing*, *leading*, and *controlling* are the four functions most often mentioned by theorists.[16]

Planning involves the setting of goals and objectives for the school

[16]See, for example, Luther Gulick and L. Urwick, eds., *Papers on the Science of Administration* (New York: Institute for Public Administration, 1937); Harold Koontz and Cyril O'Donnell, *Principles of Management*, 5th ed. (New York: McGraw-Hill, 1972); Jesse B. Sears, *The Nature of Administrative Process* (New York: McGraw-Hill, 1950).

and district and the developing of blueprints and strategies for their implementation. *Organizing* involves the bringing together of human, financial, and physical resources in the most effective way to accomplish goals. The *leading* function has to do with guiding and supervising subordinates. Plans of organizations are implemented by people, and people need to be motivated, expectations need to be defined, and communication channels need to be maintained. The fourth administrative process, *controlling*, refers to the administrator's evaluation functions and includes reviewing, regulating, and controlling performance, providing feedback, and otherwise tending to standards of goal attainment and internal-maintenance responsibilities of administration, with some attention to external adaption. Maintaining the school's cultural-pattern responsibilities are typically neglected by those who write about administrative processes.

CRITICAL ADMINISTRATIVE SKILLS

Still another way in which administration can be examined is by identifying competencies and skill areas necessary for carrying out the processess of administration. Robert L. Katz has identified three basic skills upon which, he feels, successful administration rests—technical, human, and conceptual.[17] Technical skill assumes an understanding of and proficiency in the methods, processes, procedures, and techniques of education. In noninstructional areas it includes specific knowledge in finance, accounting, scheduling, purchasing, construction, and maintenance. Usually, technical skills are more important to administrative and supervisory roles lower in the school hierarchy. The department chairperson or grade-level supervisor, for example, needs far greater command of technical skills relating to instruction than does the principal. The business manager needs a more technical command of accounting procedures and computer uses than does the superintendent.

Human skill refers to the school administrator's ability to work effectively and efficiently with other people on a one-to-one basis and in group settings. This skill requires considerable self-understanding and acceptance as well as appreciation, empathy, and consideration for others. Its knowledge base includes an understanding of and facility for adult motivation, attitudinal development, group dynamics, human need, morale, and the development of human resources. Human skills seem equally important to administrative and supervisory roles throughout the school heirarchy. Regardless of position, all adminis-

[17]Robert L. Katz, "Skills of an Effective Administrator," *Harvard Business Review*, Vol. 33, No. 1, (1955), 33–42.

trators work through others; that is, they use human skills to achieve goals.

Conceptual skill includes the school administrator's ability to see the school, the district, and total educational program as a whole. This skill includes the effective mapping of interdependence for each of the components of the school as an organization, the educational program as an instructional system, and the functioning of the human organization. The development of conceptual skill relies heavily on a balanced emphasis of administrative theory, knowledge of organizational and human behavior, and educational philosophy. Usually, conceptual skills are more important to roles further up the organizational hierarchy. The superintendent may not know much about the technical aspects of teaching youngsters with learning disabilities to read, but must know how this piece of the puzzle fits and interacts with other aspects of operating the school district.

Figure 1–1 summarizes aspects of the job of educational administration. The four critical administrative responsibility areas are listed on the left margin, and the four critical administrative processes on the top margin. Together they form a sixteen-cell two-dimensional grid for

FIGURE 1–1
Mapping the job of educational administration

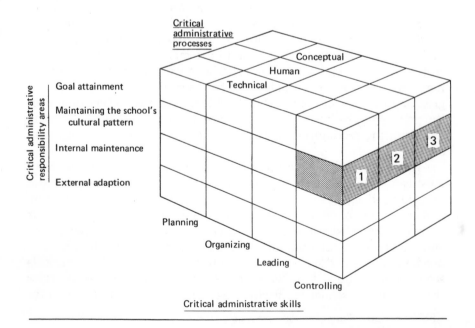

mapping administrative activity. The shaded cell in Fig 1–1, which marks the intersection of maintaining cultural patterns with the controlling functions, might be illustrated by an administrator who is surveying community attitudes toward a particular school policy or program. The grid becomes three demensional when the three critical administrative skills are added. In surveying community attitudes, for example, the administrator needs to know the technical rudiments of survey conducting and reporting. Human skills will be needed in obtaining public participation in the project and in resolving disputes which might be evident in the survey. Conceptually, the administrator needs to understand the implications of the intended and unintended consequences of the survey on educational program planning, the school's public relations program, and other factors. Additional insights into the role and function of educational administrators, which highlight needed competencies, specific tasks, and descriptions of how administrators actually spend their time, are provided in later chapters.

EDUCATIONAL ADMINISTRATION AS EDUCATIONAL LEADERSHIP

Before proceeding further into this introduction to educational governance and administration, we consider specifically the important topic of educational leadership and its relationship to administration. As one proceeds through the book, it will become increasingly clear that administrative responsibilities are vast and encompass a variety of roles and an array of problems and issues—many of which seem not to be clearly or directly related to education.

Increasingly, for example, educational administrators are portrayed as managers. School boards and community publics demand sound fiscal management and expect the school to be run in a business-like fashion. Indeed, such topics as cost-effectiveness, accountability, fiscal integrity, efficiency, wage administration, and personnel policy capture increasingly larger shares of the headlines in education these days. Rivaling the manager image of education administration is that of politician. On the local scene, for example, communities are more diverse, expectations and demands for resources are more ambiguous and vocal, power and authority are more diffuse, and public participation in the affairs of the schools is more intense. At a broader level, the strengthened role of state education departments, the increased federal influence through mandated legislation and the courts, and the shifts in school funding patterns which afford to federal and state levels greater responsibility are further reinforcers of the politician image for educational administration.

MANAGERIAL, POLITICAL, AND EDUCATIONAL ROLES

Though many decry the emergence of managerial and political roles in educational administration, the inescapable realities of modern educational administration require that administrators understand and articulate these roles. But, to borrow a metaphor from management, the "bottom line" for educational administrators remains *educational leadership*. Management roles, therefore, while critically important, are not central. Indeed, they exist only to support and complement educational leadership roles.

By the same token, political roles are supplements to and supporters of statespersonship roles. Both leadership and statespersonship have qualities beyond what presently is; they suggest a vision of what is desirable and good, and a determination to marshal organizational energy in this direction. Leaders and statespersons, however, cannot be aloof from or ignorant of managerial and political roles. But good management and good politics are not in themselves sufficient.

Perhaps the point can best be made by focusing in detail on the leadership aspects of educational administration and contrasting these with good management. Levitt, for example, describes management as follows:

> Management consists of the rational assessment of a situation and the systematic selection of goals and purposes (what is to be done?); the systematic development of strategies to achieve these goals; the marshalling of the required resources; the rational design, organization, direction, and control of the activities required to attain the selected purposes; and, finally, the motivating and rewarding of people to do the work.[18]

The administrator as manager, according to this view, is concerned with such questions as, what should be accomplished and how are best results achieved? Certainly these are important considerations in the effective operation of schools and school districts. But, as Zaleznik points out, "it takes neither genius nor heroism to be a manager, but

---

[18]Theodore Levitt, "Management and the Post Industrial Society," *The Public Interest*, Summer 1976, p.73.

rather persistence, tough-mindedness, hard work, intelligence, analytical ability and, perhaps most important, tolerance and good will."[19]

From a management perspective, educational administrators are viewed as professional managers. Like other professionals, they possess certain insights and technical skills which have great instrumental value. Give an engineer the specifications you require, for example, and this person will provide the blueprint for action. Similarly, the professional medical practitioner responds to a particular diagnosis with a predetermined and standardized treatment. In our case, provide a professional administrator-manager with outcomes to be achieved, and this person will engineer organization and talent in that direction. We defined administration in its management sense earlier as the science and art of achieving organizational objectives in a fashion which is cost-effective and which obtains sufficient teacher and consumer satisfaction to ensure their continued participation and support.

Educational leadership, by contrast, is a more expansive concept which includes concern for the worth of objectives and their impact on school and society. Whereas professional administration suggests a utilitarian quality (what are the best means to achieve given ends), educational leadership suggests a normative quality (how adequate are the ends themselves). Beyond concern for the value of objectives and the overall mission of the school, leadership evokes a quality of living and attractiveness which moves individuals and organizations beyond the ordinary in their zeal, commitment, and work habits. As Zaleznik suggests, leaders

> are active instead of reactive, shaping ideas instead of responding to them. Leaders adopt a personal and active attitude toward goals. The influence a leader exerts in altering moods, evoking images and expectations, and in establishing specific desires and objectives determines the direction.... The net result of this influence is to change the way people think about what is desirable, possible, and necessary.[20]

In sum, the professional administrator is likely to view his or her role as that of one who finds out what consumers want from the schools and who delivers educational services accordingly. The educational leader, by contrast, is very much concerned with the issues of purpose and direction. Neither alone is sufficient, for the educational administrator will need to bring to his or her work both a vision of what ought to be and knowledge of the means to achieve these ideals.

[19]Abraham Zaleznik, "Managers and Leaders," p. 68.
[20]*Ibid.*, p. 71.

QUALITATIVE ASPECTS
OF LEADERSHIP

Having established that educational leadership requires good management, but that good management itself is not sufficient, let us examine more closely the nature of leadership. Starratt, for example, suggests that, in addition to management skill, the leader brings to his or her work extra qualities of vision, intensity, and creativity.[21] Leaders are concerned with a vision of what is possible and desirable for them and others to achieve, and a vision of the significance of what they are presently doing. The leader engages in organizational activities with great energy and brings to the job an intensity of desire, commitment, and enthusiasm which sets him or her apart from others. The leader brings to the organization and its work a certain freshness of thought, a commitment to new ideas, and belief in creative change. Concentrating on the qualities of vision, intensity, and creativity, Starratt believes that leaders can be distinguished from others as follows:

    1. Leaders work beneath the surface of events and activities, seeking a deeper meaning and deeper value. They are able to identify the roots of meaning in the ebb and flow of daily life in schools and, as a result, to provide students, teachers, and community members with a sense of importance, vision, and purpose above the seemingly ordinary and mundane.

    2. Leaders bring to the school a sense of drama in human life that permits one to surface above the dulling routine which often characterizes day-by-day activity. They see the significance of what a group is doing and could be doing. They have a feel for the more dramatic possibilities inherent in most situations and are able to urge people to go beyond the routine, to break out of the mold into something more lively and vibrant.

    3. Leaders are able to communicate their sense of vision by words and examples. They use language and symbols which are easily understood but which also communicate a sense of excitement, originality, and freshness.

    4. Leaders provide opportunities for others to experience their vision and sense of purpose so that others come to share in their ownership.

[21]This section follows closely Robert J. Starratt, "Apostolic Leadership," Jesuit Commission on Research and Development Workshop, San Jose, Calif. June, 1977. See also Robert J. Starratt, "Contemporary Talk on Leadership: Too Many Kings in the Parade?" *Notre Dame Journal of Education*, Vol. 4, No. 1 (1973), 5–15; Starratt, "What lies Ahead —The Best of Times, The Worst of Times," Chapter 17 in T. J. Sergiovanni and R. J. Starratt, *Supervision: Human Perspectives Second Edition* (New York: McGraw-Hill, 1979).

5. Leaders are able to transform their vision, intensity, and creativity from idiosyncratic or personal meanings into goals, structures, and processes for the school. Ideas became programs, visions become goals, and senses of commitment from others become operating structures. Indeed the leader translates qualities of leadership into characteristics of the school as an organization.[22]

In sum, leaders are able to grasp the deeper meaning and value of seemingly common events, translate these into a dramatic sense of purpose and vision, convincingly communicate both meaning and purpose to others, obtain their commitment and sense of partnership, and articulate these qualities into organizational goals, structures, and programs. Managerial skills remain important, for once programs are identified, they need to be effectively and efficiently articulated.

THE SUBSTANCE OF LEADERSHIP IN EDUCATION

Qualities of leadership are universal to all organizations. Hospital, business, military, governmental, and educational administrator-leaders, for example, bring to their respective organizations common qualities of vision, intensity, and creativity. The substantive aspects of leadership, on the other hand, have to do with the unique and central context of the work of a particular organization. Educational program, curriculum and instruction, teaching and learning, and supervision and evaluation are the central concerns of schools, and these comprise the substance of educational leadership.

One dysfunction of recent trends toward pressuring educational administrators to assume more managerial and political roles is that these have become central, displacing educational roles. Goodlad describes this trend as follows:

Recent years have been harrowing ones for school administrators. We have yielded to the pressures and temptations of becoming experts in fiscal and personnel management, public relations, collective bargaining, and the political process. Few of us are trained or experienced in any of these, even though we must take responsibility for them. . . . It is now time to put the right things at the center again. And the right things have to do with assuring comprehensive, quality educational programs in each and every school under our jurisdiction.[23]

[22]Propositions about leadership are adapted from Starratt, "Apostolic Leadership."
[23]John I. Goodlad, "Educational Leadership: Toward the Third Era," *Educational Leadership*, Vol. 35, No. 4 (1978), 322.

Continuing, Goodlad feels that serious steps need to be taken to reverse this trend.

> One step is to check our present perspectives regarding what is central to our work. If, in so doing, we conclude that collective bargaining, balancing the budget, and informing the public are central, something has gone amiss. These are the conditions surrounding, complicating and, perhaps, endangering our jobs. We ignore them at our peril; we would be well advised to attend special institutes or workshops so as to be thoroughly updated on the issues and our role in dealing with them. But to put these matters at the center, often for understandable reasons of survival and expediency, is to commit a fundamental error which, ultimately, will have a negative impact on both education and one's own career. Our work, for which we will be held accountable, is to maintain, justify, and articulate sound, comprehensive programs of instruction for children and youth.[24]

Certainly Gooodlad's arguments are persuasive, but keeping matters of educational program central to one's roles will not be easy. A first step is to make a commitment to educational leadership, viewing managerial and political roles as important to educational leadership but not as ends in themselves.

What can one expect from making a commitment to educational leadership? Some evidence exists that such a commitment is at the heart of noticeable differences between effective and ineffective educational administrators. In a study of effective and ineffective elementary school principals conducted by Becker and his associates, principals of effective schools had the following characteristics in common:

> 1. Most did not intend to become principals. Most indicated that they had intended to teach, but were encouraged to become principals by their superiors.
>
> 2. Most expressed a sincere faith in children. Children were not criticized for failing to learn or for having behavioral difficulties. The principals felt that these were problems that the school was established to correct; thus the administrators emphasized their responsibilities toward the solution of children's problems.
>
> 3. They had an ability to work effectively with people and to secure their cooperation. They were proud of their teachers and accepted them as professionally dedicated and competent people. They inspired confidence and developed enthusiasm. The principals used group processes effectively; listened well to parents, teachers, and pupils; and appeared to have intuitive skill and empathy for their associates.

[24]*Ibid*, p. 326.

4. They were aggressive in securing recognition of the needs of their schools. They frequently were critical of the restraints imposed by the central office and of the inadequate resources. They found it difficult to live within the constraints of the bureaucracy; they frequently violated the chain of command, seeking relief of their problems from whatever sources that were potentially useful.

5. They were enthusiastic as principals and accepted their responsibilities as a mission rather than as a job. They recognized their role in current social problems. The ambiguities that surrounded them and their work were of less significance than the goals they felt were important to achieve. As a result, they found it possible to live with the ambiguities of their position.

6. They were committed to education and could distinguish between long–term and short–term educational goals. Consequently, they had established philosophies of the role of education and their relationship within it.

7. They were adaptable. If they discovered something was not working, they could make the necessary shifts and embark with some security on new paths.

8. They were able strategists. They could identify their objectives and plan means to achieve them. They expressed concern for the identification of the most appropriate procedures through which change could be secured.[25]

These characteristics suggest that effective principals were certainly concerned with good management and politics; but clearly, educational leadership was of paramount concern. To repeat, a fundamental assumption underlying this book is that managerial and political roles, no matter how important they seem to the success of educational administration, must be judged on the basis of how they serve educational leadership aspirations of administration. Indeed, this is the yardstick by which one assesses the usefulness and appropriateness of further administrative study in such areas of law, finance, facilities, politics, organizational behavior, and other topics.

EDUCATIONAL ADMINISTRATION AS AN EMERGING PROFESSION

Educational administration has a short history, and only since World War II has it shown signs of establishing itself as an emerging profession. The years 1946 and 1947 are often considered as the critical beginning of this emergence. It was during this period that the American Association of School Administrators (AASA) received a report

[25]Gerald Becker et al., *Elementary School Principals and Their Schools* (Eugene, Ore: University of Oregon, Center for the Advanced Study of Educational Administration, 1971), p.233.

from its planning committee urging a long-range commitment to the professionalization of educational administrators. This committee recommended that AASA work to improve preparation programs in administration at colleges and universities, to encourage school boards to develop more adequate standards for the selection of superintendents, and to become more active as an organization in the general professional affairs of education. The 1947 annual AASA conference was characterized by initial planning for the formation of the National Conference of Professors of Educational Administration (NCPEA). Its members, professors and others involved in the preparation of administrators at colleges and universities, met that summer in Endicott, New York and produced a landmark report entitled *Educational Leaders: Their Functions and Preparation.*

Three years later the emerging profession of educational administration was to receive an enormous boost—the development of the Cooperative Program in Education Administration (CPEA). Founded as a result of a Kellogg Foundation grant and of planning by the AASA, the National Association of Rural Superintendents, the Council of Chief State School Officers and University Professors, CPEA resulted in the establishment, by 1951, of regional centers at eight American universities.[26] The purposes of these centers were:

1. to improve preparation programs for preservice training of potential administrators and in-service training of administrators already in the field;

2. to develop greater sensitivity to large social problems through an interdisciplinary approach involving most of the social sciences;

3. to disseminate research findings to practicing administrators;

4. to discover new knowledge about education and about administration; and

5. to develop a continuing pattern of cooperation and communication among various universities and colleges within a region and between these institutions and other organizations and agencies working in the field of educational administration.[27]

[26]University of Oregon, Stanford University, University of Texas, University of Chicago, Ohio State University, George Peabody College for Teachers, Columbia University, and Harvard University.

[27] *Toward Improved School Administration: A Decade of Professional Effort to Heighten Administrative Understandings and Skills,* W. K. Kellogg Foundation, Battle Creek Michigan, 1961, p. 13, An Account of CPEA activities can be found in Hollis Moore Jr., *Studies in School Administration.* (Washington, D.C., AASA, 1947). See also, W. R. Rlesher and A. L. Knoblauch, *A Decade of Educational Leadership,* National Conference of Professors of Educational Administration, 1957.

Educational administrators often claim a professional status higher than that of teaching, and with some justification. Teaching, for example, is a prerequisite occupation to administration. Though teaching is an occupation characterized by "ease of entry"[31] administrative positions are fewer in number, in greater demand, and more difficult to obtain. Academic and professional requirements for certification are more advanced and build upon preliminary training as a teacher. Further, unlike teaching, administration is a male-dominated occupation with more latitude and fewer scheduling constraints. These occupational characteristics permit administrators to have greater visibility in the community. Administrators attend luncheons, have golf–business meetings, and enjoy other privileges normally reserved to the male-dominated, recognized professions—*but these are deceptive indicators of professionalism*.

Recently the Bicentennial Commission on Education for the Profession of Teaching of the American Association of Colleges for Teacher Education (AACTE) developed a composite of generally accepted criteria associated with the recognized professions.[32] These characteristics, listed below, can be used to assess the extent to which educational administration measures up to professional status.

1. Professions are occupationally related social institutions established and maintained as a means of providing essential services to the individual and the society.

2. Each profession is concerned with an identified area of need or function (e.g., maintenance of physical and emotional health, preservation of rights and freedom, enhancing the opportunity to learn).

3. The profession collectively, and the professional individually, possess a body of knowledge and a repertoire of behaviors and skills (professional culture) needed in the practice of the profession; such knowledge, behavior, and skills normally are not possessed by the nonprofessional.

4. The members of the profession are involved in decision making in the service of the client, the decisions being made in accordance with the most valid knowledge available, against a background of principles and theories, and within the context of possible impact on other related conditions or decisions.

6. The profession is organized into one or more professional associations which, within broad limits of social accountability, are granted autonomy in control of the actual work of the profession and the conditions which sur-

[31]Lortie, *School Teacher*, p. 17.

[32]Robert B. Howsam, et al., *Educating a Profession* (Washington, D.C.: American Association of Colleges for Teacher Education, 1976).

A significant outgrowth of CPEA activity was the establishment in 1956 of the University Council for Educational Administration (UCEA). Thirty-three major universities throughout the country with preparation programs in educational administration formed the initial membership nucleus. The purposes of UCEA were to improve the preservice and inservice education of school administrators, stimulate and conduct research, encourage innovation through development projects, and disseminate materials growing out of research and development activities. Originally located at Columbia University, UCEA moved its headquarters staff to Ohio State University in 1959, where it remains today with a membership of about forty-seven universities.

The UCEA had a profound effect on building an identity among professors of educational administration and indeed on improving their training. Further accomplishments included developing a knowledge base in the social and management sciences for preparing administrators. The UCEA has also served as a public forum on behalf of the academic community in influencing federal and state policy decisions relating to educational administration. Other landmark developments during this formative period were the publication in 1964, by the National Society for the Study of Education, of a yearbook devoted to the relationship of the behavioral sciences to educational administration[28] and the establishment of the Center for the Advanced Study of Educational Administration (CASEA) in 1964 at the University of Oregon.

In 1968 the AASA established the National Academy for School Executives (NASE). Modeled after similar advanced inservice arms of other professions, the Academy offers intensive workshops, seminars, and other activities designed to keep superintendents in touch with current developments and issues and up to date in current concepts and skills. Activities of the Academy are highly regarded, as evidenced by wide attendance, expanding programs, and the awarding of academic credits by several universities to administrators who participated in Academy programs.

The 1970s can be characterized as a plateau in the academic side of the development of educational administration as a profession. Several of the original members of UCEA, including two CPEA sites, have dropped from this organization. Training programs for educational administrators in many major universities have been curtailed. Enthusiasm and excitement for educational administration seems to have

[28]Daniel Griffiths, ed., *Behavioral Science and Educational Administration*, 63rd Yearbook, National Society for the Study of Education, 1964.

leveled off. Sources of funding for research, training, and development declined dramatically in the 1970s and have now reached a new but lower level. These events can be explained in part by economic conditions nationally and by changes in policy priorities at the federal level —an important source of money for the academic community—and in part by pessimistic administrative-need estimates as a result of declining student enrollments in the public schools. Universities, foundations, and governmental funding sources are typically reluctant to invest in low-growth, zero-growth, or negative-growth educational programs. But part of the slowdown in financial support and in enthusiasm can be attributed to insufficient responsiveness to changing conditions. It may be that the field has gone as far as it can by pursuing its present course and tradition, and that renewed support and enthusiasm for the academic side of the profession awaits a change in direction. Increased interest in such issues as public policy, the broader politics of education, and the school as a political system, among academics involved in preparing administrators, has produced some encouraging stirrings. The emergence in universities of academic departments of educational-policies studies as additions to or replacements for traditional departments of educational administration are considered by some to be evidence of shifts in interests and emphasis among scholars. What seems important in these recent developments is not necessarily the newly founded "solution," but that the profession is dissatisfied enough to search for new avenues of inquiry.

AASA, with approximately 18,000 members, remains the most influential professional organization for administrators. Superintendents dominate this organization, and though principals and other administrators are not excluded, they typically identify with more specialized professional groups such as the National Association of Secondary School Principals, (NASSP) the National Elementary School Principals Association (NESPA), the Association of School Business Officials (ASBO), and similar organizations for supervisors, personnel administrators, and others. Unlike teachers, who are bound together in the two-million-member National Education Association (NEA) or the smaller but influential American Federation of Teachers (AFT), educational administrators lack a strong national voice and strong rallying organization. Changes can be expected in this situation as administrators feel the need to maintain a strong, unified, professional interest in the face of increased concentration of power over education at the state and federal levels, and of increased influence of teachers on school boards at the local level. In California, for example, the recent establishment of an umbrella organization for all administrative groups, The Association of California School Administrators,

may well suggest the surfacing of a national trend toward developing more unified administrative groups. The Association for Supervision and Curriculum Development (ASCD) in recent years has grown to an organization of some 33,000 professionals in part by appealing to all groups to join together around a common interest—educational quality. Perhaps their success is a harbinger of further efforts to unite not only administration but all educational professionals in a common cause.

Beginning in 1964, AASA required the completion of a two-year graduate program in educational administration as a condition for acceptance into membership. This requirement was later rescinded, and for many this action indicates a step backward in developing educational administration as a field of professional practice. The issue of professionalism is considered in the next section.

MEASURING UP AS A PROFESSION

Occupations recognized as professions enjoy more prestige and other benefits than their ordinary brethren. Traditionally only a small number of occupations are considered as recognized professions. *Designating* an occupation as a profession and being *recognized* as a profession are not the same. The designation of professional is used more democratically today to refer to almost any organized occupation as a way to separate this group from amateurs. If licensing, advanced training, and a guild membership are occupational requirements, then claim to the professional designation is even stronger.

Some designated professions, such as nursing, social work, and teaching, are striving hard to join the ranks of the recognized professions. Certainly further along on this continuum than barbering, baseball, piloting, and plumbing, these "emergent" occupations are referred to by occupational sociologists as semiprofessions.[29] In differentiating between recognized professions and semiprofessions, Etzioni notes that "their training is shorter, their status is less legitimated, their right to privileged communication less established, there is less of a specialized body of knowledge, and they have less autonomy from supervision or societal control than 'the' professions."[30]

[29]See for example, W. J. Goode, "The Theoretical Limits of Professionalization," in Amitai Etzioni, ed., *The Semi-Professions and Their Organization: Teachers, Nurses, Social Workers* (New York: The Free Press, 1969) and Dan C. Lortie, *School Teacher: A Sociological Study* (Chicago: The Universtiy of Chicago Press, 1975).

[30]Etzioni, *The Semi-Professions*, p. V.

round it (admissions, educational standards, examination and licensing, career line, ethical and performance standards, professional discipline).

7. The profession has agreed-upon performance standards for admission to the profession and for continuance within it.

8. Preparation for and induction to the profession is provided through a protracted preparation program, usually in a professional school on a college or university campus.

9. There is a high level of public trust and confidence in the profession and in individual practitioners, based upon the profession's demonstrated capacity to provide service markedly beyond that which would otherwise be available.

10. Individual practitioners are characterized by a strong service motivation and lifetime commitment to competence.

11. Authority to practice in any individual case derives from the client or the employing organization; accountability for the competence of professional practice within the particular case is to the profession itself.

12. There is relative freedom from direct on-the-job supervision and from direct public evaluation of the individual practitioner. The professional accepts responsibility in the name of his or her profession and is accountable through his or her profession to the society.[33]

Though educational administration measures up fairly well to most of these standards, some difficulties and omissions are apparent. As the introduction to educational governance and administration unfolds in this book, patterns of hits and misses with the criteria will become apparent. Difficulties in meeting criterion 6, for example, have already been suggested. Though a number of professional organizations for administrators exist, they are by no means united into one policy-making and influencing umbrella organization. Further, certification legally rests in the hands of the State through its jurisdictional prerogatives over university training programs. In recent years the states have exercised greater control and closer supervision over university training programs, and now hold the balance of power in certification decisions. Signs exist that teachers—initially through legislated majority membership on state certification boards, and then probably through the development of quasi-legal but autonomous boards—are the heir apparents to certification power. Presently, state certification boards are responsible not only for establishing and maintaining teacher certification criteria, but that of other certified educational professionals such as administrators and counselors. If present trends continue, a distinct possibility exists that decisions affecting administrative certification will be made by teachers.

[33] *Ibid.*, pp. 6–7.

Criteria 11 and 12 are particularly difficult to meet because of the legal structure of education and the organizational characteristics of schools. Administrators are professionals in legally sanctioned organizations with many bureaucratic characteristics—all of which suggest a form of accountability different from that of the more entrepreneurlike professional occupations.

NEGATIVE EFFECTS
OF PROFESSIONALISM

Americans largely feel that the professionalization of anything makes it better. Beneath the glamour and material benefits associated with educational administration achieving status as a recognized profession, however, are a number of possible negative, unanticipated consequences for schools and communities. Emergent professions, for example, attempt to develop a definition, role, and function distinctly different from that of other occupations working in the same area, particularly those with lower organizational status. To do otherwise endangers their claim to distinctiveness and special importance. This could result in administrators spending less time in teaching, with students, in classrooms, with curricula, and in the community, and more time tending to such management tasks as running the school properly. Another unanticipated consequence of emerging professionalism might be to give increased attention to the maintenance and development of a professional image at the expense of serving people. Rights and prerogatives of position, status, protocol, and propriety can get in the way of helping, sharing, serving, and problem solving. As professions mature to full recognition, these issues of arrogance and aristocracy versus public service seem to become less pronounced.

CHARACTERISTICS
OF ADMINISTRATORS

In this section a selected demographic profile of educational administrators is provided. The intent of the profile is to afford a glimpse of what administrators are like and provide a benchmark for examining administrative careers in the readers' area of most likely employment. Most of the information on the superintendency is summarized from an AASA research study conducted in 1969/1970.[34] Though changes

---

[34]Stephen Knezevich, ed., *The American School Superintendent: An AASA Research Study* (Washington, D.C.: AASA Commission on the Preparation of Professional School Administrators, AASA, 1971).

could be expected in a study conducted today, this study bears a remarkable similarity with earlier studies of the superintendency, suggesting some stability in administrator characteristics.[35]

What are School Superintendents Like?

The average age of superintendents who participated in the 1969/1970 AASA study was forty-eight years. The average superintendent obtained his first teaching job at age twenty-four, moved into an administrative-supervisory position at thirty and became a superintendent at thirty-six, logging a total of twelve years in this role. Rural and small town accounted for 85 percent of the backgrounds of superintendents in 1969/1970. In districts with 100,000 or more students, however, only 60 percent claimed a rural or small-town background. Though this percentage is still high, it suggests that urban superintendents have background characteristics significantly different than the national profile.

Popular impressions to the contrary, superintendents as a whole are not a highly mobile group. The 1969/1970 study shows that the vast majority of American superintendents (75.5 percent) confine their superintendency career to about two different school districts. The figure was 70.7 percent in an AASA 1958/1959 study.[36] Further, nine out of ten superintendents spend their entire professional career in only one state. Indeed, for the most part, school superintendents can be characterized as locals. The picture changes a bit for school districts with 25,000 or more students. One out of ten of these superintendents have served in five or more school districts. It is these cosmopolitan few who seem to account for highly mobile impressions of the superintendency career. As a result of a recent study of the superintendency in Illinois covering the period from 1960 to 1976, Burlingame estimates, contrary to the AASA study, that roughly 16 percent of Illinois superintendents will change jobs each year and, further, that districts with *fewer* than 500 students will account for the highest turnover pattern.[37] The local image of the superintendency, however, is sustained by Burlingame's study; indeed, he finds that about two of three Illinois superintendents are place-bound. Further, those who move go to new districts of the

[35]See for example, AASA, *Professional Administration for American Schools*, 38th Yearbook (Washington, D.C., AASA, 1960).

[36]*Ibid*.

[37]Martin Burlingame, "An Exploratory Study of Turnover and Career Mobility of Public School District Superintendents in the State of Illinois for 1960–1976" (Springfield, Illinois: Select Committee on School District Organization, Illinois Office of Education, August 1977), Reference Document Number C 128.

same type, size, and geographic region. When mobility occurs, it is horizontal rather than vertical.

In 1969/1970, 55 percent of the superintendents reported the masters degree as their highest degree, 13 percent the specialist degree or Advanced Certificate, and 29 percent the doctorate. The larger the district, the more likely it was that the superintendent had the doctorate. Most who pursued the doctorate began studying at age thirty-three, though superintendents in districts with student enrollments of over 25,000 begin doctoral study earlier.

THE STATUS OF WOMEN
IN ADMINISTRATION

The status of women in the superintendency during the 1969/1970 year was bleak. Fully 98.7 percent of the superintendents who participated in the AASA study were men. No women were represented among the 137 superintendents of school districts with student enrollments above 25,000, and only 20 percent of the remaining 1,266 superintendent participants were women. In a 1975 statistical report issued by the U.S. Department of Health Education and Welfare (HEW) only 65 of the 13,037 superintendents in the country were identified as women.[38]

The general distribution of women across all roles in education continues to suggest staffing patterns based on sex stereotypes. Figure 1–2, for example, shows that though over 60 percent of teachers are women, they account for only a negligible percentage of junior- and senior-high principals and assistant principals. Note also the domination of women in such stereotyped roles as librarian and nurse. Comparatively, women fare better in elementary school administrative positions—but that figure may be deceptive, as shall be discussed in the following section.

Women and the Elementary School
Principalship

A 1968 study of the elementary school principalship conducted by the then Department of Elementary School Principals of the National Education Association[39] suggests that though women are in elemen-

---

[38] *The Condition of Education, 75th ed.*, (Washington, D.C.: National Center for Education Statistics, U.S. Department of Health, Education and Welfare, 1975), p. 173.

[39] Administrative groups, once departments of NEA, have since become independent groups such as the National Elementary School Principals Association and the National Association of Secondary School Principals.

FIGURE 1–2
**Percentage distribution of full-time public school instructional staff,
by sex: 1972–73**

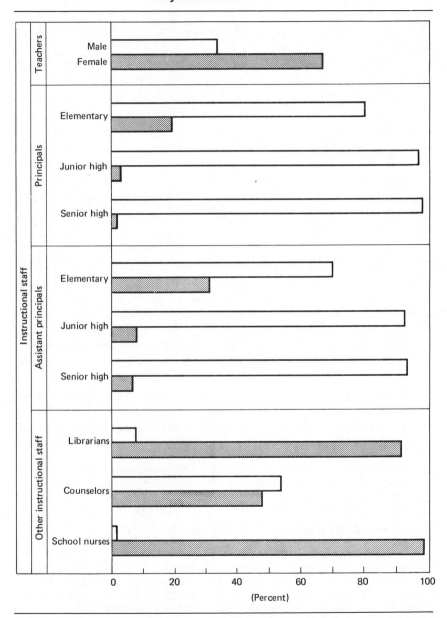

Source: *The Condition of Education 75th Edition.* National Center for Education Statistics,
U.S. Department of Health, Education and Welfare, 1975, p. 71.

31

tary school administrative posts in numbers, their position is eroding.[40] As in the case of the superintendency study, this study shows only minor differences from the one conducted by the principal's association in 1958, suggesting a strand of stability in the demographic character of the principalship. Previous studies were conducted as well in 1928 and 1948.

In 1928, 55 percent of the principals were women. This percentage decreased to 41 percent in 1948, to 38 percent in 1958, and was only 22 percent in 1968. Seventy-one percent of the male supervising principals were under fifty years of age (median age forty-three), while 77 percent of the female supervising principals were under thirty-five, as compared with 2 percent of their male counterparts.[41] In a separate 1976 study of Illinois administrators, Carver found that though there were 102 women elementary principals age fifty-six years or older, less than 100 women teachers with administrative certificates were available from the prime age group (under thirty-six) to replace these women principals upon retirement.[42]

When asked why they chose the principalship, 20 percent of all the principals who participated in the national study indicated that they preferred administration and supervision over classroom teaching, 17 percent indicated that they needed a larger income, 30 percent considered the principalship to be especially important, and 30 percent were encouraged to take the principalship by the superintendent's office. Fifty-six percent of the female supervisory principals (as opposed to 16 percent of the men) took the principalship because they were encouraged to do so by the superintendent's office. This statistic is of interest in light of a recent study of the principalship which found that the most

[40]Information summarized in this section is abstracted from *The Elementary School Principalship on 1968 . . . A Research Study* (Washington, D.C.: Department of Elementary School Principals, National Education Association, 1968). This discussion follows Thomas J. Sergiovanni and David Elliot, *Educational and Organizational Leadership in Elementary Schools* (Englewood Cliffs, N.J.: Prentice-Hall, 1975), pp. 11–13.

[41]Mildred Bledenknapp and Jacob Goering, "How Masculine Are Male Teachers?" *Phi Delta Kappan*, Vol. 53, No. 2 (1971), 115.

[42]Fred D. Carver, "Administrative-Certification and Training in Illinois" (Urbana, Ill.: The Department of Administration, Higher and Continuing Education. University of Illinois, March 1976), Mimeo. For additional studies on women in administration see, Martin Burlingame, "Women in Illinois School Administration 1963-64 to 1975-76," (Urbana, Ill.: Department of Administration, Higher and Continuing Education, University of Illinois), Mimeo; and Stefen Krchniak, "Entry into School Administration by Women in Illinois: Facts and Dynamics" (Springfield, Ill.: Management Services Division, Illinois Office of Education, 1977).

effective principals had intended to teach but were encouraged to become principals by their superiors.[43]

The number of principals surveyed with master's or higher degrees has risen from 16 percent in 1928, 67 percent in 1948, and 82 percent in 1958, to 90 percent in 1968. Majors in graduate school were elementary school administration (47 percent), secondary school administration (4 percent), general school administration (20 percent), elementary school supervision and curriculum (10 percent), elementary school instruction (7 percent), and academic major (5 percent). Thirty-three percent of the female supervising principals had graduate majors in elementary supervision, curriculum, and instruction, as opposed to only 13 percent of the men.

These descriptions stongly imply that since 1928 the elementary school principalship has moved from a role open to all who could qualify to one dominated by men. There are few indications that we might see a reversal of this trend in the immediate future. Indeed, with only 2 percent of female principals under thirty-five and 77 percent over fifty, male domination seems relatively stable. Aside from issues of sex stereotyping and discrimination, with male domination it appears that fewer principals are prepared primarily in the areas of supervision, curriculum, and instruction. One might also infer that, since more female principals report being coaxed out of the classroom, male domination suggests that fewer principals will be oriented to or primarily identified with classroom life.

In a recent study of women administrators in Illinois, Pancrazio notes that women were better represented as elementary and high school principals in 1950 than today. She notes that the most significant decline was in elementary schools, where women accounted for 42 percent of the positions in 1952 but only 14 percent in 1976.[44]

Large numbers of men, the increased number of advanced degrees, and the popularity of majors in administration suggest that the elementary school principalship, as is similar with other educational administrative roles, is being increasingly professionalized as an entity separate from teaching. What is not known at this point is what effect professionalization of the principalship has on the effectiveness of the elementary school as an educational and socializing agency.

The plight of women in educational administration has not gone

[43]Gerald Becker et al., *Elementary School Principals and Their Schools* (Eugene, Ore.: University of Oregon, Center for the Advanced Study of Educational Administration, 1971) p. 2.

[44]Sally Buckley Pancrazio, " Women Administrators," *Illinois School Board Journal*, Vol. 45, no. 5 (1977), 27.

unnoticed by the profession. The UCEA, for example, provides extensive help to women and minorities seeking positions in educational administration. A computerized placement service is available through their organization. AASA's Office of Minority Affairs offers similar programs. This office, for example, recently received a Ford Foundation grant which will enable it to offer special increased employability workshops for women seeking superintendencies. Further, once women are employed, the office will provide on-site support teams to furnish guidance as needed. A typical support team would consist of an experienced superintendent, specialists in curriculum, business, and personnel, as well as a fifth person knowledgeable about problems of the individual employing district.[45]

SUMMARY

In this chapter a general overview of educational administration was provided. Administration was generally defined as the process of working with and through others to efficiently accomplish school goals. It was noted that some theorists prefer to define administration with a greater emphasis on deciding rather than doing. For them, administration is the art and science of decision making. Typically, a distinction is made between administrative and leadership behavior. Administrative behavior suggests operating within organizational structure and processes, and leadership behavior emphasizes the initiation of new structures, procedures, and goals. Though the distinction provides some advantages, a number of disadvantages were cited.

Chris Argyris' conception of organizational core activities was used to define four critical responsibility areas for educational administration: responsibility for *maintaining cultural patterns* is concerned with protecting and nurturing school and community tradition and cultural norms; responsibility for *goal attainment* is concerned with defining objectives and mobilizing resources to obtain them; responsibility for *external adaption* is concerned with school adjustment to its external environment; and responsibility for *internal maintenance* is concerned with structural coordination of different parts of the districts, and building a sense of loyalty and commitment among staff and students to the school. It was noted that, though difference in emphasis among schools exists, all four critical needs must be provided for to some degree by all schools and school districts.

[45]See for example, *Sex Equality in Educational Administration* (Arlington, VA: American Association of School Administrators, 1975) for specific suggestions to educational administration for improving sex-equality policy.

Administration was also defined as a process of functions. *Planning, organizing, leading,* and *controlling* were identified as the functions most often cited by authorities. Planning involves the setting of goals and the development of blueprints and strategies for their implementation; organizing involves the bringing together of human, financial, and physical resources; leading involves guiding, motivating, and supervising subordinates; and controlling involves evaluating performance.

Three critical administrative skills were identified: *technical, human,* and *conceptual.* Technical skills assume an understanding of and proficiency in the processes, procedures, and techniques of education and administration. Human skills refer to the ability to work effectively with others as an individual and on a group basis. Conceptual skill includes the ability to view the school as a whole, to understand the interdependent nature of its parts, and to determine meanings which result from administrative decisions. Critical responsibility areas for administration, critical administrative processes, and critical administrative skills were then used as building blocks to map the job of educational administration.

The relationship between educational leadership roles and responsibilities and those of management and politics were then discussed. Despite pressures for educational administrators to give more attention to functioning as manager and politician, it was pointed out that these roles are not ends in themselves, but exist to serve educational ends.

Educational administration was then examined as an emerging profession, and a brief historical account of its development was provided. It was noted that though the field developed rapidly during the 1950s and 1960s, the 1970s were marked by a growth plateau. A number of reasons were cited for this slowdown in development, including economic constraints, shifting priorities in federal and state policy, and declining student enrollments. Part of the slowdown was attributed to insufficient responsiveness to changing conditions by the educational-administration profession and by the educational-administration academic community.

The extent to which educational administration measures up to professional status was then examined. It was noted that though the field measured up to most professional standards, important difficulties exist which stem from the legal and organizational structure of education and from public accountability. Though professionalization of any occupation is typically seen as desirable, some negative consequences of increased professionalization of education administration were discussed. The chapter concluded with a selected demographic profile of the superintendency and the elementary principalship, including as part of the discussion the status of women in administration.

STUDY GUIDE

Can you recall the meaning of the following terms? Discuss them with a class colleague and/or apply them to your school-community setting.

administration as decision making
administration versus leadership
administrative processes
conceptual skills
designated professions
external adaption
goal attainment
human skills

internal maintenance
management
maintaining cultural patterns
professional criteria
recognized profession
technical skills
traditional values

SUGGESTED ACTIVITIES

1. Develop a list of national professional organizations in education. For each organization, identify its major purposes, target audience, and requirements for membership. What state and local affiliates exist for each organization? How do these organizations overlap in purpose, point of view, and membership, and how do they differ?

2. Many authorities advocate a common-cause type organization for education capable of attracting members from a variety of special-interest groups. If you were to develop such an organization in your state, what would be its purposes and how would you propose the organization be structured and governed?

3. What are the requirements for obtaining certification as an administrator or supervisor in your state? What certificates are offered? How do teacher organizations and other professional groups, state departments of education, and universities each influence the certification process? What are the purposes of licensing educational-administrator professionals? Can you identify disadvantages to present certification practices and procedures?

4. Write a short essay on how school board members and community members view educational administrators. To help sharpen your perceptions, attend school board meetings, study letters to the editor which have been written in the last few months, interview PTA or PTO leaders and members, and visit informally with friends and acquaintances.

SELECTED READINGS

American Association of School Administrators, *Profile of the Administrative Team*. Washington, D.C.: American Association of School Administrators, 1971.

CAMPBELL, ROALD F., and L. JACKSON NEWELL, *A Study of Professors of Educational Administration: Problems and Prospects of an Applied Field*. Columbus, Ohio: UCEA, 1973.

——, EDWIN BRIDGES, and RAPHAEL NYSTRAND, *Introduction to Educational Administration* (5th ed.), Boston: Allyn & Bacon, 1977.

CUBAN, LARRY, *Urban School Chiefs under Fire*. Chicago: University of Chicago Press, 1976.

HEMPHILL, JOHN K., JAMES M. RICHARDS, and RICHARD E. PETERSON, *Report of the Senior High School Principalship*. Washington: National Association of Secondary School Principals, 1965.

KIMBROUGH, RALPH, and MICHAEL NUNNERY, *Educational Administration: An Introduction*. New York: Macmillan, 1976.

KNEZEVICH, STEPHEN, *Administration of Public Education* (3rd ed.), New York: Harper & Row, Pub., 1975.

——, *The American School Superintendent*. Washington, D.C.: American Association of School Administrators, 1971.

MARCH, JAMES G., "American Public School Administration: A Short Analysis," *School Review*, February 1978, pp. 217–248.

MAYHEW, LEWIS B., *Educational Leadership and Declining Enrollment*. Berkeley: McCutchan Publishing Corp., 1974.

National Education Association, Department of Elementary School Principals, *The Elementary School Principalship in 1968*. Washington, D.C.: National Education Association, 1968.

2

THE DEVELOPMENT
OF THOUGHT
IN EDUCATIONAL
ADMINISTRATION

A general overview of educational administration was provided in Chapter 1. This overview included definitions of administration, a consideration of administrative critical responsibility areas, processes, and tasks associated with administration, and an analysis of educational administration as a field of professional practice. Special attention was given to the importance of educational leadership roles. This chapter is concerned with the intellectual heritage of educational administration. Administrators and other professionals practice their art from certain perspectives or accepted ways of operating which are directly related to the development of thought in their respective fields over time. It is for this reason that professional practice in any field can be better understood by examining its intellectual heritage.

In many school districts across the country, patterns of organization and administration are remarkably similar, and a fair amount of reliability can be seen in administrative actions across these districts. Personnel and student-policy manuals, for example, tend to read the same, and teacher-board contracts are strikingly similar. School structure and management arrangements strike a familiar cord as one moves from state to state and place to place. But though many similarities exist in organization and management structure, differences still exist among schools, particularly in the style of administration and in the tone or climate of the school as an organization. With respect to certain administrative issues—how schools should be organized, for example—professional-practice norms have arisen which seem to govern administrative actions. For other issues—the extent to which teachers should be involved in decision making, for example—less agreement is evident and more diversity in practice can be observed. Norms tend to be more fixed as one goes up the ladder of abstraction to issues of how schools should be organized, structured, and governed, and less fixed as one moves down to such issues as proper administrative behavior, organizational climate, and educational-program administration. These latter concerns seem more directly related to assumptions and beliefs of individual administrators regarding such management issues as control, participation, authority, and the nature of humans, and are therefore more susceptible to differences.

Much can be learned about patterns of agreement and disagreement among administrators by examining the major strands of thought from which practice norms emerge. Such norms and the standard behaviors which accompany them are more common in the established professions such as medicine, law, and science. In these fields, best practice in a given situation seems to be defined as that which exemplifies the normative response of most professionals for that situation. Practitioners are judged by their ability to respond reliably to similar problems. In determining medical malpractice, for example, the emphasis is more on whether the practitioner followed standard professional procedures than on his or her basic competence. Similarly, in the research professions a scientist evaluates a research report on the basis of its meeting accepted standards for research design and on its consistency to accepted theory. In the legal profession, law tradition dictates that governmental policies emerge logically in accordance with established case-law precedents, with present circumstances often being secondary. Among administrators, an administrative action is evaluated by peers for compatibility with such management norms as proper documentation, and an administrator is considered careless for not putting directions and decisions in writing.

MODELS OF ADMINISTRATIVE PRACTICE

In the more established professions, and to a lesser extent in educational administration, frames of reference, models, or paradigms govern professional practice. The terms *frames of reference, models,* and *paradigms* are used by theorists to refer to systematic ways of thinking and to other approximations of reality which help to more fully understand this reality. Generally, *frames of reference* refer to mini-views, *models* to intermediate views, and *paradigms* to macro-views. For the purpose of discussion, the term *model* will generally be used to encompass the three. Models are systematic approximations of reality. They come complete with a convincing internal logic, set of assumptions, postulates, data, and inferences about some phenomena. Sometimes models are formal and explicit, but often models are implicit—and indeed, are articulated unknowingly by administrators. Models determine what problems are critical for a particular profession and provide the practitioner with a theoretical framework for understanding and dealing with problems. Models underlying the administration of special education, for example, emphasize remediation of difficulties rather than prevention. Thus special-education administrators are more likely to be concerned with the critical problem of learning disabilities in urban youth than with poor nutrition of pregnant women in urban areas, though the first seems causally related to the second.

Models undergirding the various professions also suggest to the practitioner certain actions or routines as being more valid than others, and suggest certain standards of proof for determining effectiveness of these methods. An administrator who operates from a "human relation" model, for example, might consider interpersonal relationships as the critical administrative priority in a school. This administrator would employ specific techniques, such as participating in decision making, to improve these relationships, and would judge his or her effectiveness by positive changes in morale of the staff. An administrator who operates from an "accountability" model might consider increased performance as the critical concern in this same school. This administrator would employ specific techniques such as management by objectives (MBO) and teaching by objectives (TBO) to improve performance, and would judge his or her effectiveness by the number of objectives achieved. The behavior and orientation of each administrator is governed by the model from which he or she is working.

Substantial changes in professional practice are not likely to occur as a result of tinkering here or there, but rather as a result of substantial shifts in the models which characterize thinking for that profession. In discussing this point, Thomas Kuhn argues that science does not change as a result of piecemeal accumulation of knowledge, but by "conceptual revolutions" which result in critical shifts in the intellectual thinking for a particular field—changes in its prevailing models or paradigms.[1] This chapter examines the development of thought in

[1]Thomas Kuhn, *The Structure of Scientific Revolution* (Chicago: University of Chicago Press, 1962).

modern administration, seeking to identify the major models which undergird the profession and the shifts in these models which help explain changes in professional practice.

MAJOR STRANDS OF THOUGHT IN ADMINISTRATION

Examining the development of thought in educational administration has its problems. The knowledge base within this field is weak, and the profession has relied heavily on concepts and ideas borrowed from other areas. Further, because of the complexity and social significance of administration in general, its intellectual roots encompass a number of diverse disciplines. Dwight Waldo, for example, noted that "indeed no discipline is without relevance for administration . . . and administrative study is relevant for every discipline."[2] To simplify matters, recent intellectual development in administration will be grouped into three major strands of thought, each of which suggests a fairly distinct model for viewing administration. One is characterized by a concern for *efficiency;* the second, a concern for the *person;* and the third, a concern for *politics and decision making.*

The efficiency period began in the early 1900s and remained popular until about 1930. Of course, prior to this time a field of administration existed and organizations functioned. But the early 1900s period marked the systematic study of administration as if it were a science, and was characterized by the development of a literature on administration and the formal study of administration at the university level. It is generally recognized that modern academic administration and contemporary professional-administrative practice were born of this period. Person models of organization and administration were predominant from about 1930 to 1960s and remain popular today in the literature and among practitioners. Politics and decision-making views span a period from the end of World War II to the present. This view is now considered by many to dominate present thinking in educational administration. Though models characterized by a concern for efficiency and a concern for the person have "had their day," they have not been replaced completely. Both enjoy advocates from the university context and from within the practicing profession; indeed, much of what the models offer remains appropriate and can be incorporated into political and decision-making views. In spite of their present popularity, political and decision-making views, too, will be replaced by

[2]Dwight Waldo, *The Study of Administration* (Garden City, N.Y. Doubleday 1955), p. 55.

others as part of the natural progression of knowledge expansion in our field.

Academic advocates of one or another model are often ideological and dogmatic about what good practice is in educational administration. Ideas from competing models are viewed negatively. Though academic battles over which view is "best" are of interest to practicing administration, most experienced administrators assume a more moderate and tolerant posture by looking for the good in all views. Therefore, as we briefly overview the three major strands of thought, keep in mind that each has features which are appropriate to certain aspects of professional practice but not to others. *Further, when used exclusively, none of the views is sufficiently comprehensive or true to be helpful.* The efficiency model, for example, can be helpful in establishing high-school scheduling routines or in developing a series of attendance or purchasing management policies. Applying insights from the same model to problems of teacher motivation, supervision, and evaluation, however, is likely to result in serious staff morale problems. As the strands of thought and inferred models are discussed and compared, therefore, keep in mind the costs and benefits of using each in professional practice. This analysis should help one to use the models as alternative possibilities, each appropriate to different aspects of practice.

CONCERN FOR EFFICIENCY

Schools today are organized and operated according to certain established principles of "good management." A division of labor exists whereby instructional and coordinative tasks are allocated to specific roles. Roles are defined by job descriptions which are clearly linked to some overall conception of what the school is to accomplish. Certain guides, such as span of control and student-teacher ratio, have been accepted to help decide the number of teachers needed and how they should be assigned. Tasks are subdivided and specialists are hired for some functions. Roles are ordered according to rank, with some enjoying more authority and privilege than others. The development of rank helps to ensure that those who are lower in the hierarchy will function in manners consistent with job expectations and goals. Day-by-day decisions are routinized and controlled by establishing and monitoring a system of policies and roles. These, in turn, ensure more reliable behavior on behalf of goals. Proper communication channels are established and objective mechanisms are developed for handling disputes, allocating resources, and evaluating personnel.

If one were given the task of building, from scratch, an administrative and organizational design for a new school system, it is likely that most of the manifestations of "good management" described above would be incorporated into the design. An organizational chart would likely be constructed, depicting an array of school roles from superintendent and staff, through principal and teacher, to students. Staff personnel such as counselors and curriculum coordinators would be included. Each would be depicted in a fashion which delineates their rank and suggests normal lines of communication within and between ranks. Each of the roles depicted on the organizational chart would be backed up by a job description which would define the role incumbent's major responsibilities and tasks. Second-grade teachers, for example, would be given responsibilities and tasks different from those of the guidance counselor, kindergarten teacher, athletic director, attendance officer, purchasing assistant, physics teacher, elementary principal, and diversified occupations teachers. Responsibilities and tasks for each role would be linked to a more grand scheme of activities directed at certain school goals and functions. Policies and roles would be developed to ensure that teachers and others would respond similarly to similar situations. A system of supervision and evaluation would be provided to ensure that each role incumbent was performing "up to par." *Par* would be defined as performing one's job in accordance with certain implicit and explicit expectations, which would be validated by extent of contribution to job objectives and school goals.

Good management, *defined in this sense,* is directed at the efficient achievement of certain ends. But efficiency cannot be accidental; it requires a great deal of deliberate and calculated planning. The ends must be clearly defined and the means carefully determined and stipulated. If means are implemented precisely according to plan, ends are likely to be accomplished efficiently. These efficiency values and ideas are widely accepted and practiced in the administration of our schools. In the section which follows, sources of these values and ideas are briefly explored.

SCIENTIFIC MANAGEMENT AND THE EFFICIENCY MODEL

Much of what is taken for granted as good management today can be traced to an era of development in administration referred to as *scientific management.* This movement contributed greatly to the establishment of professional management in general and of educational administration in particular as a unique field of study and a distinct professional career. Frederick Winslow Taylor is credited as the founding father of the scientific-management movement. Taylor's impact on organization and management in education is now a matter of record, and will only be briefly reviewed.[3]

In his *Principles of Scientific Management,* published in 1911, Taylor offered four principles which were the foundation for his science of work and organization.[4] The first was to replace intuitive methods of doing the work of the organization with a scientific method based on observation and analysis to obtain the best cost-benefit ratio. He felt that for every task a *one best way* should be determined. The second principle was to scientifically select the best person for the job and train this person thoroughly in the tasks and procedures to be followed. The third principle was to "heartily cooperate with the men" to ensure that the work is being done according to established standards and procedures; the fourth, to divide the work of managers and workers so that managers assume responsibility for planning and preparing work and for supervising. Taylor's ideas quickly found their way into the study and practice of educational administration. Franklin Bobbitt, an educator of the period and an advocate of scientific management, stated:

> In any organization, the directive and supervisory members must clearly define the ends toward which the organization strives. They must co-ordinate the labors of all so as to attain those ends. They must find the best methods of work, and they must enforce the use of these methods on the part of the workers. They must determine the qualifications necessary for the workers and see that each rises to the standard qualifications, if it is possible; and when impossible, see that he is separated from the organization. This requires direct or indirect responsibility for the preliminary training of workers before service and for keeping them up to standard qualifications during service. Directors and supervisors must keep the workers supplied with detailed instructions as to the work to be done, the standards to be reached, the methods to be employed, and the materials and appliances to be used. They must place incentives before the worker in order to stimulate desirable effort. Whatever the nature or purpose of the organization, if it is an effective one, these are always the directive and supervisory tasks.[5]

[3]Raymond, Callahan, *Education and the Cult of Efficiency* (Chicago: University of Chicago Press, 1962).

[4]Frederick, Taylor, *The Principles of Scientific Management* (New York: Harper & Row, 1911. Reprinted by Harper & Row in 1945.

[5]Franklin, Bobbitt, "The Supervision of City Schools: Some General Principles of Management Applied to the Problems of City School Systems." *Twelfth Yearbook of the National Society for the Study of Education* (Bloomington, Ill, 1913).

For the next three decades, basic concepts and strategies of the efficiency model were applied to the broader question of administration and organizational design by many European and American writers. Henri Fayol offered a universal list of good-managment principles which became very popular.[6] These included division of work, authority, and responsibility, discipline, unity of command, and unity of direction. Gulick and Urwich offered the principles of unity of command, span of control, and matching of people to the organizational structure.[7] They were advocates of division of work, not only by purpose, but by process, person, and place. Scientific management did not offer a theory of administration and organization as such, but a set of principles and simple injunctions for administrators to follow. Efficiency was to be maximized by defining objectives and outputs clearly, by specializing tasks through division of labor, and—once the *best way* is identified —by introducing a system of controls to insure uniformity and reliability in workers' tasks and to insure standardization of product.

The following principles of management offered by Fayol are examples of the efficiency literature of administration in the management of schools—all of which are still used today in various degrees:

1. *Division of work* based on task specialization should be practiced. Jobs should be broken down into small parts and grouped in a fashion which permits individuals to work on only a limited number.

2. *Authority* should be clearly delineated so that responsibilities of each worker are known and their relationships to others worker, up, across, or down the hierarchical chain, are clear.

3. *Discipline* should be established in the sense that superiors (administrators and teachers, in our case) have a right to expect deference and obedience from subordinates.

4. *Unity of command* should be practiced as a mechanism for clearly delineating authority relationships. Fayol believed that an employee should receive direction from and in return be accountable to only one superior. (One of the arguments often cited in opposition to team-teaching plans is that the traditional authority structure of the teacher and students becomes confused and students are not sure to whom they "belong.")

5. *Unity of direction,* whereby each objective should be accompanied by a specific plan for achievement of a specific group of people who would be accountable for achieving that objective.

[6]Henri, Fayol, *General and Industrial Management,* trans. Constance Storrs (London: Sir Isaac Pitman and Sons, 1949).

[7]Luther, Gulick., and L. Urwick, eds., *Papers on the Science of Administration* (New York: Institute of Public Administration, 1937).

6. *Subordination of individual interest* in favor of those of the organization and of the work group should be encouraged.

7. *Remuneration* should be fair but routinized so that unreasonable over-payments are avoided. The standard salary schedule, for example, is considered better than merit pay.

8. *Centralization* of decision-making should be practiced to permit proper coordination, with judicious decentralization accompanied by proper controls when needed.

9. *Scalar chain,* as a mechanism for defining the line of command and flow of communication from the highest to lowest rank, should be practiced.

10. Material and social *order* should be the rule to ensure that everything and everyone is in the proper place.

11. *Equity* should be practiced, in the sense that justice should govern administrative action.

12. *Stability* of tenure of personnel is desirable and should be sought.

13. *Initiative* should be encouraged at all levels of the organization.

14. *Esprit,* in the form of harmony and unity of workers, should be encouraged.[8]

Some would argue that the first ten of Fayol's principles contradict the last four. Equity, stability, initiative, and esprit are likely to suffer in the absence of more flexibility and greater distribution of authority.

Lyndall Urwick, a British scholar of the day, developed a summary view of the state of the art by reviewing the works of Taylor, Fayol, and others and by identifying twenty-nine principles of efficient management—or elements of administration, as he called them. In his words,

> the fact that these principles collected from the writings of half a dozen different people, many of whom made no attempt to correlate their work with that of others, can be presented in a coherent and logical pattern is in itself strong evidence that there is a common element in all experience of the conduct of social group, that a true science is ultimately possible.[9]

The twenty-nine principles are shown in Figure 2–1. The principles are validated as appropriate elements of administration and evaluated for effective articulation on the basis of their contributions to and accomplishment of efficiency in work and organization. Efficiency principles persevere today as strong considerations in curriculum development, in selecting educational materials, in developing instructional systems,

[8]Fayol, *General and Industrial Management,* pp. 20–40.
[9]Lyndall, Urwick, *The Elements of Administration* (New York: Harper & Row, 1943), p. 118.

FIGURE 2-1

Twenty-nine principles which comprise the elements of administration.

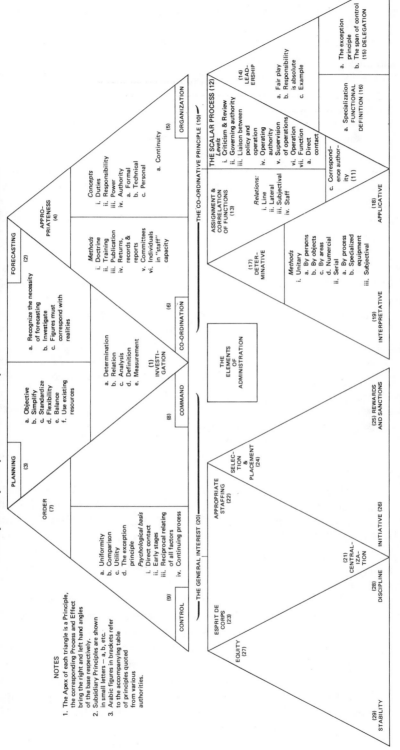

Source: Lyndall Urwick, *The Elements of Administration.* New York: Harper & Row, 1943, pp. 118–19.

47

and in other aspects of educational administration. Scientific-management thinking has weathered ups and downs for three quarters of a century, and today enjoys a resurgence in education. Fueled by demands for accountability, economic recession, and political conservatism in our society, and by advancements in management techniques (such as operation research, system analysis, and computer systems), earlier scientific management has emerged into a new, more sophisticated form. In education this neoscientific or modern scientific management offers such efficiency ideas as performance contracting, behavioral objectives, state and national assessment, cost-benefit analysis, Management by Objectives (MBO), Planning Programming Budgeting Systems (PPBS), and Management Information System (MIS), each prescribed to maximize educational reliability and productivity at decreased costs. Neoscientific management shares with older versions of the efficiency model heavy management reliance on norms of rationality as it pursues accountability, control, and efficiency, and seeks greater reliability in the organization and operation of schools.

Traditional scientific-management control mechanisms such as face-to-face supervision, however, are replaced in neoscientific management by more impersonal, technical, or rational control mechanisms. It is assumed, for example, that if visible standards of performance, objectives, or competencies can be identified and measured, then the work of teachers and that of students can be better controlled by holding them accountable to these standards, thus insuring greater reliability, effectiveness, and efficiency in performance. In 1977, for example, the number of states with some form of competency requirement for high school graduation increased from 16 to 26, a sign of the resurgency of scientific management ideas.

Scientific-management theories provide administrators with a rational model from which to work. The rational model assumes that the educational administrator is capable of identifying objectives, arranging the work and instructing workers accordingly, supervising in a fashion which ensures that work will be done properly, and evaluating performance and products against original objectives. The issue of motivating workers is handled similarly. Since it is assumed that persons are primarily motivated by economic and other extrinsic incentives, they will do that which brings them the greatest extrinsic gain. Workers can be controlled by manipulating these incentives. Applications of scientific-management thinking and the rational model are perhaps most easily recognized in the organization and instruction of many classrooms. Decisions with respect to class objectives, assignments, activities, and supervision of students are made unilaterally by teachers. Students are evaluated against class objectives, and grades are the primary incentive offered to students. If the curriculum is programmed in sufficient detail, teachers play a minor role in this process, that of following and giving directions, and are themselves supervised and evaluated according to scientific-management principles by administrators.

BUREAUCRATIC THEORIES AND THE EFFICIENCY MODEL

Though principles of scientific managements were enthusiastically adopted in both industry and education, they were not a full-fledged theory of organization and administration. The German sociologist Max Weber proposed a pure form or idealization of an organization which he called *bureaucracy.*[10] This idealization was in the form of a set of structural properties and characteristics such as hierarchy, division of work, rules, and procedures. Further, impersonality and objectivity were suggested as management principles in dealing with workers such as teachers and students. In the interest of efficiency, an organization should have a well-defined *hierarchy* of authority, with jobs and offices defined with reference to jurisdiction and location; a *division of work* based on functional specialization; a system of *rules* which spell out the rights and responsibilities of workers; a system of *procedures* for dealing with categories of activities within areas of responsibility; relationships characterized by *impersonality;* and a reward structure based on technical *competence.*

Bureaucratic thinking refined the norms of rationality and certainty that were characteristic of scientific management. It was assumed that all aspects of the organization, from its objectives, technical requirements, and work flow, to the details of its organizational structure, could be defined and organized into a permanent grand design. All that remained was to find people who could be programmed into this design. According to Weber,

the fully developed bureaucratic mechanism compares with other organizations exactly as does the machine with the non-mechanical modes of production . . . precision, speed, unambiguity, continuity, discretion, unity, . . . these are raised to the optimum point in a strictly bureaucratic administration. . . .

[10]Max, Weber, "Bureaucracy," in Max Weber, *Essays in Sociology,* trans. and ed. H. H. Gerth and C. W. Mills (Oxford University Press, 1946); Reprinted in Joseph Litterer, *Organizations: Structure and Behavior.* (New York: John Wiley, 1969). Max, Weber, *The Theory of Social and Economic Organization,* trans. A. M. Henderson and T. Parsons, ed. T. Parsons (New York: Free Press, 1947).

> The individual bureaucrat cannot squirm out of the apparatus in which he is harnessed ... in a great majority of cases, he is only a single cog in an ever moving mechanism which prescribes to him an eventually fixed route of march.[11]

Bureaucracy shares with scientific management the assumptions of rationality and economic conceptions of humans. Persons are primarily motivated by economic (or other extrinsic) concerns, and work to maximize their economic gain. But economic gain is under control of the organization, and the person is to be engineered and controlled by this organization. The individual rationality of scientific management is replaced by organizational rationality as defined by standard operating procedures, formal organization charts, job descriptions, policy manuals, and other organizational routines. It is this impersonal quality of organizational rationality which suggests the metaphor *mechanistic* when one speaks of bureaucratic theories.

Mechanistic images view the school as a well-oiled machine capable of rationally organizing human talents for the production of services to clients. Goals are not the issue, having presumably been either decided by some higher authority or implied from organizational arrangements. Rather, the attention of administrators is on discovering the most rational structure and the most efficient work routines for achieving these goals. Impartiality, objectivity, and order are further administrative concerns. For these reasons, the rational structures sought by administrators are formalized into standardized and reliable arrangements. The major problem for administrators is how to handle diverse inputs in a fashion which produces a standard outcome. Consider the typical secondary school with its monolithic curriculum, standard teaching, common expectations, and uniform grading practices. Here youngsters with different needs, abilities, and interests are processed *similarly* in accordance with *identical* standards in pursuit of *common* goals. Comprehensive high schools offer some relief by offering students programmatic choices such as vocational or college prep, but once a student is properly tracked or elects a course, standard processing resumes.

The traditional organizational chart depicting roles and relationships within the school structure is a representation of many of the values of bureaucratic thinking. One such chart is illustrated in Figure 2-2. In such charts care is taken to clearly define roles and establish specific lines of communication and authority. It takes only limited experience in schools, however, to realize that, in spite of the organiza-

[11]Weber, Ibid., 1946. pp. 34–37.

tional chart's rational conception, an informal organization tends to develop and function—which, if accurately mapped, would be at odds with the formal organization.

Bureaucracy remains a part of the image of most educational organizations, and its advocates work diligently to incorporate its principles of order and certainty. Though the relatively harsh conception of humankind typically associated with this efficiency model may not fully characterize the relationships which generally exist between administrators and teachers, this conception remains ubiquitous as applied to students. Indeed, as one might well predict from bureaucratic thought, the lower one is in the organizational hierarchy, the more he

FIGURE 2–2
An example of a school district organizational chart

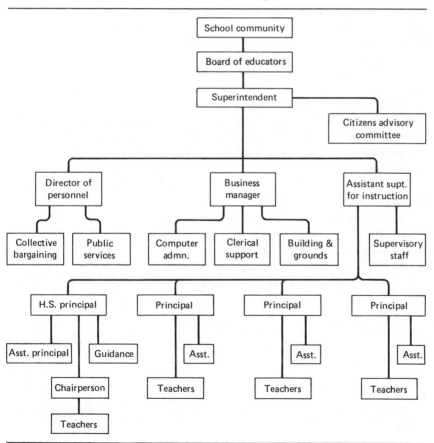

or she will be seen as fitting the underlying assumptions of human characteristics of the efficiency model.

CONCERN FOR THE PERSON

The emphasis in both scientific-management and bureaucratic theories is on increasing efficiency of the entire school organization as it achieves its goals. Bureaucracy emphasizes structuring the organization properly, defining roles, and assigning functions. Scientific management emphasizes the development of control systems which can engineer the work to ensure standard output. In each case, certain aspects of organization and administration are emphasized and better understood, but other aspects are neglected or given only secondary status. Neither scientific-management nor bureaucratic thinking give adequate attention to the human side of life in educational organizations. Such issues, for example, as individual personality and human needs, and such conditions as job satisfaction, motivation, and morale seem clearly secondary.

By the 1930s an effective counterforce on behalf of the human side of enterprise was to emerge. This force was later to evolve into a distinct pattern of thought about administration which we label as the *person model*. The metaphor *organic* is used to describe person views. The analogy is that of a biological organism capable of feeling and growing but also capable of ill-health if not properly nurtured. Maintenance and nurturance of the human organization are important concerns of administrators who operate within the person model. The building blocks to organizational health are individuals and their needs and groups of individuals. According to this view, an ideal school is one characterized by highly motivated individuals who are committed to school objectives from which they derive intrinsic satisfaction. These individuals are linked together into highly effective work groups. The work groups are characterized by commitment to common school objectives, by group loyalty, and by mutual support. Whereas scientific management and bureaucracy emphasize *task* specialization, person views emphasize *person* specialization. Task specialization requires the careful sectioning, dividing, and assigning of work by those in authority. Person specialization permits individuals to function as experts who enjoy discretionary prerogatives and who are influenced more by client needs and their own expert abilities than by carefully delineated duties and tasks. Person views will be divided into two phases, human relations and human resources, with the latter being an extension and further development of the former. Let us first consider human relations.

HUMAN RELATIONS AND THE
PERSON VIEW

The benchmark most frequently mentioned as the beginning of the human relations movement in administration is the work of the research team which operated from 1922 to 1932 at the Cicero, Illinois, Hawthorne plant of the Western Electric Company. This research team, headed by Elton Mayo and Fritz Roethlishberger, sought to determine the relationship between such physical factors as level of lighting at the work place, rest periods, and length of the work day on increased performance of workers.[12] They found that regardless of whether physical conditions such as lighting, rest periods, and length of the workday were positively or negatively varied, production continued to increase. They finally concluded that changes in physical job conditions did not result in increased production; rather, such increases seemed to result in changed social conditions of the worker. Changes in worker motivation and satisfaction were most often credited with increased production. These, in turn, seemed related to more democratic patterns of supervision used by the researchers and others during the experiments. Relative to existing conditions, workers received unprecedented attention from researchers, were able to easily socialize with other workers, and had some say in deciding working conditions. These conditions, in turn, seemed to have resulted in higher motivation and commitment levels, greater effort at work, and higher production records for persons involved in the Hawthorne experiment.[13]

Elton Mayo's work is of particular importance to the development of this movement. His extensive interview studies at Western Electric revealed that workers subjected to more efficiency-oriented management suffered from acute alienation and loss of identity. As a result of his work, Mayo offered a set of assumptions to characterize people, which were quite different from those of efficiency management. He suggested that persons are primarily motivated by social needs and

[12]Frederick, Roethlisberger., and William Dickson, *Management and the Worker*. (Cambridge, Mass.: Harvard University Press, 1939).

[13]The phenomena of working hard because of the feeling of participating in something very special and very new has come to be known among the research community as the "Hawthorne effect."

obtain their basic satisfaction from relationships with others. He maintained that management had robbed work of meaning, and therefore meaning must be provided in the social relationships on the job. On the basis of his interviews, Mayo also concluded that persons are more responsive to the social forces of their peer group than to extrinsic incentives and management controls. And finally, a person's identity and loyalty to management and organization depended upon his or her ability to provide for self-social (interaction and acceptance) needs.[14]

Humane leadership principles which took into account the social group, satisfaction of workers' social needs, and psychological manipulation of workers through counseling were examples of management to be gleaned from the historic Hawthorne studies.

The now famous analysis and comparison of Theories X and Y by Douglas McGregor is a good representation of human-relations thinking. McGregor believed that Theory-X and Theory-Y managers behaved differently because they had internalized two very different theories of management. Theory X was comprised of assumptions and propositions generally associated with efficiency views of administration. Theory Y, on the other hand, had a higher regard for the value and potential of the person. The assumptions and propositions of theories X and Y are listed below.[15]

Theory X

1. *The average human being has an inherent dislike of work and will avoid it if he can.*

2. *Because of this human characteristic of dislike of work, most people must be coerced, controlled, directed, threatened with punishment to get them to put forth adequate effort toward the achievement of organizational objectives.*

3. *The average human being prefers to be directed, wishes to avoid responsibility, has relatively little ambition, wants security above all.*

[14]Elton Mayo, *The Social Problems of an Industrial Civilization* (Boston: Harvard Graduate School of Business, 1945).

[15]The genesis for these assumptions is McGregor's essay, "The Human Side of Enterprise," which appears in Warren G. Bennis and Edgar H. Schein, eds., *Leadership and Motivation: Essays of Douglas McGregor* (Cambridge, Mass.: M.I.T., 1966), p. 5. The essay first appeared in *Adventure in Thought and Action*. Proceedings of the Fifth Anniversary Convocation of the School of Industrial Management, M.I.T., Apr. 9, 1957. The article has been reprinted in *The Management Review*, vol. 46, No. 11 (1951), 22–28.

Theory Y

1.   *The expenditure of physical and mental effort in work is as natural as play or rest.* The average human being does not inherently dislike work. Depending upon controllable conditions, work may be a source of satisfaction (and will be voluntarily performed) or a source of punishment (and will be avoided if possible).

2.   *External control and the threat of punishment are not the only means for bringing about effort toward organizational objectives. Man will exercise self-direction and self-control in the service of objectives to which he is committed.*

3.   *Commitment to objectives is a function of the rewards associated with their achievement.* The most significant of such rewards, e.g., the satisfaction of ego and self-actualization needs, can be direct products of effort directed toward organizational objectives.

4.   *The average human being learns, under proper conditions, not only to accept but to seek responsibility.* Avoidance of responsibility, lack of ambition, and emphasis on security are generally consequences of experience, not inherent human characteristics.

5.   *The capacity to exercise a relatively high degree of imagination, ingenuity, and creativity in the solution of organizational problems is widely, not narrowly, distributed in the population.*

6.   *Under the conditions of modern industrial life, the intellectual potentialities of the average human being are only partially utilized.* [16]

Human-relations thought is often criticized for overemphasizing human social needs at the expense of needs for accomplishment and responsibility. As a result, a person's social needs were often considered separate from other concerns more directly related to the tasks of the organization. It was assumed that as long as a worker was happy and comfortable, he or she would show little interest in the policy decision affecting his or her work.

HUMAN RESOURCES AND THE PERSON VIEW

Human relations began to mature with the work of Kurt Lewin as he sought to link human behavior more closely with such environmental factors as role expectations and organizational climate. His social-

---

[16]Douglas McGregor, *The Human Side of Enterprise* (New York, McGraw-Hill, 1960) pp. 33–34, 47–48.

systems view of persons in organizations provided a more complete picture of reality.[17] The writings of Abraham Maslow, Douglas McGregory, Chris Arygris, Warren Bennis, and Rensis Likert became the new tenets as human-relations thought matured. These theorists had academic credentials in social psychology or in the new interdisciplinary field at the time—organizational psychology.[18] Some authors would refer to this maturity of human relations as *human resources,* to suggest the change of emphasis from social needs of individuals at work to needs expressed as a desire for more intrinsic satisfaction from increased organizational responsibility and from achievement of organizational goals.[19]

Human-resources theorists agreed with earlier human-relations writers that an efficiency model typically resulted in loss of meaning in work. But this loss was not attributed to neglect of a person's social needs as much as to his or her inability to use talents fully. Certainly social needs were not to be denied, but a person's capacity for growth and challenge were the needs which received the greatest attention by human-resources theorists.

The nature of interaction between personality and organization became the key focus of study. Human-relations theorists viewed personality and organization as being hopelessly in conflict and sided with personality. Efficiency theorists shared this view, but its advocates sided with organization. Human resources recognized personality and organization conflict, but did not view it as inherent. According to this view, the two were to be integrated, with workers receiving maximum satisfaction and enrichment from achievement at work, and work in turn reaching new levels of effectiveness because of worker commitment to organizational goals.

Human resources urged that shared decision making, joint planning, common goals, increased responsibility, and more autonomy were the sorts of power-equalization strategies to be developed by educational administrators. Motivation was to be intrinsic because jobs were to be interesting and challenging. Job enrichment was advocated as a

[17]Kurt Lewin, *Field Theory in Social Science* (New York: Harper & Row. 1951).

[18]See, for example, McGregor, *The Human Side of Enterprise* and Rensis Likert, *The Human Organization* (New York: McGraw-Hill, 1967) For examples, c.f., books in educational administration identified with this era: see Jacob Getzels, James Lipham, and Roald Campbell, *Administration as a Social Process* (New York Harper & Row); Thomas Sergiovanni and Fred D. Carver, *The New School Executive: A Theory of Administration.* (New York: Dodd Mead, 1973, Harper & Row, 1975).

[19]See, for example, Raymond E. Miles, "Human Relations or Human Resources?" *Harvard Business Review,* Vol. 43, No. 4 1965) and Thomas J. Sergiovanni and Robert J. Starratt, *Supervision Human Perspectives,* 2nd ed. (New York: McGraw-Hill, 1979).

TABLE 2-1

Comparing human relations and human resources views

Human relations model	Human resources model
Attitudes Toward People	
1. People in our culture, teachers among them, share a common set of needs—to belong, to be liked, to be respected.	1. In addition to sharing common needs for belonging and respect, most people in our culture, teachers among them, desire to contribute effectively and creatively to the accomplishment of worthwhile objectives.
2. While teachers desire individual recognition, they more importantly want to *feel* useful to the school and to their own work group.	2. The majority of teachers are capable of exercising far more initiative, responsibility, and creativity than their present jobs or work circumstances require or allow.
3. They tend to cooperate willingly and comply with school goals if these important needs are fulfilled.	3. These capabilities represent untapped resources which are presently being wasted.
Kind and Amount of Participation	
1. The administrator's basic task is to make each teacher believe that he or she is a useful and important part of the team.	1. The administrator's basic task is to create an environment in which subordinates can contribute their full range of talents to the accomplishment of school goals. He or she works to uncover the creative resources of subordinates.
2. The administrator is willing to explain his or her decisions and to discuss subordinates' objections to the plans. On routine matters, he or she encourages subordinates in planning and in decision making.	2. The administrator allows and encourages teachers to participate in important as well as routine decisions. In fact, the more important a decision is to the school, the greater the administrator's efforts to tap faculty resources.
3. Within narrow limits, the faculty or individual teachers who make up the faculty should be allowed to exercise self-direction and self-control in carrying out plans.	3. Administrators work continually to expand the areas over which teaches exercise self-direction and self-control as they develop and demonstrate greater insight and ability.
Expectations	
1. Sharing information with teachers and involving them in school decision making will help satisfy their basic needs for belonging and for individual recognition.	1. The overall quality of decision making and performance will improve as administrators and teachers make use of the full range of experience, insight, and creative ability which exists in their schools.

57

TABLE 2-1 (cont.)

2. Satisfying these needs will improve faculty morale and will reduce resistance to formal authority.	2. Teachers will exercise responsible self-direction and self-control in the accomplishment of worthwhile objectives that they understand and have helped establish.
3. High faculty morale and reduced resistance to formal authority may lead to improved school performance. It will at least reduce friction and make the administrator's job easier.	3. Faculty satisfaction will increase as a by-product of improved performance and the opportunity to contribute creatively to this improvement.

Adapted from Raymond E. Miles "Human Relations or Human Resources?" *Harvard Business Review*, vol. 43, no. 4, pp. 148–163, 1965, exhibits I and II.

means to build into the jobs of students and teachers increased opportunities for experiencing achievement, recognition, advancement, opportunities for growth, and increased competence. Human-resources theories reflected not only an interest in people at work, but also a new regard for their potential. Teachers, for example, were to be considered as professionals well able to respond to these progressive, optimizing ideas. In education, such organizational concepts as team teaching, family grouping, open space, school within a school, open corridor, integrated day, and multi-unit are often based on human resources-concepts. In Table 2-1 assumptions basic to human-relations views and human-resources views are summarized and compared.

Person views of administration, particularly human-resources, place a great deal of emphasis on autonomy, inner direction, and the desire for maximum self-development at work. As long as these conditions hold for teachers at one level and for students at another, then the optimizing characteristics of these views are likely to work. But the desire for universal self-actualization and the centrality of the work setting in one's life are debatable. In speaking of this issue, Robert Dubin notes that

> work, for probably a majority of workers, and even extending into the ranks of management, may represent an institutional setting that is not the central life interest of the participants. The consequence of this is that while participating in work, a general attitude of apathy and indifference prevails. . . . Thus, the industrial worker does not feel imposed upon by the tyranny of organizations, company, or union.[20]

[20]Robert Dubin, "Industrial Research and the Discipline of Sociology" in Proceedings of the 11th Annual Meeting. Industrial Relation Research Association, (Madison, WIS, 1959), p. 161. as quoted in George Strauss, "Some notes on Power Equalization," in Harold J. Leavitt, ed, *The Social Science of Organization*. (Englewood Cliffs, N.J.: Prentice-Hall, 1963), p. 48.

And George Strauss cautions:

1.   Although many individuals find relatively little satisfaction in their work, this may not be as much of a deprivation as the hypothesis would suggest, since many of these same individuals center their lives off the job and find most of their satisfactions in the community and the home. With these individuals, power-equalization may not liberate much energy.

2.   Individuals are not motivated solely to obtain autonomy, self-actualization, and so forth. With various degrees of emphasis, individuals also want security and to know what is expected of them. Power-equalization may certainly stir up a good deal of anxiety among those who are not prepared for it, and at least some individuals may be reluctant to assume the responsibility that it throws upon them.

3.   Power-equalization techniques are not too meaningful when management needs no more than an "adequate" level of production, as is often the case when work is highly programmed. Under such circumstances the costs entailed by modification in job design and supervisory techniques may be greater than the gains obtained from increased motivation to work.[21]

A further criticism of person views, which applies as well to efficiency theories, is their internal-to-the-organization emphasis. By focusing almost exclusively on individual and group issues, the larger social, political, and legal contexts of educational administration are underemphasized and often ignored. This issue will be explored further in our discussion of the political and decision-making model of administration.

THE
RATIONAL-MECHANISTIC-ORGANIC
METAPHORS

Metaphors associated with particular strands of intellectual thought in educational administration reveal a great deal about the values and behavior patterns of administrators. Indeed a metaphor is a *link* between scientific language and the real world; a means of getting from *fact* about organization and administration to *value* in the form of beliefs and opinions which are the basis of actual practice decisions. Let us examine the metaphors most frequently associated with efficiency and person views of educational administration. The rational metaphors associated with scientific management suggest a calculating image of humans programmed to make decisions which

[21]Strauss, *Ibid.,* p. 267.

optimize their self-interests. There is a robot or computer-oriented quality to these metaphors. Given proper engineering through planning, establishing clear objectives, delineating and structuring tasks, and providing rewards linked to specific objectives, teachers and students are likely to respond in predictable ways.

Mechanistic metaphors conjure machine images of how schools function, and they differ from rational metaphors only in levels of analysis. Mechanistic metaphors emphasize the rational structuring and functioning of organizations to efficiently achieve objectives, as opposed to only the rational programming of the work of individuals. to efficiently achieve objectives. By carefully assigning responsibilities and hierarchies of authority, by developing clear and distinct job descriptions, by implementing standard operating procedures and policies for programming decisions—making and governing behavior, and by uniformly applying standards, a logical, objective, and predictable lifestyle will emerge within the school to ensure standard results.

The organic metaphors associated with person views portray the organization as a biological entity which needs to be kept healthy on the one hand and growing on the other. Maintaining a healthy organizational climate and providing for the growth needs of teachers and students are of the highest priority. One aspect of organizational health is the psychological success of its members. The practices of promoting good relations, maintaining trust and confidence, promoting shared control and responsibility, and using conflict-resolution techniques are the proper nutrients to keep this biological-like organization healthy and growing. Health and growth, much like fertilizer and proper soil conditions for plants, are expected to pay dividends in increased performance by individuals on behalf of the school.

One test of a good metaphor is whether it generates other metaphors which provide additional descriptions of the phenomena under consideration. Opponents of a particular view, for example, generate *negative* metaphors to dramatize their points of view. Critics of person views, for example, view administrators who reflect these views as being "missionaries" or "do-gooders." These critics are in turn seen as being "dehumanizing" or "robot-like" in character. Advocates of person views are concerned about organizational "health" of schools and how to promote it. Their critics, on the other hand, are concerned about lack of direction, and want schools to be more "businesslike" and "accountable." Structure is seen by one group as "stifling growth," and the lack of structure by the other group as "anarchistic," "inefficient," and "unbusinesslike."

Interestingly, the ideas basic to each strand of thought are neutral. It is the metaphors they generate, the going from fact to value, which often results in the dogmatic taking of sides on the issues. Metaphors aside, the field of educational administration would benefit by better integration of several views (a theme of the next chapter, as the concept of contingency theory is explored). In the next sections, a third, more recent view of organization and administration in education is discussed, a view which needs to be understood as a complement to, not a competitor with, the other views.

POLITICAL AND DECISION-MAKING VIEWS

Political thinking represents a recent and important development in the literature of educational administration. In many respects, this view of organization and administration represents a major change in thinking—a significant paradigm shift. Four critical emphases distinguish political and decision-making views from those which emphasize efficiency or the person.

> 1. Whereas each of the other views were primarily concerned with forces, events, and activities internal to the school as an organization, the political and decision-making views are concerned with the dynamic interplay of the organizations with forces in its external environment.

The school, for example, is viewed as an open rather than closed system, and therefore as an integral part of its larger environment rather than as a bounded entity isolated from its environment. As an organization the school receives inputs, processes them, and returns outputs to its environment. Since inputs are typically diverse (youngsters differ in ability, for example) and output demands contradictory (the school is expected to maintain tight control over youngsters but at the same time teach them self-responsibility and initiative), there is constant interplay between school and environment. The nature of this interplay is political, as issues are resolved, bargains struck, and agreements reached. Internally, the school is comprised of interdependent subunits and groups, each with self-interests which compete with others. Each of these subunits is affected as others are affected, and together they comprise an array of mini-open systems subject to the same laws of political behavior which characterize the schools larger organizational-environmental interplay.

> 2. Whereas the emphasis in other views is on the administration of policy decisions, the emphasis in political and decision-making views is on policy development.

Political and decision-making views do not consider goals as givens to be administered. Goals are considered to be highly unstable and constantly changing. Therefore, understanding the process of bargaining in the development of goal consensus and understanding the sensitivity of such agreements to external forces are considered important. Further, the notion that educational administrators typically have little control over these forces, and at best play a brokerage role in the development of goal consensus, is central. For these reasons, analysis of goal development and building coalitional strategies for gathering and holding together sufficient support for goals are far more central to political thinking than is mere implementation.

3.   Whereas the other views seek to suppress, program, gloss-over, or resolve conflict, conflict is considered as both natural and necessary in political and decision-making views.

Conflict resolution is an important concern to theorists and practitioners who work from the person model; indeed, to them conflict is considered as pathological. Since finding and using "the one best way" are characteristics of both rational and mechanistic models, advocates of efficiency also regard conflict as a deviation to be corrected. Contrast these images of conflict with those of Victor Baldridge, which follow:

Conflict is natural, and is to be expected in a dynamic organization. Conflict is not abnormal, nor is it necessarily a symptom of a breakdown in the organization's community.

The organization is fragmented into many power blocs and interest groups, and it is natural thay they will try to influence policy so that their values and goals are given primary consideration.

In all organizations small groups of political elites govern most of the major decisions. However, this does not mean that one elite group governs everything; the decisions may be divided up, with different elite groups controlling different decisions.

Formal authority, as prescribed by the bureaucratic system, is severely limited by the political pressure and bargaining tactics that groups can exert against authorities. Decisions are not simply bureaucratic orders, but are instead negotiated compromises among competing groups. Officials are not free simply to order decisions; instead they have to jockey between interest groups, hoping to build viable compromises among powerful blocs.

External interest groups have a great deal of influence over the organization, and internal groups do not have the power to make policies in a vacuum.[22]

---

[22]J. Victor Baldridge, "The Analysis of Organizational Change: A Human Relations Strategy Versus a Political Systems Strategy," R&D memo #75 (Stanford: Stanford Center for R&D in Teaching, Stanford University, 1971), p. 14.

The emphasis in political and decision-making views is on policy formulation. This emphasis in turn requires debate over appropriate goals, values, and strategies. Conflict is considered a natural outgrowth of the process, and indeed is seen by advocates of this model as a sign of organizational *health* rather than organizational pathology.

4. Whereas each of the other models assumes norms of rationality in decision-making, political theories are not based on such norms.

This particular characteristic is related to each of the other three that distinguish political and decision-making views from person and efficiency models. Since it is assumed that goals are not given but negotiated, and since the interplay within the organization and between the organization and its environment is viewed as based on bargaining, then the rational pattern of establishing clear goals—and subsequently programming individual and organizational behavior to maximize these goals—is suspected by advocates of political and decision-making views. With respect to the organic model, the rational pattern of building a core of common values and commitments among workers is also suspected. In the political and decision-making view, a "satisficing" image of man and organization is offered as a substitute for the more traditional rational images. School administrators, for example, do not seek optional solutions to the problem they face, but seek solutions that will satisfy a variety of demands. Thus, not the best reading program for children, but the one which is easier for teachers to implement and which costs less, is selected.

Political and decision-making views began to receive attention by administrators in the late 1950s as scholars from political science and the decision sciences systematically began to give study to the problem of organization and administration. As with each of the other models, this group first gained strong acceptance among those interested in business organizations and business administration, and later became the dominant strand of thought in educational administration. Herbert Simon's now classic, Nobel-Prize-winning work, *Administrative Behavior: A Study of Decision-Making Processes in Administrative Organization,* first published in 1945, is considered by many as the forerunner of this movement.[23] In Simon's view, the limits of rationality

have been seen to derive from the inability of the human mind to bring to bear upon a single decision all the aspects of value, knowledge, and behavior that would be relevant. The pattern of human choice is often more nearly a stimulus-response pattern than a choice among alternatives. Human rationality

[23]Herbert J. Simon, *Administrative Behavior* (New York: Macmillan, 1945).

operates, then, within the limits of a psychological environment. This environment imposes on the individual as "givens" a selection of factors upon which he must base his decisions. However, the stimuli of decision can themselves be controlled so as to serve broader ends, and a sequence of individual decisions can be integrated into a well-conceived plan.[24]

Later, in a classic critique of the efficiency models of organization, Herbert Simon and James G. March discussed not only the cognitive and affective limits of individual rationality, but the limits of rationality implicit in the detailed organizational designs characteristic of bureaucratic theories.[25]

In recent years, James G. March and his colleagues have turned their attention to the analysis of educational organizations. Characterizing educational organization as "organized anarchies," they identify three distinct, important, and troublesome features of educational organizations, which seem to justify the anarchy label.

First, their goals are problematic. It is difficult to specify a consistent set of goals. Instead, goals seem to shift over time; they seem to vary from one part of the school to another; they seem to be stated in terms that are hard to translate into action. There is conflict over goals, and the conflict is not resolved easily. Although it is sometimes possible to impute goals to the organization by observing behavior, such imputations appear often to be unstable or to define goals that are not acceptable to all participants in the organization. The decision process seems to reflect more a series of actions by which goals are discovered than a process by which they are acted upon. Speeches on goals express platitudes that are not useful administratively.

Second, their technologies are unclear. Although we know how to create an educational institution, to staff it, and to specify an educational program for it, we do not know much about the process by which it works, It does work, at least in some senses. Students seem to change. Moreover, we can duplicate our results. If we recreate the procedures in a new school, they will often have approximately the same outcomes. But we have remarkably little capability for designed change in the system. We do not, in general, know what will happen if we make changes; we do not in general, know how to adapt the standard system to non-standard students or situations. New occasions require a new set of trial-and-error procedures, either in the school or in an experimental laboratory.

Third, participation in the organization is fluid. Participants come and go. Students, teachers, and administrators move in and out. There is even more turnover in other participants or potential participants. Parents, individually and collectively, are erratic in their involvement; community leaders some-

---

[24]*Ibid,* 2nd ed., pp. 108–109.

[25]John March, and Herbert Simon, *Organizations* (New York: John Wiley, 1958).

times ignore the schools, sometimes devote considerable time to them; governmental agencies are active, then passive. All of the potential actors in the organization have other concerns that compete with the school for their attention. Thus, whether they participate in the school depends as much on the changing characteristics of their alternatives as it does on the characteristics of the educational organization involved.[26]

Certainly this description of schools challenges conceptions implicit in the more traditional theories of administration and organization.

Graham Allison's classic analysis of governmental decision-making during the Cuban Missile Crisis of 1962 is often used by theorists to contrast ideas derived from political and decision-making theories with the more traditional rational and mechanistic models.[27] In that study, Allison showed that the particular model internalized by the analyst governs his or her explanation of the crisis and its associated events. In explaining organizational events using the political-theory model, Allison notes that one assumes events to occur as a result of diverse groups, each bargaining to improve its own position. Leaders of organizations are not seen as a monolithic group, but rather, each in his own right as a player in a highly competitive game known as politics. This game of politics is played by bargaining in regularized ways among players in the hierarchy.

Actions emerge neither as the calculated choice of a unified group nor as a formal summary of leaders' preferences. Rather the context of shared power but separate judgments concerning important choices determines that politics is the mechanism of choice. Note the *environment* in which the game is played: inordinate uncertainty about what must be done, the necessity that something be done and crucial consequences of whatever is done. These features force responsible men to become active players. The *pace of the game,* hundreds of issues, numerous games, and multiple channels—compels players to fight to "get others' attention," to make them "see the facts," to assure that they "take the time to think seriously about the broader issue." The *Structure of the game*—power shared by individuals with separate responsibilities—validates each player's feeling that "others don't see my problem," and "others must be persuaded to look at the issue from a less parochial perspective." *The rules of the game*—he who hesitates loses his chance to play at that point, and he who is uncertain about his recommendation is over-powered by others who are sure—pressures players to come

[26]David M. Cohen, James G. March, and J. P. Olsen, "A Garbage Can Model of Organizational Choice", *Administrative Science Quarterly,* Vol. 17, No. 1 (1972).

[27]Graham T. Allison, "Conceptual Models and the Cuban Missile Crisis," *The American Political Science Review.* Vol. 63, No. 3 (1969) 689–718.

down on one side of a 51–49 issue and play. The *rewards of the game*—effectiveness, i.e., impact on outcomes, as the immediate measure of performance—encourages hard play.[28]

Central to this view is the building of coalitions in order to reach sufficient agreement and concentrate sufficient authority to be able to function. March, for example, suggests that organizations should be viewed as political coalitions, and administrators as political brokers.[29] As a political coalition, the form, shape, and structure of a school as well as its goals and missions are negotiated. He further notes that within the organization, individuals frequently join together into sub-coalitions. Coalition members in schools would include teachers, chairpersons, supervisors, administrators, janitors, students, the school board, the PTA, the teacher's union, the central office, volunteers, interest groups, regulatory agencies, and municipal departments.

Schools, according to this view, are concerned with a set of potential and actual participants which makes demands on the system.[30] These demands are the price the system must pay if it wishes to maintain the coalition as relatively domesticated—that is, as being able to carry on an acceptable pattern of interaction with the system. Demands take the form of money, attention, involvement, personal treatment, and other resources deemed important by coalition members. Demands are sometimes complementary and sometimes contradictory. When contradictory, meeting demand *A* makes difficult meeting demand *B*. Consider a group of parents who want the school to stress its educative function of teaching responsibility and self-discipline on the one hand and maintain its custodial function of student control on the other.

If the school cannot maintain some semblance of coalition with important members, it is likely that competing coalitions will be established outside of accepted patterns of interaction. As competing coalitions gain in strength, they replace established coalitions. A principal who loses the support of only a few teachers and parents can survive. But as the number of disenchanted teachers or parents increases, or if the two smaller groups gain enough strength by joining forces, the principal is replaced and the school's social order disturbed.

---

[28]*Ibid,* p. 710.

[29]James G. March, "The Business Firm as a Political Coalition." *The Journal of Politics, Vol. 24 (1962).*

[30]This discussion follows that which appears in Thomas J. Sergiovanni and Fred D. Carver, *The New School Executive, A Theory of Administration Second Edition.* (New York: Harper & Row, 1980) Chapter 4, "Administrative Values and Decision-Making."

Administrators, according to this view, try to use the organization to maximize their own interests and needs. They face the problem of selecting a coalition of participants so that demands required as price for participation do not compromise the return they seek. A principal who seeks support from teachers for a program of staff development, at the cost of losing access to teachers' classrooms, might find that the trade-off jeopardizes not only his immediate intent but his future options as well. A cost-benefit analysis is conducted whereby the administrator assesses whether the benefits accrued by participating in a coalition with person *A* justify the demands which must be provided.

March suggests that the coalitional nature of organizations is political in four critical ways. "First, the focus of attention shifts from the owners (and their objectives) to the actual, operating organizers of the coalition—whoever they may be."[31] Schools in particular are public organizations with few rules governing who can play the game of bargaining, and since many of the players are *outside* of direct authority of administrations (tenured teachers, parents, alumni, the mayor, juvenile sections of the police department, NAACP, citizens for basic education, etc.), bargaining cannot be avoided. "Second, the theory emphasizes the non-uniqueness of short-run solutions to the coalition problem. At any point in time, there are a number of possible coalitions that are viable (that is, their total value exceeds their total cost of maintenance)."[32] This phenomenon encourages the establishment of *ad hoc* coalitions and permits administrators some latitude in maintaining favorable coalitions by making them tenuous. The administrator as a broker is sensitive to which coalitions have long-term implications and which are more expendable. Further, the cost of dissolving today's coalition against possible loss of future participation by individuals cannot go unnoticed. "Third, the theory does not solve the problem of conflict by simple payments to participants and agreement as a superordinate goal. Rather it emphasizes the importance of policy demands and payments and of sequential rather than simultaneous mediation of demands."[33] Demands differ and no standard payoff can assure a happy array of coalitions. Dealing with conflicting demands is a political process. Conflict, however, is often managed by separating conflicting goals and payments. The high school principal who works with the counseling department at 9 A.M., the college-prep academic departments at 10 A.M., and the distributive-education department at 11 A.M. is dealing with conflicting interests sequentially.

[31]March, "The Business Firm," p. 674.

[32]*Ibid.*

[33]*Ibid.*

"Fourth, the theory emphasized the importance of institutional constraints on the solution of coalition problems."[34] Active and potential participants in coalitions are not free to make any demand they wish, and administrators are limited in payments available. Coalitions are struck within institutional boundaries on the one hand and environmental constraints on the other. Budgetary constraints, codes of ethics, case-law policies and other administrative precedents, and the school-code are examples of constraints on coalition demands and payments. According to this bargaining model, the administrator as broker uses constraints in managing coalitions to his favor.

Much remains to be learned about the constructive use of conflict in organizations and about the bargaining role of the school administrator. Recognizing first that conflict can have constructive consequences for schools is in itself an important contribution of the political and decision-making view of schools. Indeed, viewing the school as a political system adds a rich dimension to understanding how schools actually operate. But as enhancing as these glimpses of reality are, serious caveats are in order. Political and decision-making views are largely descriptive, not prescriptive. They attempt to describe and understand what is actually occurring rather than what should be occurring, and these are important undertakings.

School administrators should not assume, however, that because events are as they are, the name of the game is only to learn the rules and play by them. *The rules themselves are at issue, and must be evaluated for goodness of fit to the unique values of the school as a particular kind of organization.* In educational enterprises, means and ends are often indistinguishable. Teachers and students alike learn as much from how we organize and behave in schools as they do from the official educational program. Management and organization are part of the school's hidden curriculum, and they teach important lessons to students.

The major features of each of the three views of administration are summarized in Table 2–2. The table provides examples of metaphors associated with each view as well as the basic unit of analysis, major concepts, authority type, and administrative prescription associated with each. Though views are presented as mutually exclusive images of organization and administration, the three actually represent alternate and overlapping lenses through which one might better understand administrative phenomena (the topic of the next chapter). In the section which immediately follows, educational administration is

[34]*Ibid.*

TABLE 2-2

A comparison of efficiency, person, and political and decision-making views of educational administration

The major view	Efficiency	Person	Political & decision-making
Sub-views	Scientific management as efficiency in work. Bureaucracy as efficiency in organization.	Human relations view of the person as a social being. Human resources view of the person as an achievement-oriented being.	Decision making within the school. Policy development in the broader school context.
Generative Metaphors	Rational Mechanistic	Organic	Bargaining
Other Metaphors	Engineering Machine Factory Assembly line Blueprint Economic person	Health Nurturance Missionary Social person Plant	Coalition Thermostatic person Trade-off Game Dealing
Basic Units of Analysis	The work flow and the organizational design	The human organization	The organization as an open system
Major Concepts	Goals and Objectives Alternatives Cost/benefit Analysis Maximizing decisions Accountability Organizational routines implicit in structure & function, role and rules and rights & prerogatives	Commitment of supportive work group to school goals. Motivation and job satisfaction	Individuals and organization as players and actors Rules of the game Stakes and interests
Authority Type	Reward, coercive, legal, position	Normative	Instrumental
Administrative Prescription	Plan, organize, control, evaluate Emphasize formalization, centralization, stratification, efficiency, production in organizational structure.	Use team administration and power-equalization strategies to develop a highly effective work group committed to school objectives.	Assume a brokerage role to build coalition among competitive and conflicting interests within the school and between the school and its environment.
Decision-Making	Humankind and organization are rationally concerned. With proper planning, organizing, controlling, and evaluating, predetermined goals can be rationally and efficiently achieved. Decision-making strategies are linear as in systems analysis.	Humankind and organization are rationally concerned. Given human capacity to value, believe, and self-actualize, it is possible to set goals and develop binding commitments to these goals. The result is higher levels of performance and greater satisfaction. Decision-making strategies are linear as in management by objectives.	Cognitive limits on human rationality and environmental constraints on organizational rationality suggest that decision making is "satisfying." Neither person nor organization seeks the best needle in a haystack, but rather, an acceptable one. Degree of acceptability is determined by bargaining.

69

viewed as an applied science, and features which separate this science from administration in general and business administration in particular are discussed.

THE SCIENCE OF ADMINISTRATION

In recent years the quest for developing a science of administration has increased, and this quest has been somewhat successful. Scholars of administration can point with pride to progress in theorizing about the nature of organizations and how they work, and about the nature of organizational and administrative behavior. Indeed, a vast literature from an array of scholarly journals is available as evidence of research-and-development efforts to expand and refine theoretical conceptions of administration and organization. Administration as a science is concerned with describing, explaining, analyzing, and predicting organizational phenomena and human behavior as they relate to the accomplishment of organizational goals. The scientific approach to administration is one of objectivity and neutrality. The focus of this approach is on the identification and articulation of principles which have wide application to administration in general. The approach therefore presents a panoramic view which includes methods of organizing, workflow, authority and power systems, leadership, control, coordination, planning/change, administrative behavior, group behavior, individual behavior, human adaptation, motivation, decision making, and others. Ultimately, those who seek a science of administration wish to examine each of these variables in cause-and-effect relationships so that action propositions may be developed to guide administrative behavior more effectively.

Scientific approaches to administration, while able to provide invaluable educational decision-making information in the form of hard knowledge, concepts, and fundamental understandings, offer little direct help in formulating operational strategies for school administrators. An important problem remains: deciding which scientific propositions are appropriate to the school. This problem is compounded by the presence of unanticipated consequences of administrative acts. Thus administration may be scientific in that one can make fairly accurate initial predictions based on theory and propositions; but administration is also artistic in the sense that once action is implemented, the variability and complexity of human behavior produce unanticipated consequences which defy systematic decision making.

The strengths of a science of administration—objectivity, neutrality, and wide applicability—are also its weaknesses. The absence of values, the lack of goal emphasis, and the difficulty in developing carry-over in particular situations require that educational administration continually assess and modify scientific propositions in the light of a value system unique to education and of goals unique to the schools. Therefore, while it would be inappropriate to ignore scientific findings, it seems equally inappropriate to accept them without evaluation and modification.

As educational administrators work with teachers and other educational professionals, they need to be sure that their leadership is consistent with the broader goals of education, rather than simply with those which will result in increased outputs. Yet the science of administration does not permit us the luxury of evaluating its propositions in terms of a value system unique to education. Herbert Simon, one of the pioneers in developing a science of administration, reminds us that belief systems have no place in science: "An administrative science, like any science, is concerned purely with factual statements. There is no place for ethical assertions in the body of science. Whenever ethical statements do occur, they can be separated into two parts, one factual and one ethical; and only the former has any relevance to science."[35] What is needed, therefore, is a view of administration which is general enough to benefit from scientific inquiry but specific enough to take into account problems of professional practice and issues of value unique to the school as a special kind of organization.

EDUCATIONAL ADMINISTRATION
AS AN APPLIED SCIENCE

James G. March has accurately referred to educational administration as being "managerially parasitic," speaking to its tendency to borrow heavily from the insights, theories, and practices associated with the organization and administration of business enterprises.[36] Superior funding and greater demand has brought business organization to the attention of scholars, and most of the literature on organization and administration has been developed with this type of organization in mind. In this section some of the differences between management in educational and other public organization and that in business organization are discussed. These differences suggest that

[35]Simon, *Administrative Behavior*, p. 253.
[36]James G. March, "Analytical Skills and the University Training of Educational Administrators," *The Journal of Educational Administration.* Vol. 12, No. 1 (1974), 43.

great care must be taken in adapting management practices from other sectors for use in schools.

It is easily recognized that, at one level of analysis, management is management. But, though public and private organizations share many features, the differences are significant. The well-known management professor Wallace Sayre has stated that "business and government administration are alike in all unimportant respects."[37] Joseph Bower of the Harvard Business School notes that "American business is an inappropriate analogy for discussing and evaluating public management. In the public sector, *purpose, organization* and *people* do not have the same meaning and significance that they have in business."[38]

Some important differences between schools, as one kind of public organization, and private organizations are contrasted below.

1.   Power over money, organization, and personnel rests in the hands of the legislature, school-code, and local school board rather than in the hands of management.

2.   Measures of progress toward goals are difficult to devise. What are the school measures of good citizenship, intellectual enrichment, problem-solving ability, independent thinking, a desire to learn, economic sufficiency, and effective family living, for example? These are contrasted with the readily understood and quantifiable economic objectives of private organizations.

3.   Public accounting to which the school is subjected is designed to *control* current expenditures, as contrasted with business accounting which tends to support future planning, research, and development.

4.   Tenure laws and civil-service laws tend to protect educational workers from the control of administrators and supervisors.

5.   School purposes and organizational processes designed to achieve these purposes are influenced indirectly by administrators through individuals and groups (a political process), rather than directly by administrators (a management process).

6.   Goals and objectives are often unclear and contradictory. The latent custodial functions of schools, for example, contradict the manifest self-actualization functions.

7.   No market exists to determine effectiveness. Expensive special-educational programs, for example, are maintained for political and legal reasons, though if subjected to a market economy, general consumer interest would not likely be sufficient to sustain them. By comparison, product lines of firms are thinned out by a market economy.

[37] As mentioned in Joseph Bower, "Effective Public Management; It isn't the same as Effective Business Management," *Harvard Business Review,* March-April 1977, pp. 131–140.
[38] *Ibid,* p. 140.

8. Resources are distributed on the basis of formula and other approximations of "equity" rather than on "merit." Allocating greater resources to "high producing" schools, for example, would be considered fraudulent.

9. Administrators work with an array of people whose careers are outside of management control.

10. Administrators are expected to accomplish goals in less time than that normally allowed to managers of business firms.

11. A tight coupling exists between means and ends, or products and processes. Schooling is a human activity with human ends.

12. Many objectives are pursued with scarce resources, as contrasted with the firm which allocates more resources to fewer—indeed, more focused— objectives.

Perhaps the most critical difference between the school and most other organizations is the human intenseness which characterizes its work. Schools are human organizations in the sense that their products are human and their processes require the socializing of humans. Further, unlike most organizations which rely on machinery and technology, schools are labor intensive. Well over 70 percent of the money spent for education, for example, goes to the educational labor force— mostly to it's nearly two million teachers.

This human intensity in educational organizations makes critically important the role of values in schooling, as Harry Broudy notes:

> The educator, however, deals with nothing but values—human beings who are clusters and constellations of value potentials. Nothing human is really alien to the educational enterprise and there is, therefore, something incongruous about educational administrators evading fundamental value conflicts. . . . The public will never quite permit the educational administrator the moral latitude that it affords some of its servants. For to statesmen and soldiers men entrust their lives and fortunes, but to the schools they entrust their precarious hold on humanity itself.[39]

For these reasons, it is best to view educational administration as a distinct applied science. This applied science relies heavily on concepts, insights, and practices from the various disciplines and from the study of organization and administration in general, but evaluates these ideas for goodness to fit to the unique value structure of educational organizations. In this process, some ideas are rejected and others accepted.

[39]Harry S. Broudy, "Conflict in Values", in Robert Ohm and William Monohan, *Educational Administration—Philosophy in Action* (Norman, Okla.: University of Oklahoma, College of Education, 1965), p. 52.

Educational administrators often confuse an applied science of administration with the development of "practical strategies." Being practical, however, often involves using the most efficient way to achieve school goals, and as such, can sacrifice means in order to achieve ends. An applied science, on the other hand, is concerned with means as well as ends, and focuses on quality of process as well as on quality of goal achievement. It is our view that *educational administration is basically an ethical science concerned with good or better processes, good or better means, good or better ends, and as such is thoroughly immersed in values, preferences, ideas, aspirations, and hopes.* Further, these are the concerns central to the concept of educational leadership.

Deciding what factors to take into account in decision making is no easy task. Choices must be made as to what theoretical concepts and other insights available from administrative science and from one's pratical experience should be selected for use, given the unique circumstances that are being faced, and what concepts and insights are appropriate, given the humanistic nature of educational enterprises. In recent years contingency theories have been offered as mechanisms or frameworks to help administrators navigate through this uncertain sea of factual knowledge and value knowledge in search of solutions which are both effective and appropriate. Contingency theories offer no easy answers, and indeed raise a number of serious problems which encumber effective and appropriate decisions. But they can be useful, and are of sufficient interest and importance to administrators today to warrant separate consideration—the purpose of the next chapter.

SUMMARY

This chapter has been concerned with the intellectual heritage of educational administration. It was suggested that administrators practice their art from certain perspectives or sets of biases which are related to the development of thought in educational administration. Efficiency, person, and political models were used to illustrate and summarize the major strands of thought affecting administrative practice. Though the models exist as objective accumulations of concepts, it is the ideological and value differences among them that add richness and controversy to the field. Metaphors such as rational, mechanistic, organic, and bargaining were used to go from facts about each model to values.

Particular attention was given to political and decision-making theories, for these represent the most recent conception of educational administration. It was pointed out that while political and decision-making images evoke a familiar ring, they are descriptive theories and are not designed to suggest administrative practice. They focus on what is the real world of administration, not what ought to be.

Educational administration was then viewed as an applied science with values and other characteristics unique to the school, as a standard by which concepts from the science of administration and those tried and true from the real world of practice are evaluated for appropriateness. This analysis includes a contrast of differences between administration of public and private organizations.

In the next and final chapter of part I, a contingency approach to organization and administration is suggested as a mechanism which can help make sense of the array of concepts and ideas available to educational administrators and can help in selecting from this array those ideas more fitting to the school administrator's unique work context.

STUDY GUIDE

Can you recall the meanings of the following terms? Discuss them with a class colleague and apply them to your school-community setting.

applied science
bargaining metaphor
bureaucratic theories
the person model
generative metaphors
human relations
human resources
managerially parasitic
mechanistic metaphor

model
neoscientific management
organic metaphor
political and decision-making
   model
professional practice norms
private management
public management
rational metaphor
scientific management

SUGGESTED ACTIVITIES

1. Interview one or two managers from a business or commercial organization, one or two public administrators, and one or two educational administra-

tors. In each case, ask them to describe how they plan, organize, control, lead, and evaluate. In what ways are their responses similar and different?

2.   Develop a working or operational definition of theory. It is often said that "there is nothing as practical as good theory." To what extent do you agree with this statement?

3.   Which of the theories and models of administration summarized in Table 2–1 best fits, as an overall picture, schools and school administrators with which you are familiar?

SELECTED READINGS

ALLISON, GRAHAM T., *Essence of Decision.* Boston: Little, Brown, 1971.

BIDWELL, CHARLES E., "School as a Formal Organization," in James G. March, ed., *Handbook of Organization.* Chicago: Rand McNally, 1965.

CALLAHAN, RAYMOND E., *Education and the Cult of Efficiency.* Chicago: University of Chicago Press, 1962.

CAMPBELL, ROALD, and GREG RUSSELL, eds., *Administrative Behavior in Education.* New York: Harper & Row, 1957.

CULBERTSON, JACK et al., *Toward the Development of a 1969–1974 UCEA Plan for Advancing Educational Administration.* Columbus, Ohio: UCEA, 1967.

DRACHLER, NORMAN et al. *Training Educational Leaders: A Search for Alternatives.* Washington, D.C.: Institute for Educational Leadership, 1976.

GRIFFITHS, DANIEL, ed., *Behavioral Science and Educational Administrator,* 63rd Yearbook, NSSE. Chicago, University of Chicago Press, 1964.

MARCH, JAMES G., and JOHAN P. OLSEN, *Ambiguity and Choice in Organizations.* Bergen, Norway: University Press of Norway, 1976.

McGREGOR, DOUGLAS, *The Human Side of Enterprise.* New York: McGraw-Hill, 1958.

SERGIOVANNI, THOMAS J., and FRED D. CARVER, *The New School Executive: A Theory of Administration* (2nd ed.). New York: Harper & Row, 1980.

SIMON, HERBERT, *Administrative Behavior.* New York: Macmillan, 1945.

3

CONTINGENCY THEORY IN EDUCATIONAL ADMINISTRATION

The last decade has produced a significant body of literature dealing with what has been called *contingency,* or *situational,* theory. Contingency theory has been very popular in many academic circles. Further, the practical nature of contingency theory affords it wide appeal among practicing administrators. Interest in the notion of contingency theory, therefore, is high.

Those who have developed contingency theory have rejected the idea that any one particular model of organization and administration is superior to others in all situations. No one best way to plan, lead, organize, motivate, control, or evaluate exists which can be used for every instance. When considering efficiency, person, or political and decision-making models, therefore, no single model can be considered superior. Instead, according to contingency theory, appropriate organizational and administrative processes and choices are contingent upon the particular character or nature of the organization itself, the environment of the organization at that particular moment, and the specific task or tasks the organization seeks to accomplish at this time.

The nature of contingency theory can be easily understood by considering an example from professional football. Whether a particular play called by the quarterback or coach is effective is contingent on a number of factors. The particular down, the field position, the score, the pattern and success rate of previous plays, the best estimate of what defense is likely, and just plain intuition are examples which must be considered. As these situational or "contingency" variables change, so should the plays called by the quarterback. Even though the quarterback and coach may have studied books on strategy, reviewed films, and scrutinized sophisticated computer analyses of opponents' strengths and weaknesses, these elements of the overall game plan do not dictate every play called. The general tendencies of opponents, such as their tendency to "blitz" on third down and long yardage, are helpful. But all this information, while helpful, is not a surrogate for the decision processes which must be undertaken. The quarterback must in the final analysis assess the actual situation and call the play from his view. His success will in large part be contingent upon matching the play with the situation at hand. The epitome of this matching is when the quarterback calls one play in the huddle, brings the team to the line, and then, in surveying the defense, changes the play at the line of scrimmage.

Educational administrators often find themselves in similar situations. For example, the game plan represents the best thinking available about problems they face. The real-life problem itself, however, does not neatly fit the game plan. The play-calling represents decisions administrators make. The decision to act in a certain way, to emphasize certain administrative and organization principles, is informed by theoretical knowledge and other factors, but is made in the light of a set of particulars. As particulars change, as the situation is redefined, so too must the decisions made be changed.

Contingency theory was spawned by two different criticisms of the traditional literature on organizations. First, administrators argued that their world of practical problems was made "too simple" by singular theories of organizational behavior or leadership. They were constantly asked to decide about the number of classes that should be taught by English teachers, the length of the lunch period for students, the need for additional or fewer supplies for teachers, and the program for parents' night at the school. When administrators turned to the field of educational administration or to academic disciplines for help in solving these and other problems, they were frustrated. Instead of helpful prescriptions, practicing administrators found conflict and confusion. These arguments among academics were produced by differing research traditions, ideological positions, and emphases. As suggested in the last chapter, models internalized by academics colored their view of the world.

Second, researchers in the fields of organizational studies increasingly discovered that what administrators did "depended" upon the conditions of the situation. Passing a school-bond referendum, dealing with an upset parent, or counseling a teacher about a discipline problem depended upon a set of circumstances. Researchers sought to systematically enumerate these conditions and their various interactions as a way of explaining factors such as leadership, decision making, or organizational structure.

To this point in time, no single contingency theory has captured the imaginations of both practicing administrators and researchers. Later in this chapter we shall examine several of these theories. Nor is it likely that any single theory will emerge. What seems more likely is that contingency theory will be used as a metatheory for guiding the sorting and classifying of readings, experiences, and reflections. The general categories of contingency theory invite the mind's eye to reconstruct the writings and empirical studies of others with the day-to-day experiences of the administrator. The categories used in contingency theory offer a checklist for handy recapitulation of a practical situation. A later section spells out one possible set of guidelines for quickly noting the major contours of a real-life situation.

Hence, this chapter treats contingency theory as a special subset of the general conceptual approach to educational administration. The discussion views contingency theory less as a theory in its own right and more as a general framework for analyzing and selecting from an array of existing theories those theoretical elements which are useful for a given circumstance. Our purpose is *not* to teach a contingency theory or to suggest that contingency theory is *the* only viable approach to understanding administration. Indeed, contingency theory does present a powerful tool for examining literature and practices in educational administration; but, as with all tools, contingency theory is suited for certain jobs, but inappropriate for others. The fatal flaw of contingency theory for educational administration is its value neutrality. By and large, the contingency approach oversells the idea of finding solutions which work rather than those which are appropriate.

CONFLICTING ASSUMPTIONS AND IDEOLOGIES

One way of coming to understand the utility of a contingency theory is to explore briefly the effects of conflicting assumptions and ideologies on educational research and practice. The last decade in education, for example, has witnessed concern and controversy about a variety of topics such as the disadvantaged child, the cycle of poverty, bilingual schooling, white flight, and failures to teach the basics or to arrest falling achievement test scores. These topics are controversial because people make different assumptions about human beings and about the capabilities of schooling. How have these assumptions determined in the past how one views educational organizations and administration?

Assumptions

Three sets of assumptions have influenced research and the practice of administration. These are assumptions about why people behave as they do, about social processes, and about linkage patterns.

Researchers and administrators often make assumptions about the factors that influence why people behave as they do. Schein, for example, has catalogued four differing sets of assumptions about people.[1] The assumptions not only classify ways researchers have viewed motivation of people, but also imply strategies for organizational management. The assumptions and relationships to job factors are summarized in Table 3–1.

The human, as a rational-economic creature, is motivated by economic incentives and seeks to maximize economic gain. When the rational-economic human fails to achieve managerial objectives, remedies include re-examining the reward plans to insure that rational-

TABLE 3–1
Management's assumptions about people

	Motivation	Relationships on job	Normal mode of response	Organizational management
Rational-Economic Man	Greatest economic gain	Passive and manipulable agent	Irrational	Neutralize and control feelings
Social Man	Social needs	Social relationships for meaningless job	Peer group	Social needs and needs for acceptance
Self-Actualizing Man	Hierarchy of needs	Maturity, autonomy, and independence	Self-motivated and self-controlled	No conflict between self and organization
Complex Man	Complex and variable	Interaction of needs and experience	Motives may vary with situation	Satisfaction and effectiveness vary with task, motivation, and managerial strategy

[1]Edgar H. Schein, *Organizational Psychology* (Englewood Cliffs, N.J.: Prentice-Hall, 1965), pp. 43–65.

economic workers can clearly see their payoff, re-analyzing job structure so that work is efficient, and re-examining the control structure so that those who loaf can be spotted and then punished or those who overachieve can be identified and rewarded.

The opposite end of the continuum is the complex human. Congruent with contingency theory, individuals are seen as complex and highly variable in their motive structure. While motives may be arranged in some type of hierarchy, the hierarchy may change over time as a result of learning, and may shift with situations. Successful managerial strategy requires the administrator to learn to value differences, be flexible, and inquire diagnostically about which motives are in play in this particular situation.

A second major way that researchers and managers have differed is in their preferences for certain social processes. Dahrendorf, for instance, argued in the late 1950s for the inclusion of conflict in sociological analysis.[2] He claimed that sociological theorists were unduly concerned with explaining uniformity, social harmony, recurrent patterns, and groups or communities isolated from others. This concern for "utopian" patterns of development highlighted stability, harmony, and consensus. Dahrendorf urged that society be examined from the point of view of conflict, change, and constraint. Such a perspective highlighted deviance, social discord, the emergence and disappearance of social patterns, and groups or communities in conflict with others. In the last few years, administrators have been urged to use conflict as a device for deliberately generating new insights about organizational problems.

A third dimension has been the patterns of interaction that researchers and managers have created. These images of social processes influence ways that problems are framed, alternatives generated, and consequences weighted. For example, Luecke and McGinn have used the same three factors (family, school, teacher) to explain student achievement, but link these factors in several different ways.[3] One model links these factors sequentially: family background affects the school the student attends, school affects the teacher assigned to the student, and teacher alone directly affects student achievement. A second model, according to these authors, does not link these factors, but indicates that all are independent. The third view links family to school and teacher: school directly affects teacher, and family, school,

[2]Ralf Dahrendorf, "Out of Utopia: A Reorientation of Sociological Analysis," *American Journal of Sociology,* 64 (September, 1958), 115–127.

[3]Daniel F. Luecke and Noel F. McGinn, "Regression Analyses and Education Production Functions: Can They Be Trusted?" *Harvard Educational Review,* 45 (August, 1975), 325–350.

FIGURE 3-1
Causal relations built into variations of the model

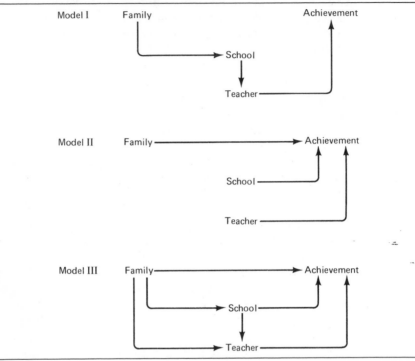

Adapted from: Daniel F. Luecke and Noel F. McGinn, "Regression Analyses and Education Production Functions: Can They Be Trusted?" *Harvard Educational Review,* 45 (August, 1975), p. 339.

and teacher all directly affect student achievement. The models are summarized in Figure 3–1.

These models suggest different research questions and administrative strategies. In the first model, researchers would ask questions about the relations between the school and family, but *not* between family and teacher. The second, on the other hand, suggests that school administrators need have little interaction with family or teachers, while the third model suggests that mutual interactions among school, teacher, and family might affect (positively or negatively) student achievement.

These three dimensions—models of humans, processes, and linkages—influence deeply the social-science researcher and the administrator. Working within disciplines which often favor elements of these dimensions, researchers frame problems, generate information, and make claims about human behavior. These claims legitimate some of the assumptions administrators make, while they upset other administrative strategies. In general, however, the conflicting claims of the academic social scientists and the findings of empirical research are of little practical guidance to the administrator. In order to be useful, these claims need to be coherently ordered.

Administrative Ideology

Those who administer in organizations have often invited researchers to help them solve problems. These "consulting" relations have been driven by needs of administrators to improve the operations of the organization. General schemes for improvement brought by researchers are helpful to administrators, but administrators themselves bring two additional dimensions to the situation: a sense of the history of the organization and a feeling for the life of the organization.

Sense of history and feeling for the life of the organization are important ingredients in coming to grips with practical situations. Too often, outside experts "miss" what is going on because they lack the intuitions of experienced administrators. These intuitions are more than just hunches or wishful thinking; they reflect tacit knowledge which practitioners have of situations.

Administrators and researchers need some sense of the forces that shaped the organization over its life history. Katz and Kahn, for instance, trace the evolution of organizations through three stages.[4] In *stage one* the organization exists as a primitive system in which people with common needs create a production structure. The one-room school, for instance, sprang from the needs of communities to educate their children. Over time the primitive system becomes a stable organization. In this *second stage*, environmental needs still exist, but the production structure has increased the need for reliability of performance. this produces a managerial structure which seeks to strengthen the production structure. Our one-room school now has four rooms, a teacher-principal, and teacher evaluation. In *stage three*, the managerial structure is linked closely to the environment to engender support, while the production system has become elaborated and focused on internal concerns. In multiple-school districts, superintendents and principals work closely with the public while teachers work with students in school settings.

This historical development stamps organizations with individual-

---

[4]Daniel Katz and Robert L. Kahn, *The Social Psychology of Organizations* (New York: John Wiley, 1966), pp. 77–84.

ized characteristics. The problem that initially created the organization is re-defined over time, pioneers are forgotten or made heroes, traditions are built, rules made, broken and remade, and reforms affected. The "way we do things around here" becomes a part of the image of the organization.

Of particular import to this organizational history is the nature of the goals sought by the organization. Schools, for example, have had some fairly constant goals and some which have changed. Reading, writing, and arithmetic persist, while driver training[5] has come and selling war bonds has gone. The tolerance for ambiguity about goals, about different meanings for goals, or the hierarchy of goals are part of the history and development of the organization which administrators sense and researchers need to know.

A second dimension that administrators bring to researchers is a feeling for the life of the organization. This feeling for or sense of the life of the organization involves predominantly the sense of repetition of events over a period of time. Mintzberg speaks of this as the "periodic patterns" which emerge when looking at executives.[6] For instance, during the closing weeks of school, the superintendent of the district presides over or appears ceremoniously at graduation ceremonies. These graduation exercises happen every year, and become an important marker for those who live and work in schools. The life of the organization has a skeleton composed of repetitive events—the opening of school, the Thanksgiving recess, Christmas vacation, spring break, and graduation.

The repetition of these events provides a sense of continuity to veterans in the organization and a sense of "social time" to newcomers. Experienced hands in schools prepare themselves for the opening few days of classes with meticulous care, knowing the importance of first impressions. The past provides a series of guideposts for dealing with recurrent events. Inexperienced teachers struggle through the last day before Christmas vacation, for instance. Having lived that day just once, these newcomers begin to plan for activities that will occupy students during that longest of school days.

Administrative ideologies include not only assumptions about the nature of human beings, senses of fundamental social processes, and linkage patterns of important factors, but also a feeling for the historical development of the organization and a feeling for the periodic pattern of life in the organization. Such a rich mixture of assumptions

[5]The interest in driver training may well have peaked with new studies now suggesting that its effectiveness in reducing accidents is suspect.

[6]Henry Mintzberg, *The Nature of Managerial Work* (New York: Harper & Row, 1973), p. 122.

about the nature of humans and of the world provides multiple opportunities for conflict, not only about what is happening, but also about what ought to happen.

It is at this point that contingency theory becomes helpful. The contingency approach, for example, suggests ways of not only identifying differing assumptions and ideologies, but also of ordering them so that discussion can be more deliberate. Nonetheless, contingency theory offers few guides for moral or ethical choices.

CONTINGENCY THEORY:
A METAFRAMEWORK

The general notion of contingency theory provides a useful framework for organizing the diverse literature of research and practice. Contingency theory, for example, provides a set of categories and relations, which permits generation not only of research problems and hypotheses but also of diagnoses and prescriptions for practical situations. This section reviews briefly works which belong to the family of contingency theory. Included are examples of contingency theories concerning leadership, organizations and environment, and managerial work.

Leadership

Leadership is considered to be a critical administrative process. Authorities agree that though schools in the same district may be organized similarly, and staff, students, and financial resources may be distributed according to formula to insure equality, schools differ in their effectiveness. A frequent explanation in educational administration is that the leadership of the principal makes all the difference. This may well be an overstatement, but few would deny the importance of quality leadership to school effectiveness. A frequent problem that leaders face is whether to stress the task or the humanistic elements. Task-oriented behavior reflects a high concern for planning, organizing, structuring, and evaluating work. Humanistic or relations-oriented behavior reflects a high concern for nurturing and developing human relationships and for general considerations of others.

Fred Fiedler's work on developing a contingency theory of leadership is addressed specifically to the problem outlined above—identifying the proper situational conditions for task and for relations-oriented leadership behavior.[7] Fiedler defines situations as the mix of three

[7]Fred E. Fiedler, *A Theory of Leadership Effectiveness* (New York: McGraw-Hill, 1967).

conditions: the quality of leader-member relations (good, moderate or poor); the nature of the task to be accomplished (structured or unstructured); and the position or power of the leader relative to the group (weak or strong). These three dimensions permit classification of situations that are very favorable, intermediate in favorableness, or unfavorable to the leader. Favorableness is defined as the extent to which the leader is able to influence the outcome of the group. Eight situations are depicted in Table 3–2. Each situation is defined by the three dimensions, and offers the leader lesser or greater opportunities for influencing group outcomes. Task leadership, for example, is more effective in situations 1, 2, 3, and 8, but would be ineffective in situations 4, 5, 6, and 7. Indeed, Fiedler concludes that very favorable and unfavorable situations are more effectively led by individuals with a task orientation. Intermediate situations, on the other hand, have highest task-group performance if the leader operates in a relationship style. Each different group situation calls for a different kind of leadership style.

Research conducted in schools, using Fiedler's contingency theory, produced another important insight: with increased experience, school principals often performed less well than principals with less experience. Fiedler suggested that experienced principals often modified their leadership styles over time. For instance, if elementary school principalships were classified as type 2 situations (favorable), the effective leadership style would be task orientation. A new principal might come to a school knowing few, if any, staff members. This principal might adopt a task-oriented style. But over time, the principal and staff would come to know one another and develop strong personal bonds; this principal would come to value these bonds and become increasingly a relationship-oriented leader. Unfortunately, as the principal becomes more relationship oriented with experience, the principal's performance will decline because of the increasing mismatch between situational factors and leadership style.

Organization and Environment

Another important issue frequently faced by educational administrators is the extent to which schools stress centralized or decentralized functions. Centralized functions stress the *integration* of the organization, while decentralized activities highlight the *differentiation* of the school. The work of Lawrence and Lorsch suggests that the correct

TABLE 3-2

A summary of Fiedler's contingency theory of effective leadership

Effective leader-ship style	Task	Task	Task	Relation	Relation	Relation	Relation	Task
	Very Favorable to the Leader			Moderately Favorable to the Leader			Unfavorable to the Leader	
Situation	1	2	3	4	5	6	7	8
Leader-member relations	Good	Good	Good	Moderate	Moderate	Moderate	Moderate	Poor
Task structure	High	High	Low	Low	High	High	Low	Low
Position power	Strong	Weak	Strong	Weak	Strong	Weak	Strong	Weak

emphasis in integration or differentiation is contingent upon the rate of organizational change desired and the nature of tasks to be accomplished.[8] Studying three different industries, they find that rapid environmental change induces high differentiation among organization subunits. The members of these organizational departments differed not only in terms of the specific tasks they performed but also in their attitudes. Specifically, across the subunits, members differed on factors such as emphasis on interpersonal skills, time perspective, and need for formalized organizational procedures.

The complexity of the environment created a complex organization. The organization then faced the problem of integrating these complex and diverse subunits. Lawrence and Lorsch examined conflict-resolution processes and found that various industries and organizations developed different strategies for resolving conflict. Stable industries in slow-changing, stable environments, for example, used top management to resolve conflicts, while highly differentiated organizations in rapidly changing environments used lower-position members whose primary purpose was to work with conflict subunits. Effective organizations are thus able to deal with environmental complexity and conflict produced by differentiation.

Managerial Work

Mintzberg proposes a contingency theory of managerial work.[9] He argues that the work of any administrator is influenced by the relations among four major variables as they interact with basic managerial roles and managerial work. His contingency view of managerial work is illustrated in Figure 3–2. The four variables are: environment, job, person, and situation. These variables influence the extent to which distinguishing characteristics of managerial work and managers' work roles are displayed in a situation. For example, Mintzberg found that all managers spent part of their time in contact with public groups, acting as a liaison for the organization. When he compared the manager of a firm that produced consumer goods to a public school superintendent, the superintendent spent more time in scheduled and clocked meetings with directors (school board) and clients. The superintendent was easily available to outsiders where the role required a liaison.

Mintzberg argues that there are eight managerial job types. These job types are present in the work of any manager, but their relative

---

[8]Paul R. Lawrence and Jay W. Lorsch, *Organization and Environment: Managing Differentiation and Integration* (Homewood, Illinois: Richard D. Irwin, 1969).

[9]Mintzberg, *The Nature of Managerial Work,* chapter 5.

FIGURE 3-2
A contingency view of managerial work

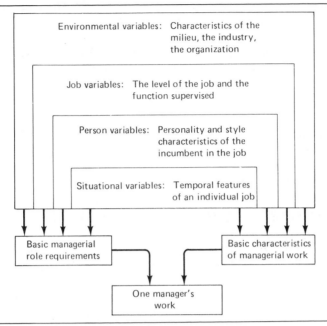

Source: Henry Mintzberg, *The Nature of Managerial Work.* New York: Harper & Row, 1973, p. 103.

emphasis depends upon the particular combination of variables present in that situation. For instance, all managers are more or less concerned with the role of *resource allocator.* In various situations, this particular aspect of the administrator's job becomes important. Superintendents, for example, become concerned with this part of their role as contract negotiations with teachers draw near. Once the contract is settled, however, the superintendent may emphasize another element in the role (liaison with community groups, for instance).

A PRAGMATIC INTEGRATION FOR EDUCATIONAL ADMINISTRATION

The studies reviewed, and many others, suggest the rich array of thinking available under the general label of contingency theory. Where does one begin in adopting a contingency-theory strategy in educational administration? What questions might one ask in building such a strategy?

This section proposes a working model of a contingency theory for school administrators. The format used is that of providing administrators with a series of questions which might be considered in analyzing a problem and forming a solution. Obviously all the questions would not be asked for every problem, but a fairly exhaustive list is provided to suggest the issues and areas which might be considered.

The working model has four purposes:

1.   to suggest to practitioners in a situation the major factors to be included and excluded from study;

2.   to suggest to practitioners in a situation the major linkage patterns to be included and excluded from study;

3.   to surface to practitioners in situations the habitual or semiconscious assumptions and ideologies which may or may not be applicable in the situation; and,

4.   to provide a way for practitioners to systematically catalogue and integrate both research studies and reflections upon experience.

Finally, the model does not pretend to be the penultimate formulation of contingency theory. What it constitutes is an attempt to think conceptually about educational administration in a manner which encourages the integration of theory and practice. This integration is suggested by the general structure of contingency theory—the sense that what administrators do in a situation depends upon a host of factors. Instead of being swamped by a never-ending list of possibilities, the proposed contingency model suggests a series of factors and relations which order inquiry in any situation. As students, practitioners, and researchers learn more about how administrators and organizations function, amendments and revisions are inevitable. This first pass is valuable as a working guide, not as a blueprint.

The working model is presented as Figure 3–3. Five major factors are seen as influencing the administrative decision for the situation. Each of these factors may be examined through a series of questions, as outlined below.

Factor 1: External Societal Environment

The following are some questions for educational administrators to consider in exploring this factor:

1.   What is the overall rate of change in the environment?

FIGURE 3–3
A possible contingency framework model for educational administrators.

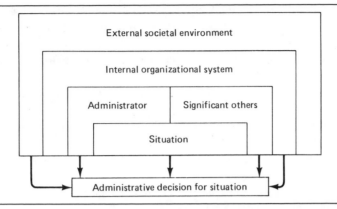

2. Are some aspects of the environment changing more rapidly than others?

3. What is the general socioeconomic status of society which comprises the environment?

4. What is the prevailing mood about growth or decline of the environment?

5. What are the demographic characteristics of the environment (urban, suburban, town, rural)?

6. What is the age structure of the environment's population (young to old)?

7. What resources are available from the environment to moderate or resolve conflict?

8. What is the history of support or criticism for educational activities in the environment?

9. What are the influences of other competing educational institutions?

10. What is the environment's general attitude toward the roles of professional organizations and unions?

Factor 2: Internal Organization Systems

The following are some questions for educational administrators to consider in exploring this factor:

1. What is the size of the school or school district?

2. Is the structure of the school relatively permanent, or does it frequently change?

3. What is the general ratio of agreement among the goals of specific individuals, to specific units, to the school as a whole?

4. What mechanisms does the school have for systematically monitoring the environment?

5. What conflict-resolution mechanism of processes are operant in the school?

6. What is the general level of resources made available to the school by the environment?

7. What is the general structure for deciding who makes decisions that affect others?

8. What are the general channels by which information flows through the school?

9. How permanent or changing are the standard procedures for dealing with normal day-to-day activities?

10. What are the capacities of the school to generate willingness to diagnosis and to generate new or different organizational goals?

Factor 3: Administrator

The following are some questions for educational administrators to consider in exploring this factor:

1. What is the general inclination of the administrator toward the primary and secondary rewards of the office?

2. What is the experience of the administrator in this role?

3. What are the general values the administrator holds about people?

4. What are the various administrative tasks which the administrator enjoys most and enjoys least?

5. What is the administrator's tolerance for ambiguity in a situation?

6. What is the general level of confidence of significant others (staff, parents, students, community) in the administrator?

7. What is the administrator's general willingness to take risks or general propensity to avoid risks?

8. What are important sources of information to the administrator about the day-to-day operations of the school and the state-of-the-art of the profession?

9. Is the administrator interested in achieving a different or higher administrative position?

10. What personal characteristics influence the administrator's general style of defining problems, generating alternatives, weighing consequences, and presenting solutions?

Factor 4: Significant Others

The following are some questions for educational administrators to consider in exploring this factor:

1. What is the orientation of the group of significant others (parents, teachers, students, etc.) toward general school goals?

2. What has been the general mode and mood of relations between significant others and administrators?

3. What is the time perspective employed by significant others?

4. Who speaks for significant others?

5. What are the relations among members in significant other groups?

6. What are the major sources of information for significant others?

7. What particular skills do significant others have?

8. What sense of independence and willingness to accept responsibility do the significant others display?

9. How do various groups of significant others view other groups?

10. What is the general sense that significant others have about their ability to affect the school?

Factor 5: Situation

The following are some questions for educational administrators to consider in exploring this factor:

1. Is there general agreement about both the existence and the general nature of a problem or opportunity?

2. What are the possible ways of resolving the problem or issue?

3. Can explanations of the problem be spread quickly and easily to others?

4. In what ways is the problem similar to and different from past practice?

5. What new resources or major redistribution of resources will be needed?

6. Is the solution to this problem one that cannot be reversed?

7. What are the relative impacts of interpersonal and intergroup relations on the problem?

8. How many people or communication channels must be involved in knowing and deciding about the problem?

9. Are changes, when proposed, generally seen as radical, as moderate alternatives, or as not advisable because of "the way things are done around here"?

10. What are the possible competing criteria for judging the worth of possible solutions?

These five factors, thus, provide for a practicing administrator in a particular situation the means for exploring that circumstance. They also suggest the intimate linkages that may exist among these factors. As such, these factors and the linkages among them do *not* constitute a contingency theory *per se,* but a set of guidelines to identify issues which might be considered by administrators. Factors and linkages suggested by the questions are expected to be different at different times and in different places. An array of strategies and solutions is needed to deal with this complex and ever-changing world.

We have now come to the heart of this chapter. Contingency theory as a metatheory provides a tool for practicing administrators—a tool which stresses the importance of exploring conceptually the multifaceted world of the educational administrator. It is not enough to consider just the environment or the immediate situation. These and other factors must be examined not only in light of past experiences but also of future goals. As metatheory, contingency theory provides help in these difficult tasks.

CONTINGENCY THEORY: STRENGTHS AND WEAKNESSES FOR EDUCATIONAL ADMINISTRATION

Contingency theory represents an important stage in thinking about the administration of schools. Thinking in this manner has several strengths; but two major weaknesses must be overcome if contingency theory is to be of great benefit to educational administrators.

Strengths

As a metaframework for the study of and reflections on administration, contingency theory has three major advantages. *First,* contingency theory lays to rest the notion that there is "one best way" to handle situations. In contrast to those who proclaim that their recipe makes the best administrative solution, the mood engendered by using contingency theory is that repeating a "pat answer" to a problem may be a fatal flaw. The sense of "it depends upon" means that there may be no one way to have a committee to approve a textbook, to obtain a favorable school board vote on a curriculum change, or to negotiate with teacher organizations about salaries and benefits.

Second, contingency theory provides an important perspective toward change. Change is a critical part of contingency theory, because slight shifts in any factor of the model often ripple through the entire system. Contingency theory alerts administrators to the pervasiveness of change, provides useful indicators for assessing the impact of change on various factors, and makes administrative thinking sensitive to balancing stability and continuity against change and emerging patterns. Administrators working from contingency theory are always alert to the relationship between "it depends on" and "the times they are a-changin'."

Third, contingency theory accentuates the multiple dimensions of the world of the administrator. The model suggests the inherent complexity of the life that administrators lead. They must be alert to the environment, to the general organization system, to their own perspectives, to significant others around them, and to situations. This multiplicity of factors contrasts sharply with simplistic how-to-do it manuals, and parallels closely the buzzing-booming confusion that often constitutes the busy world of administrators. Contingency theory and its multi-factor and multiple-relations perspective provides clues about why administrators never have enough time to get all their work done.

Weaknesses

Contingency theory has two major weaknesses. *First,* contingency theory implies that if administrators are alert to situations, they will be able to make good decisions. By tending to business, administrators are able to stay on top of situations and will make a series of good decisions about small problems. Where contingency theory may fail, however, is in the implicit assumption that a series of well-made decisions about small situations will automatically lead to a good big decision. Taking care of a host of small details somehow constitutes the production of a good, single, comprehensive outcome.

It seems reasonable to suggest that the minute and the detailed are important, but it also seems reasonable to suggest that administrators need to have larger visions of their roles, organization, and environment. These big pictures seem essential because series of small decisions often do not lead to sound major decisions. Examples of rigid adherence to detail or to following orders, without any sense of the total pattern developing, are all too commonplace. Where means become ends in themselves, distortions about human purpose abound.

Second, contingency theory has a general sense of value neutrality. Existing conditions—factors such as the environment, organization, or significant others—can be taken as givens which must be reacted to.

Strategies for change which stress normative shifts in these factors can be ignored. Administrators using contingency theory can be seduced into being only reactive barometers of the ways current winds are blowing.

These two criticisms are potential. In the field of educational administration, we suggest a deliberate stress upon the moral vision and commitment needed to deal with a complex situation. As a purposive organization, schools seek to deliberately change their students. While a series of good experiences are important, administrators cannot ignore the need to deliberately reflect upon ways of integrating the host of school experiences into a larger perspective. Equally, schooling has long-range consequences in terms of shaping the characteristics of the environment in coming years. Educational reform is normatively oriented: we seek to make the world a better place, not just a comfortable one.

SUMMARY

This chapter has stressed the utility of contingency theory as a metaframework for organizing research and reflection about educational administration. Contingency theory suggests the importance of understanding empirical research, of assumptions made by researchers about human beings, of fundamental social processes, and of relations among factors. Contingency theory underscores the importance of reflections by practitioners about the history and life of their organizations. As a metaframework, contingency theory can be used to generate a series of questions about factors and relations. Finally, educational administrators may find useful the attack of contingency theory on those who offer simplistic solutions. They must be wary of the lack of moral vision which can result from blind adherence to a reactive contingency model.

STUDY GUIDE

Can you recall the meanings of the following terms? Discuss them with a class colleague and apply them to your school-community setting.

metatheory	environment and differentiation
contingency theory	situational variables
models of man	societal environment
linkage patterns	organizational system
organizational evolution	significant others
"social time"	change
effective leadership style	value neutrality

SUGGESTED ACTIVITIES

1.   Break the class into several small groups, and ask the groups to deal with a problem—for example, should their school district expend course offerings for very gifted students. In the discussions, ask a recorder for each group to note the influence of differences in the districts—for example, how size, resources of human talent, or finances influence the various solutions proposed. Ask the recorders to "generalize" some of the key factors.

2.   Using Fiedler's theory of leadership effectiveness, speculate about the relationship between school superintendents and school boards. Consider factors such as the newness of the board or the superintendent, the types of issues which come to school boards, and pressures on the board from various segments of the community.

3.   Using the proposed model, examine minutely and in great detail a single problem in your present employment situation. For example, your school may be facing declining enrollments. After this consideration, systematically vary one major element in the environment and "trace" its effect on the other factors—for example, a "baby boom."

4.   Take any single factor in the proposed model. Reflect about your own practical experiences, and develop new questions or modify existing ones. Now, review one or two articles which appear to bear on this factor. Once again, develop new questions or modify existing ones. Finally, arrange to interview one or two administrators in your district. In the interviews discuss with them their experiences on this factor. Once again, develop new questions or modify existing ones.

SELECTED READINGS

BLAU, PETER M., and RICHARD A. SCHOENHERR, *The Structure of Organizations.* New York: Basic Books, 1971, chapters 6–8.

CHILD, JOHN, "Organizational Structure, Environment and Performance: The Role of Strategic Choice," *Sociology,* 6 (January, 1972), 1–22.

DILL, WILLIAM R., "Environments as an Influence on Managerial Autonomy," *Administrative Science Quarterly,* 2 (March, 1958), 409–443.

HALL, RICHARD H., *Organizations: Structure and Processes* (2nd ed.). Englewood Cliffs, N.J.: Prentice-Hall, 1977, chapters 11–12.

LITWAK, EUGENE, "Models of Organizations which Permit Conflict," *American Journal of Sociology,* 76 (September, 1961), 177–184.

Introduction to Governance in Education

4

THE SCHOOL
AS A
POLITICAL
ORGANIZATION

Twenty years ago it would have been heresy to characterize the school as a political organization; today it raises few eyebrows. For one thing, schools have changed in ways that make it more difficult to maintain the fiction that education is nonpolitical. A dramatic surge of education legislation at both the state and federal levels, controversial court cases, and more contested school-board elections are just a few of the ways the political nature of schools is brought to our attention.

Equally important, our view of what is "political" has broadened. Take, for example, the three situations sketched below. Each describes an issue in the realm of education which will be resolved according to certain political processes.

1. The superintendent of Teagarden District, faced with declining enrollments and a deficit budget, has just informed the board of education of his decision: Rock Bottom Elementary School should be closed next year. A coalition of neighborhood parents and teachers has launched a vigorous campaign to pressure the board to keep the school open.

2. The education committee of the state senate has been holding hearings on a bill which would mandate a minimal competency test for all graduating seniors in the state. The state chapter of the National Association of Secondary School Principals and the National Education Association are both working to have the bill defeated, but legislators have detected strong public

support in most districts. The Governor, facing re-election this November, has given the bill his unqualified support. The state Superintendent of Education is seeking to have the bill amended to give local school districts an option of whether or not to institute the program.

3.   The principal of Kenworth Junior High School has been directed by the district office to review discipline policy at her school. A delegation of black parents recently visited the superintendent, expressing their dismay at the large number of suspensions meted out. They noted that a high proportion of the suspensions were given to black students, and questioned the educational soundness of this kind of discipline. Why, they wanted to know, were their youngsters being singled out? And how could the students learn anything if they were not permitted to come to school?

Each of these situations finds people in disagreement about what should be done in some area of educational policy. When such disagreement becomes substantial and public, we call it a political *issue.* Issues are the starting point in our analysis of the political process. Without them there would be no need for politics. And one measure of the worth of a political system is how sucessfully it deals with issues that arise. As you can see in each of the three cases above, some kind of resolution is needed.

So when we say that the school is a political organization, we do not necessarily mean that it is a focal point for partisan politics, with Democrats and Republicans squabbling over educational matters. Nor do we mean it in quite the same sense as the disgruntled citizen who complains that "it's just all politics!" Schools are political in the sense that they, along with most other organizations, confront and respond to essentially political questions. What objectives should be emphasized? How will scarce resources, such as money or teaching talent, be allocated among various programs? And, in the memorable phrase of Harold Lasswell, "Who gets what, when, and how?"[1]

RECONCILING INTERESTS:
THE PROBLEM OF COLLECTIVE
CHOICE

If everyone agreed upon what outcomes are desirable from schooling, making educational policy would be a lot simpler. But disagreement over what constitutes an appropriate education is natural within any complex society. We have been socialized to value different things. Even more obviously, we hold different positions and play different

[1]Harold D. Lasswell, *Politics: Who Gets What, When, How* (Cleveland: Meridian Books, 1958).

roles within our society, which may lead us to take different positions on educational questions. Recent Gallup polls of the American public, for instance, found that

> low-income citizens are far more likely to resist increasing school taxes than middle- and upper-income citizens (1970);
>
> parents of parochial school children are more likely to favor giving government tax money to church-related schools than parents of public school children (1970);
>
> whites are less likely than non-whites to favor proposals for tax-appointed child-care centers for all pre-school children as part of the public school system (1976);
>
> citizens over age fifty are more likely to favor promotion of children from grade to grade only after they have passed an examination than are younger citizens (1978).[2]

None of that is very surprising. These and most other differences of opinion between segments of the American public are readily understandable. Somehow they have to be reconciled, however, if we are to get on with the business of educating children.

The most difficult challenge in the area of government and politics is to find the best way to arrive at _collective choices_ in the face of differences. Individual choices are difficult enough, as anyone who has vacillated between two new automobiles, or two careers, knows very well. With collective choice, however, there is the additional complication that various individuals in the collectivity will prefer different outcomes and propose different ways of achieving them. In the case of schools, some students care very little about having a strong girls' athletic program while others care very much. Some parents want almost exclusive emphasis on the three R's, while others favor expanding art education and still others believe it is the auto-mechanics program that needs more teachers and more equipment. Many teachers are concerned about obtaining smaller class sizes; the local chapter of the taxpayers' association may propose larger classes. While almost everyone believes that some kind of an organizational effort is required to educate children, not everyone has quite the same view of what constitutes an _appropriate_ education, or what kind of system will bring it about.

In short, educating youngsters for productive lives in the twentieth

[2]Results of Gallup Poll surveys of beliefs about education have appeared in the _Phi Delta Kappan_ annually for the last ten years. The findings cited here are from the February 1970, October 1976, and September 1978 issues of that journal.

century requires organization, and organizations require governance. Governance includes such things as setting some priorities among possible objectives of the organization, allocating resources to meet these objectives, and coordinating the activities of members of the organization in order to accomplish the objectives more effectively.

Individuals or groups who want different outcomes from a social process are said to have different *interests*. For many years we have tried to sustain the myth that everyone wanted the same thing from the educational system and that, thus, there are no separate interests in this area. Today we see more clearly that the interests of academically talented students, the academically disadvantaged, parents, teachers, taxpayers, employers, professional administrators, and nonacademic staff may not coincide. Old myths may still comfort us at times, but we must not allow them to obscure our vision when we set about analyzing the educational policy process.

David Truman, a political scientist who wrote a classic volume on political interest groups, defined interests simply as "shared attitudes."[3] Unfortunately, *attitude* is a rather imprecise term in social psychology. We would twist Truman's definition of *interest* just a bit to make it a *preferred outcome*. Individuals who agree upon which outcomes they prefer may be said to have the same interest in a certain issue area such as education. The important thing, whether we are dealing with shared attitudes or shared preferences about outcomes, is that no policy maker, administrator, or social scientist can unilaterally decide what is in another individual's interest. Only that individual can determine what outcomes he or she prefers.

There are a number of natural interest groups in education that make their own distinctive demands upon the school system. Much of the attention of policy makers, all the way from principals, superintendents, and school-board members to state and federal officials, is devoted to reconciling the competing demands of these interests. Where the difference of opinion is traceable to some mistaken belief about what will happen if a certain policy alternative is adopted, convincing evidence that that particular fear (or hope) is groundless should help. Much of policy research in education attempts to provide better knowledge about the probable consequences of certain policy changes.

More often, however, the disagreement is over questions of value. There is no simple way for any school administrator to decide who is right and who is wrong on questions of this type. Resolutions which

[3]David B. Truman, *The Governmental Process: Political Interests and Public Opinion* (New York: Knopf, 1951), p. 34.

leave all parties reasonably satisfied (or at least not at each other's throats) may be the best we can hope for. It is the process of finding, presenting, and justifying these resolutions that characterizes the political process. The goal is not so much to come up with the "right" answers by some ideological standard, as it is to come up with resolutions which keep all of the people affected as satisfied as possible.

While there is no magic formula for finding such resolutions, we can all think of ways which would strike us as arbitrary, unjust, or just plain foolish for arriving at collective choices. On the other hand, there are methods of reconciling differences which are widely viewed as legitimate in our culture. Four time-honored ways are listed below.

Persuasion   Given time and the requisite skills of persuasion, some members of the collectivity may simply be able to convince others that their goals, or ways of reaching them, are preferable. The aim, in this case, is consensus upon the best choice among all those involved.

Authority   Consensus, however, is not always possible. Individuals in certain positions may be granted the authority to make some decisions for the collectivity. School board members, for example, enjoy the authority to make many collective choices by virtue of the position they occupy within the school district. Superintendents have the authority to resolve some other kinds of issues on their own. Persons are usually chosen by election or appointment for such positions of authority.

Voting   On the theory that no one person is wise enough or even-handed enough to make choices for the collectivity, votes may be taken to obtain a more representative expression of individual interests. This is the form of collective decision making used by most legislative bodies.

Bargaining   Parties may simply negotiate their differences until a resolution is found which is acceptable to everyone. Not all disagreements are negotiable, because bargaining assumes that a possible resolution exists which leaves all parties better off than they would have been if no agreement had been reached. The most notable example of bargaining in education today is the formal process of collective bargaining used by teachers' organizations and school boards in many districts to settle the terms of employment for teachers.

As we have already noted, none of these means of reaching a collective choice is without its problems. Most decisions of educational governance (as within other areas) are made by one or another—and often a mixture—of these four processes.

A CLOSER LOOK AT "POLICY"

Organizations control the actions of individuals within them by making and enforcing *policy*. For our purposes we may define a *policy* as any authoritative communication of expected behavior for individuals in certain positions under specified conditions. Thus, the principal who issues a memorandum saying that "no teacher should leave the building before 3:45 P.M. on school days" has fashioned a policy. So has the superintendent who directs principals not to suspend pupils for more than three days without board approval, or the state legislature that passes a law requiring minimal competency tests to be given before high school graduation.

An older notion of *policy* reserved the term for statements of major goals or far-reaching programs. According to this view, school boards, state legislatures, and congress established policy, while school administrators simply carried out their wishes. Careful observation of the policy process, however, indicates that that distinction is largely imaginary. Many actors, including teachers, principals, and superintendents, as well as students and parents, are intimately involved in the process of shaping policy as well as carrying it out.

It is hard to imagine any very complex organization operating effectively without some policies in force. All organizations, including schools, face certain recurring problems. All that is needed, it would seem, is for members of the organization to sit down and consider impassionately how best to deal with a familiar problem when it occurs again; they will surely be able to think up a way of handling the problem that will serve the ends of the organization better than if every employee were left to his or her own devices. Furthermore, it will usually be to the advantage of the organization if that problem is dealt with in the same way each time it recurs. Aside from promoting effectiveness and consistency, policies protect those who follow them. Put yourself in the position of an English teacher who conscientiously assigns reading books only from a list approved by a district-wide committee. Any complaints from parents about a book on that list can be neatly parried by pointing a finger at the committee that approved the book. Woe and behold the teacher who strays beyond the approved list, however, when irate parents descend upon the principal.

The German sociologist, Max Weber, saw bureaucracy as a sort of ideal type of organization, and placed a great deal of importance on written policies and regulations.[4] In an age when personal favoritism

[4]See, for example, H. H. Gerth and C. Wright Mills, *From Max Weber: Essays in Sociology* (New York: Oxford University Press, 1958, a Galaxy Book), chapter 8.

was far more prevalent than today, making an organization into a sort of impersonal machine seemed like a good idea. At least it would reward according to merit rather than to who you were or who you knew. Weber was not, we hasten to add, as sensitive to some of the more vexing aspects of modern bureaucratic organization as we are today. But he had a point: Organizations, just as people, should strive to be as rational as possible. First, get your objectives clearly in mind, then calmly determine what policies would be most likely to achieve them. It was surely something that a few reasonable men and women, working together, could accomplish. Or was it?

Today we are aware of so many more complexities in the process of making policy that we are no longer sure. Some, such as Charles Lindblom, would argue that policy making seldom proceeds in a very rational manner. Lindblom painted a picture of an organization which, instead of finding optimal solutions to problems, staggered uncertainly toward marginally better ways of handling them.[5] He called it the method of "successive approximations."

Gone was the notion of wise men sitting around solving recurring problems for all time. Replacing it was a notion of fallible human beings, limited in their ability to see very far ahead, unable to examine all conceivable alternatives, settling for the first suggestion that promised to yield better results than the present policy. Lindblom and others who saw the same kind of limitations upon rational policy-making, became known as the incrementalists, and Lindblom himself dubbed his view the process of "muddling through."[6] We will want to examine these newer formulations of the decision-making process in more detail in Chapter 14.

Reflect, for a moment, about what goes into changing a policy. All of the kinds of activity outlined below are usually present, often behind the scenes.[7]

Reaction to Existing Policy   Someone, somewhere, expresses dissatisfaction with the way things are currently being done. If that dissatisfaction strikes a responsive chord, a policy issue will have been created.

[5]David Braybrooke and Charles E. Lindblom, *A Strategy of Decision: Policy Evaluation as a Social Process* (New York: Free Press, 1970), pp. 123–124.

[6]Charles E. Lindblom, "The Science of Muddling Through," *Public Administration Review*, 19 (1959), 79–88.

[7]An excellent introductory discussion of the concept of policy and policy stages is Charles O. Jones, *An Introduction to the Study of Public Policy*, 2nd ed. (North Scituate, Mass: Duxbury Press, 1977). Norman C. Thomas, *Education in National Politics* (New York: D. McKay, 1975), pp. 172–217, applies his own formulation of policy stages to federal decision making.

Proposal of Alternatives   Someone proposes an alternative way of handling the problem. Often more than one alternative will be proposed. Compromise proposals may combine elements of previously suggested alternatives.

Influencing the Outcome   Various actors try to increase the probability that their preferred alternative will be adopted, by influencing others to support it or to oppose other alternatives.

Authoritative Decision   Some person or group who has been vested with authority in this matter decides which alternative to adopt. They may, of course, decide to stick with the old policy.

Complying with the New Policy   Individuals whose behavior is supposed to be changed by the new policy either comply or refuse to comply with its prescriptions.

Enforcement of the New Policy   In most cases someone will be designated to check to see if the new policy is being obeyed and to take steps to enforce it if it is not.

Several generalizations become apparent as we contemplate this list. First, there is a lot more to the process than simply sitting back and making wise decisions. Generations of students of policy have been preoccupied with the behavior of authorizing bodies—why legislatures vote the way they do, or why a governor vetoes a bill, for example. By looking more closely at the policy process, we see that other kinds of behavior may be just as important. The ability to register dissatisfaction with present policy strenuously enough to get authorities to recognize it as an issue and to move it onto their agenda is an extremely important aspect of the process.[8] Some individuals and groups are very skilled at this, while others have difficulty even getting their discontents publicly acknowledged. Similarly, the creative act of inventing new policy alternatives or developing ingenious compromises which satisfy all interests is a crucial part of the process. Finally, we need to know more about the two kinds of behavior which characterize the implementation process: compliance, and administration which aims to assure compliance. If no one complies with the new policy, it has not accomplished very much.

Depending upon the resources and skills they possess, different individuals and groups will participate in the process in quite different ways. Some groups specialize in creating issues by mobilizing opposi-

---

[8]For an insightful account of this part of the policy process, see Robert W. Cobb and Charles D. Elder, *Participation in American Politics: The Dynamics of Agenda-Building* (Boston: Allyn & Bacon, 1972).

tion to existing policies. Other groups and individuals have the resources to create new proposals, draft legislation, or hammer out compromises. Others may be adroit administrators able to get everyone quickly into line with a new policy.

There is one problem with any portrayal of the various stages of the policy process. The list gives a misleading appearance of orderliness. In the real world a lot of influence behavior and even deliberation by the authoritative decision body may already have occurred when someone suddenly proposes a brand new alternative which changes things drastically. That new proposal may, in turn, be effectively vetoed by a powerful interest group whose leaders urge their members not to comply if the new proposal becomes policy. And so the process goes, careening wildly from proposal, to reaction, to influence behavior, to more proposals. It is useful, we think, to suggest the variety of activities that go into the policy process; but our list does not serve as a very accurate guide to the sequence of events. Furthermore, the process is neverending. As soon as any new policy comes into being, people affected by it will start evaluating. When dissatisfaction surfaces, a new issue has been forged and the process begins again.

INFLUENCE, POWER, AND AUTHORITY PATTERNS

At the heart of politics is the idea of some individuals or factions prevailing over others by obtaining policies closer to their own preferences. The mysteries of influence, power, and authority have intrigued social scientists for centuries. We are still far short of a satisfactory understanding of how these processes work, and some of our problems can be traced simply to a lack of uniformity in the way we use the terms. We will confine ourselves to the three most used terms—*influence, power*, and *authority*—but the reader should be aware that the distinctions we make are not the only ones possible.

Let us start with the simplest case: Two individuals, Mr. X and Mr. Y. We will say that X has exercised *influence* over Y whenever Y's behavior is different from what it would have been without the presence of X. That kind of definition is broad enough to cover everything from passing the salt at Mr. X's request to handing over all your money at the point of Mr. X's gun.

There are, however, two special cases of *influence* which are especially helpful in analyzing political processes. The first of these is *power*, which is usually defined as a kind of influence in which sanctions are employed. More precisely, a power relationship exists when

X influences Y by setting up a contingency in which better things will happen to Y if he follows X's wishes. Bribery, blackmail, and armed robbery are all clear cases of the exercise of power, but there are also many legitimate ways to exercise power in most organizations. A superintendent's intimation that principals who help most in pruning the district budget will be first in line for future promotions is one example. Another is the threat of a strike by the local teachers' organization in their efforts to obtain a higher salary schedule.

Looking at power in this simple way reveals several things. For one, if Y wants nothing that X can offer and is not threatened by anything X can do, there is no way X can exercise power over Y. It is also worth noting that X's threats or promises will be effective only to the extent that they are *believed* or judged *credible* by Y. Thus, one necessary step on X's way to power is to establish credibility as one who carries out his promises and threats. Finally, most exercise of power requires the control, and frequently the expenditure, of resources. This is most obvious in the case of bribery, but almost any exercise of power entails what Harsanyi called "opportunity costs" to the person exercising power.[9]

A *political resource*, then, might be thought of as anything which may be useful in influencing other individuals or groups. An individual who successfully resists offers of money may yield to promises of increased status or prestige. One skill of many "political" individuals is the ability to sense the vulnerabilities of other political actors and select the right kind of resource to exert power. Some interest groups enjoy an abundance of potential political resources which may be used in the exercise of power, while others suffer from a distinct shortage of resources. The unequal distribution of political resources in all societies is one of the hard facts of political life.[10]

So far, we have been discussing the simple case of *interpersonal* power, or power relationships between people. The relevance of this to school systems is not difficult to see. Teachers exercise power over students, on each other, and against their administrators. By the same token, school administrators, board members, custodians, and pillars of the community may attempt to influence each other through the use of political resources. Not all power in organizations, however, is interpersonal.

[9]John C. Harsanyi, "Measurement of Social Power, Opportunity Costs, and the Theory of Two-person Bargaining Games," *Behavioral Science*, 7 (1962), 67–80.

[10]Robert A. Dahl, *Modern Political Analysis, 3rd ed.* (Englewood Cliffs, N.J.: Prentice-Hall, 1976), pp. 56–57.

The extension of the concept of power—and, more generally, influence—to organizations which make extensive use of policies to control the behavior of individuals is straightforward. If a policy is effective in controlling the behavior of someone in the organization, it follows that anyone who influences the substance or implementation of that policy will have exercised influence, albeit indirectly, over the behavior of others. If we can identify the people who have impact upon the shape of policy and the way it is enforced, we can be confident that we have found the "influentials" in the organization.

The other special case of influence is *authority*. In this case, Y complies with the demands of X, not because of threats, promises, or even gentle persuasion, but because he recognizes the legitimate right of X to make those demands of him. Now Y may grant X that right for any of several reasons, but the reason of most interest to organization theorists is the *position* which X holds in the organization. If we are school principals, there are certain things we do just because the person who wants us to do them happens to be superintendent.

In considering authority relationships, we speak of subordinates and superordinates. In a sense, the subordinate suspends critical judgment as to the merit of the superordinate's request. It is even possible that the subordinate will comply with an order that he or she does not agree with. Formal authority relationships are an important part of any organization, including schools, but there may also be informal authority patterns—such as the tradition in some schools that younger, inexperienced teachers should defer to the wishes of older, more experienced hands in such things as the classroom assignments of students or the curriculum design.

There is a subtle, murky relationship between authority and power. An authority figure, such as a policeman, relies to the extent possible upon his authority rather than his gun; but there is usually the specter of power backing up authority. The advantage of using authority, rather than power, is that it costs little or nothing. But authority requires a period of socialization during which subordinates learn and internalize the desired authority patterns. We can all remember such lessons about the authority of our parents, or the policeman at the corner, when we were children. Boot camp in the military is as much an attempt to instill appropriate reactions to authority as it is a physical-training and skill-development exercise. Officers want the lines of authority well ingrained, to avoid having to rely upon persuasion, or even power, in a crisis situation. Similarly, students, teachers, administrators, board members, bureaucrats, and legislators are all part of the intricate authority patterns which exist in public education. Each goes through a socializing experience, learning what he or she has a right to expect from each of the others.

COMMUNITY POWER STRUCTURE

One of the questions that has engaged political analysts for many years is how one can most accurately describe the structure of influence relationships in the American system. Two broad camps have spent years defending their point of view and attacking the other. The first of these views, labeled "power elite" theory, postulates a single ruling elite which makes, or at least colors significantly, most of the major collective choices faced by the society. Stated in fullest form by C. Wright Mills, the captains of industry, government, and the military make the major, highest-level decisions for the society, based upon a more or less common set of values and ample opportunity for interaction among themselves.[11] Mills does not contend that middle-level decisions (which would probably include most education policy) are made by the power elite, but that they may be constrained and shaped by the grand lines charted by the ruling elite.

Floyd Hunter, a sociologist who developed a "reputational" approach to the study of power, supported elitist theory from yet another angle. In a seminal community-power study of Atlanta, Georgia, Hunter found that a business-oriented group of top policy makers determined the general direction of community affairs.[12] While there is no necessary implication of a conspiracy, it is clear from his description that these men had a common outlook upon the world, their society, and the opportunity to interact in deciding the affairs of the city.

At about the same time, the political scientist Robert Dahl was studying the power structure of New Haven, Connecticut.[13] Dahl broke down the governance of New Haven into "issue areas" (e.g., political nominations, urban redevelopment, and public education), then he observed the activities of individuals in each of these areas to try to ascertain who was exercising influence. His conclusion was that the power structure of New Haven was "pluralist," with competing elites arising in each issue area. Futhermore, he found little overlap in the

---

[11]C. Wright Mills, *The Power Elite* (New York: Oxford University Press, 1956); see especially chapter 12.

[12]Floyd Hunter, *Community Power Structure: A Study of Decision Makers* (Garden City, N.Y.: Anchor Books, 1963), p. 111.

[13]Robert A. Dahl, *Who Governs: Democracy and Power in an American City* (New Haven: Yale University Press, 1961).

composition of these elites from one issue area to the next. It was a conclusion that obviously did not square with Hunter's, and a great deal of energy has gone into trying to settle the dispute over the two versions of community power structure.

With the benefit of hindsight, two interpretations appear obvious. First, there is no compelling reason why all cities should have the same kind of power structure. Perhaps Atlanta and New Haven were just very different kinds of cities politically. Second, it is possible that the strikingly different methodological approaches used by the two scholars accounted for at least part of the discrepancy. If we ask general questions about who exercises power in this city, the argument goes, a power-elite group will probably emerge composed of individuals whose names appear frequently in the press and who have an established reputation for being prime movers in the community. If, on the other hand, you observe activity in a particular interest area, you may become aware of competing interests locked in apparent conflict, but may miss any indications of a power elite.

While the issue has never been resolved, out of it came a heightened appreciation that "Who exercises power?" is not the only important question to be asked about governmental systems. In recent years, there has been a steady shift to the equally important question of *who benefits* from public policy programs. It may, after all, matter very little who is responsible for setting education policy in either New Haven or Atlanta, unless the kinds of programs which result benefit some interests more than others.

The analogue of the community-power controversy in education is the dispute over who exercises power in local school districts. Is there a single, identifiable, community elite which influences education policy in most communities by informal and sometimes covert means? Is the education profession itself a sort of power elite in school matters, imposing its own values upon the community?[14] Elected school boards would be little more than symbolic bodies in this case, usually rubber-stamping the initiatives of the superintendent of schools. Or, as the pluralists would have it, is the realm of education simply another issue area which spawns its own competing interests, each trying to get its own preferences established as policy?

As with communities, it is entirely possible that some districts operate one way while others are structured the other way. Yet, the last two decades have witnessed the emergence of a number of orga-

[14]See, for example, L. Harmon Zeigler and M. Kent Jennings with G. Wayne Peak, *Governing American Schools: Political Interaction in Local School Districts* (North Scituate, Mass: Duxbury Press, 1974), p. 6.

nized interests in education, each making demands upon the system. Certainly at the federal and state levels, and to an increasing extent at the local level, there is conflict and competition among these interests in pressing their claims. Any analysis of educational policy which ignores the existence and activity of these interests misses a great deal of the process of educational governance. In the rest of this chapter we shall examine several of the more important of these interests.

THE INTERESTS OF STUDENTS
AND PARENTS

The most likely place to begin our search for major interests in education would seem to be with the highest-stake players in the game —students and their parents. Although not all students want precisely the same range of outcomes from their education, in some respects, we can think of them as having a collective interest in the educational process. A preponderance of students everywhere, for example, might rally to the cry of less arbitrary treatment, more conscientious, understanding, and competent teaching, fewer invasions of privacy, better employability upon graduation, or more freedom of expression.

Unfortunately for students, they are a classic example of an almost powerless interest. They enjoy few of the political resources that traditionally influence policy. Money, status, experience with the political process, contacts, organizational skills—all are in short supply among students' groups. Furthermore, students are often in a vulnerable position when it comes to pressing for change in the status quo. Grades, promotion, and letters of recommendation have all been used at one time or another in retaliation against student activists who work too strenuously to change educational policy.

Even if powerless as individuals, can students at least exercise influence through their student governments? We think not, in most cases. However useful student governments have been in teaching leadership skills and democratic norms (and even that can be debated), they have done little to change school policy. Student-council sponsors and school administrators typically listen politely to students' proposals, tolerate the innocuous, and veto the potentially harmful, knowing full well that they, not the students, will be held accountable for the outcome. Spontaneous student groups that occasionally arise at the secondary and higher education level are plagued with rapid turnover in leadership, which renders the development of expertise and continuity difficult. The time available to most students simply does not permit in-depth understanding of many policy issues or following them through to their resolution.

The one variety of power which, on occasion, has been used effectively by students is the power to disrupt. The classroom of uncooperative adolescents trying to "break in" a demanding neophyte teacher, or the large student protest groups on campus in the late 1960s and early 1970s, operate on the principle that the ability to make their discontents known is the first step toward changing policy. Sometimes just creating an issue is enough to get the ball rolling your way. Still, protest alone is a crude tool with which to try to shape educational policy to your liking on a day-to-day basis.

One of the historic functions of the judicial system in the United States is to protect individuals, and classes of individuals, who have little power to defend their own interests. Not many years ago, students were routinely sent home from many schools if their hair was too long or their jeans did not have a belt. Student-authored stories in the school newspaper might be censored by school officials. Suspension from school was sometimes meted out arbitrarily and without recourse to appeal.

In recent years the courts have increasingly turned their attention to the rights of students. Landmark cases, many engineered by the American Civil Liberties Union, have affirmed students' rights to dress as they like, print what they want in student newspapers, and express themselves as they please on public issues as long as the educational process was not substantially disrupted. The right to due process of law was strengthened in matters of search and seizure and in disciplinary proceedings. We will be looking more carefully at some of these constitutional questions in Chapter 7.

Parents, also, might be expected to represent their children's interests in educational matters, and to some extent they do. Lay control of education is still an important norm in the U.S., and professionals ignore the proprietary attitude of parents at their own peril. The private telephone call from parent to school administrator about some problem experienced by a son or daughter frequently gets results. That is one of the aspects of our educational system that leaves Europeans shaking their heads. Still parents have difficulty organizing effectively to bring collective pressure to bear upon school policy makers. They are not a very cohesive group when it comes to education policy. Once in a while, an issue will come along that will galvanize a group of parents into action. It may be reading books branded as "obscene, atheistic, and un-American" that stirs them, as in Kanawha County, West Virginia back in 1974. Closing a school building, instituting a new busing program to achieve racial balance, instituting a new sex-education program, banning (or permitting) corporal punishment, or closing down the athletic program have done the trick elsewhere. But more usually, parents find themselves in disagreement about what the proper course of action should be, uncertain of how to make their feelings known, or simply too far removed from the central issues to worry much about having an impact upon policy.

The most noteworthy attempt to organize parents in the United States has been by the National Congress of Parents and Teachers. Most elementary and secondary schools today have a local unit of this organization, or perhaps a parent-teacher organization unaffiliated with the national PTA. The majority of local units are content to assume a supportive posture with respect to educational policy, steering safely clear of most controversial issues. They may, of course, endorse school-tax-increase elections when called upon, finance new warmups for the track team or a set of encyclopedias for the school library, while extolling the virtues of American public education in general—and the local schools in particular—at every opportunity. That is an important role, but not one which lends the PTA or its leaders great influence in determining the course of educational events within a community.

At the state and federal level a subtle shift of role occurs. State PTA organizations command respect in most state capitals. As the legislature and governor grapple over education legislation, including the all-important funding of school-aid formulae, PTA lobbyists may be much in evidence. In Washington, the PTA is also usually to be found on the side of higher appropriations for education, and may take strong positions on controversial legislation such as the tuition-tax-credit proposals debated in 1978. The national office also orchestrates campaigns on student-welfare issues designed to appeal to most parents and alienate few. Crusades against child pornography and the prevalence of sex and violence in TV programming have been launched in recent years.

A new type of organization, the National Committee of Citizens in Education, has for several years been attempting to recruit parents into the fight for the rights and welfare of students. Styling itself as an advocacy group in the same vein as the consumer-protection groups, NCCE collected testimony about public education from parents, students, teachers, and experts in a series of hearings held in major cities across the nation. Positions which emerged from these hearings were pressed upon Congress and various Washington agencies in an attempt to influence policy. While it is still too early to assess the long-range impact of this venture, it may represent the best avenue available today for parents who want to stand up and be counted on controversial issues.

TEACHERS AND THEIR
ORGANIZATIONS

Nowhere has the power structure of education changed more rapidly than in respect to the role teachers are playing in the development of policy. For well over a century, teachers in this country have been organizing to further the cause of education and, in the process, to advance their own interests in the realm of school politics. In the last two decades the movement has gathered steam rapidly. Some would argue that teachers and their organizations are destined to become the dominant force in education policy in the years ahead, if they have not already.

While we find students and their parents at something of a disadvantage in attempting to shape the nature of their schools, teachers probably enjoy more organizational advantages than any other interest group. Most of the traditional political resources (e.g., numbers, experience, affluence, status, inside information, and political skill) are available to teachers. By virtue of the fact that they spend most of their working lives in schools, teachers also have an incentive to shape education policy, which may be missing in interests further removed from the scene. In order to gain a better picture of how teachers have exploited these strengths through their organizations, we will look briefly at each of the two large teacher organizations in the U.S.

The National Education Association and
the American Federation of Teachers

By far the oldest (1857) as well as the largest (over 1,886,000 members) of our current teacher organizations, the NEA has a long and venerable past. Advertising their organization as a professional association rather than a union, its leaders worked in the early years for their vision of a highly professional educational system, with teacher-welfare issues playing a relatively minor role. Administrators as well as teachers were welcomed into the fold. For years, in fact, NEA leadership positions were dominated by school administrators and university professors, who enjoyed more visibility and the luxury of being able to attend professional meetings.

In the late 1800s and early 1900s the NEA was about the closest thing this country had to a national education policy. Even as late as the 1950s, the pronouncements of the NEA and the U.S. Office of Education were almost indistinguishable.

Yet, there was a conservative cast to NEA activity in the first 100 years of its existence. Its membership was largest in southern and rural parts of the country. A long-term alliance with the American Legion reinforced its staid character. Eschewing the strike and most other militant tactics as "unprofessional," NEA affiliates attempted to persuade school boards with reason and facts provided by the state and national organizations. The concept of collective bargaining with the board smacked too much of unionism.

The American Federation of Teachers, on the other hand, made no apologies about being a union. From its earliest days in Chicago, it was clearly identified with the American labor movement. It did not, however, sanction the use of strikes in school matters. Growth was slow through the 1920s and 1930s. One turning point came when, in 1944, an AFT local in Cicero, Illinois signed a collective-bargaining agreement with the board of education; another in 1947, when the Buffalo Teachers' Federation struck for higher salaries despite their parent organization's no-strike policy. Although the AFT maintained its official ban on strikes for a time, it became clear that striking locals could expect sympathetic treatment from the national union.

The AFT traded upon its union connection with the AFL/CIO, especially in the large metropolitan districts where teachers were less likely to be squeamish about labor affiliation and labor tactics. Competition between the upstart AFT and the NEA developed in several states and culminated in a showdown in the New York City schools. By 1960, the AFT had launched a major organizing drive in New York, focused upon its largest local—the United Federation of Teachers (UFT)—in New York City. A bitter strike in that year had done much to create an atmosphere of militancy and to catapult Albert Shanker into the forefront of the teacher movement. A scheduled vote the following year on which teacher organization should represent New York teachers at the bargaining table was instrumental in shaping the teacher movement for years to come.

To understand why that was so, and much that has happened since then, we need to know a little about the nature of the competition for membership between the AFT and the NEA. The advent of collective bargaining had changed the rules of that game so that it was no longer just a matter of trying to interest as many teachers as possible in the monthly journal and the high-sounding objectives of the organization. For collective bargaining to work, some bargaining agent has to be designated to bargain for all the teachers. No self-respecting school board is going to want to bargain simultaneously with two or three organizations, arriving at separate agreements with each of them. Any district that was considering collective bargaining, then, would have to have an election to determine the "sole bargaining agent" for teachers.

While both the NEA and AFT had local organizations in New York schools, it was the nature of collective bargaining that precipitated the showdown.

The NEA had recognized the challenge. While their membership figures were still several times greater than those of the AFT, the metropolitan battle grounds ahead would be more difficult for the NEA. Furthermore, there was a shift of mood among American teachers toward bolder, more militant tactics, which might make the AFT attractive to many. Within a relatively short period of time, the NEA had revised its long-standing policies against collective bargaining and teacher strikes, and had gently expelled school administrators—now suspect, with the turn toward adversary processes like collective bargaining—from the fold. Yet, despite a major effort in New York, the NEA lost. AFT victories in other large cities swelled their membership to over 446,000 by 1976. The competition between the two groups is still intense, although they have become even closer in their positions on major issues and tactics.

Three changes in the power structure of education have been brought about by the growing teacher movement. First, a larger proportion of teachers are politically knowledgeable and politically active today than a generation ago. More are members of one or the other of the major organizations, and these organizations have played a part in the politicization of the American teaching profession. Teachers today are more likely to see their interests as somewhat distinct from those of taxpayers, administrators, board members, parents, or even students. Their political awareness has resulted in substantial gains, relative to other professions, in compensation and working conditions. By material standards, the organization of American teachers has paid off, even after taking into account annual dues paid by a member to local, state, and national units of the organization.

Second, the nature of collective bargaining, which is rapidly supplanting older board-controlled methods of arriving at teacher salaries and working conditions, has fundamentally changed the way in which resources used for education are allocated. Professional administrators and elected board members used to have a monopoly on that process. Today, in many districts, every item on the proposed budget for next year will have to be justified to representatives from the teachers' bargaining agent sitting across the table before a contract between teachers and the district will be forthcoming. The strike, of course, remains the ultimate threat used by teachers in this process. But one should not underestimate the effect of having negotiators arguing the teachers' case, who know as much about the district's financial situation as the business manager and who may know even more about trends in surrounding districts, the state, or the nation. Those are powerful resources which have channeled an increased share of the educational dollar into the pockets of teachers and have provided more job security, better working conditions, or more favorable teaching climates for teachers.

Third, there has been, since the establishment of collective bargaining in many districts, a subtle shift in authority relationships within a school district and in the way schools are viewed by people on the outside. Teachers no longer project the image of good-hearted samaritans who, despite low salaries and miserable working conditions, teach just for the love of children. They are unlikely to accept direction from school administrators as uncritically as they once did. They may draw the line more quickly than before, the line beyond which they will not go in the performance of their duties. They are increasingly skeptical of the efficacy of teacher training provided by colleges and universities, and are eager to have a hand in developing their own training programs.

These are perfectly natural reflexes in the process of becoming a stronger profession. The changes, however, may have contributed to a more recent shift in public attitudes toward schools. With teachers bargaining hard and looking out for themselves, the public seems less inclined to give its once almost automatic approval to school-tax increases. The days when almost anything done in the name of education would be looked upon favorably by the public appear to be over. Public support for education leaders continues to be high, by comparison with most other social and political institutions (see Figure 4–1), but has declined in recent years (see Table 4–1).

TABLE 4–1
National ratings of public schools by local residents

	1974	1975	1976	1977	1978
A or B rating	48%	43%	42%	37%	36%
C, D or Fail rating	32	44	44	44	49
Don't know/no answer	20	13	14	19	15
	100%	100%	100%	100%	100%

Question: Students are often given the grades A, B, C, D, and FAIL to denote the quality of their work. Suppose the *public* schools themselves, in this community, were graded in the same way. What grade would you give the public schools here—A, B, C, D, or FAIL?

Source: George H. Gallup, "The 10th Annual Gallup Poll of the Public's Attitudes Toward the Public Schools," *Phi Delta Kappan* (September 1978), p. 35.

FIGURE 4–1
**Confidence of the public in people running institutions in the U.S.
1973 to 1977**

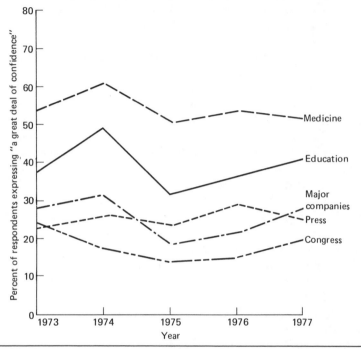

"I am going to name some institutions in this country. As far as the people running these institutions are concerned, would you say you have a great deal of confidence, only some confidence, or hardly any confidence at all in them?"

Source: The Condition of Education 1978 (National Center for Educational Statistics) and National Opinion Research Center, University of Chicago, General Social Survey.

OTHER EDUCATION INTERESTS

Our discussion of students', parents', and teachers' discernable interests in educational matters barely scratches the surface. There are literally scores of interest groups in American society which seek to influence educational policy. Ethnic and religious minorities, as well as various economic interests, are active on selected educational issues. There are also a host of professional groups seeking to advance the cause of their particular niche in the educational establishment.

There was a time when we bragged that America was really a collection of minorities. Yet, there is little point in denying that today an English-speaking, Anglo-Saxon, Protestant majority dominates the culture of American schools. The language of instruction in most cases is the majority language; the history that is taught emphasizes the development of Western civilization; the school calendar is built around the religious holidays of the Christian majority. The difficulty for the minority child in adjusting to the sometimes alien culture of the school, along with the economic, social, and academic disadvantage of many minority students, has made the representation of their interests in educational policy matters a critical concern. Blacks, Chicanos, American Indians, Puerto Ricans, Chinese, Japanese, Jews, and the Amish, among others, have all felt the heavy hand of the dominant majority at one time or another.

The largest single minority issue in the postwar period has been the racial desegregation of schools. The historic role of the National Association for the Advancement of Colored People (NAACP) in the court case which led to the 1954 *Brown* v. *the Board of Education of Topeka* decision is well documented. Other groups, including the Urban League, the Southern Christian Leadership Conference (SCLC), and Jessie Jackson's PUSH, have articulated the interests of black school children. The American Indian Movement (AIM) has recently attacked the Bureau of Indian Affairs which directs the federal effort in Indian education, and tribal councils have pushed for changes in both public and government schools where Indian children are enrolled. Chicano interests have been instrumental in obtaining substantial federal aid for bilingual, multi-cultural programs in districts with heavy Mexican-American populations. On the religious front there are also organizations with interests in education, including the National Catholic Education Association which has attempted to modify the relationship between public and private education.

Nor does the list of educational interests end with minorities. The business community has a vital interest in the public schools, principally as a training ground for literate, skilled, hard-working employees and managers. At the national and state level, the Chamber of Commerce expresses keen interest in manpower projections, the labor market, and technical and vocational education programs in the schools. At the community level, the business interests connect with schools in a somewhat different way. Rotary International, Kiwanis, the Lions Club, and other business-oriented service groups take a proprietary interest in the development and prosperity of the community; schools are one obvious element in their ability to sell the community to new residents, businesses, or industry. Their ideas about how those schools might be improved are usually available to school administrators who may have been invited to join one or another of the clubs. Taxpayer associations, on the other hand, are in evidence in most states and large cities, and may actively oppose increases in education funding.

Historians of education have frequently stressed the influence of two less obvious kinds of institutions upon education policy. The Ford Foundation, the Rockefeller Foundation, and the Carnegie Corporation are only the most familiar examples from an array of charitable foundations spawned by large, private corporations. While their habit of giving money away for educational programs and research provides the parent corporation both a tax shelter and excellent public relations, their impact upon American education has also been significant. Over the years, most have developed an organizational independence of their parent industries that makes it difficult to say whose interests they serve, on balance. Many of their more notable initiatives (e.g., the Carnegie Corporation's sponsorship of an influential study by James B. Conant, which precipitated a national wave of school-district consolidations, or the Ford Foundation's advocacy of community action programs to break the cycle of poverty, which led to Project Head Start) have been reformist in character.

The accrediting association has also had a decided effect upon American schools. These private professional organizations came into being largely to assure universities and prospective employers of the quality of the high schools and colleges that their applicants had attended. On-site inspections by accrediting associations have encouraged many schools to bring their staff, course offerings, or procedures into line with the standards required for accreditation. Those standards were usually arrrived at by professionals, and the charge is frequently made that accrediting associations have reinforced the already tight grip of professional educators over the direction of public education, at the expense of public influence.[15]

We shall reserve more extensive treatment of specific interest groups at the state and federal level for Chapter 6. We should warn in advance, however, that the number and variety of professional groups maintaining lobbyists in Washington, D.C. is sobering. America has been called a nation of groups, and the educational establishment is doing its part to perpetuate that image. Guidance counselors, English teachers, publishing firms, universities, school superintendents, educational researchers, teacher educators, and even an organization of Chief State School Officers, have advocates on the spot looking out for

[15]Joel Spring, *American Education: An Introduction to Social and Political Aspects* (New York: Longman, 1978), pp. 198–201.

their interests. It is a system that encourages noisy, sometimes rancorous, debates on most educational issues. It is also a system which attempts to minimize the probability that any significant interest in American education will go unnoticed or have its claims upon the educational system ignored.

SUMMARY

In any complex policy system, issues arise from time to time about the best course of action to be followed. Various interests will have different policy preferences on these issues. Their differences must be reconciled through a collective decision arrived at politically. School systems are not exempt from this process, and thus, in this broad sense, they are political organizations.

Processes for reaching collective decisions include persuasion, authority, voting, and bargaining. Most issue resolutions, in fact, involve a mixture of these processes. The policy which eventuates will authoritatively prescribe the behavior of certain actors in the system. Thus, policy is a means by which authorities may attempt to control the behavior of other actors. A policy may serve to make the organization operate more effectively or with greater consistency, or to protect individuals who faithfully follow its prescription.

Policies usually change only after dissatisfaction is expressed in some quarter. Once the issue is on the agenda, alternatives will be proposed and weighed amidst influence attempts aimed at gathering support for preferred alternatives and defeating others. Authoritative enactment of one alternative will result in a new policy. Two important aspects of the policy-change process remain, however. Will the target individuals comply with the prescribed behavioral change? If not, who will enforce the new policy, and how? Only after a new policy has been implemented will substantive changes in the operation of the organization take place.

Interests in the educational process include those of students, parents, teachers, taxpayers, and minorities, among others. Political resources useful for increasing the adoption of preferred policy alternatives are unequally distributed among these interests. The most apparent recent change in the power structure of education has been the effective organization of teachers bargaining collectively with authorities at the local, state, and national levels.

STUDY GUIDE

Can you recall the meanings of the follow terms? Discuss them with a class colleague and apply them to your school-community setting.

political issue   political resource
political interest   policy
collective decisions   policy formulation
influence   policy implementation
power   collective bargaining
authority

SUGGESTED ACTIVITIES

1. Organize your class to arrive at a better discipline policy than the one under attack in the introduction to this chapter (situation 3). Designate members of the class to play the roles of administrator, teacher, minority parent, student, and others. As the actors in this role-playing session develop an alternative discipline policy, other members of the class should see if they can detect behavior (1) expressing dissatisfaction with existing policy, (2) proposing new alternatives, (3) influencing the position of others, (4) enacting the new policy, (5) complying with the new policy, and (6) enforcing the new policy.

2. Interview a small sample of teachers, administrators, parents, or students to determine what they perceive as the most important policy issues confronting school governance in your community.

3. Identify an important minority in your community, and discuss with the leaders of one of their interest groups any problems they have experienced with the educational system.

4. Discuss as a class what different values or priorities are likely to be implicit in a debate over whether or not elementary schools should be closed due to enrollment declines.

5. Comment upon this statement: "There is a right way and a wrong way to educate children. A good school administrator reviews research findings to determine the right way, then makes necessary changes in the school to make sure the right way prevails."

SELECTED READINGS

DAHL, ROBERT A., *Modern Political Analysis*, 3rd edition (Englewood Cliffs, N.J.: Prentice-Hall, 1976).

JONES, CHARLES O., *An Introduction to the Study of Public Policy*, 2nd edition (North Scituate, Mass.: Duxbury Press, 1977).

MANN, DALE, *Policy Decision-Making in Education: An Introduction to Calculation and Control* (New York: Teachers College Press, 1975).

MILLS, C. WRIGHT, *The Power Elite* (New York: Oxford University Press, 1959).

WIRT, FREDERICK M. and MICHAEL W. KIRST, *The Political Web of American Political and Social Foundations of Education* (Berkeley, Ca.: McCutchan, 1975).

5

POLICY MAKING
IN THE
LOCAL
SCHOOL DISTRICT

here is a tendency among some teachers to view educational policy as something too distant and too abstract to make much difference in their classroom. Isn't it, after all, that special relationship between students and teacher that is at the heart of the educational enterprise? How can long debates in school board meetings or decisions handed down from the superintendent's office affect that relationship very much? Let the politicians govern and administrators administer; the essence of education will be little changed.

A moment's reflection upon the crucial nexus of student and teacher in the classroom leads us to question that assessment. First, and perhaps most basic, we must ask who, out of all those who might want to, will be allowed to teach in that classroom. What kind of person will be charged with the educational development of those children? What qualifications will he or she have? What kind of experience? What professional training? Which of a number of "qualified" candidates will get the job? What happens when a teacher starts interacting with children in the classroom may be largely a function of who has been chosen as teacher. Those kinds of decisions are still left largely to the local policy process, and there can be little doubt that they fundamentally affect the nature of the educational process.

Nor does that teacher have complete control of what will be taught once he or she has been hired. Subtle pressures may be brought to bear upon the elementary teacher to emphasize math this year, as opposed to social studies. School or district-wide testing programs may obligate the teacher to "cover" certain subject areas. Nor do teachers at the secondary level have complete control over what they teach. The assistant superintendent for instruction may rule that calculus cannot be taught next year because too few students have indicated an interest in it. Reassignment of teachers from primary to secondary teaching specialties is not unheard of. Teachers of Spanish may find themselves teaching English when district needs so dictate.

How the teacher goes about the job will also depend upon previously made policy decisions. What kinds of resources will be made available? Will the textbook ordered three years ago by a predecessor have to be used again simply because it has been budgeted for a five-year life span? What is available in the way of microscopes or analytic balances for the science laboratory? Is there a school library, and if so, can the teacher order whatever supplementary materials are deemed necessary? Will prompting from administrators or fellow teachers encourage a phonics approach to reading, the use of manipulatives in mathematics, or a "discovery" approach in social studies? How much time is provided for preparation and development of those creative ideas that we all get from time to time but just do not have time to work out?

There is also a myriad of contextual and organizational factors that may dramatically effect the interactions of teachers and pupils. Is the classroom we have been visualizing one among ninety in a suburban high school of 3,000 students, or one of four in a small rural school? Are there eighteen students in the class, or forty? Are only the most academically talented students found in this class, or is a cross-section of the student body represented? If it is a secondary school, how long will class periods be? Thirty-five minutes? Forty-five? Fifty-five? Will a split lunch schedule mean that the class has to be interrupted in the middle to send students off to the cafeteria? Will school buses whisk some children away to homes in distant corners of the community immediately after the last class period, depriving them of an opportunity to try out for the track team or go over least common multiples one more time with the math teacher? What ground rules, procedures, and support will be available to our teacher when the inevitable occurs and some student is insubordinate or creates a disruption in the classroom?

Each of these questions can be answered only if one knows something about the educational policy-making system within the local district. Despite the encroachment of state and federal regulations and programs, there is still remarkable latitude for the local district to provide its own answers to questions of this type. The objectives which are emphasized and the manner in which available resources are allocated to meet these objectives significantly shape the classroom relationship between teacher and student. In this chapter we will be looking at the way these objectives are transformed into policy within the political system of the local school district.

THE LOCUS OF AUTHORITY
AT THE LOCAL LEVEL

Providing a general map of the formal structure of authority in making educational policy is not too difficult. Despite numerous exceptions across our fifty states and the local school districts within them, a general pattern prevails. A state grants certain legal authority to a board of education, usually elected, to provide a public school system in that area. The school board hires a superintendent of schools to manage the day-to-day affairs of the district. Building principals and teachers are also hired, with the authority to exercise some discretion with respect to policy at their levels.

For our purposes it will be helpful to think of educational policy at five different levels. In the classroom, teachers set their own policy across a surprising range of topics. Within fairly broad limits, most teachers can establish their own grading policy, classroom-discipline policy, select their own textbooks, and structure their learning activities in the way they believe will be most effective. The discretion of the American teacher on questions of this kind is in sharp contrast to the French system, for example, where many more questions of classroom operation are addressed in directives emanating from the ministry of education.

Just above the classroom level is the building level of policy. Principals of American schools enjoy their own authority to create policy in certain realms. Policies promulgated from the principal's office typically concern some of our most fundamental educational questions, such as what courses will be offered, how students are to be assigned to classes, discipline and promotion policy, and how the student's time in school will be scheduled.

At the district level, the school board, along with the superintendent and his or her assistants, will determine policies meant to apply to all buildings in the district. Principals, as well as teachers and students, may be constrained by district policy. A decision to bus students to combat racial segregation would involve more than one school and would usually be taken at the district level. Similarly, decisions to develop an interscholastic girls' athletic program or to reduce the teaching force in response to a district-wide enrollment decline would, in most instances, be made at the district level.

Important policy, then, is made at the classroom, school-building, and district levels, and it is the manner in which those policies evolve that we will address in this chapter. We will save our discussion of the other two policy levels—the state and federal levels—for Chapter 6. There is, however, one point that will already be apparent. Issues arise not only over the substantive questions of educational policy, but over the procedural question of which level is the appropriate level for the resolution of any given policy issue. Heavy-handed principals stir the ire of teachers who are convinced that they can resolve many issues better at the classroom level. Some of the best principals fight for more and more independence from the district office to fashion policy in their school as they think best. Superintendents are capable of high indignation when the state legislature mandates a program that restricts their own options. And the top education officials at the state level often join with district superintendents and board members in decrying the attempts of their federal counterparts to mold American schools in accordance with national priorities.

Proponents of local control argue that most educational policy questions should be decided at the lowest possible level. Only then can decisions take account of all of the idiosyncratic features of the particular locale in question. Proponents of more centralized approaches to policy point out that when the interests of people beyond the confines of the local unit are significantly affected, a collective decision at a higher level is in order. Only a higher-level decision can acknowledge the interests of all parties involved. In an increasingly mobile and interdependent society, matters of literacy, sex education, driver training, degree requirements, special education, and equity are concerns which transcend district boundaries.

POLICY MAKERS AT THE LOCAL LEVEL

Teachers do not spring to mind when one starts listing policy makers in education. We forget just how much policy is made, sometimes on the spot, by teachers in a classroom. Yet, many of the problems that inexperienced teachers have stem from not having their own classroom policy worked out to apply to the scores of problems that confront them each day in the classroom. By the same token, students devote much of their spare time discussing, testing, and complaining about each teacher's way of handling recurring situations in the classroom. Is homework assigned regularly? Collected? How much talking is permitted in class? What about gum chewing? Are pop quizzes to be expected? Will tardy students be reported to the office? Can missed work be made up? Will too much (or too little) exuberance in class result in a detention? These are not inconsequential questions in the education of youngsters, and in most cases the teacher is granted undisputed authority to run the classroom as he or she wants within rather broad limits. In larger schools where coordination is deemed important, grade-level chairpersons (elementary) or subject-matter department chairpersons (secondary) may supervise the determination of some intermediate-level policy questions such as the selection of textbooks or the adoption of a common approach to a subject across classes.

That part of the teachers' role which includes policy making is important in one other sense. In U.S. education, principals are recruited from the ranks of teachers, superintendents from the ranks of principals, and many (but not all) state and federal authorities from the ranks of superintendents. While the career administrator may have a slightly different view of the enterprise from each new vantage point, earlier experiences as policy maker at a lower level lend some perspective.

Even as teachers exercise authority within the classroom, their influence over educational policy outside the classroom has been expanding. In their professional role, teachers now assert themselves on a panoply of educational questions that used to be the private preserve of administrators and board members. Take, for example, the practice in many districts of involving teachers in personnel decisions about the appointment or retention of teachers and administrators.[1] That is a major responsibility that can quickly reshape a school. Teachers a few decades back would have had little part in these decisions. Furthermore, the influence of teachers, through their professional organizations, upon salary schedules, class size, school calendars, or reduction-in-force clauses, has changed the tenor of district policy making so markedly that we will discuss the advent of collective bargaining separately, later in this chapter.

If one is to believe a frequent finding in educational research, the building principal may be the most crucial single position in the educational enterprise. While it is often difficult to ascertain the effects that

---

[1]For an informed view of the variety of areas in which the influence of teachers has been expanding, see Marshall O. Donley, Jr., *Power to the Teacher: How America's Educators Became Militant* (Bloomington, Ind.: Indiana University Press, 1976).

a superintendent, or even teachers, have upon the system, study after study has indicated that this or that program succeeds in schools where it has the active and enthusiastic support of a competent principal, and fails in schools where that support is lacking.[2] Not only are the principal's substantive decisions apt to make a difference, but the style of the principal may set the tone for the entire school. Those who look with disdain upon the contributions of administrators (and there are many teachers who do) would do well to contemplate the overwhelming evidence that principals make a difference.

Despite the ability of the principal to shape such consequential matters as the array of course offerings or the extent of parent involvement in the school, principals have lost ground as authorities in recent years. While teachers have been demanding more say in how the building should be run, directives from the district office, as well as guidelines and forms from the state capital and Washington, D.C. have multiplied.

Atop the local school administrative heirarchy sits the district superintendent of schools. It is a position that demands all of the administrative skill and political wisdom one can muster. The successful superintendent is expected to detect potential trouble spots before they become major problems. Bold, innovative district-wide programs will usually come about only at his or her initiative. Disagreement among building principals must be resolved, and mountains of paperwork spawned by state and federal agencies must be tended to. Annual budgets will have to be prepared, defended, and deftly steered through the board. The superintendent is at once that board's agent and its expert, but is also the leader of the professional staff and the most visible single official in the district.

In many matters, a memorandum from the superintendent is sufficient to establish district policy. On broader questions requiring board approval, the superintendent may still have a hand in virtually every stage of the policy process from identifying the problem and getting it on the agenda, to proposing alternatives, lining up support, and seeing that the new policy is communicated and enforced. When support for the educational program is high, the superintendent will thrive; when support crumbles, the superintendent is usually the first to pay the price.

For most foreign observers, however, the most remarkable feature

[2]See, for example, Mark Chesler, Richard A. Schmuck, and Ronald Lippitt, "The Principal's Role in Facilitating Innovation," in J. Victor Baldridge and Terrence Deal, eds., *Managing Change in Educational Organizations: Sociological Perspectives, Strategies, and Case Studies* (Berkeley, Calif.: McCutchan, 1975), pp. 321–327.

of American education is the local board of education. This unique institution shoulders the ultimate legal responsibility for the education of children in the district. Perhaps more important, political account-ability rests with the board members; for, in most districts they are elected for two- or three-year terms in nonpartisan, at-large, elections. While the size of boards and the electoral arrangements vary consider-ably throughout the nation, a seven-member board with two or three members elected each year is the modal case. It will meet once, twice, or perhaps several times a month, depending upon the size of the district, the wishes of the superintendent, and the press of political issues.

Much of what the board does is specified by state law, but there is enormous discretion as to how active its members wish to be and on which issues. The approval of a budget and the appointment of new teachers are powers usually delegated to the board by state law. But the board also has the formal authority to bring about major changes in district policy in virtually any area of the educational program. From the earliest days of American history, the notion has prevailed that education was too important to leave to the experts. The doctrine of lay control developed as a tacit acknowledgement that community values should be a strong, perhaps dominant, force in deciding how schools will educate our children. Just how well boards of education have fulfilled this mission of keeping schools in line with community sentiment is the subject of lively debate.

As with all collective decision systems featuring shared responsibil-ity, there is considerable potential for tension between superintendents and boards. Extreme cases can be found, to be sure, where a board simply does the bidding of the superintendent, or where the superin-tendent follows the lead of the board on every major matter. But their roles are different, and in many cases, beneath the air of cordiality, there is an edginess about prerogatives.

One might assume that the board and the superintendent were somewhat mismatched whenever their judgments about appropriate courses of action diverge. It is true that superintendents seldom win thirty-year service pins by openly confronting the elected officials who appointed them and have the power to dismiss them. Still, there are some pretty good cards in the superintendent's hand as well. First, as a full-time professional constantly meeting with other school adminis-trators, teachers, and students, the superintendent will become aware of most problems before board members do. Second, the superintendent can draw upon the resources of his or her administrative and profes-sional staff to propose alternatives to a policy that is not working. Board members frequently have neither the time nor the expertise to work out an alternative proposal in detail. Third, in arguing for his or her proposal, the superintendent will have the benefit of much more detailed information about the day-to-day operation of the schools. And fourth, while the board members may speak with the authority that accrues to elected officials, the superintendent wears the mantel of expert. On certain kinds of questions, his or her pronouncements are not likely to be challenged by anyone in the room. Finally, should the board be anything but unanimous in its opposition to the superintendent, its larger numbers may turn into a liability. An adroit superintendent can marshal the evidence in the most advantageous way possible to support his or her position, without much fear of direct contradiction from subordinates. But any board member, in attempting to present a case for or against the proposal, may find his or her position neutralized by the board member who speaks next.

The superintendent's leverage works best when things are going smoothly. A major issue that drags on, the rise of widespread public dissatisfaction, the loss of board confidence, all may find the board quickly becoming the dominant force. Furthermore, as we shall see later in this chapter, some have argued that even in quiet times the board may be far more influential than it appears. To better understand what makes a board tick, it will be necessary to look more closely at the political side of American school boards.

SCHOOL BOARD POLITICS

One indication of the special place education has enjoyed in the political history of the United States is that, in the vast majority of districts, a separate governmental structure, largely insulated from the rough and tumble partisan politics of municipal government, has been erected. The school board has symbolized the importance of lay control, as mentioned earlier, but it has also served to reinforce the local, nonpartisan nature of educational policy.

Just how representative is the typical school board of the electorate it represents? In interviews with 490 school board members from 82 districts conducted in 1968, Zeigler and Jennings compared them with a national sample of the American electorate drawn that same year. In general, they found that board members were somewhat more likely to exhibit qualities traditionally valued in American society. To put it another way, women, racial minorities, the young, and the elderly were all under-represented; the well-educated, well-employed, Republican, Protestant, regular church-going, long-term residents of the community were over-represented (see Table 5–1).

TABLE 5-1
Social and economic comparison between board
members and general public[a]

Characteristics	General public	Board members
Sex:		
Males	48%	90%
Females	52	10
Race:		
Whites	89	96
Nonwhites	11	4
Age:		
Under 40	37	24
40–59	39	63
60 and over	23	13
Years Lived in Community:		
0–15	47	20
16–over	52	80
Education:		
Less than 12 grades	41	7
12 grades	32	22
1–4 years college	23	47
Graduate and professional school	4	25
Income:		
Under $7,500	56	10
$7,500–19,999	39	54
$20,000 and over	6	36
Occupation:		
Professional and managerial	30	66
Other	70	34
Home Ownership:		
Yes	66	93
No	34	7
Political Party Identification:		
Democratic	46	40
Independent	30	16
Republican	24	44

[a]Percentages should be read down the columns. The percentages for each characteristic within each sample will total 100% except for rounding error.

Source: Adapted from L. Harmon Zeigler and M. Kent Jennings, *Governing American Schools* (North Scituate, Mass: Duxbury Press, 1974), p. 28.

It is a long and perhaps unwarranted inferential leap to suggest that because school board members come disproportionately from the more advantaged segments of society, they do not adequately represent the interests of the disadvantaged in educational matters. When asked to identify "the most important problem facing education in this school district," the need for more money was mentioned most often by both board members and their constituents, with concern over the quality and compensation of teachers, racial integration, educational standards, and governance following in that order. In fact, the agenda for board members appeared much the same as for the public, with the exception of board members' slightly greater reluctance to cite racial conflict as a problem, and their greater preoccupation with governance problems including lack of public participation and board-superintendent relations.[3] Most surprising, however, was the finding that while board members' concern over school racial problems was highly related to whether constituents in their districts saw it as a problem, there was virtually no relationship between board members' concern over teaching quality or educational standards and similar concern on the part of their constituents.[4]

Even where board members and their constituents agree on what the major problems are, there is no guarantee that they will agree about how to handle them. Zeigler and Jennings found moderately high agreement between board members and their constituents on such items as whether or not prayers should be used in schools, whether there is too much or too little federal control over local education, and whether teachers should have a stronger voice in educational policy. On the other hand, board members' views about the appropriateness of the federal role in school integration or the right of teachers to strike, bore little relationship to the views of their constituents. Across the country as a whole, board members were somewhat more opposed to prayers in public schools, to giving teachers the right to strike, to giving teachers a stronger voice, to federal control over local education, and to state control over local education than was the national sample of constituents. They were, however, more favorably disposed to the federal government taking the lead in school integration.[5]

These findings leave us with a mixed interpretation of the representativeness of American school boards. While board members nation-

[3]L. Harmon Zeigler and M. Kent Jennings with Wayne G. Peak, *Governing American Schools* (North Scituate, Mass.: Duxbury Press, 1974), p. 128.

[4]Ibid., p. 128.

[5]Ibid., p. 137.

wide do not accurately reflect the social, education, racial, economic, and demographic characteristics of the public, their general sense of which problems are most pressing appears to be much the same as that of the public. Within any given district, moreover, board members are likely to reflect community sentiment as to whether or not general societal problems (e.g., the importance of racial problems in the schools) deserve a place on the policy-making agenda. Community concerns are not as apt to be reflected by board members in their assessment of more distinctly educational problem areas. On school-policy preference questions, there is little evidence that board members systematically depart from the views of the general public, except for a discernable tendency to jealously guard their own decision-making prerogatives against encroachment from teachers on the one hand and state and federal agencies on the other. Correlations between the views of board members and their constituents range from almost no relationship on some issues to moderately high relationship on others. The worst that can be said is that on some issues it would be difficult to predict the position a board would take simply by knowing the preferences of constituents in that district.

There remains a possibility that the picture snapped by Zeigler and Jennings of school board members has changed in the last decade. The manner in which candidates are recruited and elected to school boards varies over time and place. To illustrate this, let us look at two fictitious cases which typify quite different selection systems, even though the formal rules are the same.

Model 1—Noblesse Oblige and the Politics of Consensus

Ted Sumner hung up the telephone and turned to face his puzzled wife.

"That was Charlie Becker. You won't believe what he wants me to do now. Seems as though there is going to be an opening on the school board. Old Jerry Rice has decided to give up his seat. Of course he hasn't announced it yet, but as president of the board Charlie wanted me to consider running. Said if it was handled right there shouldn't be much opposition."

"You told him no, I hope. You were complaining just the other day about how you haven't had much time with the family since Joe left the firm. You don't need this on top of everything else."

"How the hell do you tell Charlie no. Besides, it's sort of expected around town that I'd take my turn when the time came. I've heard several people mention it."

Ted didn't tell Charlie no, but he didn't say yes for awhile either. In the next week or two, several other members of the school board urged him to take the plunge. It would amount to only a couple of nights a month, and Frankton needed people with his judgment on the board. Finally, as the filing deadline approached and no other candidate appeared, Ted agreed to run.

As an unopposed candidate, Ted's campaign created few shock waves. He spent a grand total of ninety-five dollars to have some campaign buttons made up. There were the obligatory rounds of service clubs and several neighborhood tea gatherings to air his viewpoints on the schools. At these affairs Ted invariably settled for a few platitudes about how Frankton needed the best schools possible and how he would do everything he could to see that those schools were run efficiently and fairly. He also wanted everyone to know that, as their representative on the board, he would listen to them. At that point he usually threw the meeting open to questions and spent the rest of the evening listening. Whenever someone tried to pin him down on an issue, he would simply plead that he didn't have all the facts yet, but they could be sure that he would weigh all sides of the question before deciding.

Ted was widely known throughout the community, and most people respected him. His bearing inspired trust. While no one, including Ted himself, knew exactly where he stood on teachers' demands for higher salaries and lower class size, the state's move toward minimal competency testing, or the superintendent's plan to phase out a special program for gifted youngsters, most agreed that he would approach these and other questions responsibly, honestly, even wisely.

On the day of the election only 28 percent of the eligible voters in the district went to the polls. As with most low-turnout elections, it was the established, well-off voters who were most likely to trudge to the polls. There was little incentive for new residents, the unemployed, minorities, or other voting groups, who might have been forces for change in Frankton's schools, to come out to vote in an uncontested election. Most of those who did vote dutifully marked their ballots for Ted Sumner and went home feeling rather noble about having fulfilled their civic duty and contributed to the future well-being of Frankton's schools.

Congratulations poured in—from other members of the school board, from the local Parent-Teacher Association president, from the teacher's organization, and from the superintendent. Ted was feeling a little noble himself. The superintendent suggested that they have lunch so that Ted could be briefed on some of the current business before the board. This would make it easier for him to plunge right in at the regularly scheduled meeting next Tuesday. Ted agreed and spent two hours over a Rueben sandwich listening to a rundown of the district's prospects and problems as seen by the superintendent.

Over the next year Ted faithfully made each of the sparsely attended biweekly sessions on Tuesday nights. On the Friday before each meeting, he received a packet of information from the district office, including the agenda of the upcoming meeting. He would always spend part of his weekend going over the material and deciding what his reaction would be to items that would be considered. School district matters became a part of his conversations with associates and the subject of occasional telephone calls from friends at night. But, for the most part, Ted had decided that the district was being capably managed. He argued rather strongly for a tougher position in bargaining with the teachers' organization that spring, and wound up on the board's negotiating team. He found little occasion, however, to go into any school, other than for award banquets or other ceremonial events.

When his wife raised questions about his plans for the future, Ted was evasive. In truth, the job was not much more of a strain than he had expected. It didn't hurt his practice any to be identified as a community leader. But sooner or later, perhaps after one more term of office, it would be someone else's turn.

Model 2—Issue-Oriented Candidates and Competitive Elections

Sarah Sandberg could hardly believe it! The evening paper said that the board of education was considering closing three elementary schools, including the one Tim went to. Several neighboring suburbs had already closed schools, but Sarah remembered perfectly well that the superintendent had assured parents that enrollments in Edgewood District would probably remain high enough to keep all schools open. George was unhappy too, but ventured that there were, no doubt, some very good reasons for closing schools these days. Sarah found a better sounding board for her indignation with a call to Jane Stewart, longtime friend, former president of the League of Women Voters, and presently serving on the PTA board with Sarah. "It's just a crime," she gasped, "to start closing buildings when they could use those classrooms so many ways. You know they'll be trying to lay off teachers next —that's the only way they can save any real money. Seems like they would cut out some of those assistant superintendents before they start closing down neighborhood schools."

"Well, Sarah," Jane half-teased, "sooner or later we're going to have to elect some people with common sense to that board. You'd make a perfect candidate."

It was George's condescending smile that made Sarah's decision final. She would challenge "those smug bastards" next fall. In the meantime she started attending every board meeting, noting who voted which way, studying every issue right along with the board members. More and more often she spoke out from the floor, especially whenever the school-closing matter came up.

By the time she declared her candidacy in September, administrators, board members, and a few teachers knew who she was and where she stood on a number of issues. Two other newcomers, similarly upset about the prospective closings, had also emerged to challenge the three incumbents up for re-election. Since the election was "at large," the three candidates receiving the highest number of votes would win seats. Sarah knew that most of the advantages would normally lie with the incumbents in such a race. But strong resentment was brewing in the community about the way the school closing was being handled. Challengers who didn't have high name-recognition among voters, or the experience of the incumbents to point to, would have to rely upon that major issue and the general feeling that it's time for a change in Edgewood School District. That would mean an active campaign to get Sarah and her message before the voters.

There was a day when Sarah couldn't have done it. But with Tim in school all day now, she could make time for telephone calls to potential supporters and spend mornings pouring over district budgets, advisory-committee reports, and state and national statistics. More than once in the weeks to come, her research would pay off in telling exchanges with opponents. She gave the impression of being not only earnest, but knowledgeable about schools. More of her personal savings account than George thought wise went into her candidacy. Television and newspapers are not very suitable advertising media for suburban campaigns; so a volunteer "Committee to Elect Sarah Sandberg" was formed to distribute handbills door-to-door with a personal touch. Large advertisements were placed in an area shopping guide distributed at supermarkets.

Everywhere Sarah spoke—at PTA meetings, the League of Women Voters, on a panel TV show—she lashed out at "rubber-stamp board members who don't do their homework and don't find out what the public wants." Then she would make her pitch for keeping every school open and organizing strong advisory councils of students, teachers, parents, and other citizens for each school building. Much to the consternation of district administrators, she visited first-grade classes, high school English classes, and special-education classes. When not observing classes, she was peppering the district business manager with questions about the state school-aid formula. Board members not up for reelection were somewhat patronizing. Several favorable letters to the editor appeared. The only area daily newspaper endorsed her candidacy, along with a host of candidates in other districts. Many citizens were at first bemused, but soon started listening. Still, Sarah was not at all sure, by election eve, whether she would be first or last in the balloting. She and her small coterie of supporters celebrated as the turnout edged toward 40 percent and it became clear that she would run second to the other leading challenger. Between them they had narrowly ousted two of the three incumbents.

Sarah's term on the school board marked a turning point for Edgewood School District. For the first time in memory, the superintendent was grilled about the details of almost everything he presented. Proposals for new programs or action started coming from the board, with requests for the administration to look into the feasibility of the idea and report back at the next board meeting. A well-orchestrated show of support for keeping schools open scuttled the tentative plans for closures. Then came the administration's quiet decision not to renew the contract of an untenured geometry teacher who had publicly declared that he was homosexual. Sarah sprang to the young man's defense and rallied at least two and maybe three other board members to her side. She argued that there was absolutely no evidence that the man's sexual preference had affected his teaching in any way. The press picked up the issue. Rumors spread about what had transpired in the board's executive sessions. Shortly after the American Civil Liberties Union started making inquiries, the superintendent renewed the contract.

Later the same year, the superintendent of Edgewood School District announced that he had accepted a position as Deputy Commissioner of Education in a neighboring state. Sarah saw to it that several of her supporters were named to the search committee for a new superintendent. "Sooner or later," she said, "we're going to have to get someone with some common sense in that job."

THREE VERSIONS OF THE POLICY PROCESS

It is one thing to paint, in rather broad strokes, the manner in which local school policy is made, but quite another thing to judge or interpret that process in terms of democratic theory. At least three major interpretations are possible. As indicated in Chapter 4, there is enough variety from one district to the next that it is doubtful that any single interpretation will do for all. But let us consider the three possibilities in turn.

The most romantic and, we daresay, the most popular version is that school policy making at the district level is the last bastion of grassroots democracy. Citizens, in this interpretation, control their schools by electing like-minded, responsive board members who chart out the future of the district by enacting policy for the superintendent and the administrative staff to implement. Board members who lose sight of citizen priorities are voted out of office. Any major problem with the schools is quickly and accurately communicated to board members, who then bring about the necessary changes. Citizens have ready access to the policy machinery and are able to keep close tabs on what is happening in the schools through their elected representatives. One presumed by-product of this grassroots democracy is a feeling of close identification with the school as an institution. This identification may be translated into support during times of need, such as tax-increase elections.

The grassroots democracy interpretation is one carefully fostered by civics textbooks and school board associations. It does have its weak points, however. Evidence to date indicates that, in general, public knowledge of and interest in education policy is lower than one might expect. For most citizens, reports of six-car pileups on the local inter-state, results of the playoffs in the NFL, and what the president is doing about inflation will be read, while the short article about last night's school board meeting goes unnoticed. It is not that the public is incapable of becoming aroused over educational issues on occasion; but the notion of very many citizens following, much less directing, the week-to-week vicissitudes of public schools is, to say the least, naive.

A second interpretation focuses upon the alleged domination of school policy making by superintendents as the salient feature. Given the inability of elected, lay board members to effectively control the routine operation of the district, proponents of this view see a professional, managerial class—headed by superintendents—which has imposed its values upon public schools. While professional educators do not all step from the same mold, they have had extensive, and to some extent common, socializing experiences. The vast majority have taught school, earned teaching and administrative credentials in teacher colleges, read many of the same books and journals, attended the same professional meetings, and committed their work lives to education. These kinds of experiences fairly effectively weed out people who believe we spend too much money on educating children. They tend to produce administrators who believe even the most severely handicapped child—physically, mentally, emotionally, economically, or socially—should have an opportunity to develop to his or her fullest potential.

Those advancing the professional-dominance interpretation of local policy making argue that professional socializing experiences have also produced a cadre of educators who feel they are so firmly in possession of truth that what parents, students, and other citizens want does not matter very much. Years of arguing about the "right" answer to many problems have left professionals less sensitive than they might be to preferences of groups and individuals in the community. A more "political" system, these critics believe, is called for, in which discontents would be aired openly, issues joined and argued out, and professional dogma challenged by representatives emerging from competitive, issue-oriented, elections.

More recently, a third interpretation of the policy process has emerged which falls somewhere between the "grassroots-democracy" and the "professional-domination" versions, even while rejecting both of them. According to this view, while citizens do not keep very careful tabs on their schools, they do elect board members who roughly reflect their most deeply held values. In a sense, these board members become the public's agents to make sure things do not get too far out of hand. While the board does not have the effective means to challenge or control the superintendent every step of the way, if things get bad enough, the board does have one ace in the hole—its power to dismiss the superintendent. Public apathy and "rubber-stamp" boards may, then, simply be symptomatic of districts where things are proceeding well and everyone is relatively satisfied. Districts in turmoil, on the other hand, are, for the most part, those where the professional leaders have strayed beyond the limits imposed by the values of board members and the public.

For those who find that process a somewhat cumbersome, inefficient way to proceed, there is some solace. William Boyd has reminded us of the old "law of anticipated reactions" and applied it to educational policy making.[6] Since superintendents know that, despite their tactical advantages over the board in day-to-day affairs, they must ultimately keep that board satisfied or lose their jobs, they will attempt to anticipate the reactions of board members to initiatives they are considering. Looking ahead, a superintendent may discern quite a range of actions that the board of education would support, and restrict his or her leadership to these programs. There may also be a number of things that a superintendent would like to do, but which are simply rejected as unfeasible given the present make-up of the board. What we wind up with, then, is a mechanism by which the board can control, or at

[6]William L. Boyd, "The Public, the Professionals, and Educational Policy Making: Who Governs?," *Teachers College Record,* 77 (May 1976), 556–558.

least limit, the behavior of the superintendent without lifting a finger. It is a very difficult mechanism to document, because it takes place without overt actions. Intuitively, however, it seems plausible that board members, by merely communicating their values to superintendents, may encourage greater attention to potential problems that might otherwise have been overlooked, or head off adventures that might ultimately have forced the board to take matters into its own hands.

COLLECTIVE BARGAINING

The largest recent change in the local educational power structure is the rapidly growing practice of negotiating formally with a teachers' organization, designated as the bargaining agent for teachers, over the provisions of a contract which will set forth the terms of their service in the coming academic year. From the standpoint of policy making, this means that decisions—not only concerning a salary schedule, but on a host of other questions as well—once made exclusively by the board of education and the superintendent are now made in a bargaining mode. From the standpoint of power relationships, the innovation has strengthened the hand of teachers at the expense of board and administration.

The legal aspects of collective bargaining will be dealt with more extensively in Chapter 9. At this point we want to examine the effects of negotiation upon local policy making. A prime concern of each of the major teachers' organizations nationally has been to obtain bargaining rights for teachers. National collective-bargaining legislation which would clarify the position and status of teachers in collective negotiation has been a priority item of professional groups for several years, but the Congress has preferred to leave it to the states. Most states have a collective-bargaining law for public employees, though several do not. But even in states where there is no collective bargaining law, the issue has been joined, and teachers in some districts have organized and bargained effectively with district authorities.

There is little mystery about how teachers have enhanced their own power vis-a-vis district authorities. You will remember that the exercise of power requires the ability to make a credible promise or threat. Once teachers established that they were willing and able to withhold their services if the board did not negotiate in good faith, the scales began to tip. Board members might claim that teachers' demands were unreasonable, but the prospect of turning children away due to a teacher strike was sobering. Where strikes did occur, parents proved perfectly capable of holding teachers, administrators, and board all responsible. Pressure quickly mounted on board members to get the thing settled and get the kids back in school where they belonged. Attempts to replace striking faculty were sometimes of dubious legality and more often simply not feasible (see Table 5-2).

The deck is not stacked entirely in favor of teachers in a strike situation, however. Successful work stoppages require substantial solidarity among teachers. If large numbers of teachers do not belong to the organization, or cross picket lines, the effectiveness of the strike is reduced accordingly. In most cases teachers will not be paid for the time they are on strike, and while strike funds may help, the salary foregone in a long strike has lowered the resolution of many teachers to hold out for a more favorable settlement. Furthermore, if a strike ends without a favorable settlement for teachers, the effectiveness of a strike threat in future years is likely to be reduced.

TABLE 5-2
Work stoppages by teachers: 1959 to 1976

Year	Number of stoppages	Teachers involved	Man-days idle during year
1959	2	210	670
1960	3	5,490	5,490
1961	1	20	20
1962	1	20,000	20,000
1963	2	2,200	2,590
1964	9	14,400	30,600
1965	5	1,720	7,880
1966	30	37,300	58,500
1967	76	92,400	969,300
1968	88	145,000	2,180,000
1969	183	105,000	412,000
1970	152	94,800	935,600
1971	135	64,600	713,000
1972	87	33,900	207,300
1973	117	51,400	620,700
1974	133	60,100	538,100
1975	218	182,300	1,419,800
1976	138	65,100	713,500

Source: U.S. Department of Labor, Bureau of Labor Statistics, *Work Stoppages in Government, 1958–68*, Report 348; 1970; *Work Stoppages in Government, 1973*, Report 437, 1975; *Government Work Stoppages*, 1960, 1969, and 1970, 1971; and unpublished tabulations.

REFERENDA

One of the legacies of the political-reform movements of the first half of this century which has had special impact upon education is the referendum. As big-city political machines and state legislatures made headlines with various kinds of corrupt practices, many states turned to three varieties of "direct democracy"—the initiative, the referendum, and the recall—as ways of keeping their elected representatives in line. Of the three, initiative and recall were destined to be used only infrequently; but the referendum, by which voters reserved the right to vote directly on certain kinds of substantive questions, became an important part of the way in which many school districts were financed.

As separate taxing units, most school boards may set tax rates for their district within the maximum set by state law. But to provide flexibility in districts where the maximum rate will not generate sufficient revenue, districts may be allowed to submit a proposal to increase taxes beyond the maximum to the voters of the district. A simple majority of those voting is usually required to approve the issue. Similarly, proposals to sell bonds as a means of financing a new building or meeting other major expenditures may require, by state law, the endorsement of the voters. Partly because of the nature of school finance, referenda and bond elections have been more common in education than in any other field of government.

The most interesting thing about referenda, other than the fact that they constitute almost the last vestige of direct democracy in the American system, is that they frequently become something more than straightforward decisions about tax rates. They may be viewed by many voters as an opportunity to hold the board and the superintendent more or less accountable for the district's fortunes. Public dissatisfaction with the state of local schools, even for reasons not directly related to the stated purposes of the referendum, will not bode well for its success. Referenda are not just a yes or no decision on tax increases, but a citizen's chance to make out his or her own report card on how well the schools have been doing.

Hundreds of studies have been done on various aspects of school referenda. Although few have systematically examined more than a single district's experience, we now have at least tentative answers to three interesting questions: Who votes in them, and why? What kind of voter is most likely to support increasing taxes for educational purposes? And what factors, in general, contribute to passage of the proposed tax increase or bond sale, rather than to the defeat of the proposal? Let us look at what researchers have found with respect to each of these questions.

In referenda, as in school board elections, it is not a cross-section of the eligible voters who actually go to the polls. Higher-status voters —the better educated, higher income, middle aged—have historically been more likely to vote in all elections, and the effect is even more pronounced in nonpartisan, low-information, local elections than in presidential elections. The two explanations most often advanced for this phenomenon revolve around the concepts of "civic duty" and "political efficacy." Higher-status individuals apparently have been more thoroughly indoctrinated in the importance of voting. They tend to view voting as a civic duty irrespective of the results of any particular election.

It may also be that higher-status individuals have a better-developed (some might even say over-developed) sense of their own ability to affect things by voting. Political scientists have dubbed this a person's "subjective sense of political efficacy" and find that it is higher in people who are economically and socially advantaged.[7] It is a plausible guess that someone who believes that their vote matters in shaping the future of the local schools will be more likely to get to the polls than another individual who believes that their vote probably will not make any difference.

The answer to the second question—Why do individuals vote for or against tax increase proposals?—is not quite the same. Here we find that younger citizens with school-age children, coming from either the skilled-labor or white-collar ranks, are most likely to support school-tax increases. There is some evidence that those recently arrived in the community are also more likely to vote yes. On the other hand, young adults without children, parents of youngsters in private schools, the elderly, professionals, and long-time community residents are more likely to oppose the increased financial burden.[8]

Once again, two kinds of explanations have been advanced by voting scholars for why people vote the way they do in nonpartisan elections such as referenda. The first of these emphasizes what Wilson and Banfield call a sense of "public regardingness."[9] While some citizens

[7]Sidney Verba and Norman H. Nie, *Participation in America: Political Democracy and Social Equality* (New York: Harper & Row, 1972), p. 19.

[8]Frederick M. Wirt and Michael W. Kirst, *The Political Web of American Schools* (Boston: Little, Brown, 1972), pp. 101–104.

[9]Edward C. Banfield and James Q. Wilson, *City Politics* (Cambridge: Harvard University Press, 1963), pp. 234–240.

are primarily motivated, even in public affairs, by privatistic, "what's in it for me?," kinds of concerns, others appear to be largely motivated by their perception of the public interest. Thus, even the elderly, wealthy property-owner without children might support school referenda just because he or she believes that education is a great opportunity for everyone and that society would be much better off if our efforts in that domain are redoubled.

There is, however, another side to voting choice, which other scholars have been quick to point out. For many, it may boil down to a calculation of whether or not the voter's own interests will be served. Following this line of reasoning, people with children who would benefit more directly should, on balance, be supportive, while those who are least able to bear the brunt of the tax increase (including renters, since tax increases are usually passed on to the tenant) should lead the opposition. Furthermore, the larger the tax increase, the more people should be inclined to vote against it. Even the economic climate at the time of the referendum may be a factor, persuading some voters to vote against another assault on their pocketbooks during times of inflationary pressure, unemployment, or recession.

To cloud the issue just a bit more, many observers have been struck by the manner in which referenda quickly become symbolic opportunities for the voter to express displeasure with almost any aspect of public, or even private, affairs. In the normal course of events, citizens have little opportunity to vent their indignation about political scandals in the statehouse, price-and-wage controls, or even uncertainty about their own jobs. A school referendum coming along at the wrong time may be a tempting opportunity for citizens to let "them" know that they cannot be pushed any further. To put it another way, a citizen has to have a pretty high regard for education and its consequences to vote against his other apparent financial interests by supporting a tax increase.

Theory about why people vote, and which way they vote, should help us list the factors that auger well for a successful referendum. Most generally, the chances for success of a referendum are higher when turnout is small. Small turnout indicates that voters with a high sense of citizen duty and "public regardingness" are about the only ones to make it to the polls. Higher turnout is often symptomatic of dissatisfaction. One or more major issues may have captured public attention and activated the privatistic interests of voters who would otherwise not have voted. As we would expect, there also appears to be an empirical relationship between the size of the increase sought, the general economic climate, and even the time of year (administrators understandably try to avoid scheduling referenda in the period just after citizens have paid last year's real-estate taxes).[10]

The successful management of a tax-increase referendum will be a feather in the career cap of the district superintendent. Teachers, the PTA and many parents, and administrators in other districts, will all applaud his or her political wizardry in extracting more revenue from the public for such a good cause. Yet, more than one superintendent has noted an awkwardness about the process. From what we have learned, it seems clear that prospects for passage will be better if the whole thing is kept rather quiet: Avoid mobilizing the opposition; ignore them if they do mobilize; play down any issues that emerge; reassure one and all that the local schools are the best schools possible, that they just need a little more money to keep them that way.

Yet, political scientists like Zeigler complain that school governance is not political enough, that some issues never are raised, that the public is not as interested or as well-informed as it should be, and exerts little guidance—even through elected board members—over the professionals running the district.[11] It is difficult to argue with suggestions that local school policy making should be more open, better publicized, and even more conflictual, if the public is to maintain its long-standing tradition of lay control in an era of strong professionalism. When dealing with referenda, however, school administrators have usually favored attempts to develop consensus over noisier battles which might serve to stimulate competing claims from various interests within the district—claims which would then have to be reconciled.

SUMMARY

While authority has shifted in recent years toward the state and national levels of educational policy making, local school districts retain sufficient discretion to dramatically shape educational programs. By looking at three local levels of policy making—the classroom, the school building, and the district—we find a surprising range of important educational decisions being made at each level.

District policy is the outgrowth of community interests as interpreted and adjudicated by the superintendent and a board of education.

[10]Wirt and Kirst, *Political Web of American Schools,* pp. 104–108.
[11]Zeigler and Jennings with Peak, *Governing American Schools,* especially chapter 3.

The relationship between superintendent and board may take many forms, but their different role definitions create a climate often characterized by underlying tension. While superintendents typically have the advantage in managing the day-to-day operations of the district, boards may still play a major role in charting the future of the district, directly through their power of appointment and dismissal and indirectly through the probability that the superintendent will attempt to anticipate board reactions to administrative proposals and to tailor major initiatives to conform to dominant values and interests represented on the board.

A recent challenge to the authority of the superintendent and board has come from teachers, in the form of collective bargaining. While ultimate authority to approve a contract with teachers may remain with the board, one effect of collective bargaining is to involve teachers much more intimately in an array of policy issues once left largely to the board.

Referenda for approval of tax increases and other educational purposes provide interesting insights into the nature and distribution of public support for education. While that support appears to be relatively high, compared with other social and political institutions, there are signs that it has declined somewhat in recent years.

STUDY GUIDE

Can you recall the meaning of the following terms? Discuss them with a class colleague and apply them to your school-community setting.

policy discretion	law of anticipated reactions
policy levels	referenda
lay control	civic duty
grassroots democracy	sense of political efficacy
professional dominance	sense of public regardingness

SUGGESTED ACTIVITIES

1. Attend a meeting of your local school board, and prepare a brief report on that session. Indicate, for example, whether agenda items were routine or controversial in nature. Who took the lead in proposing policy changes? Is there evidence that different board members are responsive to different

interests in the community? How much public involvement in the deliberations did you observe?

2.   Talk with a small number of local citizens about their school board and administration. Attempt to gauge their feelings about how adequately the superintendent and board are performing their duties. Also attempt to gain, as diplomatically as possible, some sense of how knowledgeable they are about their representatives on the board and about any major school policy issues.

3.   Obtain a copy of the current contract negotiated by teachers in a nearby district with their board of education. What items other than salary are included in the contract?

4.   Send a delegation to talk with the business manager of a local school district. The group should ascertain the current tax position of the district, and report back to the class. Is a tax-increase referendum a possibility in the near future? Is the current political climate favorable for such a move? Why, or why not?

SELECTED READINGS

CRONIN, JOSEPH M., *The Control of Urban Schools: Perspective on the Power of Educational Reformers* (New York: The Free Press, 1973).

DONLEY, MARSHALL O., JR., *Power to the Teacher: How America's Educators Became Militant* (Bloomington, Indiana: Indiana University Press, 1976).

IANNACCONE, LAURENCE and FRANK W. LUTZ, *Politics, Power and Policy: The Governing of Local School Districts* (Columbus, Ohio: Charles E. Merrill, 1970).

KOERNER, JAMES, *Who Controls American Education? (Boston: Beacon, 1968).*

NUNNERY, MICHAEL Y. and RALPH B. KIMBROUGH, *Politics, Power, Polls, and School Elections* (Berkeley, Calif.: McCutchan, 1971).

PETERSON, PAUL E., *School Politics Chicago Style* (Chicago: The University of Chicago Press, 1976).

ZEIGLER, L. HARMON and M. KENT JENNINGS with G. WAYNE PEAK, *Governing American Schools: Political Interaction in Local School Districts* (North Scituate, Massachusetts: Duxbury Press, 1974).

6

THE INFLUENCE
OF STATE
AND FEDERAL
GOVERNMENT
ON EDUCATION

W hen it comes to nostalgia, profes-
sional educators hold their own with sports fans and old-time radio
buffs. The "good old days" (for administrators who have been around
that long) are likely to refer to an era sometime before World War II
when county superintendents held sway over a good part of the educational system of the nation. Thousands of one-room schools still dotted
the countryside, and more youngsters dropped out of high school than
finished.[1] But teachers seldom were mugged in the corridors, poverty
was viewed as a fact of life rather than a social pathology, and the term
racial balance had not yet been coined. A superintendent could go for
weeks, even months, without hearing from the state office of education.
What happened in Washington was the talk of the town, but it did not
affect schools very much.

In fact, county and district superintendents could often do as they
pleased, as long as it did not bruise local sensibilities, exhaust local
finances, or violate a few general canons of state law. According to the
state, schools had to be provided, and children had to be in them until
the end of their compulsory school years. Teachers had to be certified,
although the certification standards were far more lenient than today.

[1]W. Vance Grant and C. George Lind, *Digest of Education Statistics, 1977–78*, National
Center for Education Statistics, Washington, D.C.: U.S. Government Printing Office,
1978, p. 14.

The manner in which tax revenues were to be set and collected was also controlled by state law. But, for the most part, local school officials had wide discretion to fashion the kinds of schools they and their folk wanted in their county and district.

Today that prototypical district has grown manyfold. Urban sprawl has nearly enveloped the once-rural townships and sections. In place of the one-room schoolhouses stand low-slung brick structures with queues of yellow school buses loading and unloading children.

What contrasts would a nostalgic administrator find today while seeking out the district offices tucked into a corner of one of these buildings? As he or she wanders through the corridors, there will be some familiar features. A clerk hovers over a file cabinet marked "credentials" which contains documents certifying district teachers. Lists of students for attendance purposes are still neatly stacked on a table, though computer printouts have replaced the old ledgers. The state school-code resides on the superintendent's desk, as always, but now rivals the metropolitan telephone directory in size.

Spread out on the desk is a large map of the district, with residential housing patterns delineated and school enrollments pinpointed by race. The district desegregation plan, drawn up three years earlier, is being revised; and the annual report to the state office, showing compliance with state and federal guidelines, is due next week. Those guidelines, an amalgam of policy set by the state board of education, by courts, and by various federal agencies, serve as a standard for determining whether the district is in compliance and, if not, what it needs to do to be in compliance. Changes in those guidelines, as well as shifting residential patterns and school enrollment decline, have made each year's review a major undertaking.

Meanwhile the business manager is completing the Title I count of children in the district who meet the criteria of "economically disadvantaged" for the compensatory education section of the Elementary and Secondary Education Act. Even minor errors in interpreting the convoluted rules and regulations applying to this report may mean thousands of dollars in federal aid lost to the district. Forms have already been collected to support the district's claim for both federal and state impacted aid, provided to partially compensate for the burden that government agencies within the district have placed upon educational facilities.

A committee of special-education teachers in the district has assembled in the conference room to discuss the implications of Public Law 94–142 in regard to the district's special-education programs. Several things are clear at the outset. This major piece of legislation requires each district to guarantee the availability of an appropriate free education for every handicapped child. That education, moreover, should be provided within the "least restrictive environment," which the state agency people interpret to mean that most special-education students should be worked into regular classroom settings. Such a program will require the development of an Individualized Educational Program (IEP) for each special-education child. The role of both special-education teachers and regular classroom teachers will be changed. But additional money is there to provide more help than ever to exceptional children—if the guidelines are followed.

The assistant superintendent for instruction, working next door, ponders what to do about the new state mandate in health education. Next year, for the first time, drug education, tobacco education, alcohol education, and sex education must be taught to all students in grades four, seven, and ten. Furthermore, the instruction must be offered by teachers certified in health education. This would seem to rule out handling the matter within the regular required physical-education courses, as had been the custom. Few of the P.E. teachers are presently qualified to teach the topics according to the new standard. Two years ago the state had sent out a directive alerting administrators to this coming change and encouraging them to prepare for it; so far, nothing has been done in this district.

Physical education teachers have their own problems anyway. Title IX of the Education Amendments of 1972, which addresses inequities between men and women in education, has been interpreted by the U.S. Office of Education as requiring that girls have the same opportunity to participate in interscholastic sports as boys have enjoyed. The district now has almost run out of time granted to bring the girls' athletic program into compliance. Girls' basketball, volleyball, and track have already been installed; cross-country and swimming are to be added this year. The boys will still be ahead, eight sports to five.

Back in the district offices, the director of guidance is reviewing several standardized tests for possible adoption as the district's minimal-competency examination in mathematics. The state office of education had supported legislation in the last session which directed each district to develop and test its own minimal-competency testing program. The substitute bill was clearly a tactic for diverting a state legislature bent upon establishing a state-administered minimal-competency graduation requirement. A district committee had been assembled to carry out the mandate, but little enthusiasm for the project itself, let alone the hard work of developing their own tests, was discernable. The committee finally decided that tests available from commercial sources should first be examined to see if appropriate ones already existed. Math was selected as the first content area for the experiment, over the objections of the two mathematics teachers serving on the committee.

State or federal guidelines also must be consulted for school lunch-program reimbursement, provision of bus transportation for outlying students, computation of the "weighted average daily attendance" for the state aid formula, even approval of bake sales, and more—the list of items in which district discretion has been narrowed by state or federal initiative has grown too long to enumerate. Today it is no longer enough for the school administrator to know what citizens in the local district want and to try to bring that about. A welter of state and federal law, court decisions, rules, regulations, guidelines, and deadlines, have changed both the local administrator's job and the locus of authority within the educational policy system. While it is still true that many vital decisions are made at the district, building, and classroom levels, it is no longer the case that intervention by state and federal government in educational matters is limited to superficial or noncontroversial matters. Indeed, one can make a strong argument to the effect that the most important *changes* in educational policy since World War II have originated at the state or federal level.

THE CHANGING ROLE OF THE STATE

Part of the recent assertiveness of the states in educational affairs can be chalked up to some dramatic changes in the nature of state governments. Since 1962, court-ordered reapportionment of state legislatures has guaranteed equal representation to citizens in urban areas, while bringing new, younger, better-educated legislators into state government. Party competition returned to areas that had previously been safe, one-party districts, and legislators became more responsive to their constituencies. The image of stodgy, antiquated legislatures meeting once every two years, bent upon keeping things the way they were, slowly gave way. More streamlined bodies sporting less-cumbersome committee structures, better-qualified staff, and annual sessions began to emerge. Part-time amateur legislators are also giving way to well-paid professional politicians who devote most of their attention to questions of public policy.

Expertise and quality staffs are indispensible when the modern state legislator confronts the hundreds of education bills that cross his or her desk in a typical legislative session. These bills may have been drafted by legislators responding to constituent pressure, by the governor's staff, by staff in the state education agency, or by any of the numerous education interest groups. Many of them will receive close scrutiny by policy analysts working for the governor, by a budget director, the state school board, the chief state school officer, and by the education committee which will first consider the bill. The level of state school aid for the next academic year will usually emerge as one of the major items on the legislative calendar; but changes in teacher tenure laws, a collective-bargaining law for public employees, minimal-competency testing, or a new special-education program may take center stage during any given session.

The hand of the governor in molding education policy has also been strengthened in recent times. Changes in state constitutions, giving more governors a four-year term of office and the opportunity to serve more than one consecutive term, have contributed to the enhancement of gubernatorial power. The governor's major opportunity to influence education policy, however, lies in his or her power of appointment and, even more importantly, in the area of fiscal authority. In most states the governor has primary responsibility for preparation of the state budget. That provides substantial opportunity for input into decisions about which new educational programs will be funded and at what level old programs will be supported. While in every state the legislature has the authority to override the governor's budget recommendations, the item veto and reduction veto powers granted the chief executive in some newly revised constitutions, and the governor's political clout, make wholesale legislative restructuring of the budget very difficult indeed.

In recent years, governors have seldom taken strong stands on substantive educational issues. The opposition of southern governors to desegregation in the early 1960s and, more recently, the positions of chief executives in Florida and Georgia on minimal-competency graduation requirements establish their potential to do so. For the most part, however, governors have been content to play the role of financial managers, leaving the advocacy and evaluation of programs to education specialists in the legislature or executive branch.

The state school board—elected in some states, but appointed by the governor in most—gives special status to education within the structure of state government. It represents, in fact, an extension to the state level of the principle of lay control of education. It also represents a distrust by reformers of partisan political resolutions in the area of education.

Few, if any, state school boards have developed sufficient muscle to hold their own in the rough-and-tumble world of state politics. Their usual functions are to legitimate the proposals of the chief state school officer and, upon occasion, to shift the focus beyond the short-term preoccupations of the current legislation session. While most policy making at the state level places little premium upon long-range planning, a state board of education can look at the broad sweep of educational issues in an attempt to establish some longer-range goals and programs. Whether these programs will be honored in the press of legislative in-fighting and gubernatorial budget-cutting is always open to question. But if state educational policy is to receive any direction beyond year-to-year decisions on specific issues, it is the state school board and the bureaucracy headed by the chief state school officer that will have to provide it.

Historically, the chief state school officer (CSSO, variously referred to as the state superintendent of schools, state superintendent of education, state superintendent of public instruction, or commissioner of education) was elected in most states; more recently, the trend is toward appointment by the state board of education. As nominal head of the state's education establishment, the CSSO's actual influence upon education policy varies widely from state to state. Most CSSOs have contented themselves with performing the maintenance functions of their office—keeping the machinery operating smoothly. Several have charted bolder courses of educational growth or reform. The incumbent of this position, whether elected or appointed, is likely to be a career educator with experience in education at lower levels.

In a very real sense, the CSSO provides the link between lay policy direction from the state board of education, the legislature, and the governor's office, on the one hand, and the thousands of professional educators throughout the state on the other. Loss of confidence from either of these sectors may make satisfactory resolution of educational issues difficult.

The chief state school officer has yet another constituency. In many states, the most fundamental change in the policy process has resulted from the growth of bureaucracies within the executive branch. The state office of education has typically been in the forefront of this development. Usually staffed by a blend of career government workers and professional educators, the sense of mission and effectiveness of personnel in this complex organization may wither under the leadership of a neglectful or politically troubled CSSO.

There are at least three important functions performed by most state offices of education. On the one hand, the agency is delegated the responsibility for regulating many aspects of education under state and federal law. Teacher certification, approval of private schools, stipulation of the number of days that schools must be in session, and accreditation of teacher-education programs are just a few of the regulatory tasks undertaken. But the agency also performs a service function, standing ready to provide consultants in each of the subject areas or for helping districts and teachers clear special hurdles, such as teaching the metric system of measurement, developing minimal competency tests, or training teachers how to "mainstream" special-education students into their classes. Local administrators may even receive assistance in preparing a proposal for federal funding of a demonstration center in reading or other projects.

Finally, state offices of education are increasingly the source of new legislative proposals. The requisite records, expertise, and political savvy are more likely to be found here than in any other single agency. Drafts of desired legislation may be ordered up by the state school board, by the CSSO, or by a department head. But the state office of education is also a likely place for the state teachers' associations, the PTA, or interested legislators to come for advice, support, and skilled assistance when seeking changes in education law. Thus, state offices of education are beginning to play a role at the beginning as well as the end of the policy process.

Few are unaware of the role that federal courts have come to play in the educational-policy process, but the extent to which state courts have also entered the fray is often overlooked. *Serrano v. Priest*, ultimately decided by the California Supreme Court, may revolutionize educational finance in that state when it goes into effect in 1981. Most other states have also felt the recent influence of their courts in educational matters. Interpretation of law with respect to collective bargaining, teacher tenure, freedom of expression, privacy, district reorganization, teacher liability, racial desegregation, and tax rates has become a significant part of the docket in many state courts.

Landmark court cases, even at the state level, usually do not just happen; carrying them through the judicial system to completion is apt to be an expensive and exhausting process. Consequently, many interest groups actively seek out the "best" case for a desired court test from their point of view, and provide much of the needed legal aid. Even the supposedly neutral judicial process is not immune to the influence of political interests.

There is an indirect, as well as a direct, effect from the rapid rise of litigation in the states. A decision as to whether striking teachers can be dismissed under the state's collective-bargaining law will establish a precedent in other similar cases that follow. That court decision may also stimulate new legislation, and will almost certainly affect the regulatory activity of the state bureaucracy. Furthermore, the state school board, the CSSO, or even the legislature will almost certainly attempt to anticipate the court's position on the constitutionality or legality of any policy they are considering. The resulting interaction of courts and other state agencies in resolving some of the most controversial issues is just one more instance of the expanded role that state government has assumed in determining educational policy.

INTEREST GROUPS AT THE STATE LEVEL

Several organized interest groups have the potential to affect educational policy at the state level. Foremost among these in most states are the state teacher associations. State affiliates of the National Education Association have long enjoyed great influence in most states, and the affiliates of the American Federation of Teachers, often bolstered by the parent AFL/CIO state offices, are also making their presence felt in many state capitols. The state association of school board members may be a natural ally of the teachers' organization on some issues, and a protagonist on others. Associations of school administrators, parent associations, and advocates of special education will bring their influence to bear upon legislators and other state officials on selected issues. In some cases, these professional groups will command the resources necessary to staff an office and will lobby for their preferred positions of issues that affect their clientele.

Lobbyists are one of the more maligned groups in American politics. The vision of strong-arm tactics and backroom deals is pervasive but overdrawn. First and foremost, lobbyists function as information sources, providing data and possible arguments to officials within the policy-making system. Such information, even if only about the position of the lobbyists groups, may sometimes enlighten a beleaguered official and inform the ensuing debate. Legislators grow to rely upon the best lobbyists as fountains of accurate, if selective, facts and persuasive debating points.

There is, of course, the specter of political power just below the surface. If political promises and threats are usually implicit, they may still be accurately perceived and influential. One important way that interest groups with substantial financial resources gain the attentive ear of a legislator or governor is by contributing to their electoral campaigns. Some major interests make it a practice to contribute to all candidates who have a chance of being elected to an influential position, regardless of their party affiliation or political philosophy, simply as a means of increasing their chances of access when the chips are down. Even groups which have little ability to deliver votes directly may endear themselves as regular contributors to a key legislator's campaign war-chest.

There are also non-education interest groups that exert substantial influence upon the resolution of educational questions at the state level. Labor unions, groups representing particular minorities, civil-rights groups such as the American Civil Liberties Union, or state taxpayers' associations may all campaign actively for or against an education bill that affects their members or the ideals they represent.

Often there will be an attempt among the various education interest groups (frequently in concert with the state office of education) to work out their differences and present a united front to the legislature and other state officials. This pattern, which Laurence Iannaccone has called the "monolithic" pattern, has most of the educational expertise in the state lined up on one side.[2] It is most effective in budgetary matters where the quest for more education dollars induces the interests to bury their differences and emphasize their common need. When that approach breaks down, the education associations may find themselves in open conflict with each other, forcing the legislators to take sides in their internecine struggle. A variant of this pattern finds the state organizations so fragmented that they constitute little effective influence upon the policy-making machinery. In states which display this pattern, local school administrators may fill the void by exercising influence directly upon legislators from their home districts.

One subtle but perceptible shift has occurred in recent years in at least a few states. Education has seemingly begun to lose its special favored position in the allocation of the budgetary pie. The rapid increase in cost per pupil (even in real dollars) during the 1960s and the increasing share of total education costs shouldered by state governments have resulted in a more searching analysis of every education line in the budget.[3] Declining school enrollments in the late 1970s and early 1980s have struck many governors and legislators as an indication that this is the time to reign-in fiscal growth in the educational realm. Whereas the relatively smaller amounts requested two decades ago were often approved more or less automatically, the competition with other policy sectors—most notably other social services such as welfare, health, and environmental concerns—is toe-to-toe and no holds barred today.[4]

[2]Laurence Iannaccone, *Politics in Education*. (New York: Center for Applied Research in Education, 1967).

[3]Grant and Lind, *Digest of Education Statistics*, 1977–78, p. 73.

[4]Ellis Katz, *Educational Policymaking 1977–78: A Snapshot from the States* (Philadelphia: Center for the Study of Federalism, Temple University, 1978), p. 41

THE FEDERAL ROLE

Still small in monetary terms, compared to the states and the local districts, the growth of the federal role in so many areas since 1960 has left few, if any, schools unaffected. While the portion of elementary and secondary expenditures footed by the federal government has paused at around 9 percent, most observers would agree that those federal agencies have received a lot for their money.

Although ample precedent existed for greater federal involvement in educational matters (there has been, in fact, an Office of Education since the late 1860s), policy makers at this level pursued a hands-off approach to most major educational issues until the mid 1950s. The two following decades were to witness a minor revolution in the posture of federal agencies and of the Congress toward our nation's schools. Three related conditions spawned events and legislation or court decisions which brought about this dramatic reversal.

The first condition was a legacy of slavery: schools racially segregated by design and residential patterns throughout the nation. By 1954 the U.S. Supreme Court was ready to declare that "separate educational facilities are inherently unequal."[5] Lower federal courts were charged with supervising and enforcing desegregation. While the results of this landmark decision were far from instantaneous, by the mid 1960s this strong precedent for federal involvement in local school affairs already existed.

The second condition was a national insecurity about the United States' position as world leader. Tension between the U.S. and the USSR ran high in the 1950s. "Cold war," "space race," and "missile gap" were slogans claiming headlines. When the Soviet Union launched the world's first earth-orbiting satellite, *Sputnik I*, on October 4, 1957, wounded national pride in the U.S. sought the source of the problem. If we had lost round one of the space race, one of the reasons must be that American schools had failed to produce scientists of sufficient stature to do the job. Congress moved rapidly to rectify that state of affairs. The National Defense Education Act, which provided, among other things, much of the funding for the most ambitious effort at curriculum development in modern history, sailed through Congress in 1958. New courses of study emerged in mathematics, physics, chemistry, and in several social-science disciplines such as geography, economics, and anthropology. The "new math," "new science," and "new social studies" were widely proclaimed.

[5]*Brown* v. *Board of Education*, 1954.

The third condition which invited federal intervention in education during the 1960s was a society which, more so than several other industrialized nations, permitted extremes of wealth and poverty. With our increasing appreciation of the extent to which poverty sapped the economic strength of the nation as well as its moral fiber, Lyndon Johnson declared a "war on poverty." One very important weapon in the arsenal would be education. Economically disadvantaged youth would be the targets of many federal programs designed to compensate for their disadvantage in an attempt to break the persistent cycle of poverty. The Elementary and Secondary Education Act of 1965 represented the first massive influx of federal dollars to inner city and other economically depressed school districts. The big money in Title I of that act left little doubt that the principle of compensatory education was now a political reality.

The three forces described above launched and shaped the federal role in education. But other not-so-incidental programs grew up beside them. School lunch and milk programs poured millions of dollars into federal subsidies of school cafeterias in the interest of improving the nation's nutrition and, coincidentally, a struggling dairy industry. "Impacted-area" aid was extended to many local districts blessed with an overabundance of children from large federal military bases or other installations. Major programs sprang up in vocational and technical education, directed at special national manpower shortages and at raising the general level of employability of the nation's youth. Pressure for bilingual-multicultural instruction in schools with large ethnic minorities brought federal funds for special teacher-training programs. These and other Washington-based initiatives brought the annual federal contibution to between 8 and 10 percent of the total cost of elementary and secondary education throughout the 1970s.

Two things are evident from this short history of the federal role in education. First, most federal incursions into the traditional preserve of the states and local districts have been attempts to use schools to help resolve "non-educational" social or economic concerns. Few programs emanated from Washington with the simple objective of improving the quality of education. Second, even though the education policy process in Washington may be best described as inchoate, the overall effects of these diverse programs have been almost without exception, to assure greater access to and equity in schooling. Federal education policy has not, unlike some other policy areas, served narrow private interests to the exclusion of a broader constituency.

One could, in fact, question whether it is even accurate to speak of "federal policy" in education. Certainly there is no single center of planning and coordination within our nation's capital. Programs which bear upon education emerge, rather, from literally dozens of agencies and congressional committees. The campaign pledge of President Carter to fashion a new Department of Education out of this polyglot of bureaus and interests assumed, perhaps naively, that greater coherence was rationale enough.

It may be possible, nevertheless, to discern some focal points for the development of educational programs in Washington. It would be tempting to start our search at the White House. In recent administrations, however, Presidents have spent little time on educational questions. Nor has any identifiable senior staff person in the White House provided much direction on education matters. Strong presidential initiative did come from the Eisenhower, Kennedy, and Johnson White Houses, but that was an era when education was seen as a cure for racial injustice, questionable national security, or poverty.[6] Today, education intrudes into presidential politics but rarely.

One consequence of this presidential neglect is that school policy questions at the federal level tend to be relatively nonpartisan. On some issues, such as the desirability of block grants rather than categorical aid, it is possible to ascertain a Republican and a Democratic position. But on most major programs the crucial controversies tend to cross party lines and be worked out in congressional committees or executive agencies.

The natural executive home for many educational programs has been in the Department of Health, Education, and Welfare (HEW). The Secretary of that largest of federal bureaucracies has substantial ability to influence the course of the federal role in education, but divides his or her time with two other policy areas as well. Some have exercised strong direction; others have been content to leave most major questions in education to middle-level policy makers at the Assistant Secretary or Deputy Assistant Secretary level. Firmly imbedded within HEW is the United States Office of Education (USOE) which is headed by the Commissioner of Education. Here, surely, we have found the nexus of educational policy making at the federal level. But Washington veterans point out that however symbolically important a strong Commissioner of Education may be for the education community, anyone in that position is destined to have difficulty in the rough and status-conscious world of Washington political life. The Commissioner is just too many rungs below powerful Secretaries and Directors in other policy areas to fare well in the scramble for federal dollars and for the attention of Congress, the President, or the media.

[6]For an engaging account of this era, see Norman C. Thomas, *Education in National Politics* (New York: David McKay Company, 1975).

Newest of the education agencies is the National Institute of Education, established by Congress in 1972 to stimulate quality educational research and incorporate research findings in policy decisions. While it is still too early to predict with certainty what role the NIE will play in policy deliberations, it appears that it may become increasingly influential at least in defining major problem areas and suggesting acceptable remedies.

If this is the mainline educational establishment in Washington, it is certainly not the whole establishment. There are countless pockets within other agencies and departments that exercise control over highly significant programs. The Office of Civil Rights has been instrumental in enforcing desegregation guidelines. Head Start, Follow Through, and Upward Bound programs make their home in the Office of Economic Opportunity. Dependents' schools on overseas military bases are administered by the Department of Defense, and many American Indian children attend schools administered by the Bureau of Indian Affairs within the Department of Interior.

In the absence of central direction of federal educational programs, the Congress assumes special importance. Congress relies heavily on its committees for careful, deliberate consideration of legislation. The Education and Labor Committee of the House of Representatives reviews many, but not all, education bills passing through that house. Carl Perkins, its venerable chairman, is one of several congressmen who have built legislative careers on their experience and expertise with education legislation. On the Senate side, the Education, Arts, and Humanities Subcommittee of the Human Resources Committee is the authorizing body for much educational legislation. In both houses of Congress, strong appropriations committees still have to provide the money to fund programs that have been authorized. Additional education specialists sit on these appropriations committees in each house.

One other forum for deliberation and scrutiny of education policy is the Office of Management and Budget, whose director works closely with the White House in paring down agency requests for each new fiscal year. Budget examiners are assigned to the various areas of education, as well as to other policy areas, and may wield considerable influence in determining whether a program will prosper or will be cut.

There is a formidable array of educational interest groups in Washington, and they tend to focus their attention upon Congress. First among them in terms of political resources comes the National Education Association (NEA), closely followed by the American Federation of Teachers (AFT). The National School Boards Association is another group able to make congressional heads turn, in part because of its organizational depth at the state and district level throughout the country. The Council for Exceptional Children and the Children's Defense Fund are illustrative of interest groups that do battle over a narrower range of issues. Increasingly, governmental units at lower levels—state offices of education, universities, and even major metropolitan school districts—have permanent lobbyists in Washington to keep watch over their particular interests as the policy process unfolds. In fact, any given education issue is apt to bring out a dozen representatives from interest groups, testifying, offering their language for congressional mark-up sessions of bills under consideration, or drafting speeches for their favorite members of congress to deliver on the floor. Sympathetic legislators may find campaign donations forthcoming and find helpful acknowledgement of their legislative insight in newsletters destined for the folks back home.

In one way, the collection of education interests is not quite so disparate as it might appear. Deliberation over educational programs at the federal level is less likely to be directed at how to make an existing (or proposed) program more educationally sound than at how much money should be provided for it. Since education is still not a major slice of the federal budget pie, most education interests share at least one wish: that the President, and the director of OMB, will be generous in the size of the piece they cut for education next year. And so it is that many of the special interest groups in the educational realm come together in the Committee for Full Funding of Education to present a united front in urging the highest possible allocations to education.

FEDERAL, STATE, AND LOCAL
RELATIONS

If one looks at the percentage of expenditures for elementary and secondary public education provided by local, state, and federal sources over the 1970s, a clear trend is visible. After the boom years of the 1960s, federal contributions have grown only slightly and unevenly.[7] The major shift has come in the increasing burden assumed by state governments and the decreasing share contributed by local districts. For the first time in history, state governments are on the verge of outspending local units in their support of public schools (see Table 6–1).

As we enter the 1980s, strong public and political sentiment exists in many states to limit both taxation and expenditures. What

[7]Grant and Lind, *Digest of Education Statistics*, 1977–78, p. 21.

TABLE 6–1
Estimated expenditures of public elementary and secondary
schools by source of funds

	1969–70	1977–78
Federal	8.2%	9.4%
State	38.6	44.9
Local	52.9	45.6
All other	.3	.1
	100.0%	100.0%
	($41.0 billion)	($82.7 billion)

Source: W. Vance Grant and C. George Lind, *Digest of Education Statistics, 1977–78*, National Center for Education Statistics (Washington, D.C.: U.S. Government Printing Office, 1978), p. 21.

effect this will have upon state-local relationships in education is uncertain. Tax-limitation legislation may take the form of limiting local property-tax revenue even more sharply than state taxation. In any event, it would appear unlikely that the trend toward greater financial responsibility for public education by the states is to be reversed in the near future.

While much of the state share is provided in the form of general state aid, there is also an increasing tendency for state governments to mandate certain programs and standards that had previously been left to the discretion of local districts. Resentment of this perceived encroachment by the state runs high in many district offices throughout the country, but the sense of loss is seldom strong enough to prompt district administrators to spurn the financial aid accompanying the mandates. A similar situation exists with respect to the federal government and the local district. Even today, federal aid makes up a relatively small portion of the total budget of most school districts. It is a large enough part, however, that few superintendents can afford to seriously contemplate rejecting federal aid for which their district may be eligible. Nor can the ultimate threat of the federal government to cut off all education funds if guidelines with respect to desegregation, or other federal programs are not met, Title IX, be taken lightly.

The form in which aid from Washington should be made available has been a divisive issue since the beginning of the federal largess. Those with specific objectives in mind argue for *categorical* grants tailored to specific programs, leaving relatively little discretion to the recipient (i.e., the state or local district) about how the money is to be used. Those who are concerned primarily with strengthening the role of state and local governments at the expense of the federal bureaucracy favor *general revenue sharing*, under which funds will be distributed by formula to states or localities, with very few restrictions upon how the money is to be spent. Between the two extremes lies the block-grant concept, wherein funds are distributed by formula for use in certain broad functional areas. Under a block grant, similar programs will be grouped into the same block. The state or local unit has more flexibility than with a categorical grant, but more restrictions than under general revenue sharing.[8]

In general, Democrats in Washington have opted for categorical grants as the most efficient way to achieve the social purposes they seek. Republicans, on the other hand, have tended to support general revenue sharing and, more recently, block grants, both out of skepticism about the equalizing objectives of many Democratic-sponsored programs and from an ideological conviction that discretion in these matters is better placed at the state and local levels. State officials, for the most part, prefer general revenue sharing or block grants, which leave them more latitude to shape programs as they wish.

Some grants-in-aid are made by federal agencies directly to local school districts. Increasingly, however, federal education agencies have realized their own real limitations in implementing and enforcing complex policy in school districts throughout the land. Given insufficient personnel and inadequate administrative channels to do the job themselves, they have turned to state education agencies to administer many federal programs. Much of the growth of state offices of education has been due to this additional responsibility. Thus, from the vantage point of the local school administrators, the state has become even more powerful, because it is often administering federal, as well as its own, policies.

THE CENTRALIZATION-DECENTRALIZATION ISSUE

Almost no one argues that what we need in education is more federal involvement and control. To the contrary, there is strong sentiment for putting the authority back in the hands of local board members and administrators. "Local control" is more than an appealing slogan. Yet, one is hard-pressed to find examples of recent vintage where either a state or the federal government has relaxed its grip on an area of educational policy and turned it back to the local districts

[8]Advisory Commission on Intergovernmental Relations, *Categorical Grants: Their Role and Design* (Washington, D.C.: U.S. Government Printing Office, 1977).

to do what they will with it. Why is it apparently so easy to centralize education policy making, and so difficult to decentralize?

First, American society is becoming more interrelated with each passing decade. In the case of education, what and how youngsters are taught in our local community today will affect people far beyond our local community tomorrow. Geographical mobility, and an interlocking economic system tie the nation together and make every community dependent in hundreds of ways upon the rest of the state or nation. Ignorance, disease, and crime no longer respect school-district or even state boundaries. In other words, issues that were once largely local issues now transcend the community and are likely to be viewed as state or national issues.

Add to that fact the observation that, in state and national political forums, minority interests that would have great difficulty carrying the day in their local communities have an opportunity to pool their efforts and affect policy in ways not available to them at home. This aggregation of minority interests has been most noticeable at the federal level, where education policy has been directed with surprising consistency at expanding the educational opportunity of blacks, Hispanics, the poor, the unemployed, and other historically disadvantaged groups.

Finally, there is a sort of political accountability which makes federal and state officials reluctant to turn over tax moneys generated at their level, with no strings attached, to local school districts. Few governors, state legislators, or chief state school officers would wish to be held accountable for the manner in which each district might spend its state aid under such conditions. Without guidelines and regulations to avoid at least the worst abuses, any future opponent would have only to point with indignation toward one or two flagrant examples of districts which accepted state aid but turned away handicapped students, maintained all-black schools, or purchased "un-American" textbooks with the money. There is a well-conditioned response among most career politicians to cover their backsides whenever funds are appropriated.

Some forces appear to be running in the other direction, toward decentralization. Instead of hoped-for economies of size which would make centralized administration more efficient, an excessively rigid, bureaucratic system has resulted. A constant stream of paperwork tries the patience of state and local officials alike. Special reasons why their particular school, district, or state should be exempted from this or that ruling are ignored.

All of this, along with the knowledge that important decisions are being made far from the classroom where they will have their effect, may progressively alienate teachers and administrators who see little opportunity to influence their own schools for the better. If that feeling grows, the vitality, experimentation, and flexibility which have become trademarks of American schools may be in jeopardy.

SUMMARY

There is little doubt about where legal responsibility for education lies. As the U.S. Constitution contains no reference to education, authority in this domain is reserved to the states and the people, under the Tenth Amendment. The issue is only slightly obscured by the fact that historically the states have passed along discretion for most kinds of policy to the local school districts which they established.

The most dramatic shift of the last two decades has found states assuming a larger share of the fiscal burden of education and, at the same time, flexing their policy making muscle in areas once left to the local districts. Involvement of the federal government in educational programs has deepened during this same period. There are several reasons for these shifts, but the dominant one is the quest for greater equality of educational opportunity, across districts and states, than can be provided by local districts relying exclusively on their own resources. Many inequities still exist, but the overall effect of state and federal intervention has been to decrease the worst discrepancies. Active advocacy by interest groups representing minorities and disadvantaged groups, and legislatures and educators dedicated to the principle of equal educational opportunity, have all contributed to this change.

Despite strong sentiment for local control of education, and frustration with bureaucratic elements of state and federal intervention, the trend toward higher-level intervention in a wide array of policy areas is well-established. Nor does there appear to be a viable formula for reversing the trend. The reasons underlying this gradual shift in the authority structure start with a more and more geographically mobile society. The case for local control would be stronger if products of a community's schools never left the community. But in a nation where youngsters from Tuscaloosa or Abilene may wind up in Birmingham, Chicago, or Sacramento, the quest for general assurance about the variety and quality of education available in all communities is strong. States, and to some extent the federal government, can attack the worst inequities even though, by exhorting, prodding, and regulating local districts, they attempt to provide that assurance.

STUDY GUIDE

Can you recall the meaning of the following terms? Discuss them with a class colleague and apply them to your school-community setting.

compensatory education
minimal-competency testing
lobbying
Chief State School Officer (CSSO)
National Defense Education Act
  (NDEA)
Elementary and Secondary
  Education Act (ESEA)

Title I
Title IX
Public Law 94–142
impacted-area aid
categorical grants
block grants
revenue sharing
local control

SUGGESTED ACTIVITIES

1. Invite a local school superintendent or business manager to address your class on the subject of "How State and Federal Government Have Changed Public School Administration."

2. Obtain a copy of the volume (usually referred to as the "School Code") compiling all state laws applicable to schools in your state. Develop a list of major areas in which the discretion of local school boards and administrators is limited by state policy.

3. Set up a task force to devise a measure of the extent to which any school district in your state is relatively advantaged or disadvantaged in its efforts to provide a quality educational program without state intervention. For example, in states where districts rely heavily upon property-tax revenue, high assessed-valuation per student might put a district in a relatively advantageous position. Now examine the effect of your state's general school-aid formula. Does state aid in your state help advantaged or disadvantaged districts more?

4. Organize a debate among members of your class on the topic, "Resolved that the federal role in education should be increased."

5. Assume that you are a staunch proponent of local control of education. Can you devise a politically and economically feasible plan for returning control of the nation's schools to local school boards? Defend your plan before designated critics in the class.

SELECTED READINGS

BAILEY, STEPHEN, *Education Interest Groups in the Nation's Capital* (Washington, D.C.: American Council on Education, 1975).

GOLLADAY, MARY A. and JAY NOELL, eds., *The Condition of Education*, 1978 edition (Washington, D.C.: National Center for Educational Statistics, n.d.).

KIRST, MICHAEL W., ed., *The Politics of Education at the Local, State and Federal Levels (Berkeley, Calif.: McCutchan, 1970).*

ORFIELD, GARY, *The Reconstruction of Southern Education: The Schools and the 1964 Civil Rights Act* (New York: Wiley-Interscience, 1969).

THOMAS, NORMAN C., *Education in National Politics* (New York: David McKay, 1975).

THOMPSON, JOHN THOMAS, *Policymaking in American Public Education* (Englewood Cliffs, N.J.: Prentice-Hall, 1976).

7

PUBLIC
SCHOOLS
AND THE LAW

Public-school districts are creatures of the state legislatures, and local boards of education govern according to the authority granted them by state law. In spite of the potential power that legislatures enjoy, they have generally granted wide-ranging power to local school boards, and local control of education has historically been fostered by this autonomy. During the last two decades, inroads into this local autonomy have taken place. State legislatures, for example, are making more demands on local school districts about how their money is spent, while the federal government has been expending categorical aid to schools in an attempt to achieve certain social objectives. In addition to this expanded legislative involvement in public schools, the judiciary has become such a sufficiently potent force in public schools that educational administrators need to have a keen eye for the legal parameters that define much of their job. Only recently have we begun to realize how powerful the law-education interface really is. Desegregation policy, for example, is being formed by a handful of federal judges across the nation.

This explosion in judicial involvement in public schools is explained primarily by the willingness of federal courts to decide public-school matters on the basis of the U.S. Constitution. The once-held doctrine that students do not enjoy constitutional rights while in school has been discarded. In fact, the judicial activist philosophy which argues that the Constitution is a flexible document that must be read with a sensitive eye for contemporary social problems undreamed of by the Founding Fathers is an important part of this development. With increasing attention given to social problems, and the apparent inability of the public schools to solve these problems, it is not surprising that the federal courts would intervene. This chapter will analyze the judicial process and identify several of the landmark decisions of the U.S. Supreme Court which affect public schools.

THE JUDICIAL PROCESS

People generally understand legislative action better than judicial action. Legislatures—whether they be federal, state, or local—pass laws which people are expected to obey. It is not so clear how judges operate. Who writes these decisions? Why does a matter get settled by courts? How does one make sense of these decisions? These are common questions.

In spite of a general ignorance about the judicial branch of government, people often employ judicial decisions—accounts of which are usually read in newspapers or popular news magazines—as authority for pressing a certain viewpoint. Because most persons prefer to follow the law, and because few other persons involved in the educational decision can authoritatively challenge the veracity of the claim made for the case, such popular accounts become persuasive arguments. For example, in discussions over tracking or leveling students, someone can raise the argument that the courts have prohibited tracking. To accept this statement on its face and thereby reject a tracking program would be a legal mistake (judgment is withheld about the educational benefits surrounding tracking). It is true that a federal judge declared tracking unconstitutional as practiced in the Washington D.C. school system because it had the effect of racially segregating students—isolating minorities into the lower tracks, with very little possibility of them attending academically rigorous courses that could prepare them to attend college.[1] But this decision does not stand for the proposition that

---

[1]Smuck v. Hansen, 408 F. 2nd 175 (1969). Cases are often cited as support for a proposition, and the citation communicates how the case can be easily located if a reader wants to read the case. To the uninitiated, cases are collected according to reporter systems, each of which has its own title and abbreviation. For example, federal district court decisions are collected in the Federal Supplement Series, abbreviated F. Supp., while the Circuit Courts of Appeal decisions are collected in the Federal Reporter, Second Series, and are abbreviated F. 2nd. State court decisions are not collected for courts of general jurisdiction (the lowest level), while the state appellate courts will be collected either under the official state title (e.g., the Illinois Reporter or the California Reporter) or

tracking, by itself—not linked with any racial discrimination, is unconstitutional. In fact, even tracking in a multiracial school is constitutionally acceptable so long as it is not done in a racially discriminatory manner. It is the unequal treatment by race that is constitutionally suspect, not the educational practice of tracking. This is just one example of how the unwary may misunderstand a judicial decision which has impact upon the educational practices of a school. This potential for misinterpretation, combined with the real impact that legislation and judicial interpretations have upon public-school administration, make it imperative to understand the legal process as well as the substantive law. Consequently, the first part of this chapter will examine the legal process, and the second part will consider several landmark U.S. Supreme Court decisions in public education.

LEGAL SOURCES OF "SCHOOL LAW"

The phrases "school law" and "education law" are used as though they describe a body of knowledge separate from the law in general. Though the context of education is a distinctive theme in school law, the mode of analysis employed cuts across a wide range of legal specialties.

School-law decisions come out of a variety of legal principles including contracts, torts, administrative law, and constitutional law; each of which involves a different mode of analysis. When confronted with a school-law issue, the initial consideration is to know what type of analysis to apply. Increasingly, a particular issue may involve several types of inquiry. For example, teacher dismissal will necessitate interpretation of the contract, an understanding of state law, and knowledge of constitutional due-process safeguards. Lawyers are trained to analyze fact situations according to these particular specializations, while educators are not. Historically, educational administrators have been able to stay abreast of statutory requirements by mastering the school code. With the explosion of constitutional cases in the past fifteen

under a regional reporter. The major legal publisher, West Publishing Co., reports state opinions by regions. For example, the Atlantic Reporter, Second Series, abbreviated A. 2nd, reports cases from Connecticut, Delaware, Maine, Maryland, New Hampshire, New Jersey, Pennsylvania, Rhode Island, and Vermont. There are seven regional reporters —Atlantic, Northeastern, Northwestern, Pacific, Southeastern, Southern, and Southwestern—that report all fifty states. The number in front of the reporter is the volume; the number following the reporter is the page number at which the decision can be found. Therefore, the Court of Appeals decision in the Hansen case can be found on page 175 of volume 408 in the Federal Reporter, Second Series.

years, however, knowledge of the school code is, in itself, insufficient. A fundamental principle of our constitutional system is that statutes, regulations, or board policies are valid as long as they are constitutional. Board policies are therefore enforceable as long as they are constitutional and authorized by state law. It is easy to see the potential power that judges hold over legislatures and school boards because of their authority to interpret constitutions.

On occasion, the particular type of legal analysis employed will dictate the definition, and probable resolution, of the problem. Consider for example the case of Mr. James, a high-school English teacher who insisted upon wearing a black arm band in school in symbolic protest against U.S. involvement in Viet Nam. As a Quaker, James felt that this protest was protected as a matter of religious freedom. After James was dismissed from his teaching position for failure to remove the arm band, his lawyer had some difficulty persuading James that a free-speech claim was the only viable basis he had for winning the case. Ultimately James did win the case, and it is acclaimed as a precedent for academic freedom.[2]

THE FEDERAL SYSTEM AND
MULTIPLE JURISDICTIONS

A fundamental principle of the federalist system is the dual authority enjoyed by states and the federal government. States have legislatures and judicial systems separate from the federal government, and much of the development in school law has come from increased involvement by the federal government, particularly the federal courts. Because the source of a decision has bearing on its authority and significance, an introduction to the structure of state and federal courts is important to determining which has jurisdiction.

Most states have a three-tiered judicial system which includes a court of general jurisdiction, a court of general review, and a court of last resort (see Figure 7–1). Small states may not have the intermediate court of review. The particular name given to each of these levels differs considerably from state to state, and can be a source of some confusion. The court of general jurisdiction may be called a *district court* or *circuit court.* It is usually organized on a county basis, and the judge or magistrate is not required to render a written opinion. Deci-

[2]James v. Bd. of Ed., 461 F. 2nd 566 (2nd Cir. 1972). For an essay documenting the personal strain and sacrifices behind this decision, see R. Harris, "A Patch of Black Cloth," *New Yorker Magazine,* June 17, and June 24, 1974, p. 37.

FIGURE 7–1
Typical three-tiered state judicial structure

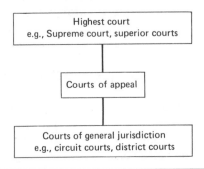

sions at this level are not published and generally have little precedential value, although they are watched with considerable interest to see what new developments are occurring. The party who loses at this level can appeal to the second level, the appellate court. Finally, the courts of last resort can accept cases on appeal. This process of selective appeal, known as *certiorari,* protects the highest court from minor or routine cases which could result in case overload.

Figure 7–2 describes the three levels of the federal court system. District courts, circuit courts of appeal, and the Supreme Court are the most important courts at each level for educational decisions. Federal district courts have general jurisdictional requirements that must be satisfied (e.g., claiming that a dispute arises between citizens of two different states involving more than $10,000, or declaring that an alleged deprivation of a protected constitutional interest has occurred) in order to use that forum. Appeals from the district courts are made to the circuit courts of appeal. At the final level of review the U.S. Supreme Court enjoys selective review. At least four of the Supreme Court Justices must agree to hear a case before it will be briefed, argued, and decided by the Court. The criteria the Justices generally use in selecting cases for review include the case's potential for developing a more precise interpretation of the law, and the case's potential for resolving conflicts that exist between different circuit courts of appeal. Although consistency under the law is an objective of the legal system, it is not always realized. For example, the circuit courts of appeal are almost evenly split on the constitutionality of school policies which regulate student hair length.[3] The Supreme Court has, on sev-

---

[3]The circuits are split 5 to 4 on the constitutionality of school policies regulating hair length. The leading cases are:

FIGURE 7–2
Three jurisdictional levels in the federal court system.

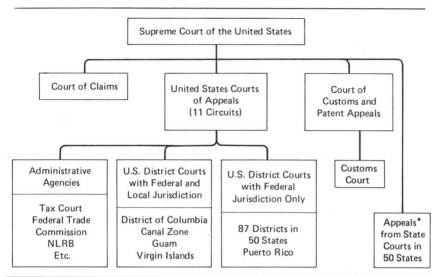

Source: "The United States Courts," House Document No. 180, 88th Congress, 1st Session.
*Appeals from state courts can be taken by the U.S. Supreme Court only if they involve matters of federal constitutional, statutory, or regulatory law.

eral occasions, refused to resolve this inconsistency. More recently, the Second and Fourth Circuits disagree with the Seventh Circuit over the constitutionality of precisely drawn guidelines to review underground publications before they are distributed. In Greenwich, Connecticut, and Richmond, Virginia, school authorities can exercise this narrow review prior to publication, while school authorities in Chicago are barred from doing so.[4] Figure 7–3 provides the boundaries for the eleven circuit courts of appeal.

State courts enjoy jurisdiction over disputes involving state legisla-

(allowing the regulations) Zeller v. Donegal School Dist., 517 F. 2nd 600 (3rd Cir. 1975); Ferrell v. Dallas Ind. School Dist., 392 F. 2nd 697 (5th Cir. 1968); Jackson v. Dorrier, 424 F. 2nd 213 (6th Cir. 1970); King v. Saddleback Junior College Dist., 445 F. 2nd 932 (9th Cir. 1971); Freeman v. Flake, 448 F. 2nd 258 (10th Cir. 1971);

(striking down the regulations) Richards v. Thurston, 424 F. 2nd 1281 (1st Cir. 1970); Massie v. Henry, 455 F. 2nd 779 (4th Cir. 1972); Breen v. Kahl, 419 F. 2nd 1034 (7th Cir. 1969); Bishop v. Colaw, 450 F. 2nd 1069 (8th Cir. 1971).

[4]Two circuits allow prior restraint—see Eisner v. Stamford Bd. of Educ., 440 F. 2nd 803 (2nd Cir. 1971) and Nitzberg v. Parks, 525 F. 2nd 378 (4th Cir. 1975), while one circuit prohibits prior restraint—Fujishima v. Chicago Bd. of Educ., 460 F. 2nd 1355 (7th Cir. 1972).

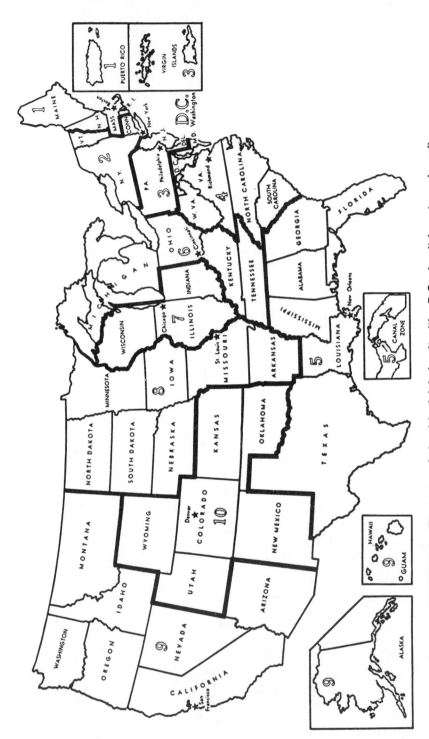

FIGURE 7-3 The eleven federal judicial circuits (the D.C. circuit is not numbered)

Source: Reprinted by permission of the West Publishing Co.

tion, the state constitution, and the U.S. Constitution. The highest level state court is the final word interpreting the meaning of state laws or state constitution, while federal courts enjoy jurisdiction over disputes involving federal legislation and the U.S. Constitution. It is possible for federal constitutional questions to move from state courts into federal courts; but beyond this, the systems try to protect the jurisdictional autonomy implicit in the federal system.

School law developed to a large extent from the expanded interpretation of the U.S. Constitution as applied by the federal judges to public schools. An alleged deprivation of a constitutional right was sufficient to get into federal court, and these federal courts were considered to be more liberal in their constitutional interpretations than the state courts. Currently the pattern seems to have shifted somewhat, with certain state courts showing a more liberal penchant in certain areas. For example, in spite of the U.S. Supreme Court's refusal to declare unconstitutional those public-school-finance schemes which are heavily dependent upon local property tax and provide widely disparate educational aid per student throughout the state,[5] several state supreme courts have declared this scheme in violation of part of the state constitution.[6] For reasons to be elaborated later, the school-law observer will want to be conscious of the particular legal claim advanced and the type and level of the jurisdiction in which the case was decided.

IDENTIFYING THE LEGAL STANDARD

A statute passed by a legislature is very different from a judicial decision rendered by a judge, although both are treated as the "law" and both influence the conduct of educational administrators. Whereas a statute is general and attempts to deal with all future circumstances, a judicial decision by necessity deals with interpreting a statute, contract, regulation, or constitution in the context of a particular dispute. The interpretation is valid for that set of facts. Judges are conscious of the precedential nature of their decisions; but the applicability of the decision is often limited by the particular facts involved in the case. The tricky part of determining the importance of a court decision is determining how broadly applicable the standard and result reached in one decision can be generalized so as to be applicable to other fact

---

[5]San Antonio Independent School District v. Rodriquez, 411 U.S. 1, 93 S.Ct. 1278 (1973).

[6]See, e.g., Serrano v. Priest II, 135 Cal. Retr. 345 (1976) and Robinson v. Cahill, 118 N.J. Supp. 223, 287 A 2nd 187 (1972), *supplemented in* 119 N.J. Super. 40, 289, A 2nd 569 (1972), *aff'd* as modified, 62 N.J. 473, 303 A 2nd 297 (1973). For a more detailed description of school finance litigation, see Chapter 9 in this book.

situations. Consequently, one cannot feel comfortable defining a general standard of conduct for schools in a particular area until several cases in that area, examining slightly different fact situations, have been decided.

Precedent is critical in the judicial process. Judges apply the judicial standard that pertains to that particular set of facts. Controversy turns on how close the set of facts in the dispute are to those in the decision as well as on the appropriateness of this standard for the facts in dispute.

Consider as an example the general question of the latitude provided teachers by the First Amendment to say and teach what they desire while in the classroom. In the 1971 case of *Mailloux* v. *Kiley*[7] the judges of a Massachusetts federal district court decided that the dismissal of an English teacher for using the word *fuck* in an eleventh-grade English class violated that teacher's constitutional right of academic freedom. The judge was satisfied that the teacher used the word as a vehicle for teaching the concept of taboo words, that some educational experts recognize this as a valid objective and a valid way of achieving it, and that the school had no regulation prohibiting it. At one point in the opinion there is a glowing statement of academic freedom.

> The Constitution recognizes [academic] freedom in order to foster open minds, creative imaginations and adventurous spirits. Our national belief is that the heterodox as well as the orthodox are a source of individual and of social growth. We do not confine academic freedom to conventional teachers or to those who can get a majority vote from their colleagues. Our faith is that the teacher's freedom to choose among options for which there is any substantial support will increase his intellectual vitality and his moral strength. The teacher whose responsibility has been nourished by independence, enterprise, and free choice becomes for his student a better model of the democratic citizen. His examples of applying and adapting the values of the old order to the demands and opportunities of a constantly changing world are among the most important lessons he gives to youth.[8]

Yet further along in the same opinion, the language seems considerably less enthusiastic about academic freedom.

> This court rules that when a secondary-school teacher uses a teaching method which he does not prove has the support of the preponderant opinion of the teaching profession or of the part of it to which he belongs, but which

[7]Mailloux v. Kiley, 323 F. Supp. 1387 (WD Mass. 1971).
[8]*Ibid.,* supplemented in 1391.

he merely proves is relevant to his subject and students, is regarded by experts of significant standing as serving a serious educational purpose, and was used by him in good faith, the state may suspend or discharge a teacher for using that method, but it may not resort to such drastic sanctions unless the state proves he was put on notice either by a regulation or otherwise that he should not use that method.[9]

In determining the application of this decision to the general question of academic freedom, it is hard to know precisely which is the controlling statement. What is the academic freedom when younger students are involved, when: the discussion topic is not related to the content of the course but nonetheless socially significant, when the school has a rule restricting what is taught, and when the material is not developed into a cohesive unit or lesson plan? The answers to these questions depend on which language from the decision is employed. And later cases make it clear that the interpretation of academic freedom is consistent with the more restrictive language.[10]

The point of this example is that court opinions must be read with careful attention to the facts. The significance of the decision must be understood within these facts, and extreme caution needs to be employed in placing much faith in more expansive language that goes beyond the confines of the fact situation.

WEIGHT OF JUDICIAL AUTHORITY

Technically, a court's decision is binding authority only within its own jurisdiction. A decision of the federal District Court of Nevada, for example, is binding only upon those persons in Nevada's jurisdiction, while the Supreme Court is binding authority for the United States. Practically, though, a court's decision may have an impact which is much broader than its jurisdiction. When issues are litigated, school administrators, among others, watch the decision with keen interest. Unless they feel strongly about the matter, they will tend to follow a course of action consistent with this result. Still, if the administration feels that the decision reached is inappropriate because of improper application of a judicial standard, the administrator may wait to have

[9]*Ibid.,* supplemented in 1392.
[10]See, e.g., Parducci v. Rutland, 316 F. Supp. 352 (ND Ala. 1970), Brubaker v. Bd. of Ed., 502 F. 2nd 973 (7th Cir. 1974). For an exhaustive analysis of academic freedom for classroom teachers, see S. Goldstein, "The Asserted Constitutional Right of Public School Teachers to Determine What They Teach," 124 *U. of Penn. L. Rev.* 1293 (1976).

the practice challenged in the district. High litigation expenses require that this decision will not be entered into lightly.

Courts do not provide advisory opinions. There must be a real dispute between at least two parties for a court to hear the arguments and render an opinion. Litigation is a costly process and, typically, persons try to avoid it whenever possible. This reluctance results in many significant legal questions remaining unanswered. Administrators can seek advisory opinions of the state attorney general or the legal staff of the state department of education, or legal advice from the school district's legal counsel, if available. Courts do not find attorney-general or state-office-advisory opinions binding or precedential in any way. Courts are most likely to show deference for decisions of equivalent or higher courts, less deference for lower court decisions, and very little, if any, deference for advisory opinions. Court decisions respect and usually describe the logical process followed by an equivalent court in another jurisdiction in arriving at its decision, but do not feel bound in any way to follow their lead. In short, courts are bound to follow the precedent of earlier decisions controlling the jurisdiction, and will look to other jurisdictions for insight about how other judges, faced with similar fact situations, may have defined and answered the issues.

ANATOMY OF A SCHOOL LAW CONTROVERSY: IMPLICATIONS FOR ADMINISTRATION

The different sources of legality that exist, the jurisdictional limitations that surround the enforceability of judicial decisions, and the difficulty of precisely identifying the legal standard which flows from the facts of the decided case are not matters of consequence to only attorneys and judges. They also critically affect many of the decisions which the school administrator makes. As an example of this, briefly consider one school-law controversy—the legality of rules restricting participation in an interscholastic sport on the basis of sex.

In the early 1970s many state high school athletic associations had rules which excluded girls from participating on boys' teams. Two Minnesota girls who desired to participate on the high school tennis, cross-country, and cross-country-skiing teams challenged the constitutionality of their exclusion. The Eighth Circuit Court of Appeal[11] agreed with the girls both because of the failure of the High School

---

[11]Brenden v. Independent School District 742, 477 F. 2nd 1292 (8th Cir. 1973).

League to show that women are incapable of competing with men in non-contact sports and because the girls were denied a chance to demonstrate their individual ability. "The failure to provide the plaintiffs with an individualized determination of their own ability to qualify for positions on these teams is ... violative of the Equal Protection Clause. ... [T]heir schools have failed to provide them with opportunities for interscholastic competition equal to those provided for males with similar athletic qualifications."[12] The decision suggested three alternatives to state high-school athletic associations: drop interscholastic sports altogether, offer membership to teams on basis of competitive skill (regardless of sex), or provide separate teams for each sex.

In 1972 Congress passed Title IX, which prohibited sex discrimination in public schools.[13] When writing the regulations for the athletics section, the Department of Health, Education, and Welfare employed the *Brenden* decision and said that single-sex contact sports are acceptable while non-contact sports must be open on a competitive-skill basis if only one team is provided. The teams may be segregated by sex if two teams are provided in the same sport. Beyond this, there must be equal athletic opportunity for all students in the school.[14]

The portion of this regulation allowing the absolute exclusion of one sex in a contact sport has been declared unconstitutional in several states. In one case, a female wanted to participate in interscholastic soccer competition but was barred because of its classification as a contact sport by the Colorado High School Activities Association. A Colorado federal district court decision declared this rule unconstitutional because, once again, it did not adequately allow for individual differences to be considered in making the soccer team.[15] Other courts have reached similar conclusions in similar cases involving female participation in contact sports.[16]

Although the law is still developing in this area, the implications for the educational administrator are clear. First, the administrator needs to watch several legal sources ranging from federal statutory and constitutional law to the state and local policies controlling the district

[12] *Id.* at 1302.

[13] *Id.* 13. 20 USC Sections 1681–1686.

[14] 45 C.F.R. Section 86.41.

[15] Hoover v. Meiklejohn, 430 F. Supp. 164 (D. Colo. 1977).

[16] See, e.g., Darrin v. Gould, 550 P. 2nd 882 (Wash. Sup Ct. 1971); Yellow Springs Exempted Village Sch. Dist. v. Ohio H.S. Ath. Assoc., 443 F. Supp. 975 (SD Ohio WD 1978) and Packel v. Pennsylvania Interscholastic Athletic Assoc., 334 A 2nd 839 (Penn. 1975).

athletic program. Second, there is some ambiguity about what the precise standard will be in a particular area of enforcement.[17] Conflicting advisory opinions have come out of two different regional enforcement offices. Another example is the ambiguity surrounding the definition that will be given the concept of *equal athletic opportunity* for enforcement purposes. Third, the administrator needs to be aware of the implications of a decision in a different jurisdiction. Are the facts and legal questions in the other jurisdiction pertinent to the local school? Finally, the example should make very obvious the time that can be involved while the judicial process laboriously works its way through the development of a standard. The administrator must be prepared for some ambiguity about the standard, and be prepared to shift or change policies if the standard goes in directions previously unforeseen. The issue will change, but the variables the administrator should consider will be fairly constant.

Chapter 8 will consider in greater detail how many of these factors involved in the judicial process might influence the school administrator's thinking. Before considering these, it will be informative to review a number of key Supreme Court decisions in the school-law area.

LANDMARK SCHOOL LAW DECISIONS
BY THE U.S. SUPREME COURT

The growth in school law which has been particularly noticeable in the past decade is based to a large extent on the willingness of federal courts to entertain constitutional claims. Following is a brief synopsis of several of the most significant U.S. Supreme Court constitutional decisions. For each of the decisions, the facts of the case and the legal principle employed by the Court in resolving the dispute are briefly described.

There are two areas of school law in which the Supreme Court has been active for over two decades, but for which it is not possible to identify a single landmark case—school desegregation and First Amendment religion. For these, an attempt will be made to describe a handful of significant cases that define the area, before moving to the more singular landmark cases.

[17]For a more complete analysis of related issues see Thurston, "Judicial Dismemberment of Title IX," *Phi Delta Kappan,* Vol 60 (April, 1979), p. 594.

Racial Desegregation of Public Schools[18]

In 1954 the Supreme Court handed down the *Brown* v. *Board of Education of Topeka* decision,[19] clearly one of the most significant decisions ever made by the Court. The plaintiffs, black students acting through their legal representatives, asked the Court to find that their racial segregation in public schools violated the Equal Protection Clause of the Fourteenth Amendment. The Court responded by overruling its own 1896 precedent that allowed "separate but equal" facilities as constitutional, and said that in 1954 separation in education could not be equal and that legally required segregation is therefore unconstitutional.

> We conclude that in the field of public education the doctrine of "separate but equal" has no place. Separate educational facilities are inherently unequal. Therefore, we hold that the plaintiffs and others similarly situated for whom the actions have been brought are, by reason of the segregation complained of, deprived of the equal protection of the laws guaranteed by the Fourteenth Amendment.[20]

As a remedy, the Supreme Court ordered the defendant school districts to desegregate.[21] Federal district courts, guided by general powers of equity, were given the responsibility to shape and determine what precise actions the local districts had to perform to achieve desegregation. This allowed the federal district courts wide flexibility in assessing the particular factors involved in the district, and in fashioning a remedial order. This broad power of enforcement and shaping of remedial action by the federal district courts has continued to the present, although it has been challenged in certain circumstances. In the 1971 *Swann*[22] decision the Court elaborated upon this judicial authority, saying that once a violation of the Constitution has been shown in the failure of a school system to eliminate racial segregation, the district court has broad powers to shape appropriate remedies.

[18]For an exhaustive description of the historical background as well as a description of the *Brown* decision, see R. Kluger, *Simple Justice: The History of Brown v. Board of Education and Black America's Struggle for Equality* (New York: Knopf, 1975).

[19]Brown v. Board of Education of Topeka, 347 U.S. 483(1954).

[20]*Id.* at 495. *Ibid.*, supplemented in 495.

[21]Brown v. Board of Education of Topeka, 349 U.S. 294 (1955). The Court waited until 1955 to order the remedy for desegregating schools.

[22]Swann v. Charlotte-Mecklenburg Bd. of Educ., 402 U.S. 1 (1971).

These appropriate remedies may include the limited use of mathematical ratios to provide a starting point for determining desired racial balances, the altering of attendance zones, and the transportation of students. This transportation has largely taken the form of busing.

More recently, in the *Dayton* case, the Supreme Court suggested that district courts match the remedial orders more closely with the particular illegal discriminatory practices the district engaged in.[23] Racial imbalance between schools, by itself, does not involve violation of the Fourteenth Amendment. Yet racial imbalance which occurs as a result of intentional segregative actions on the part of the school board is unconstitutional, and federal district courts have the responsibility of determining what board actions, if any, display this improper segregative intent. From this the courts can establish a remedy to decrease the racial segregation which resulted from an improper board action.

Despite the *Brown* decisions, the racial segregation of students increased. The Civil Rights Act of 1964, commonly known as Title VI,[24] was passed by Congress, with enforcement powers in HEW, to enhance desegregation by tying federal funds to school-district desegregation efforts. Enforcement of Title VI continues.[25]

At the constitutional level, judicial desegregation orders can be given only if it can be proven that official state action—state legislation or school board policies—has the effect of segregating students by race. Consequently the courts have continually distinguished *de jure* and *de facto* segregation. *De jure* segregation occurs because of some official action on the part of the state, municipality, or school district, and is prohibited by by the Fourteenth Amendment. *De facto* segregation is deemed to have occurred because of private, non-governmental forces, and is outside the reach of the Fourteenth Amendment. The *Brown* cases spoke to state-mandated segregation, and the attempt to remedy segregation focused initially in those states which had legislated segregation. It was not until 1973 that the Supreme Court found sufficient evidence of unconstitutional intent and purpose by a school board in

[23]Dayton Bd. of Education v. Brinkman, 97 S. Ct. 2766 (1977).

[24]The substantive language of Title VI of the Civil Rights Act of 1964 reads, "No person in the United States shall, on the ground of race, color or national origin, be excluded from participation in, be denied the benefits of, or be subjected to discrimination under any program or activity receiving Federal financial assistance." (402 USC Section 2000d). Regulations were promulgated for Title VI. (See 45 C.F.R. 80, et.seq.)

[25]The Department of Health, Education and Welfare has come under recurring criticism for not actively enforcing Title VI. In Adams v. Richardson, 480 F. 2nd 1159 (DC Cir '73), HEW was ordered to enforce Title VI more diligently.

a region which had not historically been legislated a dual school system.[26] This decision in Denver, Colorado, marked the beginning of constitutional enforcement of racial desegregation throughout urban areas of the north, touching such cities as Boston, Detroit, Indianapolis, and Springfield, Illinois.

The Denver Board of Education was found to have engaged in the purpose or intent to segregate because of its policies in regard to building new schools, gerrymandering attendance zones, using mobile classrooms, writing certain student-transfer policies, transporting students, and assigning faculty and staff on identifiable racial bases. Because of the showing of the board's segregative intent in these new schools, the burden of proof shifted to the school district to show that the disproportionate racial composition of the inner-city schools was not also the result of school-board policy. The board's argument that it followed a simple policy of neighborhood schools was rejected, and the matter returned to the federal district court to develop a district-wide remedy. The practical effect of *Keyes* has been that where segregative intent can be shown in a portion of the district, it is likely that the racial imbalance of whole district will be considered illegal. This will trigger a desegregation remedy which usually involves most, if not all, schools within the district. As discussed above, the Court appears to have retreated from this standard in the *Dayton* decision, in which it argued that the remedy shaped by the district court should stick closer to the precise illegal actions of the school board and not be so quick to develop district-wide remedies.

> The duty of both the District Court and of the Court of Appeals in a case such as this, where mandatory segregation by law of the races in the schools has long since ceased, is to just determine whether there was any action in the conduct of the business of the school board which was intended to, and did in fact, discriminate against minority pupils, teachers or staff.... If such violations are found, the District Court ... must determine how much incremental segregative effect these violations had on the racial distribution of the Dayton school population as presently constituted, when that distribution is compared to what it would have been in the absence of such constitutional violations. The remedy must be designed to redress that difference, and only if there has been a system-wide impact may there be a system-wide remedy.[27]

[26]Keyes v. School District No. 1, Denver, Colo., 413 U.S. 189 (1973).

[27]Dayton Bd. of Ed. v. Brinkman, 97 S. Ct. 2766 at 2775. In applying this criteria in a subsequent decision, the Supreme Court held that the Dayton Board of Education had not adequately removed the vestiges of the racially segregated system that existed prior to 1954. Consequently, the Court affirmed an order for a district-wide desegregation busing plan. Dayton *Bd. of Ed* v. *Brinkman*, —U.S.—, 47L.W. 4944(1979).

Desegregation remedies have been difficult to develop where the school district is basically one race, thereby providing no possibility for integrated schools. This is apparent in some of the major northern cities where the black population has become increasingly predominant.

One obvious alternative which would achieve greater racial balance would be to join the predominantly white cities into the school-desegregation plan. The Supreme Court rejected this remedy for Detroit and its suburbs in *Bradley* v. *Milliken.*[28] The Court said that the school districts were to be treated as integral public units, and that they could not be joined into any remedy unless they could be shown to have engaged in action that led to the racial composition of their district. The Court could not find any such illegal action on the part of these districts or the state as a whole, and consequently removed them from the Detroit desegregation remedy. To the extent that the population patterns in the suburbs and the urban area are the result of some intended governmental action, a remedy could be imposed which would cut across city boundaries.[29]

First Amendment Religion Cases: Separation of Church and State[30]

The First Amendment provides that "Congress shall make no law respecting an establishment of religion, or prohibiting the free exercise thereof. . . ." The Fourteenth Amendment has incorporated this language and applies it to the states and their subdivisions. The precise meaning given to these words has been the source of considerable litigation and numerous Supreme Court opinions. This litigation usually involves either the constitutionality of some religious practice in the public schools or the constitutionality of some public aid to parochial schools. The scope of this chapter does not permit an exhaustive

[28]Milliken v. Bradley, 418 U.S. 717 (1974).

[29]In Bradley v. Milliken "II," 97 S. Ct. 27 (1977) the Court approved a remedy which required extra state support for the Detroit public schools to support various programs designed to maximize the desegregation effort.

[30]Defining the First Amendment boundaries between church and state in the public-school context has consumed a lot of the Supreme Court's attention. Following are a few of the cases in the area which are beyond the scope of this chapter: (Release time for religious instruction) McCollum v. Bd. of Education 333 U.S. 203 (1948), and Zorach v. Clauson, 343 U.S. 306 (1952); (prayer in school) Engel v. Vatale, 370 U.S. 421 (1962); (free transportation to parochial school students) Board of Education v. Allen, 392 U.S. 236 (1968); (public aid to private schools, generally) Meek v. Pittinger, 95 S. Ct. 1753 (1975), and Wolman v. Walter, 97 S. Ct. 2593 (1977).

overview from each area; therefore, one representative Supreme Court opinion from each area will be examined.

In 1963 the Supreme Court rendered an opinion, based on two different lower-court opinions, about whether the reading of the Bible and the Lord's Prayer at the beginning of the school day violates the Establishment Clause of the First Amendment. In one case a Unitarian family challenged a Pennsylvania statute requiring Bible reading, without comment, at the opening of each school day, although any child could be excused with parental permission. In the other case, an atheist challenged a similar Baltimore rule providing Bible reading or the Lord's Prayer. Both plaintiffs testified that the Bible readings conveyed religious doctrines which were contrary to their own religious beliefs—the Unitarians about the literal meaning of the Bible purveyed in these exercises; and the atheists about the emphasis on belief in God as the source of all moral and spiritual values.

The Supreme Court framed the following test for measuring whether a requirement violates the Establishment Clause of the First Amendment:

> What are the purpose and the primary effect of the enactment? If either is the advancement or inhibition of religion, then the enactment exceeds the scope of legislative power as circumscribed by the Constitution. That is to say that to withstand the strictures of the Establishment Clause there must be a secular legislative purpose and a primary effect that neither advances nor inhibits religion.[31]

The Supreme Court held that both situations involved religious exercises because of the basic part the Bible plays in religious belief. These exercises violate the religious beliefs of the plaintiffs and are therefore unconstitutional. It is unimportant to the Court that the plaintiffs can be dismissed from the exercises, since that still imposes a religious burden. Nor is it important that these are relatively minor encroachments. The principle of religious neutrality must guide inclusion of practices in the public schools so as not to infringe on the religious beliefs of people attending the school. "In the relationship between man and religion, the State is firmly committed to a position of neutrality."[32]

Next, let us consider the question of public aid to parochial schools. Rhode Island and Pennsylvania had statutes which provided aid to parochial schools. Most simply stated, Rhode Island would pay up to 15

[31]Abington S. D. v. Schempp, 374 U.S. 203 at 222.
[32]*Ibid.*, supplemented in 226.

percent of the salaries of teachers of secular subjects in nonpublic elementary schools. In addition to certain limitations upon the salaries and per-pupil expenditures not exceeding those in public schools, the law required teachers to agree by written oath to not teach a course in religion while receiving these salary supplements. Pennsylvania authorized the State Superintendent of Public Instruction to buy certain secular educational services from nonpublic schools for the actual costs of teachers' salaries, textbooks, and instructional materials for certain restricted courses in mathematics, modern foreign languages, physical science, and physical education which are found in the curricula of public schools.

In considering the constitutionality of these parochial statutes, in *Lemon* v. *Kurtzman,* the Court stated three tests. "First, the statute must have a secular legislative purpose, its principal or primary effect must be one that neither advances nor inhibits religion, . . . finally, the statute must not foster 'an excessive government entanglement with religion'."[33] Although the Court accepted the legislation as having a valid secular intent, both statutory schemes were found unconstitutional because of excessive entanglement between government and religion.

In the Rhode Island program the Court was cognizant of the religious character and purpose of Roman Catholic elementary schools, which were the only beneficiaries of salary supplements. The Court emphasized the high percentage of nuns in these schools who, although they would not qualify for salary supplements, represent the pervasive religious atmosphere which the legislation cannot avoid. In addition to concern over the substantial religious character of these church-related schools, the Court expressed fears of entanglement necessitated by attempts to enforce the legislation. It would be very difficult to know the extent to which a teacher was engaging in religious or secular instruction.

The Pennsylvania program was found to be excessively entangling for the same reasons plus two additional defects. First, the cash payments and subsidies going directly to the parochial schools involve the worst form of entanglement. This type of aid is much more entangling and difficult to audit than the previous types of aid—textbooks and transportation—which were upheld as constitutional because the students or parents received the benefits. Second, the Court voiced concern over the potential political divisiveness inherent in competing for resources. The political activity inherent in such campaigning for or against increased support for parochial schools will, the Court fears,

[33]Lemon v. Kurtzman, 403 U.S. 602 at 612–613.

find peoples' votes closely aligned with their faith. And it was this political division along religious lines which the Court thinks was one of the "principal evils against which the First Amendment was intended to protect."[34]

Teachers and Free Speech: *Pickering* v.
Board of Education, 391 U.S. 563
(1968).

An Illinois school district passed a multi-million-dollar bond issue in 1961 to build two new schools, and returned to the voters in 1964 for passage of an increase in the tax rate for educational purposes. The voters rejected this referendum in both May and September, 1964. Shortly after this second defeat, Marvin Pickering, a teacher in the district, wrote a "letter to the editor" which appeared in the local newspaper, criticizing the school board's management of the 1961 bond proposals and the way the board had subsequently allocated these resources. He felt that too much of the money was spent developing athletic facilities. Pickering also charged the superintendent with attempting to prevent teachers in the district from opposing or criticizing proposed bond issues.

Pickering was dismissed from his teaching position because of this letter. He was charged with having made numerous false statements in the letter and with damaging both the board and the school administration by their publication. The board was concerned about the disruptive effect that such a letter would have upon staff morale and felt that a general deterioration of education would occur in the schools. The Illinois Supreme Court upheld the dismissal, and Pickering appealed to the U.S. Supreme Court on the grounds that the dismissal amounted to an unconstitutional infringement of his First Amendment free-speech rights.

In hearing this claim, the Court stated the general balancing test to be used in such cases. "The problem . . . is to arrive at a balance between the interests of the teacher, as a citizen, in commenting upon matters of public concern, and the interest of the State, as an employer, in promoting the efficiency of the public services it performs through its employees."[35] Applying this stan-

---

[34]*Ibid.,* Supplemented in 622.
[35]Pickering v. Bd. of Ed., 391 U.S. 563 at 568.

dard, the Court found Pickering's letter to be minimally disruptive. The criticism of the board and superintendent did not involve a close working relationship that may require personal loyalty or confidence. Because of the distant relationship between the parties and the inability of the district to provide evidence that the letter did, in fact, have a detrimental impact upon the educational enterprise, the district's interest in firing Pickering was minimal. It is inconsequential that some factual errors existed in Pickering's letter. Because the errors made were matters of public record, and not something particularly in the realm of Pickering's professional expertise, the board could best counter the inaccuracies by providing the correct information in another letter. The letter involved a matter of public interest, and a school employee could not be denied the right to speak out on such a matter.

Students and Symbolic Protest: *Tinker*
v.
Des Moines Independent Community School District

A group of adults and students decided to demonstrate their objection to U.S. involvement in Viet Nam by wearing black arm bands during the Christmas holiday season. Aware of this plan, the principals of the Des Moines schools met and adopted a policy which would allow that any student who refused to remove the arm band would be suspended indefinitely until the student returned without the arm band. The policy was applied to three Tinker children who refused to remove their arm bands and were suspended from school. The Tinker family filed suit in federal district court, seeking an injunction ordering the school not to suspend students for wearing the black arm bands. The case reached the Supreme Court, which had to decide the extent to which the constitutional free-speech protections applied to students in public schools.

Justice Fortas, writing for the majority of the Court, penned the oft-quoted sentence now famous in school-law cases. "It can hardly be argued that either students or teachers shed their constitutional rights to freedom of speech or expression at the schoolhouse gate."[36] Later in the opinion, Justice Fortas elaborated upon this constitutional protection that students enjoy in school.

[36]Tinker v. Des Moines Independent Community School District, 393 U.S. 503 at 506.

In our system, state-operated schools may not be enclaves of totalitarianism. School officials do not possess absolute authority over their students. Students in school as well as out of school are "persons" under our Constitution. They are possessed of fundamental rights which the State must respect, just as they themselves must respect their obligations to the State ... [Students] may not be confined to the expression of those sentiments that are officially approved. In the absence of a specific showing of constitutionally valid reasons to regulate their speech, students are entitled to freedom of expression of their views.[37]

This is lofty, high-sounding language, and the particular constitutional rights being claimed need to be litigated separately to know if they will, in fact, be protected in public schools. But the *Tinker* decision did provide a constitutional protection for symbolic speech of the arm-band variety as long as there was no disruption which jeopardized the orderly environment of the school. In fact, a simple allegation by the school principal that disruption would follow the symbolic protest was insufficient grounds for limiting the free speech. The school must protect the student right to engage in this symbolic protest, and can limit such speech only when it becomes too dangerous or too expensive to protect. Because the Des Moines principals could not show any factual basis for alleged disruption that would follow the wearing of the arm bands, the district was enjoined from suspending any students for wearing arm bands, and ordered that any reference to the suspensions be withdrawn from the Tinker childrens' student records.

Student Suspensions and Procedural Due Process: *Goss* v. *Lopez*

During a period of widespread student unrest, approximately eighty students were suspended for up to ten days from the Columbus, Ohio, public schools. These suspensions were made pursuant to an Ohio law that empowered a public-school principal to suspend up to ten days or expel a pupil for misconduct. Under this law parents must be notified of the suspension or expulsion within twenty-four hours and be given reasons for the action. In the case of an expulsion, the student and parents are entitled to a hearing

[37] *Ibid.*, supplemented in 511.

before the board of education, while suspended students are entitled to no such hearing. Nine of the suspended Columbus, Ohio
students challenged the constitutionality of this statute as violat-
ing the Fourteenth Amendment due-process clause because they
were suspended without a hearing. They sought invalidation of
this statute and the removal of all references to each suspension
from their records.

Justice White, writing the majority opinion for the Supreme
Court, undertook a two-step analysis in declaring the statute unconstitutional. First, he determined that removal of a student
from school for a period of up to ten days was a serious deprivation. These suspensions "could seriously damage the students'
standing with their fellow pupils and their teachers as well as
interfere with later opportunities for higher education and employment."[38]

Having identified a deprivation, Justice White then had to
decide what minimal level of procedures are constitutionally required to accompany the suspension. Although suspensions are
not as damaging as expulsions—which require a written notice
and opportunity for a formal hearing before the board of education—suspensions must be accompanied by a lower-level notice
and hearing.

> Students facing temporary suspension have interests qualifying for
> protection of the Due Process Clause, and due process requires, in
> connection with a suspension of ten days or less, that the student
> be given oral or written notice of the charges against him and, if
> he denies them, an explanation of the evidence the authorities have
> and an opportunity to present his side of the story. The clause
> requires at least these rudimentary precautions against unfair or
> mistaken findings of misconduct and arbitrary exclusion from
> school.[39]

Minimal procedural safeguards require that oral notice and
oral hearing be provided in a student suspension. The two can be
given simultaneously. The administrator can tell the student
what he is charged with, and then ask if he has anything to say
about the charge. If there is no information given to doubt the
veracity of the charge, the student can be suspended. Where a
question is raised about the validity of the charge, the administrator needs to seek more information. This notice and hearing

[38]Goss v. Lopez, 419 U.S. 565 at 575.
[39]*Ibid.,* supplemented in 581.

should be provided prior to the suspension, but can be put off until after the suspension where the continued presence of the student jeopardizes the health or safety of other students or threatens to disrupt the academic process. In such circumstances the necessary notice and hearing should follow the suspension as soon as possible.

Non-Tort Liability of School Board Members: *Wood* v. *Strickland*

Two tenth graders were expelled from school for having "spiked" a punch which was drunk at an extracurricular meeting sponsored by the home-economics class and attended by students and parents. The spiking was not discovered until the home economics teacher heard rumors of it after the meeting; and the girls admitted doing it when questioned. The teacher brought the matter before the board of education, seeking their expulsion. After two hearings the girls were expelled for the rest of the semester.

The Supreme Court remanded the case to determine the appropriateness of the expulsion and whether or not it complied with procedural due-process standards. The importance of the *Wood* decision transcends the particular facts by establising a standard of liability for which school-board members might be sued for depriving someone of their constitutional rights. Justice White, writing for the majority, rejects malice as the sole standard of constitutional liability. Under the malice standard, a school-board member would be liable only when it could be shown that the board member had knowingly or recklessly deprived the student of a constitutional right. The *Wood* decision broadens liability to include those deprivations of constitutional rights which the school-board members should have known.

> [A]n act violating a student's constitutional rights can be no more justified by ignorance or disregard of settled, indisputable law on the part of one entrusted with supervision of students' daily lives than by the presence of actual malice. To be entitled to a special exemption from the categorical remedial language of Section 1983 in a case in which his action violated a student's constitutional rights, a school board member, who has voluntarily undertaken the task of supervising the operation of the school and the activities of the students, must be held to a standard of conduct based not only on permissible intentions, but also on knowledge of the basic, un-

questioned constitutional rights of his charges.... Therefore, ...
we hold that a school board member is not immune from liability
for damages under Section 1983 if he knew or reasonably should
have known that the action he took within his sphere of official
responsibility would violate the constitutional rights of the student
affected, or if he took the action with the malicious intention to
cause a deprivation of constitutional rights or other injury to the
student.[40]

This standard puts new teeth into constitutional safeguards,
and places additional responsibility upon school-board members
—and probably school administrators—to know what the Constitution requires. School-board members are not liable for predicting the future cause of constitutional law, but they will be liable
for "such disregard of the student's clearly established constitutional rights that his action cannot reasonably be characterized
as being in good faith."[41]

Constitutionality of Corporal Punishment: *Ingraham* v. *Wright*

Two junior-high students in one Dade County school received
exceptionally harsh discipline. One student, for example, testified
that he was out of school eleven days, suffering a painful
hematoma from a paddling in the principal's office where two
assistant principals pinned him face down across a table while the
principal administered at least twenty licks. Another student testified to being paddled several times, resulting in painful, although nonpermanent injuries. On at least two occasions
punishment was administered in spite of the student's denial of
alleged wrongdoing. The Supreme Court focused on two issues:
1. Does the Eighth Amendment's prohibition against "cruel
and unusual punishment" apply to an extremely harsh case of
corporal punishment in a public school? Justice Powell, writing
for the majority, asserted that the "cruel and unusual punishment" prohibition of the Eighth Amendment had been applied
only to criminal punishment, and was therefore inapplicable to
sanctions applied in schools. In response to the rather anomalous

[40]Wood v. Strickland, 420 U.S. 308 at 321–322.
[41]*Ibid.*, supplemented in 322.

situation this conclusion creates—where school children could be beaten mercilessly without constitutional redress while the Eighth Amendment would protect convicted criminals from a similar punishment—Justice Powell emphasizes the existing family and community support system for the child as well as the openness of the public school to distinguish the student from the incarcerated criminal. Abuses of corporal punishment in the school are to be managed through civil and criminal liability, not a constitutional standard.

2. Does the Fourteenth Amendment require minimal procedural safeguards to accompany the punishment? Although the majority opinion finds that corporal punishment amounts to a deprivation of liberty, Justice Powell believes that existing criminal and civil liability provides sufficient safeguards to protect the student. Departure from these traditional safeguards and requirement of advance procedural safeguards would add to the cost of disciplining students with no apparent benefit.

The *Ingraham* decision is important for schools and school districts because of what it omits rather than what it states. First, the decision focused exclusively on constitutional issues. Although the Eighth and Fourteenth Amendments were held inapplicable to public-school corporal punishment, the status quo is maintained. State laws and school-board policies can still be framed which will limit or prohibit corporal punishment.

Second, the Court did not address the questions of appropriateness of corporal punishment in public schools. This is an educational debate which will need to be raised at state or local policy-making levels, in which administrators will continue to have a central role.

Third, if schools decide to employ corporal punishment in their discipline schemes, they have a range of options regarding procedural safeguards to accompany it. For reasons of educational soundness as well as insurance against criminal or civil liability, districts may require that certain precautionary procedures accompany corporal punishment.

SUMMARY

Judicial decisions play an increasingly important role in shaping school policies. In accepting the importance of the judiciary, the school administrator must understand the legal process as well as the substantive requirement of certain landmark decisions. Important variables in the legal process include identification of the legal standard, application of the standard to different facts, and the jurisdiction of the deciding court.

Landmark cases are important because they develop, elaborate, or —on occasion—put to rest various principles of constitutional law. These cases demonstrate the range of school issues that have been approached through a constitutional interpretation. Desegregation and school prayer are two cases in which Supreme Court decisions affect the operation of public schools. In addition, the Supreme Court has decided cases which recognize the First Amendment right of teachers to speak out on matters of public debate, and the First Amendment right of students to engage in nondisruptive symbolic protest. Fourteenth Amendment due process has been applied to short-term student suspensions, while corporal punishment was declared not to be a violation of the Eighth Amendment's prohibition of cruel and unusual punishment. School-board members can be found personally liable for actions taken which deprive someone else of a clear constitutional right. Beyond these individual cases, educational administrators have been faced with several developing legal principles that have generally restricted the range of options available in administering the schools. This has necessitated increased consultation with lawyers. Chapter 8 will therefore consider the part that lawyers play in the development of educational practice and will consider briefly those critical areas of school law—such as due process, affirmative action, student rights, and collective bargaining—that shape the operation of public schools today.

STUDY GUIDE

Can you recall the meanings of the following terms and cases? Discuss them with a class colleague and apply them to you school-community setting.

legal sources	*Brown* v. *Bd of Educ. of Topeka*
federal system	*Keyes* v. *School Dist. No. 1*
multiple jurisdictions	*Abington S. D.* v. *Schempp*
United States Courts of Appeals	*Lemon* v. *Kurtzman*
judicial precedent	*Pickering* v. *Bd. of Educ.*
advisory opinions	*Tinker* v. *Des Moines Ind. Comm.*
	S. Dist.
	Goss v. *Lopez*
	Wood v. *Strickland*

SUGGESTED ACTIVITIES

1. Assume that you are an educational administrator involved in a discussion with someone over a particular school policy, and the other person refers to a particular judicial decision as the basis for requiring a particular course of action by you. What questions, if any, would you ask about the judicial decision in order to assess its importance? Why?

2. The Supreme Court has interpreted various sections of the Constitution to apply to public schools. Following is a list of constitutional sections and accompanying areas of application to public schools. Can you identify the appropriate standards in greater detail as they apply to public schools?

Fourteenth Amendment, Equal Protection Clause—Desegregation

First Amendment, Religion Clause—Prayer and Bible Reading

First Amendment, Free Speech—Student in School

First Amendment, Free Speech—Teacher Out of School

Fourteenth Amendment, Due-Process Clause—Student Suspension

Eighth Amendment—Corporal Punishment

Constitution, generally—Non-tort liability for depriving someone of their constitutional rights.

3. Read one of the complete Supreme Court decisions described in the chapter. Identify the critical facts involved in the case, and state precisely the legal issue(s) before the Court.

SELECTED READINGS

ALEXANDER, KERN, RAY CORNS, and WALTER McCANN, *Public School Law: Cases and Materials.* St. Paul, Minn.: West Publishing Co., 1969.

GOLDSTEIN, STEPHEN R., *Law and Public Education: Cases and Materials.* Indianapolis: Bobbs-Merrill, 1974.

HAZARD, WILLIAM R., *Education and the Law* (2nd ed.). New York: The Free Press, 1978.

KEMERER, FRANK and KENNETH DEUTSCH, *Constitutional Rights and Student Life.* St. Paul: West Publishing Co., 1979.

MUIR, WILLIAM K., *Prayer in the Public Schools: Law and Attitude Change.* Chicago: University of Chicago Press, 1967.

PETERSON, LEROY, RICHARD ROSSMILLER, and MARLIN VOLZ, *The Law and Public School Operation*. New York: Harper & Row, 1969.

REUTTER, E. EDMUND, JR., and ROBERT R. HAMILTON, *The Law of Public Education* (2nd ed.). Mineola, N.Y.: Foundation Press, 1976.

8

LEGAL
CONSIDERATIONS
IN THE
ADMINISTRATION
OF PUBLIC SCHOOLS

The descriptions of several land-mark Supreme Court decisions in Chapter 7 should indicate the impact of law upon public schools. These constitutional decisions are supplemented by countless statutes, regulations, and judicial interpretations thereof. Beyond question, contemporary school administrators from superintendents to assistant principals must understand that their roles are much more precisely defined by the law than was true for their predecessors. School administrators today still enjoy wide-ranging discretion, but the legal parameters defining the limits of this descretion must be appreciated.

Increased judicial involvement in the public schools is clear. The potential personal liability of the school administrator for depriving someone's constitutional rights, combined with a generally heightened awareness in the population about their rights, are sufficient reasons for the school administrator to know some school law. In addition to this, an administrator will need to be able to weigh the validity of claims that a certain recommended course of action is legal or illegal. But with the competing demands on the administrator's time and the increased proliferation and complexity of school-law decisions, it is unreasonable for the administrator to stay abreast of the current cases and their implications for the school. (Even if the administrator could stay current, there may be circumstances—usually involving a situation where "expert advice" is needed to persuade someone—when the administrator will need legal advice.) This chapter will examine two quite different aspects of this interaction of schooling and law. The first section of this chapter will examine the place of legal considerations in developing educational policy. Particularly significant is the relationship between the administrator and the legal advisor. The second section will briefly describe several key substantive areas of the law that have affected the way administrators must act. Legal areas such as student rights, due process, affirmative action, and collective bargaining affect the way schools operate—although there is disagreement over the extent of effects.

OBTAINING SOUND LEGAL ADVICE

Before considering various mechanisms for getting legal advice, it is necessary to make explicit an underlying assumption about the role of educational administrators. Administrators need to be generalists. They cannot have the legal expertise of a lawyer, the systems expertise of a computer specialist, or the financial expertise of a school finance specialist. Certain administrators will need to develop particular specialties as part of their job. Assistant superintendents of personnel, for example, will need to be familiar with affirmative-action law, business managers need special understanding of school finance, and principals need to understand student rights. Still, these administrators are generalists.

The *administrator as generalist* has a particular meaning. The school administrator acts as a generalist in a leadership sense rather than in the "paper shuffling" way of a contemporary bureaucrat. Whereas the bureaucratic generalist coordinates the paper flow between different parts of the organization, the leader-administrator knows enough about the particular specialties relating to education to be able to evaluate the quality of the advice and know how to apply it to the schools. The leader-administrator has a conception of quality education, and whether specializing in the educational program, curriculum and instruction, teaching and learning, or supervision, the administrator is able to evaluate this advice from the perspective of maximizing the quality of education.

There are three general avenues open for school administrators to receive legal advice, with a number of variations on each. First, there is a communication system between administrators that can provide information. The system can be formal (membership in organizations or subscription to periodicals) or informal (talking to other administrators on the phone to inquire about practice in their schools). Second, administrators can seek interpretation and advice from state officials. States differ on the mechanisms through which this advice is available. Some states make advisory opinions available through the attorney general's office, while other states advise through the legal office of the state office of education. In addition, the state may place particular responsibility on regional superintendents for managing legal inquiries. If the regional superintendent does not know the answer, the question will be directed to the appropriate state legal advisor. Finally, the district may have direct contact with its own legal counsel. For the very large urban school districts, this means keeping attorneys on staff who are full-time employees of the district. Since this arrangement is quite expensive, districts will opt for keeping attorneys on retainer, or hiring them for specific tasks. A retainer means that the district pays a certain fee to get access to legal advice. The precise cost of this retainer will vary depending on the level of services which are receivable under it. Often a district will have a retainer to cover ongoing legal advice, and will pay additional for any court appearances or official legal actions that are made for the district. For example, the district will receive, under the retainer fee, advice on how to manage a teacher dismissal. But if the case goes to court, the district will pay additional fees to cover court preparation and appearance time. Districts that do not keep legal counsel on retainer will nonetheless have to hire an attorney for certain tasks such as property transactions that require one. There are comparative advantages and disadvantages for these three sources of legal services. Access to counsel on retainer is speedy but expensive, while reliance on other administrators is cheap but unreliable. Advice from the official state source is probably fairly reliable but of questionable accessibility. Administrators will have to decide what balance to reach in these trade-offs.

Regardless of the source of legal advice, it must be evaluated. The administrator will need enough knowledge about the law to know initially what questions to ask. Several things should be kept in mind when ruminating over legal advice. There are, of course, certain situations in which the administrator does not evaluate or second-guess the attorney. For example, once the board of education has voted officially to sell an old building, the administrator will not oversee the technical process that the attorney goes through in transfering title. Administrator evaluation of legal advice comes in those situations where the advice affects the educational system and will potentially influence educational policy in the district. There are several factors the administrator will want to weigh when considering the attorney's advice. This evaluation will be important both for the quality of the advice as well as for understanding it sufficiently to be able to communicate about the matter to others.

First, have the attorney explain the legal sources which lead to the result. Is it based on a statute, or regulation, or constitutional interpretation? Is the interpretation of the statute being made by the attorney, or are there cases which support this interpretation? The analysis begins with legal sources; therefore, it is important to identify the source involved.

Second, if a court is involved in the legal interpretation, compare the facts of that case with the facts involved in your district. Will the legal principle enunciated in the other case still be controlling for your district? The educational expertise of the administrator can help elaborate important differences between fact situations that might call for different legal principles. For example, assume an assistant superintendent for personnel calls the board attorney to ask whether it is legal for the district to make extracurricular duty assignments to teachers without additional pay. The attorney answers that it is, and there is a case in your state and cases in other states to support this conclusion. The assistant superintendent who took this advice at full face value without further inquiry into its legal basis would likely put more reliance on it than the assistant superintendent who asked and was told that the litigated case involved only those extracurricular assignments requiring minimal time—such as patrolling toilet areas and collecting tickets at athletic events. Although the same principle might apply for more time-demanding assignments such as coaching or yearbook supervision, the assistant superintendent will probably be somewhat more cautious in developing a course of action.

Third, consider the jurisdiction in which the controlling decision came from. Is it a mandatory precedent for your district? Would another court be likely to follow this court's lead? Are there sufficient educational and legal grounds to suggest that a different result may be reached?

Finally, the administrator will want to be alert for any educational preferences that the lawyer may personally have that are mixed in with the legal advice. The attorney should be making only a legal recommendation which the administration will apply to the educational context of the district. Unless the administrator examines the basis for the advice, it will be hard to tell how much of the advice comes from personal preference. In some of the easy situations, the attorney will be able to recommend a specific course of action. In other situations, where the law is not so clear or where the conduct of a third party is undetermined, the legal advice will come as a series of options. Each of the options may have different chances of success with different price tags. The administrator will then use this information from the lawyer, along with other information, to develop a strategy or course of action. It is important to remember that the legal advisor is one tool or source of information which the administrator has at his or her disposal. And although advice and counsel are important tools for the successful operation of the school, the administrators and the board of education, not the legal counsel, operate the school.

Lawyers, in one sense, can be used as tools by the school administrators. They can be used, for example, as the "fall guys" to blame when a particular distasteful or politically unpopular course of action has to be taken. Or, they can be hired to stall a certain inevitable result. But this view of lawyers and the law should not be confused with the developing body of school law that shapes to a large extent the context of the way schools operate. Administrators need to be alert to ways of shaping the movement of this developing doctrine so that it is conducive to good education, while not trying to resist those areas of the law that are already settled. For example, protracted resistance to desegregation is a misguided tactic that begets additional problems. To a large extent, the way public schools view the authority of the courts—and this includes challenging legislative or constitutional guidelines when there are valid educational and legal reasons for doing so—will say much about how schools can expect the public to follow their lead in compulsory education. Legal counsel can be both a resource of information and a tool for achieving certain objectives, but the quality of utilization will depend to a large extent on the wisdom of the administrator.

SUBSTANTIVE AREAS OF THE LAW
WHICH AFFECT ADMINISTRATION
OF PUBLIC SCHOOLS

Although legal considerations touch many decisions that school administrators will make, there are several areas that have changed dramatically over the past fifteen years. This section of the chapter considers student rights, due process, affirmative action, and collective bargaining, all areas which have recently emerged and which significantly influence the professional lives of educational administrators. Legal parameters of these areas will be briefly defined and questions will be raised about their impact upon public schools.

Student Rights

The phrase "student rights" received wide publicity in the early 1970s, in the period of student activism protesting U.S. involvement in Southeast Asia. Much of this activism spilled over to public schools, and the nearly absolute authority of school officials to control student conduct was challenged. Simply put, "student rights" refers to that conduct or status of students which cannot be subject to regulation by public-school authorities. This limitation upon school authority can come either through a constitutional interpretation or through a state-law interpretation that limits the area of discretionary authority which school officials enjoy. Although an exhaustive cataloguing of student rights is beyond the scope of this chapter, students are protected by the First and Fourteenth Amendments in a number of ways. As we saw in Chapter 7, students cannot be suspended for engaging in symbolic, nondisruptive protest or without appropriate procedural safeguards. Students cannot be required to participate in flag-salute or pledge-of-allegiance ceremonies,[1] even though the school may hold such exercises. And haircut regulations are enforceable in only about half of the United States.[2] The remainder of this section will consider two particular examples of student rights in greater detail: the right of students to publish and distribute underground newspapers, and the enforceability of regulations prohibiting married students from participating in extracurricular activities.

Underground Newspapers

Underground newspapers refer generally to those materials which students write, publish, and distribute on campus, and are distinguishable from school-sponsored newspapers.[3] It is legal for schools to restrict the time, place, and manner of distribution of such newspapers

[1] West Virginia State Ed. of Education v. Barnette, 319 U.S. 624, 63 S. Ct. 1178 (1943). Justice Jackson wrote in the Barnette opinion, "If there is any fixed star in our constitutional constellation it is that no official, high or petty, can prescribe what shall be orthodox in politics, nationalism, religion or other matters of opinion, or force citizens to confess by word or act their faith therein."

[2] See chapter 7 in this book.

[3] A broader definition of underground newspapers would include any materials distributed by students on campus. This could include literature distributed on behalf on non-school–sponsored organizations. For a case striking down a blanket prohibition of such literature as being too broad a prior restraint, see Hernandez v. Hanson, 430 F. Supp. 1154 (D. Neb. 1977).

so as to avoid disruptions to the educational process. Obviously this restriction cannot be used as a subterfuge to bar all such publications.

Beyond this, there is a split of authority between several circuit courts of appeal about the legality of imposing a prior restraint upon their distribution. The Seventh Circuit Court of Appeals prohibits any prior restraint.[4] Schools may punish students for distributing improper material—for example, obscene or defamatory material—but they cannot screen these materials prior to distribution. The Second Circuit[5] and Fourth Circuit[6] Courts of Appeal allow a limited amount of prior restraint. Prior restraint is allowed in school regulations only when substantial justifications for such restraint are precisely defined and the procedures for making these determinations and reviewing any decisions to restrain distribution are adequate. These two standards are not as far apart as they appear, because it has proven very difficult for school districts to write sufficiently narrow prior-restraint policies. Consider, for example, the Arlington, Virginia, policy limiting distribution of underground newspapers.

> ... [Posters, pamphleting, newspapers or newsletters] should conform to journalistic standards of accuracy, taste, and decency maintained by the newspapers of general circulation in Arlington; they shall not contain obscenity, incitements to crime, material in violation of law or lawful regulation, or libelous material. Any student or student group intending to distribute written material shall submit a copy of the text of such material to the school principal as soon as the text of such material is available, but in no case less than one school day prior to the day of intended distribution, without permission of the principal.[7]

The suspension of a student for not complying with this board policy was overturned. The policy did not satisfy the narrow prior restraint requirements because the standards to be applied were not identified with sufficient specificity nor were the procedural appeals described narrowly enough. The standards of "accuracy, taste, and decency" were improperly vague. These terms, as well as the meaning of "obscene" or "libelous material," need greater precision. In addition, the procedures for appealing the decision must be specific and short so that the appeal cannot drag on for a long period of time. It may be nearly

[4]Fujishima v. Bd. of Education, 460 F. 2nd 1355 (7th Cir. 1972).

[5]Eisner v. Stanford Bd. of Education, 440 F. 2nd 803 (2nd Cir. 1971).

[6]Nitzberg v. Parks, 525 F. 2nd 378 (4th Cir. 1975); Baughman v. Freienmuth, 478 F. 2nd 1345 (4th Cir. 1973); Quarterman v. Byrd, 453 F. 2nd 54 (4th Cir. 1971).

[7]Leibner v. Sharbaugh, 429 F. Supp. 744 at 747 (E.D. Va. 1977).

impossible for a district to write a sufficiently narrow policy to comply with this prior-restraint standard. Students enjoy broad First-Amendment publication rights in the public schools, something that may well not be popular with all citizens.

Married Students and Extracurricular Activities

Historically, school boards and school administrators often took the view that the public schools were the guardians of morality, and that one way to uphold certain moral standards was to exclude persons who engaged in what was considered undesirable behavior from participating in extracurricular activities. For example, a school district might have a policy restricting married students. "Married students, or those who have been married, are in school chiefly to meet academic needs and they will be disqualified from participating in extracurricular activities and Senior activities except Commencement and Baccalaureate." Further, school districts without policies of their own could be bound by rules of state high-school athletic associations. Such a state rule might read "Students who are or have been at any time married are not eligible for participating in intraschool athletic competition."[8] If the district wanted to compete in interscholastic athletics it would be obligated to comply with all the rules of the state association.

Generally, prior to 1970 these rules were enforced when challenged.[9] Schools were viewed as having broad discretion in molding appropriate student behavior. Also since students did not enjoy any guaranteed right to participate in extracurricular events, they had no grounds to challenge exclusion because of marital status.

After 1970 these exclusionary rules were increasingly challenged, and the courts unanimously struck them down.[10] The judicial decisions agreed that schools could decide whether or not to offer extracurricular activities, but having decided to offer them, they could not limit participation on the basis of marital status. Though it may be appropriate for school authorities to discourage teenage marriages, exclusion is not a

[8]These two rules are taken from Indiana High School Athletic Association v. Raike, 329 N.E. 2nd 66 (1975).

[9]See, e.g., School Dist. of Waterloo v. Green, 147 N.W. 2nd 854 (Iowa '67) and Kissick v. Garland Ind. School Dist., 330 S.W. 2nd 708 (Tex Cir. App. Dallas 1959).

[10]See, e.g., Moran v. School Dist. No. 7, Yellowstone County, 350 F. Supp. 1180 (D.C. Mont. 1973); Davis v. Meek, 344 F. Supp. 298 (D.C. Ohio 1972); Holt v. Shelton, 341 F. Supp. 821 (M.O. Tenn., 1972); Haas v. South Bend Comm'y School Corp., 298 N.E. 2nd 495 (S. Ct. Ind. 1972); Bell v. Lone Oak Ind. School Dist., 507 S.W. 2nd 636 (Tex Cir. App. Texarkana, 1974); Indiana H.S. Ath. Assoc. v. Raike, 329 N.E. 2nd 66 (Ind. 1975).

viable method of doing so. Such a rule is unconstitutional without a more specific showing of how the married student's participation is going to morally taint unmarried students.[11] "Insulating athletic competition from the baleful influence of high school students who may or may not have married in haste will not pass constitutional muster, because there is no fair and substantial relationship between such a prohibition and the desired objective of wholesomeness in interscholastic competition."[12]

This rationale which limits the authority of school officials to regulate participation of students because of some trait or status has been applied beyond marital status. Pregnant girls cannot be excluded from school or extracurricular activities (unless participation might be harmful to the pregnant girl or others participating).[13] Nor can mentally retarded students be excluded from public school.[14] Some school officials may complain about the perceived erosion of their absolute authority, but it is hard to fault the fairness of these decisions.

Because of the potential liability that may result from depriving a student of a constitutional right, it is important for school administrators to know these rights.[15] Beyond this, it is hard to evaluate the extent to which the existence of student rights has affected the quality of education. Certainly much of the enthusiasm has gone out of student rights as it was portrayed in the early 1970s, and with increased con-

[11]Some courts reach the same conclusion relying on state law instead of the Constitution. Under this analysis, officials are not authorized by the State to sanction private conduct such as marriage, and therefore such rules are invalid. For a complete description of this type of analysis see Goldstein, "The Scope and Sources of School Board Authority to Regulate Student Conduct and States: A Non-constitutional Analysis," 117 *U. PA. L. Rev.* 373 (1969).

[12]Indiana H.S. Ath. Assoc. v. Raike, 329 N.E. 2nd 66 at 79.

[13]See Title IX, Sec. 86.40.

[14]See, e.g., Pennsylvania Association of Retarded Children V. Commonwealth of Pennsylvania, 334 F. Supp. 1257 (E.D. PA. 171)—this was a consent decree, and PL 94-142, mandating special education.

[15]In Picha v. Wielgos, 410 F. Supp. 1214 (N.D. E.D. IL., 1976) the district court found the principal liable for monetary damages for denying 3 female students their Fourth-Amendment rights when he ordered a body search in school for drugs, upon a tip from the police. In Carey v. Piphus, 545 F. 2nd 30, the Seventh Circuit Court of Appeals held the principal liable for monetary damages for suspending the student without appropriate procedural safeguards. On appeal, the U.S. Supreme Court (46 *U.S. Law Week* 4217) revised the Seventh Circuit decision, holding that monetary damages could be awarded under the Wood v. Strickland standard of constitutional liability only to the extent the plaintiff students could show actual or real damages from their improper expulsion. This standard will have the effect of decreasing the impact of *Wood.* Still, the awarding of attorney fees under the Civil Rights Attorneys Fee Act will provide considerable incentive for school districts to respect student rights.

cern over student discipline, the notion of student responsibility is becoming linked with student rights. There is one argument that says that the creation of these student rights has opened up education, providing access to more students on a fairer basis, in an atmosphere more conducive to the free and open exchange of ideas. Critics of this position argue that, in spite of all this rhetoric about student rights, the nature of schooling has changed very little. The absolute control of classrooms by teachers has not changed, and these so-called student rights are so tangential to the main schooling function that they are meaningless. The answer to this argument is not easy or forthcoming, but it should spark any potential administrator to think more seriously about the rationale behind student rights and question the extent to which these legal principles are consistent with goals and organizational structure of public schooling.

Fourteenth-Amendment Due Process

The due-process clause of the Fourteenth Amendment ("No state shall deprive any person of life, liberty or property without due process of law") has been one of the major sources of public-school litigation. The interpretations made of this one constitutional sentence have made administrators conscious of following procedures. This section will briefly describe the judicial analysis made in deciding due-process cases, and then describe its application to students and faculty members.

Since 1973[16] the courts have generally applied a two-tiered analysis to any alleged deprivation of due process.[17] First, the Court asks if there has been a deprivation of a liberty or property interest. These terms are quite general, but there has been a developing body of case law defining these terms. (The meaning of liberty and property will be described more fully in the student and faculty sections following.) If no deprivation exists, then the inquiry ends and no procedural safeguards need to be provided. Yet, if a liberty or property deprivation is found, the Court asks a second question. Given this deprivation, what level of procedural safeguards must be minimally provided to protect the threatened interests?

[16]This analysis was first employed in Bd. of Regents of State Colleges v. Roth, 408 U.S. 564, 92 S. Ct. 2701 (1972).

[17]In a handful of cases the Supreme Court has applied a different due-process analysis. When a rule or regulation applies an inflexible standard, this can, on occasion, be challenged as an irrebuttable presumption. This has been applied, for example, striking down a rule requiring all pregnant teachers to stop teaching at the fifth month of pregnancy. Cleveland Bd. of Education v. LaFleur, 414 U.S. 632, 94 S. Ct. 791 (1974).

No mechanical formula exists for determining appropriate procedural safeguards. The court is guided by a general conception of due process being equated with fairness, and the level of procedures should be provided which will fairly surround the deprivation and protect the various interests involved.

Justice Frankfurter described this notion of due process as fairness. "It is not a technical conception with a fixed content unrelated to time, place and circumstances ... due process is not a mechanical instrument. It is not a yardstick. It is a delicate process of adjustment."[18]

The procedures provided to the defendant charged with breaking the criminal law are used as a benchmark when less serious matters are involved. The criminal defendant is entitled to the following procedures:

1. written notice of the alleged violation and adequate time to prepare a defense

2. right to be represented by counsel

3. right to hearing by impartial tribunal

4. right to compel witnesses to attend and testify

5. right to confront and cross-examine adverse witnesses as well as presenting own friendly witnesses

6. a record of the proceedings be kept

7. decision based on the information presented during the hearing.

Courts have systematically rejected attempts to require procedural due-process safeguards for students or faculty members equal to those provided in a criminal trial.[19] Nonetheless, these procedures stand as the benchmark for determining what level of procedures is necessary for the particular deprivation. Consider how this analysis has been employed for students and faculty members.

Due Process of Students

As described in chapter 7, the Supreme Court ruled in the *Goss* and *Ingraham* decisions that short-term suspensions and corporal punishment, respectively, deprived students of liberty and property. The procedures due in both circumstances are quite different. Short-term suspensions must at least be accompanied by oral notice and oral hear-

---

[18]Joint Anti-Fascist Refugee Committee v. McGrath, 341 U.S. 123 (1951), concurring opinion.

[19]See, e.g., Linwood v. Bd. of Educ., 463 F. 2nd 763 (7th Cir. 1972).

ing, while corporal punishment can be given without any procedural safeguards. The Court held that the existence of other remedies for abuse of the corporal punishment sufficiently protected the children.

Although there is no Supreme Court decision involving a student expulsion, there are a number of lower federal court decisions. The level of procedural safeguards provided in expulsions includes written notice of the alleged misconduct, a right to appear before the board of education (or its authorized representative) and tell the story, and a right that the decision made by the board of education be based on the information provided in the record. Beyond this there is disagreement between judicial districts about the nature of the factual presentation of evidence. For example, some courts require that all adverse testimony made against the accused come from the actual witnesses,[20] while other courts allow school administrators to give the testimony of other witnesses.[21] Because technical rules of evidence are not necessary, hearsay evidence like this may be allowed, but it is difficult to allow the defendant-student to meaningfully engage in cross-examination. Courts also differ on the extent to which the defendant will be able to develop his or her case, ranging from full right of cross-examination and presenting one's own witnesses, to merely allowing one's own witnesses to testify and make a statement.

There is disagreement over whether the defendant has a right to be represented by someone in the hearing—by counsel or by someone else, possibly a friendly teacher. Some jurisdictions will uphold the banning of these representatives to avoid adversarialness,[22] while other courts will allow counsel to be present to help students present a better case.[23]

The concept of notice requires that the charges be sufficiently specific that the student will know precisely what conduct is deemed undesirable. As an example, one district-court decision found the expulsion notice defective for using such general language as "your son ... continutes to conduct himself in an irresponsible and disruptive manner" and "he has been deliberately defiant of reasonable requests by teachers" without providing more specific information about approximate dates and sufficient detail to identify the student's inappropriate behavior.[24]

[20]See, e.g., Tibbs v. Bd. of Educ., 114 N.J. Super. 287, 276 A. 2nd 165 (N.J. Superior 1971).

[21]Boykins v. Fairfield Bd. of Educ., 492 F. 2nd 697 (5th Cir. 1974).

[22]In Madera v. Bd. of Educ. of City of New York 386 F. 2nd 778 (2nd Cir. 1967), a student with discipline problems was determined to have no right to representation by counsel in a guidance conference to determine his appropriate educational placement.

[23]In Givens v. Poe, 346 F. Supp. 202 (W.D.N.C. 1972), a student-expulsion hearing was deemed to constitutionally require legal representation of the student.

[24]Keller v. Fochs, 385 F. Supp. 262 at 266 (E.D. Wis. 1974).

Due Process of Faculty

The due-process analysis is widely applied in faculty-dismissal challenges. The leading case in the area outlines a general definition of liberty or property interest, the existence of either of which will act to trigger procedural safeguards for the dismissal.[25] A property interest exists when a person has some objective claim to a job or source of money. Welfare payment which is provided by statute is a protected property right, and one could not be taken off of welfare without certain procedural safeguards provided to satisfactorily show that the recipient no longer qualifies.[26] For teachers, the primary sources of property derive from the contract and tenure status, which is simply a continuous contractual status provided by state law. Consequently a teacher can not be dismissed from a contractual status (during the course of a contract term, for non-tenured teachers; nonrenewal, for tenured teachers) without accompanying procedural safeguards.

A liberty interest exists when one's reputation or honor in the community is damaged or when one's opportunity to obtain equivalent employment is foreclosed. These potentially significant avenues to due process have been all but closed by a number of court decisions. For example, non-renewal of non-tenured teachers for incompetency does not involve a liberty interest, regardless of how other people in the community or other potential employers might view it.[27]

The property interest is the most significant way for teachers to trigger constitutional due process. If this is triggered, the teacher can expect to receive written notice of the dismissal charges specifying reasons for dismissal, an impartial hearing, right to be represented by counsel, right to present testimony, and can expect that the decision be based on the evidence presented in the hearing. The teacher can be dismissed without pay prior to the hearing; but if the teacher wins, reinstatement with back pay to the time of dismissal is the usual remedy. Probably the most important part of due process is the way it acts to shift the burden of proof. When one has a protected liberty or

[25]Bd. of Regents of State Colleges v. Roth, 408 U.S. 564, 92 S. Ct. 2701 (1972).

[26]Goldberg v. Kelly, 397 U.S. 254, 90 S. Ct. 1011 (1970).

[27]Dismissals in the following cases were not violations of liberty interests: Collins v. Wolfson, 498 F. 2nd 1100 (5th Cir. 1974)—simple reduction in teaching staff; Ferris v. Special School Dist., 367 F. Supp. 459 (D. Minn. 1973)—dismissed for being "defensive, rude, argumentative and sullen"; and Gray v. Union City Educ. Dist., 520 F. 2nd 803 (9th Cir. 1975)—dismissed for insubordination. Compare these with Wellner v. Minn. State Jr. College, 487 F. 2nd 153 (8th Cir. 1973)—accusation placed in teacher file that teacher was a racist held to deprive that teacher of a liberty interest, and Stewart v. Pearce, 484 F. 2nd 1031 (9th Cir. 1973)—where a stigma was found because of a suggested mental incapacity of a teacher, and an ensuing psychiatric examination was ordered.

property interest, the employer-school-district has the responsibility for pleading and proving the incompetence, immorality, or whatever other cause might exist for dismissal. Yet if no such protected interest exists, the teacher may be dismissed at the end of the existing contractual term, and the teacher has the burden of showing that the dismissal was based on protected constitutional grounds.

A distinction can be made between *substantive* and *procedural* due process. Procedural due process refers to those required procedures, such as notice, which must be complied with. Substantive due process goes beyond the technical procedures, inquiring into the fairness of the actual regulation or decision. For example, a board could abide by the technical procedural requirements in a teacher dismissal and still render a decision that is contrary to all testimony presented. This would violate substantive due process while complying with procedural due process. At least one circuit court of appeals uses the same analysis in determining what substantive due-process safeguards are required as for procedural due process.[28] For example, a nonrenewal of a nontenured teacher for allegedly arbitrary and capricious grounds does not rise to substantive due-process protection, because no liberty or property interest is involved.

States have the authority to add any procedural safeguards to the constitutionally required minima. Consequently, when determining what procedures need to be provided in a certain circumstance, the administrator needs to be aware of state law as well as constitutional interpretations for the jurisdiction.

Due Process As a Management Style

Clearly, school administrators need to know what constitutional due process is required for certain actions taken with staff and students. Failure to follow such minimal procedures could jeopardize the administrative decision regardless of its actual soundness. But it is unclear how significant these procedural requirements have been in improving the quality of administrative decisions. It is possible to argue that, at least for students, the due-process requirements are so minimal that almost any administrator will be operating at this basic level.

Beyond this, it is possible to conceive of due process as a rational

[28]Jeffries v. Turkey Run Consolidated School Dist., 492 F. 2nd 1 (7th Cir. 1974). Other circuits have reached a different result—allowing that substantive due process can be violated without considering procedural due process. See Drown v. Portsmouth School Dist., 451 F. 2nd 1106 (1st Cir. 1971), and Ahern v. Bd. of Educ. of School District of Grand Island, 327 F. Supp. 1391 (D. Neb. 1971), affirmed 456 F. 2nd 399 (8th Cir. 1972).

decision-making process that could be employed as a management style. Due process is the attempt to connect factual data and information with a general standard. What facts exist to support the alleged teacher incompetency? What facts exist to support the alleged student misconduct? This movement between factual evidence and appropriate general standards characterizes much administrative decision making. Consequently, it is possible to view due process both as a constitutional standard and as a rational decision-making model.

Affirmative Action

School districts have had to become increasingly aware of various statutory and constitutional prohibitions against discrimination. This area of anti-discrimination law, euphemistically known as affirmative action, is based on a variety of different legal sources. Although a detailed description of all these sources is beyond the scope of this book, the major anti-discrimination legal sources that can affect public schools are described in Table 8-1.

Enforcement of these legal sources minimally involves a number of procedural steps including self-evaluations, assurances of nondiscrimination, establishment of a complaint-processing procedure, and the filing of certain statistical information.[29] It is hoped that these laws realize the laudable nondiscriminatory goals that they intend. Yet it is often not precisely clear what specific action is required in a certain situation, and this disagreement between the enforcement agency and the defendant can lead to litigation.

Administrators certainly feel the hand of federal and state affirmative-action regulations and statutes upon them. Self-evaluation task forces and statistical reports are two of the most prominent aspects of this anti-discrimination effort.

The extent to which these affirmative-action programs have eliminated or reduced discrimination is unclear. They have unquestionably raised the consciousness about discrimination and have reduced the more flagrant types of discrimination. Yet, beyond this, the effect of these affirmative-action programs is probably very closely connected with the political and social factors of the community. It is clear that these affirmative-action programs provide an additional source of legal intervention in the school. Administrators need to know these legal sources, to know what technical requirement must be met, and to

[29]Proposals were made in 1978 by President Carter to centralize many of the anti-discrimination enforcement offices, thereby enhancing particularly the Office For Civil Rights within the Department of Health, Education, and Welfare.

TABLE 8-1
Major anti-discrimination legal sources

Title VI, 42 U.S.C. Section 2000(d), *et. seq.*

Title VI prohibits discrimination on the basis of race. It is enforced by the Office for Civil Rights (OCR) and its violation can lead to withdrawal of federal funds. OCR works to obtain compliance short of removal of funds, and has been active in the Deep South, the border states, and urban areas of the North and West.

Title VII, as amended in 1972, 42 U.S.C. Section 2000(e), *et. seq.*

Title VII prohibits an employer from discriminating against his employees or applicants for employment "because of such individual's race, color, religion, sex or national origin." Since 1972 this statute has applied to public schools. Complaints are processed through the Equal Employment Opportunity Commission, and remedies available include back pay and reinstatement.

Title IX, Education Amendments of 1972, 20 U.S.C. 1681, *et. seq.*

Title IX prohibits sex discrimination in public schools. The regulations, promulgated in 1975, specify practices which are prohibited by schools relating to both students and employees. Violation of the statute can lead to loss of federal funds.

Rehabilitation Act of 1973, Section 504, as amended 9 U.S.C. Section 793.

This act, and the 1977 regulations promulgated thereunder, prohibits discrimination against the handicapped. Regulations cover both students and employees in programs or activities which receive or benefit from federal financial assistance. Noncompliance can result in loss of federal funds.

Age discrimination in employment Act of 1967, 29 U.S.C. Section 621, *et. seq.*

This act prohibits discrimination against employees, or prospective employees, between ages forty and seventy. Noncompliance can result in back pay and job reinstatement.

The Constitution

The Constitution, particularly the equal protection clause, and to a lesser extent the due process clause of the Fourteenth Amendment, can be used to reach discriminatory activity. They are particularly important for racial discrimination, and can be used on occasion when other suspect classifications are involved.

State Laws

Many states have a number of laws prohibiting certain discriminatory practices. These laws backstop many of the federal statutes, but nonetheless are important as separate sources of compliance and involve potentially large investments of paperwork.

---

decide to what lengths compliance will take them. It also means that the school will need to be able to obtain legal counsel when it believes it is being asked to do more than the statute or regulation requires and more than it believes is educationally defensible.

Collective Bargaining

Public-employee collective bargaining has increased dramatically during the past fifteen years, and nowhere has this been more evident than in the public schools. Teachers' salaries have improved dramatically during this period. Also, teacher-administrator relations have experienced a new militancy. Some observers feel that this teacher power comes at the expense of administrator discretion and authority.

Unlike private-sector collective bargaining, which is governed by federal statute,[30] public-employee collective bargaining is determined by state law. There are a number of different mechanisms that states use for collective bargaining. Some states have a statute which applies to all public employees, while other states have a separate statute applying exclusively to teachers. Some states do not allow collective bargaining, while other states allow local boards of education to decide the extent to which they want to engage in collective bargaining. See Table 8–2 for a description of the status of collective bargaining in each of the fifty states.

Because collective bargaining is controlled by state law, it is impossible to make general statements about it in the same way that one can for federal statutes or federal court decisions. Nonetheless, there are several components of any collective-bargaining relationship that deserve attention. Each of these components will be briefly identified.

1. What Is The Appropriate Bargaining Unit?   This involves two sub-questions. What groups are to be included in the bargaining unit? There has been a tension between a desire for a narrowly identifiable group and a wish to keep the total number of bargaining units small. The trend now is to a small number of large units, with only a few units for the school districts to negotiate with. It is generally accepted that all teachers K–12 will be part of the same bargaining unit for the district. The harder question is whether persons with certain administrative positions, like assistant principals and department chairpersons, can belong to this bargaining unit. Also, do substitute teachers have a sufficiently common interest with teachers to belong to the unit?

[30]The National Labor Relations Act covers private employers and is administered by the National Labor Relations Board.

TABLE 8-2

States with mandatory laws fully or partially covering
elementary/secondary (K-12) education personnel

Meet and confer			
Professional		*Classified*	
Connecticut	Kansas*	Kansas*	
Delaware	Nebraska	Missouri	
Idaho	Vermont		

Collective bargaining			
Professional		*Classified*	
Alaska	Nevada*	California	New Hampshire
California	New Hampshire	Florida*	New Jersey
Florida*	New Jersey	Hawaii	New York
Hawaii	New York	Indiana	Oklahoma
Indiana	North Dakota*	Iowa*	Oregon
Iowa*	Oklahoma	Maine	Pennsylvania
Maine	Oregon	Maryland**	Rhode Island
Maryland	Pennsylvania	Massachusetts	South Dakota
Massachusetts	Rhode Island	Michigan	Vermont
Michigan	South Dakota*	Minnesota	Washington
Minnesota	Washington	Montana	Wisconsin
Montana	Wisconsin	Nevada*	

States with no mandatory collective bargaining laws covering education personnel			
Alabama	Illinois	North Carolina	Utah
Arizona	Kentucky	Ohio	Virginia
Arkansas	Louisianna	South Carolina	West Virginia
Colorado	Mississippi	Tennessee	
Georgia	New Mexico	Texas	Wyoming

* "right to work" state.
** 12 of 23 counties covered; Baltimore has separate procedures.
Source: This material appeared as part of a Table in D. Ross's '76 Update: Collective Bargaining in Education, A Legislator's Guide, (Denver: Education Commission of the States, 1976), pp. 5-6. Reprinted by permission of Education Commission of the States.

Various states answer these questions differently. The second question involves what mechanism is used in determining the bargaining agent for the unit. If there is a statute governing the collective bargaining, it will usually specify the appropriate election procedures, and the administrator need only know what these are.

    2. What Is The Scope Of Negotiations? What topics or subjects are negotiable? These questions distinguish between negotiable and non-negotiable items. The former need to be bargained over in good faith, while the latter are not subject to resolution by the collective-bargaining process. Again, the state statute and custom will play a decisive part in determining what is negotiable.

An important principle underlying collective bargaining is that boards have the power to enter into contracts only to the extent that the legislature has given them such authority. This results in occasional conflicts with the collective-bargaining process. Courts will not enforce contracts which are made without proper legislative authority. For example, the Illinois Supreme Court refused to enforce contractual provisions calling for additional procedural safeguards before a non-tenured teacher could be dismissed. The nonrenewal of the teacher's contract was made by providing timely notice, and even though the district did not comply with additional contractual evaluation procedures, the court affirmed the dismissal.[31] The New Jersey Superior Court used a similar analysis, saying that the State Education Law took precedent over the Employer-Employee Relations Act, in determining the authority of a board of education to bind itself to an extended-total-disability-leave contractual provision.[32] Consequently, in order to know what the scope of bargaining is, one must know the state education code as well as the teacher bargaining law.

3. What Are The Unfair Labor Practices Which The Employee And Employer Organizations Are Prohibited From Engaging In? The statute will specify certain practices which are prohibited. These are practices such as interference by the employer with the creation of a bargaining unit, which threaten the integrity of the collective bargaining process itself.

4. What Are The Powers Of The Public Employee Relations Board? Where a statute creates collective bargaining for public employees, an administrative agency is usually created as well, which has the responsibility for monitoring and enforcing the act. The exact powers of this agency, as well as its name, will vary from state to state. Where it exists, it provides an important source of authority and information about public-employment bargaining.

5. What Methods Of Impasse Resolution Are Available When The Bargaining Parties Reach An Impasse? States vary considerably in the

[31]Illinois Ed. Assn. Loc. Comm'y H.S. Dis. 218 v. Bd. of Ed., 62 IL. 2nd 127, 340 N.E. 2nd 7 (1975).
[32]Bd. of Ed. of Township of Piscataway v. Piscataway Maintenance and Custodial Association, 152 N.J. Superior 235, 377 A. 2nd 933 (1977).

approaches utilized in settling an impasse. Still, it will probably involve one or a combination of the three most common approaches: mediation, arbitration, or neutral fact-finding. Mediation involves the participation of some neutral third party who becomes actively engaged in the bargaining process and who, through cajoling or discussing, can get the parties to agree. Arbitration also involves a neutral third party who listens to the proposals and recommends a settlement. The arbitrator operates more from a quasi-judicial role than a bargaining role. The arbitration finding can be binding or nonbinding. A neutral fact-finder will collect facts and information, usually on one issue of the contract, and will report on these findings.

6. What Recourse, If Any, Does The School Board Have When The Bargaining Unit Strikes? In almost all states, strikes by public employees are illegal. Beyond this simple statement there is considerable difference between states about what it takes to enjoin the strike and get the teachers back to work. The issue of confronting a teacher strike, and knowing whether to seek an injunction or to allow the strike to keep the schools closed, involves a difficult balancing of legal, economic, and political considerations.

Superintendents and other school administrators who are involved in the collective-bargaining process will need to know their particular state collective-bargaining laws and the answers to these six questions. Beyond this, most administrators in any district which has a negotiated master contract will have to be conscious of the contractual language that sets limits and requirements to their jobs. The contract becomes the critical factor in defining employer-employee relations.

Considerable disagreement exists about the significance of collective bargaining for the school administrator. Certainly the contract formalizes the relationship between employee and employer. Some argue that this is positive for the educational process in that it forces administrators to recognize teachers in a professional light. Others argue that it makes the public school exist for the benefit of teachers, not students. There is a widespread belief among administrators that these contracts limit their power and authority to operate schools. Administrators may, in fact, still enjoy very wide degrees of discretion and authority. But it is at least clear that in order to be effective, administrators must understand and operate within the confines of the contract. Yet this contractual formality does not mean that the administrator will be any more or less effective; it merely describes the changing job description of the contemporary school administrator.

SUMMARY

With increasing legislative and judicial demands made upon schools, it is likely that educational administrators will need to think about some legal aspect when making an educational decision or when developing education policy. Often the administrator will need to evaluate advice from a lawyer and be satisfied with the correctness of the advice and the extent to which it provides a satisfactory educational result. Evaluation of the legal advice will involve identification of the pertinent legal source, comparison of facts in litigated cases with facts involved in the question, identification of the judicial jurisdiction, and awareness of educational aspects of legal advice.

There are four areas in which legal considerations have become critical: student rights, due process, affirmative action, and collective bargaining. Cases and statutes are sufficiently critical in these areas that administrators need to be aware of them. They limit, to a certain extent, the range of actions that administrators had enjoyed in the not-too-distant past. Although some people may feel that these new limits restrict administrators too much it is rather that administrators must know e legal parameters so that they can exercise the considerable disc...ion that they still enjoy.

STUDY GUIDE

Can you recall the meaning of the following terms? Discuss them with a class colleague and apply them to your school-community setting.

retainer
student rights
underground newspapers
procedural due process
liberty or property interest
substantive due process

affirmative action
collective bargaining
bargaining unit
scope of negotiations
impasse resolution

SUGGESTED ACTIVITIES

1. Identify a legal dispute that has developed in a school district with which you are familiar. How, in your assessment, did the legal intervention affect the

educational decision? How do any of the participants in the dispute feel about the relationship of the legal issue and the quality of education in the district?

2.   Interview a school administrator to find out the extent to which student rights, affirmative action, due process, and collective bargaining affect the administrator's job.

3.   How do school districts in your state obtain legal advice?

4.   There is a story about a mythical small town in which there was barely enough business to support one lawyer, but a second lawyer came to town, and they both prospered. School law has been one of the growth areas in legal practice during the past decade, and a larger number of attorneys specialize in school law. This specialization means increased legal fees, which are borne largely by school districts. To what extent have legal fees increased during the past ten years in any school district with which you are familiar?

5.   To the extent that some of the Supreme Court rulings are unpopular with a large portion of community sentiment, the school administrator is often in a difficult position. The administrator needs to respect the law, but also has to be sensitive about local community norms. This dilemma has historically occurred with the Bible-reading and school-prayer decisions as well as with the hair-length decisions in certain federal circuits. How would you try to handle this administrative dilemma?

6.   In your judgment, to what extent has student-rights litigation affected public education? If you believe there have been changes, are they attributable more to changes in the students or changes in the schools?

SELECTED READINGS

ALEXANDER, KERN, RAY CORNS, and WALTER McCANN, *Public School Law: Cases and Materials.* St. Paul, Minn.: West Publishing Co., 1969.

GOLDSTEIN, STEPHEN R., *Law and Public Education: Cases and Materials.* Indianapolis: Bobbs-Merrill, 1974.

HAZARD, WILLIAM R., *Education and the Law* (2nd ed.). New York: The Free Press, 1978.

O'NEIL, ROBERT M., *Discriminating Against Discrimination.* Bloomington, Ind.: Indiana University Press, 1975.

PETERSON, LEROY, RICHARD ROSSMILLER, and MARLIN VOLZ, *The Law and Public School Operation.* New York: Harper & Row, 1969.

REUTTER, E. EDMUND, JR., and ROBERT R. HAMILTON, *The Law of Public Education* (2nd ed.). Mineola, N.Y. Foundation Press, 1976.

9

THE CHANGING FACE OF SCHOOL FINANCE

Financial considerations permeate most educational decisions to an extent not experienced during the student expansion days of the late 1960s and early 1970s. The degree of financial expertise necessary for administrators differs widely depending on the particular administrative position. Obviously, the assistant superintendent of business will be obligated to know the subtleties and nuances of the state-aid formula and other aspects of school finance, whereas an assistant principal will not need to know any technical finance information. Nonetheless, with both the emphasis on tight resources and the desire of many districts to decentralize budget-making responsibilities to include building administrators in planning the budget, it is more important for educational administrators at all levels to understand the principles of school finance. This chapter provides a brief overview of school finance, moving from the more traditional approach where revenue sources and variations on state-funding formulas are described, through a consideration of the legal challenges to these financing schemes that have been taking place during the past decade, to an examination of more recent developments in school finance.

FUNDING PUBLIC SCHOOLS

As we have seen in earlier chapters, public education is primarily a function of the state. Local school districts enjoy only that discretionary authority and power which the state legislature delegates. Historically, for the most part, state legislatures generously delegated this power to the local school districts. Accompanying the delegation was almost total responsibility of the local school district to finance its own public school system. Table 9-1 shows the revenue receipts of the public schools by level of government for approximately the past fifty years. Since we are interested in the changing source of public-school revenues, the dollar figures are current, not having been changed to compensate for inflation. The trend described in this table is clear. Support from local sources, as a percentage of total public-school financing, has dropped markedly, although local sources still provide more revenue than either federal or state sources. The percentage of total support has increased markedly at the state level and, to a lesser extent, at the federal level.

Closer examination of these three governmental sources of public-school revenues reveals that different types of taxation are relied upon to provide the major revenues at each level of government. Table 9-2 identifies the money collected for various taxes at each level of government and the percentage that this amount represents of the total revenues. Federal revenue flows primarily from income taxes, individual and corporate, while state revenues depend largely on sales taxes and the local revenues depend almost exclusively on property taxes.

Each of these taxes has a different impact. Consequently, it is important for policy makers to seriously consider how revenues will be generated, which taxes will be utilized, and where the tax revenues will be allocated.

PRIMARY TAX SOURCES

As a general principle of taxation most people would accept the notion that persons in equal positions should pay equal taxes. Yet this notion eludes simple application, because people are not in equal positions (they have different levels of wealth and income and different personal needs) and because of the difficulty of allocating certain costs which all persons enjoy at a similar level. For example, national defense falls evenly on all societal members regardless of how the costs are allocated among individuals. Because various taxes have different

TABLE 9-1

Revenue receipts of public elementary and secondary schools from federal, state and local sources: United States, selected years 1929–30 to 1976–77[a]

Year	Federal		State		Local (including intermediate)[b]		Total[c]	
	Amount	Percent	Amount	Percent	Amount	Percent	Amount	Percent
1929–30	7.3	.4	353.7	16.9	1,727.6	82.7	2,088.6	100.0
1939–40	39.8	1.8	684.4	30.3	1,536.4	68.0	2,260.5	100.0
1949–50	155.8	2.9	2,165.7	39.8	3,115.5	57.3	5,437.0	100.0
1959–60	651.6	4.4	5,768.0	39.1	3,326.9	56.5	14,746.6	100.0
1969–70	3,219.6	8.0	16,062.8	39.9	20,984.6	52.1	40,226.9	100.0
1976–77[d]	6,105.9	8.2	32,267.2	43.4	35,997.6	48.4	74,370.6	100.0

[a]In millions of dollars.

[b]Includes a relatively small amount from nongovernmental sources (gifts and tuition and transportation fees from patrons, for example). The relative insignificance of these sources is exemplified by the fact that these sources accounted for only 0.4 percent of total revenue receipts in 1967–1968.

[c]Note: Because of rounding, details may not add to totals.

[d]Estimated

Source: National Center for Education Statistics, U.S. Dept. of Health, Education and Welfare, *Digest of Education Statistics: 1976 Edition* (Washington, D.C.: U.S. Government Printing Office, 1977), p. 71; and *Statistics of Public Elementary and Secondary Day Schools, 1976* (Washington, D.C.: U.S. Government Printing Office, 1977), p. 42.

TABLE 9-2

Tax revenue, by source and level of government: 1960, 1970, and 1975[a]

Type of Tax and Year	Federal Amount	Federal Percent	State Amount	State Percent	Local Amount	Local Percent	All government Total[c]	All government Percent of Total
Individual Income								
1960	40,715	94	2,209	05	254[b]	01	43,178	38.2
1970	90,412	89	9,183	09	1,630[b]	02	101,224	43.5
1975	122,386	85	18,819	13	2,635[b]	02	143,840	43.4
Corporate Income								
1960	21,494	95	1,180	05	—[b]		22,674	20.0
1970	32,829	90	3,738	10	—[b]		36,567	15.7
1975	40,621	86	6,642	14	—[b]		47,263	14.3
Sales and Gross Receipts								
1960	12,603	52	10,510	43	1,339	05	24,452	21.6
1970	18,297	38	27,254	56	3,008	06	48,619	20.0
1975	21,090	30	43,346	61	6,468	09	70,905	21.4
Property								
1960	—	0	607	04	15,798	96	16,405	14.5
1970	—	0	1,092	03	32,963	97	34,054	14.6
1975	—	0	1,451	03	50,040	97	51,491	15.5
Other Taxes and Licenses								
1960	2,191	34	3,530	55	692	11	6,411	5.7
1970	4,544	37	6,695	54	1,173	09	12,413	5.3
1975	6,088	34	9,897	54	2,166	12	18,151	5.5
Total								
1960	77,003	68	18,036	16	18,081	16	113,280	100.0
1970	146,082	63	47,962	20	38,833	17	232,877	100.0
1975	190,185	57	80,155	24	61,310	19	331,650	100.0

aIn millions of dollars.

bCorporation included with individual income.

cNote: Because of rounding totals may not agree.

Source: Bureau of the Census, U.S. Department of Commerce, *Statistical Abstract of the United States* (Washington, D.C.: U.S. Government Printing Office, 1977), p. 281.

social consequences, it is intriguing to think about the impact of and reaction to a national defense policy based on local property tax rather than on individual income tax. Different social consequences are involved for each tax. After briefly describing the four taxes, we will consider a number of economic criteria which will elaborate some of the important differences between these forms of taxation.

Income Tax

The income tax is sufficiently pervasive that it needs little description. The tax is based on the principle that income earned during the year is subject to tax. Income is distinguished from currently held assets or property. For example, interest earned on money in a savings account is taxable, while the principal in the account is not income. Although the concept of income tax is quite simple, the mechanism developed to actually determine one's income-tax liability is complicated because of other tax considerations involved. Although detailed examination of these are beyond the scope of this chapter, a few examples will be illuminating. For example, a number of deductions and tax credits ranging from business expenses and moving expenses to child-care costs, are provided. Each of these is allowed because of the general principle that certain expenses were incurred as a necessity to generate income. Beyond this there is a special investment-tax credit, which allows a tax credit for the purchase of new or used equipment which has a depreciable life of longer than three years. This tax advantage, which might under certain circumstances be called a loophole, is included as an incentive to purchase new equipment and thereby stimulate the economy. Also, interest on municipal bonds is not treated as income. This is done to encourage the purchase of municipal bonds at a lower rate of interest than other bonds.

Both corporations and individuals are subjected to income taxation. Most states have income taxes, and some states also allow local municipalities to collect income taxes.

Sales Tax

Forty-five states currently have a general sales tax, and several states permit some local governments a local sales tax. New York City, for example, has had a higher sales tax than New York State for some time. This tax is based on the sale of the good or commodity at the retail level. Services are not taxed. The purchaser pays the tax, while the seller is responsible for transferring the tax revenues to the government taxing authority. States vary in what they include as taxable. For example, medicines and food are not taxed in some states.

Excise Taxes

Excise taxes are direct charges or taxes levied on particular items. The best-known excise taxes are those charged for gasoline, cigarettes, and liquor. The purposes of these taxes vary from purely attempting to raise revenues to trying to affect consumption habits. Gasoline taxes are presently used to provide some maintenance and construction money for highway travel. Yet in a few years gasoline taxes might be raised drastically to discourage gasoline consumption. Many states appear willing to tax cigarettes and alcohol at high rates without any concern about the possible consequence of pricing someone out of consumption.

Property Taxes

In most states property tax is a major support source for funding public schools. Property tax is premised on the notion that one pays a tax on the property owned. Theoretically, the property may range from one's house and land to any belongings like a car, farm livestock, stocks and bonds, and savings accounts. A legal distinction exists between real property, which includes the land and any physical improvement upon it, and personal property, which includes any personal belongings such as checking accounts or animals, which are not attached to the land. Some states assess and tax both personal and real property, while other states assess and tax only real property. This is further confused by the distinction between individual and corporate property. One state may assess and tax corporate personal property but not individual personal property. Even though states vary considerably in what is included in their property taxation, we will focus on an example of individual real-property taxation.

Although the principle of taxing the value of real property is simple, the implementation of the principle is more difficult. Assessment provides the greatest problem. All real property has to be given an assessed valuation. The fundamental principal that all real property is unique necessitates the use of judgment in valuing property. The touchstone for valuing property is its real market value, the value of this property if it were to be sold today. This is easier when dealing with types of real property that are sold often and are easily valued. Some items, like large industrial plants, are hard to value because the market for them is very special. Sometimes determination of replacement cost can be used as an alternative method of evaluation. With this method, the assessor asks what it would cost to build this plant today.

The assessed value of property is usually pegged at a certain percentage of its real market value or replacement cost. For example, Illinois has assessed valuation pegged at 33 1/3 percent of real market value. some states allow property of various types to be classified at differential rates of full market value. For example, Arizona assesses utilities at 50 percent, commercial and industrial property at 27 percent, agricultural land at 18 percent, and residential property at 15 percent of full market value.

Uniformity of assessment is a big problem with the property tax. This partly results from the fact that many assessors are elected officials and are therefore anxious to avoid increased assessments. Consequently, assessed valuations tend to have trouble keeping up with the rapid increase in real market value of the property resulting from inflation. Historically this was not such a major concern, because so long as all property within the local government taxing unit—whether it be municipality, school district, or county—was treated the same, it was irrelevant how the property in another taxing unit was being assessed. With many states providing state aid to schools based to some degree on the assessed valuation of each district, it becomes imperative that assessment practices become standardized on a statewide basis. As a consequence, some states have applied property assessment ratios in an attempt to standardize assessment valuation practices throughout the state.

The tax rate to be applied to the assessed value of the property is determined by state law, voter referendum, or a combination of both. For example, it is common for states to allow a certain tax rate to be applied to the assessed valuation. If the governing board wants to exceed this limit, approval of the voters in the district must be officially obtained. Tax rate is usually either described as a percentage or as a millage. M mills = 0.1 percent. Therefore, a tax rate of 245 mills or 24.5 percent would generate the same amount of property tax dollars. Certainly districts can tax at a rate lower than the maximum amount allowed by law. Determination of tax rate (t) is simply calculated by dividing the amount of money needed (Mn) from local property taxes by the local tax base—total assessed valuation of the district—(B).

$$t = \frac{Mn}{B}$$

If the tax rate calculated is higher than the maximum rate allowed by law, the district must fall back to the legal maximum. This tax rate is added to tax rates of other services such as fire and police protection, and then charged against the property owners. The property owners pay the tax, and it is channeled to the appropriate governmental agency.

CRITERIA FOR EVALUATING DIFFERENT TAXES

In order to get a broader perspective on these primary tax sources it is necessary to briefly describe several criteria of taxation. Examples of differential impact will be included in the description.

Equity of Tax Burden

Although it would be quite simple to determine the total tax liability and distribute this equally between all taxpaying units (the family, for example), this would have drastically different effects among families. Consequently, equity of taxation is viewed more generally as equality of taxation according to one's ability to pay. Grossly stated, this means that persons of equal ability to pay should be taxed equally while persons of differing ability to pay should be taxed different amounts. Income and income differences are generally employed as indicators of ability to pay.

Equity of tax burden is often described in terms of the tax's regressivity or progressivity. The critical variable is the tax paid as a percentage of income. If the tax paid as a percentage of income increases, it is progressive; if it decreases, it is regressive; and if it remains unchanged, it is proportional. Figure 9-1 provides a graphic illustration of this relationship. There are two beliefs built into this concept of equity. First, as indicated above, ability to pay should be a principle of equalizing the taxation load. Second, there is a belief that as income increases less of the money has to be used for consumption of necessities and more can be saved or used for nonessentials. Combined with this is the belief that someone using money for savings or the purchase of nonessentials is in a better position to pay taxes than someone paying for essentials.

By definition, the progressive personal income tax is progressive because the rates of taxation increase as the taxpayer moves into higher rates of taxable income. Non-income based taxes such as sales and property taxes, although technically proportional, have the potential of being regressive because of the often tenuous connection between the item being taxed and the current income available to pay the

FIGURE 9–1
Relationship between tax rate and income for progressive, regressive, and proportional taxes

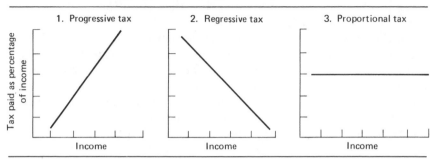

tax. Consider an example with a general sales tax. Technically the sales tax is proportional because all persons, whatever their income, will be paying the same tax rate. Yet as higher-income persons save more money, they have to spend proportionately less of their money, and consequently pay a lower sales-tax rate when considered against the total income available to them. It is in this latter sense, therefore, that the sales tax is considered regressive. It is a generally held view that property tax operates in a regressive manner much as the sales tax. Although many property owners have the income to pay the property tax, there are also low-income property owners for which the tax is regressive because they pay a much higher percentage of income for property tax than wealthier persons do. This view has been challenged, partly on the grounds that it is misleading to consider annual income as a true measure of wealth for regressivity.[1] Some persons may have small incomes for a year, but over the larger time frame have more income. Therefore, it is argued that indictment of property tax for being regressive may be misleading.

Neutrality

The neutrality criteria argues that imposition of a tax should not distort the economic picture. The open marketplace should dictate the appropriate allocation of resources, and the perfect tax would not affect this. The tax should not affect spending patterns, work incentives, or

[1]See, for example, Henry T. Aaron, "A New View of Property Tax Incidence" (Washington, D.C.: The Brookings Institution, 1974), and Mason Gaffney, "The Property Tax is a Progressive Tax," *Proceedings of the National Tax Association,* 64 (1971) 408–426.

anything else. Abstractly, taxes can reach a high degree of neutrality if they are broadly based and uniform. Excise taxes on cigarettes and alcohol are probably most clearly unneutral to the extent that states differ in the levels of taxation and that they encourage utilization of other stimulants which are not taxed. The other taxes are neutral by general definition, but they may not be neutral as to their effect as specifically legislated. For example, the specific definitions of what can be counted as deductions and credits for federal income-tax purposes affect the way people will spend their money. This is an important criterion which needs to be left to careful examination of each particular tax, and is beyond the scope of this chapter.

This neutrality standard often conflicts with attempts in lawmakers' minds to achieve certain social objectives in the process of raising tax revenues. An excise tax on liquor is a prime example of how a state might have a high tax rate to discourage consumption while also hoping to generate revenues to fund state projects.

Yield

These forms of taxation are important most simply because they provide the major tax revenues. Although the various excise taxes are less prolific, the income, sales, and property taxes provide the major sources of revenue for federal, state, and local governments respectively.

Closely related to yield is a tax's dependability. With the budget process requiring long periods of planning and projection, the dependability of tax revenues is an important factor in matching projected expenditures. One index of dependability is elasticity. A tax is said to be elastic if it grows more rapidly than the gross national product. Sales tax is moderately elastic, increasing or decreasing revenue at about the same rate of fluctuation in the gross national product. The federal personal income tax, because of its progressive nature, is the most elastic of these taxes. As personal income increases, people move into higher tax brackets, and the federal government taxes at higher rates. This is true regardless of whether the increase stems from inflation or from a real increase in personal income.

Excise taxes tend to be inelastic because of the inelastic nature of the commodities to which they are linked. It is unlikely, for example, that one's cigarette consumption will double if one's income doubles. Property-tax revenues have historically been inelastic, if we assume that the actual tax rates are held constant. This is explained by the tendency of assessed valuation to lag behind the growth of GNP and the increase in real market value of the property. To the extent that assessed valuation of property more closely tracks real market value than it has historically, and to the extent that this property value increases faster than its growth of GNP, property tax revenues will be elastic. If we consider elasticity of property taxes to include increased tax rates, then property taxes have in fact been quite elastic. During a period of rapid growth in the gross national product, or high inflation rate, elasticity is desirable as a way of achieving greater tax sources. Yet in a slow economic period, inelasticity is desirable because of its steady flow of tax revenues despite the drop in GNP.

Cost of Administration

Taxes which are convenient, simple to understand, and cheap to administer are preferable. Excise and sales taxes are easy to pay and fairly simple to administer. Property taxes require expenditures to keep the assessment roles up to date and to manage the collection. Income taxes are by far the most confusing and expensive to monitor. States are able to save some administration costs by using much of the information taken from the federal forms.

ALLOCATING FUNDS TO PUBLIC SCHOOLS

Now that we have examined the various sources of taxation, we can consider how money gets allocated to public-school districts. As we saw in Table 9–1 this was of little concern in the past, since most, if not all, of the public-school revenues came from local revenue sources. But as local governments were not able to provide total support, it became more important to decide how best to allocate these federal and state resources. This has been done predominantly through either categorical grants or the general state-aid formula, of which four different theoretical models will be briefly described.

Categorical Grants

Categorical grants provide money to public schools to be used for particular purposes. The federal government distributes most of its school aid in this fashion. For example, Title I funds provide compensatory education while Title VII provides, among other things, money for additional reading instruction. School districts need to apply for these categorical funds, but there are also mandated programs which are at least partially funded through categorical aid. P.L. 94–142 is such a law, requiring education for all handicapped children. It remains to be seen whether Congress will fund this bill at the 100-percent level for each fiscal year, as the original legislation prescribed.

State departments of education also fund schools through categorical grants. During the 1975 1976 school year, almost 17 percent of the fifty-state total of educational resources was categorical.[2] Common examples of state categorical grants include special education, student transportation, and textbooks. It is possible for those state categorical grants to be a drain on public-school revenues, for two reasons. First, they often are not funded at the full 100-percent rate. Consequently, districts need to pick up the unfunded expenditures out of the general fund. Second, a district may have to carry the expenses of these programs for a year before it will be reimbursed. This may exacerbate any cash-flow problems that a district may have.

General State Aid

Most of the state revenue that local districts receive is channeled through the general state-aid formula. Unlike the categorical aid, this money has no programmatic strings attached to it, and can be used for financing any part of the district's educational programs. Although the precise state-aid formulas will vary markedly, there are really four models that need to be understood at this juncture: flat grants, fixed-unit equalizing, percentage equalizing, and full state funding. Actual state-aid formulas will typically involve combinations of or adjustments on these models.

States have generally increased the level of support through the general aid formulas during the past decade. One simple reason for this has been the need to increase the amount of money that local districts receive beyond what can be provided through the local property tax. The general aid formula also guarantees a certain minimal level of educational expenditures throughout the state. This will be elaborated in latter sections of this chapter dealing with the constitutional challenge to school finance.

Flat Grants

Flat grants allocate a fixed amount per some educational measure. The two critical considerations involved with the flat grant are what

---

[2]Esther O. Tron, *Public School Finance Programs, 1975–1976*, U.S. Dept. of Health, Education and Welfare, Office of Education (Washington, D.C.: U.S. Government Printing Office, 1976), pp. 14–15.

the criteria of allocation will be and what level of funding will then be provided.

For the most part, flat grants have been allocated to students, and various weightings have often been introduced to differentiate the costs involved in educating different classes of students. The two important variables in this weighting system are the establishment of different classifications and the determination of the weightings to be given each classification. One traditional example has been to allocate different weights to different grade levels of students. For example, high-school students (Sd) would be weighted 1.25; elementary students, grades 1–8 (Ed), 1.0; and kindergarten students, 0.5. Under this formula, the district could determine its total weighted enrollment (Wd):

$$Wd = 0.5K = 1.0Ed = 1.25Sd$$

Dollars received by the district from state aid under this weighted enrollment would be allocated proportionately to the total state weighted enrollment:

$$Dd = \frac{Wd}{W}A$$

Dd = Dollars received by the district

W = Total state weighted enrollment

A = State appropriation

Weighting classifications can be made on a wide variety of criteria. For example, Illinois has a weighting for density of poverty students who reside in the district. A student who falls below the Title I poverty standard will be counted more than students above the poverty level. This is provided because it is believed that students from poor backgrounds need more services from schools than middle-class students. It is also possible to give different weightings to various special-education classifications and vocational education programs.

Historically, flat grants have been funded at low levels by the state. Part of this can be explained by philosophical differences over what funding level is needed to provide the essential education. In addition, economic factors have often caused states to fund the flat grants at low levels, regardless of what the educational preference might be.

Fixed-Unit Equalizing Grant

The principle at the heart of the fixed-unit equalizing grant is that a certain minimal level of support, or foundation, will be provided for each student in the state so long as the taxpayers are willing to tax at least at some qualifying level. This guaranteed foundation level will be paid by the state beyond what the local district can raise through imposition of the qualifying tax rate.

$$Dd = Nd \; f\text{-}r \; Vd$$

where Dd = dollars received by district from state

Nd = number of pupils in district

f = dollar level of foundation

r = qualifying tax rate

Vd = valuation of tax base of district

Assume that the state has set a foundation level of $500 per pupil and a qualifying tax rate of 1 percent. Two districts each have 1,000 students, but district A has a tax base of $20,000,000 while district B has a tax base of $40,000,000. Both districts will receive $500,000 in total, although the amounts from state and local sources will differ. District A will receive $200,000 from local sources and $300,000 from state sources, while district B will receive $400,000 from local sources and $100,000 from state sources. Under this formula, districts can generate additional money by taxing at rates higher than the qualifying tax rate. Note the differential impact this has for districts of different tax bases. Using the same districts A and B, assume they are both taxing at 1.5 percent. District A will receive $600,000 ($500,000 from the fixed-unit equalizer computation plus $100,000 from additional 0.5 percent times $20,000,000) while District B will receive $700,000 ($500,000 as figured above plus $200,000 from additional 0.5 percent times $40,000,000). As this example shows, considerable disparity can exist between wealthy and poor districts (measured by property wealth) under fixed equalizing, particularly when the foundation level and the qualifying tax rate are kept at low levels.

Percentage Equalizing Grant

A third approach to funding public education is to guarantee all districts, regardless of their variation in property wealth, equal access to equal dollars. Percentage equalizing, one of the ways of doing this, equalizes expenditures per pupil between districts. This is done basically by guaranteeing each district the same equalized assessed valuation behind each student. The following formula provides the mechanism for accomplishing this:

$$Dd = (1 - X \frac{Vd}{V}) \; Ed$$

Dd = Dollars received by the district from state aid

X = Arbitrary constant between 0 and 1

Vd = Assessed valuation per pupil in the district

V = Assessed valuation per pupil in the state

Ed = Expenditures of the District (pupils multiplied by per pupil expenditures)

In order to see how the percentage-equalizer grant operates, let us assume that we have two districts of markedly different wealth, both of which want to provide $1,000 per pupil. Assume that District A has an assessed valuation per pupil of $20,000, while District B has an assessed valuation per pupil of $60,000. Statewide assessed valuation per pupil is $40,000. Both districts have 1,000 students, and the arbitrary constant is 0.5. (The arbitrary constant is used as the controlling mechanism for the level of state support to be provided.) Both districts will have the same total expenditures of $1,000,000 ($1,000 per pupil X 1,000 pupils), but the source of these resources will be quite different. District A will receive $750,000 from the state because of the formula:

$$Dd = (1 - 0.5 \times \frac{20,000}{40,000}) \, \$1,000,000$$
$$= .75 \times 1,000,000 = \$750,000$$

The other $250,000 will come from local sources.

District B will provide a larger share of its revenue because of its higher property wealth. The state will provide $250,000 under the formula:

$$Dd = (1 - 0.5 \times \frac{60,000}{40,000}) \, \$1,000,000$$
$$= .25 \times 1,000,000 = \$250,000$$

$750,000 will be paid from local sources. Although district B has to pay from local taxes triple what district A has to pay, the tax rate will be exactly the same. The tax rate, determined by dividing the amount of local expenditure by the district tax base, will be 1.25 percent for both districts.

$$\text{tax rate of district A} = \frac{250,000}{20,000,000} = 1.25\%$$

$$\text{tax rate of district B} = \frac{750,000}{60,000,000} = 1.25\%$$

As districts alter their tax rate, total expenditures will change; but under percentage equalizing, a tax rate will produce the same amount of money regardless of the wealth of the districts.

It is possible under either fixed-unit or percentage equalizing for extremely wealthy districts to have negative state aid. For example, under the percentage equalizer any district with more than twice the average state assessed valuation (assuming the fixed constant is 0.5) will have negative state aid. Theoretically this means that the local district would have to send money to the state. Although this would maintain the integrity of the formula across all districts, it has not been politically feasible to get this legislated. Wisconsin did have this negative state aid as part of its school-finance reform package, but it was declared unconstitutional.[3]

FULL STATE FUNDING

The principle behind full state funding is that the state assumes primary responsibility for funding education, and that all children in the state will be funded the same. The state might employ different funding criteria to meet different educational needs that students have, but all students in the state within each classification will be treated equally. Variations in tax rates are not allowed under full state funding. The state would be responsible for levying taxes (including a standard property-tax levy) and then distributing this money throughout the state. Theoretically, the state would not have to assume any additional control over local schools; but practically, larger levels of state funding often mean increased accountability by the state. In addition, it has been difficult to legislate a maximum property tax rate which would deny the option for a district to raise additional revenue if it desires to do so. Yet, as we will see, one of the effects of the so-called taxpayer revolt against high property taxes has been the move toward full state funding.

In actuality, state finance formulas involve a combination of several factors from various models. Table 9–3 provides an example of the range of factors included in various finance formulas. The state formulas, as creatures of the state legislatures, are made from both theoretical principles and political realities. Consequently, state-aid formulas will often advantage certain districts, usually those with greater property wealth. Because of the inequity fostered by most state-aid formulas, constitutional challenges were raised in a number of states. These constitutional challenges have provided judicial mandates for some

[3]Buse v. Smith, 74 Wis. 2nd 550, 247 N.W. 2nd 141 (1976).

legislatures to alter their state formulas, while other states have revised formulas partially from fear of litigation. One cannot appreciate the current status of school finance unless one understands the rudiments of this litigation.

CONSTITUTIONAL CHALLENGES
TO STATE SCHOOL AID FORMULAS:
SERRANO AND ITS PROGENY.

The constitutionality of California's system of financing public schools, with its heavy reliance on property wealth, was challenged under both the U.S. and California equal-protection clauses. Table 9-4 demonstrates the property-wealth disparities that existed between certain California school districts. Notice, for example, the two Kern County schools. Because of the tremendous disparity in property wealth behind every student, residents of Rio Bravo can tax themselves at about one-third the amount that residents of Lamont Elementary tax themselves; yet, Rio Bravo students receive almost triple the per-student expenditures of Lamont students. This disparity between wealth and effort, and the whimsical effect it has on determining the quality of education students receive, is the heart of the constitutional challenge in *Serrano* vs. *Priest*.[4] Relying on both the equal-protection clause of the Fourteenth Amendment of the U.S. Constitution and a similarly worded equal-protection clause in the California Constitution, the California Supreme Court ruled in the 1971 *Serrano* case that, as a matter of law, reliance on the property tax to fund public schools which had such a disparate effect on per-pupil expenditures was unconstitutional. The case was then remanded to a lower court to decide whether the facts actually existed as alleged before the California Supreme Court. The *Serrano* decision had a dramatic effect throughout the United States, as all states except Hawaii relied on the property tax in basically the same fashion. A flurry of cases appeared in other states, using the same *Serrano* challenge to overturn state finance formulas. School finance schemes in Kansas,[5] Michigan,[6] Arizona,[7] New Jersey,[8]

---

[4]Serrano v. Priest, 5 Cal. 3rd 584, 487 P. 2nd 1241 (1971).

[5]Caldwell v. Kansas, Civ. No. 50616 (Dist. Ct. Aug. 30, 1972).

[6]Millikin v. Green, 389 Mich. 1, 203 N.W. 2nd 457 (1972), *vacated* 390 Mich. 389, 212 N.W. 2nd 711 (1973).

[7]Hollins v. Shofstall, Cir. No. C-253652 (Ariz. Super. Ct., June 1, 1972), rev'd. 110 Ariz. 88, 515 P. 2nd 590 (1973).

[8]Robinson v. Cahill, 118 N.J. Super. 223, 287 A. 2nd 187 (1972), *supplemented in* 119 N.J. Super. 40, 289 A. 2nd 569 (1972), *aff'd as modified,* 62 N.J. 473, 303 A. 2nd 273 (1973).

TABLE 9–3
Salient characteristics of six state school aid formulas, January, 1978

	Equalization approach[1]		Measure of Local Ability to Support Schools	Estimated 1976–77 Expenditures per Pupil in Average Daily Attendance[5]
	Foundation Program	Guaranteed Tax Base (G.T.B.)		
Massachusetts		Percentage equalizing, state share is 35% of average wealth district minimum support level 15%, maximum 75%.	Property valuation per pupil.	N/A[6]
Florida	$827 per weighted FTE (full-time equivalent) pupil. RLE: 6.4 mills.[2]		Property valuation per FTE pupil. State modifies aid through the use of a cost-of-living index.	$1594
South Dakota	$12,150 per classroom unit. RLE: 18 mills on non-agricultural property. 13 mills on agricultural property.		Property valuation	$1385
New Mexico	$900 per weighted pupil in ADM.[3] RLE: 8.925 mills plus federal impact aid (P.L. 874).		Property valuation per pupil. Uniform levy of 8.925 mills plus P.L. 874 revenue and revenue from sale of vehicle license plates.	$1476
New York	$1400 per weighted pupil in ADA[4] RLE: 15 mills.		Property valuation per pupil.	$2527
Washington	$600 per weighted FTE pupil. Chargeback in-lieu-of-tax receipts. 1% of real estate excise tax, plus other forest-related and public utility fees and funds.		Property valuation per pupil.	$1951

[1] These are descriptive labels only, and do not necessarily indicate the EXTENT of equalization. Less than full funding if an equalization program may change the parameters indicated.

[2] RLE is Required Local Effort, a local tax which must be levied. The local funds raised by the RLE are subtracted from the total foundation funds to determine the state aid for a district.

[3] ADM is average daily membership.

[4] ADA is average daily attendance. WADA is Weighted ADA.

TABLE 9–3
Continued

			State aid program compensates for				
Grade Level Differences	Exceptional Education	Compensatory Education	Bilingual Education	Density/Sparsity or Small Schools	Declining Enrollment	Capital Outlay and/or Debt Service
	100% excess cost reimbursement for 11 categories up to 110% of state average per pupil cost.	Three programs funded at current year's expenditure levels for approved projects.	Excess cost reimbursement.			50% to 75% of approved projects depending upon district wealth and type of district.
Grade Weight K–3 1.234 10–12 1.1	Sixteen weighted categories in foundation program. 222.301 weighted FTE pupils funded in 1977–78.	An amount is distributed as categorical aid based upon the number of students in lowest quartile on statewide assessment tests.	An unfunded transitional categorical program.	Sparsity factor exists but is unfunded.		State distributes both flat grants and funds based on a district's proportion of state calculated unmet capital need.
1 Classroom Grades Unit for K–8 21.85 pupils in ADM 9–12 19.54 pupils in ADM	State appropriation for special education allocated proportionally on number of FTE special education students. Approximately $400 per FTE.			Small school districts (few students) need fewer pupils to earn classroom unit.	If elementary or secondary pupil decline exceeds statewide average decline, pupil count is average of preceding 2 years.	
Grade Weight 1–3 1.10 4–6 1.00 7–12 1.25	Four weighted categories.		FTE pupils weighted 1.3 in foundation program.	Schools with less than 200 pupils; districts with less than 400 pupils; districts with over 10,000 ADM but less than 4000 ADM per high school qualify for additional aid.		Guarantee of $35 per mill per pupil for up to 2 mills; other by application.
Secondary pupils weighted 1.25.	Handicapped pupils weighted 10 except for secondary and compensatory education pupils.	Pupils scoring below maximum competence in statewide test weighted 1.25, statewide 23% of pupils are below minimum competence levels. Weighting is based on averages of tests given in 1971 and 1972.	Grants from Department of Education.		Indirectly through use of save-harmless provisions for operating aid.	Reimbursement of approved building costs debt service on percentage equalizing formula.
	Reimburse approved excess costs.	Grants for compensatory bilingual. Indian preschool and reentry.	See Compensatory Education.	Remote and necessary elementary schools less than 100 pupils; high schools less than 250 pupils. Pupils receive additional weighting of from .002 to 2.000.	Additional compensation for districts with declines in excess of 4% or 300 students will be used in 1978–79.	Approved projects on percentage equalizing basis, with 50% aid in average wealth district; minimum 20%, maximum 90%, uniform space criteria is basis of need.

[5]Current expenditure excludes capital outlay, interest in school debt, summer school, community services, adult programs, and libraries. *Source:* Fall 1977, Statistics of Public Elementary and Secondary Day Schools, Advance Report, National Center for Education Statistics, U.S. Dept. of Health, Education, and Welfare.

[6]N/A = Not Available.

Source: School Finance at a Third Glance, Education Finance Center, Education Commission of the States, 1978. Reprinted with permission.

TABLE 9–4
Comparison of selected tax rates and expenditure levels
in selected California counties, 1968–1969

County	ADA[a]	Assessed value per ADA	Tax rate	Expenditure per ADA
Alameda				
Emery Unified	586	$100,187	$2.57	$2,223
Newark Unified	8,638	6,048	5.65	616
Fresno				
Colinga Unified	2,640	$ 33,244	$2.17	$ 963
Clovis Unified	8,144	6,480	4.28	565
Kern				
Rio Bravo Elementary	121	$136,271	$1.05	$1,545
Lamont Elementary	1,847	5,971	3.06	533
Los Angeles				
Beverly Hills Unified	5,542	$ 50,885	$2.38	$1,232
Baldwin Park Unified	13,108	3,706	5.48	577

[a] ADA is average daily attendance.

Source: *Serrano* v. *Priest*, 96 Cal. Rpt'r. 601 (1971) at 612, 487 P. 2nd 1241 at 1252, fn. 15.

Texas,[9] and Minnesota[10] were declared unconstitutional. The Texas decision, *Rodriquez* vs. *San Antonio Board of Education,* was based exclusively on the Fourteenth Amendment equal-protection clause of the U.S. Constitution. On appeal, the U.S. Supreme Court reversed the federal district court decision on the grounds that it could find neither a suspect classification nor a fundamental interest involved in the facts. Where the *Serrano* court and Texas federal district court had found differential levels of school-district property wealth to be a suspect classification, the U.S. Supreme Court could not find in the record of the case a connection between the property wealth of the district and the individual wealth of persons living in the district. Individual wealth (or poverty) had been found to be a suspect classification for purposes of equal protection in earlier cases (for example, striking down a poll tax), but here the court could not find the connection between property wealth and individual wealth. The Court also refused to declare education to be a fundamental interest. At least the Court refused to declare a per-pupil expenditure which cost less than the amount paid in another district to amount to a deprivation of a fundamental interest. It left open the question whether the failure of a state

[9] Rodriquez v. San Antonio Indep. School Dist., 337 F. Supp. 280 (W.W. Texas 1971), *rev'd.* 411 U.S. 1 (1973).

[10] Van Dusartz v. Hatfield, 334 F. Supp. 870 (D. Minn. 1971).

to provide any education would amount to a deprivation of a fundamental interest. This analysis, combined with the historical role the state has played in controlling and funding public education, persuaded the U.S. Supreme Court to uphold the Texas school-finance scheme as constitutional.

Immediately following the Rodriquez decision it appeared that the challenge to state finance systems might be dead. Arizona and Michigan quickly reversed their earlier decisions. But this turned out not to be the case. Several state supreme courts declared their state-aid formula unconstitutional solely on the basis of language in their state constitution. California affirmed its earlier decision solely on the equal-protection language in its Constitution.[11] In order to comply with the California Supreme Court, the legislature needs to revise the school-aid scheme so that, at minimum, equal tax rates will provide equal dollars regardless of level of property wealth.[12]

The New Jersey Supreme Court interpreted language in the New Jersey Constitution that the state legislature provide a "thorough and efficient system of free public school"[13] be equated with equal educational opportunity. Under this standard of equal educational opportunity, the New Jersey Supreme Court invalidated the New Jersey school-finance system and ordered the legislature to develop a new school-aid formula.[14] This decision has been tantalizing because it has shifted from the fiscal neutrality standard of *Serrano* to a suggestion that the equal-educational-opportunity standard must examine the educational outcomes, not just an equalization of resources. "The Constitution's guarantee must be understood to embrace that educational opportunity which is needed in the contemporary setting to equip a child for his role as a citizen and as a competitor in the labor market."[15] Yet, in a later opinion, the New Jersey Court was not able to elaborate or refine its definition of equal educational opportunity to require a student-needs assessment. The court did not insist upon student differentiation for determining allocation, but did accept a a type of fiscal neutrality.[16] This case marks an important shift in school

---

[11]Serrano v. Priest II, 135 Cal. Rptr. 345 (Dec. 30, 1976).

[12]For a short description of the difficult financial and educational considerations facing legislators devising a school-aid formula to comply with *Serrano,* see J. Pincus, "The Serrano Case: Policy for Education or For Public Finance?" 59 *Phi Delta Kappan* 173 (Nov. 1977).

[13]New Jersey Constitution, Article VIII, Section 4, Paragraph 1 (1947).

[14]Robinson v. Cahill 62 N.J. 473, 303 A. 2nd 273 (1973).

[15]*Id.* at 295.

[16]See Robinson v. Cahill IV, 339 A. 2nd 193 (1975); Robinson v. Cahill V, 355 A. 2nd 129 (1976), and Robinson v. Cahill VI, 358 A. 2nd 457 (1976).

finance, away from fiscal neutrality to an attempt to develop other standards. The New Jersey court backed away from these standards, but commentators[17] and other litigation[18] attempt to move the judicial standards to accept different student needs as the basis of determining public-school financing. With this background we can conclude the chapter with a brief survey of the critical issues in school finance that are receiving the most attention.

CURRENT ISSUES IN SCHOOL FINANCE

The social, political, and financial milieu that education presently occupies differs drastically from the expansion, boom years of the late 1960s and early 1970s. The effect of these changed conditions has been to shift attention to many of the conditions themselves. In addition, the concepts of equity and efficiency have matured and are producing different questions than they did in the boom years.

A number of factors have combined to put a serious cost squeeze on schools generally. Following is a brief description of the most salient factors.

Inflation

Inflation has been particularly hard on public schools because its effect on expenses has outreached its effect on revenues. This is partly due to the high inflationary costs of energy, which schools generally cannot avoid, as well as the relentless upward push on salaries. The revenue coming to the schools has not increased as rapidly. Inflation has pushed property values up, but not at quite the same rate as the inflation of expenses in the schools. As inflation continues we can

---

[17]See, e.g., Robert Linquist and Arthur Wise, "Developments in Education Litigation: Equal Protection," 5 *Journal of Law and Education* 1 (January 1976). The authors review litigation in school finance to argue that needs assessment is the way finance litigation must proceed. "This evolving right [to an equal educational opportunity] is based on the precept that once a state undertakes the provision of education, a child's educational needs must be accurately assessed and met. In other words, the classification or educational-needs definition of equal educational opportunity is emerging as the dominant legal principle." (p. 53)

[18]Levittown v. Nyquist (408 N.Y.S. 2nd 606, Sup. Ct. 1978) involved a claim that certain property-wealthy cities were penalized under the New York State aid formula because it did not take into account the high absenteeism and concentration of students with special needs within the district.

expect increased scrutiny of the productivity levels of district employees, something which is beginning to receive serious attention in the private sector of the economy.

Taxpayer Revolt[19]

The passage by California voters of Proposition 13 in June 1978—which limited the property tax as a revenue source, by constitutional amendment—sent shock waves to educators throughout the nation. Although similar propositions were not as successful in other states in the November 1978 elections, there is nonetheless a deep-seated restiveness about the high level of taxation which promises to be ominous for the future funding of public schools. Two different approaches characterize the movement to limit taxation. One approach, fostered by Jarvis and Gann, calls for limits on property taxation as a constitutional amendment. Proposition 13, the California version of this approach, set a maximum tax on property of 1 percent of fair market value, limited growth in assessment to no more than 2 percent per year, and required the state legislature to have at least a two-thirds vote to substitute new state taxes for lost local revenues. A second approach, supported by the National Tax Limitation Committee, calls for cuts in public spending as well as taxation relief. The major focus is to impose spending limitations by tying growth in government expenditures to something like the cost-of-living index. This should then be accompanied by tax relief, including property-tax relief, while not jeopardizing the bond and credit ratings of state and local governments.

These two approaches, which reflect a populist concern over high taxes and the quality of public services purchased by these taxes, are on a direct collision course with the well-organized elitist groups that have pushed school-finance reform in most states through legislation and court changes. This reform has been accomplished, generally, through a leveling-up process in which most school districts received additional money in the process of increasing the equity of distribution. This kind of reform cannot continue under the conditions called for by the tax reformers.

If the tax-reform movement is successful in cutting taxes, public schools will certainly be faced with reduced resources. The implications

[19]For an introduction to Proposition 13 and its effect, see the following articles in the *Phi Delta Kappan:* Joan Baratz and Jay Moskowitz, "Proposition 13: How and Why It Happened" (Sept. 1978, p. 9); James Guthrie, "Proposition 13 and the Future of California's Schools" (Sept. 1978, p. 12); Michael Kirst, "The New Politics of State Education Finance" (Feb. 1979, p. 427).

of such cutbacks are uncertain at best, and will certainly vary from state to state. Nonetheless, it is instructive to look at California in the wake of Proposition 13 to get a sense of some of the implications. Because California had a multi-billion dollar surplus in its state treasury, money was diverted to schools to cushion the impact of massive cuts in property-tax revenue resulting from passage of Proposition 13. Still, school districts had their budgets cut anywhere from 9 to 15 percent from what had been budgeted. In addition, state legislation froze all employee cost-of-living increases which had been negotiated for the year. Consequently, support of schools has become primarily a state responsibility in California. For example, state support to schools will increase form 40 to 45 percent in 1977/1978 to 65 to 70 percent in 1978/1979, while local support will drop from 50 to 55 percent to 21 to 28 percent during the same period. Although this rapid shift to state responsibility for education should make it easier to realize the *Serrano* objectives, it will come at the expense of a general leveling down of schools. And with limits on property-tax rates, citizens will no longer be able to pass a referenda to support education at higher levels. Additional money, if it is to be raised, will have to be generated through different sources. Obviously such reductions will decrease the flexibility that districts have on the way they spend their money. This will be a powerful incentive for administrators, school-board members, and state education officials to much more consciously scrutinize the cost-effectiveness of their operations.

Finally, this rapid shift from shared responsibility for financing public schools to state assumption has major implications for local control and the governance of public schools as they presently exist. For example, it does not take much imagination to think of such conditions as statewide collective bargaining, statewide salary schedule for teachers, and even a statewide ratio controlling the number of administrators per district. The shift in amount and source of school funding will have major implications for the future governance and make-up of public schools.

Decreasing Student Population

Public-school enrollment has peaked, and will continue to decline for the next several years. This has the effect of decreasing revenues, since most state-aid formulas are tied to student enrollment. It also means that the competition for public-school dollars will increase. Already it is possible to see increased competition with senior-citizen programs over financial aid.

Declining Support for Public Education

Although there is no way of substantiating this claim, there seems to be an increased suspicion about public schools and whether they deserve more support. After watching fairly massive infusions of money into schools in the early 1970s combined with declining test scores, the public is wary of believing that additional money will be the answer to solving school problems.

Categorical and Mandatory Programs

An increasing number of categorical and mandatory programs at both the federal and state levels demand resources formerly used from general state aid. Earlier in the chapter, categorical grants were discussed. It is not unusual for these grants to be funded at less than 100 percent, while the local district is nonetheless expected to provide full compliance. Beyond the categorical grants, school districts are mandated to perform certain tasks for which they receive no reimbursement. For example, Title IX of the Education Amendments of 1972, which prohibits sex discrimination in public schools, the 504 regulations of the Rehabilitation Act of 1973, which prohibit discrimination against the handicapped, and most desegregation requirements carry certain compliance requests with no provision for reimbursement. This money must come from the general aid fund, and further tightens the financial screws within the regular educational program.

These factors account for much of the cost squeeze facing public schools, and much time and thought in school finance focuses on dealing with these factors and their implications. For example, is it desirable to link increased financial support from the state with increased state demands? Are there ways to protect schools from the wrath of property-tax payers without foregoing the value of such property tax? What are the limits of mandating social reforms through public schools? Beyond these immediate questions, school finance is still concerned with issues of equity and efficiency, although the focus for both has changed.

EQUITY IN FUNDING

Equity is a philosophical concept connoting similarity of treatment. As noted earlier, it is one of the important criteria for evaluating different tax sources. Equity has been used almost interchangeably with equality and equal educational opportunity when describing various funding formulas. It is in this domain of various funding formulas that the concept of equity is being pushed the farthest. Two areas related to equity in school funding are developing rapidly. First, the notion of fiscal neutrality, where equivalent tax efforts in different districts will provide equivalent revenues, is being challenged. Some commentators urge that its insistence upon equal dollars per tax rate is inequitable. To this way of thinking, the critical factor is need, viewed from the perspective of either the district or the students being educated. Urban school districts argue that because of greater tax burdens which cities must bear and with which the school tax must compete, and because of the generally lower socioeconomic background of its student bodies, urban districts need more money. A variation of this position argues that student need is the critical factor. School funding should provide sufficient resources for schools to meet at least some basic minimal needs of all students. And because students come to schools at drastically different levels of preparedness and capability, the funding formula will need to be flexible. Another way of describing this shift in thinking is to use the economic concepts of input and output. The focus of school finance is shifting from questions of input —the amount of resources which school districts receive, to questions of output—the effect that schooling has on students. This move to considering student needs and focusing on outputs has run headlong into the same difficult measurement problems which have bogged down statewide competency-testing programs. Elaboration of student needs as a viable way of rethinking school financing must wait for developments in the student-measurement field.

A second line of research challenges one of the basic assumptions of fiscal neutrality, calling it into suspicion. The tax effort is the central variable in fiscal neutrality, and it is based on the persuasive notion that school districts, just as individuals, may have variable preferences for the amount of public education they desire to pay tax for. Consequently the tax rate can serve as an index of the level of education desired, and the state funds will be tied accordingly to this. It is generally accepted that districts wealthy in assessed valuation also tend to be wealthy according to income. Recent research suggests that ease of effort in raising tax rates is substantially higher in wealthy districts than it is poorer districts.[20] Tax rate on assessed valuation, therefore, may not be a sound test of a district's desire to purchase education. This

[20]Walter McMahon, Faculty Working Paper no. 475, "A Broader Measure of Wealth and Effort for Educational Equality and Tax Equity" (Urbana-Champaign, Ill.: University of Illinois, College of Commerce and Business Administration, 1978).

suggests that support and tax effort need to be moved away from property valuation and placed more broadly on income as well. Development of a more precise and more neutral measure of tax effort can have implications for financing public schools and the equity of appropriations.

Intimately associated with the equity issues are very serious questions of political feasibility. During the early 1970s when the major finance reform was achieved in the country, many states had surplus funds they were willing to spend on public schools. The cry for increased equity could be met by increasing funds for everyone. Some districts simply received more than others. The mood and climate has sufficiently changed so that any future reforms very likely will come with little extra money. Consequently, some districts will need to be cut back if others are to gain. This political climate may dictate the most serious obstacle to increased equity in school funding.

EFFICIENCY IN FUNDING

Efficient use of educational resources is a common theme for both the proponents and critics of the present spending practices. One of the approaches to better measuring efficiency has been the educational production function. The production-function analysis attempts, by means of statistical regression analysis, to indicate the relative importance of certain inputs—ranging from the characteristics of the students to the variables in the schooling process itself—in explaining the achievement of certain desired student outputs, usually defined as certain levels in standardized reading or math tests. The desired result of these production functions is to more satisfactorily isolate certain school variables to indicate what the appropriate mix of variables might be in order to maximize the desired output at least expense.[21] To date, the production-function studies have not proven very effective in identifying the most significant variables for realizing savings.

Production-function studies depend to a very large extent on aggregating large amounts of data, with the intention that the significant

[21]The most famous production-function study was done by James Coleman, et al., *Equality of Educational Opportunity* (Washington, D.C.: U.S. Government Printing Office, 1977). Another example of a production-function study can be found in Eric A. Hanuschek, *The Value of Teachers in Teaching* (Santa Monica, Calif.: Rand Corporation, 1970). For more descriptive articles about the production function see Henry M. Levin, "Measuring Efficiency in Educational Production", *Public Finance Quarterly*, vol. 2, no. 1 (Jan. 1974), pp. 3–24; and Elchanan Cohn, *The Economics of Education* (Lexington, Mass.: Heath 1972), chapter 8, "Input and Output in Education," pp. 235–70.

relationships will be demonstrated statistically.[22] As the production-function analysis has not proven particularly useful in making practical cost decisions, there is reason to question the appropriateness of this massive aggregation of data necessary to make the regression analysis. Instead, it is possible that the best way to shed light on cost relationships and efficiency is more at the micro-economic level. This is what is being done in cost-effectiveness analysis, where a particular educational program or expenditure can be scrutinized to determine its degree of effectiveness and the appropriate allocation of resources.[23] Cost-effectiveness analysis attempts to optimize the educational output while minimizing the educational expenditures. In order to do this, the various inputs are carefully identified according to their price while the educational outputs are identified according to some measurable standard. Cost-effectiveness analysis involves examination of alternative ways of mixing inputs to achieve the same level of outputs. The purpose of cost-effectiveness analysis, then, is to aid the decision maker in choosing among feasible alternatives on a basis of least cost and greatest effectiveness. Motivation to employ cost-effectiveness analysis or something like it will be considerably enhanced if resources dwindle and public confidence in education declines.

SUMMARY

Financial support of public schools still depends on various taxes, each enjoying different strengths and weaknesses. These taxes are then allocated according to state-aid formulas to supplement dollars raised through local property taxation. The constitutional challenges brought against several state formulas did much to change the distribution of

[22]Although most production-function studies aggregate data, this is not necessary. For example, see Anita A. Summers and Barbara L. Wolfe, *Equality of Educational Opportunity Quantified: A Production-Function Approach* (Philadelphia: Department of Research, Federal Reserve Bank of Philadelphia, 1975).

[23]Several cost-effectiveness studies have been done. See, e.g., Henry M. Levin, "A Cost-Effectiveness Analysis of Teacher Selection," *Journal of Human Resources*, 5, no. 1 (Winter, 1970), 24-33; Office of Education Performance Review, State of New York, *School Factors Influencing Reading Achievement: A Case Study of Two Inner City Schools* (Albany, N.Y., 1974); Barbara Wolfe, *A Cost-Effectiveness Analysis of Reductions in School Expenditures: An Application of an Educational Production Function* (Madison, Wisconsin: University of Wisconsin, Institute for Research on Poverty, 1976). For a more elaborate discussion of cost-effectiveness and a survey of the literature, see Richard Rossmiller and Terry Geske, *Economic Analysis of Education: A Conceptual Framework*, Theoretical Paper No. 68 from Wisconsin Research and Development Center for Cognitive Learning, U. of Wisconsin, Madison, Wisconsin, 1977.

public-school support dollars. In spite of large increases in public-school support, inflation, declining enrollment, increased mandated programs, and resistance to high property taxes raise questions about continued adequacy of this public-school support. Questions of equity and efficiency focus the educational-finance research on better appropriation of financial resources for schools.

STUDY GUIDE

Can you recall the meaning of the following terms and cases? Discuss them with a class colleague and apply them to your school-community setting.

income tax	categorical aid
sales tax	flat grant
property tax	fixed unit equalizing
excise tax	percentage equalizing
assessed valuation	full state funding
real market value	*Serrano*
a mill	*Rodriquez*
tax regressivity	Proposition 13
tax progressivity	fiscal neutrality
neutrality of taxation	tax effort
elasticity of taxes	cost-effectiveness analysis

SUGGESTED ACTIVITIES

1.   Examine the revenue sources for a school district with which you are familiar. To what extent do they rely on federal, state, and local sources of revenue?

2.   Has a court case or state legislation within the past decade affected the financing of education in your state? What has the impact been?

3.   To what extent, if any, has the taxpayer revolt occurred in your district? What effect has it had upon the operation of the schools?

SELECTED READINGS

BENSON, CHARLES S., *The Economics of Public Education* (3rd ed.). New York: Houghton Mifflin, 1978.

COONS, JOHN E., WILLIAM H. CLUNE III, and STEPHEN SUGARMAN *Private*

Wealth and Public Education. Cambridge, Mass.: Belknap Press of Harvard University Press, 1970.

GARMS, WALTER L., JAMES W. GUTHRIE, and LAWRENCE C. PIERCE. *School Finance: The Economics and Politics of Public Education.* Englewood Cliffs, N.J.: Prentice-Hall, 1978

HERBER, BERNARD P., *Modern Public Finance: The Study of Public Sector Economics.* Homewood, Ill: Richard D. Irwin, 1975.

JOHNS, ROE L., and ALEXANDER KERN. *Alternative Programs for Financing Education,* Volume V of *National Educational Finance Project.* Gainesville, Florida, 1971.

JOHNS, ROE L., ALEXANDER KERN, and JORDON K. FORBIS. eds., *Planning to Finance Education,* Volume III of *National Educational Finance Project.* Gainesville, Florida, 1971.

JOHNS, ROE L., ALEXANDER KERN, and DEWEY H. STOLLAR, eds., *Status and Impact of Educational Finance Programs,* Volume IV of *National Education Finance Project.* Gainesville, Florida, 1971.

JOHNS, ROE L., ALEXANDER KERN, and RICHARD ROSSMILLER, eds., *Dimensions of Educational Need.* Volume I of *National Education Finance Project.* Gainesville, Florida, 1969.

JOHNS, ROE L. et al. *Economic Factors Affecting the Financing of Education.* Volume II of *National Education Finance Project.* Gainesville, Florida, 1970.

JOHNS, ROE L., and EDGAR MORPHET, *The Economics and Financing of Education: A Systems Approach* (3rd ed.). Englewood Cliffs, N.J.: Prentice-Hall, 1975.

PART
III

The Context of Work in Administration

10 ✓

ADMINISTRATIVE TASKS

Alittle more than sixty years ago the vast majority of Americans were educated in public- school districts composed of a single teacher in a one-room school. Today nearly three of every four American pupils are enrolled in school districts with more than 3,000 pupils. School districts of the 1980s are complex organizations, made up of an array of administrative and instructional tasks and roles. To a casual observer, modern school districts may seem a hodgepodge of different people bearing strange titles and doing odd bits and pieces of work. In contrast to the teacher of a one-room school, organizing modern school districts requires constructive and creative plans to efficiently and effectively integrate the talents and trainings of many different specialists.

This chapter introduces a range of administrative tasks typical of modern school-district organizations. Chapter 11 continues in the same vein by discussing key administrative roles found in schools. This overview is conscious of the fact that entire books are written on single administrative tasks, and entire careers are spent mastering a single administrative role. Specifically, the tasks to be outlined in this chapter include: school-community relations; pupil personnel; curriculum and instruction; staff personnel; physical facilities; business management; staff development; and evaluation. The administrative roles of superintendent, principal, and central-office staff will be briefly sketched in Chapter 11.

The complexity of modern school districts generates points of tension and conflict between and among administrative roles. Tension and conflict, as well as integrating mechanisms such as role expectations and team administration, will be discussed in the concluding portion of Chapter 11.

AN OVERVIEW OF MODERN SCHOOL DISTRICTS

The organizational complexity of school districts has increased rapidly in the last thirty years.

Table 10–1provides some figures on size of districts and number of professionals by category for the years 1959/1960 through 1973/1974. Careful study of Table 10-1 suggests several major points. First, the actual number of school districts declined more than 50 percent from 1959/1960 to 1973/1974, but the number of teachers and the number of principals, respectively, increased nearly 40 percent. Using simple averaging, in 1959/1960 there were 33.4 teachers per district and 1.6 principals per district. In 1973/1974 there were 128.8 teachers and 6 principals per district. Equally, increases in other categories of personnel, such as consultants or supervisors of instruction, librarians, guid-

TABLE 10-1

Selected information on school districts,
schools and staff, 1959–60 to 1973–74

School year	School districts	Elementary schools		Secondary schools
		Total	*1-teacher*	
1959–60	40,520	91,853	20,213	25,784
1963–64	31,705	77,584	9,895	26,431
1967–68	22,010	70,879	4,146	27,011
1973–74	16,730	65,070	1,365	25,906

			Staff			
School year	*Classroom Teachers*	*Principals (including assistants)*	*Consultants or Supervisors of Instruction*	*Librarians*	*Guidance and Psychological Personnel*	*Other Nonsupervisory Instructional Personnel*
1959–60	1,354,958	63,554	13,775	15,816	15,173	755
1963–64	1,567,974	72,634	18,718	23,769	29,622	3,860
1967–68	1,863,967	85,507	29,005	33,838	46,381	12,548
1973–74	2,155,448	100,465	37,738	44,242	65,069	22,493

Source: Mary A. Golladay, *The Condition of Education: 1976 Edition*, NCES–7600 (Washington, D.C.: U.S. Government Printing Office, 1976), Table 1.16 (abridged) and Table 6.2 (abridged).

ance and psychological personnel range from nearly 300 percent to nearly 3,000 percent. In 1959/1960, for example, most districts did not have any of these additional personnel categories. In 1973/1974, on average, districts had several individuals fulfilling these roles.

Table 10–2 provides a more detailed analysis of the numbers of professionals by roles in various size school districts. The figures are for all fifty states as of Spring, 1970. In examining this table note that the wide range and the broad representation of assignments in the American public schools is awesome. The vast majority of schools have the following, either on regular assignment or on call: supervisors of instruction, reading teachers, teachers of handicapped, librarians and media specialists, counselors, school-community workers or social workers, nurses, psychologists and psychometrists, speech/hearing specialists/pathologists, teacher aides, and secretaries. In general, as the number of pupils increases, the availability of specialists increases. Despite this general finding, the levels of services provided in smaller elementary and secondary schools does not lag far behind services found in schools with larger enrollment.

Tables 10–1 and 10–2 suggest one other characteristic of staffing in American schools. Staffing patterns appear to be influenced by a complex mixture of professional specializations, numbers of students, and general economic conditions. As professional knowledge has matured, we are better able to bring to bear research findings and practical wisdom on the problems of children. This best of professional practice has often been hastened by rapid increases in the numbers of students. Finally, the generally sound and expanding economy of our nation since World War II has provided the resources necessary for this task. With the prospects in the next decade of fewer students and resources for education, we could see marked shifts in the staffing of American schools.

Thus, in contrast to school districts of the 1900s or those of the early 1940s, school districts of the 1980s are larger in size and staffed with more varied and specialized personnel. These specialists offer services directly to students and classroom teachers as well. Viewed from any angle, most current school districts are complex organizations.

ADMINISTRATIVE TASKS

Despite the complexity of personnel and the array of roles found in modern school districts (or other complex organizations such as businesses, military forces, or religious groups), many experts have argued that administration consists of a set of persistent tasks. Fur-

TABLE 10-2

Percent of public schools with selected assignments available on regular assignment or available on call: 50 states and D.C., spring 1970[a]

Type of assignment	All schools	All elementary schools	All secondary schools	Enrollment 599 or less		Enrollment 600-999		Enrollment 1,000 or more	
				Elementary	Secondary	Elementary	Secondary	Elementary	Secondary
Principals[b]	96.7	96.8	97.2	95.5	93.2	100.0	100.0	100.0	100.0
Assistant Principals	27.2	14.7	64.0	9.0	34.3	20.7	77.2	76.6	91.3
Supervisors of Instruction	62.5	67.4	53.0	66.1	34.8	70.5	59.8	72.8	70.7
Other Administrative Staff	42.2	38.6	50.8	37.8	39.5	42.2	52.1	31.8	64.4
Classroom Teachers	99.6	99.9	100.0	99.8	100.0	100.0	100.0	100.0	100.0
Preprimary Teachers	45.5	59.2	6.3	53.6	10.9	73.9	5.0	69.9	1.6
Resource Teachers	29.6	32.0	25.0	28.5	24.8	38.4	20.0	53.6	29.5
Reading Teachers	67.6	67.8	69.8	64.5	67.9	75.1	66.6	82.3	75.0
Teachers of Handicapped	58.0	55.8	64.4	51.2	52.1	66.9	69.3	69.0	76.2
Other Instructional Staff	83.4	84.9	83.4	82.0	74.9	93.8	86.0	80.1	92.1
Librarians and Media Specialists	82.2	79.3	90.6	75.7	88.3	88.9	88.3	84.4	95.8
Audiovisual Specialists	48.0	50.5	46.2	46.8	30.9	59.9	51.0	58.4	62.0
Counselors	62.1	50.5	93.0	48.4	87.0	53.1	95.1	72.2	99.0
Placement Officers	16.2	16.0	18.5	14.6	12.2	18.9	18.0	22.1	31.7
School Community Workers, Social Workers	57.2	58.7	57.6	58.0	46.9	60.7	59.8	59.5	69.6
Other Instructional Services Staff	39.9	39.1	46.9	36.4	47.0	45.2	35.2	49.2	57.0
Nurses	90.0	91.9	86.4	90.7	79.9	95.1	90.5	93.8	91.3
Psychologists and Psychometrists	76.2	80.1	72.9	78.1	66.1	84.6	66.3	86.7	87.5
Speech/Hearing Specialists/Pathologists	73.8	78.0	66.1	78.2	60.1	78.1	60.7	75.7	78.6
Physicians	48.0	48.1	50.1	45.7	43.6	58.0	48.0	60.9	60.4
Psychiatrists	41.5	41.2	45.2	40.2	38.7	43.1	51.0	45.5	48.6
Dentists	34.3	35.3	33.9	36.0	32.4	33.0	30.2	36.5	39.1
Dental Hygienists	21.6	22.2	20.7	17.6	14.6	32.5	21.4	40.6	28.2
Dietitians	33.3	33.1	37.4	31.5	36.9	38.0	30.7	32.6	44.0
Physical Therapists	11.6	10.0	15.8	10.1	19.5	11.0	10.0	3.5	16.0
Other Health Services Staff	9.0	9.4	7.5	11.2	5.4	5.2	12.4	4.5	5.9
Teacher Aides	53.8	58.0	42.4	54.9	36.5	62.7	40.6	82.8	51.7
Library Aides	41.9	38.3	48.8	37.0	40.3	39.6	52.3	51.5	55.2
Health Aides	26.5	27.8	26.3	29.7	31.9	23.2	18.6	21.4	25.7
Other Aides	24.1	26.2	20.1	24.8	12.6	27.8	17.1	42.4	32.5
Clerks	33.9	30.0	43.2	22.5	26.4	47.3	39.7	57.5	68.2
Secretaries	83.7	80.0	94.1	75.3	91.7	93.2	98.4	83.1	93.4

a Elementary and secondary schools, by enrollment size

b Percent of schools having principals on regular assignment only.

Source: Leslie J. Silverman and Forest Jewell, *Staffing Characteristics of Elementary and Secondary Schools, Spring 1970*, 74-216 (Washington, D.C.: U.S. Government Printing Office, 1974), Table A-1.

ther, these experts maintain that these persistent tasks must be accomplished by the administrative sector of an organization if that organization is to survive.

In the field of educational adminstration, the 1950s and early 1960s witnessed debate about the number and nature of these tasks.[1] This debate was taxonomic, not theoretical; that is, the participants sought to describe and to classify what they believed to be the tasks of educational administration. In general, experts were not interested in empirical descriptions of what administrators actually did on the job, what practicing administrators thought they were doing, or research efforts to explain and predict what administrators actually did on the job. As Fisk noted, the development of a list of administrative tasks presented a useful set of criteria for the development and evaluation of professional improvement, even if these ideals were never achieved.[2] These tasks were normative: they constituted what experts believed to be the moral imperatives of administering an educational organization.

The discussion in this period also hinged on whether the listing of tasks should be all- inclusive or restrictive. Miller, for example, argued that there were serious flaws in listing all the responsibilities of school administration.[3] Such a list became too general and too all-inclusive. Equally, restrictive definitions which sought to exclude some tasks faced the problem of becoming too specific and not inclusive enough. Miller suggested that the key characteristic of administrative tasks was its integrative nature. The central tasks of administration were those which involved integrating the purposes of education with administrative activities into a unified pattern.

Discussions of administrative tasks have persisted to the present for two important reasons. First, such discussions provide an arena for linking what people value with what people do. Discussions of what tasks administrators ought to do provide compass points for evaluating behaviors. Second, such discussions are important in determining what ought to be done in the preparation of administrators. Tasks that are

---

[1]For example, see the following: Roald F. Campbell, Edwin Bridges, and Raphael O. Nystrand, *Introduction to Educational Administration*, 5th ed. (Boston: Allyn & Bacon, 1977), pp. 116– 157; Ralph B. Kimbrough and Michael Y. Nunneny, *Educational Administration: An Introduction* (New York: Macmillan, 1976) pp. 164–193; and Van Miller, George R. Madden, and James B. Kincheloe, *The Public Administration of American School Systems,* (New York, Macmillan, 1972) pp. 105–342.

[2]Robert S. Fisk, "The Tasks of Educational Administration" in Roald Campbell and Russell Gregg, eds., *Administrative Behavior in Education* (New York: Harper & Row, Pub., 1957) pp. 201–227.

[3]Van Miller, "Four Definitions of Your Job," *Overview,* I (November 1960), 50–51.

seen as worthwhile by trainers are pushed to center stage, and administrators concerned with fulfilling these tasks in day-to-day activities are displayed as role models for aspirants. For reasons such as these, the discussion of administrative tasks appears as a persistent element in the study and practice of educational administration.

The remainder of this chapter briefly elaborates eight tasks to which all administrators in schools attend. Some administrators spend greater or lesser amounts of time on one or more of these tasks. (These differences will be discussed in some detail in the next chapter's discussion of roles.) To some extent, school administrators deal with the following tasks: (1) school-community relations; (2) pupil personnel; (3) curriculum and instruction; (4) staff personnel; (5) physical facilities; (6) business management; (7) staff development; and, (8) evaluation. The first six tasks are fairly well defined in the literature of educational administration and in practice. Staff development and evaluation, though in the past considered parts of other tasks such as curriculum and instruction of staff personnel, are treated separately because of their importance given the nature of problems faced by administrators in recent years and our best estimates of future concerns.

School-Community Relations

This major task has the dual purposes of obtaining and maintaining community support for school programs *and* of assuring that the community is fully involved in activities of the school. The first purpose is more easily understood and readily accepted by schools. The second purpose, though often stated as part of a school's philosophy under the rhetoric that "the school belongs to the people," is typically less obvious in actual school programs.

Actual patterns of school-community relations, for example, often take the form of a planned public-relations program. This approach views participation of the community in school affairs as a privilege rather than a right, and is geared to providing a best-foot-forward image through a program of controlled information. "The natural intent of PR is to control the communication in such a way that the best is emphasized. It is also a natural part of PR for encouraging participation of the client, but in ways acceptable to the school."[4] This statement by Fantini is meant to describe what he sees as the weakness of current PR programs, not to advocate them. He continues, "Under a successful PR program, the parent is made to *feel* that the school has things under

[4]Mario Fantini, "Community Participation: Many Faces, Many Directions," *Educational Leadership,* 29, no. 8 (1972), 677.

control, that the parent can *feel* confident that the child is in good hands. If parents and other community residents feel confident, there is usually little reason for any other kind of participation."[5] Increasingly, the PR approach is becoming a less viable approach to school-community relations for two reasons. In the first place, PR is not working very well. People are less apt to buy what the school packages and sells; and educational equivalents to Ralph Nader have made the public increasingly suspicious of the often glib PR approach. Second, the PR approach denies parents the right to become full partners in the schools—a condition of increasing importance for educational effectiveness.[6]

Ideally, school-community relations are characterized by partnership, participation, and conversation *with* the public as well as communication *to* them. The major task of school-community relations may be subdivided into five subtasks. The subtasks provide substance to the general task.

1: Assisting the community to contrast its current sense of what schools do and ought to do with other conceptions of education. This may well be the classic role for the educator— one who seeks to teach the community not only what it desires but also raise the aspiration level of the community about what schools ought to do. In the last decade or so, for example, definitions of equal educational opportunity have expanded to include females and ethnic groups. These are examples of fulfillment of this subtask.

2: Interpreting the educational program to the community. This subtask highlights the dissemination of accurate information about the programs and activities of the school to the community. The use of various media, ranging from bulletins to be carried home by pupils, to newspaper, radio, and television stories, is encouraged. Citizens have a need to know about what is happening in their schools.

3: Working closely with official representatives of the community. Most frequently representatives include members of the board of education, members of parent groups, members of various booster or activity clubs, and representatives of neighborhood associations. Representatives become important vehicles for spreading reliable information and weighing support for discussing and then enhancing aspirations of the community about their schools.

[5] *Ibid.*

[6] Thomas J. Sergiovanni and David Elliott, *Educational and Organizational Leadership in Elementary Schools* (Englewood Cliffs, N.J.: Prentice-Hall, 1975), Chapter 12, "More than School-Community Relations."

4: Working with administrators of other human services. School people work closely with those interested in the physical and mental health and welfare of the community, and particularly its youth. By linking together various agencies bent upon helping the young, school administrators can play a key role in mounting combined attacks on problems created by family, economic, or social conditions.

5: Explaining the community to the professional staff. Discussions about community history, its economic base, its social, political, and religious life may help professional staff in dealing with problems they confront. Such discussions can provide tests for thinking about changes or provide explanations for why things are done certain ways.

Of particular concern is the development and maintenance of open lines of communication. On the one hand, schools develop lines for transmitting information to the community. On the other hand, schools seek information from the community. Surveying parents and others in the community by seeking opinions and advice on matters of importance is therefore a frequent practice. Exhibit 10–1 represents a typical questionnaire which might be sent to parents to elicit their advice and opinions. This questionnaire provides the superintendent and school board with an evaluation of the districts' educational program (the curriculum and instruction task area), and also suggests to parents characteristics of what a good school and district could be. Question 6 of Part I, for instance, suggests the importance of parental involvement; question 7 of Part II stresses the need for close parental ties with teachers, building, and district. Inspection of the questionnaire reveals that it is multi-purposed, and provides important information on several tasks of administration.

EXHIBIT 10-1
Parent Questionnaire

Dear Parents:

The schools in our community really belong to you, the parents. Therefore, your reactions and your thoughts are needed by us to make better decisions and plans. Please help us improve the school system by completing the following questionnaire, based upon your experiences. The questionnaire need not be signed, and someone will be available to assist you, should you need help. PART I—OVERALL REACTION—of the questionnaire should be filled out only once. PART II—BUILDING REACTION—should be completed for every school in which you have children enrolled. Thank you for your cooperation.

PART I—OVERALL REACTION

Indicate beside each of the following statements how much you agree or disagree with the statements by placing a mark (X) in the blank. If you have more than one child in our school district, base your answers on a combination of their school experiences this year.

	Agree Strongly	Agree	Disagree	Disagree Strongly
1) This school district places enough importance on basic skills and academic achievement of students.	_____	_____	_____	_____
2) Given the resources available, the schools have been managed effectively.	_____	_____	_____	_____
3) I am pleased with the education my child is receiving in school.	_____	_____	_____	_____
4) The school facilities (building, equipment, play areas, etc.) meet my child's needs.	_____	_____	_____	_____
5) As a parent, I favor the merit pay system which bases salary increases on a teacher's overall performance.	_____	_____	_____	_____
6) Parents have an opportunity to become informed about school programs through school publications, the local press and meetings with teachers and administrators.	_____	_____	_____	_____
7) As a parent, I have opportunities to express my feelings about my child's education.	_____	_____	_____	_____
8) Student bus services are satisfactory.	_____	_____	_____	_____

9) The student lunch program meets my child's needs. _____ _____ _____ _____

PART II—BUILDING REACTION

Part II of the questionnaire should be completed for each building in which you have a child enrolled. If you have more than one child in this school building, base your answers on a combination of their experiences in this school.

	Agree Strongly	Agree	Disagree	Disagree Strongly
1) My child likes school this year.	_____	_____	_____	_____
2) In this school, my child has well qualified and effective teachers.	_____	_____	_____	_____
3) In this school, my child is learning at a satisfactory rate skills in the basic areas of:				
Mathematics	_____	_____	_____	_____
Science	_____	_____	_____	_____
Social Studies	_____	_____	_____	_____
Language Arts (composition and oral communication)	_____	_____	_____	_____
Music	_____	_____	_____	_____
Art	_____	_____	_____	_____
Physical Education	_____	_____	_____	_____
Foreign Language	_____	_____	_____	_____
Related Arts	_____	_____	_____	_____
4) In this school, class sizes have insured sufficient individual attention for my child.	_____	_____	_____	_____
5) I am satisfied with the amount of homework my child has at this school.	_____	_____	_____	_____
6) In this school, my child's teachers seem sincerely concerned about how well he or she is doing.	_____	_____	_____	_____

7) In this school, parent-teacher conferences have provided me with helpful information about my child's progress.   _____   _____   _____   _____

8) The student discipline standards in this school are acceptable.   _____   _____   _____   _____

9) The report card used is helpful in communicating my child's progress.   _____   _____   _____ · _____

10) The new study skills program assists my child in learning how to study, plan and organize his work.   _____   _____   _____   _____

11) Existing classroom exposure to family life and health education information meets my child's needs.   _____   _____   _____   _____

12) Additional student services, i.e., speech therapy, learning disabilities and psychological counseling are meeting my child's needs.   _____   _____   _____   _____

PART III—ADDITIONAL COMMENTS

If you have any additional comments about the schools, please make them here.

Source: Frederic H. Genck and Allen J. Klingenberg, *The School Board's Responsibility: Effective Schools Through Effective Management* (Springfield: Illinois Association of School Boards, 1978), pp. 88–90.

Pupil-Personnel Services

Both quantitative and qualitative aspects of providing pupil-personnel services should be considered.[7] On the quantitative side, the school is required to maintain a fairly elaborate system of pupil accounting, to maintain records, and to report information to various agencies at the local, state, and federal levels. State funding of public schools is, for example, linked to records of the number of students who attend classes daily. Careful records need to be kept to obtain this funding. We leave to your imagination the havoc which might be created by accidental errors in reporting attendance to the state, particularly errors which result in overpayments by the state.

Records of student progress, racial and sex data for certain federal projects or to meet affirmative action guidelines, and information on student discipline occurrences and actions are examples of other mandatory record keeping. More recently, school and community census data and periodic projections of student enrollments have become important in planning school openings or closings and in projecting staffing needs.

Qualitative aspects of pupil personnel have to do with providing direct services to students. Table 10–2, for example, suggests that these services cover a variety of roles and seek to help students adjust better to the school, develop more effectively as social and emotional persons, become better learners, and develop skills for dealing with their future beyond high school. Large numbers of professionals with titles such as social worker, guidance counselor, vocational-college counselor, nurse, and school psychologist are available to provide assistance.

Despite the presence of an array of qualitative specialists, they are often hindered by insufficient administrative and clerical support. Instead of working with students, these professionals spend a large amount (and sometimes most) of their time on quantitative aspects of pupil personnel. More specially, they often spend too much time collecting, processing, and reporting information. This, in turn, seriously impairs their ability to provide direct, qualitative services to students. Proper administration of this task area seeks to balance both quantitative and qualitative dimensions.

Three major subtasks can be identified as presently dominating activity in the task of pupil personnel.

1: Establishing and maintaining a system of recordkeeping. States and districts vary greatly, but most require that records of students

---

[7]See, for example, Stephen J. Knezevich, *Administration of Public Education*, 2nd ed. (New York: Harper & Row 1975), Chapters 16 and 17.

include items such as courses taken and credits earned, days absent, times tardy, and records concerning health problems. These are accounting matters of significance to districts because they may be coupled with state funding and because of the need of parents and students to present accurate educational credentials.

2: Developing a fair and equitable system of student discipline. This system should be able to handle problems ranging from minor behavior incidents in classrooms, through disruptive behavior at school events, to illegal acts such as alcohol or drug use. In the last few years, this aspect of pupil personnel has received increased attention as courts have required the use of due process, and as the level of violence in school has seemingly accelerated. Many schools and districts have developed elaborate and formalized procedures for student discipline.

3: Providing special assistance to pupils. These activities and programs range from providing nurses and physicians for school-related illness or injury, to day-care centers for the children of high school students. Most frequently these services involve the counseling and guidance staff of the school and district, either directly in working with students or as a clearing-house for referring students to specialized personnel or agencies.

Curriculum and Instruction

This task area involves a wide array of specialists, including in many districts highly specialized subunits dealing with generic processes such as reading, and academic disciplines such as mathematics. This task involves five subtasks.

1: Development of a philosophy of education, and objectives consistent with that philosophy. The involvement of many individuals from diverse backgrounds and with many points of view is often necessary to this subtask. Curriculum and instruction discussions involve implicit and explicit views of the past history of humankind, the meaning of present events, and our efforts to shape the future.

2: Construction of programs to fulfill these objectives. This subtask spans activities such as reviewing textbooks and other instructional materials, preparing educational materials for students, developing curriculum guides, and visiting with others about successful practice. Coherent programs rest upon our understanding of such diverse elements as psychology of learning, the attention and motivational span of pupils, and the influence of pictures and graphs on the ability of students to comprehend lessons.

3: Constant appraisal of curriculum and instruction. This evaluation activity involves re-examination of objectives to determine their relevance, assessment of materials to determine if the desired objectives are being achieved, and analyses of various indications of the success or failure of curriculum and instruction programs. These indicators should include efforts to ascertain the relative success or failure of programs on several standards. A single indicator, such as gain or loss on a standardized score, or general increase in interest in a subject, is far too slender a reed for the appraisal of most, if not all, programs.

4: Engender a climate which displays a readiness for change. The evaluation of curriculum and instruction takes place most profitably in an arena which incorporates evaluation results in efforts to improve curriculum and instruction. The feedback mechanism between evaluation and improvement provides such opportunities to examine and analyze the health of the school and of its curriculum and instruction component.

5: Provisions of support and materials to curriculum and instruction activities. Support often involves providing teachers and others with released time or summer opportunities to work on curriculum development. It may also involve the use of consultants, travel to other schools or to professional meetings, or simply the use of a secretary for a few hours to type letters requesting information or materials. Materials themselves are vital components of curriculum and instruction activities; planning and preparation can be sabotaged by the failure of an administrator to purchase needed materials or to insure their arrival when required.

For rather obvious reasons, we will not discuss in detail these five subtasks. We will, however, sample a set of issues related to the first subtask—the development of a philosophy of education and objectives consistent with that philosophy. Debate exists over educational objectives. No one philosophy of education exists. Despite statements of official objectives made by local districts or state curriculum guides, teachers have enough discretionary power to teach what they wish, and they typically do. Often what is taught is less the result of a deliberate revolt against official objectives and more related to what materials are available. Students also influence what is taught by shows of enthusiasm or disinterest. Parents or other community groups are not at all bashful in suggesting, asking for, or demanding the inclusion or exclusion of certain topics. In sum, although most districts can display a paper model of the district's philosophy, objectives, and curricula, the day-to-day curriculum remains in the minds and hearts of the individuals involved.

We suggest that these day-to-day activities be labeled an individual's *educational platform*. Since individual teachers and administrators will have their own platforms, curriculum development can be viewed as a political process in which conflict must be managed and negotiated decisions must be reached.

Clearly the administrator who has some sense of what he or she believes, of the territory upon which he or she stands, and of the aspirations toward which he or she strives will be advantaged in the process of curriculum development. The development of an educational platform, therefore, can be helpful in informing judgment and guiding decisions. Indeed, in the political process which more accurately describes curriculum development, educational leadership and state personship require that the administrator come to grips with his or her platform.

Starratt has identified ten elements, and has provided some questions for each which administrators should consider in building platforms for themselves.

1. The aims of education—Here it would help to set down, in order of priority (if possible), the three most important aims of education—not simply education in the abstract, but education for the youngsters in our school system.

2. Major achievements of students this year—Bringing these aims down to more specific application, identify the major achievements of students that one deals with desired by the end of the year. (For example, some might put down mastery of some academic skills up to a certain level; others might put down the acquisition of certain basic principles which would govern behavior; others might put down more personal achievements, such as increased self-awareness or self-confidence, or trust and openness.)

3. The social significance of the student's learning—Here one might find that he or she emphasizes learning for entering the world of work; others might focus more on the utilization of learning for good citizenship; still others might focus on the acquisition of the cultural heritage of our civilization. This element may also draw a response which denies any direct major social significance to the student's learning because of a predisposition to view the individual in a highly individualistic sense.

4. The image of the learner—This element tries to uncover attitudes or assumptions about how one learns. Is the learner an empty vessel into which one pours information? Some may view the learner in a uniform way—as though all learners are basically the same and will respond equally to a uniform pedagogy. Some may use "faculty" psychology to explain how students learn. Still others will differentiate among various styles and disposi-

tions for learning which point to a greater emphasis on individualization of learning.

5.   The value of the curriculum—This element touches upon attitudes about what the student learns. Some will say that the most important learnings are those most immediately useful in "real" life. Others will say that any kind of learning is intrinsically valuable. Others would qualify that latter position and consider some learnings, such as the humanities or the school subjects to be intrinsically more valuable, because they touch upon those more central areas of our culture. Others would claim that the learning of subjects has value only insofar as it sorts out people of different abilities and interests and channels them in socially productive directions. Some might even claim that the curriculum helps youngsters to understand God better.

6.   The image of the teacher—What basically is a teacher? Is a teacher an employee of the state, following the educational policies and practices dictated by the local, state, and federal government? Or is a teacher a professional specialist whom a community employs to exercise his or her expertise on behalf of youngsters? Or is a teacher a spokesperson for tradition, passing on the riches of the culture? Or is a teacher a political engineer, leading youngsters to develop those skills necessary for the reform of their society? This element tries to elicit assumptions about the role of the teacher.

7.   The preferred kind of pedagogy—This element should be fairly clear. Will the teacher dominate the learning experience? Some assume that inquiry learning is the best way to teach. Others assume that each discipline lends itself better to some forms of pedagogy than others and that, therefore, the discipline will dictate the pedagogy. Some would opt for a much more permissive, student-initiated learning enterprise. While there would understandably be some reluctance to focus on *one* pedagogical approach to the exclusion of all others, nonetheless, we usually tend to settle on two or three as the more effective approaches.

8.   The primary language of discourse in learning situations—This element frequently concerns the levels and quality of learning involved. Does the language focus on precision of verbal definitions or the precise measurement of phenomena, or does it rather stress imaginative relationships? Frequently the difference between the question "How do you feel about that?" and the question "What do you think about that?" reveals a basic orientation toward the kind and level of learning being emphasized. Frequently a metaphor that is used gives away some underlying attitude, whether it be concerned with exact precision, the moral use of knowledge, or artistic sensibility.

9.   The preferred kind of teacher-student relationship—This element involves the quality of interpersonal relationships preferred by the teacher and student. Some would prefer a very caring kind of relationship in which the "needs of the whole child" are attended to. Others would prefer much more distance, leaving the personal needs of the students for someone else to attend to, stressing more the academic discipline. Still others would be very nondirective, allowing the spontaneous, felt needs of the child to direct the relationship, with the teacher being more of a resource person. Others might

prefer a group orientation in which the teacher works primarily to facilitate the work of the group.

10.   The preferred kind of school climate—Here, some of the organizational considerations would come into play. This element concerns a constellation of factors such as schoolwide and classroom discipline, student pride in the school, faculty morale, the openness of the school community to divergent life styles, expressive learnings, and individualistic ways of thinking and behaving. Some would opt for order and predictability. Others would prefer a more relaxed climate, perhaps more boisterous but also more creative and spontaneous. This element would be very much related to what is valued in the curriculum and to the social consequences of learning.[8]

An examination of these elements and questions suggests that the reason for coming to grips with the issues of an educational platform is not to arrive at a definitive answer, but to clarify one's own convictions and unspoken assumptions about education, to open the door for thoughtful and analytic discussions, and to provide thoughtful rigor to one's stances about educational issues.

These ten elements and attendant questions also suggest the prospective and competencies required in a variety of administrative areas. They suggest, for example, the critical necessity of efforts to understand how learning takes place in classroom settings.

Staff Personnel

The task area of staff personnel is in a state of flux. The more traditional interests—recruitment and retention of staff, and helping staff to function more effectively on behalf of school objectives—have been challenged by collective bargaining and reductions in force (RIFs) created by declining enrollments. Four major subtasks formally dominate the staff-personnel task area.

1: Development, elaboration, and revision of staff-personnel policies. With the coming of collective bargaining, such policies have come to be included in the collective bargaining agreement or contract. Staff-related policies cover a variety of topics including issues such as payment for non-school activities, seniority, and work load.

2: Assessing and meeting personnel needs. In the early 1960s this meant the development of policies and procedures involving recruitment, screening, selection, appointment, and orientation of new

[8]Thomas J. Sergiovanni and Robert J. Starratt, *Supervision: Human Perspectives,* 2nd ed. (New York: McGraw-Hill, 1979), pp. 226-228.

staff members. These policies and procedures are still important in some districts; but in most, the late 1970s and early 1980s have seen policies developed for releasing personnel, and now include such topics as job status of non-tenured teachers, hire-back procedures, efforts to make consistent teacher-pupil ratios across all subjects and schools in a district, pay procedures, benefit plans, and more. Policies such as these, and their attendant procedures, provide ways for meeting the personnel needs of the district by insuring the selection of well-trained personnel and the just treatment of staff.

3: Development of policies and procedures for evaluation of teacher effectiveness.   The arena of professional development of teachers includes not only patterns and procedures of supervision of instruction, but also methods available for teachers to enhance their skills through inservice training. In many districts these areas have become parts of the collective-bargaining agreement. At a minimum, staff personnel should be aware of the criteria used in their evaluation, the expertness of supervisors, and the resources available for remediation of perceived deficiencies. All too often, for example, the use of simple checklists of teacher characteristics for evaluation have had little effect on professional development of teachers. A variety of evaluative techniques should be used in assessing teacher effectiveness, and a wide range of inservice options should be available to assist teachers in professional growth.

4: Development of policies and procedures for the use of paraprofessional assistance.   Certified non-certified personnel have become an integral part of instruction in many school districts. The largest category is teacher aides, but many districts have library and health aides as well. Conditions of employment, rights and responsibilities, and pay and retention policies of aides, for example, should be clearly elaborated.

A basic foundation for these various subtasks is an administrative commitment to helping professionals grow in their intrinsic satisfaction from school employment. Of course, specific elements of this commitment may be assigned to specialists, but the responsibility for growth rests upon those with general supervisory responsibility. How teachers are treated, for example, the extent to which they are consulted, the amount of authority delegated to them, the extent to which they find work interesting and challenging, the opportunities they have for success, the recognition they get for a job well done, and the extent to which they are regarded and treated as competent professionals are the sorts of factors which contribute to intrinsic job satisfaction and enhanced performance. There is a growing literature on the subject of job enrichment which speaks to some of these issues.

One important strand of these discussions has been the linkage between job characteristics and work motivation. Hackman and Oldham, for example, identify certain core job dimensions which they find contribute to critical psychological states of the worker. These states, in turn, result in certain personal and work outcomes. The "job characteristics" model is presented in Figure 10–1.

The core job dimensions of Hackman and Oldham include skill variety, task identity and task significance, autonomy, and feedback. The more these dimensions are evident in the job, the more critical the psychological states of the workers, including meaningfulness, responsibility, and knowledge of results, are experienced positively. An increase in autonomy, for example, leads to a greater positive psychological state of experienced responsibility for outcomes of the work. These increases in experienced responsibility in turn lead to increases in factors such as low absenteeism and turnover, higher internal work motivation, and high- quality work performance.

FIGURE 10–1
The job characteristics model of work motivation

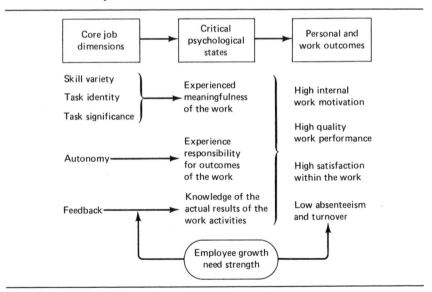

Source: J. R. Hackman and G. Oldham, "Motivation Through the Design of Work: Test of a Theory," *Organizational Behavior and Human Performance,* 16 (1976) 256.

Keeping professional employees in effective service is a common core in the staff-personnel subtasks. Job enrichment ideals, such as those suggested by Hackman and Oldham, require efforts beyond those of any particular office or administrator. A coherent set of personnel policies, for example, contribute directly and indirectly to the ideal of effective service. Personnel policies which provide for the core dimensions of jobs, for example, enhance work effectiveness by enhancing the job of educational professionals.

Physical Facilities

With reductions in force and declining enrollments, the traditional post-World War II problem of constructing new schools has paled before the task of closing schools. Despite this shift in emphasis, two subtasks dominate the task of physical facilities.

1: Effective operation of school facilities. This involves planning and completion of routine housekeeping, provision of supplies and materials for minor repairs, hiring of competent and reliable personnel, and training of personnel in the best methods of operations and the most effective uses of energy. The maintenance of clean classrooms, halls, and eating areas provides not only an important atmosphere for students and faculty, but also is critical for health and safety reasons. The appearance of buildings and grounds is an important source of pride for all members of the community.

Of increasing importance is the efficient use of current energy sources and intelligent planning for the use of new energy sources. Many school buildings are being re-insulated, increased efforts are made to conserve or recycle energy producing materials, and deliberate choices are made in cutting all energy costs. Some newer buildings are using solar energy sources, particularly in the "Sun Belt" states. Some are exploring the use of power as generated by wind or underground geothermal sources. Energy use and conservation is an emerging theme of the effective operations of schools in the 1980s.

2: Planning for physical facilities. In general, planning for most districts in the 1980s will involve issues of school closings and remodelings. The issues surrounding the closings of schools quickly transcend the mere counting of students, teachers, and classrooms. They involve the effect of closings on the neighborhood, the problems linked with transportation of pupils, and a host of other concerns about the implications of school closings. Many, for instance, are concerned with the "dumping" of buildings, arguing that our nation will experience another "baby boom" by 1995. Critics of this argument counter that *even if* we experience such a boom, we have no assurance that schools as they are now located will be near this new crop of youngsters. Various experts predict alternative futures including different assessments of the possibility of changes in child-bearing and different patterns of geographic locations of these new families. Finally, the general wisdom of school closings does not apply to growth situations in some of the "Sun Belt" states or in some suburbs of larger cities. These districts may require the skills associated with the early "boom" of the 1950s and 1960s. Nonetheless, the overall picture for the next decade is one of declining enrollments.

Many communities face issues of remodeling schools as they decide about closings. These discussions often produce conflicts as some members of the community wish to see their school remodeled and not closed, while others wish no remodeling done until precise population trends can be developed. Such discussions require careful development and dissemination of factual information, efforts to check rumors, and decision processes which involve as much community participation as is feasible.

Business Management

An example of one important contribution of business management is the projection of revenues and expenses in future years. Table 10-3 is an example of a five-year financial projection. The projection makes assumptions about increases in costs (6 percent) and about the rapidly increasing deficit of the district. Beginning with a positive balance in 1977/1978, by 1981/1982 the deficit will exceed one million dollars unless new revenue is found.

Unfortunately, this example involving rapidly increasing costs fueled by inflation, stable tax revenues, and increasing budget deficits may ring all too true to many in education. Under these conditions, the efficient business manager becomes an important part of the administrative team. The business manager must present to other administrators critical information about the financial future of the district. The task of business management involves four important subtasks.

1: Understanding the sources of revenues for the school district.
The district receives funds primarily from local and state tax revenues, and from federal programs. Opportunistic business administrators are able to provide maximum funds for their districts by following closely the revisions in qualifications for funding, shifts in definitions of categories of programs, personnel or district needs, and changes in taxing procedures. Such activities insure that efforts by various levels

TABLE 10–3
Five-year financial projection

Assumes cost increases of 6 percent per year.

	1977–78	1978–79	1979–80	1980–81	1981–82
Free Cash Balance (Deficit)–July 1	$ 297,000	$ 108,000	$ (145,000)	$ (468,000)	$ (895,000)
New taxes for new year	1,722,686	1,794,000	1,869,000	1,918,200	1,987,000
State assistance	170,000	175,000	180,000	185,000	190,000
Other income	345,000	350,000	355,000	360,000	365,000
Total estimated cash	2,534,686	2,427,000	2,259,000	1,995,200	1,647,000
Estimated expenditures	2,426,400	2,572,000	2,727,000	2,890,800	3,064,500
Estimated ending balance (deficit) June 30	108,286	(145,200)	(468,000)	(895,600)	(1,417,500)

Source: F. H. Genck and Allen J. Klingenberg, *The School Board's Responsibility: Effective Schools through Effective Management* (Springfield: Illinois Association of School Boards, 1978), p. 111.

of government to provide funds for schooling are not thwarted by the ignorance of local school-district officials.

2: Preparing the school budget. In most districts, the preparation of the budget involves nearly all district personnel. Initially, individuals submit proposals for their needs for the coming school year. These estimates are aggregated by school and by function by the business administrator. These preliminary estimates are contrasted with probable revenues available for the coming year. Rarely do revenues exceed proposed expenditures. A second round of estimates is then generated, usually suggesting top limits for expenditures. These estimates are again aggregated, and a proposed budget is drawn up and submitted to other district administrators and the school board for discussion.

3: Monitoring of expenditures in light of the approved budget. This subtask involves purchasing materials and supplies under competitive bidding, and providing storage and distribution of materials and supplies. Also involved in this subtask are record-keeping, accounting and auditing procedures, and the hiring and training of personnel. The business administrator is responsible for creating a staff of personnel who use their skills and talents to acquire the best materials available under the constraints imposed by the budget. In many states, regulations determine the qualifications of personnel, purchasing practices, and bookkeeping, auditing, and reporting procedures. Increasingly in many districts, these procedures are done on computers.

4: Management of services by non-certified personnel. These services may include transportation, pupil safety, food, insurance, debt services, and legal advice. Depending upon the size of the district, these services may literally run into the millions of dollars. They require the business administrator to become involved in a number of different activities, all of which are essential for support of the schools' instructional staffs and students.

SOME EMERGENT TASK AREAS

Staff development and evaluation are areas which have always been of concern to educational administrators. Staff development, for example, has been typically subsumed under the staff personnel task area, and evaluation under the curriculum and instruction task area. Events in recent years, notably demands for accountability, declining budgets, and shrinking numbers of students, have placed sufficient pressure on schools to require that these subtasks be moved to center stage. Increasingly, universities, for example, are preparing specialists for both staff development and evaluation positions. Districts of even moderate size are increasingly employing specialists, as resources permit. We propose, therefore, to consider staff development and evaluation as two additional task areas in their own right.

Staff Development

The increased interest in staff development results, in part, from the realization that a serious consequence of declining student enrollments and teacher surpluses in most areas is staff stability. Jobs in many areas of the country and in many teaching areas are hard to find. Mobility among teachers seems to be declining. Indeed, some argue that the teacher who is lucky enough to land a teaching position will not have the opportunity to easily leave that position. Staff stability, combined with a further realization that we have a relatively young and inexperienced teaching force, means that many districts will have the same teachers for twenty-five or more years.[9] Staff development has become a matter of urgency for schools who face this problem and who hope to keep a teaching cadre growing in competence and excitement about their work over the course of a long and rewarding career.

[9]See, for example, Martin Burlingame, "Their Hearts Were Young and Gay: The In-Service Needs of an Inexperienced Teaching Force," in Louis Rubin, *The In-Service Education of Teachers: Trends, Processes, and Prescriptions* (Boston: Allyn & Bacon, 1978), pp. 155-161.

Staff stability has also re-accentuated the problems of preservice education. The profession has always recognized that while newly graduated teachers came to their positions with fire and enthusiasm, they were not fully developed professionals. Louis Rubin, for example, points out that:

> a teacher prepares to teach by spending four or five years at a training institution. There, in the existing order of things, he or she learns a sampling of all accumulated information, something about the theory of education, and a few prescriptions regarding the art and science of teaching. Even if this preparation were adequate, and it clearly is not, the training can become outdated in a very short time. Indeed, the moment teachers leave the training institution they embark upon a rapid journey to obsolescence. The eye of research may soon detect cracks in the foundation of old theory, lighten what were once dark voids, and illuminate new educational requirements. The social sciences are only now beginning to probe deeply into the dimensions of human interaction. And we have recently come to realize, with incredible lateness, that schools can teach children to be failures as well as successes. Beyond affective considerations, the continuous modernization of substantive knowledge is an accepted fact. It has often been noted, and with good reason, that the teacher who has not studied, say biology, during the last five years no longer knows the subject. The odds are therefore good that such a teacher will fill students with misconceptions. Preservice training alone, then, cannot produce great teaching.[10]

The increasing importance of staff development raises several important issues for the education profession. For example, should staff development be viewed as an administrative responsibility, as a responsibility of the teaching staff, or as something teachers do individually for themselves? While there is no easy answer, a brief outline of an answer to these questions may suggest that different emphasis produce different patterns of responsibility.

Traditional staff development is an administrative responsibility. Here, programs are formally planned, implemented, controlled, and evaluated by administrators. Usually this type of staff development assumes that the problem under consideration is a deficiency in knowledge of some kind. Teachers are seen as passive learners, exposed to a logically structured set of learning activities. For example, teachers may be seen as lacking in understanding of new audio-visual techniques or the use of pocket calculators to teach math. Responsibility for traditional approaches to staff development is closely linked to personnel administration.

[10]Louis J. Rubin, "The Case for Staff Development," in Thomas J. Sergiovanni, ed., *Professional Supervision for Professional Teachers* (Washington, D.C.: Association for Supervision and Curriculum Development, 1975), p. 34.

The notion that the teaching staff should be responsible for staff development is the nub of the emergence of teacher centers. The program of the center, for example, is typically planned, implemented, controlled, and evaluated by the teacher center board, the majority of whom are teachers. Usually teacher center programs assume that individual teachers have particular skills and knowledge which can be shared with fellow workers. This process of sharing not only enriches the practical tricks-of-the-trade that all teachers possess, but also becomes an important forum for thoughtful analyses of the teaching-learning process. For example, the sharing of a technique for teaching the social effects of the Civil War may lead to discussions of how students should be assisted in thinking about the role of violence in American life. Responsibility for teacher centers falls heavily on teachers.

Much of staff development in the past has been the selection of courses and degree programs by *individual* teachers. Teachers may informally plan their own inservice training by selecting from the marketplace of courses offered by colleges and universities. Or, they may seek admission to programs planned by professors and university departments which result in advanced degrees and professional certification. Such an informal approach stresses the intensity of personal involvement, stimulation of interest by contacts with meaningful associates, and translation of learnings into classroom practices. The responsibility for the success or failure rests squarely on the shoulders of the individual.

It seems likely that in the 1980s all three of these avenues will be traveled. Staff development will be such an important function for most districts that administrators will continue to be involved in traditional programs, teacher groups will evolve even more effective mechanisms than teacher centers, and individuals will be even more conscious of their needs and opportunities.

Evaluation

Since the mid-1960s, education has been put to the evaluation test. With the advent of increased federal dollars there came increased federal demands for evaluating the effectiveness of these new programs. For example, Titles I and III of the Elementary and Secondary Education Act of 1965 required that each project must be evaluated, and that these evaluations be reported to the federal government. Equally, many citizens became concerned that their property-tax dollars were not being used in the best possible way in the schools. They demanded that evidence be produced, that schools be accountable for their activities.

Educational administrators had evaluated programs, expenditures, and school performance for many decades prior to the 1960s. Evaluation in task areas such as curriculum and instruction were common. What is new about the recent press for evaluation is the emphasis on formal planning, systematic sampling, accurate instruments, and easily understood results. It seemed as though the older, informal evaluations which rested upon professional wisdoms and intuitions were to be replaced by accurate, scientific data.

The decade since 1965 witnessed a continuing press for evaluation and a growing sophistication about the conduct of evaluation. Citizens' groups, tax-payer associations, legislatures, and many parents continued to worry about the costs and quality of education and to demand some sense of what was happening in schools. Modern educational evaluators and administrators, meanwhile, learned that conducting evaluations was a difficult business. This difficulty rested on two pillars: the assessment of worth, and the types of evaluation models possible.

The issues involved in the evaluation of the worth of educational programs are many and complex, remaining beyond the scope of this introduction. What should be noted, however, is that educational evaluation is focused on the search for those particular values in a particular situation which help actors make decisions. For example, teachers decide among textbooks; principals choose between methods of evaluating teachers; and school board members decide among possible policies about teacher leaves of absence. These are not casual decisions; they impact the opportunities of students and teachers. Hopefully, evaluation makes clearer to those who must decide, the relative worth of options available.

In the following section a discussion of types of evaluation models currently available appears. Popham has suggested that four major types of evaluation models can be identified:

Goal-attainment models

Judgmental models emphasizing intrinsic criteria

Judgmental models emphasizing extrinsic criteria

Decision-facilitation models.[11]

The goal-attainment models view evaluation as the determination of how well programs achieve their goals. For example, if these models were used to evaluate a program in consumer education, the achievements of students on measures such as objective tests, simulations of

[11]W. James Popham, *Educational Evaluation* (Englewood Cliffs, N.J.: Prentice-Hall, 1975), p. 22.

buying products such as automobiles, and actual situations would be contrasted against a set of specified goals. Many of these goals might be stated as behavioral objectives. A leading proponent of goal-attainment models has been Ralph W. Tyler.

Judgmental models emphasizing intrinsic criteria stress the importance of professional judgments. Intrinsic criteria are those inherent in the object to be judged—for example, the degree of training of the faculty would be a criterion for evaluation of the school's faculty. Intrinsic criteria are at the core of evaluations carried on by accreditation associations. The North Central Association, for example, selects representatives of various professional groups to evaluate a school and its program. The evaluative criteria provided by the association are intrinsic, focusing on the number and quality of courses offered, the sequence of student academic programs, and the number and quality of books in the school library.

Judgmental models emphasizing extrinsic criteria emphasize the effects of the program to be evaluated. Intrinsic criteria are concerned with the quality of the process. Extrinsic criteria evaluate the product. Models which emphasize extrinsic criteria vary widely. Michael Scriven, for instance, has stressed that evaluations should not be concerned with the rhetoric of goals provided by instructional planners, but should examine exactly what is happening in instructional programs. Rather than accepting what designers say, evaluators should devise measurement devices for capturing what is happening to students. Robert E. Stake, in a different vein, has emphasized that evaluators should compare what is intended to what is actually observed. This model also stresses that evaluation is a process of description and judgment which occurs at the beginning, during, and at the end of an educational program. Judgmental models such as those of Scriven and Stake stress the need for powerful tools of description and subtle means of judgment about the many products of instructional activities.

Decision-facilitation models stress the accumulation and presentation of evaluative information to a decision maker or a decision-making body. In contrast to other models, decision-facilitation models emphasize that evaluators should avoid determining the worth of educational programs. That province is the responsibility of the school principal, for example, or the school board. One decision-facilitation model is the discrepancy-evaluation model of Malcolm Provus. The model compares the standards of a program to the actual performance of that program. Differences (discrepancies) between standards and performance are noted. Decision makers can then use discrepancy information either to change performance or to change standards. Evaluators may indicate with test information, for example, that fourth-grade students have difficulty grasping the notion of "light years" in a unit on space science. The decision maker in this case may be the science coordinator for the district, who uses this evidence to decide that this concept will be put off until the sixth-grade science curriculum.

There can be little doubt that the next decade or so will see continued press for evaluation, continued sophistication in evaluation methods and models, and ongoing debate about ways of assessing the worth of educational programs. Educational administrators at all levels will become more and more involved in formal evaluation processes and concerned about using evaluations to improve educational offerings.

SUMMARY

This chapter provided an overview of six traditional administrative tasks and two emerging tasks. This overview suggests the complexity of modern school districts and the expertise required in their administration. Administrators must attend to the relationship between school and community, the needs of pupils and staff, the issues of curriculum and instruction, problems of physical facilities, the efficient business management of schools, increased concern over staff development, and more attention to the evaluation of instructional programs.

Such a wide range of tasks is sorted by most districts into a number of distinct roles. In the next chapter we discuss a few of these roles. Underlying these different roles, nonetheless, are some of the important administrative tasks we have reviewed.

STUDY GUIDE

Can you recall the meanings of the following terms? Discuss them with a class colleague and apply them to your own school-community setting.

staffing patterns
tasks as normative criteria
planned public relations
parent questionnaire
qualitative pupil services
educational platform
collective bargaining

job enrichment
critical psychological states
financial projections
staff development
evaluation models

SUGGESTED ACTIVITIES

1. Select any single task and review how your school district deals with this task. Is it, for instance, assigned to a single individual in the district, or is it delegated to several individuals? Compare your district to those of your class colleagues.

2. Obtain from your district copies of items such as budget projections, enrollment projections, and possible curriculum projects. In what ways do these projections of the future support Miller's argument that the key task of administration is integrative?

3. Interview the individual responsible for pupil-personnel services in your district. Use as a guide the tasks presented in the chapter. After the interview, revise the key subtasks to incorporate interview materials.

4. Discuss with your colleagues the implications of Hackman and Oldham's model of core job dimensions in educational roles such as student, teacher, principal, or superintendent.

5. Plan an evaluation of one of the curriculum areas in your school or school district (e.g., social studies) using any two of the evaluation model processes. Compare and contrast how information would be collected and analyzed with each.

SELECTED READINGS

KAUFMAN, R. A., *Educational Systems Planning.* Englewood Cliffs, N.J.: Prentice-Hall, 1972

KNEZEVICH, STEPHEN J., *Administration of Public Education* (3rd ed.). New York: Harper & Row, 1975.

LANDERS, THOMAS J., and JUDITH G. MYERS, *Essentials of School Management.* Philadelphis: W.B. Saunders, 1977.

MILLER, VAN, GEORGE R. MADDEN, and JAMES B. KINCHELOE, *The Public Administration of American School Systems* (2nd ed.). New York: Macmillan, 1972.

11 ✓

ADMINISTRATIVE ROLES

$\mathbf{I}$t is rare today to find a school district with a single administrator who is completely responsible for accomplishing all eight tasks of administration. Most districts consciously organize to divide these tasks among several trained individuals. In this chapter, attention shall be on the administrative roles found in many school districts. These roles include the superintendent, principal, and central-office staff. These are, obviously, not the only roles to be found in school districts. A glance back at Table 10–2 should dispel any thoughts along that line. These roles, however, have been foci for much of the thinking in educational administration and illustrate suitably the general operations of many districts.

This chapter begins with a brief discussion of types of administrative roles, reviews the roles of superintendent, principal, and central-office staff, and concludes with a brief discussion of tensions and mechanisms for integrating administrative activities.

CLASSIFICATION OF ADMINISTRATIVE ROLES

Administrative roles may be divided into generalist and specialist, and line and staff categories. Generalists deal with all or most of the eight administrative tasks, while specialists deal with one or two tasks.

Superintendents and principals are generalists because they oversee all eight administrative tasks, while most central-office personnel are specialists because they deal with one or two tasks only. Line personnel have formal authority to make decisions, while staff are advisers to line personnel. In general, and with notable exceptions, superintendents and principals are line generalists. Central-office administrators are staff specialists. But as central-office administrators, they do have line authority and generalist responsibility over the staff specialists in their working units. Consultants who work in a central-office unit are examples of such staff specialists.

An illustration may sharpen these distinctions. Figure 11–1 displays part of the administrative staff of a typical mid-sized school district. The line authority in the district comes from the electorate and

FIGURE 11–1
Abbreviated organizational chart of a school district administrative staff.

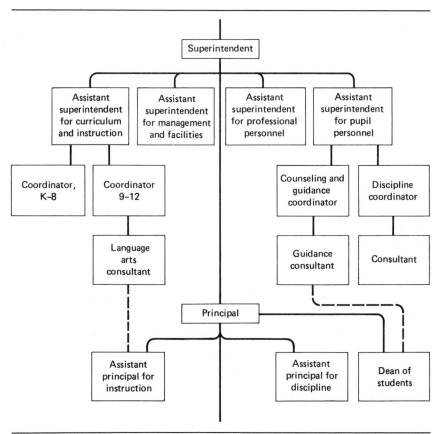

the school board to the superintendent. The line authority of the superintendent provides formal authority to the school principal. Various administrators on the central-office and school-building staff receive line authority for their special areas. Individuals such as the assistant superintendent for pupil personnel are staff officers to the superintendent, but carry line authority over members of their staff, such as counseling and guidance coordinator.

Such arrangements and distinctions are not arbitrary. Line officers are charged with formal authority. Given the power to decide, they need to consider all facets of an issue. Staff officers are charged with providing expert advice. They are advocates for their field of expertise, believing that their expert knowledge should be decisive for line administrators. The tensions created between expertise and broad needs of the organization can provide a healthy atmosphere for creative debate and discussion, or it may result in unhealthy conflict. After a discussion of some key roles, we shall return to a discussion of maintaining a healthy atmosphere.

SELECTED ADMINISTRATIVE ROLES

The Superintendent of Schools

The role of superintendent of schools involves three major components. Superintendents are the chief executive officers of boards of education, the symbols of the schools to the community, and the professional leaders of their staff.

As chief executive officers of boards of education, superintendents are responsible for implementing the policies and achieving the goals established by the board. Superintendents are responsible to the board for the successful accomplishment of all eight administrative tasks. As the single individual responsible for the general operations of the district's schools, the superintendent faces awesome responsibilities.

Superintendents, for example, often delegate specific responsibilities to individual or organizational units; but they retain ultimate responsibility. This responsibility requires superintendents to adopt a generalist posture. Superintendents thus "sit at the head of the table," receiving various assessments of situations from the perspective of various specialists. It is their responsibility to weigh this advice, to sort the relevant and critical from the irrelevant and fleeting, and to see the school district as a totality. As chief executive officers, they must seek to systematically integrate all administrative tasks.

Superintendents are thus called upon to balance the need for improvements in curriculum and instruction, for instance, against the need for expenditures on physical facilities. They face problems of settling disputes about the handling of pupils in discipline cases in light of school-community relations. In each of these instances, and in many more that could be recounted, superintendents must seek to sift and weigh the relative importance of administrative tasks.

As symbols of education to their communities, superintendents must be advisers to and willing partners with their boards of education. As they communicate their visions of what needs to be done to improve the community and its schools, they are resources for raising the aspiration level of the community. These suggestions are weighed by the representatives of the people, the board of education. In the dialogue which may follow, superintendents and boards have opportunities to enhance the range of educational benefits available to the community. Superintendents are resources to the community, not only in terms of raising the performance required of educational institutions, but also in linking education to wider societal trends.

For instance, for a number of years schools have provided students opportunities to visit museums, to attend traffic courts, to examine industrial plants, and even to travel abroad for study. These and other such activities suggest to the community the richness of life associated with educational activities to be found in their schools. These opportunities not only become a source of community pride but also enrich the lives and expectations of those who live in the community.

Superintendents, finally, are professional leaders of their staff. This leadership is best seen as superintendents enunciate the goals of the system in deeds as well as in words. Nothing is more disheartening to a staff than to hear their superintendent speak positively for a project, and a few days later to receive a notice from him or her that lack of funds has killed the project. As professional leaders of staff, superintendents must maintain a posture which provides fertile ground for the intellectual discussion of educational goals and practices. All too often, members of the staff see their superintendents as checkbook balancers, little concerned with educational problems or debates.

Educational leadership, however, is not the sole possession of the superintendent. A vital and vibrant profession sparks its members to worry about why they do things as they do, to ponder about the nuances and meanings of current happenings, and to take a lively interest in shaping the future. As generalists, seeking to find creative and integrative balances among competing demands and needs, superintendents are critical elements in the intellectual life of the profession. To see them only as managers is to ignore their potential for broad visions about education.

These larger expectations are often translated into job descriptions for superintendents. Exhibit 11–1 provides an example. The job description delineates the major responsibilities of the superintendent, establishes line functions, and lists the primary tasks the superintendent as generalist must oversee. In this example, the superintendent works with two associate superintendents, four other central-office administrators, and twenty-one principals to accomplish thirteen primary duties. A review of these duties suggests that many will be accomplished by staff members of the administrative team. It is also clear from the statement of basic responsibilities that the superintendent is *the* line officer of the district.

EXHIBIT 11-1
A Superintendent's Job Description

BASIC RESPONSIBILITY

The Superintendent is Chief Executive Officer, responsible for overall planning, operation, and performance of the district. He provides staff support and recommendations to the Board with respect to decision-making, policies and planning, and is the Board's agent in all relationships with the staff. He selects, organizes, and gives leadership to the management team, oversees planning, staff development, and reward systems throughout the district, and ensures adequate operational and financial control.

REPORTS TO Board of Education

SUPERVISES Associate Superintendents (2)
Director of Planning and Analysis
Director of Public Relations
Administrator of Business Services
Administrator of Educational Services
Principals (21)

PRIMARY DUTIES

1) Establish and maintain a constructive relationship with the Board of Education based on appropriate performance and financial information. Guide and aid the Board in its effective operation through competent staff support and through development of his and the Board's skills in working together effectively.

2) Establish programs and practices for the constructive relationship of the district with its community on a school and district level.

3) Direct and coordinate district planning to ensure educational programs and performance in line with community needs and desires. Ensure sound planning of financial, facility, and enrollment requirements for the future. Prepare and recommend an annual budget consistent with long-range plans and appropriate to community financial resources.

4) Recommend district purposes, objectives, policies, and decisions as required, supported appropriately with information, analysis and conclusions presented to the Board and to the public.

5) Organize, staff, and give leadership to the management team as required to meet district objectives. Plan and execute a management development program appropriate to realizing the district's educational objectives.

6) Establish and maintain constructive relationships throughout the district at all levels, including community, parents, students, teachers, staff, and Board.

7) Ensure the development and operation of adequate recruiting, selection, appraisal, and compensation systems to meet district objectives.

8) Develop the competence of teachers, staff, and management to the maximum extent possible in the best interests of the individuals involved and to meet district objectives.

9) Establish a performance monitoring system incorporating test data results and consumer judgments to meet the needs for performance information throughout the organization.

10) Establish financial and operating controls adequate to safeguard the district against misuse of funds or unnecessary operations, and to ensure fair value for all expenditures.

11) Provide leadership to the district and community in developing, achieving, and maintaining high educational standards, sound programs, and good performance.

12) Ensure that district operations meet all legal requirements.

13) Oversee staff negotiation and contract administration.

KEY WORKING RELATIONSHIPS

1) Work with the Board of Education to ensure effective Board operations, district policies, objectives, decisions, and performance in line with the public interest.

2) Maintain effective relationships with and among staff at all levels of the organization.

3) Ensure a healthy relationship of the district with its community.

4) Represent the district as required and appropriate in various community, association, and government activities.

Source: Fredrich Genck and Allen J. Klingenberg, *Effective Schools Through Effective Management* (Springfield, Ill.: Illinois Association of School Boards, 1978), pp. 62–63.

The Principal

Principals are also line generalists. In many ways, their role involves major components similar to superintendents. While they obviously are not the chief executive officer of their school board, they are the chief executive officer of their building. As with superintendents, they are important symbols to their communities of the schools, and professional leaders of their buildings' staffs.

As chief executive officer of their school buildings, principals are involved in communicating to and organizing with their staff the plans and intentions of the school board and superintendent. Principals are major information sources for their staff. In most districts principals attend school-board meetings where they watch, and sometimes participate in, the deliberation and making of policy. Often they are called upon to provide specific information or to give responses to possible policy initiatives. Principals work with their staff to organize the operations of the building to implement these policies. They face the problem of translating larger notions about what should be done into the daily activities and routines of their assistants.

Principals also serve as the immediate symbols of the school to their building's attendance area. They are most often the first individuals contacted when something does not go well in their schools. Principals hear complaints about teacher behaviors, instructional programs, and extracurricular activities. They must carefully assess the worth and merit of these criticisms, sorting the biased and destructive from the honest and constructive. In turn, these criticisms must be transmitted to members of the faculty in an individualized and positive manner. By using community suggestions and criticisms, principals may enhance relations between school and community.

But communication is not a one-way street. Principals equally have the responsibility for explaining and defending the program of the school and behavior of the faculty to the community. In this posture, principals are agents of education, working with community members to think carefully about what schools and educators do. This process may well involve efforts to simply describe what is going on in the school. It may include conscious attempts to explain differing philosophies of education, or it may result in impasses which must be resolved by deliberations of the school board and central office.

As professional leaders of their building's staff, principals not only set a tone for the building, but also seek to bring district resources to bear on staff improvement. Some scholars view the principal as the climate setter in his or her building. The climate of a building may be warm, open, friendly to thoughtful discussion and changes, and professionally enriching. The climate also may be cold, closed, hostile to thoughtful debate and change, and professionally arid. The chief generators of climate in most buildings are principals. Halpin and Croft suggest three important dimensions of school climate are (1) authenticity of principals' and group members' behavior, (2) satisfaction with both social needs and task accomplishment and (3) latitude with which both the leader (principal) and group members can initiate leadership acts.[1]

Principals also are involved in linking their staff to the resources available in other parts of the school district. This linking may involve keeping a card file of members of the community who are valuable resource people, or telephoning an assistant superintendent for curriculum and instruction and requesting a consultant to help a beginning teacher with lesson preparation. In these many and varied situations, principals serve as information resources for their schools. They become important repositories of information about kinds of aid available to their staff. Of particular importance is their knowledge about and assessment of the capabilities of specialists available from the central office of the district. In this capacity, principals can bring district resources to bear on particular problems of a school.[2]

As with the superintendent, many districts develop job descriptions for their building principals. Exhibit 11-2 illustrates a different way of describing the role of the principal. This analysis of the principal's role stresses five general responsibilities. These responsibilities underscore the line-generalist characteristics of the principalship. The description suggests the wide range of tasks the principal must deal with, the wide-ranging number of contacts the principal must maintain, and the importance of the role to the management of the building and the education of children.

EXHIBIT 11-2
The Responsibilities of the Principal

The work of the principal can be classified into various categories both for convenience in description and for clarity. The following outline is a way of presenting such a classification based on our concept of the principalship as a special class of management:

---

[1]Andrew W. Halpin and Don B. Croft, *The Organizational Climate of Schools* (Chicago: Midwest Administration Center, University of Chicago, 1963).

[2]Daniel E. Griffiths, David L. Clark, D. Richard Wynn, and Laurence Iannaccone, *Organizing Schools for Effective Education* (Danville, Ill.: The Interstate, 1962), 157–221; and Seymour Tilles, "The Manager's Job: A Systems Approach," *Harvard Business Review,* 41 (January–February, 1963), 73–81.

1. Developing and Implementing the Educational Program
   a. Organizing the school for instruction (establishing and clarifying role relationships) (establishing the operational framework)
   b. Curriculum development (goal setting, planning learning experiences, allocating resources)
   c. Program supervision, including instructional material, equipment and supply procurement and allocation
   d. Program evaluation
2. Instructional Staff Development
   a. Teacher and related staff placement, assignment, transfer
   b. Orientation
   c. Evaluation, retention, dismissal
   d. Selection
   e. In-service growth
   f. Establishment and maintenance of wholesome school climate, in line with sound labor relations principles
3. School Community Relations
   a. Identifying the school community and the various constituencies and agencies
   b. Communication with school clientele (students, parents, other citizens) (interpreting the school)
   c. Gauging community educational interests and support
   d. Developing community interest and support for responsive educational programs
   e. Interpreting the community to school staff
4. Supportive Services and Programs
   a. Pupil personnel services
   b. Finance and fiscal record keeping and reporting
   c. School plant maintenance
   d. Auxiliary services (food service, health, pupil transportation)
   e. School office management
5. Relation of the School to the School System
   a. Interpretation of policy procedures and data, including union agreements
   b. Representation, interpretation, and advocacy of the school
   c. Identification and utilization of available personnel, material and services
   d. Articulation, horizontal and vertical (pupil and staff placement and transfer) (program development)
   e. Referral and appeal

To attempt to rank the functions or classes of functions in order of importance is to seek frustration and would indicate a serious lack of understanding of the nature of schools and schooling and their place in society.

These classes of activities are interrelated and interdependent. None may be slighted if the school is expected to be effective in promoting pupil learning and development.

Source: James R. Tanner, "Management Development of School Principals: A National Priority," in Norman Drachler, ed., *Training Educational Leaders: A Search for Alternatives* (Washington, D.C.: Institute of Educational Leadership, George Washington University, 1976), pp. 106–107.

Central Office Personnel

The various specialists assembled at district level differ sharply in specific subtasks. Some may be concerned solely with district purchasing and bidding procedures, others may consult with teachers about language arts programs, and a few may worry about the routing of buses. Specific subtasks may vary, but central office personnel generally share three characteristics: they are specialists; they coordinate activities with line personnel; and they provide important services to the district.

As specialists, central-office personnel are required to know a good deal about a narrow segment of education. They are trained as experts in a particular field, and the titles they bear reflect this training. We expect, for instance, that dietitians, physical therapists, social workers, supervisors of instruction, librarians, audiovisual specialists, and language-arts consultants know a great deal about the present state of their respective arts and professions. When asked, these specialists are expected to know.

These specialists are also expected to coordinate their activities with those of line personnel. As experts, central-office personnel are biased in terms of their orientation to defining and to solving problems. As specialists, they know the problems they are capable of dealing with. Unfortunately for line personnel, problems rarely come in neat packages that correspond with a particular speciality. Several specialists may be called upon to diagnose and to prescribe a single situation. In such cases, these specialists may disagree. It is at this point that line generalists must help coordinate the activities of several staff specialists. In such situations, specialists may have to work in collaboration with others to solve problems. These collaborative efforts may involve

293

modifying slightly some of the specialists' views of situations. These instances also provide opportunities for specialists to assess the wisdom of their specialization, and the problems of setting too sharp a boundary on the activities of their profession.

The services provided by specialists rest upon their knowledge and their ability to coordinate their skills with others in solving problems. As resources for their districts, specialists may use their unique training and skills to enrich the district. They may also define their efforts in ways which deny the district opportunities to creatively attack problems. Ideally, line generalists work to create an atmosphere or climate in which the initiative of specialists is prized. Specialists, in turn, see their work as part of a collaborative team effort.

One brief example may clarify this point. A large school district became concerned about the problems of keeping an inventory of supplies available to teachers. Such items as paper, ditto masters, maps, and chalk were either gone early in the year or seemed to overflow at the end of the school year. The problem was raised and discussed at a conference of assistant superintendents. In turn, the assistant superintendent for curriculum and instruction mentioned the problem casually to a young assistant in charge of data processing. The assistant suggested that in her night-school course on computers they had just studied a new inventory method which might "fit" this problem. An informal meeting with the associate superintendent for business resulted in approving the new program. Within two weeks, the inventory of supplies was put on the computer, and instant information was available on the status of teacher's supplies for all district personnel.

Hence, specialists provide important services essential to the fulfillment of educational purposes in school districts. To make these general and abstract claims more specific and concrete, the next three sections examine the roles of curriculum-and-instruction specialists, supervisory specialists, and personnel-administration specialists. The final touch of realism in this section is a portfolio of job descriptions found in operating school districts.

Curriculum and Instruction Roles

Roles such as supervisor, curriculum coordinator, director of secondary education, associate superintendent for instruction, and assistant principal for instructional services are specifically designed to facilitate direct, specialized, and concentrated efforts in improving the quality of curriculum and instruction. From our perspective, these roles are central to the core mission of the educational enterprise—

teaching and learning. Nonetheless, these functions cannot be success-fully completed unless others, such as the director of personnel or the business manager, provide adequate material and administrative sup-port. In complex organizations such as modern school districts, core and support roles are interdependent.

Those who work directly in the area of curriculum and instruction deal directly with the roles of teacher and principal. Teachers, as they function in their roles, make curricular decisions in their classrooms while creating learning environments and teaching. The principal is also responsible for making curricular decisions and creating a school climate which enhances learning. Hence, there are clearly overlapping functions in these three roles.

Each of these roles also has contacts with a variety of others who have a stake in their effectiveness. Curriculum-and-instruction special-ists—principals and teachers, for instance—all wish children to learn in a humane and effective way; but principals may be more concerned about parental complaints than teachers, for example. Figure 11–2 suggests the relation between functions and contacts in a number of curriculum-and-instruction roles. The overlapping nature of the role responsibilities and of the respective network of contacts and relation-ships suggests that full harnessing of the potential each role offers to the improvement of instruction requires a great deal of cooperation and teamwork. As Figure 11–2 illustrates, the teacher could receive help from five other sources, or could be torn in five different directions. This schematic underscores our earlier discussions of the need for coordination and cooperation.

The Supervisor's Role

Those who work in curriculum and instruction with particular emphasis on supervision can be differentiated from other administra-tive roles by such characteristics as (1) heavy reliance on expertness as an educational program leader and instructional leader, (2) the neces-sity of living in two worlds and speaking two languages, and (3) limits imposed on their authority.[3]

Supervisors in education are expected to be experts in the produc-tion system of their organizations. A high-school principal can get along quite well with only a conversational acquaintance with class-room organizational patterns, problems, and prospects, but a depart-ment chairperson needs a more detailed perspective to be successful.

[3]Thomas J. Sergiovanni and Robert J. Starratt, *Supervision: Human Perspective* (New York: McGraw-Hill, 1979), pp. 17–22.

FIGURE 11–2
Curriculum and instruction role responsibilities and relationships

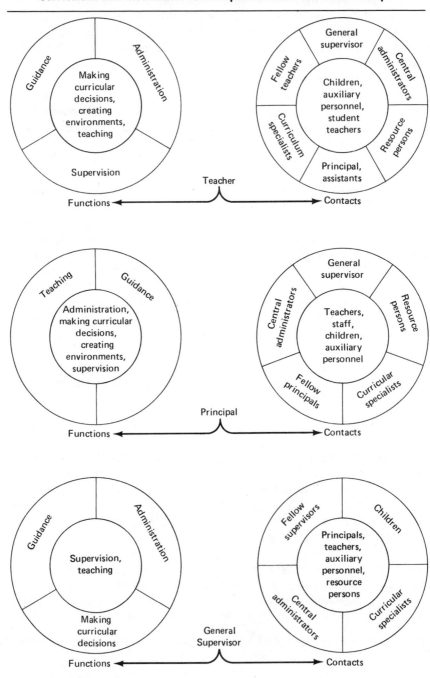

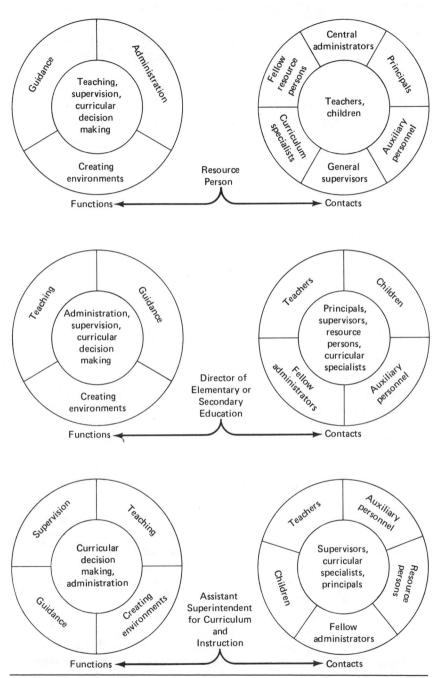

Source: Arthur J. Lewis and Alice Miel, *Supervision for Improved Instruction* (Belmont, Calif.: Wadsworth, 1972), pp. 49–50.

Supervisors are expected to be experts in educational and instructional matters. As such, their work exhibits a high concern for such functions as

Curriculum and teaching objectives

Educational program content, coordination, and scope

Alternatives and options

Curriculum and teaching innovation

Structured knowledge

Grouping and scheduling patterns

Lesson and unit planning

Evaluating and selecting learning materials

Patterns of teacher and student classroom influence

Developing and evaluating educational encounters

Teaching styles, methods, and procedures

Classroom learning climates

Teacher, student, and program evaluation.

A second characteristic differentiating supervisory from other roles is the necessity of speaking the languages of both teachers and administrators. Most teachers and most administrators operate from different perspectives, perspectives which can often make one unintelligible to the other. Even though most administrators have been teachers previously, they have been cast into a different arena and subjected to different pressures. They often have difficulty in understanding the problems teachers face. Teachers, on the other hand, view the school from a limited, often unrealistic, perspective. Their perspective is frequently accompanied by an unsympathetic view of the administrator and his or her role. Supervisors are forced to live in both worlds and to mediate difficulties in communication and perspective between the two worlds without alienating either (no small order!).

A third characteristic involves limitations placed on the supervisor's authority: Supervisors are often considered "staff" rather than "line" officers, though admittedly the difference between the two is more muddled than neat. As such, they rely heavily on functional authority conferred by their knowledge as educational and instructional leaders and on personal leadership characteristics as sources of authority to influence both teachers and administrators. Effective administrators rely similarly on functional authority, but this is enhanced or backed up by formal authority derived from their more clearly superordinate position in the heirarchy.

TABLE 11–1
Summary of task areas *Descriptive not normative*

Task descriptor	Ranking	Percent of respondents indicating involvement in task area
In-service programs	1	94
Program evaluation	2	90
Staff meetings	3	83
Developing standards	4	75
Community relations	5	71
Budget	6	69
Teacher supervision	7	67
Federal programs	8	62
Teacher evaluations	9.5	59
Testing	9.5	59
Other categories	11	34
Teacher negotiations	12	21

Source: Adapted from Donald J. Christensen, "The Curriculum Writer Today," in Charles A. Speiker, ed, *Curriculum Leaders: Improving Their Influence* (Washington, D.C.: Association for Supervision and Curriculum Development, 1976), p. 55.

These characteristics of supervisory roles mean that, often, role occupants become involved in a wide-ranging array of activities. In a survey of curriculum-and-supervisory workers conducted by Christensen under the auspices of the Association for Supervision and Curriculum Development, twelve areas emerged as the most frequently mentioned descriptors of the curriculum-supervisory worker's tasks. Descriptors and the frequency with which they were mentioned are summarized in Table 11–1. Supervisory personnel were heavily involved in in-service programs, staff meetings, developing standards, and program evaluation, as might be expected; but some were involved as well in teacher negotiations. Some might suggest that involvement in budget (70 percent), community relations (71 percent), and federal programs (62 percent) is surprising; others might suggest it is common. This widespread involvement of supervisors underlines their expertise, their bridging of multiple perspectives, and the centrality of curriculum-and-supervisory tasks to the work of the school.

The Role of Personnel Administrator

It is frequently claimed that education is a "labor intensive" occupation. In contrast with other occupations which might be technically or machine intensive, education, and particularly teaching, is carried out by large numbers of personnel. Despite technological advances

299

such as computer-assisted instruction, the work of schools is based on the labors of craftspersons. School budgets illustrate the large investment in professional salaries—up to 75 percent of many district budgets.

The importance of the personnel administrator in such a labor-intensive occupation is obvious. The many facets of this important task are beyond this text, but a brief examination of two aspects of the role may shed light on its importance. The aspects of our interest are collective bargaining and staff-hiring practices.

Collective bargaining is the process in which representatives of teachers and the school system negotiate jointly an agreement (contract) over a specific period of time (one to three years). This agreement defines the terms and conditions of employment. The process of bargaining is demanding in time, and is both tedious and complicated in operation. Castetter's analysis of the process of collective negotiations is found as Figure 11–3. From preparation for a new cycle of negotiations to evaluating an ending cycle, the success of collective negotiation depends heavily on the leadership of personnel specialists.

Consider also the host of guidelines which must be recognized by the personnel administrator when hiring personnel. As illustrated in Table 11–2, the employing district must be careful of what it asks of prospective employees. As the second column suggests, there are lawful inquiries. But the third column points out possible unlawful practices. The purpose of Table 11–2, obviously, is not to adjudicate what are lawful or are not lawful practices. It does, however, point out how complex the personnel function is today.

The complexity of collective bargaining and hiring highlight the arguments for centralization of this important role. Except in the smallest district, the arguments of Castetter for a specialized personnel role seem convincing:

1. The significance of people to the success of the enterprise warrants the status and role of a major function in the central administration.
2. The superintendent of schools cannot personally devote the time, energy, and thought required to plan, organize, and direct the function.
3. Line administrators are not qualified by training and experience to administer the range of personnel activities illustrated in Figure 11–3.
4. Centralization of the function enhances the possibility of securing greater uniformity in interpretation and implementation of personnel policies and procedures.
5. Decentralization of personnel activities is not conducive to unified personnel planning, coordinating, and control.
6. The increasing size of school systems, the emerging problems (for example, collective negotiations), the growth of nonprofessional staffs and increas-

FIGURE 11-3
The Collective Bargaining Process

Subprocesses	Related Activities
Prepare for Collective Negotiations	Responsibility assigned for collection and analysis of pertinent data. Roles of board, superintendent, principals, personnel director defined.
Select Negotiating Team	Negotiating team selected. Responsibility and authority clarified.
Plan Negotiations Strategy	Decisions made concerning negotiations objectives
Develop Negotiations Tactics	Decisions made as to means by which objectives are to be achieved.
Negotiate Agreement	Formal agreement reached concerning relationship between system and negotiating group for specific period of time.
Administer Agreement	Contract implemented by both parties. Appeals system applied when disputes over contract arise.
Appraise Collective Negotiations Process	All facets of collective negotiations process reviewed to improve its operation.

Source: William B. Castetter, *The Personnel Function in Educational Administration* (New York: Macmillan, 1971), p. 332.

ing employment of para-professional personnel in school systems make complete decentralization of the personnel function impracticable.

7. Expertise required in the formulation of personnel policies and processes is not usually possessed by personnel in school attendance units.[4]

The general acceptance of these ideas about the centralization of the personnel function, nonetheless, still leaves important questions

[4]William B. Castetter, *The Personnel Function in Educational Administration* (New York: Macmillan, 1971), p. 47.

301

TABLE 11-2
General guidelines to lawful and unlawful employment practices

Types of inquiries of job applicants typically made by employers in selection	Lawful practice(s) related to inquiry	Possibly unlawful practice(s) related to inquiry
1. Name	Inquiry as to full name.	Inquiry into any title which indicates race, color, religion, sex, national origin, or ancestry.
2. Address	Inquiry into place and length of current and previous addresses.	Specific inquiry into foreign addresses that would indicate national origin.
3. Sex		Any inquiry that would indicate sex.
4. Religion-creed		a) Any inquiry to indicate or identify denomination or customs. b) May not be told this is a Protestant, Catholic, or Jewish organization. c) Request of a recommendation or reference from someone in clergy.
5. Birthplace of national origin		a) Any inquiry into place of birth. b) Any inquiry into place of birth of parents, grandparents, or spouse. c) Any other inquiry into national origin.
6. Race or color		Any inquiry which would indicate race or color.
7. Citizenship	a) Whether or not a U.S. citizen. b) If not, whether intends to become one. c) If U.S. residence is legal. d) If spouse is citizen. e) Require proof of citizenship after being hired.	a) If native-born or naturalized. b) Proof of citizenship before hiring. c) Whether parents or spouse are native-born or naturalized.
8. Age	a) Request proof of age in form of work permit issued by school authorities. b) Require proof of age by birth certificate after hiring.	Require birth certificate or baptismal record before hiring.
9. Photographs	May be required *after* hiring for identification purposes.	Require photograph *before* hiring.
10. Education	a) Inquiry into what academic, professional, or vocational schools attended. b) Inquiry into language skills, such as reading and writing of foreign languages.	a) Any inquiry asking specifically the nationality, racial, or religious affiliation of a school. b) Inquiry as to what is mother tongue or how foreign-language ability was acquired, unless necessary for job.
11. Relatives	Inquiry into name, relationship, and address of person to be notified in case of emergency.	Any inquiry about a relative which is unlawful (e.g., race or religion inquiries).
12. Organization	a) Inquiry into organization memberships, excluding any organization the name or character of which indicates the race, color, religion, sex, national origin, or ancestry of its members. b) What offices are held, if any.	Inquiry into all clubs and organizations where membership is held.

TABLE 11-2   Continued

13. Military service	a) Inquiry into service in U.S.Armed Forces. b) Rank attained. c) Which branch of service. d) Require military discharge certificate after being hired.	a) Inquiry into military service in armed service of any country but United States. b) Request military service records.
14. Work schedule	Inquiry into willingness to work required work schedule.	Any inquiry into willingness to work any particular religious holiday.
15. Other qualifications	Any question that has a direct reflection (i.e., can be shown to be job related) on the job to be applied for.	Any non-job-related inquiry that may present information permitting unlawful discrimination.
16. References	General personal and work references not relating to race, color, religion, sex, national origin, or ancestry.	Request references specifically from clergymen or any other persons who might reflect race, color, religion, sex, national origin, or ancestry of applicant.

Source: Richard W. Beatty and Craig Eric Schneier, *Personnel Administration: An Experiential Skill-Building Approach* (Reading; Mass: Addison-Wesley, 1977), pp. 458–459.

unanswered. To whom, for instance, should the personnel administrator report? And, what alternative arrangements can be made in smaller districts? The answers to these and other issues are addressed by more specialized books dealing specifically with the personnel function. For our purposes, the questions suggest the importance of the role of personnel administrators.

A Portfolio of Other Administrative Roles

We feel a sense of frustration in trying to discuss in detail the array of roles found in modern, complex school districts. To maintain the introductory nature of this book, we have touched on such roles as superintendent and principal, but ignored those such as business manager, plant maintenance, or special education administrator.

Included in this section is Exhibit 11-3, a portfolio of sample job descriptions for some roles, which provides useful information for understanding how each particular role fits into and contributes to the functioning of the entire district. These descriptions should be examined on the following dimensions: What specific specialized knowledge is essential to this role? How are these specialists coordinated not only with other staff specialists but also with line generalists? What important services do these specialists bring to the educational mission of the district?

EXHIBIT 11-3
Portfolio of Administrative Role Descriptions*

ASSISTANT SUPERINTENDENT FOR BUSINESS

The Assistant Superintendent for Business shall be directly responsible to the Superintendent of Schools and is delegated responsibilities in those areas related to the conduct of school business affairs. He shall:

Attend all meetings of the Board of Education except when his own election, tenure, efficiency, or remuneration is being considered;

Exercise line-staff supervision of the activities of the directors or supervisors of School Plant, Maintenance and Buildings and Grounds, Cafeteria and Food Service, and Transportation;

Be responsible for supplying financial and related data for all county, state, and federal reports, maintain files and records of same, and audits of reports for submission to such authorities;

Be responsible for the collection and audit of revenue, for auditing claims and disbursing monies, and accounting for all funds administered by the Board of Education;

Be responsible for the administration of internal audits;

In cooperation with the Superintendent, the Assistant Superintendent for Personnel and Pupil Personnel Services and the Assistant Superintendent for Instruction be responsible for budgetary development and control;

Act as a purchasing and disbursing agent for the Board of Education within the limits of the budget, including supervision of persons assigned as purchasing agents;

Aid the Assistant Superintendent for Personnel and Pupil Personnel Services in recommendations to the Superintendent of all non-professional personnel;

Be responsible for the maintenance of an adequate and correct system of records pertinent to income and expenditures, encumbrances, payrolls and payroll deductions, teacher and municipal employee retirement, debt service, titles, contracts, abstracts, insurance, tuition and other as deemed necessary;

Be responsible for accurate and current inventory records of all school property and equipment;

In cooperation with the staff, assist in planning for new buildings and additions;

Be responsible for maintenance of effective liaison and communication with architects and contractors concerned with school buildings and facilities;

Be responsible for rental of school facilities;

Be responsible for the storage and distribution of all supplies and equipment;

Perform all other duties necessary to his office and such other duties as may be fixed by the Board of Education or the Superintendent of Schools.

ASSISTANT SUPERINTENDENT FOR PERSONNEL AND PUPIL PERSONNEL SERVICES

The Assistant Superintendent for Personnel and Pupil Personnel Services shall work directly under the supervision of the Superintendent of Schools and report directly to him. He shall:

Be responsible for cross conferring with other assistant superintendents relative to Personnel and Pupil Personnel Services functions;

Develop and administer personnel policies;

Prepare job descriptions and specifications for any position to be used by the district, drawing on the advice of administrative personnel appropriate to the position;

Establish a program for recruitment of personnel;

Search for and screen through applicants for positions, drawing on the assistance of administrative personnel where vacancies exist in the final selection of candidates to be recommended to the Superintendent for employment;

Handle all assignments and requests for transfers, consulting appropriate administrative officers when needed;

Provide administration for all sick leave, personal leave and professional leave and travel requests;

Provide management for substitute personnel, including available rosters and files;

Administer all designations of salaries, in accordance with the salary policies of the district, drawing assistance from whatever position necessary;

Provide counseling relative to retirement;

Develop and administer procedures for hearing of grievances, drawing assistance from district personnel and personnel organizations;

Provide assistance in negotiations to the Office of Superintendent;

Develop budget estimates related to personnel and administer personnel budgets in cooperation with the Assistant Superintendent for Business;

Maintain adequate personnel records;

Assist in developing in-service programs for personnel;

Assist in programs of public information relative to personnel and personnel activities;

Perform any other duties related to personnel functions that may be delegated by the Superintendent;

Prepare all required reports, local, state, and federal, related to pupil enrollment and attendance;

Oversee activities related to pupil absenteeism and fee delinquencies;

Administer necessary pupil transfers;

Provide coordination of psychological, social work and guidance services and maintain close cooperation with other administrative personnel who draw on such services;

With the assistance of other administrative personnel, provide a continuing evaluation of the effectiveness of Pupil Personnel Services.

DIRECTOR OF HEALTH, SAFETY, PHYSICAL EDUCATION, AND ATHLETICS

The Director of Health, Safety, Physical Education and Athletics is directly responsible to the Assistant Superintendent for Instruction. He shall:

Plan a curriculum for grades kindergarten through twelve in health, physical education, and safety;

Provide supervision and coordination of such curriculum;

Provide consultative services to the Superintendent, Assistant Superintendent for Instruction, Directors and Principals in the area of health, physical education, and safety;

Plan the location and maintenance of all physical education equipment;

Recommend the supplies and equipment to be purchased;

Be responsible for a program of in-service education for teachers in the area of physical education;

Plan and supervise all afterschool and Saturday intramural and interschool physical education activities;

Work directly with the department chairman and consultants in physical education to improve the instruction in their areas;

Cooperate with the City Recreation Department in planning and supervising city and school interrelated program;

He shall serve as Athletic Director and be responsible for schedules, officials, transportation, supervision of games, purchasing equipment, care of equipment, care of playing fields and gyms; supervision of coaching staff. He shall advise in development of new facilities, publicity, conducting the tournaments, eligibility of players, medical care, and insurance;

Work cooperatively with principals to coordinate the interscholastic and athletic program;

Be directly responsible to the Assistant Superintendent for Instruction.

DIRECTOR FOR TALENTED

The Director of the Program for the Talented is expected to:

Serve under the guidance and supervision of the Assistant Superintendent for Instruction;

Be responsible for the successful operation of the reimbursement program including preparation of the proposal for submission to the State of Illinois and submission of appropriate reports and claims;

Operate in-service training programs for professional staff members to increase their familiarity with, and use of, the methods and materials used in the program;

Select and procure appropriate materials to be used in the program;

Report periodically to the Assistant Superintendent for Instruction concerning the progress and the problems in the program. A concise, written annual report should be submitted by May 1 of each school year with information concerning who was served, how, when, staff members involved, major successes, major problems, approximate cost, and recommended changes in program and/or personnel, if appropriate;

Cooperate with administrators and teachers in Champaign schools participating in the program to develop and evaluate programs;

Provide for both ongoing and annual evaluations of the reimbursement programs with recommendations for modification where appropriate;

Provide for dissemination of the content and the methodology used in the program, where this is deemed desirable;

Perform such other duties in connection with the talented program as may be assigned by the Assistant Superintendent for Instruction.

DIRECTOR OF BUILDINGS, GROUNDS, AND MAINTENANCE

He is directly responsible to the Assistant Superintendent for Business who shall receive his reports and exercise supervision over his activities;

He shall have general supervision of all engineers, custodians, and all maintenance employees. Immediate supervision resides in the principal;

He shall be responsible to the Superintendent and the Assistant Superintendent for Business for the management of all school properties and be responsible for the repair and upkeep of these properties;

He shall assist the Superintendent of Schools, the Assistant Superintendent for Business, and the Principal in all matters of property management to the end that the best possible physical properties may be provided for the children of the school system;

He shall recommend to the Assistant Superintendent for Personnel and Pupil Personnel Services, all employees under his direction;

It is the duty of the Director of Maintenance to see that all fire hazards are eliminated;

He must work with the local fire department and the insurance inspectors and comply with their requests as far as possible;

He shall be responsible in cooperation with the Assistant Superintendent for Business for the maintenance, repair, alterations, and improvements of school buildings and grounds;

He shall be responsible in cooperation with the Assistant Superintendent for Business in developing orientation programs and an inservice training program for the custodial staff;

He shall be responsible for the maintenance, repair and use of all operating equipment.

*Role descriptions included in this portfolio are from a school district serving a midwestern city of approximately 75,000 people. The district includes some rural and suburban satellite areas as well.

In this description of roles, and in the earlier discussion of tasks in Chapter 10, the emphasis has been on the creation of an atmosphere in which administrators work together to define problems and generate solutions. In many, if not most, cases, people do work together; but there are also points of conflict and tension. These points, as well as devices for reducing dysfunctional consequences of conflict and tension, deserve examination.

GENERATION AND RESOLUTION OF TENSION AND CONFLICT

Those who believe that educational administration is enhanced by the analysis of administrative tasks and the specification of administration have been challenged by two sets of criticisms. The first set of critics have worried about the all-inclusive nature of this approach. Some have charged that administrators are required to do everything, without proper regard for setting priorities. In the tasks-and-roles approach, administrators appear to be effective if they are completing a long checklist of activities or checking off elements of the job description. What is lacking is the sense of what tasks or parts of roles must be fulfilled at a particular moment in the life of the school.[5] Certain tasks, priorities, or elements of roles may be important today. The tasks-and-roles approach does not facilitate rank ordering by priorities or tasks which must be done now versus those which can be put off until tomorrow; the tasks and roles approach ignores the contingencies of the situation.This criticism suggests an inherent source of conflict in the tasks-and-roles approach. Members of the organization may agree on the listing of tasks, but differ sharply on the priorities of tasks. They may quarrel about which of those elements of their roles need elaboration or about those needs which must be met today. Priorities are the problem, and are not created by listing tasks or roles.

A second set of criticisms has relied on actual studies of organizations to suggest that organizations are rife with conflict. Dalton, for instance, analyzed conflict between staff and line officers.[6] Staff officers and line officers got into conflicts because (1) staff officers were ambitious and wanted line authority, (2) staff officers felt their ideas should be accepted without criticisms by line officers, and (3) staff officers resented line officers who controlled staff promotions. These conflicts obviously impaired successful operations of both line and staff units, and hindered cooperation between these units.

In another study, Mechanic suggested that lower-ranked organization members had considerable power over higher ranked members.[7] Subordinate members gained power because supervisors were dependent on them for access to persons, information, and other organizational resources. Low-ranking participants with expert knowledge, for instance, could deny this knowledge to superiors. Such seeming insubordination might be tolerated because of the difficulty of replacing experts. Equally, lower-ranked members gain power when superiors are not interested in a particular job, and simply turn the job over to subordinates. These and other empirical studies suggest that what goes on in organizations is not a mere reflection of job descriptions or of task analyses.

These two criticisms of the tasks-and-roles approach suggest the

[5]Thomas J. Sergiovanni, *Handbook for Effective Department Leadership: Concepts and Practices in Today's Secondary Schools* (Boston: Allyn & Bacon, 1977), pp. 31–41.

[6]Melville Dalton, "Conflict Between Line and Staff Officers," *American Sociological Review,* 15 (1950), 342–351.

[7]David Mechanic, "Sources of Power of Lower Participants in Complex Organizations," *Administrative Science Quarterly,* 7 (1962–63), 349–364.

need of organizational members to consciously consider mechanisms for resolving conflicts over priorities and resolving tensions among organizational participants. A number of mechanisms have been developed, but our attention will be fixed on only two means of resolving tensions and conflicts: role expectations and administrative teams.

One integrating mechanism has been the conscious effort to develop clear expectations about the tasks associated with various roles. These expectations are developed from a number of sources such as training programs, inservice development activities, job descriptions, formal discussions with other role occupants, and informal discussions with others. For example, principals learn what principals are to do in graduate programs leading to their certification, in workshops staged by their districts, from administrative handbooks furnished by their districts, in chatting with other principals, and in discussions with parents, students, and teachers about how they are doing or ought to be doing their job as principal. These expectations develop not only senses of what obligations exist for fulfilling the role, but also what tension and conflict surround the role. For instance, principals know that a part of their role involves evaluating teachers, even though this evaluation can produce conflict and tension.

A second mechanism is the deliberate designing of administrative teams.[8] These teams, comprised of superintendent, central-office staff, and principals, are formally constituted groups created by boards of education. As teams, they avoid the older notions of an authoritatian superintendent while emphasizing the roles and responsibilities of team members.

Though superintendents remain the final authority, the team concept spells out the decision-making domains of members of the team. These careful delineations force team members to be clear about decisions in which they can most effectively participate as terminal decision makers. For example, team members may wish a clearer policy about who may discuss collective bargaining negotiations with media persons. This spelling out also clarifies situations in which members of the team have purely advisory functions.

The concept of *administrative team* suggests not only a careful delineation of specific role responsibilities but also a sense of active and creative participation in the organization. Members have a forum for discussion of their beliefs about priorities, and a procedure for knowing if their beliefs will be advisory or final in decisionmaking. Team mem-

[8]American Association for School Administrators, *Profiles of the Administrative Team* (Washington, D. C.: AASA, 1971); and Richard Wynn, *Theory and Practice of the Administrative Team* (Arlington, Va.: National Association of Elementary School Principals, 1973).

bers also have opportunities for resolving conflicts between line and staff, or superordinate and subordinate. Careful delineation requires that as conflicts or tensions develop, team members may wish to evaluate both the procedures used for resolving conflicts and those utilized when establishing areas of responsibility. Instead of conflict or tension creating blockages in organizational activities, conflict or tension may trigger evaluation and change of team procedures.

Some empirical evidence suggests benefits of an administrative team. Schmidt, for example, found in a sample of secondary-school administrators that job satisfaction increased as they were provided opportunities to be creative, to experiment with new programs, and to explore new areas for their achievement.[9] No team could guarantee such conditions, but the general notion of *team* underscores not only the delineation of responsibilities but also the opportunities for personal and professional growth.

The development of administrative teams suggests the viability of integrating administrative tasks and roles for modern, complex school-district organizations. In themselves, task-and-role descriptions are normative checklists for administrators. Tasks provide senses of what administrators, either individually or in teams, ought to do. Roles provide normative expectations for actors and team members. In combination, administrative tasks and roles provide guidelines for training new administrators, establishing job descriptions and role expectations, and helping to conceptualize administration as a team effort.

There is one integrative mechanism which most authorities would reject: absolute authority. The excuse of "obeying orders" has no place in the administration of schools or in the practice of education. Fortunately, educational professionals do not face the simple choice of either obeying or being insubordinate. Professional knowledge and professional values dictate thoughtful compliance, not blind obedience. A commitment to team administration can help reach this ideal.

SUMMARY

This and the preceding chapter have briefly elaborated major tasks and roles of educational administrators. Such an approach contends that administration of educational institutions consists of the completion of a number of vital tasks. Tasks, in turn, are usually assigned to

[9]Gene L. Schmidt, "Job Satisfaction among Secondary School Administrators," *Educational Administration Quarterly,* 12 (Spring, 1976), 68–86.

roles. Generalists are responsible for overseeing these tasks, while specialists have the unique knowledge necessary for the accomplishment of specific tasks. The roles of superintendent, principal, and central-office personnel were briefly examined. Some sources of conflict and integrating mechanisms were noted.

Our general feeling is that while the tasks-and-roles approach has some value, it presents a limited view of educational administration. Of particular importance to educational leadership is the ability to set priorities. The task-and-roles approach helps enumerate what priorities could be, but lacks a way of deciding what priority should be paramount at what moment. Because of this flaw, the elaboration of tasks and roles, though helpful, is insufficient in accurately describing what administrative work in education is or should be.

STUDY GUIDE

Can you recall the meanings of the following terms? Discuss them with a class colleague and apply them to your own school-community setting.

generalist	building climate
specialist	job description
line	staff-line conflict
staff	lower participant power
formal authority	administrative team
chief executive	role expectations

SUGGESTED ACTIVITIES

1. Generate a portfolio of job descriptions from your district and those of your colleagues. Examine the various roles in terms of issues such as line-staff relations, sources of possible conflict and integration, and needed expert knowledge.

2. Interview your district superintendent to explore the mechanisms used by your district to coordinate the work of staff specialists. For example, are committees used to get the insights and differences of various groups? Are inservice training programs aimed at clarifying and deepening role expectations?

3. From your local college or university, obtain copies of the courses required for various educational specialists—for example, curriculum coordina-

tors, school psychologists, or business managers. Compare and contrast these curricula. Does your college or university require general courses for these specialists, or may they pursue only specialized courses? What problems does the planning of curricula for specialists create for the development of integrating mechanisms such as administrative teams?

SELECTED READINGS

GETZELS, JACOB W., JAMES M. LIPHAM, and ROALD F. CAMPBELL, *Administration as a Social Process*. New York: Harper & Row, 1968.

KIMBROUGH, RALPH B. and MICHAEL Y. NUNNERY, *Education Administration: An Introduction*. New York: Macmillan, 1976.

MINTZBERG, HENRY, *The Nature of Managerial Work*. New York: Harper & Row, 1973.

SAYLES, LEONARD R., *Managerial Behavior: Administration in Complex Organizations*. New York: McGraw-Hill, 1964.

SERGIOVANNI, THOMAS J., and FRED D. CARVER, *The New School Executive: A Theory of Administration* (2nd ed.). New York: Harper & Row, 1980.

12

THE WORK OF EDUCATIONAL ADMINISTRATORS: A DESCRIPTIVE VIEW

Books are written in professional fields such as educational governance and administration for a variety of reasons. Informing, explicating, exploring, and describing are examples. Typically included among reasons to write these books is to improve the field in question. Authors want to make things better, and professional books usually prescribe best ways of operating, or propose a series of axioms and propositions designed to make things better.

In fields such as education, where values and ethics are of particular importance, normative models and theories are popular.[1] These are concerned with what one ought to do; with determining actions which are designed to produce the best solutions. A normative view of educational administration is depicted in Figure 12–1. Here it is assumed that choices are made by administrators to maximize certain desirable values and objectives. The educational administrator, being faithful to certain value statements and committed to certain objectives, uses the financial, human, and material resources available to him or her to achieve goals in accordance with a maximum cost/benefits exchange, and in a manner which ensures organizationally desirable behavior. Teachers, administrators, students, school boards, parents, and others are expected to think and act first on behalf of what is viewed as good for the school and its objectives. To this end, the administrator per-

---

[1] See for example, Thomas J. Sergiovanni and F. D. Carver, *The New School Executive: A Theory of Administration,* 2nd ed. (New York: Harper & Row, 1980).

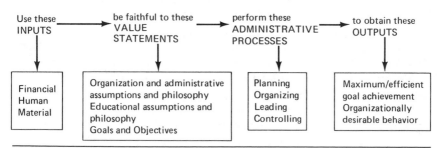

FIGURE 12–1
A normative view of educational administration

Following the Decision-rule "Choices are made to Maximize Values and Objectives,"
An Educational Administrator <u>should</u> behave as follows:

Use these INPUTS	be faithful to these VALUE STATEMENTS	perform these ADMINISTRATIVE PROCESSES	to obtain these OUTPUTS
Financial Human Material	Organization and administrative assumptions and philosophy Educational assumptions and philosophy Goals and Objectives	Planning Organizing Leading Controlling	Maximum/efficient goal achievement Organizationally desirable behavior

---

forms certain processes such as planning, organizing, leading, and controlling.

NORMATIVE THEORIES AND MODELS

Normative theories and models have a number of advantages. They specify what should be done. They challenge individuals who are involved with the school to place highest priority on moral rather than instrumental values; on what is just and good rather than on what is expedient or profitable; on what is most effective rather than on some lesser good. They facilitate the development of theoretical structures for understanding ideal administrative functioning. They help to set goals, to reach agreement on future directions, and to develop plans for future action. And they set the standard for improving present levels of organizational and administrative functioning. Despite these important advantages, normative theories and models fail to capture the world and work of administration as it really is. By contrast, *descriptive* models and theories are concerned with what is; with accurately describing the activities and events they represent.[2] In this chapter a descriptive view of the world and work of administration is presented.

A DESCRIPTIVE VIEW
OF EDUCATIONAL ADMINISTRATION

Normative views of administration assume a level of rationality which underplays such realities as internal organizational politics, the

---

[2]See, for example, Henry Mintzberg, *The Nature of Managerial Work* (New York: Harper & Row, 1973).

larger political environment within which schools function, the actual distribution of power and authority, the pressures which administrators face to manage conflict, the compromises which accompany this effort, and the human limits on choices which administrators make. Normative views, for example, assume that organizational participants will act first on behalf of the school, with self-interest being clearly secondary. Reality, however, suggests that events occur as a result of diverse groups, each bargaining to improve its own position.[3] Decisions are made and outcomes achieved as a result of compromise, coalition, competition, and confusion. Bargaining is the activity which dominates this process.

Some theorists, such as James G. March, suggest that viewing organizations as coalitions rather than rational collectivities of individuals, groups, and agencies is a more accurate representation of the real world.[4] In the coalition view, the distribution of authority is not always as clear and rational as it seems by examining an organizational chart. Those lower in the heirarchy often develop informal power bases more powerful in some areas than superiors. Many outside groups over which the school has no formal authority are active and influential participants in school affairs. Each of these internal and external groups makes demands on the school and its administrators. Demands take such forms as money, attention, involvement, and personal treatment. Sometimes demands from competing groups are complementary and sometimes contradictory. When contradictory, meeting one demand makes it difficult meeting another. Consider, for example, a group of parents who want the school to stress the teaching of responsibility and self-discipline, on the one hand, and to maintain its custodial function of student control, on the other. These are contradictory expectations for administrators. Administrators, according to the coalition view, try to use the organization to maximize their own interests and needs. They face the problem of selecting a coalition of participants so that demands required as price for participation do not compromise the returns they seek. A principal who seeks support from teachers for a program of staff development at the cost of losing access to teachers' classrooms might find the trade-off as jeopardizing not only to his or her immediate intent but to future options as well. An informal cost-benefit analysis is conducted whereby the administrator assesses whether the benefits accrued by participating in a coalition with a particular person or group justify the demands which must be provided.

[3]Graham T. Allison, "Conceptual Models and the Cuban Missile Crisis," *The American Political Science Review,* 63, no. 3 (1969) 689–718.

[4]James G. March, "The Business Firm as a Political Coalition," *The Journal of Politics,* 24 (1962).

A key difference between normative and descriptive theories and models is that in the latter it is assumed that administrative choices are made to satisfy constraints rather than to maximize objectives. As depicted in Figure 12–2, the educational administrator is conscious of and interested in value statements and goals important to his or her organization, and desires to perform administrative processes in an ideal way; but these are *mediated* by such realities of organizational life as politics, the press for conflict resolution, limits on rationality,[5] and the distribution of power and authority. Satisfactory goal achievement and self-serving behavior tend to be more accurate descriptions of outcomes as the administration seeks to satisfy these constraints. Normative and descriptive views of the administrative processes are compared below.

Planning, in the normative view, assumes rationality, optimization, and loyalty to the school, over self-interest. Further, the focus is on anticipated consequences and stated goals. By contrast, the descriptive model acknowledges the existence of "satisficing" and self-serving behaviors and the presence of unanticipated consequences.

Organizing, in the normative view, assumes that form follows function and that administrators design organizations to achieve maximum effectiveness. By contrast, descriptive views acknowledge that orga-

FIGURE 12–2
A descriptive view of educational administration

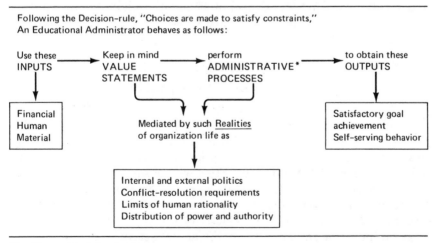

*See Figure 11–1 for details.

[5]Limits on human rationality and their effects on educational decision-making are discussed in Chapter 13 of this book—"The Decision-Making Process."

nizational decisions are made to resolve conflicts, that organizations change slowly, and indeed that often, perhaps typically, function follows form.

Leading, in the normative view, assumes that jobs should be designed in a fashion which motivates teachers and students, that intrinsic rewards are important, that creativity and innovation are desirable, and that rewards should be linked to performance. By contrast, the descriptive view acknowledges the importance of extrinsic rewards, the tendency to reward "don't rock the boat" schools and work groups, and the fact that often performance has very little to do with rewards in education.

Controlling, in the normative view, assumes that a rational accountability system based on ideal objectives can be developed. By contrast, the descriptive view acknowledges that control mechanisms concentrate on aspects that are visible to various school publics and that can be described and measured with ease.

Accounts of gaps between normative and descriptive views of educational administration are not cause for alarm, providing that the supply of both views is rich and abundant. Presently, abundance and richness characterize the normative literature but not the descriptive literature. A need exists, therefore, for theorists to focus more talent and attention to mapping and describing the real world and work of administration. In the sections which follow, the work of Henry Mintzberg is discussed and elaborated.[6] His landmark research in the tradition of the "Work-Activity School of Thought" in administration provides a start for developing this rich and abundant descriptive view of educational administration.

THE WORK-ACTIVITY SCHOOL

Most research in organization and administration tends to be deductive. Conclusions are inferred from general principles. The principles themselves are based on assumptions or premises. The work flow of deductive research is as follows: Start with assumptions or premises; theorize; extract propositions; state and test hypothesis; analyze results; draw conclusion; re-evaluate premises; and re-define theory, thus repeating the process. The work-activity school, on the other hand, relies on inductive research. Here, the actual activities of administrators are studied systematically. Diary methods which record actual work of managers and actual distribution of how their time is used; activity sampling whereby through actual observation the researcher

[6]Mintzberg, *Nature of Managerial Work.*

records activities of administrators at random intervals; and structured observation whereby administrators are observed over extended periods of time are the techniques typically employed. In work-activity research, conclusions are drawn and theoretical statements are inferred only when they can be supported by empirical evidence.

Work-activity research strives to develop an accurate description of the characteristics and content of administrative work. The descriptions help answer such job characteristics questions as where do administrators work, how long do they work, what means do they use to communicate, how do they handle and send mail, and what work patterns exist day to day and week to week? The descriptions help answer as well such job-content questions as what do administrators actually do, what activities do they carry out, and why? Categorizations of job content help one to infer the actual roles that administrators assume.[7] Often these roles are in sharp contrast to the roles administrators should perform.

THE NATURE
OF MANAGERIAL WORK:
MINTZBERG

A role can be defined as a set of integrated behaviors associated with an identifiable positon. Following the thinking of the work-activity school, determining administrative roles requires that one have an accurate picture of the content of administrative work. What an administrator actually does determines his or her real administrative roles. In Mintzberg's extensive structural-observation study of five executives (one a school superintendent), he sought to describe the content of administrative work.[8] Work-content descriptions were then used to infer a number of critical administrative roles which, Mintzberg suggests, characterize the nature of managerial work.

The managerial activities recorded suggested ten administrative roles which could be grouped into three major categories: (1) *interpersonal,* containing figurehead, leader, and liaison roles; (2) *informational,* containing monitor, disseminator, and spokesperson roles; and (3) *decisional,* containing entrepreneur, disturbance-handler, resource-allocater, and negotiator roles. These roles are further examined below, and discussed within the context of educational administration.[9]

---

[7]*Ibid.,* pp. 22–24.

[8]*Ibid.,* pp. 230–277.

[9]This discussion of managerial roles follows closely Mintzberg, *Nature of Managerial Work,* pp. 54–99.

Interpersonal Roles

Interpersonal roles require that the administrator be involved either directly or indirectly in the activities of others. This set of roles takes a great deal of an administrator's time. Though demanding, many role activities included here seem only remotely connected to the central job of administering a school. Some of the roles are symbolic, as in the case of *figurehead*. Others are more directly involved in the work of the school, as in the case of *leader*. Still others are more political in nature, as in the case of *liasion*. But all are critically important to an administrator's success and to the welfare of the school. Slighting any of the three interpersonal roles can cause problems. All are highly visible roles which lend themselves to easy evaluation by students, teachers, parents, other administrators, board members, and various segments of the community public.

The most basic and simple administrative role is that of the *figurehead*. This role requires that administrators, because of their formal authority and high status, perform a number of duties, most of which on the surface seem to have little direct connection with the information-processing and decision-making work of the school. But they are important, as any educational administrator will attest.

Consider the hours that a high school principal spends at basketball and other games, pep rallies, proms, school plays, picnics, honor society ceremonies, and other events of this sort. Add to this the chores of greeting visitors, leading school tours, attending school-community meetings, hosting social events, and such requirements as being available to parents and other community members whose requests and complaints seem never satisfied unless attended to by the top person. Consider also such responsibilities as the signing of documents, letters, and reports prepared by others on the staff which require his or her general imprimatur as head of the school, and we begin to sense the flavor of the figurehead role. Though superficiality often characterizes this role, it is carried out with a tone of sincerity befitting the status and dignity which the administrator brings to an event. The superintendent receives a call of complaint from a parent about a teacher attentively and sympathetically, only to privately refer the complaint to the principal. The superintendent reads a series of warm and personal statements of commendation for several students at an awards assembly for parents, having only just met the students and reading from a script prepared by the guidance counselor.

Though the figurehead has received only slight consideration in the literature of administration, the leader role has received extensive attention. As leader, the administrator sets the tone or climate of the school. The focus of this role is on the interpersonal relationships which exist between the leader and those being led. The administrator, for example, uses his or her formal authority to achieve better integration between the needs of teachers and the goals of the school. The administrator does this through such leadership-role activities as directing, guiding, developing, motivating, evaluating, correcting, and rewarding subordinates. This role is also manifested in such administrative tasks as recruiting, selecting, training, promoting, and dismissing subordinates.

Unlike the leader role, which focuses on vertical relationships between the administrator and others, the liaison role focuses on horizontal relationships. Like the figurehead role, this role has been virtually ignored in the literature of administration. The liaison role involves the web of relationships that the educational administrator maintains with groups and individuals outside the school. As George Homans has pointed out, the higher a person's social rank in a group or organization, the more frequently he interacts with persons outside his group or organization.[10] Thus the liaison role is likely to be more visible in administrative activities of the superintendent of schools than in those of the department chairperson or grade-level supervisor. By the same token, this chairperson or supervisor is likely to exhibit the liaison role more frequently than teachers. The network of contacts which are the fruits of liaison activities is cultivated by joining important community organizations, engaging in social activites, and attending conferences. "Keeping in touch" with important others, "building bridges" with influential groups, "making contact" with the right people, and "keeping the channels open" to all who can impact the school are the benefits sought by the administrator. Thus, this external linkage system can be both a source of information and a source of political support.

Informational Roles

Mintzberg suggests that in exercising his informational roles the administrator is akin to a nerve center which receives information of various types from an array of sources, processes this information by rejecting, altering, or approving, and disseminates this information to others in his organization. The nerve-center metaphor suggests the central postion which administrators occupy in receiving and moving information. This influential and advantageous vantage point at the organizational nerve center results from the administrator's unique

[10]George C. Homans, *The Human Group* (New York: Harcourt Brace Jovanovich, 1950), p. 186.

access to external information (liaison role, for example) and his or her access to internal information derived from his or her formal authority (leader role). Three informational roles are identified by Mintzberg to characterize administrative activity associated with this nerve-center position; the *monitor* role, through which the administrator becomes informed about the school and its environment, and the *disseminator* and *spokesperson* roles, through which the administrator transmits information to others inside and outside the organization.

As monitor, the administrator seeks information from others, and on the other hand is bombarded by information from others which helps in understanding what is going on within the school and the school's environment. Information received by the chief executives who Mintzberg studied fell into five categories:

1.   Information about the progress of *internal operations* and events gleaned from reports, meetings, informal conversations, and observational tours of his organization.

2.   Information about *external events* concerning parents and other community groups, other schools, political, civic and governmental agencies, and new developments in education.

3.   Information derived from the *analysis of reports* on various issues. Reports come from a variety of solicited and unsolicited sources. Some are internal reports; others are policy memoranda from the state department of education or the federal government; still others arrive in the mail from state universities, professional associations, and seemingly endless other sources.

4.   Information gleaned from conferences, formal and informal meetings, and other sources which helps the administrator to better understand significant *ideas and trends* from the environment which touches his or her organization.

5.   Information brought to the administrator in the form of, or as a result of, *pressures* and demands from a variety of sources.

Much of the information obtained and processed in the monitoring role is simply transferred into the organization or passed on to others outside the organization. In the disseminator role, the administrator passes into the organization both factual (what is) and value (what ought to be) information. Exactly what information to pass, in what detail, to whom, and how often, can pose significant problems for the administrator. Since most of the information he or she has is stored in memory, it generally requires verbal dissemination, and this can be a time-consuming process. Therefore, in the interest of conserving time, not all of the relevant information gets passed down to subordinates, and this in turn effects the nature and quality of their work. To ensure that subordinates better meet his or her standards, the administrator can increase the amount and kind of information disseminated, but at the risk of role overload. As Mintzberg characterizes this dilemma, "Hence the manager is damned by his own information system either to a life of overwork or to one of frustration. In the first case, he does too many tasks himself or spends too much time disseminating verbal information; in the second case, he must watch as delegated tasks are performed inadequately, according to his standards, by the uninformed."[11] Though normative views of administration espouse the maximum flow of information and require that the administrator settle for none less than top performance, evidence from the real world suggests that, of necessity, not all the available information is disseminated, and administrators do settle for less than best.

In the spokesperson role the administrator transmits information out to the school's environment. The administrator is expected, for example, to speak on behalf of the organization, to lobby for the organization, to serve as a public-relations figure, and to represent the organization as an expert. Two groups need to be kept informed: the organization's set of key influencers as defined by legitimate authority, and the array of publics who by virtue of the political process exert influence on the school. With regard to the first group, for example, department chairpersons are obliged to keep principals informed of department activities and, similarly, school superintendents are obliged to keep school boards informed. The second group to whom the spokesperson role is addressed is vast, but typically includes parents, business groups, teacher organizations, state department representatives, suppliers, newspaper reporters, and potential employers of graduating students.

In executing the spokesperson role the administrator is required to have accurate and up-to-the-minute information about the organization and its environment. Further, the information needs to be disseminated in a dignified and credible manner. The administrator must therefore be an expert on the affairs of the organization, and be able to activate this expertness in a commanding and convincing manner. The information roles are summarized and illustrated in Figure 12–3.

The Decisional Roles

The third set of administrative activities identified by Mintzberg involves the making of significant decisions. Decisional roles are typi-

[11]Mintzberg, *Nature of Managerial Work,* p. 75.

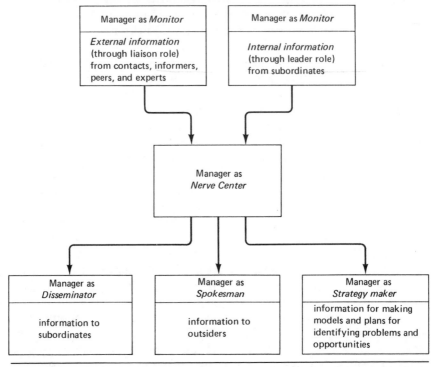

FIGURE 12–3
The manager as information processing system

Manager as *Monitor*	Manager as *Monitor*
External information (through liaison role) from contacts, informers, peers, and experts	*Internal information* (through leader role) from subordinates

Manager as
Nerve Center

Manager as *Disseminator*	Manager as *Spokesman*	Manager as *Strategy maker*
information to subordinates	information to outsiders	information for making models and plans for identifying problems and opportunities

Source: Henry Mintzberg, *The Nature of Managerial Work* (New York: Harper & Row, 1973), p. 72.

cally considered to be at the heart of administrative work and to be a natural outlet of the administrator's formal authority and strong access to information. Formal authority and access to information are important sources of power which legitimize the administrator's decision-making prerogatives. On occasions where the former can be successfully challenged, the latter is sufficiently strong to ensure these prerogatives. Though the normative literature speaks often of the value of shared or participatory decision making, Mintzberg was impressed with the extent to which the executives he studied were in command of the decision-making process. He notes that they were substantially involved in all significant decisions made by their organizations. He further suggests that, contrary to normative views which prescribe rational and goal-maximizing decision making, the administrators he studied tended to "satisfice."[12] They were inclined to accept courses of action which were "good enough" rather than best. Indeed, decision making might better be viewed as a "science of muddling through"[13] rather than a rational science.

Four decisional roles were identified by Mintzberg; *entrepreneur, disturbance handler, resource allocator,* and *negotiator.* In the entrepreneur role the administrator initiates and designs programs intended to improve the organization. To this effort he or she is constantly scanning the organization, being alert to problems. Once problems are identified, a program is begun which may directly involve the administrator further, or more typically, which requires delegating to others. As this program is implemented, the administrator is constantly called upon to authorize and approve activities of subordinates. The administrator maintains supervisory control and retains responsibility for all design decisions associated with the program.

As an entrepreneur the administrator initiates action of his or her own will; but as a disturbance handler, is forced into situations—some of which may well be beyond his or her control. A teacher strike, cafeteria fight, student insurrection, or false fire alarm might be examples of disturbance crises to which the administrator must respond. But many other instances are less dramatic and require more long-range attention. Handling competition among elementary schools or high-school departments for scarce resources, deciding which school will be closed, settling on a reduction-in-force policy, constantly reassigning students in an effort to meet desegregation commitments, and dealing with personality clashes among staff members might be examples.

The disturbance-handling role often receives more notice than other administrative roles because of the suddenness with which disturbances tend to emerge, the presumption of high stakes at risk by those involved, emotional overtones, and the general urgency felt to get things resolved. Therefore, though activities associated with other roles may be more important, they take a back seat as the administrator is pressed into the disturbance-handling role.

In any organization, resources such as time, money, materials, equipment, and human talent must be allocated. When an administrator is involved in making decisions about significant organizational resources, he or she is behaving as a resource allocator. This role was evidenced in the Mintzberg study in three essential ways—scheduling

---

[12]Herbert A. Simon, *Models of Man* (New York: John Wiley, 1957), p. 204.

[13]Charles E. Lindblum, "The Science of Muddling Through," *Public Administrator Review,* 19 (1959). See, for example, our Chapter 14, "The Decision-Making Process," for a contrast of rational and non-rational decision models.

time, programming work, and authorizing decisions by others. As the administrator schedules time, he or she communicates to others what is important and what is not. Issues of low priority, for example, do not command much of the administrator's time. By programming work, the administrator controls and schedules the time of others. In effect, he or she decides what will be done, by whom, and under what conditions; therefore ensuring that high-priority issues are attended to. Human resources are allocated toward ends considered important. By authorizing action, the administrator maintains control over significant decisions made by subordinates, again ensuring that time and energy are used in a manner considered appropriate. Budget control is, of course, still another facet of the resource allocating role of administrators. There is no doubt that the administrator is aware of the power implicit in controlling the allocation of organizational resources. Further, he or she shows little hesitation in exercising this power.

The administrator as negotiator is the final decisional role identified by Mintzberg. In exercising this role the administrator: represents the group or organization as it negotiates with other units within the organization (one department with another, one school with another); negotiates with identifiable subgroups associated with the organization (the teachers' union); and negotiates with outside agencies (accrediting teams, park district, mayor's office). This role is difficult to delegate because other partners to the negotiation often refuse to settle for substitutes, demanding typically to negotiate with the chief administrator.

Table 12–1 contains a summary description of each of the ten administrator roles identified by Mintzberg and the administrative activities associated with each role, and it comments on the attention that each role has received in the literature of administration.

VARIATIONS IN ADMINISTRATORS' WORK

The literature in administration suggests that role activities are more similar than different across administrative jobs in different kinds of organizations and across administrative jobs within the same organization. Each of the ten roles we discuss are likely to be present to some degree in virtually all administrative positions. Differences, therefore, would be in emphasis rather than in kind. Though all of the roles can be identified in the activities of both elementary and secondary school principals, for example, different combinations of roles will likely be emphasized.

Hierarchical level within an organization also seems to influence the combinations of role emphasis one observes. Chairpersons, principals, and superintendents engage in each of the roles, but some are emphasized more than others, depending upon level. The leader role might be dominant for chairpersons; resource allocator, for principals; and spokesperson, for the superintendent of a given district. Size of school, complexity of educational programs, expectations of teachers and community, and the personal idiosyncrasies of individual administrators can also be expected to influence the emphasis given to activities of each role.

Mintzberg noted in his study that the activities and work conditions of the school superintendent he studied differed somewhat from those of non-educational administrators.[14] The superintendent's work, for example, was characterized by greater formality and more scheduled meetings. The meetings often took place in the evening. The superintendent met more frequently than did others with the school board and, particularly, with the parents. He also experienced more formal authority requests and relied more on analysis in the form of written reports. The greater flow of information to and from government agencies was another important difference noted.

Further research is needed to map out the specific role descriptions which typify various educational administrative jobs and settings. We are able in a very general sense, however, to speak of clusters of role emphasis and of the administrative styles they represent. Mintzberg suggests eight such styles, each of which emphasizes a certain combination of key roles. These are summarized below.[15]

Administrative Style	Key Roles
contact person	liaison, figurehead
political administrator	spokesperson, negotiator
entrepreneur	entrepreneur, negotiator
insider	resource-allocator, leader
real-time administrator	disturbance handler
team administrator	leader
expert administrator	monitor, spokesperson
new administrator	liaison, monitor

The contact person, for example, spends a great deal of time outside the organization. The liaison and figurehead roles dominate. Activities which characterize this style are doing favors for others, winning fa-

[14]Mintzberg, *Nature of Managerial Work,* pp. 262–264. Indeed, though similarities existed, each of the executives studied did exhibit some unique characteristics.
[15]*Ibid.,* p. 127.

TABLE 12–1

A summary of administrative roles and activities*

Role	Description	Identifiable activities from study of chief executives	Recognition in the literature
Interpersonal			
Figurehead	Symbolic head; obliged to perform a number of routine duties of a legal or social nature	Ceremony, status requests, solicitations	Sometimes recognized, but usually only at highest organizational levels
Leader	Responsible for the motivation and activation of subordinates; responsible for staffing, training, and associated duties	Virtually all managerial activities involving subordinates	Most widely recognized of all managerial roles
Liaison	Maintains self-developed network of outside contacts and informers who provide favors and information	Acknowledgments of mail; external board work; other activities involving outsiders	Largely ignored, except for particular empirical studies (Sayles on lower- and middle-level managers, Neustadt on U.S. Presidents, Whyte and Homans on informal leaders)
Informational			
Monitor	Seeks and receives wide variety of special information (much of it current) to develop thorough understanding of organization and environment; emerges as nerve center of internal and external information of the organization	Handling all mail and contacts categorized as concerned primarily with receiving information (e.g., periodical news, observational tours)	Recognized in the work of Sayles, Neustadt, Wrapp, and especially Aguilar
Disseminator	Transmits information received from outsiders or from other subordinates to members of the organization; some information factual, some involving interpretation and integration of diverse value positions of organizational influencers	Forwarding mail into organization for informational purposes, verbal contacts involving information flow to subordinates (e.g., review sessions, instant communication flows)	Unrecognized (except for Papandreou discussion of "peak coordinator" who integrates influencer preferences)

328

TABLE 12-1 Continued

Role	Description	Identifiable activities from study of chief executives	Recognition in the literature
Spokesman	Transmits information to outsiders on organization's plans, policies, actions, results, etc.; serves as expert on organization's industry	Board meetings; handling mail and contacts involving transmission of information to outsiders	Generally acknowledged as managerial role
Decisional			
Entrepreneur	Searches organization and its environment for opportunities and initiates "improvement projects" to bring about change; supervises design of certain projects as well	Strategy and review sessions involving initiation or design of improvement projects	Implicitly acknowledged, but usually not analyzed except for economists (who were concerned largely with the establishment of new organizations) and Sayles, who probes into this role
Disturbance Handler	Responsible for corrective action when organization faces important, unexpected disturbances	Strategy and review sessions involving disturbances and crises	Discussed in abstract way by many writers (e.g., management by exception) but analyzed carefully only by Sayles
Resource Allocator	Responsible for the allocation of organizational resources of all kinds—in effect the making or approval of all significant organizational decisions	Scheduling; requests for authorization; any activity involving budgeting and the programming of subordinates' work	Little explicit recognition as a role, although implicitly recognized by the many who analyze organizational resource-allocation activities
Negotiator	Responsible for representing the organization at major negotiations	Negotiation	Largely unrecognized (or recognized but claimed to be nonmanagerial work) except for Sayles

Source: Henry Mintzberg, *The Nature of Managerial Work* (New York: Harper & Row, 1973), pp. 92–93.
* F. J. Aguilar, *Scanning the Business Environment*. N.Y.: Macmillan, 1967; G. C. Homans, *The Human Group*. N.Y.: Harcourt Brace Jovanovich, 1950; R. E. Newstadt, *Presidential Power: The Politics of Leadership*. N.Y.: John Wiley, 1960; A. G. Papandreou, "Some Basic Problems in the Theory of the Firm." B. F. Haley, (ed.) *A Survey of Contemporary Economics*. Homewood, Ill. Irwin Vol. 2, pp. 183–219; L. R. Sayles, *Managerial Behavior: Administration in Complex Organizations*. N.Y.: McGraw-Hill, 1964; W. F. Whyte, *Street Corner Gang, Second Edition*. Chicago: University of Chicago Press, 1955; H. E. Wrapp, "Good Managers Don't Make Policy Decisions." *Harvard Business Review*. Vol. 45, 1967, p. 91–99.

vors in return, building a friendship network of support, giving speeches, and attending a variety of functions. The emphasis is on public relations and the intent is to build favorable linkages with important individuals and groups outside the organization who are in a position to influence the organization. School-community-relations literature and practices reflected the contact-person style popular during the 1950s and 1960s.

The political administrator also spends a great deal of time and energy with outside groups and individuals, but not for superficial, polite, or ceremonial public-relations reasons. This type of administrator, caught in a complex web of controversy, enters the outside arena with the intent to reconcile conflicting forces acting on the school. Key roles here are those of spokesperson and negotiator. Though the contact-person style is popular with administrators in more stable and homogeneous communities (small towns, isolated suburb), conditions are such in most school environments that now administrators are likely to assume the political-administrator style to a greater degree.

The administrator as entrepreneur seeks opportunities for change and for introducing programs within the school. Entrepreneur and negotiator roles characterize this style. This style was particularly popular during the 1960s as we experienced a period of expansion and innovation in education, and it still thrives today in communities and settings where administrators continue to enjoy strong professional prerogatives. The increased political nature of educational policy making now being experienced in many school districts, however, makes this style more difficult to articulate.

Insider administrators are primarily concerned with the operation and maintenance of smoothly running schools. Working primarily from resource-allocator and leader roles, they concentrate on overseeing school operations, nurturing and developing internal programs, and supervising the staff. Many elementary and secondary school principals can be characterized as insiders. Sometimes the insider is the second in command, responsible for running the school or district, letting the superintendent or principal tend to outside affairs.

Real-time administrators are insiders of a different sort. They are primarily interested in internal maintenance, and focus on day-to-day problems. They are constantly busy with "putting out fires," and seem to have a "finger in every pie." Disturbance handler is the dominant role. In schools where discipline is a serious problem, school security is tenuous, or other constant crises exist, the administrator may be forced into this style.

The team administrator is also oriented to the inside, but his or her interest is in building a highly effective, cohesive work group characterized by high morale and mutual support among teachers. By comparison, other roles are overshadowed by the attention that team administrators give to the leader role. This style suits many principalships, particularly those of smaller schools not characterized by strained labor-management relations and where informal organizational designs dominate.

Expert administrators are those who, in addition to assuming administrative responsibility, continue to participate in the specialized work of the school. Special-education and art supervisors, teaching principals, and department chairpersons might be examples. Key roles here are monitor and spokesperson.

The last administrative style discussed by Mintzberg is one *new* to the job. Lacking a network of contacts and sufficient information, the *new* administrator emphasizes liaison and monitor role activities. "The decisional roles cannot become fully operative until he has more information. When he does, he is likely to stress the entrepreneur role for a time, as he attempts to put his distinct stamp on his organization. Then he may settle down to be one of the other managerial types—contact man, insider or some other type."[16]

SUMMARY

Our intent in this chapter was to provide readers with a glimpse of the real world and work of administration. Relying on the work of Mintzberg and others of the work-activity school, ten administrative roles characteristic of most administrative jobs were identified. The roles were grouped into three major categories: interpersonal, informational, and decisional. It was observed that despite the presence of the roles in most jobs, differences could be found based on the emphases which each of the roles received. Eight administative styles were identified, each resulting from a distinct combination of role emphasis. The focus of this chapter is on the "real" rather that the "ideal," the "is" rather than the "ought." This descriptive emphasis, where administrators have to satisfy constraints, is in contrast to the more common normative view of administration, where it is assumed that administrators behave to maximize objectives. Though the balance in the literature is clearly in favor of normative views and the need is great to

[16]*Ibid.,* p. 129.

enrich the descriptive literature, a caveat is in order. Administrators cannot be seduced by the descriptive literature into willy-nilly acceptance of affairs as they are, and behave accordingly. This positon would gravely distort the concept of leadership. But neither can administrators ignore the realities of their world. To do so would result in a naïve and ineffectual articulation of leadership. What is needed is a better balance and integration of both views, and this need suggests a likely future for research-and-development efforts in educational administration.

STUDY GUIDE

Can you recall the meaning of the following terms? Discuss them with a class colleague and apply them to your school-community setting.

administrative styles	organizations as coalitions
decisional roles	organizations as rational
descriptive theory	collectivities
informational roles	role
interpersonal roles	role emphasis
normative theory	work-activity school

SUGGESTED ACTIVITIES

1. Prepare a chart or other illustration which compares normative and descriptive aspects of administrative work.

2. Select several positions in a typical school district (chairperson, principal, director of instruction, superintendent, etc.) for study and analysis. For each position determine which of the roles exhibited in Table 12–1 seem dominant.

3. Write a paragraph or two for each role, describing the extent to which you feel comfortable with displaying the behaviors associated with the role.

4. Prepare a brief report on stress in administration. Discuss the extent to which such practices as physical exercise and meditation can contribute to stress management.

SELECTED READINGS

BARNARD, CHESTER, *The Functions of the Executive.* Cambridge: Harvard University Press, 1938.

CROSS, RAY, "The Principal as Counterpuncher," *The National Elementary Principal,* 2, no. 2 (1975), 26–29.

MARCH, JAMES G. "American Public School Administration: A Short Analysis," *School Review,* February 1978, pp. 217–250.

MARCH, JAMES G. "Analytical Skills and the University Training of Educational Administrators," *Journal of Educational Administration,* 12 (1974), 17–44.

MINTZBERG, HENRY, *The Nature of Managerial Work.* New York: Harper & Row, 1973.

SLOAN, A. P., *My Years with General Motors.* Garden City, N.Y.: Doubleday, 1963.

SORENSON, T. C., *Decision Making in the White House.* New York: Columbia University Press, 1963.

WOLCOTT, HARRY J., *The Man in the Principal's Office.* New York: Holt, Rinehart & Winston, 1973.

13

PLANNING
AND
TIME MANAGEMENT
IN EDUCATION

Though educational administrators speak often among themselves about the nature and characteristics of their work, only recently has research grown in this area. Such research is not yet extensive; but even in its preliminary stages, descriptions which emerge strike a chord of familiarity among practicing administrators. As suggested in our discussion in Chapter 12, job-characteristics questions refer to where administrators work, how long they work, what means they use to communicate, and what work patterns emerge day to day and week to week. This is in contrast to job-content questions from which administrative roles are inferred.

This chapter examines some of the characteristics found common to the work of administration, and considers the ways in which administrators can increase their control over the work context. The analysis of planning and time management as a means to gain control is sobering, however, for such concepts are typically oversold and this leads to disappointment among practitioners. One outcome of this chapter is the suggestion that though administrators can increase their control over events to some degree, much of the nature of their jobs will remain beyond their grasp. To the optimist, this is cheering news, for finding an extra hour a day or increasing discretion by 15 percent over how one can spend his or her time can have a significant effect on administrative and organizational effectiveness. This chapter begins by examining some of the emerging research that attempts to map the characteristics of administrative work.

THE CHARACTERISTICS
OF ADMINISTRATIVE WORK

In a recent study of educational administrators of new educational programs, Sproul found that words such as "local," "verbal," "choppy," and "varied" were used most often to describe the typical administrative workday.[1] The subjects of Sproul's research were administrators of programs considered innovative, such as heading a high-school urban career-education or a regional bilingual-education consortium.

Choppiness, for example, was evidenced by the presence of many activities of brief duration. The composite administrator in Sproul's study engaged daily in fifty-six activities, each averaging about nine minutes in duration, and sixty-five events, each averaging six minutes. Events were described as periods of time one minute or longer during which administrators used one medium such as a phone, meeting, individual conversation, memo, or letter to work on one purpose. Activities were collections of events devoted to one purpose. This distinction, according to Sproul, was forced by numerous interruptions that characterized the administrator's work day. Conceivably, without interruption, each activity could be completed by one event. Choppiness, then, is reflected in the vast array of events and activities of short duration which characterize the work day. This choppiness is illustrated in the following excerpt from Sproul's field notes:

> Manager A is sitting at his desk writing a letter of recommendation about one of the students in his program for her college applications (20 min.). Teacher 1 comes in and asks him to have a student project form reprinted because the supply is running low (1 min.). Teacher 1 leaves and the manager resumes writing the letter of recommendation (1 min.). Teacher 2 comes in (the manager 3.5 hours earlier had asked the secretary to tell this teacher to see him) and the manager asks him about his behavior toward one of his students. (Earlier in the day the manager had received a call from an angry parent complaining that teacher 2 had mistreated her child.) After the manager hears Teacher 2's side of the story (he had heard from the student

[1]Lee S. Sproul, "Managerial Attention in New Educational Systems." Paper prepared for seminar on Organizations as Loosely Coupled Systems, University of Illinois, Urbana, Nov. 13–14, 1976.

earlier), he cautions the teacher about "not kidding around too much with kids who might not understand" (18 min.). The secretary enters with letters that must be signed right away in order to go out in the afternoon mail (1 min.). After signing them, the manager continues writing the letter of recommendation (1 min.). Teacher 3 brings in a list of students chosen to fill out a district-wide questionnaire about "career awareness." Only half of the listed students, who had been randomly selected by the district computer from fall enrollment registers, were still enrolled in the program. The teacher and manager replace the names of the no-longer-enrolled with the names of "kids who will be around tomorrow," the day the questionnaire is to be administered (5 min). Teacher 3 leaves and the manager resumes working on the letter of recommendation (5 min).[2]

Consider below the other work characteristics identified by Sproul. She notes that on a composite basis,

1. Seventy-five percent of the workday was spent locally in the program office.

2. Seventy-eight percent of the workday was spent in *verbal* interaction, mostly in personnel interaction (66%) and telephoning (11%). Wolcott, in his study of an elementary school principal, estimated that 76 percent of the workday was spent in verbal interaction.[3]

3. The average number of different topics in a given day to which the administrator attended was 26. Because of this *variety,* each topic received on the average only 20 minutes of attention.

Similarly, Mintzberg, in his study of five executives including a school superintendent, finds the work of administrators characterized by brevity, variety, and fragmentation.[4] He notes that the majority of administrative activity is of brief duration—often taking only minutes. The variety is not only great but often without pattern or connectedness, and typically is interspersed with trivia. The administrator, as a result, is required to shift moods and intellectual frames frequently and quickly. These characteristics suggest a high level of superficiality in the work of administration.

Mintzberg further notes that because of the open-ended nature of his job, the administrator is compelled to perform a great amount of

[2]Sproul's field notes of April 27, 1976, as quoted in *Ibid.,* p. 5.

[3]Harry J. Wolcott, *The Man in the Principal's Office* (New York: Holt, Rinehart & Winston, 1973).

[4]This section follows Henry Mintzberg, *The Nature of Managerial Work* (New York: Harper & Row, 1973), pp. 29–53.

work at an unrelenting pace—a further contributor to superficiality. Free time is only rarely available, and job responsibilities seem inescapable. A 1965 study of the secondary-school principalship revealed that principals studied spent fifty, often sixty, hours a week on job activities.[5] A 1971 study of the superintendency suggest a work week in excess of sixty hours for about one-half of the superintendents studied.[6] Evening and weekend work was common to the superintendency.

The administrators in Mintzberg's study demonstrated a preference for live action and for verbal means of handling this action. The current and active elements of the job were preferred over the abstract, technical, and routine. Visiting personally, talking on the telephone, and formal and informal conferences were the common strategies. Because of the propensity for verbal interaction, much of the business of the organization remains unrecorded and stored in the administrator's memory, making delegation and shared decision making difficult. The administrator is overloaded in exclusive knowledge about the organization, and in meeting commitments on his time as others seek this information. It is difficult to keep on top of events and in control of organizational activities, and seemingly, no mechanisim exists to relieve him or her of responsibilities. Faced with the apparent requirement that he or she be involved in most everything, the recourse is to treat work activities with a distinct superficial flair.

As Laswell suggests, "The man who keeps on top of his responsibilities is likely to suffer from chronic fatigue and exasperation, and unless he has an exceptional natural constitution, a quick mind, and selective habits of work, he falls further and further behind."[7]

Though educational administrators are likely to find the description of their world of work familiar, this familarity does not lessen their anxiety over what often seems an impossible dilemma. Understandably, attempts are made to bring order to one's administrative life of apparent confusion; to seek control over one's work activities. This search for order and control is what makes discussions of planning-and-time-management theories and models so appealing to educational administrators.

[5]John Hemphill, James Richards, and Richard Peterson, *Report of The Senior High-School Principalship* (Washington, D.C.: The National Association of Secondary School Principals, 1965).

[6]Stephen Knezevich, ed., *The American School Superintendent: An AASA Research Study* (Washington, D.C.: AASA Commission on the Preparation of Professional School Administrators, AASA, 1971).

[7]Harold D. Laswell, *A Pre-View of Policy Sciences* (New York: Elsevier North-Holland, 1971), p. 34.

TIME AS A SCARCE RESOURCE

Time is a scarce resource in the sense that any future allocation of time is diminished by the amount allocated to present activities. Further, since the number of activities which can be simultaneously tended to is limited, time spent on one activity results in neglect of others. But time distribution is a social-psychological concept as well as one in economics. Symbolically, how an administrator uses time is a form of administrative attention with meaning to others in the school. It is assumed that an administrator gives attention to the events and activities he or she values. Spending a great deal of time on interpersonal relationships, educational program objectives, building student identity with the school and its programs, or in some other area, communicates to teachers and students that this sort of activity is of worth to the administrator and school. As others learn the value of this activity to the administrator, they also are likely to give it attention. Administrative attention, then, can be considered a form of modeling for others who work in the school. Through administrative attention, the principal contributes to setting the tone or climate of the school and communicates to others the goals and activities which should enjoy high priority.

The social-psychological effects of administrative attention tend to occur whether or not they are intended. An elementary-school principal might, for example, *espouse* an educational platform which suggests a deep commitment to building a strong educational program sensitive to individual needs of students, taught by a happy and commited faculty, and supported by his or her school-community. But this platform is likely to be ignored in favor of the one which students, teachers, and parents infer on the basis of administrative attention. Protestations to the contrary, if most of his or her time is spent on busy office work and on administrative maintenance activities, observers will learn that "running a smooth ship" is the goal of real value to the principal and school, and will likely behave accordingly.

In sum, administrative attention not only has obvious management effects when considered in an economic sense as a scarce resource, but has social psychological effects as well. The potency of administrative attention is the reason why discussions of planning and time management are important.

PLANNING IN EDUCATION

Most authorities agree that educational leadership requires administrators to give adequate attention to planning. Indeed the good principal, it is often said, plans in advance what to do, how to do it, and when to do it. Further, this planning helps him or her to organize the means to achieve these ends, to provide the necessary personal leadership to others who will ultimately carry out the plans, and to evaluate progress. In this sense, planning is a rational and deliberate attempt to carefully map out the future.

Elsewhere in this book we have suggested that organizational life is not as rational as one might like, and that administrative behavior is limited by human characteristics of administrators as persons and by political, financial, and other constraints which define the administrator's work context. In accord with this view, James G. March likens decision making in organization to a "garbage can." Various school problems and solutions are deposited in this can, though typically solutions are only loosely connected to the problem.[8] Given the garbage-can metaphor, March and his associates would suggest that a better image of planning and decision making is one which assumes that *solutions exist which must be matched to problems*. It is often presumed, for example, that a group of teachers who adopt a teaching program, such as mainstreaming instruction in the arts with the traditional academic program (a solution), do so in response to a *problem—* such as neglect of the arts in the curriculum. But what may really be the case is that *the problem is invented* to accommodate the preferences, training, and beliefs of the teacher (solutions). The "garbage can" metaphor and other images which portray the non-rational nature of decision-making are considered further in Chapter 14.

Planning of any duration or in any detail, according to this view, may well be an academic exercise with marginal utility to educational administrators. Perhaps a more balanced position would be to accept the limitation of planning suggested by March and his associates, but to view them as limitations to an otherwise purposive and rational-striving process.[9] Planning should best be viewed as an important and helpful process which can improve effectiveness. But at the same time, one needs to acknowledge that the planning process is limited by human frailty and the political process.

One example of a rational perspective on planning in education is that referred to generally as systems analysis. As a construct around which one might organize one's thinking, systems analysis offers a number of benefits. But too often, systems analysis underplays human

[8]See, for example, Michael Cohen, James March, and Johan Olsen, "A Garbage Can Model of Organizational Choice," *Administrative Science Quarterly*, 17 (March 1972), pp. 1–25.

[9]See, for example, Thomas J. Sergiovanni and Fred D. Carver, *The New School Executive: A Theory of Administration*, 2nd ed. (New York: Harper & Row, 1980), chapter 14.

and political limitations and thus assumes an unrealistic posture of rigidity and infallibility. A discussion of systems planning is considered below.

SYSTEMS ANALYSIS

Systems thinking focuses attention on the complex of interdependencies which exists between parts and the processes required to identify predictable relationships among these parts. The systems analyst is interested in breaking the whole into its interdependent parts and understanding how the parts effect each other and the whole. When his or her tools are applied to planning in administration, the following steps are typically followed:

1. The assessment and justification of needs in terms of validity criteria lead to the structuring of new goals and/or redefinition of existing goals.

2. The definition of goals stimulate policy formulation and the resulting policy decisions establish performance requirements which are assigned to management.

3. Management must analyze performance requirements in order that it can define a complete array of performance specifications which can be used to explain the performance requirements.

4. The specifications are classified and categorized according to levels of organization and a hierarchy of performance objectives can be defined in measurable terms.

5. Performance objectives are the fundamental basis of plans-each plan outlines a course of action and details appropriate management controls.

6. Plans must be verified in terms of the performance context and the action sequence (strategy) which has been developed to accomplish the objective.

It should be noted that a plan is the best alternative solution which will fully satisfy the specifications. A strategy, on the other hand, embodies the communication elements (information, education, and motivation) required to make the plan work in terms of required compromises, adaptations, adjustments, and concessions.

7. A strategy which has been validated through feedback and control is a reliable management procedure for the achievement of objectives.

8. The establishment of a management procedure facilitates the achievement of performance consistency in spite of the internal and external constraints on performance.

9. The resulting performance can be evaluated to determine the effectiveness of performance in terms of previously specified criteria and specifications.

10. The achievement of desired levels-of-performance proficiency produces change. Such change will produce new needs, which, when justified, will stimulate the formulation of new goals, and the cyclic phenomenon will continue.[10]

The steps raise significant questions and issues which should be attended by educational administrators. But if the steps are taken literally as a rigid blueprint for action, some problems become apparent. These problems are shared as well by other planning systems characterized by such "engineering" characteristics as preciseness, formality, rigidity, rationality, and step-wise or linear processes.

1. The problem of reductionism

Systems analysis requires that problems and problem components, goals and goal components, and inputs and input components, be reduced to their lowest denominators before they are dealt with. Problems are decomposed into subproblems, and subproblems are then solved more or less independently. Total solution to major problems, then, take the form of collections of smaller solutions, or subsolutions. Major problems, however, are often obscured and the "forest is often missed because the trees are in the way."

2. The problem of overplanning and overcommitment

One hazard of defining objectives too specifically, of deciding on narrowly defined alternatives, of establishing rather clear-cut procedures and arrangements for implementing alternatives, and of creating specific structures and forms to facilitate these arrangements is that the mold remains long after its usefulness or desirability diminishes. Building an educational facility to carefully match a specific educational program, for example, can continue to mandate this program long after interest in it has passed.

3. Emphasis on mechanistic dimensions

Systems-analysis techniques, if taken literally, are by definition geared to bring out highest production at lowest cost. Production, in order to meet the demands of strict systems analysis, usually takes some quantifiable form, such as how many students graduate, how many points on an achievement test, how many dropouts. Other, often

[10]Donald R. Miller, "Policy Formulation and Policy Implementation in an Educational System," in Richard Kraft, ed., *Strategies for Educational Planning* (Tallahassee, Fla.: Educational Systems Development Center, Florida State University, 1969), p. 25.

more important objectives and outcomes are neglected because they are difficult to operationalize and seem not to easily fit the systems model.

4. Reduction of discretion

Systems analysis, if applied literally, is an extreme form of centralization which increases control of top management. In this sense, system analysis is a form of management control which can decrease discretion of teachers and other professional workers. The result of this decrease, according to Gerald Bell, is an increase in rigidity; a decrease in vertical communications; an increase in administrative coordination; a decrease in self-control and group supervision; a decrease in voluntary, internal, or professional compliance; a decrease in satisfaction and consideration; and ultimately a decrease in goal attainment —the reason for adopting system techniques in the first place.[11]

CAUTION IN PLANNING

Planning is an essential requirement in building administrative effectiveness. But hazards exist as one plans.[12] Of particular concern is adopting a highly formalistic planning strategy which does not match the unique characteristics of schools. Several studies do demonstrate that in many cases formal planning can be more effective than informal planning. One study, for example, shows that business organizations with formal planning procedures outperformed those which relied on informal planning on such performance indications as earnings on common equity and earnings per share.[13] Another study shows a 130 percent increase in profit for formal-planning–oriented business organizations as compared with 59 percent over the same period for those who relied on informal planning.[14] Studies of this sort are often viewed as convincing by policy makers in this day of accountability and cost-benefit analysis. But similar evidence in favor of a formal-planning

[11]Gerald Bell, *Organization and Human Behavior: A Book of Readings* (Englewood Cliffs, N.J.: Prentice-Hall, 1967), p. 101. The cooperative-system approach is an alternative system strategy which permits discretion at lower organizational trends. See Sergiovanni and Carver, *The New School Executive.*

[12]See for example, Sergiovanni and Carver, *The New School Executive.*

[13]Stanley Thune and Robert House, "Where Long-Range Planning Pays Off," *Business Horizons,* August 1970.

[14]David Herold, "Long Range Planning and Organizational Performance: A Cross-Validation Study," *Academy of Management Journal,* March 1972.

emphasis in *public* organization does not exist. As a rule of thumb, the more structured the organization, the more standardized and reliable the work process, the more agreement on goals, the more obvious and refined the technology, the more insulated the organization from its environment, and the more authority vested in management, then the greater the gain in emphasizing formal planning. Contrasting these characteristics typical of business organization with those of schools and other public organizations presented in Chapter 2 suggests that *informal* planning strategies are more appropriate to the school.

A PRACTICAL APPROACH
TO PLANNING

Perhaps the greatest benefits of planning occur at the micro-level as individual administrators attempt to manage their own time more effectively and organize their workdays in better accord with school objectives. In this section a number of suggestions are offered as to how individual administrators might plan more effectively and achieve better utilization of time. The ideas presented, we believe, need to become a natural part of one's administrative style, and this goal is not achieved suddenly. In many respects, combining one's present career in education with preparation for an administrative career is sufficiently hectic to simulate, in a small way, the conditions one is likely to encounter on the administrative job. Thus, as one finds himself or herself in an introductory course in administration, this might be an opportune time to give the issue of micro-planning and time management attention, and to incorporate some of its features in one's own academic and professional life.

What follows, then, is a discussion of a relatively simple and informal approach to planning that is not dependent on larger or coordinated effort by others in the school. The essential parts of the planning process are illustrated in Figure 13-1.

As suggested in Figure 13-1, goals are desired ends or future status.[15] Plans differ from goals in that they suggest the general strategies or means to reach some future state. Activities are the more detailed steps and processes required to reach our goals. In a sense they represent the content of the plan—the specific means by which a strategy is implemented. Goals, plans, and activities are the planning components most often taken into account by administrators. Two

---

[15]This section follows Thomas J. Sergiovanni, *Handbook for Effective Department Leadership Concepts and Practices in Today's Secondary Schools* (Boston: Allyn & Bacon, 1977), pp. 250–257.

FIGURE 13-1
The planning process

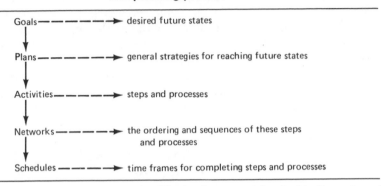

Source: T. J. Sergiovanni, Handbook for *Effective Department Leadership Concepts and Practices in Today's Secondary Schools* (Boston: Allyn & Bacon, 1977), p. 251.

additional components, networks and schedules, seem underemphasized in practice.

A network is the ordering and numbering of activities in sequence, thus showing more clearly what needs to be done and why. Developing an activity network becomes more important as the number of activities in the plan increases. Eight or more activities, for example, might well be the sign that a network is needed. The ordering and numbering of activities can be done most simply by developing a flow chart as follows:

This example shows that each activity must be completed in sequence. Typically, however, activities to be completed do not lend themselves to such single sequencing. Figure 13-2, for example, illustrates a number of other, more complex networks.

Most components of the planning process are concerned with the "what" and "how" of planning. Scheduling is concerned with the "when" of planning. Signs that an administrator may be slighting the scheduling aspect of planning are (1) being short of time after one begins an activity, (2) using the desk calendar as the only scheduling device, (3) scheduling only one week at a time, (4) being unable to combine a number of different activities, and (5) finding that one's planned activities are out of sequence with the plans of others.[16]

Networks become schedules when time frames are added. Scheduling is little more than putting dates and deadlines on activities which

[16]*Ibid.* pp. 252–253.

FIGURE 13-2
Examples of networks

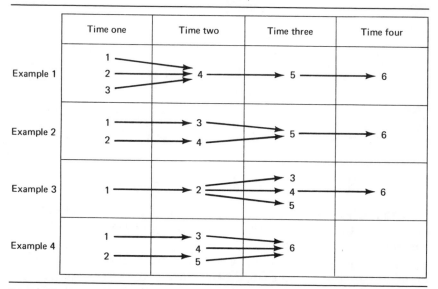

	Time one	Time two	Time three	Time four

Source: Thomas J. Sergiovanni, *Handbook for Effective Department Leadership Concepts and Practices in Today's Secondary Schools* (Boston: Allyn & Bacon, 1977), p. 253

are part of one's plans. The networks illustrated in Figure 13-2, for example, become network schedules when dates are added. Consider, for example, a principal who is asked to give an oral report on a special school program to the board of education. He or she decides to develop a network of activities and to determine the timing of these activities. As the presentation is planned he or she identifies and orders the following activities:

1. Develop report objectives.
2. Interview teachers involved in the program.
3. Review evaluation reports.
4. Write the report in the form of an oral presentation.
5. Have illustrations drawn.
6. Make transparencies.
7. Have report typed.
8. Rehearse report.
9. Give report.

FIGURE 13–3
A network schedule

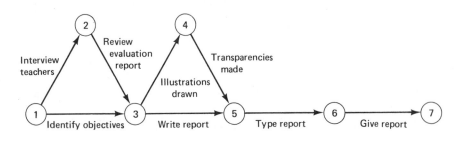

Source: T. J. Sergiovanni, *Handbook for Effective Department Leadership Concepts and Practices in Today's Secondary Schools* (Boston: Allyn & Bacon, 1977), p. 256.

The administrator then draws a network such as illustrated in Figure 13–3 to show the relationship between activities and the order in which they must be accomplished.

By casting this network over a calendar, or by estimating the number of days each step will take, the network is converted to a network schedule. Time estimates and calendar-casting techniques are shown together in Figure 13–4.[17] Schedules help answer such simple but important questions as, when should the project begin; how much time will each step or activity take; what difficulties might one encounter in meeting deadline; how much leeway exists between activities or steps;

FIGURE 13–4
Time and calendar casting network schedules

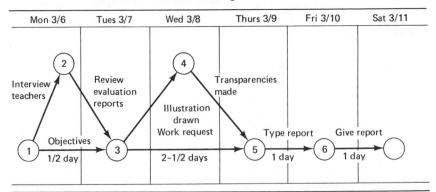

[17]More sophisticated means for determining time-frames exist. See for example, Ralph A. Van Dusseldorp, Duane Richardson, and Walter Foley, *Educational Decision-Making Through Operations Research* (Boston: Allyn & Bacon, 1971).

is it important to stay on schedule; and must each activity begin immediately after the previous activity?

TIME MANAGEMENT

Finding sufficient time to plan and to articulate one's plans is a task of no small consequence. Most administrators are already working long hours and are expending maximum effort at work. To suggest that one find *additional* time or *new* sources of energy to meet present and new job demands is not reasonable. But working hard or working long hours and *working effectively* are not the same. An administrator might be at the limit of his or her investment in energy and time, yet still increase effectiveness by managing time more efficiently. Time-management experts, for example, often speak of "working smarter, not harder."

Our caveats with respect to planning apply as well to this discussion of time management. Time management can help increase effectiveness, but the gains are likely to be modest. Even the most effective administrators are in control of only a small part of their time. One is in control when he or she decides how the time will be used, has descretion over this time, and uses it in accord with his or her judgment. One is not in control when one is reacting to situations and conditions determined by others, or when one is engaged in routine organizational tasks and demands programmed by the larger bureaucratic and political environment within which he or she works. An ideal split of discretionary and non-discretionary time is one-third—two-thirds. But most educational administrators control less than one-third[18] and probably 10 to 20 percent might be a more accurate estimate.

Obtaining more discretionary time is only one stage in increasing effectiveness. Using their time wisely is the second stage. In Peter Drucker's words:

> Effective executives concentrate on the few major areas where superior performance will produce outstanding results. They force themselves to set priorities and stay with their priority decisions. They know that they have no choice but to do first things first—and second things not at all. The alternative is to get nothing done.[19]

---

[18]See, for example, Wolcott, *The Man in the Principal's Office.*
[19]Peter Drucker, *The Effective Executive* (New York: Harper & Row, 1967), p. 24.

Setting priorities requires that one has a clear understanding of the major components of his job and some sense of how they relate to expectations of the school or district or an educational agency. In attempting to identify these components and how they relate to school purposes, one needs to spend *less* time examining stated objectives and public lists of critical job components and *more* time in *inferring* the real component and objectives from careful study of what an administrator does and how he or she allocates time to these tasks and activities. A first step, therefore, in beginning a time-management program is to keep a detailed log of ones activities over a period of several weeks. The inconvenience of recording what it is that you are doing, with whom, for how long and why, every fifteen minutes or so is well worth the effort. In analyzing a time log, ask such questions as:

1.   What actual objectives and priorities can be inferred and how do they compare with my stated objectives and priorities?

2.   Do results obtained from different classes of activities justify the amount of time spent?

3.   What tasks and activities could be delegated without loss of effectiveness, and what tasks and activities should be retained?

4.   When others are involved in your work; what is the purpose of the involvement? Is involvement necessary? Are you using the time of others effectively?

In reviewing your time log, be conscious of omissions as well. What tasks and activities are not appearing as frequently as they should? Since total hours is likely to be fixed, any addition of time given to certain tasks and activities require that others receive less. The goal of time management is, therefore, one of redistribution.

THE PRINCIPLE OF VITAL FEW

Earlier in this chapter superficiality was suggested as a prime hazard of the nature of administrative work. Variety, brevity, and fragmentation were the work characteristics which contributed to superficiality. The administrator's propensity for verbal action, whereby much of the knowledge of the school is stored in memory, thus making the administrator's presence often indispensable, was cited as another contributor. If superficiality is to be managed, the administrator will need to seek a balance between issues which require full concentration and attention and those which can be slighted. Mintzberg suggests that issues faced by an administrator can be handled in one of three ways. First, the great majority can be delegated, even though the administrator realizes if time was unlimited he or she could deal with many of these issues better than anyone else. Second, the administrator can deal personally with some issues, but in a marginal way. That is, superficiality remains a characteristic of involvement. Marginal involvement suggests authorizing and approving actions of others, receiving reports, and helping to set objectives for the work of others. Responsibility for details, however, remains with others. Third, the administrator gives special attention to certain issues—typically those considered most important, complex, variable, volatile, and most likely to have long-range effects on the school and its work.[20]

Educational administrators are likely to *overestimate* the number of issues which must be placed in the third category, thus requiring special administrative attention. Many management experts, for example, suggest that only about 25 percent of the issues faced by administrators could be classified as vital, with the remaining 75 percent being trivial by comparison.[21] These experts often refer to "Pareto's Law" as the genesis of the "vital few" and "trivial many" principle. In 1906 the Italian economist Vilfredo Pareto suggested that economic inequality was due in part to the unequal distribution of human resources in society, and could be predicted mathematically.[22] Applied to financial and business situations, "Pareto's Law" suggests, for example, that approximately 75 percent of the wealth of a nation is in the hands of 25 percent of the people. As another example, 25 percent of the physical assets of a firm account for 75 percent of the firm's value. Though the 25:75 ratio is only an approximation, the main point is that only a vital few account for most of the value, and the trivial many for the remaining value. One popular example often used to illustrate the principle is to ask one to list the value of all his or her possessions. Typically, a few items account for most of their total worth.

In applying "Pareto's Law" to the work of administrators, it is likely that most of one's effectiveness results from only a few of the activities in which one engages. By treating all activities the same, the vital-few activities are slighted and the trivial many get administrative attention beyond their worth in effectiveness to the school. One popular technique suggested to educational administrators as a method for helping to sharpen their focus, and that of subordinates, on the vital few, is Management By Objectives (MBO), the topic of the next section.

[20]Mintzberg, *Nature of Managerial Work*, p. 179.

[21]For a lengthy, popular discussion of the principles of "vital few" and "trivial many," see Joseph Juran, *Managerial Break Through* (New York: McGraw-Hill, 1964).

[22]Vilfredo Pareto, *Manuale di economia politica, con una introduzione ulla scienza social* (Milan: Societa Editrice Librarie, 1906).

MANAGEMENT BY OBJECTIVES

Introduction of the concept of Management by Objectives (MBO) to administration is generally attributed to Peter Drucker.[23] Management by objectives is a process whereby senior and junior administrators, or administrators and teachers together, identify common goals, define major responsibility areas for each role, determine results expected within a particular time frame for each role incumbent, and use expected results as guides for making operating decisions and taking measurements for assessing contributions of persons involved in the process. To some, MBO is a philosophy of administration which includes such assumptions as, it is important to identify the important goals and objectives and the vital-few activities and events most likely to contribute to these goals and objectives for each role or position in the school. Further, administrators, supervisors, and teachers should participate together in this process of identification. According to this view, MBO is considered as a form of participatory decision making, a mechanism for exchanging information, and as a vehicle for building goal awareness and commitment. To others, MBO is viewed as an administrative-control technique designed to increase top administrative control over the goals and activities of lesser administrators, supervisors, and teachers. The common features of both MBO views are: goal setting by subordinates in interaction with superordinates, planning strategies for achieving these goals, and reviewing performance.

When viewed as a philosophy, features of MBO are articulated differently than when viewed as an administrative-control mechanism. In goal setting, more reliance is placed on superordinates and subordinates together deciding on goals. Subordinates are rarely free to set any goal, but the emphasis is nevertheless on mutually establishing goals. Further, the nature of dialogue which accompanies goal setting permits goals to be viewed more as hypotheses of direction rather than immutable specifications. When appropriate, goals are set more precisely; but preciseness is not in itself valued. Subordinates are afforded a great deal of freedom in deciding on implementation strategies. To MBO advocates, this freedom builds a sense of responsibility for, commitment to, and ownership in one's work, which encourages one to work harder and to experience more intrinsic satisfaction from work. Performance review is typically pointed toward previously agreed-upon objectives, their relationship to events and activities which comprise one's implementation plan, and behavior of the subordinates. Since much of the specifics of the process emerge as a result of interac-

[23]Peter Drucker, *The Practice of Management* (New York: Harper & Row, 1954).

tion between superordinates and subordinates, all three are evaluated. New goals, for example, might be discovered and stated goals abandoned as a result of performance review. During each of these phases, subordinates are viewed as being capable of accepting responsibility and participation in the process.

When viewed as an administrative control technique, MBO seeks to bring about greater standardization in outputs, and reliability in performance among subordinates. Goals are set with greater precision with superordinates assuming the dominant, often exclusive, role in this process. Often the goals are linked to some master plan for the school district as a whole. Implementation strategies are often predetermined as well. In schools with a highly structured and highly coordinated curriculum, teachers engaging in this process are not likely to have much choice in how they will pursue certain instructional goals. But where discretion is possible, it is permitted and encouraged. Since objectives are set with determination and precision, evaluation is rarely exploratory. Performance is judged on the basis of the link to achieving these predetermined objectives. MBO, in this view, seems less concerned with identifying and decision making, and more concerned with monitoring and evaluating. The administrative-control view of MBO is more formal than its philosophy counterpart, and is typically accompanied by forms and other records to document the process. This paperwork is noticeably reduced in the MBO-as-philosophy view.

Critics of the philosophy view point out that what results is not MBO at all, but merely a process for getting together to discuss issues of goals, strategies, and evaluation. Further, the process is sufficiently ambiguous that conflict is avoided, hard decisions are not made, and a *laissez-faire* attitude prevails. Critics of the administrative-control view point out that the major purposes of MBO are ignored. True participating decision making, for example, does not exist, and no dialogue occurs about goals and strategies—which in itself, they would argue, is a form of evaluation. Further, because of demands for preciseness and concerns for standardization and reliability in evaluating, the "trivial many" are emphasized. The key assumption here is that the "vital few" are often more difficult to articulate and to measure with precision.

The issues are not insurmountable, and MBO has sufficient potential to warrant that they be resolved. The philosophy-of-MBO view, for example, is weakened because it is often not accompanied by some administrative structure. The administrative-control view, on the other hand, is weakened by its emphasis on techniques and procedures as opposed to people and purposes. An ideal MBO program is one with sufficient structure to permit one to comment with some confidence on past effectiveness, present effectiveness, and future effectiveness.[24] These in turn require that the MBO formats be open and participatory enough to permit such administrative activities as appraisal, coaching, and dialogue. Appraisal is needed to determine past effectiveness, coaching to improve present effectiveness, and dialogue to determine future goals, purposes, and actions.

SUMMARY

This chapter examined some of the characteristics found common to the work of administrators, and considered ways in which administrations might increase control over the work context. Studies by Sproul suggested that such characteristics as "local," "verbal," "choppy" and "varied" dominated the typical administrator's workday. Mintzberg found the work of administrators characterized by brevity, variety, and fragmentation. Both conclude that these characteristics suggest a high level of superficiality in the work of administrators.

It was noted that time is a scarce resource which requires careful allocation. Further, administrative attention was an important signal communicated by administrators to others, indicating what is of value to them. Though often the administration does not intend to communicate by his or her pattern of attention, the message is received by others anyway. Planning and systems thinking were critically discussed as the common remedies offered by experts to bring order to confusion, and rationality to superficiality. Though merits of planning and systems analysis were presented, shortcomings and caveats were emphasized. Time management in general, and the principle of vital few in particular, were then examined. The chapter concluded with a discussion of management by objectives as an administrative control technique and as a point of view or philosophy of administration.

STUDY GUIDE

Can you recall the meaning of the following terms? Discuss them with a class colleague and apply them to your school-community setting.

[24]W. J. Reddin, *Managerial Effectiveness* (New York: McGraw-Hill, 1970), p. 276.

administrative attention
"engineering" characteristics
"garbage can" metaphor
management by objective
network
network schedule

planning process
principle of vital few
systems analysis
time management
work characteristics

SUGGESTED ACTIVITIES

1.   Outline arguments for and against management by objectives. Give attention to the qualities of MBO which can improve administration and school performance, and reasons why MBO can fail.

2.   Keep a careful record of how you spend your time at work for one week. Make entries in a time log which detail events and activities engaged in, and beginning and ending times. Which of the events and activities seem most important in contributing to your overall effectiveness? Compare the time spent on these activities with time spent on all others. To what extent does the "principle of vital few" apply to your analysis?

3.   Conduct a shadow study of one or two administrations, each for one or two days. Meet the administrator upon his or her arrival at work in the morning, and shadow the person for a complete working day (and evening if necessary). Try recording your observation by writing a statement every ten minutes or so (keep the same time interval throughout the day) which best describes what the administrator is actually doing, with whom, and on what topic or issue.

4.   A major theme of this chapter is that "planning should be viewed as an important and helpful process which can improve effectiveness, but at the same time one needs to acknowledge that the planning process is limited by human frailty and by the political process." Give examples which illustrate this statement.

SELECTED READINGS

DRUCKER, PETER, *The Effective Executive*. New York: Harper & Row, 1967.

IMMEGANT, GLENN, *An Introduction to Systems for the Educational Administrator*. Reading, Mass.: Addison-Wesley, 1973.

MARCH, JAMES G., "Model Bias in Social Action," *Review of Educational Research*, 42 (1973), 413–429.

ORDIONE, GEORGE, *Management by Objectives*. New York: Pitman, 1965.

SPROULL, LEE, STEPHEN S. WEINER, and DAVID B. WOLF, *Organizing an Anarchy*. Chicago: University of Chicago Press, 1977.

WEICK, KARL E., "Educational Organizations as Loosely Coupled Systems," *Administrative Science Quarterly*, 21 (1974), 1–18.

14

THE
DECISION-MAKING
PROCESS

Many theorists have posited decision making as the core of the administrative process. Most practicing administrators would agree, suggesting that their time is consumed by activities such as preparing to make decisions, the actual making of decisions, and implementing tasks and procedures dictated by prior decisions. In numerous areas of concern, from textbook selection to public involvement in issues to budget preparation, educational administrators are involved in deciding. Few would quibble about the importance of decision making, particularly in roles such as superintendent or principal.

Controversy, nonetheless, has surrounded efforts to describe and to analyze administrative decision making; and indeed, since the late 1940s intensive debate has enriched the study of this subject. This chapter provides an overview of much of that debate. It begins by examining the attack on the notion that decision making involves the simple processes of defining a problem, creating alternative solutions, testing these alternatives, and then selecting the best. As this simple notion of "rationality" has been debated, differing models of decision making have emerged. The second section examines some of these new and different models of administrative decision making. The third section explores briefly how administrators may manage the decision-making process, and examines the issue of efficiency in decision-making situations. The chapter thus provides a sense of the issues involved in the last four decades of study of decision making.

THE CALCULATIVE DECISION MAKER

The most commonly taught and generally held image of decision making is the calculative. Calculative decision making is purposive—the decision maker decides what should be done, scans all possible alternatives, weighs the consequences of these alternatives, and then chooses the alternative which provides the greatest benefit for the smallest cost.[1] Being calculative is the chief definition of *rationality*.

A graphic device used by the calculative decision maker is the decision tree. Here, "pictures" of decision situations permit decision makers to examine several alternatives, the likelihood of various consequences, and to present choices clearly. For example, Figure 14–1 is

FIGURE 14–1
Decision tree

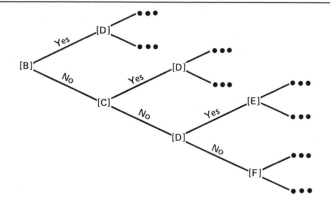

B. Do I have sufficient information to make a high quality decision?
C. Is the problem structured?
D. Is acceptance of·decision by subordinates critical to effective implementation?
E. If I were to make the decision by myself, is it reasonably certain that it would be accepted by my subordinates?
F. Do subordinates share the organizational goals to be attained in solving this problem?

Source: Victor Vroom and Arthur Jago, "Decision-Making as a Social Process: Normative and Descriptive Model of Leader Behavior." Technical Report No. 5, Organizational Effectiveness Research Programs. Office of Naval Research N0014-67-A-0097-0027, May 1974, p. 39.

[1]Graham T. Allison, *Essence of Decision: Explaining the Cuban Missile Crisis* (Boston: Little, Brown, 1971), pp. 10–38.

a section of a larger decision tree developed by Vroom and Jago. The larger decision tree was developed as a way of deciding which of five decision-styles are appropriate in various situations.

To use a decision tree, start at the statement of the problem which is placed on the left side of the page. Then, move across the tree from left to right by answering the questions with either yes or no. In Vroom and Jago's decision tree, for instance, different answers lead to different questions (e.g., a yes at D leads to E, while a no leads to F). For the calculative decision maker, the use of a decision tree creates a powerful means for examining alternatives, consequences of choices, and relative costs or benefits of choices.[2]

Criticisms of the Calculative Decision Maker

Despite the appeal of this image of decision making, much debate has centered on the veracity of the calculative model of decision making. Three major criticisms have surfaced: first, human beings have limited calculative powers; second, the environment of individuals and organizations is often uncertain; and third, individuals and groups *in organizations* do not decide in a calculative manner. These criticisms are considered below.

1. Limited calculative powers   In a series of important studies, Nobel-prize winner Herbert Simon and his colleagues have raised serious questions about the calculative decision maker.[3] Their criticisms may be condensed into three major questions.

First, administrators face a host of problems at any instant. *Which of these many problems capture the attention of the decision maker?* Principals, for example, often face situations where they must deal with an irate parent, a sick child, a telephone call, and the need to get a supplies request out, almost simultaneously. How do principals decide which problem they will attend to at a particular instant, knowing full well that other problems also need immediate attention? The issue for the decision maker may not involve stating the problem, but deciding which of the many immediate problems must be dealt with.

The calculative solution to this question has been to stress planning

[2]See also Victor Vroom, "Leadership Revisited," in Eugene Carr and Frederick Zimmer, eds., *Man and Work in Society* (New York: Van Nostrand Reinhold, 1975), pp. 220–234.

[3]This account is drawn from James G. March, "Business Decision Making," in Harold J. Leavitt and Louis R. Pondy, eds., *Readings in Managerial Psychology* (Chicago: University of Chicago Press, 1964), pp. 447–456; and Herbert A. Simon, "Theories of Decision-Making in Economics and Behavioral Science," *American Economic Review,* 49 (June 1959), pp. 253–283.

activities. What administrators need to do in such situations is to plan ahead and establish long-range goals. But, in studying the behavior of administrators in a number of different settings, Simon and others found that day-to-day problems and situations dominated administrator activities. Administrators spent literally all their time tending to daily business and to immediate crises. A small amount of time was spent on short-range planning: almost no energy was spent on long-range planning. Administrators dealt with immediate issues, with limited awareness of long-term goals or consequences of their actions.

Second, administrators must invest time, effort, and resources in solving a problem. *How much time, energy, and other resources should the decision maker invest in resolving any single problem?* To return to our harrassed principals, they may answer the telephone, tell the irate parent to have coffee and wait for one moment, send the sick child to the nurse, and have the secretary fill out the supplies form. In order to decide which of these activities to undertake, principals would be forced to examine in detail the consequences of each of these activities, and then weigh these consequences to see which is most important. The time, energy, and general effort needed to generate this amount of information would be tremendous.

The calculative solution to this problem is to divide work among a number of specialists, and to have these specialists provide possible alternatives and consequences to the decision maker. Simon suggested that administrators were conscious of and sensitive about the costs associated with generating and analyzing all this information. The amount of time, energy, and resources which could be consumed in finding out all there was to know about any single incident, issue, or topic appeared unlimited. There seemed to be a point at which decision makers found out enough about the situation to make a decision, even if they knew that more information was available. Some point exists, Simon argued, at which obtaining information from specialists cost too much. Knowing everything could mean knowing more than you really wanted or needed to know.

Third, most problems have multiple solutions. *What criterion or criteria should be used in solving a problem?* Some might feel, for instance, that the principal's first duty is always to the child; hence, harried principals should deal with the child personally. Others would suggest that parents, especially if they are truly irate, should receive immediate attention.

The calculative decision maker seeks the one best solution, balancing costs and benefits. In his research, Simon found that instead of searching for the best possible solution, decision makers often accepted "satisfactory" solutions. Administrators simply did not create decision trees or seek all possible solutions, rank order them from best to worst in terms of likely consequences, and find out all pertinent information. Instead, decision makers had a sense of what would probably work in the situation, and accepted the first alternative closest to that generally satisfactory solution. While success might raise the level of satisfaction, and failure lower it, search for alternatives declined sharply once a solution was found near the existing satisfaction level. The criterion for a solution was that it was satisfactory in that situation at that time.

The research of Simon and his colleagues raised serious doubts about the universality of the calculative decision maker. Administrators, Simon found, choose deliberately to limit their attention to some problems, rarely find out all they need to know about situations, and base their solutions on "satisfactory" results.

2. Environmental uncertainty   A second major critique of the calculative decision maker has examined the issues of the likelihood of consequences occurring.

Suppose that a school board and superintendent decide to seek a tax referendum to increase the district's operating budget. In their deliberations the board and superintendent are able to explain certain consequences of the event with complete and accurate knowledge ("certainty"). If the election passes, for example, then the supplies budget for each teacher will increase by ten dollars. The board and superintendent are also able to discuss the probability of some consequences occurring with reasonably accurate knowledge ("risk"). They may know that two of every three elections in their area have been successful this year. Finally, these decision makers may have no accurate knowledge about the probability of an event, such as a blizzard, occurring on election day ("uncertainty"). There may also be sharp disagreement among board members over the impact of a new collective bargaining agreement on the attitude of possible voters. Even after careful discussion, and with reasonable calculation about some events, there seems no "best" or even "decent" estimate of what may happen. They are "uncertain" about what may happen.

Researchers have studied decision making under conditions of certainty, risk, and uncertainty for the last three decades.[4] The calculative

[4]Marcus Alexis and Charles Z. Wilson, *Organizational Decision Making* (Englewood Cliffs, N.J.: Prentice-Hall, 1967), pp. 148–162; and Dennis J. Palumbo, "Organization Theory and Political Science," in Fred I. Greenstein and Nelson W. Polsky, eds., *Handbook of Political Science, Volume 2: Micropolitical Theory.* (Reading, Mass.: Addison-Wesley Publishing, 1975), pp. 335–350.

decision maker operates best under conditions of certainty and of risk, as long as probabilities are accurately known. Under such conditions the calculative decision maker can develop a decision tree which presents either clearly evident choices ("certainty") or choices which have definite probabilities ("risk"). The odds, so to speak, may be the result of experience or of educated guesses. However, the conditions of uncertainty upset the calculative decision maker. Unfortunately, Simon and others argue, decision makers frequently have no accurate knowledge about the probability of consequences occurring. Many administrative decisions deal with "uncertainty."

3. *Organizational behavior* The calculative decision maker easily translates into the chief administrator of the typical organization. The superintendent, for instance, is responsible for structuring the school district central office, for detailing rights and responsibilities of other administrators, and for coordinating decision activities. By viewing the school district as a pyramid with the superintendent at the apex, important decisions remain under the calculative control of the superintendent. Building principals, for example, might arrange for the scheduling of school activities, but the superintendent could override these decisions if he or she felt that it would benefit the entire district.

Many students of organizational behavior have severely criticized this image of organizations as a pyramid. Dill has pointed out that lower-level personnel are frequently forced or seek to assume roles and responsibilities which they are not assigned.[5] Thus, principals often become involved in campaigns to improve the image of the schools in the entire district, even though their particular school may be highly respected. Equally, there are cases when improvisation has proved beneficial to a district. We are all aware of the importance of displaying "initiative."

Dill also points out that problems have a way of changing as they move through the organization. Those at higher levels are influenced not only by how lower participants define problems, but also by the importance they attach to them. In schools, for example, teachers, vice-principals, and principals may all be concerned about discipline— but in very different ways. Teachers may worry about their classrooms, vice-principals may be concerned about maintaining an orderly school environment, and principals may fret about the impact of discipline on parental support. Each participant is worried about the problem of

[5]William R. Dill, "Varieties of Administrative Decisions," in Harold J. Leavitt and Louis R. Pondy, eds., *Readings in Managerial Psychology* (Chicago: University of Chicago Press, 1964), pp. 457–473.

discipline, but each would worry about different aspects and propose different solutions for the problem.

Dill states further that when organizations are seeking to decide, anybody who can help is called upon. Instead of maintaining a strict pyramid, devices such as committees or task forces are used to break down barriers between various departments and between low- and high-level personnel. Curriculum committees in many districts involve individuals from different subject areas, different schools, and different roles as ways of obtaining information and assisting in decision making.

Finally, Dill notes that most organizations have informal patterns of influence and authority which do not fit neatly on any organizational pyramid. In many districts, veteran teachers are often consulted informally about possible courses of action. These consultations not only draw upon the wisdom and experience of these teachers, but also make them aware of what is happening. By being abreast of developments, these veterans will not be surprised and perhaps will not resist the effects of an impending decision.

The consequences of Dill's line of reasoning are clear. In organizations, lines of authority and responsibility frequently become clouded. Sometimes this confusion is created by different ways people see problems; sometimes confusion is a deliberate device to generate new and different solutions. Regardless of the intent, organizational members and organizational leaders lose control of the calculative process. Factors such as informal processes or special committees upset normal calculative procedures. Often, these organizational processes appear more political than calculative, more bent on gaining power than on finding right answers.

Research over the last three decades has tarnished the image of the calculative decision maker. Though the calculative model is still discussed widely in the popular literature as if it offered the only way for viewing all decision making, scholars are increasingly skeptical of this claim. Studies of the self-imposed limits on calculation, of conditions of certainty, risk, and uncertainty, and analyses of actual decision making in organizational settings, suggest a limited use for the calculative model. The model is simply not an accurate description of how educational administrators typically make decisions.

If administrators are not completely calculative decision makers, how then do they make decisions? Certainly one response is that human beings are brutish creatures, driven by ignorance and any number of mortal sins. A better response would be to examine the various types of decision situations and multiple strategies that decision making can take. Instead of arguing that there is one best way to make decisions, educational administration literature should be sensitive to the need for several modes of decision making.

OTHER MODES OF DECISION MAKING

In this section, three other modes of decision making will be examined. The intent is to provide an overview of alternative modes of decision making which have been examined by researchers and discussed by practitioners over the last four decades. These alternative modes may be brought to bear on situations when the calculative model is less appropriate.

An extended example may prove helpful. As the superintendent of a seven-school elementary district, a group of parents from Applewood Elementary approached you last evening at a public meeting. They were upset because recently published achievement test scores in reading had shown Applewood's average to be below district average. As one mother summed up the situation, "We want those scores raised, and those teachers to get with it. We will support any reasonable teacher requests. But we want the scores raised."

At the scheduled principals' and central-office administrators' meeting this morning, you raised this issue for discussion. Sharp, and often bitter, disagreements quickly developed. Some dwelt on the incompetence of teachers, the abuses and fallibility of test scores, and the wrongheadedness of parents. Others stoutly defended teachers, tests, and parental concerns. As you moved the meeting on to the next agenda item, one principal cynically remarked; "We sure are in agreement on that problem, aren't we?" She shyly winked, and then busied herself for the next topic.

It is now evening, and as superintendent you are trying to sort out these events. Your reflections about these discussions are that four distinct positions emerged. They are:

1. *agreement* over the steps needed to remedy the situation (assist teachers in the reading program through activities such as inservice) and *agreement* about goals to be achieved (raise the average Applewood reading-achievement-test score);

2. *disagreement* over the steps needed to remedy the situation (teachers need assistance, versus teachers as competent and well-trained, versus teachers should be replaced by reading specialists) and *agreement* about goals to be achieved (raise reading-test score);

3. *agreement* over the steps needed to remedy the situation (assist teachers in reading program, through activities such as inservice) and *disagree-*

ment about goals to be achieved (raise average reading-test scores, versus enhance enjoyment of reading, versus using tests that better measure reading);

4. *disagreement* over the steps needed to remedy the situation (teachers need assistance, versus teachers as competent and well trained, versus teachers should be replaced by reading specialists) and *disagreement* about goals to be achieved (raise reading-test scores, versus enhance enjoyment of reading, versus using tests that better measure reading).

As superintendent, you have been trained in the calculative model. In the four situations you have defined, the calculative-decision model will work only in the situation where there is agreement about both steps needed and goals to be achieved. Where there are disagreements about means and disagreements about ends, or both, the calculative mode will not apply. How should decisions be made in the other three situations?[6]

Disagreement about Means, Agreement about Ends

What strategies for decision making can be applied in situations where there is disagreement about means but agreement about ends?

Several researchers believe that this pattern occurs most frequently in collegial organizations. Collegial organizations, such as schools, hospitals, and research-and-development laboratories, are staffed by professionally trained workers who have definite goals, but who may differ on means. Teachers, for instance, are professionally trained to accept certain general educational goals. They may differ sharply on precise ways of attaining these goals and on the precise nuances of goals, but general agreements exist about treatment of students, standards of conduct, and professional bearing.

Davis suggests that a key element in the administration of collegial or professional organizations is the sense of mutual contribution of participants.[7] Expecting that participants probably will disagree over means, the orientation of administrators should be toward integration and teamwork. Hence, the superintendent should expect teachers to agree in the value of teaching students to read, but anticipate disagree-

[6]The following account is based on James D. Thompson and Arthur Tuden, "Strategies in Decision-Making," in Fremont J. Lyden, George A. Shipman, and Morton Kroll, eds., *Policies, Decisions, and Organizations* (New York: Appleton-Century-Crofts, 1969), pp. 310–330.

[7]Keith Davis, "Evolving Models of Organizational Behavior," in Keith Davis, ed., *Organizational Behavior: A Book of Readings* (New York: McGraw-Hill, 1974), pp. 4–15.

ments over issues such as phonics, which texts are best, and the worth of differing methods of enhancing comprehension. Administrators, thus, should create opportunities for discussion, exchange of opinions and information, and efforts to team the activities of several individual teachers.

Thompson and Tuden indicate that in collegial organizations there is a strong norm that all members have the right to participate in decisions influencing their professional activities. Equally, some individual discretion is permitted even after the ultimate choice is made by the majority.

Schools appear to be organizations where this type of decision making is common. The bulk of decisions made by administrators deal with situations involving professionally trained colleagues. These colleagues generally assume vast responsibility for the work they do, are counted upon to be self-disciplining, and find much of their rewards in the self-actualizing characteristics of their work. Under such conditions, faculties become important decision-making bodies in which professional information is shared, professional judgment exercised, and the majority of colleagues establish general standards about conduct and practice. Individuals retain some discretion in both means and ends, but a professional consensus sets the general boundaries of acceptable means and valuable goals.

Agreement about Means, Disagreement about Ends

Two rather distinct versions of decision making exist under conditions of agreement about means but disagreements about ends.

In contrast to viewing administrative decision making as a rational science, Lindblom has argued that administrators actually operate from a science of "muddling through."[8] In this provocative line of thinking, he argues that means and ends are closely intertwined. Any effort to define a single goal or objective results almost immediately in disagreement. Even if a goal can be prescribed, disagreement emerges quickly about sub-objectives. It is prudent, then, for administrators to agree about a policy without ever being too clear about what is the most appropriate objective. These muddled through policies, in fact, turn out to be the incremental changes made to existing policies.

Lindblom's formulation has been sharply criticized by some authorities. Others support his contention that incrementalism describes

[8]Charles E. Lindblom, "The Science of Muddling Through," *Public Administration Review,* 19–20 (spring, 1959), 79–88.

accurately the compromises and bargains made in decision making. Each new proposal to a problem is examined against desired objectives, with the knowledge that what is desired may itself change during consideration. Muddling through a problem affects the level of desired aspiration of the decision maker, suggesting that the desired goal must be either downgraded or upgraded, depending on conditions. For Lindblom, muddling through is the appropriate strategy for deciding in complex situations.

A second version of decision making where agreement exists on means but not on ends views organizations as if they were political bodies. Allison develops a model which proposes that what organizations do is the result of bargaining within the organization.[9] Decisions that organizations reach are not calculated solutions to problems, but are the results of conflict, compromise, and confusion. Members representing various departments in the organization bargain among themselves about what the organization should do. These sessions are enlivened by the fact that the distribution of power and influence is not equal among departments, and that patterns of distribution are not fixed, but change over time.

Representative bodies, such as legislatures, city councils, or school boards, can display both these patterns. Most discussions of policies which must be decided involve not only bargaining among various participants, but also shifting aspirations about what can or cannot be accomplished. These bodies frequently seek not only to make all the facts of a situation known, but also to adhere to the principle that ultimate preference is decided after bargaining by vote of the majority.

Incrementalism of Lindblom and political bargaining of Allison assume that groups or individuals can find reasonable means while ignoring or downplaying differences over goals. Hence, we would expect to find that political bodies would place great emphasis on agreeing about means to be used, even though participants would differ sharply on goals. In legislation, for example, rules that govern debate are important means which all agree to, even though the goals debated may sharply separate legislators.

Disputes about ends occur less frequently in collegial organizations such as schools. The training and experience of professional employees provide senses of the goals of the organization. Goals often form constellations, such as the well-being and enhancement of the client, the enrichment of best practice and advancement of knowledge, and the self-actualization of the professional. Such constellations suggest that educational goals are complementary, not adversial.

Despite the general sense of goals of education instilled by profes-

[9]Allison, *Essence of Decision,* pp. 144–184.

sional training, this sense often does not exist among school board members. The consensus developed by years of professional training and experience about ends and about the values of disputes over means is a rare commodity for most school board members. This suggests that much of the deliberations of school board meetings fits well the image of a representative, political body. As noted in earlier chapters, in the last two decades the politics of education, and of the school board, has become an important theme in the practice and study of education. One perspective for looking at school boards, then, is to study agreements and disagreements about means and ends.

Disagreement about Means and Ends

From the calculative model, it is correct to suggest that no decisions can be reached when there are disagreements over both means and ends. Nonetheless, two different ways of responding to these conditions have been explored: charisma, and a garbage-can model of decision making.

The notion of charisma became part of the vocabulary of American life in the 1960s. But its intellectual origin can be found in the early 1900s in the works of Max Weber. Working in his native Germany from 1890 to 1920, Weber produced a remarkable series of studies in the field of sociology. His works examined bureaucracy, law, religion, and capitalism; they are still widely read and discussed by thinkers in those fields.

Central to Weber's work is the concept of charisma. While Weber discusses this notion in several works, his analysis in his works on sociology of religion present a clear picture of the charismatic individual. The bearer of charisma, the prophet, proclaims a religious doctrine or divine commandment. Weber then notes that:

> prophetic revelation involves for both the prophet himself and for his followers . . . a unified view of the world derived from a consciously integrated and meaningful attitude toward life. To the prophet, both the life of man and the world, both social and cosmic events, have a certain systematic and coherent meaning. To this meaning the conduct of mankind must be oriented if it is to bring salvation, for only in relation to this meaning does life obtain a unified and significant pattern.[10]

For Weber, the prophet or charismatic leader is able to provide a view of the world which creates agreements about means, ends, or both. The pattern of meaning permits followers to create understandings, and

[10]S. N. Eisenstadt, ed., *Max Weber: On Charisma and Institution Building*. (Chicago: University of Chicago Press, 1968), p. 266.

thus to operate in other decision modes. Problems of disagreement are overcome by some new or different, and obviously inspired, view of the world.

If our superintendent truly faced a situation in the district of disagreement over both ends and means, as a charismatic leader the superintendent might offer a new vision of what education is about. It is doubtful that many superintendents have such charisma, or most educators, for that matter. Superintendents, however, do seek to inspire teachers and other administrators to larger visions of their professional responsibilities. For instance, in the late 1960s many in education expanded their image of schooling to include "disadvantaged" children, just as in the 1970s we have included the "handicapped." These extensions represent larger and different views of the world of schooling.

A very different solution exists for resolving the issues of disagreement over both means and ends. In their analysis of university decision making, Cohen, March, and Olsen found disagreements over ends and means common.[11] They labeled universities "organized anarchies," and suggested that organizational choice in the university was best described by a garbage-can model of decision making.

Since organizational participants such as administrators, faculty, and students disagree about both means and ends, how are decisions reached? Cohen, March, and Olsen suggest that problems and solutions are simply dumped into a "garbage can." This metaphor highlights the notions that various individuals and groups create problems and generate solutions. There is no common agreement among participants about what constitutes either the means or ends to be used in evaluating solutions or problems. Hence, the mix of problems and solutions in the garbage can is continuously being arranged and rearranged. Often problems are not solved; they just go away. Often solutions are put in place, even if there is no problem. Most frequently, garbage-can decision making involves either grabbing the first easily available solution ("oversight") or ignoring a problem until a solution comes along which solves another problem ("flight").

An example may help clarify this model. Many high schools have a combination cafeteria–student-recreation room. Students frequently petition the administration to install a juke box in this area (solution). The rationale offered for this solution is that a problem exists—the area is littered with trash, students are rowdy, some smoking is starting in the area. Hence, because of this problem, a solution is needed

[11]Michael D. Cohen, James G. March, and John P. Olsen, "A Garbage Can Model of Organizational Choice," *Administrative Science Quarterly,* 17 (March 1972), 1–25.

immediately. These petitions to the administration claim that student morale will be increased, and student control will be solved by the juke box. Some might argue that the "solution" of a juke box came first, and that students then had to find a problem or some problems to match this solution. These cynics would also hope that administrators do not make this decision by oversight.

Both charisma and the garbage-can model try to explain decision making when disagreements exist over both means and ends. These modes of decision making fly in the face of the calculative decision-making model. They are, nonetheless, useful for examining some of the decision-making behavior in schools. There are charismatic crusades to reconstruct our views about children, schooling, and teaching. There also are cases where the garbage-can model applies to decision making in schools, and instances of oversight and flight.

In summary, the study of decision making over the last four decades has been an intellectually stimulating field. Research has sharply delimited the calculative model of decision making and produced an interesting array of differing decision-making models. A brief summary of these is presented as Table 14–1.

MANAGING THE DECISION-MAKING PROCESS

The recurring theme of this chapter has been that the calculative image of decision making, though offered in abundance to educational administrators, is not an accurate portrayal of the complexity of the actual decision-making process. Several alternatives to that model

TABLE 14–1
Different decision-making modes

| | | Goals | |
		Agreement	*Disagreement*
Means	*Agreement*	1. Calculative decision maker 2. Decision tree	1. Muddling through 2. Political representative bodies
	Disagreement	1. Collegial organizations 2. Integrative leadership	1. Charisma 2. Garbage can model

have been examined. In this section, we shall note briefly how educational administrators may actually manage the decision-making process. Again, the intent is not to prescribe some ideal "right" way, but to describe actual administrative behaviors.

Efforts to analyze agreement or disagreement about both means and ends ought to be a part of every administrator's activities. These activities involve deliberate efforts by administrators to create agreements over means, ends, or both. Rather than passively accepting the world as it is, administrators may deliberately use tactics to change the conditions surrounding decision making and to improve efficiency in making decisions. In the next sections we will deal with some of the issues of administrative tactics and efficiency.

Administrative Tactics[12]

One time-honored administrative tactic is the creation of a deliberately short time line. This is most frequently done by giving teachers or others twenty-four hours to reach a decision. The press of time creates conditions which reduce the examining of many alternatives, force artificial agreements on means and ends, and generate feelings of comradeship in tackling and defeating an impossible situation.

A second common device is the elimination of all but a very few alternatives. Usually this is achieved by an administrator suggesting that only so much money is available, or that school board members will not buy wild ideas, or that the community is not ready for too new an idea. Once again, the restriction of alternatives creates areas of agreement which might not exist under less restricted conditions.

A third administrative tactic is to obtain "early on" commitment to reaching a solution to the problem. The administrator then seeks consciously to make this commitment the highest priority in discussions. Such a tactic is an integral part of muddling through or political bargaining, and a critical element in dealing with several competing groups.

Another device is to generate a consensus on ends, often by creating deliberately vague and ambiguous phrases or slogans. These flourishes of campaign oratory are not the sole province of politicians seeking office. They are important strategies in crystallizing consensus about certain issues and in creating favorable images not only of the school but also of teachers and administrators. These broad appeals may induce productive activity which over time generates agreements on specifics that currently do not exist.

[12]Adopted from Thompson and Tuden, "Strategies in Decision Making," pp. 326–328.

A fifth administrative tactic is to break a single complex situation into a series of discrete situations. Usually this tactic involves assigning these discrete situations to separate decision units. Such a tactic runs the risk that units may produce a series of bad decisions; but this option seems at least as preferable as prolonged and unproductive conflict. This tactic creates a series of mini-calculative decision models.

A final device is the deliberate upsetting of agreements by an administrator to provoke constructive conflict. The extreme emphasis of the calculative model on agreement and the dysfunctions of conflict has been attacked in the last twenty years or so. At times, the growth of individuals and the effectiveness of organizations are enhanced by conflict. Bower, for example, points out that conflict leads individuals to defend their choices by presenting as cogently as they can all information which supports their position.[13] Both the extent and quality of information increases in periods of healthy conflict.

Let us return for a moment to our harrassed superintendent and the problems about reading scores. The superintendent might, for example, create deliberate deadlines for the school principals to come up with a "solution" to the reading problem. Or, the superintendent might deliberately generate a conflict situation, claiming that the district should have only one reading philosophy, and demanding that the principals create this philosophy quickly. These and other tactics suggest an important point about decision making: administrators are not simply pawns to be pushed around; they possess important resources for reshaping decisions.

These and other tactics are means of administering the decision process. This management involves controlling the strategies to be applied in decision situations. This line of reasoning argues that administrators need to be conscious about whether they are making "the" decision or creating conditions for others to make "the" decision.

Redundancy and Efficiency

A second practical concern deals with the administrators' sensitivity to the values of redundancy and efficiency. Most, if not all, decision making literature lauds the value of efficiency, contrasting efficient methods to waste, extravagance, and duplication. Efficiency most often means the calculative model. The general argument of this section is to suggest that there are important limitations to the criterion of efficiency.

[13]Joseph Bower, "The Role of Conflict in Economic Decision-Making Groups: Some Empirical Results," *Quarterly Journal of Economics,* 79 (May 1965), 263–277.

The positive role of redundancy in organizations and decision making needs highlighting. There are clear positive values in redundancy in organizations, especially when those organizations deal with human beings. Landau, for instance, argues that the dual braking system of a car is a useful example of valuable redundancy.[14] If the cost of error is high, such as a brake failure, then organizations, and automobiles, should be arranged so that when a single part fails, the entire system does not fail. In the dual braking system of a car, when one part fails a single system fails; but an entirely separate and different system is not affected, and the driver is able to operate the car. Since the cost of an error could mean the loss of a human life, a dual breaking system seems a reasonable investment. The parallel with educational organizations seems evident.

In human organizations, a good example of a system filled with redundancies is our federal government. The legislative, judicial, and executive systems often deal with the same issue. Senators and representatives propose differing ways of dealing with educational problems, for example. Members of the executive branch—agency officials, members of the executive staff, and the president—offer counter-proposals. Increasingly, the courts and judges are brought into discussions of educational problems. Such a sloppy procedure involves seemingly endless redundancy. Checks and balances, action and reaction, become part of a confusing pattern of competing redundancies.

Or so it would seem if our sole criterion was efficiency. But our federal system seems to thrive because of this redundancy. Instead of being built in such a way that the failure of any single part results in the collapse of the system, the system persists and is adaptive and flexible even if we have a weak president, an ineffective legislature, or a corrupt judiciary. Landau suggests that planning human organizations where units are closely linked together and which have no redundancy built into the system is an example of administrative brinkmanship.

Those who administer schools are dealing with human beings. The costs of error can be very high. Hence, we need to be conscious of ways of creating useful redundancy. While this redundancy may strike some as inefficient, for those who could be affected by a breakdown in a tightly linked system, redundancy seems worthwhile. For example, suppose a student is viewed by a single teacher as a potential scholarship winner. It may seem a waste of time to check with others about this evaluation, but a thorough investigation may suggest either that

[14]Martin Landau, "Redundancy, Rationality, and the Problem of Duplication and Overlap," *Public Administration Review,* 29 (July/August 1969), 346–358.

the teacher was too favorable or that additional evidence can be marshaled to support the student's application. Equally, inputs of parental groups, community groups, and school-board members may indicate the necessity of strengthening certain aspects of a new program in social studies. These diverse sources suggest the need to build certain redundancies into the program so that if students miss one lesson they will not miss the entire course. There are important redundancies built into much of the curriculum of our schools.

SUMMARY

Practicing administrators need to be conscious of the several models of decision making and the general situations of their application, of the tactics for managing the decision situation and strategy, and of the values of redundancy in organizations. These concerns reflect the limited usefulness of applying a single calculative model to all decision situations, the capabilities that administrators have for shaping decisions, and the necessity to indicate limits on the value of efficiency in schools.

STUDY GUIDE

Can you recall the meanings of the following terms? Discuss them with a class colleague and apply them to your own school-community setting?

calculative decision maker	muddling through
decision tree	political bargaining
limited calculative powers	charisma
certainty	garbage-can model
risk	oversight
uncertainty	flight
collegial organization	redundancy

SUGGESTED ACTIVITIES

1. Discuss with colleagues reasons why social scientists since the late 1940s have become more and more critical of the calculative decision model.

What events, for example, in domestic policy in the United States might have tarnished this model?

2.　Visit a school-board meeting in which you deliberately attempt to classify decisions into the cells created by Table 14–1. Be alert to differences that may exist between members and between the board and the superintendent. In light of that meeting, which of the four cells best represents school-board decision making.

3.　Imagine that you have been asked to speak to a group of fellow educators about the relations between means and ends in American education. Outline two speechs: the first describes American education in terms of disagreement over means but agreements on ends; the second describes American education in terms of agreement over means and disagreement over ends. Discuss with your colleagues the differences and similarities in these two presentations.

4.　You may wish to review Chapter 3 and the materials on contingency theory. Reflect on the relations which exist between contingency theory and decision making, considering, for example, how changes of agreement on means may influence the decision-making situation.

SELECTED READINGS

BROSS, IRWIN D. J., *Design for Decision.* New York: Macmillan, 1953.

CALLAHAN, RAYMOND E., *Education and the Cult of Efficiency.* Chicago: University of Chicago Press, 1962.

COHEN, MICHAEL D., and JAMES G. MARCH, *Leadership and Ambiguity: The American College President.* New York: McGraw-Hill, 1974.

HELLER, FRANK A., "Leadership Decision Making and Contingency Theory," *Industrial Relations,* 12 (May 1973), 183–199.

THOMPSON, JAMES D., *Organizations in Action.* New York: McGraw-Hill, 1967.

PART IV

Deciding
on an
Administrative
Career

15

PERSONAL GOALS, TRAITS, AND THE EDUCATIONAL-ADMINISTRATION CAREER

Throughout this book we have sought to introduce readers to educational governance and administration as fields of study and professional practice, and settings for public-policy development in education. This chapter focuses specifically on the prospects of choosing educational adminstration as a lifelong career. Readers who are now pondering this career choice should find the chapter personally helpful. Readers with non-career interests in educational administration should find the chapter of some assistance in understanding better the sorts of persons likely to choose this particular career line and some of the consequences of this choice.

Career planning is a personal process which requires a great deal of self-analysis. Abstract discussions of career opportunities and career-planning procedures are helpful, but not adequate substitutes for self-analysis. In this spirit, an experential approach is used in this chapter to assist readers in self-analysis. One section of the chapter, for example, is designed to help assess job-related personality traits and examine them for suitability to a career in administration. Readers are asked to respond to a Self-Description Inventory and to analyze their scores across several dimensions in comparison with a set of norms associated with managerial success in general. A second section of the chapter asks readers to evaluate a set of competencies, identified as important to the technical aspects of an administrative role, on two dimensions: their present level of competence, and the extent to which they are likely to enjoy working in each listed competency area. A third section asks readers to focus on one's life and career goals, comparing these with a career in educational administration. The intent of these experiences is to provoke thought, stimulate thinking, and increase self-awareness as one considers choosing a career. *None of the exercises, therefore, should be considered as a definitive yardstick described to scientifically determine whether a person should or should not commit himself or herself to an educational administration career.* Happiness and success are the two important concerns as one considers a particular job. For example, readers should critically examine their own interest, dispositions, and capabilities against the demands and rewards of a career in educational administration on both counts. Will I be happy as an educational administrator? Am I likely to be successful as an educational administrator?

AN OVERVIEW OF JOB
OPPORTUNITIES

The old adage is that there will always be a need for good school administrators. But beyond this truism, traditional jobs in educational administration are at present not abundant. Traditional jobs refer to those associated with administering the schools over the years. Principals and assistants, superintendents and assistants, and specialists such as business managers, curriculum administrators, and personnel administrators are examples. Caught in a squeeze between declining student enrollments and subsequent school closings on the one hand, and continued interest in consolidating smaller into larger school districts on the other, demands for jobs such as these are, for the most part, on a replacement rather than expansion basis.[1]

More recent public-school administrative and supervisory job designations, however, seem on the increase, particularly in larger districts. Special-education administrators, specialists in systems analysis, collective-bargaining experts, finance administrators, school-community relations coordinators, and staff-development experts are examples. These jobs are in response to such environmental pressures

[1]Many exceptions to this replacement trend in employment patterns exist. Expansion hiring still occurs, for example, as population shifts within states and between states. Many suburban areas that are not landlocked are building schools and hiring staff as their urban neighbors close schools and reduce staff. Nationwide, population shifts from many of the northern states to the sun-belt areas create similar imbalances in the overall employment picture.

as increased special-education legislation, more detailed and abundant planning and reporting requirements from state and federal level agencies, growing unionism, fiscal stringency and accountability, increased pressure for public participation in school governance, and the consequences of staff stability in a relatively tight job market for teachers.

In the years ahead, public interest in expanding the role and function of the principal, the autonomy of the local school site, and the governance authority of its local citizens-advisory committee, may well increase as citizens and educators seek a response to countering the increased centralization of education trend. Local school autonomy— or school-site management, as this trend is coined by some in the United States[2] —is suggested as a means to bring better balance between lay participation in school governance and professional control of schools, and between both these local characteristics and state and federal control. This trend could alter the job picture somewhat, suggesting decreases in the number and type of central-office position and increases in the number of building-level administration and supervisors.

Though local school autonomy remains a likely future for educational governance, this ideal does not now and in the future will probably not substantially alter the increased concentration of jobs at the state level. State education bureaucracies will continue to grow in size, power, and influence. Many state agency jobs are more technical than administrative (a bilingual expert, as opposed to a special-education supervisor), but most include administrative and supervisory responsibility, as the state works with local school districts and other public agencies at all levels of government. Further, many of the technically oriented and administratively oriented jobs require that incumbents have training in such special areas of administration and governance as policy analysis, decision-making, economics and school finance, planning, and educational business management. The federal government, through such agencies as the Department of Education, offers similar (though by comparison with state governments, markedly fewer) job opportunities in Washington, D.C., and in regional offices throughout the country.

Not to be overlooked are jobs as educational administrators and

---

[2]Local school autonomy is a concept long practiced in Britain, where the school head traditionally assumes a strong leadership position in matters of educational policy and school-community relations. Recently James Guthrie and his associates have developed the concept of school-site management, offering a more detailed perspective of local school governance and a more thorough analysis of the financial and political implications of such a design.

administrative specialists in the various professional organizations for administrators and supervisors, and in local, state, and national teacher association or union organizations. These organizations require quality leadership and rely heavily on many of the administrative specialities such as finance, public policy, and personnel administration. Finally, higher-education careers in community- and senior-college administration, or clinical or research-oriented professors in educational administration and policy, are other possibilities.

THEORIES OF CAREER CHOICE

The literature on career development, counseling, and choice is vast. Vocational psychologists, counselors, personality theorists, and sociologists have been active in trying to understand the vocational decision-making process, and in attempting to identify the requirements which will help determine if one will be happy and successful in a particular job. As one can expect, numerous theories have been proposed and a number of approaches have been developed to assist professional career counselors in their work.

In an effort to provide a summary of various approaches to career counseling, Samuel Osipow suggests a four-category grouping.[3] Trait-factor theories, the first category, assume that a fairly direct matching of an individual's abilities and interests with specific job opportunities can be accomplished. Sometimes vocational tests, such as the Strong Vocational Interest Blank and the Kuder Preference Record, and aptitude tests, such as the Guilford-Zimmerman, are used to assess interests and abilities and match them to specific jobs. Very few career counselors rely *only* on the trait-factor approach, though this approach typically plays a role in most of the other models of career counseling.

A sociological model based on chance comprises a second view of career choice and development. According to this approach, circumstances beyond an individual's control typically contribute significantly to career choices, and to subsequent development once a career track is chosen. Being at the right place at the right time, and recognizing opportunities as they develop, are unquestionably factors which contribute to one's career choices, and their opposites to career frustration.

Self-concept theory represents a third grouping of career counseling thought. Osipow suggests that the central theses of this approach

[3]Samuel Osipow, *Theories of Career Development* (New York: Appelton-Century Crofts, 1968).

are that one develops a more clearly defined self-concept as he or she grows older, although this definition varies to conform with the changes in one's view of reality as correlated with aging; one develops images of the occupational world which are compared with this self-image in trying to make career decision; and the adequacy of the career decision he or she makes is based on the similarity between self-concept and the vocational concept of the career eventually chosen.[4]

The fourth grouping suggested by Osipow includes personality theories of vocational choice. Common to personality theories is the assumption that individuals choose a job or career because they see potential in that choice for satisfying their needs. Some theorists from this group contend that individuals with similar personality characteristics choose certain jobs. A corollary assumption offered by others is that exposure to a job over time modifies the personality characteristics of the worker. Thus teachers, administrators, pilots, or surgeons come to share many personality characteristics.

It is difficult to view these groupings of career theory as being independent of one another. Indeed, each approach shares some of the characteristics of the others, and all contribute somewhat to career choice and development. In the sections which follow, trait-factor, self-concept, and personality approaches will receive further attention.

IDENTIFYING MANAGERIAL TALENT

Educational administration is a separate and distinct field of study and professional practice.[5] Nevertheless, the general processes of administration in the United States and other Western cultures are universal. Administrators in educational, business, government, hospital, and other organizations, for example, are engaged in planning, organizing, communicating, decision making, influencing, coordinating, and evaluating.[6] Some of these processes may receive more emphasis in one setting than another, but all are present to some degree in all administrative settings. This similarity makes it possible to speak about gen-

[4]*Ibid.* p. 11.

[5]See our discussions of educational administration as an applied science in Chapter 2 for an elaboration of differences. Figure 1–1 in Chapter 1, on the other hand, suggests characteristics common to all administrative enterprises.

[6]See, for example, Russell Gregg, "The Administrative Process," in Ronald Campbell and Russell Gregg, ed., *Administrative Behavior in Education* (New York: Harper & Row, 1957); Jesse Sears, *The Nature of the Administrative Process* (New York: McGraw-Hill, 1950); and Henri Fayol, "Administration industrielle et generale," in Constance Starrs, *General and Industrial Management* (London: Sir Isaac Pitman & Sons, Ltd., 1949).

eral patterns and levels of traits, personal qualities and abilities required for success in administrative jobs wherever they may be.

In this section, we are interested in these universal characteristics of administrative success. Readers are invited to respond to the Self-Description Inventory, which is designed to assess traits and abilities necessary for success in administration. This inventory was developed by Edwin Ghiselli as part of his twenty years of research searching for a link between such traits and managerial success.[7] Working with managers in an array of ninety business and industrial organizations, Ghiselli found that one's supervisory ability was the most important quality necessary for success. Intelligence, self-assurance, and decisiveness were traits also linked to managerial success in his study. Further, such personality characteristics as high need for achievement and self-actualization and low need for security were identified as predictors of managerial success.[8] These characteristics were described as follows:

> *Supervisory ability*   The capacity to direct the work of others and to organize and integrate activities in a manner which enhances group goals. *This characteristic was most strongly linked to success for the group of managers studied by Ghiselli.*
>
> *Intelligence*   The capacity to judge, reason, deal with ideas, abstractions, and concepts. The ability to learn, to be insightful, to analize, and to synthesize.
>
> *Decisiveness*   The readiness to make quick decisions with self-confidence. A decisive decision-maker, for example, feels that it is better to make a decision than to beg the issue; that it is difficult to gather all of the facts about an issue; and that action is important. Further, the decision maker believes that hesitation often turns minor problems into major ones.
>
> *Self-Assurance*   The extent to which an individual perceives himself to be effective in problem solving, to be sound in judgment, and to have faith in his ability to cope with a variety of situations.
>
> *Need for achievement*   The extent to which a person seeks responsibility and prestige associated with a high position. Ghiselli speaks of this need as *occu-*

[7]Edwin E. Ghiselli, *Explorations in Managerial Talent* (Pacific Palisades, Calif.: Goodyear, 1971).

[8]Ghiselli studied 306 managers from an array of ninety business-type organizations ranging from finance and insurance, to transportation, communication, utilities, and manufacturing. The managers ranged in age from twenty-six to forty-two and geographically represented all of the regions of mainland United States and Hawaii. The 306 managers do not constitute a representative sample of executives and administrations in the United States, but nevertheless, sufficient variation existed in Ghiselli's sample to suggest that the study has a good deal of generalizability.

pational achievement and defines it somewhat differently than the "need for achievement" associated with David McClelland's work.[9]

Need for self-actualization The extent to which a person seeks opportunities to utilize talents to the fullest extent on activities of importance and in which achievements are seen to have consequences for society.

Low need for job security Those concerned with job security work to establish their positions. Protection of job and status are important, as are seeking safe assignments and avoiding situations which lend themselves to evaluation. The familiar is "good," the unknown is "bad." *Those with a low need for job security are less concerned with these conditions.*

Each of the traits associated with managerial success comprise subscales of the Self-Description Inventory.[10] The supervisory-ability subscale, for example, estimates a respondent's capacity to direct the work of others and to organize and integrate activities in a fashion which enhances the attainment of work-group goals.

The Self-Description Inventory should not be considered as a definitive yardstick designed to scientifically determine whether a person should or should not commit himself or herself to a career in educational administration, but instead, should be considered as a feedback instrument which can provide a general indication of one's disposition toward a career in administration in general.

It may be, for example, that decisiveness is less important in educational administration because of the press for lay participation, the complexities of state regulation, and the distribution of authority among an array of individuals and groups. Further, the inventory provides information more appropriate to traditional line positions than to the more specialized staff position, such as systems analyst and finance expert, or to positions associated with research and development activities in universities or state government.

THE SELF-DESCRIPTION INVENTORY

The Self-Description Inventory, with directions, appears as Exhibit 15–1. Exhibit 15–2 contains the scoring keys for subscales identified by

---

[9]See for example, David McClelland *et al.*, *The Achievement Motive* (New York: Appelton-Century-Crofts, 1953), and David McClelland, *The Achieving Society* (Princeton, N.J.: D. Van Nostrand, 1961).

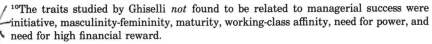
[10]The traits studied by Ghiselli *not* found to be related to managerial success were initiative, masculinity-femininity, maturity, working-class affinity, need for power, and need for high financial reward.

The purpose of this inventory is to obtain a picture of the traits you believe you possess, and to see how you describe yourself. There are no right or wrong answers, so try to describe yourself as accurately and honestly as you can.

In each of the pairs of words below, check the one you think *most* describes you.

1. ✓ capable
___ discreet

2. ✓ understanding
___ thorough

3. ✓ cooperative
___ inventive

4. ✓ friendly
___ cheerful

5. ___ energetic
✓ ambitious

6. ___ persevering
✓ independent

7. ___ loyal
✓ dependable

8. ✓ determined
___ courageous

9. ___ industrious
✓ practical

10. ___ planful
✓ resourceful

11. ___ unaffected
✓ alert

12. ___ sharp-witted
✓ deliberate

13. ✓ kind
___ jolly

14. ✓ efficient
___ clear-thinking

15. ✓ realistic
___ tactful

16. ✓ enterprising
___ intelligent

17. ✓ affectionate
___ frank

18. ___ progressive
✓ thrifty

19. ✓ sincere
___ calm

20. ✓ thoughtful
___ fair-minded

21. ✓ poised
___ ingenious

22. ___ sociable
✓ steady

23. ✓ appreciative
___ good-natured

24. ___ pleasant
✓ modest

25. ___ responsible
✓ reliable

26. ___ dignified
✓ civilized

27. ___ imaginative
✓ self-controlled

28. ✓ conscientious
___ quick

29. ✓ logical
___ adaptable

30. ✓ sympathetic
___ patient

In each of the pairs of words below, check the one you think *least* describes you.

31. ____ stable
    ✓ foresighted
32. ____ honest
    ✓ generous
33. ✓ shy
    ____ lazy
34. ✓ unambitious
    ____ reckless
35. ____ noisy
    ✓ arrogant
36. ✓ emotional
    ____ headstrong
37. ____ immature
    ✓ quarrelsome
38. ____ unfriendly
    ✓ self-seeking
39. ✓ affected
    ____ moody
40. ✓ stubborn
    ____ cold
41. ✓ conceited
    ____ infantile
42. ____ shallow
    ✓ stingy
43. ____ unstable
    ✓ frivolous
44. ____ defensive
    ✓ touchy
45. ____ tense
    ✓ irritable
46. ✓ dreamy
    ____ dependent
47. ✓ changeable
    ____ prudish

48. ____ nervous
    ✓ intolerant
49. ✓ careless
    ____ foolish
50. ✓ apathetic
    ____ egotistical
51. ____ despondent
    ✓ evasive
52. ____ distractible
    ✓ complaining
53. ____ weak
    ✓ selfish
54. ____ rude
    ✓ self-centered
55. ____ rattle-brained
    ✓ disorderly
56. ____ fussy
    ✓ submissive
57. ✓ opinionated
    ____ pessimistic
58. ____ shiftless
    ✓ bitter
59. ✓ hard-hearted
    ____ self-pitying
60. ____ cynical
    ✓ aggressive
61. ____ dissatisfied
    ✓ outspoken
62. ____ undependable
    ✓ resentful
63. ✓ sly
    ____ excitable
64. ____ irresponsible
    ✓ impatient

Source: Edwin E. Ghiselli, *Explorations in Managerial Talent* (Santa Monica, Calif.: Goodyear, 1971), pp. 139–141.

EXHIBIT 15-2
Selected Scoring Keys: The Self-Description Inventory

This and the following list give the correct responses for each of the various scales. The first number is the item number and the last number is the weight or score of the item. T means the top adjective of the pair is the correct response, and B means the bottom adjective is correct.

Supervisory Ability	Intelligence	Need for Security	Self-Assurance
4 B2	3 B4	3 T2	2 B2
5 T2	4 B2	7 B1	7 B1
14 B3	8 T2	8 T1	11 B1
15 B3	9 B1	11 T2	12 T2
21 T2	10 B2	12 B1	13 T1
23 T3	12 T2	14 T1	16 B2
25 T3	13 T2	18 B1	18 T2
27 T3	16 B4	20 T1	20 T1
30 T2	19 B2	21 T1	22 B1
31 B3	22 B1	27 B3	24 T2
33 B1	24 T1	31 T2	25 T2
34 T2	25 T3	36 B1	26 T1
35 T4	27 T1	37 B2	27 B1
36 B1	34 B1	45 T1	30 B1
41 T3	35 B1	49 T1	31 B2
42 T2	37 B2	53 B1	33 B2
44 B1	39 T2	57 T1	37 T1
49 B2	40 B2		38 B1
50 T2	41 B4		41 B2
51 T2	42 T2		42 B1
54 T1	43 T1		43 T2
56 B3	45 T1		46 T1
60 T2	46 B3		50 T2
61 T2	47 B1		51 T2
	48 B2		53 T2
	50 T3		56 B1
	52 B1		57 T1
	53 T2		58 T1
	54 T3		59 B2
	55 T4		60 T2
	58 T2		62 T1
	59 T1		
	60 B1		
	61 B1		
	62 T1		
	64 T2		

Decisiveness	Achievement Motivation	Need for Self-Actualization
1 T2	1 B1	3 B2
8 T1	2 B3	8 T2
9 T2	3 B3	11 B1
10 B1	6 T4	12 T2
12 T2	7 T2	14 B2
16 T2	20 B4	21 B2
19 T2	25 T3	26 T1
22 T2	26 T3	33 B2
24 T2	27 T3	36 T1
26 T2	32 B3	49 B1
30 T1	41 B5	56 B1
34 T3	47 B2	60 T1
38 T1	49 B4	
42 B1	50 T3	
45 B1	53 T6	
50 T2	55 T6	
53 T1	59 B4	
57 T1	61 T2	
60 T2	63 T3	
61 T2	64 T2	
63 T1		

Source: Edwin E. Ghiselli, *Explorations in Managerial Talent* (Santa Monica, Calif.: Goodyear, 1971), pp. 142–144.

Ghiselli as related to managerial success. In scoring for supervisory ability, for example, be concerned only with responses to questions listed for that subscale in the scoring key (questions 4,5,14,15, and so on). The correct response for question 4, using the supervisory-ability score key, is B, and this response is worth two points. If you choose "cheerful" (B for bottom response) as opposed to friendly (T for top response), award yourself two points. A top response to question 5 ("energetic as opposed to ambitious") earns an additional two points. The sum of points earned for all of the items listed in the scoring key for a particular subscale is your score for that subscale. Higher scores for all the subscales *except job security* are related to managerial success. On the job-security subscale, lower scores are better predictors of managerial success.

Exhibit 15-3 provides norms for each subscale. The norms were developed by Ghiselli in such a way that it is possible for respondents to compare their scores with a cross-section of the adult male and

EXHIBIT 15-3
Selected Norms: The Self-Description Inventory

Supervisory Ability		Intelligence		Self-Assurance		Decisiveness	
Score	Percentile Rank	Score	Percentile Rank	Score	Percentile Rank	Score	Percentile Rank
43	99	56	99	39	99	32	99
43	98	55	98	38	98	31	97
41	97	54	97	37	96	30	95
40	93	53	96	36	94	29	90
39	89	52	93	35	91	28	85
38	85	51	90	34	87	27	79
37	80	50	86	33	82	26	72
36	76	49	82	32	74	25	65
35	72	48	77	31	65	24	59
34	67	47	72	30	56	23	50
33	61	46	67	29	47	22	41
32	55	45	62	(28)	39	21	34
31	48	44	57	27	33	20	28
30	43	43	53	26	27	19	22
29	37	42	49	25	22	18	15
28	32	41	44	24	18	17	12
27	28	40	40	23	14	16	9
26	23	39	35	22	9	15	6
25	19	38	30	21	7	14	4
24	15	(37)	26	20	6	13	3
(23)	9	36	22	19	5	(12)	2
22	8	35	19	18	4	11	1
21	6	34	16	17	3		
20	5	33	14	16	2		
19	3	32	12	15	1		
18	2	31	10				
17	1	30	8				
		29	6				
		28	5				
		27	4				
		26	3				
		25	2				
		24	1				

EXHIBIT 15-3 cont.

Achievement Motivation		Need for Self-Actualization		Need for Security	
Score	Percentile Rank	Score	Percentile Rank	Score	Percentile Rank
58	99	17	99	19	99
57	98	16	98	18	98
56	97	15	94	17	97
55	96	14	87	16	94
54	94	13	78	15	87
53	91	12	68	14	78
52	88	11	54	13	68
51	84	10	34	12	61
50	81	9	20	11	52
49	77	8	11	10	44
48	73	7	4	9	37
47	69	6	2	8	26
46	64	5	1	7	17
45	60			6	10
44	56			5	5
43	51			4	1
42	46				
41	39				
40	35				
39	30				
38	26				
37	23				
36	21				
35	19				
34	17				
33	15				
32	13				
31	12				
30	10				
29	9				
28	7				
27	5				
26	4				
25	3				
24	2				
23	1				

Source: Edwin E. Ghiselli, *Explorations in Managerial Talent* (Santa Monica, Calif.: Goodyear, 1971), pp. 145–147.

female population employed in the United States. A score of 34 on the supervisory ability subscale, for example, converts to a percentile ranking of 67. This means that a person scoring 34 is higher on this quality than 67 percent of the adult work population but lower than 33 percent of that same group. Comparing your scores with the norm group can provide you with a general indication of how you compare with others in the traits Ghiselli found to be related to *general* managerial success.

CONSIDERING COMPETENCIES
IN ADMINISTRATION

University preparation programs in educational administration are in part designed to provide students with specific competencies they will need to function as administrators on the job. Competency development, of course, is not the only aspect of such preparation programs. Most programs are interested as well in the statespersonship components of administrative roles in education. Thus the programs give much, often most, of their attention to providing future administrators with a sound grasp of administrative and organizational theory, an understanding of the workings of our political system, a sound educational philosophy, and a commitment to a set of values which provide one with the basis for developing long-term educational management platforms. It is this emphasis on conceptual skills which equips a person for a career in educational administration.[11] Without this emphasis, a preparation program would at best provide students with only job-entry training.

Nevertheless, administrative behavior implies action, and administrative action requires that one possess certain technical skills as well as those considered more conceptual. Unlike conceptual skills, which often defy precise definition, the technical skills are easier to articulate. Often the technical skills required to function in a given job are listed as competencies for that role. Similarities will exist in the competencies required for different administrative roles, but important differences exist as well. Department chairpersons for example, might be expected to regularly use the latest clinical supervisory techniques in working with teachers, but not the superintendent of schools. On the other hand, the superintendent might be expected to regularly prepare and present testimony on matters of school finance to state legislative committees, but not the chairperson.

[11]See our discussion of administrative skills which appears in Chapter 1.

A list of competencies associated with the secondary-school department chairperson's leadership roles is provided in Exhibit 15–4.[12] This is an ideal list of competencies and therefore should not be viewed as a standard for qualification for a position. *The list represents the level of competence one needs to achieve as one strives throughout one's career to attain maximum professional potential.* Similar lists are available for other administrative roles.[13] Such lists can be used to help you plan your formal course of study as you pursue a university preparation program. Formal programs, however, can contribute only so much. Responsibility for filling the gaps will depend on your participating in school-district inservice, attending professional conferences, and planning an independent program of professional development. Competency lists are specific enough to enable one to estimate the extent to which he or she is likely, or not likely, to enjoy engaging in particular activities. The hallmarks of a sound career decision are future success *and* enjoyment.

Exhibit 15–4 lists and arranges competencies for the secondary-school chairpersonship in a fashion which permits self-analysis. For purposes of illustration, assume that you are interested in a position as department chairperson. For each competency, indicate whether you are satisfied with your present level of performance in this area, if you need additional help, and if you think you will enjoy regularly engaging in this sort of activity. You might wish to add, revise, or delete this list as you review competencies for such roles as elementary or seconday school principal or central-office specialist. Share your responses to the first two questions for each competency with a colleague or supervisor at work. Responses to the third question require serious reflection. If you responded no to many or most of the items, it may be helpful to review your aspiration for a career in educational administration with family members or other confidants. *Remember, the list is ideal and represents a blueprint for setting targets and making plans for career-long professional growth.*

[12]This list is adapted from Thomas J. Sergiovanni, *Handbook for Effective Department Leadership Concepts and Practices in Todays Secondary Schools* (Boston: Allyn & Bacon, 1977), pp. 13-18. The Competencies were originally developed by Ben Harris and John King, *Professional Supervisory Competencies: Competency Specification for Instructional Leadership Personnel.* Special Education Supervisory Project, University of Texas at Austin, Rev., 1975; and Lloyd McCleary and Kenneth McIntyre, "Competency Development and University Methodology," in *The Principals Search* (Washington, D.C., National Association of Secondary School Principals, 1972), pp. 53–68.

[13]See, for example, Jack Culbertson, *Performance Objectives for School Principals* (Berkeley, Calif.: McCutchan Publishing Corp. 1974), and Delwyn Haroldson, "What is the Principalship?—A Study of the Competencies and Functions of the Elementary School Principal," Doctoral Dissertation, University of Idaho, 1974.

EXHIBIT 15-4
Sample Competencies for Chairpersons

	I AM SATISFIED WITH MY PRESENT LEVEL OF COMPETENCE IN THIS AREA		I NEED ADDITIONAL HELP ON THIS		I THINK I WILL ENJOY THIS ACTIVITY	
	YES	NO	YES	NO	YES	NO
EDUCATIONAL LEADERSHIP						
1. *Setting Instructional Goals* Given a mandate to clarify major goals of instruction, you can lead groups of parents, citizens, specialized personnel, teachers, and pupils through a series of discussions, presentations, training sessions, and other experiences to produce a report showing some of the most important instructional goals on which there is agreement.	✓					
2. *Designing Instructional Units* You can design instructional units which specify targets and objectives, instructional sequences, a variety of appropriate teaching/learning activities, materials, and evaluative procedures.			✓			
3. *Developing and Adapting Curricula* Having secured innovative curricula developed outside the school or district, you can adapt the curricula to meet the needs of a student or student group, and make them available to local personnel for use in guiding instructional planning.	✓					

390

EXHIBIT 15-4 cont.

	Competence Level Satisfactory		Need Additional Help		Activity Sounds Enjoyable	
	YES	NO	YES	NO	YES	NO
4. *Evaluating and Selecting Learning Materials* Given expressed needs for learning materials, you can develop a set of evaluative criteria and procedures to determine the quality, utility, and availability of learning materials, and can organize and conduct review sessions where teachers and other personnel can apply the criteria to new materials and make recommendations for acquisitions in needed areas.	✓					
5. *Evaluating the Utilization of Learning Resources* Given an array of learning resources currently available for use, you can design and conduct a study to determine the extent and appropriateness of their utilization, and based on the results of that study, can make recommendations for the improved utilization of specific learning resources in specific ways.			✓			
6. *Producing Learning Materials* Given learning needs and a curricular design to meet those needs, you can arrange for the production of the necessary learning materials to complement, fulfill, and/or enhance the aims of the curriculum.			✓			
7. *Supervising in a Clinical Mode* Given a teacher experiencing difficulties within a classroom, you can lead the teacher through a clinical cycle			✓			

EXHIBIT 15-4 cont.

	Competence Level Satisfactory		Need Additional Help		Activity Sounds Enjoyable	
	YES	NO	YES	NO	YES	NO
using classroom observation data, non-directive feedback techniques, and various planning and in-service experiences to produce significantly improved teacher behavior.						
8. *Planning for Individual Growth* Given a teacher and data concerning various facets of his/her on-the-job performance, you can assist the teacher in establishing individual professional growth plans which include objectives for change in classroom practices, a schedule of experiences sequenced for continuous stimulation and growth, criteria specified for interim and terminal evaluation, and a specified period for accomplishing the objectives.			✓			

SUPERVISORY LEADERSHIP

1. *Building a Healthy Climate* ✓ You know and are able to employ model(s) that identify organizational conditions important to the building of self-actualization in the staff and the satisfaction of ego needs of individuals.

2. *Team Building* You know ✓ about and are able to employ procedures for establishing organizational goals, clarifying roles, planning and otherwise providing structure in order for individuals to relate to each other in cooperative and supporting ways.

EXHIBIT 15-4 cont.

	Competence Level Satisfactory		Need Additional Help		Activity Sounds Enjoyable	
	YES	NO	YES	NO	YES	NO
3. *Resolving Conflict* You know about and are able to work through conflict situations with students, parents, teachers, and others related to school activity involving role conflict, value conflict, goal conflict, and interpersonal conflict.	✓					
4. *Making Decisions* You know about and are able to apply decision-making models, and, through participatory procedures, develop with the students and staff rational approaches to problem solving; focusing both on problem content and on process.	✓					
5. *Planning and Organizing Meetings* You know about and are able to plan and operate meetings which are effective because they get the job done and at the same time build staff identity and commitment to group decisions.	✓					
6. *Recruiting and Selecting Personnel* You know about and are able to engage in a variety of selective recruitment activities, and can secure a list of several possible applicants from various sources, can systematically secure and validate relevant information on the applicants by conducting personal interviews, by checking with previous employers, and by using other selection procedures, and can prepare a set of	✓					

EXHIBIT 15-4 cont.

	Competence Level Satisfactory		Need Additional Help		Activity Sounds Enjoyable	
	YES	NO	YES	NO	YES	NO

recommendations for filling the vacancies with the applicants who will best fulfill job requirements.

7. *Assigning Personnel* You know about and are able to analyze the needs, expectations, and composition of existing staff groups in various units, and, based on that analysis, you can prepare and justify recommendations for assigning and reassigning staff members to positions for optimum educational opportunity.

8. *Bringing About Change* You know about and are able to build a change strategy which takes into account human factors helping or hindering change, level of acceptance needed from teachers for successful implementation and a realistic appraisal of the amount and kind of influence you have as a change facilitator.

ORGANIZATIONAL
LEADERSHIP

1. *Revising Existing Structures* Having determined the strengths and weaknesses of an existing organizational structure, you can propose carefully reasoned or research-supported changes, which may include the alteration of assignments, of the use of staff time, of the

EXHIBIT 15-4 cont.

	Competence Level Satisfactory	Need Additional Help	Activity Sounds Enjoyable
	YES NO	YES NO	YES NO

required reporting patterns, or of the allocation of resources to improve efficiency, productivity, and morale, and, in so doing, improve efficiency.

2. *Assimilating Programs* Given a successful instructional program operating within a department, center, classroom, or other unit, you can design a plan for the smooth integration of the entire program or selected components thereof into a larger system, prepare a time-table and assignments for the transferring of responsibilities, and assure that the instructional improvement evidenced in the program is continued in the system to which it is transferred.

3. *Monitoring New Arrangements* Given the task of implementing a new organizational arrangement, you can determine reporting procedures, compare actual operations with planned developments, and when necessary, make recommendations to modify operations to bring them into agreement with formulated plans.

4. *Developing a Staffing Plan* Given a new project proposal which specifies budget, general objectives, and operational procedures, you can describe essential staff positions to be filled, develop job descriptions

EXHIBIT 15-4 cont.

	Competence Level Satisfactory		Need Additional Help		Activity Sounds Enjoyable	
	YES	NO	YES	NO	YES	NO

for each, and specify the competencies required of the individuals who will fill the positions.

5.   *Informing the Public*   You can establish, promote and maintain favorable impressions of public school programs among community members by disseminating school information through the public media, by speaking to public and school groups, by conferring with parents and other interested individuals, and by meeting, as necessary, with community groups and leaders.

6.   *Student Discipline*   You can establish adequate control of the student body and provide necessary disciplinary rules with the help and cooperation of teachers, parents and students.

7.   *Policies and Procedures* You know about and are able to establish a system of policies and procedures, linked to and justified by educational goals and purposes, which facilitates and frees teachers to work more effectively and which sets high standards for that work.

ADMINISTRATIVE LEADERSHIP

1.   You know about and are able to employ managerial planning tools and procedures in administering your department.

EXHIBIT 15-4 cont.

	Competence Level Satisfactory		Need Additional Help		Activity Sounds Enjoyable	
	YES	NO	YES	NO	YES	NO
2. You can organize, supervise, and manage the financial affairs of the department.	✓					
3. You are familiar with the projected budgetary needs of your school, including salary, operation and maintenance costs.	✓					
4. You know the financial situation of your school and can analyze cost by student, grade, by total enrollment, by number graduating, and by number failed or dropping out. You are aware of implications for your department.	✓					
5. You can plan the department's educational program in accordance with the available facilities and equipment.	✓					
6. You can apply rational decision making models and procedures in the administration of department programs.	✓					
7. You are able to keep accurate records of purchasing needs, inventories, expenditures and other business functions.	✓					

Source: Adapted from Thomas J. Sergiovanni, *Handbook for Effective Department Leadership Concepts and Practices in Today's Secondary Schools* (Boston: Allyn & Bacon, 1977), pp. 14-18. The competencies are adapted from lists developed for administrators and supervisors by Ben Harris and John King, *Professional Supervisory Competencies, Competency Specification for Instructional Leadership Personnel*. Special Education Supervisor Training Project, University of Texas at Austin, Rev., 1975; and Lloyd McCleary and Kenneth McIntyre, "Competency Development and University Methodology," in *The Principal's Search* (Washington D.C.: National Association of Secondary School Principals, 1972), pp. 53–68.

LIFE GOALS AND CAREER PLANNING

It is no secret that administrative positions are demanding in time, commitment, and talent of those who seek them. No systematic link exists, however, between the presence or lack of health and happiness and positions of responsibility such as educational administration. Some studies suggest that greater responsibility at work increases opportunity for many to experience greater intrinsic satisfaction from work and greater satisfaction in general.[14] Others point out the stresses and strains on health and family which can accompany increases in job responsibility.[15] Probably the effects of increased upward mobility are too idiosyncratic for generalizing. A critical factor, nevertheless, is the extent to which one is able to find satisfaction in his or her career on the one hand and accommodate the career interests to the needs and requirements of other life goals.[16]

Some individuals prefer to avoid thinking about what they value in life and what they hope to achieve as private persons and as public professionals. The pursuit of one goal can result in the neglect of others, and some would rather avoid than face up to goal conflict. Without committing oneself to goals, a person cannot fail. Avoiding the goal issue then, avoids the issue of success and failure. We believe it is important for one to face up to what his or her job is and what it can become, and to come to grips with what one seeks and values in life

[14]See for example, Lyman Porter, "Job Attitudes in Management: Perceived Deficiencies in Need Fulfillment as a Function of Job Level." *Journal of Applied Psychology,* 47 (1963), 386–397.

[15]See for example, Lotte Bailyn, "Career and Family Orientation of Husbands and Wives in Relation to Marital Happiness," *Human Relations,* 23 (1970), 97–113; P. Evans, "The Price of Success: Accomodation to Conflicting Needs in Managerial Careers." Doctoral Dissertation, MIT, 1974.

[16]Satisfaction with one's career choice is a slightly better predictor of longevity than is overall happiness. Consider the following quotations from the massive and well known study *Work in America* as reported by Donald Sanzotta in his book *Motivational Theories and Applications for Managers* (New York: AMACOM, 1977) p. 5, p. 6.

In an impressive 15-year study of aging, the strongest predictor of longevity was work satisfaction. The second best predictor was overall happiness. These two socio-psychological measures predicted longevity better than a rating by an examing physician of physical functioning, or a measure of the use of tobacco, or genetic inheritance. Why is job satisfaction perhaps one of the best ways of extending the length of life? . . .

Research findings suggest that *physical* factors may account for only about 25 percent of the risk factors in heart disease, the major cause of death. That is, if cholesterol, blood pressure, smoking, glucose level, serum uric acid, and so forth, were perfectly controlled, only about one-fourth of coronary heart disease could be controlled. Although research on this problem has not led to conclusive answers, it appears that work role, work conditions, and other social factors may contribute heavily to this unexplained 75 percent of risk factors.

both personally and professionally. This is the sort of painstaking analysis which can help you decide if you should pursue a career in educational administration. To assist in this effort, an abridged version of a personal and career-planning exercise, developed by David Kolb, Irwin Rubin, and James McIntyre, is provided for your use.[17] The exercise, complete with instructions, appears as Exhibit 15–5.

EXHIBIT 15-5
Life Goal Inventory

The purpose of this inventory is to give you an outline for looking at your life goals systematically. Your concern here should be to describe as fully as possible your aims and goals in all areas of your life. Consider all goals that are important to you, whether they are relatively easy or difficult to attain. Be honest with yourself. Having fun and taking life easy are just as legitimate life goals as being president. You will have a chance to rate the relative importance of your goals later. Now you should try to just discover *all* of the things that are important to you.

To help make your inventory complete, we have listed general goal areas on the following pages. They are:

A. Career satisfaction
B. Status and respect
C. Personal relationships
D. Leisure satisfactions
E. Learning and education
F. Spiritual growth and religion

These categories are only a general guide; feel free to change or redefine them in the way that best suits *your own life*. The unlabeled area is for whatever goals you think of that do not seem to fit into the other categories.

Directions: First fill out your own goals in the various sections of this inventory, making any redefinitions of the goal areas you feel necessary. Ignore for the time-being the three columns on the right-hand side of each page. Directions for filling out these columns appear at the end of section G.

A. CAREER SATISFACTION

Your goals for your future job or career, including specific positions you want to hold.

---

[17]David Kolb, Irwin Rubin, and James McIntyre, *Organizational Psychology: An Experiential Approach,* 1st ed. (Englewood Cliffs, N.J.: Prentice-Hall, 1971).

Individual Redefinition:

Specific Goals	Importance (H, M, L)	Ease of attainment (H, M, L)	Conflict with other goals (yes or no)
1.			
2.			
3.			

B. STATUS AND RESPECT

To what formal and informal groups do you want to belong? What are your goals in these groups? To what extent do you want to be respected by others? From whom do you want respect?
Individual Redefinition:

Specific Goals	Importance (H, M, L)	Ease of attainment (H, M, L)	Conflict with other goals (yes or no)
1.			
2.			
3.			

C. PERSONAL RELATIONSHIPS

Goals in your relationships with your colleagues, parents, friends, people in general.

Individual Redefinition:

Specific Goals	Importance (H, M, L)	Ease of attainment (H, M, L)	Conflict with other goals (yes or no)
1.			
2.			
3.			

D. LEISURE SATISFACTIONS

Goals for your leisure time and pleasure activities—hobbies, sports, vacations; interests you want to develop.
Individual Redefinition:

Specific Goals	Importance (H, M, L)	Ease of attainment (H, M, L)	Conflict with other goals (yes or no)
1.			
2.			
3.			

E. LEARNING AND EDUCATION

What would you like to know more about? What skills do you want to develop? To what formal education do you aspire?

Individual Redefinition:

Specific goals	Ratings		

F. SPIRITUAL GROWTH AND RELIGION

Goals for peace of mind, your search for meaning, your relation to the larger universe, religious service, devotional life.
Individual Redefinition:

Specific goals	Ratings		

G. OTHER PERSONAL GOALS

Definition:

Specific goals	Ratings		

DIRECTIONS FOR RATING GOALS

Now that you have completed the inventory, go back and rate the importance of each goal according to the following scheme:

H—Compared to my other goals this goal is very important.

M—This goal is moderately important.

L—A lot of other goals are more important than this one.

According to the following scheme, rate each goal on the probability that you will reach and/or maintain the satisfaction derived from it.

H—Compared with my other goals, I easily reach and maintain goal.

M—I reach and maintain this goal with moderate difficulty.

L—It would be very difficult to reach this goal.

In the last rating space, write whether or not (Yes or No) the goal is in conflict with any of your goals. Then fill out the Goal Conflicts sheet which follows.

Goal Conflicts

List the goals that are in conflict with one another. Which ones are the most serious? Which will require your personal attention to be resolved?

1.

2.

3.

4.

5.

Anticipating Conflicts

One of the major deterrents to goal accomplishment is the existence of conflict between goals. The person who ignores the potential conflicts between job and family, for instance, will probably end up abandoning goals because of the either/or nature of many decisions.

The cross-impact matrix is one method of anticipating possible conflicts. List your goals on both axes of the matrix in order of priority (Goal 1 is first on both horizontal and vertical axes). The next step is to estimate the potential impact of the vertical goal statements on the horizontal, using the following symbols:

(+) for a helpful impact ("working on Goal 1 will help me with Goal 3")

(–) for a hindering impact ("working on Goal 2 will make it more difficult to accomplish Goal 5")

(0) for no impact of any kind

Think about your goal statements carefully as you do this. Try to think of all possible conflict situations and enter them.

THE CROSS-IMPACT MATRIX*

	Goal 1	Goal 2	Goal 3	Goal 4	Goal 5	Goal 6	Goal 7	Goal 8
Goal 1								
Goal 2								
Goal 3								
Goal 4								
Goal 5								
Goal 6								
Goal 7								
Goal 8								

List conflicts in order of importance:
1.
2.
3.
4.
5.

*This portion of the personal and career planning exercise is from Kolb *et al.*, *Organizational Psychology*, 2nd ed. (1974), p. 307.

Removing Obstacles

What personal shortcomings will keep me from achieving my goals?

1. _____

2. _____

3. _____

4. _____

What obstacles in the world will keep me from achieving my goals?

1. _____

2. _____

3. _____

4. _____

What can I do to eliminate or lessen the effect of any of these obstacles or shortcomings? (Note that you need not eliminate the block entirely. Anything you can do to lessen the force of the obstacle will start you moving toward your goal.)

OBSTACLE   WHAT CAN I DO ABOUT IT?

_____   _____

_____   _____

_____   _____

_____   _____

_____   _____

_____ _____

_____ _____

_____ _____

_____ _____

_____ _____

What specific things can I do which will move me toward my goal?

1. _____

_____

2. _____

_____

3. _____

_____

4. _____

_____

5. _____

_____

_____

Circle the one which you are going to emphasize the most.

Who can help me achieve my goals?   *What will I ask of them?*

1. _____   _____

                                 _____

                                 _____

                                 _____

                                 _____

2. _____   _____

                                 _____

                                 _____

                                 _____

                                 _____

Source: This personal and career planning exercise is an abridged version from David Kolb, Irwin Rubin, and James McIntyre, *Organizational Psychology: An Experiential Approach* (Englewood Cliffs, N.J.: Prentice-Hall, Inc., 1971), pp. 277–288. © 1971. Reprinted by permission.

QUALIFYING FOR A POSITION

Obviously, one's career-decision problems are not solved by engaging in exercises of the sort outlined in previous sections. But such analyses can help to clarify both what is desirable and what is possible as one considers a career in educational administration. In this section some thought is given to qualifying for a position after a career decision is made.

Chance plays an important role in any career decision and in subsequent career development. In a tight job market such as we are now experiencing, one needs to plan strategies for making chance work. Enrolling in a university educational-administrative training program and obtaining a state certifying license for an administrative role and a graduate degree are necessary *but not sufficient* for subsequent employment. You now need to become employable by increasing your chances of being in the right place at the right time and by developing attractive qualifications and interests over and above formal licensing requirements. Work on the latter increases your visibility among potential employees and provides you with a reputation as being a desirable prospect—both of which contribute to the former.

You can help increase your employment chances by becoming acquainted with the professors you have for courses and other training experiences in your university training program. Professors should know of your serious interests in a career, since many students sample courses from educational-administration curricula without intending to pursue this career. Show your leadership talents by engaging in class assignments and seeking class responsibility. Be sure that your academic advisor knows of your interests and talents.

You should also consult with administrators in your district about your interests. Take advantage of on-the-job opportunitites to learn more about and express an interest in educational administration. View committee work and attending meetings as opportunities. Working out a part time *unpaid* internship with your present school or school district can be helpful in obtaining needed experience, as well as providing an opportunity to demonstrate your leadership talents and your commitment to educational administration.

Seeking formal semi-administrative responsibilities can also be helpful. Some responsibilities, such as those of department chairperson or athletic director, are considered prestigious and encompass a great deal of responsibility; others, such as student-activity, attendance, or media coordinator, may be viewed as less important; but all should be considered as opportunities. A job well done at this level can increase one's chances for promotion. District-wide committee work provides a means for becoming acquainted with teachers and administrators in other schools and with personnel at the central office. Successful district-wide committee chairpersonships increase one's chances for promotion within the district, and help build the kind of record that potential employers elsewhere find attractive.

In districts characterized by accepting and cooperative teacher association-union and administrator-board relationships, leadership responsibilities with the teacher organization can be helpful in career advancement. Obviously insurgent and belligerent teacher-organization behavior will not be viewed with favor; but, assuming a level of civility, responsible teacher-organization leadership is often viewed as an asset in seeking an administrative position. Demonstrated community interest in the form of knowledge about community life and active leadership in some aspect of this life, are typically viewed as very desirable by potential employers. Quality of participation may well be more important than quantity on this count. One is less impressed with membership in an array of organizations than with *active* participation in selected community activities.

Not to be overlooked in qualifying for an administrative position is attention to one's responsibilities as a teacher. Neglect of one's classroom responsibilities and general carelessness in, or disdain for, assuming one's role as a teacher is likely to close the door to an administrative position regardless of how strong the other indicators seem. No direct relationship exists between the quality of one's teaching performance and subsequent success as an administrator; thus, excellence in teaching is not usually viewed as a prerequisite. Administrators and school boards, however, do require a responsible and conscientious teaching record coupled with evidence of at least average, and preferably above average, teaching ability. *Ability is used here in an artistic sense and refers to one's performance capabilities—as opposed to cognitive knowledge about educational philosophy, principles of pedagogy, and educational sociology and psychology. On these cognitive dimensions, a high level of mastery is usually assumed to be a prerequisite for administrative positions.*

Perhaps one way of summarizing these suggestions for improving one's employability is to asume that you are evaluating a candidate for a principalship position. What information might you require about this candidate? What clues, for example, might you seek in estimating the extent to which this person has sufficient knowledge of, interest in, and motivation to be a good principal?

SUMMARY

This chapter was designed to help readers focus realistically on the prospects of choosing educational administration as a lifelong career. Though some emphasis was given to discussing career opportunitites, the chapter assumes that career planning is a process which requires self-analysis. In this spirit, an experiential approach was used. Readers were asked to respond to a self-descriptive inventory designed to help assess job-related personality traits; to a competency checklist designed to suggest needed skills in administration and to provide evaluative information on one's present level of competency for each skill and on the likelihood that one would enjoy engaging in that sort of activity; and to a career and life-planning inventory designed to raise issues about what is really important in one's life.

On several occasions readers are reminded that the activities should not be considered as definite yardsticks designed to scientifically determine one's suitability to educational administration. Rather, the purpose of engaging readers in these activities was to stimulate thinking and to increase self-awareness as readers ponder educational administration as a possible career choice.

STUDY GUIDE

Can you recall the meaning of the following terms? Discuss them with a class colleague and apply them to your school community setting.

competencies in administration	job success
goal conflict	life goals
job opportunities	local school autonomy
job satisfaction	managerial success traits

SELECTED READINGS

CARLSON, RICHARD O., *School Superintendents: Careers and Performance.* Columbus, Ohio: Chas. E. Merrill, 1972.

CULBERTSON, JACK, and STEVEN HENLEY, *Preparing Administrators: New Perspectives.* Columbus, Ohio: University Council for Educational Administration, 1962.

JACKSON, PHILIP, "Lonely at the Top: Observations on the Genesis of Administrative Isolation," *School Review*, May 1977, pp. 425-432.

LEVINSON, HARRY, *Executive Stress.* New York: Harper & Row, 1970.

OSIPOW, SAMUEL, *Theories of Career Development.* New York: The Meredith Press, 1968.

INDEX

411

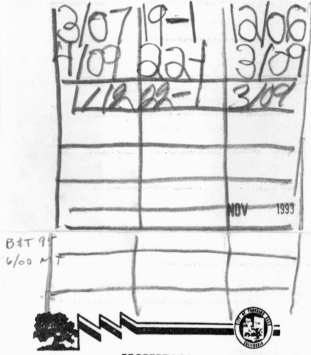

No More
"Nice Girl"

No More "Nice Girl"

Power, Sexuality and Success in the Workplace

ROSEMARY AGONITO, PH.D.

BOB ADAMS, INC.
PUBLISHERS
Holbrook, Massachusetts

Published by Bob Adams, Inc.
260 Center Street
Holbrook, Massachusetts 02343

ISBN: 1-55850-244-0

Printed in the United States of America.

J   I   H   G   F   E   D   C   B   A

This publication is designed to provide accurate and authoritative information with regard to the subject matter covered. It is sold with the understanding that neither the
publisher nor the author is engaged in rendering legal, accounting, or other professional advice. If legal advice or other expert assistance is required, the services of a
competent professional person should be sought.

COVER DESIGN: Marshall Henrichs

331.4133

Dedicated to my sisters

Dr. Mary Antoinette Ampola
whose pioneering spirit, accomplishments,
and generosity I treasure
and
Mary Angela Morgan
whose quiet courage I greatly admired
and whose memory I cherish

Contents

Introduction

I've met countless women in the work force of all races, young
and old, in my eleven years as a gender equity consultant and
trainer, and as a college professor of philosophy and director of
women's studies. Their stories have appalled me and made me
sad, inspired me and made me hopeful. Their stories were my
story and others' stories—a kind of universal set of experiences
with the same substance but different forms.

What women in the workplace have in common is a
lifetime of struggle against barriers, some overt and blatant,
some subtle and almost imperceptible, like a quiet gnawing
inside that won't show itself and won't go away. The most
obvious barriers are external in the people, situations, and
systems around us. Those that are most obscure lie deep
within ourselves, the result of a lifetime of messages programming our thoughts, feelings, and memories, conscious
and nonconscious.

The hardest thing for working women in and out of the
home, next to recognizing the exact nature of such barriers, is
knowing what to do about them. While the women's movement struggles for women's basic rights, each working woman
must interact one-on-one with people in a sexist world—the
underminers and the supporters, the vicious and the indiffer-
ent—while simultaneously battling the hidden enemies within
herself.

I write this book not to contribute more ideas to the women's movement or reach the already converted. I make no claim to contribute new ideas or to speak to intellectuals or academics. Rather, this book is geared to action—action of an individual sort. I write this book to help working women deal with the personal, professional, and structural sexism encountered day in and day out in small affronts and in great offenses. I write it because everywhere I go, I see that feminism has not yet reached the daily lives of most women, who still confront the enemies inside and out feeling very alone, who have not yet experienced the supportive bond of sisterhood advocated by the women's movement.

As many feminists have recognized (from Mary Wollstonecraft to Gloria Steinem), our lack of self-esteem as women lies at the heart of the darkness of sexism. But I do not think that women can be talked into self-esteem, into feeling good about themselves. We feel good about ourselves, very simply, when we *act* in ways that make us feel good about ourselves. Just as I cannot feel successful without concrete accomplishments, or free without the ability to act on my own choices, I cannot feel good about myself if my actions are self-effacing, controlled, passive, or masochistic.

Behavior changes are difficult in the best of times because most patterns of behavior grow from a lifetime of repetition and habituation. Fundamental behavior changes may occasionally follow conscious insights, but normally this happens in moments of "conversion," of profound and shattering insights. For instance, my partner, Joseph, read Pete Singer's *Animal Liberation*[1] years ago and never ate meat or fish again. It happens.

But for most of us, such overnight conversions are rare. Most serious behavior changes reflect a persistent effort, a slow process of growth and change. Each of us has to start where we are.

Feminist theory, process, and practice, like all great movements, are far ahead of their time. The pace of feminism's vision outstrips its ability to reach most people, who lack the means, the affiliations, the time, or even the desire to follow its shattering implications. Feminism frightens people because it challenges the core of our beliefs and being, because it calls us to alter the very structure of our lives. This is true of those who stand to gain as well as those who stand to lose from the movement. Yet there is no question in my mind that most women are hungry for feminist insights, although they don't encounter it much in the ordinary course of their lives. Too often, when they do, it's in the perversions of the media.

This book attempts to reach especially those women in the work force who are struggling day after day with assaults on their dignity, with barriers recognized and unrecognized, with burdens of children and work, with bread-and-butter issues, with survival itself. . . .

The most immediate problem, as I see it, lies in our inadvertent cooperation in our own oppression. While I hear awful stories of how women are treated everywhere I go, especially in the workplace, I don't hear many women telling me that they dealt very well with that treatment or, for that matter, that they dealt with it at all. Instead, I hear story after story of passive nonresponses by women, peppered with an occasional story of a bitter, aggressive lashing-out at the offender. Now and then I'm heartened by the story of a positive, assertive response but sadly, they are too few.

I certainly understand those nonresponses. I've done my share of passive role-playing in the game of life. We all have. This passivity fits our lifelong conditioning as females. We are being "Nice Girls," just as we're trained to be. We don't talk back and we don't fight back. We don't want to hurt anybody's feelings and, above all, we don't want people to stop "liking us." Our upbringings have taught us that being connected with the people around us is our top priority.

Beyond conditioning lies the fear of consequences. Vulnerable as we are, consequences, real or imagined, also paralyze us into inaction. But we pay a terrible price for being Nice Girls. Passivity tells the perpetrator that we don't mind, that his or her behavior is acceptable, or that we don't care enough to object. It serves to embolden the perpetrator and encourages more, and often escalating, abuse. Acting like doormats, or just habitually going along because it seems easier, erodes our standing as autonomous individuals, as human beings, in our eyes and in the eyes of others.

There's little question that women understand what's happening (with the exception of the occasional woman who, despite all evidence to the contrary, swears *she's* never been discriminated against). *But most women genuinely don't know how to deal one-on-one with the offender.* What's worse, women see this as a monumental, almost impossible task, when it really is not. So we act like Nice Girls, even though it's to our detriment.

This is no small matter. Being able to stand up for ourselves, to say no, and to insist on being treated with dignity, is the absolute beginning of change for women. Without doing so, we cannot hope for self-esteem and self-confidence. It becomes hard to take ourselves seriously and hard for others to take us seriously. We experience ourselves as powerless, so we accept, at some deep level, the conventional wisdom that we are inferior.

We know from past experience that we will not simply be given respect, equal opportunity, power, or anything else without insisting on them. As individuals and as a group, women must struggle to be taken seriously, to change the practices and systems we object to, and to end the daily and lifelong oppression of sexism. People like Nice Girls, but liking them is not the same as respecting them.

Too often we look for others to do it for us—to win us rights, to end discrimination, to change the world. Certainly collective action provides a vital basis for change. But the world won't change in any meaningful way unless we change our small piece of it. A lasting revolution in the whole comes from a million revolutions in the parts that make up that whole.

The women's movement is not an abstraction; it's women moving—each of us moving, one by one. If I can't deal with the clown who's putting me down with a dirty joke, the boss who doesn't give me important assignments, the colleague who steals my ideas, or the guy who patronizes and trivializes me, I can't expect the women's movement to change my life in any fundamental way. If I feel stuck in a low-paying, dead-end job, or my boss won't promote me despite all my accomplishments, or my family isn't sharing the menial burdens of life while I juggle career and children, or if I feel too afraid to risk starting a business of my own, no Prince (or Princess) Charming will save me. In the final analysis, I save myself or I don't get saved.

I certainly don't mean to suggest that we are totally alone and isolated in our struggles against sexist barriers. We're not. Countless people, both women and men, are fighting those battles every day. Sometimes the barriers encountered are so great that they can't be overcome by individuals alone. But much of what must be changed in our lives can only be changed by each of us individually, with or without the support of others.

This book is a simple call to action for women everywhere, especially women in the workplace. It seeks to empower women to stand up for themselves—to understand that if we begin to tackle the small affronts, we can move with confidence against the great offenses. Only by refusing to cooperate with sexism can we ever hope to approach simple equity, let alone attempt systemic change in society.

Dealing effectively with everyday sexism involves three steps:

1. We need to understand the nature of the barriers. (What's *really* going on here?)

2. We need to see the connections between all the seemingly disparate events in our lives that comprise systemic sexism. (How does sexual harassment relate to the fact that women don't get paid or promoted the

way men do? How does what happened to me as a child relate to my passive behavior on the job? How does the beer commercial with the sexy nymphette relate to the trivializing and patronizing behavior women experience with so many men? How does what's happening to the woman next to me relate to me?)

3. We need to *act* in a self-affirming, self-respecting way, regardless of the barriers.

In the process, we'll win sometimes and we'll lose sometimes. But win or lose, we'll be in control, in a way that we could never, ever, be if we're passive recipients of objectionable behavior, if we're perpetual Nice Girls. Each time we stand up for ourselves, it becomes easier and easier, and we feel better and better about ourselves. And each time, it gets harder and harder for the perpetrator to act with impunity under the cloak of silence.

• • •

This book shares our stories—my story and those of the women I've met and worked with over the years. I share these stories, many of them very private, so that we can better understand the nature of the barriers we're facing and make the connections between the seemingly disparate events in all our lives. Along with the stories, I share what I've learned about the simple act of standing up for myself, especially how it can be done in a way that is not self-destructive. While these strategies are certainly not a panacea—and each woman will have to decide for herself whether they are applicable in her particular circumstances—they are offered in the spirit of change and hope for a brighter future.

Our story is one of movement from unwitting cooperation in our own oppression to independence and self-affirmation. Our story, despite all its sadness, anger, and despair, is one of hope for change through action that begins in each of our daily lives—grassroots change in the most serious sense of the word.

This work owes a great deal to the women I have known. Their stories have taught me what human endurance is really about, what it means to survive and persist in the face of obstacles large and small, and how sheer determination can prevail against the most difficult or impossible odds.

The stories and incidents I share of other women are anonymous stories. Their names and places have been changed to protect their privacy, and because their stories could easily be, and often are, our stories. I thank all of these women.

Mindful that each generation of women builds on the accomplishments of the women who struggled before them, I also thank the women I've known only through their works: those nameless women of ancient Rome who fought to end the tradition that gave men the right to put their wives to death, the millions of women worldwide who were executed as witches because they did not stay in their place, the early feminists of the eighteenth and nineteenth centuries who stood up for themselves in the face of obstacles that defy imagination, the countless poor women throughout history who have always worked outside the home to feed themselves and their families. . . .

I thank those men, too, who throughout history, stood against their peers and the conventions of their day, to speak out for the humanity of women. In my own life and work, I have known good men working to make things right and to support women's efforts, at home and in the workplace.

I thank the women whom I've known only through their books and works. Without these women I do not know who I would have become—Andrea Dworkin, Robin Morgan, Shulamith Firestone, Marilyn French, Gloria Steinem, Marge Piercy, Mary Daly, Kate Millett, Elizabeth Cady Stanton, Matilda Joslyn Gage, Mary Wollstonecraft, and others. And I thank the few I've been privileged to meet like Florence Howe, Wilma Scott Heide, Midge MacKenzie, Tillie Olsen, Karen DeCrow, Bella

Abzug, and Betty Bone Schiess.

On a more personal note, I thank my spouse of over three decades, Joseph Agonito, who has been able to grow with me in my feminist metamorphosis and to contribute to women's studies in his own right as a teacher, writer, and producer of documentaries. While our long partnership, enduring in a sea of divorce, surely qualifies us as dinosaurs, it also testifies to the ability of women and men to respect, support, and care about each other, despite serious setbacks.

My mother I can never thank enough. Although she spent most of her life enduring one hardship or another, she managed to buffer my sisters and me from the worst emotional tyrannies of the patriarch in our lives.

Finally, I thank my editors at Bob Adams, Inc., for their help and support—Bob Adams, Brandon Toropov, and especially Laura Morin, whose help and suggestions I found valuable at every step of the way.

CHAPTER 1

External Barriers

The "Nice Girl" Syndrome

I've come to realize over the years how important it is to work through our childhood experiences to achieve self-understanding. Who we are, why we made our particular life choices, how our daily actions and responses to the world are shaped, and most important, where we are headed—these secrets lie buried in childhood, waiting to be uncovered.

Whether painful or joyful, such discoveries can empower each of us by widening our understanding and giving us the opportunity to build on, neutralize, or repudiate the early influences on our psyches. In the ongoing process of creating a future for ourselves centered around work and personal relationships, this scrutiny of "growing up" is invaluable in mapping our choices in that future.

The discovery of who I was growing up can free me to pursue what I really want out of life, especially if that turns out to be different from what I, as a woman, have been conditioned to pursue. It can free me from the destructive, programmed responses drilled into each of us as Nice Girls, responses that lie at the heart of our conditioning.

Being a "Nice Girl" means putting ourselves last. It means pleasing others at all costs, accommodating *their* needs and wants—even when their agendas harm us. By striving always to

17

be liked and accepted (which psychologists have long known to motivate women), we suppress our own desires and feelings, our own belief systems and values, to accommodate those of others.

As Nice Girls we don't want to hurt anybody's feelings, so we don't talk back and we don't fight back, even when under siege. We go along; we take it. Metaphorically, the Nice Girl smiles too much, becoming a person whose whole being has frozen into a perpetual grin.

Long-suffering and uncomplaining, the Nice Girl is ever dutiful. But being dutiful is defined as playing by somebody else's rules, rules that we had no say in creating. It means conforming to traditional ideals of womanhood, even when those ideals are hopelessly out of synch with the realities of our lives. Most of all, the Nice Girl syndrome entails passivity and deference. Instead of *acting*, we are forever *reacting*. Instead of helping ourselves, we wait to be rescued, like Cinderella and Rapunzel, who need a Prince Charming to come into their lives.

In the workplace, the Nice Girl stance has serious consequences, rendering us inconsequential, powerless, and dependent. Since we primarily accommodate the agendas of others, we are not taken seriously and are often exploited. All the while succeeding in our careers requires qualities opposed to being a Nice Girl—independence, assertiveness, creativity, competence, power. . . . Yet when we don't behave like Nice Girls, we are called "bitches." The result in the workplace is a schizoid existence that tears us in opposite directions. We want to "make it," but find it hard to shake free of our conditioning.

Being a Nice Girl is ultimately a state of perpetual childhood. This stance is incompatible with being a mature person, with being a powerful individual who is committed to a serious role in the workplace and the world.

Of course, not all women are Nice Girls and those who are have internalized the mindset to varying degrees. But the problem is widespread and affects women of all races and ethnic groups. For these women, it is critical to shed the powerless Nice Girl persona in order to be treated fairly in the workplace. How I've learned to do this is the story of my life.

The Roots of the Barriers in Childhood

My unease over how the world feels about females goes back to my earliest memories. My mother wanted a boy but ultimately had three girls. As the second child, I bore the brunt of that disappointment. She already had one daughter; her next child *had* to be a son, even though, by her own admission, my father didn't care one way or the other.

The story was told and retold throughout my childhood. When I "leapt" out of her womb—that was the way she told it—the doctor announced my mother had had a girl. So great was her disappointment, my mother roundly scolded the doctor for delivering a child of the wrong sex to her. To calm her, the doctor suggested that she could give me a boy's name—why not "George" or "Georgianna" since I had entered the world on George Washington's birthday. My mother was inconsolable and told the doctor what he could do with "George."

By the time her third child joined the family, Mom grudgingly reconciled herself with her fate. It was not to be. She had failed to deliver the valued baby boy to her husband.

I never much liked hearing the story of my birth, although my relatives and the other adults who visited our home laughed every time Mom recounted the incident. That was a good while back, but not much has changed. Today we argue about pre-natal gender selection and the ethics of aborting children of the undesired sex. The first question we still ask at birth is "Is it a boy or girl?" as if this is the single most important piece of information about a newborn.

As an Italian immigrant, my mother did her best, but her culture's expectations, stereotypes, and superstitions about women imprisoned her. A vivid memory of canning vegetables late one summer persists in my mind to this day. I always helped stuff the bottles with tomatoes, pears, pickled eggplants, and the rest. But when I was fourteen, something changed. As my mother readied the rows of bottles, I innocently approached to help, as usual. But to my surprise, she blocked my approach.

"Don't you have your period?" she asked sternly.

She knew I did. It was my first and I was embarrassed because she asked the question with my father present. Touching anything connected with the canning process, I learned, was forbidden during menstruation—my touch would spoil the food.

"But I'll wash my hands," I protested.

It didn't matter, my mother said. I would still contaminate everything.

I was very hurt by the lesson of my "impurity," one I was to relearn again and again as I grew older. Like many other women, I discovered that most, if not all, major religions have some notion of the inherent impurity of women because they menstruate. And many people still won't vote for a female president because they think menstruation makes women unstable and unfit. A colleague at a liberal arts college where I taught once argued, very seriously, that women should not be leaders of anything because their periods make them erratic, emotional, and unreliable.

Other lessons stand out in my mind as well.

I learned very early as a child that people think girls need protection from a host of unspoken threats in the world. All that meant to me growing up was that I couldn't do certain things because I was a girl.

It also occurred to me pretty early that women didn't occupy many powerful positions in society. The people elected as president and vice president of the country were consistently men, and with a rare exception, so were the senators and representatives, the president's cabinet, the religious leaders and priests, the business leaders, and the top educators.

This lack of female leaders particularly bothered me, al-.

though I didn't understand why at the time. Perhaps it was because holding center stage always appealed to me, as did being in charge.

When I was in elementary school, the most visible position for a student was handing out, and then collecting, the attendance sheets from each classroom. Everybody saw you twice a day, and, wow, were you important.

Liking center stage as I did, I aspired to this job and won it in the fifth grade. Becoming an attendance sheet collector was the high point of my elementary school career. I never thought about the fact that these teacher's helpers were always girls—like the kids who stayed after school to clean the blackboards and erasers.

Second to that prestigious position, in my mind, came the job of safety guard at the school crossings. Those kids got to wear splendid white belts that crossed over their chests and wrapped around their waists. They protected people, just like firefighters and police officers. And they were boys.

Well, I aspired to be a safety guard too, despite my gender. Achieving that honor in addition to my appointment as attendance sheet collector made me heady. Was there no end to what I could accomplish?

But I never could figure out why the other kids, especially the girls, called me a showoff. They didn't call the boys show-offs. In high school, when I became president of all the clubs I joined, they told me I was too bossy (the youthful equivalent of the managerial bitch?). I thought I was just doing my job; anyway, they never called the boys bossy.

I also remember how the girls and boys lined up separately in grade school. Boys here, girls there. I guessed that this meant we were different and we ought to stay with our own. I didn't like that either.

School and studying were exciting for me as I grew up. But I remember thinking how sad it was that throughout history women never seemed to do anything—at least, if they did, nobody was telling us. The men, of course, were forever exploring uncharted lands, building civilizations, and founding new countries. And the women? I assumed, as the other kids probably did, that the women stayed home all the time, keeping house and raising babies. That's what my mother did, and it didn't seem like much fun to me.

Mom was the quintessential mother—Italian mothers often are. She sacrificed, took care of everybody else's needs, never seemed to have any needs of her own, waited on Pop, and mostly worried about everything. In so many ways, my mother was the epitome of a Nice Girl.

Motherhood got good press back then, of course. The magazines, the radio (we didn't have a television yet), the school textbooks, even the nuns at religious instruction (who didn't exactly qualify as experts) advocated the joys of motherhood. To me, motherhood didn't seem too different from a job as a domestic servant—except you didn't make any money of your own.

The Church also promoted motherhood. Self-effacement, service to family and church, self-sacrifice, and self-denial defined the good woman. Since marriage was expected and contraception and abortion forbidden, it seemed to me, as a young woman, that involuntary motherhood was a woman's lot. I didn't like that either.

Career Choices

When it came time for my older sister to graduate from high school, she announced her decision to become a doctor. My father was appalled. Mom loved the idea, but she kept quiet.

"What do you want to be a doctor for? You'll only get married and have kids!" Pop growled.

He ranted and cursed and said no way was a daughter of his going to college. It was a waste of money.

In a marvelous show of courage, my sister held firm. Those were contentious times in the family, but my sister won a scholarship and headed for the university. It took a few years for Pop to accept the idea, and then only grudgingly. That broke the ice for me because I had always naively assumed I would go to college, since school was the joy of my life.

Unlike my sister, however, I didn't have the foggiest notion of what I wanted to be. All the women I knew about were mothers, teachers, nurses, waitresses, or secretaries—besides, movie stars, that is, whose pictures we girls exchanged the way boys swapped baseball cards.

When I entered college, I enrolled in the math-science major. It seemed the logical thing to do. In high school I excelled in math and science, took every math and science course offered, was president of the math club (the original all-male club), and finally graduated at the top of my class. To this day, I do not understand why, within weeks, I dropped out of the math-science major and enrolled in humanities. Maybe it had something to do with the fact that all the math-science teachers and most of the students were male, while all my girlfriends were studying humanities. My own lack of direction was probably another significant factor. I later found out from Betty Friedan's *Feminine Mystique*[2] that this is common among women since they are raised to focus primarily on marriage and family.

Despite my achievements, I felt caught between the cultural imperatives of motherhood and my personal imperative of doing something important with my life in a broader social context (the way men seemed to). It was a false dichotomy, of course; both are important. But even as a young person I was able to discern that society did not reward motherhood the way it rewarded public achievement—and I understood that we reward what we value.

In any case, I had no tools or role models for translating my personal imperative into career realities. So I waited for something important to happen to me. The obvious dawned on me slowly. Nobody really thought that I, as a woman, would ever do anything really important. If a woman did accomplish something, she was considered an aberration, more like a man than a woman. I still get angry at phrases like, "You think like a man," "You hit the ball like a man," and "You're as good as any man."

All along the way, I kept encountering sexist attitudes and stereotypes. In graduate school, one of my professors learned that I was planning to marry a man I had met there.

"Well, now she's got what she came for," he told my classmates.

That hurt. Devoted to my studies, I wondered why anyone would think I was in grad school prowling after men.

Around the same time, my sister confronted other forms of sexism. With her top academic credentials, she had been "allowed" into medical school under a reverse quota system; no more than seven women (along with one minority) were allowed admission to that particular male club. Of course, no righteous outcry rose from the white males about the discriminatory practice of quotas then.

In her anatomy class, the professor routinely interspersed pornographic slides of naked women among the academic slides of lumbar spines and hip bones. He joked about doing it to keep the class's attention.

When I finished my doctoral program, the department chair announced that he had the perfect job for me, one that would fit my "circumstances." The job turned out to be part-time teaching in college. My circumstances? Motherhood. Despite the fact that I had spent four years as an undergraduate, two years earning a master's degree, and five years working for a doctorate, he thought a part-time job would be perfect for me!

When I was hired at my first real college teaching job as an assistant professor of philosophy, the department chair told me he especially liked the fact that I was married with children. I guess that made me seem less threatening, like a Nice Girl.

"It'll make it easier for you to fit in here," he said. Single women were apparently suspect.

One of the first male faculty members I met informed me unabashedly that, "Women can't do philosophy. They don't think abstractly." I could never figure out if he was flatly denying my ability or assuming I was a female aberration.

The students certainly thought I was an aberration. After my first philosophy lecture to a huge auditorium of students, a young man approached me. "I can't believe you're a woman; I didn't know philosophers were women. But your lecture was really good anyway," he said.

It seems that it wasn't just my feelings and self-esteem that were hurt by these attitudes; my pocketbook was too. The lone woman economist on staff initiated a salary study to determine if men and women were being paid equitably. We weren't. The study revealed that it cost the women on faculty an average of about $2,000 per year just to be women, all other things being equal. In the seventies, $2,000 was a bundle. The news incensed us women, but in truth, we suffered a much smaller pay differential than most women elsewhere.

Years later, when I'd had enough of academia ("pits of political striving," someone once called it), I left to start my own business. The world outside hadn't gotten much better. Lots of women were jumping the corporate ship because they weren't paid what they were worth, couldn't get promoted to the top, or were forced to conform to a male standard that made no sense to them. So they started their own businesses.

Despite the rapid increase in their numbers, resistance to women business owners remained. One man told me he knew lots of guys "who would *never* do business with a woman!"

"After all," he asked, "if *you* had a choice of doing business with a man or a woman, who would you choose?"

When I said, "a woman," he dismissed me as a feminist. That was the mid-eighties, and by then feminism had become the new "F" word.

Meanwhile, raising a daughter and a son in a sexist society

wasn't easy either. Despite the women's movement working full-steam, and affirmative action ostensibly spreading across the landscape, the day-to-day lives of girls and women remained virtually the same. My daughter didn't aspire to being school attendance collector; they had disappeared. She did aspire, for a fleeting moment, to become a doctor. But one day she came home upset. The other kids had told her flat out that she couldn't be a doctor because she was a girl.

When my daughter decided she'd like to try her hand at carpentry, a struggle of major proportions began. No other girls were registered to take the carpentry course, and she couldn't talk any of them into doing it with her. They thought she was crazy. The prospect of being the only girl in an all-male class with a male teacher, in a program designed by and for men, seemed overwhelming. In the end, the encouragement and prodding of her feminist parents came to nothing in the face of the barriers as she saw them. She gave up carpentry before she began it.

My visits with administrators and teachers at my children's school proved even less fruitful. I would tediously page through the textbooks, noting the endless sexist examples, pictures, and approaches. I'd try to convince the staff that these books had to be changed. "These books condition young people to buy into stereotypes of girls and boys," I'd say. "They limit the options of girls and encourage their passivity and low self-esteem." The staff would nod their heads in mock agreement, but the same textbooks kept coming home year after year while my notes about the stereotypes became increasingly copious.

Understanding the Stereotypes

I've grappled a great deal over the years with the phenomenon of stereotyping (categorizing people based on their membership in a group). We all do it, even those would-be innocents who claim in all seriousness, "I'm not sexist! I'm not racist! I'm not . . ."

While a good deal of stereotyping is certainly deliberate, most stereotyping, I'm convinced, is nonconscious (that is, the nervous system processes information without one's awareness).[3] Hundreds of years of attitudes are so deeply ingrained, so automatic, that they seem natural.

I came to understand these things much better when I was conducting the research for my first book on the history of ideas about women. Sexist attitudes about women, I found, stem from ancient beliefs rooted in both conventional wisdom and philosophical tradition. The chief idea among these is that women are not fully human. This belief has been argued throughout the centuries, based on the premises that women either lack something that defines humanity or that they have too much of something that interferes with their humanity.

What is it we're supposed to lack that makes us less than human? Rationality (especially abstract thought), moral character (lack of deliberative powers to assess right and wrong), and physical strength (the male physique is the model of the human form). And what do we supposedly have too much of that interferes with our humanity? Too much emotion (clobbering our ability to think) and too much sexuality (making us more akin to animals than humans)!

Historically, this belief that women are somehow less than human and therefore inferior to men led logically to a host of conclusions we still encounter today:

- Women are weak.
- Women are emotional and cannot be trusted with important matters.
- Women are irrational, illogical, and indecisive.
- Women do not make good leaders.
- Women exist to serve others, especially men.
- Women belong in the domestic sphere with children.
- Women should be attached to and protected by men.

- Women are not interested in success and power.
- Women are temptresses—sexual creatures who under-
  mine men.
- Women are petty and vain.

These attitudes about women have historically shaped,
among other things, the mandate that women must behave as
Nice Girls. Being Nice Girls presumably compensates for our
weaknesses, keeps us in our place, protects us, and limits our
ability to wreak havoc on men.

Unfortunately, these stereotypes constantly color people's
expectations of women, which, in turn, affect their daily behavior. For example, if I believe, consciously or nonconsciously,
that women are emotional and do not make good leaders, I'll
expect women to perform poorly in positions of responsibility.
When a particular woman applies for an executive position, my
bias will incline me to look more favorably at the male appli-
cant. I will act accordingly.

The process is not particularly conspiratorial (although
sometimes it can be). Rather it's like a filter over everyone's
mind, preventing women from being taken seriously. Disengag-
ing the filter takes a lot of doing.

The fact that stereotypes are so often nonconscious makes
it especially hard to deal with them. The misdeeds that result
are not particularly visible to the perpetrators. What to do about
stereotyping makes most women—and disabled people, and
people of color, and lesbians and gays, and on and on—crazy.
It's *not* easy.

However, armed with an understanding of the process, we
can raise consciousness and help people call stereotypes into
question. I like to draw an analogy with chairs. Typically, we sit
in chairs automatically. If I enter a meeting room with chairs
around a conference table, I sit.

But I don't have to sit. I could lie on the floor, remain
standing, get up on the table. I don't; I sit. And I do so without

being aware of the process.

I don't consciously assign categories to the objects in the room (this is a wall; this is a floor; this is a window). Rather, my mind nonconsciously identifies the objects and my expectations about them (chairs are more comfortable than standing; chairs will support my weight; people expect me to sit in chairs). Then I proceed to behave appropriately toward the chair (I sit in it; I don't eat it)—all nonconsciously.

Stereotypes work in the same way. As long as they remain "behind the scenes" in the mind while affecting behavior, it's very difficult to call them into question, especially since people don't believe they exist. But the task is not impossible.

Loosening the Filter

Returning to the chair analogy, what would make me question my nonconscious categorizations and expectations such that my behavior toward chairs changes? Anything that challenges the legitimacy of the expectations will bring it all to the conscious level. If the chair collapses under me, for example, my expectations will be called into question. The next time I'm about to sit, I'll most likely think about it first, shaking and testing the chair before I sit down.

Stereotypes are challenged in similar ways. Women who behave differently than the stereotypes call them into question. Protests (marches, sit-ins, strikes) also force people to examine their attitudes, even when their initial response is negative. Of course, many people behaving in nonstereotypical ways will produce a long-term change of attitudes more quickly than a single woman.

For my part, if I want people to stop judging and treating me in stereotypical ways, I know I can't buy into those stereotypes or act them out. If I dress in sexually provocative ways at the office, I'm reinforcing the filters on other people's minds that cause them to see women as sex objects. If I constantly talk about my family on the job, I'm reinforcing the belief that women are family-oriented to the point where it distracts them from work.

But this puts the burden of change on women, some women angrily respond. Yes, because women have a vested interest in change, not men. It's a sad fact of life that oppressed people always have to struggle for change; it's never handed to us by those who have a vested interest in the status quo.

Unfortunately, the filter circles women's minds as well, since we've internalized all those stereotypes. So they appear natural to us, too. That's why women routinely act out the stereotypes, making it that much harder to disengage the filter in their minds and everyone else's.

I remember the time I hired a computer consultant to do the layout for one of my projects. She ran her business from an office at her home, so that's where I went to finalize the layout. As she ushered me into her office, we met her husband and small son.

"Do you want me to watch Bobby?" he asked.

"That's OK, I'll take him," she answered and took Bobby by the hand as we descended into her office. The whole time we worked, little Bobby crawled on and off his mother's lap, whimpered, diverted her attention repeatedly, and touched everything in sight, including the layouts. It was annoying and distracting, and I certainly didn't get her undivided attention, despite paying $40 per hour for her time.

Here was a professional woman, wanting to be taken seriously as a business owner, yet acting out the biggest stereotype women entrepreneurs face every day: women really are mothers first, and running a business is something they do on the side to make a few dollars.

A fantasy that emerged in the early days of the women's movement involved women being able to bring their children to the workplace. It was the ultimate "I can have it all" fantasy—full-time employment and full-time motherhood at the same time, in the same place. But despite an occasional article alleging that this or that woman had succeeded in raising her child in the office, the concept was a disaster. It is simply not possible to give our undivided attention to our work (we are, after all, taking payment to do just that) and to engage in child-care at the same time. Infants and children are not programmable. They are unpredictable—quietly self-absorbed one moment, crying and demanding attention the next. It's not fair to the child or the employer—and it's certainly not fair to us.

While many of us buy into the stereotypes inadvertently, plenty of women have cracked the filter in their own minds. One woman who runs a successful construction company constantly deals with skeptical clients. When they find out the owner of the firm is a woman, they start to back off.

Understanding what she's up against, Arlene's first agenda is to demonstrate the depth of her knowledge and skills in construction. On meeting a potential client, she immediately launches into a technical discussion about some aspect of the work they want done. They quickly get the message: she knows what she's doing.

"It saves my time and theirs," she explains.

Playing against the stereotype works well for her and helps loosen the filter on the minds of others.

Loosening the filter in others in any permanent way necessarily involves raising their consciousness about stereotypical thinking. But we won't feel comfortable doing that while playing the Nice Girl role.

The "Flush Out the Stereotypes" Strategy

When confronting stereotypes in others, I find that needlessly making people defensive and angry often serves to entrench stereotypical attitudes because they can dismiss the messenger. Usually there are better ways to approach people blinded by filters they don't know they have.

It's important to recognize that people who operate on stereotypes (*all* of us, to some degree or other) have genuine concerns resulting from the stereotypes. These concerns may be totally unfounded, but I, as the object of the concerns, have to deal with them.

If I suspect that stereotypes lie behind a behavior I object to, I find it helpful to approach the offending party. I try to avoid making it a women's issue initially, because that often makes people defensive, and the message gets lost. Rather, I try to educate the person and change behavior by drawing out the stereotypes. Getting the stereotypes out on the table enables me to deal with them up front.

But isn't this approach being "nice" all over again? No. Refusing to be a Nice Girl doesn't mean I have to behave like a bulldozer or in a self-destructive manner. Nor does it mean that I have to hurt someone's feelings. There is a middle ground— talking to the offender as an equal who expects to be treated with respect. Refusing to be a Nice Girl requires a self-respecting, assertive approach; simply put, I stand up for myself.

My "Flush Out the Stereotypes" technique works like this:

1. I identify the stereotypes that may be influencing the behavior I want stopped.

2. I reflect on the concerns that may underlie those stereotypes.

3. I talk to the person I suspect is doing the stereotyping.

4. I discuss the behavior as a professional concern, not as a women's issue.

5. I try to draw out the stereotypes behind the behavior by getting the person to discuss his or her concerns.

6. Once the concerns are out in the open, I address them.

For example, a friend of mine was not assigned to manage an important project she had expertise in and had worked toward for some time. Extremely upset, she had nonetheless reacted like a Nice Girl, accepting it quietly and passively because she didn't want to offend her boss or the man who received the assignment. She suspected she wasn't awarded the assignment because of her gender, but didn't know what to do about it.

I shared with her my Flush Out the Stereotypes strategy. Together, we assessed the stereotypes and concerns that might be at work in her boss's thinking and came up with a number of possibilities.

1. The project involved extensive travel. Stereotype: *Women don't want to travel; they prefer to be with their families.* Boss's concern: *If I assign the project to a woman, travel will be a significant problem.*

2. The project involved a great deal of overtime. Stereotype: *Women won't put in the time because they must be with their families.* Boss's concern: *If I assign the project to a woman, she won't have enough time to do the job right because of family demands.*

3. The project involved working with male colleagues. Stereotype: *Women do not manage men well; men prefer to work under other men.* Boss's concern: *If I assign the project to a woman, productivity will suffer and dissension may result.*

4. The project involved numerous critical, hard decisions. Stereotype: *Women aren't tough enough to deal with critical decisions.* Boss's concern: *If I assign the project to a woman, the hard choices won't be made and the whole project will suffer.*

5. The clients of this project were "heavy hitters" from a Fortune 500 company. Stereotype: *Women can't deal with the big boys; the big boys don't want to work with women.* Boss's concern: *Business will be lost.*

After our discussion, Mary reflected, "Wow! If I thought someone wouldn't travel or invest enough time, couldn't handle the crew or clients, and couldn't make tough decisions, I wouldn't appoint him or her either. But I *can* do all of those things."

"Then go talk to your boss," I suggested. "Chances are he didn't consciously deny you the job because you're a woman—it's worse than that: he probably didn't consider you at all. It's that filter on his brain! Try to see if you can get him to admit his concerns and then you can deal with them."

Mary took my advice, and later described the encounter. Surprised to learn she had wanted to manage the project, her boss said the following sorts of things: "I didn't realize you'd want to be considered. I didn't think you'd want to travel, what with the kids at home. . . . I figured Bob would be great for the assignment all around—he works so well with the crew. . . . Bob's used to making tough decisions. . . . He interacts well with those guys from X Corporation. . . ."

Mary was able to address every one of his points:

"Yes, I want to be considered for all important projects in my area of expertise. . . . I'm very interested in my career development. . . . Travel is definitely not a problem for me; I enjoy traveling. . . . I've worked with the guys on that crew for two years. We respect and know each other well. . . . I've been dealing with the clients from X Corporation for the last six months and there's never been a problem. . . . Here's a list of the tough decisions I've had to make since I joined this firm. . . . Bob's a good person, but my expertise in this area would have served you well because . . . ."

Mary ended the conversation by firmly stating that she expected to be evaluated as a professional in the future and that she looked forward to directing the next important project in the area of her expertise.

Had Mary accused her boss of sexist behavior, he probably would have become defensive and angry. Mary would not have been able to make the points she needed to make, which challenged his thinking about her (and women in general) in a fairly serious way. One thing is clear: Mary's boss will never think of her in the same old way again. Being a Nice Girl had gotten her nowhere.

Workplace Barriers Everywhere

These days it's my job, as a gender equity consultant, to know what's happening to women. And I know that the barriers women encounter at every level are still great. Their form has changed somewhat, but the substance is the same.

The biggest career obstacles start early. Young women are still tracked, subtly and not so subtly, into work traditional for their sex. Today, the vast majority of women work in traditional careers—the women in these pink-collar jobs generally have it rough. They endure low wages, low status, and powerlessness. That childcare is the lowest-paying professional work in the United States really says something about the way we value women's work—and children, for that matter.

People show surprise when I share the general results (anonymously, of course) of the assessments I often do in my consulting work. When I ask women to rank the barriers they encounter on the job, if any, the lists are remarkably consistent.

Women at all levels rank lack of credibility, trivializing behavior, and stereotyping as some of the most serious problems they confront in the workplace. But at the top of the list, no matter what the women do, emerges career-advancement barriers. This always shocks people because they assume most women aren't interested in success, that female ambition only applies to a few management types.

Well it doesn't. As far as I can see, women in all kinds of jobs—blue, pink, and white collar—desire to grow and advance in their work. Toiling in dead-end jobs is not something women desire any more than men.

I travel a great deal, meeting women from urban, suburban, and rural areas as I deliver my specially designed programs. These are not the fifties or sixties anymore, but the women still have their stories of trivialization, limitations, stereotypes, violence, and outright discrimination—except for those few who keep insisting, in the face of all reality, that they've never been discriminated against.

- A rural woman, determined to become an auto mechanic, was trying to cope emotionally with the frowns, the disapproving looks, the exclamations of, "Why do you want to do *that*?"

- A management woman was at a loss about how to deal with her boss, who had explained that she didn't get a promotion because the men don't want to work for "a girl." She saw a lawsuit as her only option, but worried that it would ruin her career; besides, it was his word against hers.

- A businesswoman was scrambling for money because she couldn't obtain a bank loan to expand her successful business, even though she had collateral.

- A teacher complained about grappling with a male-oriented curriculum that excludes the contributions of women throughout history.

- A nurse felt angry at the disdain of the doctors she works with and may jump the medical ship, as have countless others.

- A secretary was upset because she had just found out that the unskilled male janitors make more money than the female clerical workers who have business school or college training.

- A woman executive accidentally discovered that the younger man she trained, who has the same job description as her, fewer credentials and less experience, makes $7,000 per year more than she does.

- A blue-collar worker in an auto plant endured an onslaught of sexual harassment from the guys, but she tried to be a "sport" about it.

- A retail sales clerk quit her job because her boss cornered her in the stockroom.

- A woman manager expressed hurt and anger because
  a couple of her colleagues implied that she had received a promotion by sleeping with "somebody up
  there." "If so many of us are sleeping our way to the
  top," she fumed, "how come there's so few of us up
  there?"

Yet all of these women had one thing in common. They
had reacted to each affront with anger inside but silence outside. They didn't stand up for themselves; they passively went
along with behavior they objected to rather than confront the
offenders. They were behaving like Nice Girls, while being torn
up inside waiting for things to somehow be made right.

Even women who seem powerful succumb to the Nice
Girl syndrome.

I recently read with interest the story of a managing director at a top Wall Street brokerage firm. For twenty years she
played by the rules, built a solid reputation, and received promotions. But at every step of the way, she discovered, the rewards given to the men on her level were consistently
greater—bigger salaries, bigger bonuses. At each discovery,
however, she held back from any form of protest, rationalizing
her plight. She was grateful for what she had (a six-figure salary) and was embarrassed to seem greedy. Next year would be
better, she kept thinking.

The situation came to a head when she finished working
on a billion-dollar merger. She received a $400,000 bonus,
while a male managing director on her level who had also
worked on the merger was given a bonus of more than $1 mil-
lion. Still she stayed, only to find herself being treated progressively worse.

Although she ran one of the firm's most profitable divi-
sions and was ranked as one of their most valuable employees,
she found herself repeatedly undermined by her male boss, excluded from significant decisions, and stripped of power in her

own division. Eventually she was forced to resign after a clash with her boss.

In retrospect, she says of her tolerance of the pay inequities and the abuse, "I was a jerk." After twenty years, she filed a lawsuit and is essentially finished in her business.

No, she wasn't a jerk. She was behaving as women have been raised to behave, like a Nice Girl—playing by male rules that discriminated against her, staying in her place, "going along." It's a model that seems to work for a while, but ultimately self-destructs.

Sometimes women make barriers for other women, too. A woman at one of my seminars, for example, asserted that women make terrible bosses. She, for one, preferred male bosses. After some heated discussion within the group, it turned out that she had never worked for a woman; she had simply heard how terrible women bosses are.

Often, without realizing it, we hold management women to a different standard than management men. We measure them by the Nice Girl model even though managerial functions require a model diametrically opposed to this model.

Women of color suffer a double burden of racism and sexism. I remember a session in which a management woman complained of being taken for a secretary. An African-American woman jumped in, "At least they assume you're a secretary! Me—I'm the janitor's wife!"

A highly skilled computer technician working for a large corporation, this woman had been sent to a corporate facility to repair a computer. When she arrived at the security gate, the guard immediately said, "You must be here for so-and-so." And he proceeded to rattle off directions for finding so-and-so.

"Wait," she interrupted. "Who is so-and-so? I don't know any so-and-so."

"He's our janitor. You mean you're not his wife? I thought you were bringing him lunch."

Everything deteriorated after that. The men in the computer area wouldn't believe at first that she was a computer technician. As she worked on the computer, they kept asking her whether she was *sure* she knew what she was doing. Apparently they couldn't grasp the notion of an African-American woman being a computer technician.

The double burden falls heavily on older women, as well, who must also contend with ageism, and disabled women, who deal with sexism and health biases. Lesbian women, perhaps, have it toughest of all.

A male participant in one of my seminars pretty much summed it up: "Women in the workplace? Forget it. They've got it *real* bad."

CHAPTER 2

Internal Barriers

Recognizing the Barriers Within

Over time, the external barriers become internalized. Pretty soon we're carrying the enemy around inside.

An enemy inside is worse than an enemy outside. It's harder to see and we never get away from it. It's a little like cancer. We don't know it's there until it's done a lot of damage.

As women, we grow up in a sexist culture as surely as men do. If we're told X is Y long enough, hard enough, and by enough people, we believe it. X is Y becomes the reality and X is X gets forgotten.

I've done my share of buying into the stereotypes and sexist expectations, although I didn't know it at the time. It took the women's movement to wake me up.

In high school I sat on the fashion board of the city's largest department store. That meant I represented my school on an advisory board of girls who met monthly and pretended to have input into the fashion industry. My blown-up portrait hung in the junior department on a wall lined with photographs of all the board members. Boys didn't sit on this or any other fashion board.

Exactly what I was doing on the fashion board is anybody's guess. As a poor kid from an Italian ghetto, fashion was hardly a reality in my family or neighborhood. I considered myself lucky if I received one new sweater and skirt a year, and that was hardly haute couture! But being "into" how you looked was *the* female imperative, and we were all into it.

The fashion board meetings every month taught us the "essentials of beauty." These turned out to be the products sold in the department store, which we were supposed to promote among our friends in school. I remember one of the lessons: every woman, however thin or fat, must wear a girdle. They put a girdle on me, too, but it was on my brain!

The cult of the "look" manifested itself in other ways. I entered the Miss Young America Pageant in high school. Lots of the sleeping beauties did; everybody aspired to be fairest of them all. Well, fairest of them all eluded me, but I came close. I ended up a finalist in the Central New York Miss Young America Pageant and my name appeared in *Seventeen* magazine. What a kick!

In college, a friend asked me about the high point of my high school years. Without hesitating, I announced that I was proudest of having been selected a finalist in the Miss Young America Pageant. That I had graduated at the top of my class academically paled in comparison. I defined myself by fairy tales, not by my accomplishments, intelligence, or talents.

She, in turn, was proudest of having been selected from all the girls to play the Virgin Mary in her church's religious pageant. She defined herself in terms of public role-playing, too.

In college, I was the original Tammy Faye Bakker. Well, almost. I helped keep the eye makeup folks in business. Small wonder, then, I'd be remembered for how I looked, not my brains.

Recently I crossed paths with an alumnus of my undergraduate college, though we didn't recognize each other at first. When we put it all together, it turned out she had been two years behind me in college. The revelation was instant.

"Oh, yeah! I remember well," she said. "You hung out with all the artsy types. Your tiny waist was the envy of all the girls.

We'd sit around and talk about it when you walked by. I was a walrus, but you—you were so svelte, and I'll never forget the plaid skirt you wore. I wanted a plaid skirt like that so badly!"

So, all those years later, I was remembered for my small waist and plaid skirt.

Another message I internalized growing up was that being attached to a male played better than being unattached. After a certain age, I began having a series of boyfriends. That was before the sexual revolution, when being attached didn't mean being "available." "Going steady," we called it.

Being alone (read, *being independent*) somehow didn't feel right. Now this phenomenon has a name: the "Cinderella Complex."[4] I still see it everywhere, especially in young women. Prince Charming is alive and well and he lurks behind the Nice Girl mandate. He's the guy girls and women are trained to believe will "save" them and take care of them for the rest of their lives. Lots of people think he's dead, but he's not.

When high school girls are asked about Prince Charming (without using the term), they overwhelmingly affirm his existence.[5] He's that special guy who has, or will, come into each of their lives and take care of them, happily ever after. Oh, sure, young women want careers now, but they don't see them as necessary. Careers, many young women think, are an option. Big Daddy isn't.

We're still into denial, but what's to be surprised about? Prince Charming is everywhere—on television, in magazines, on soap operas, in romance novels, in music, in movies . . . . Even the "working girl" and prostitute get a Prince Charming on the big screen, but only if she's a "pretty woman." Too bad reality intrudes at some point in the lives of most women.

Looking back, I can see my life, like that of most women, was schizophrenic. I moved along two different, not-so-parallel paths at the same time. Actually, they were incompatible. One followed a serious direction, oriented toward accomplishments, and required me to use my intellect. The other moved along a frivolous path, trivialized my talents, and required a suspension of thought. Since the frivolous path was the imposed norm for women, pursuing the other took hard work, like running up a long, steep mountain.

Along the way, it's very easy to self-sabotage. In fact, self-sabotage is built into the traditional norm for women. Historically, a self-centered woman is an oxymoron. Men, on the other hand, are mostly trained to be self-centered. We can laugh all we want at the feminine equals masochism theory. But "feminine" is a social construct and that's how we're raised. Still.

Those of us who lived through the fifties know it when we see it, and we see it in the 1990s. Biological clocks ticking, cooing babies, and motherhood. Even the lesbians I know want babies!

Now, never mind that the world is splitting at the seams from overpopulation, the divorce rate is 50 percent, single motherhood is *the* formula for poverty, and the "mommy track" spells trouble for a woman's career. Women want it all, and having it all seems to mean having babies, no matter what else is or isn't happening in our lives.

In my day, we didn't call it "having it all"; it just came with the territory. If you married, which you did, you had babies. It was a package deal, even if you worked outside the home.

As a young woman, I was pretty clear about not wanting to be Mother Hubbard, although I wanted Prince Charming. Of course, women didn't *say* that they didn't want kids, not out loud. Come to think of it, I've only met two women in my whole life who actually said "I don't want children."

It isn't as though all women are happy with motherhood. Far from it. And it isn't as though all women can afford children. Far, far from it. And it isn't as though all women have the emotional resources or tolerance to raise children—or that all women have a Prince Charming to support the process.

One of my neighbors some years back had five children. Each morning she would dress and feed them, send them outside, and lock the door. They got fed, but otherwise the house was off-limits to them.

I've heard plenty of women bemoan the fact that they had children—afterwards. Ask older people, women and men, if they're glad they had children, and a surprising number say no. When Ann Landers asked her readers, they flooded her with no's.

So why do we keep having babies? Because we've internalized the message well: motherhood is next to sainthood.

I'm certainly not objecting to motherhood; I am a mother.

I am objecting to the incredible pressure on women to have babies. The pressure begins with the ubiquitous doll in earliest childhood and dogs women into menopause. I am objecting to the concept of universal motherhood, to the idea that a woman *must* be a mother to be whole and fulfilled—an idea that, sadly, we *still* internalize to the core of our being.

Motherhood is a very serious business that should be entered into only with the greatest thought and care. Yet everywhere I go, I find it to be an automatic assumption. To put it mildly, motherhood will affect everything in a woman's life, including her personal relationships, her ability to grow and develop her talents, to function in the broader social context, to engage in the work of her choosing, to be free, and certainly to have a career.

Although many studies have revealed the serious impact of motherhood on women's career aspirations, I have found one study to be particularly compelling. A longitudinal study of high-school valedictorians followed these young women and men to determine whether they had fulfilled their career aspirations.[6]

The study found that despite the fact that female valedictorians typically outperform their male counterparts academically, their chances of fulfilling their career aspirations are slim. Why? Because the women make continual accommodations to the expectation of motherhood (while in college) and to motherhood itself. Their self-esteem and ambition drop while in college, unlike the men.

While the men largely lived up to their ambitions, the women had all compromised their career expectations in some serious way (by dropping out of college or professional school, by accepting traditionally female occupations contrary to their original choices, by settling for fewer degrees than planned). If this happens to the brightest women, we can only imagine what is happening to the rest of us.

Am I suggesting these young women should not have become mothers? Of course not. I am suggesting that the automatic assumption of motherhood as something every women will do and the failure to work through the impact of motherhood minimize women's chances of making enlightened choices.

Yet almost nobody is raising the hard questions about motherhood, especially with young women. To criticize motherhood in any sense is taboo, despite what's at stake. Even feminists have largely backed off the hard questions about motherhood, given the fierce backlash.

When I married, I had one child and adopted another. Looking back, the timing of the kids was awful; they came along at precisely the wrong times. But *I* was largely responsible for those "wrong" times—I and a church that convinced me the rhythm method not only worked but was the only moral form of birth control.

My pregnancy put me to sleep for nine months. Before that, I had spent a wonderful, though financially difficult, six months trying to realize my dream of being a writer. I had written a number of articles and even gotten one accepted for publication, along with a nice check. It was the first year since I was fifteen years old that I didn't have to trek off to a job and school. I loved putting in long days writing. So why did I stop my progress dead in its tracks by getting pregnant? I didn't write another word for years.

The timing of the second child was even worse. I knew I

didn't want to sleep through another nine months of my life or put my body through another pregnancy again. But at the same time, stopping at one child seemed foreign to both my Italian and American cultures. So how to do it without doing it became the question.

Adoption presented itself as the answer. It was the mid-sixties and my activist sentiments were being stirred. What better way to legitimize an adoption than to "save" a foreign child? We tried for a Vietnamese child, but that proved impossible. So we petitioned for a Korean orphan through the Pearl Buck Foundation.

At the time, I was well into my doctoral studies and working as a graduate teaching assistant—an enormously demanding schedule. I enjoyed my work, was exploring exciting areas in philosophy of mind, and for the first time, was clear about my future direction: to become a university professor.

Needless to say, bringing another child into the family was not easy. Indeed, my studies *were* disrupted, although I managed to get myself back together after a while and finish my doctorate.

The two conflicting tracks pulled me in two directions. Or maybe Matina Horner would have found me an interesting subject for her fear of success/self-sabotage studies.[7] Not that I understood any of this at the time; I had no conscious sense of the inner forces driving me. At any rate, I didn't make things easy for myself! That was obvious.

Most of the women I know don't make things easy for themselves. We play out the scripts written for us on a stage of somebody else's choosing, without fully understanding what is happening to us.

No, I'm not blaming the victim. Our victimization is not of our doing, and frankly, I don't care whose fault it is. Blaming gets us nowhere! The issue for me has become to stop being a victim. My message to women is that we need to figure out what is going on and *do* something about it. *No one else will do something about it for us.*

Dealing with the external barriers, in many ways, is easier than dealing with the enemy within. The system has co-opted us beautifully, bringing us to the point where *we* choose the options "they" want us to choose. By being Nice Girls who do what's expected of us, we cooperate in a system that limits and even destroys us as autonomous adults. Usually we're not aware that we're doing it, which makes it all so insidious and hard to deal with.

The Sleeping Beauty myth is partly true: we fall asleep in our youth. But it's not Prince Charming who'll wake us. It's the kiss of enlightenment we desperately need, and nobody else can give us that, although others can provide the tools. We need to commit to that search ourselves.

Consciousness-raising it used to be called. In the 1970s it was the rage, but it never reached more than a handful of women, relatively speaking.

The enemy within women takes many forms: devaluation of self, low self-esteem, negative self-talk, guilt, rejection of opportunities, fear of taking risks, resignation, dependency, and ultimately, abandoning responsibility for our own lives—or trying to. The choice to abdicate responsibility is itself a choice. But victimization is not in our genes, and anatomy need not be destiny. Since we are conditioned to be victims, we can be conditioned to reject victimization. Since we are conditioned to self-sabotage, we can be conditioned to self-respect.

Everywhere I go, I catch glimpses of the enemy within women. When I train entrepreneurial women, one of the biggest challenges is to get them to charge a decent price for their products or services. Self-devaluation translates into low prices because they don't factor in the real value of their time and they don't believe anyone will think they're worth it.

In starting my own business, it's a lesson I learned the hard way. My first prospective corporate client expressed serious interest in my consulting. We had two conversations and things were moving along nicely. Then they asked me to send my fee schedule and I never heard from them again. I found out later that they took one look at my fees, which I had set too low, and concluded I couldn't be any good.

It's a vicious cycle: others devalue me as a woman, so I devalue myself. My devaluation of myself, in turn, reinforces their devaluation. So I unwittingly become part of the problem of perpetuating the stereotype or attitude. When entrepreneurial women learn this lesson and raise their prices, they invariably get taken more seriously.

The same revelations occur when I work with management women. One woman suddenly realized she had, early in her career, started refusing the more challenging and risky assignments.

"Why did I do that?" she asked, amazed at herself looking back.

Or there's the manager who angrily told her boss that her family came first *no matter what.* He had asked her to put in some extra time on a project. Then she fumed ever after because she didn't get promoted.

It's the classic trap of "either/or" thinking. Why must a person's family or career come first, no matter what? Making family top priority, without exception, is as extreme (and stereotypically female) as the traditional corporate demand that one's job comes first, no matter what. *Both* can be important without one habitually shortchanging the other.

False Expectations and Self-Sabotage

False expectations can be self-sabotaging too—expectations of ourselves and the world out there. By the time we reach adulthood, sex-role conditioning, along with social and familial structures, have shaped us into Nice Girls.

It's not that anybody ever sat us down and said, "Now these are the stereotypes of women . . . and here are the things you must do to conform to other people's expectations that women act like Nice Girls."

Instead, countless images rain down on us from the day we're born, insidiously altering our perceptions. They come from the toys (Barbie is still the best-selling toy for girls), from Saturday-morning cartoons, from school, from children's movies, from parents, from peers, from stories, from fairy tales. . . .

Snow White, Sleeping Beauty, Cinderella, Rapunzel—all the same! Prince Charming falls in love with a dead woman (Snow White), or a comatose woman (Sleeping Beauty), or a powerless woman (Cinderella, Rapunzel). Never mind what a strange guy the prince is, kissing dead and comatose women. The message is clear: passivity, powerlessness, and catatonia in women turn men on; the only good woman is a "dead" woman.

And watch out for other women! Potential princesses are victims of jealous, conniving women, especially older women (wicked stepmothers, witches, even mean-spirited sisters). Men, on the other hand, save women (but only Nice Girls—young, pretty, passive ones).

Over time, we are habituated to behave like Nice Girls (even though the behavior leads to victimization), to try to look a certain way (even though physiologically it's impossible for most women), to be mothers (even though many women— crack addicts, child abusers, and so on—have no business being mothers), and to be perfect mothers (otherwise we'll get blamed for whatever happens to our children).

Unfortunately, being a Nice Girl entails passivity and powerlessness. False expectations about how we should look lead to self-loathing. The expectation that all women should be mothers locks many women into inauthentic lives, not to mention the pain inflicted on their children and the destruction wrought on an environment already reeling from overpopulation. Perfectionism consumes inordinate time and energy and sets us up to fail.

One of my friends was growing in her career in banking, receiving raises and promotions. When a big management promotion came her way, she turned it down because she wanted to have children (or so she thought). She didn't want to be encumbered by a management position, although she loved her work.

But she had unrealistic expectations about what having a family means; it's not trouble-free, happily-ever-after. She fell into the false dichotomy of "either/or," quitting her job after the birth of her first child because she thought the child was all she needed in her life.

These days she's a nervous wreck, chasing after two kids, working part-time without benefits, and complaining about not having a moment to call her own. She keeps threatening to "run away from home," and she's dead serious.

False expectations about the workplace hurt us, too. Maybe it's because nobody takes young women aside and says "This is how it is." Or maybe it's because we bring the same romantic notions about our personal lives to the world of work. Whatever the reasons, we carry a series of myths into the corporate world.[8]

Chief among these is the myth of meritocracy: the belief that people are judged and recognized on their performance and ability. This goes along with the myth of reward: the belief that if a person works hard and does a good job, she'll be recognized and rewarded.

I constantly talk to women who complain about working hard and doing a good job but not obtaining the raises or the promotions. They indignantly protest the fact that so-and-so received the promotion because of whom he or she knew, as if this is some kind of revelation! They treat it as an aberration from the norm and are furious. They refuse to understand or acknowledge the reality of politics in all aspects of life, personal and professional.

Yet people interacting with people *are* the essence of any workplace, and relationships between people *are* political.

Of course, hard work and accomplishments are important; most successful people, including women, have a solid track record of accomplishments. But connections between people are important, too.

How ironic that we women, who focus on relationships, cling to these myths about what counts and doesn't count in the workplace. At its core, politics is the art of dealing effectively with people through compromise and consensus. Furthermore, if power is the ability to influence people and shape events, then without politics, power is unattainable.

Women tend to dismiss workplace politics as something negative, and often it is practiced as such. We confuse the destructive ways people frequently use politics with the essence of politics, which is positive. So we wash our hands of it and withdraw from connecting with all but a few of our chosen friends. But we ignore or scorn workplace politics at our own peril; in doing so, we abdicate power to others.

The enemy within holds us back, keeps us from following our dreams, or replaces those dreams with fantasies. Like the woman in one of my career-development programs, a divorced mother of two, a high school graduate, who married too young and is raising her children alone. When I met her, Margo was eking out a living cleaning other people's houses. But she had a dream—to become the owner of a domestic cleaning business with employees.

It was clearly within Margo's grasp. She had a client base that she could easily expand, given the ample demand and lack of competition in her area; she just had no idea how to go about it. But she took the first step by enrolling in our intensive three-week career-development program, faithfully attending every day. Funded by the state, the program was a great opportunity, since it was tuition-free and offered free childcare, free lunch, and transportation reimbursement.

During the course of the program, it became clear that a handful of women were interested in exploring small-business ownership, Margo being chief among them. To accommodate Margo and the others, we arranged funding to offer a free, intensive entrepreneurial training program for the women.

On the day of the entrepreneurial program, Margo never showed and never called. A few weeks later, she phoned at the last minute to say she wouldn't be attending her individual career counseling session either.

With no visible reason for Margo's dropping out that her friends could see, it seems the enemy within struck again—low self-esteem, fear of risk, rejection of opportunity, resignation. All of this was reflected in the way Margo engaged in negative self-talk, constantly putting herself down.

Margo's back to eking out a living cleaning other people's homes. The chains on her spirit are apparently too strong to break, even with help, at least for the time being.

Then there's Sue, a young welfare mother from a rural area who's also a single parent. Sue's dream was to become an auto mechanic, get off welfare, and support herself and her children. She applied to a trade school in a city forty miles away that accepted her. She was eligible for free training and could continue receiving public assistance. Her mother was supportive and willing to relocate to watch the children while Sue attended training. Moving the forty miles seemed the only obstacle, but the trade school provided help in finding housing.

Sue went, looked for housing, decided it was not quite right for her. So she retreated back to her small town, abandoning the whole venture.

At some point we have to stop being victims.

Betty is a classic case of failure to take responsibility for her life. A talented and educated young woman who dreamed of starting her own business, she got lost somehow. She had one child, then another, and another, then a fourth, a fifth, and a sixth.

Despite the warnings of her friends that she should not give up her dreams, Betty abandoned herself totally to her family. That's always dangerous, because giving too much means people take too much. Her husband continued to grow and do exciting things in the world. Betty reduced herself to a servant-drudge. As her family grew, so did her frustration.

We could all see it happening and tried to help, but nobody could make Betty's life choices for her. Betty suffered a severe, early mid-life crisis characterized by deep depression. She made demands on her husband to fill her life and her unrealized dreams. They nearly divorced.

Somehow, Betty had become so paralyzed that she could no longer take any steps to help herself, although opportunities had presented themselves. She was encouraged to explore running a small business in her chosen field, to attend a seminar in starting a business, to team up with friends who also wanted to start a similar business. She did nothing.

Money was never the problem. She just found it difficult to use it to help herself. Today she continues, frustrated but resigned for the moment, because her analyst has taught her to "adjust." Betty now shrugs her shoulders and says, "This is who I am—a mother." What she cannot admit is that motherhood alone has not fulfilled her life, and that the denial of her own needs and aspirations has had serious consequences.

Young women, for all their apparent self-assurance, also carry the self-destructive enemy within. When I talk to adolescent girls about the epidemic of teen pregnancy and the threat of AIDS, they too shrug their shoulders. I'm repeatedly told they don't insist on condoms because the guys don't like to use them! Get real sisters!

My friend, an African-American administrator in a predominantly Latino and African-American city school, laments her difficulties in encouraging young women to think about self-sufficiency and career goals.

"When I urge them to study hard so they can support themselves in the future," she says, "they tell me not to worry—they're going to marry a rich man."

Sure!

A former student of mine, Michele, works with inner-city

girls and young women, pregnant teens, and young women at risk for AIDS. A young African-American woman who's been through it all herself, she identifies with these young women. Although Michele understands why, she despairs over their obsession with boyfriends.

"They think a guy who will love them is the answer to it all," she moans. "Reaching them is very hard."

College doesn't seem to help much either. Research indicates that young women still mostly major in boyfriends.[9] Career goals and friendships with other women apparently take a back seat to the search for Mr. Right. Patriarchal power continues to mold female aspirations and accomplishments.

At the same time, our capacity for denial is strong. During a recent workshop I led, a group of women were discussing the overriding importance of a man in the lives of young women. A college senior in the group protested that it was not true.

I found her protests fascinating in light of her own story. After four years of hard work earning a degree in business management, honors grades, and a reputation as a bright young woman committed to her work, she was planning to marry immediately after graduation. The conditions of the marriage involved moving to a remote rural area where, by her own admission, there was no possibility of a career in her field. She was planning to work as a waitress and give up everything she had worked for to follow the man in her life. Yet this young person denied, in all seriousness, that women still do such things! She apparently had no sense of the connections between her own choices and the problems that plague women.

Sometimes the enemy within causes us to turn on other women. Growing up, I remember the old Italian women talking in hushed tones about a bad woman in their village back home who got what she deserved. They used the Italian word for prostitute to describe her, but I knew from the way they said it that she wasn't really a prostitute.

I was a teenager before the story finally made some sense.

It was one of those simple stories on the surface; its pain and layers of meaning never appeared when people talked about it.

It seems my aunt's husband was carrying on an affair with a married woman in the village. When my aunt learned of the affair, she determined to end it, one way or the other.

One day she went to the other woman's house, ostensibly to talk to her. At some point when the woman wasn't looking (the story is not entirely clear) my aunt took a rope from her pocket and twisted it around the neck of her husband's mistress. Only when she thought the woman was dead did she stop.

The story always ended with thanks to God that the woman had survived after all. It wasn't that they were glad the woman's life had been spared. No, she deserved to die, they said. Instead, they shook their heads and sighed in relief because my aunt would have gone to jail for life had she succeeded in the gruesome business.

I remember being very angry when I finally understood what had happened.

"But why did she try to kill the *woman*?" I asked my mother.

My mother missed the point of the question. "Because she tried to take a married man from his wife. She had no business doing that!"

"But why didn't my aunt try to kill her husband?" I persisted. "*He* betrayed her."

My mother just shrugged her shoulders as if to say, "What do you expect of men?"

It made me angry that women, too, used a double standard, although I couldn't articulate it at the time. Now I understand better how the double standard, another hidden enemy within, is internalized, becoming part of our thought processes.

Connie's Story
Sometimes the hidden enemy within can be fatal. The most independent and self-assured woman I ever met, or so I thought,

was a dear friend and colleague. An economist, a college professor, a Ph.D., a community activist, and an involved feminist, Connie radiated a wonderful personality, always upbeat, always laughing, always surrounded by friends who couldn't help but feel good around her. Indeed, I've never known a person about whom more people said, "She's my best friend."

An unspeakable shock gripped all of us when Connie's body was washed ashore on the lake she loved. She had neatly placed her diary, with its suicide note as the last entry, on the dining room table. Then she had filled her pockets with rocks, rowed out to the middle of the lake that had been her backyard for years, and jumped in.

Frantic speculation followed Connie's death. Had the prednisone she took for her asthma plunged her into a depression? Had the purchase of her first home and accompanying financial worries triggered her suicide? Had the impending marriage of her friend Roger, who had a close relationship with her for years, pushed her over the edge? None of it made any sense.

I understood a little better only years later after rereading Connie's diary. I share her private reflections to help women understand the depth of conditioning that results in a profound lack of self-esteem lurking in our souls, regardless of our accomplishments. I could see the stories of all the women I worked with rolled into one. At the heart of those stories lies a problem of self-valuation, an inner core of low self-esteem that plagues even the most self-assured woman. We all suffer this hidden enemy within. How could it be otherwise, growing up and living in a culture that systematically devalues females?

One theme begins and ends Connie's diary, spanning her teen years, when her first love was killed in a car accident, to her death: a fear—an obsession, really—of being alone. It surprised me when I first read it, for she was always surrounded by friends.

Connie's "downward spiral" as she put it in her diary, began just seven days before her death with an unlikely event.

"On April 1, I appear to have pulled down the emotional structure of my life by closing on a house." She goes on to say that although she originally thought of the purchase simply as "obtaining pleasant lodgings," that quickly changed. "Now I feel queasy and depressed and futile and worthless. Mostly my initial response involved the financial commitment. But in turn, my sense of worth got involved."

So begins a series of probing questions about the value of her person and her work—all answered in the negative. Her many achievements are obliterated in a swirl of irrationality.

Although a highly respected and sought-after teacher, Connie concludes that she offers nothing worthwhile to students, only "stale and underthought arguments."

Although the most supportive and caring friend a person could ever hope to know, she berates herself for supporting her friends "very inadequately." She even suggests people may be "relieved" at her death.

Although one of the keenest and most analytical minds her colleagues had known, she refers to herself as an impostor, "an intellectual fraud with a Ph.D. by personality."

Although she led one of the richest, most activism-oriented lives I've known, she questions, "What do I do with my time?"

Again the theme of aloneness runs through her frantic and constricting search.

"Does my lack of a mate reflect this narrowness?"

"So here I am, at 43, with only a cat as daily companion." Connie apparently blamed herself. "Having the worst taste in men since Mary, Queen of Scots, has made me very wary."

Of the house, she says, "At this moment it seems exactly the wrong thing, burdensome property, with no one to share the experience."

Later she agonizes over "how to sign off."

"Trouble is," she continues in an increasingly tortured scrawl, "there is no great message here. Just another fuddled spinster unable to maintain a sense of sanity."

Despite all her great achievements in life, despite her strong feminism, Connie reduced herself to a stereotype, to evaluating her life in the traditional way women are measured—not by individual accomplishment, but by her relationship, or lack of it, to a man. In truth, she was tormented by the same hidden enemies that stir within most women, except that all her demons conspired together at a moment of vulnerability to destroy her.

Yvonne's Story

A young woman I met some years ago epitomizes, in a very ordinary way, how hidden enemies within can conspire to bring us low if we fail to be vigilant. Yvonne started her career as an entry-level manager. Although she lacked business management experience, her credentials were strong—an MBA from a respected business school, academic honors, and lots of extracurricular work in business organizations and publications.

During her first year on the job, Yvonne put in long hours, worked hard, and volunteered for extra projects. She thought her strength lay in her ability to focus on the tasks to be accomplished and "keep her nose to the grindstone." A dedicated worker who loved what she did, Yvonne prided herself on avoiding office politics and on her determination to do her own work without relying on help from others.

At the end of her first year, Yvonne told me how pleased she was with her accomplishments. She felt certain her boss would be hard-pressed to find anyone like her.

A short time later, she confessed her devastation when she was not given a raise. Others, she said, who seemingly did less work and spent more time in the politics of the company, received raises and promotions.

As time passed, she became increasingly disillusioned, complaining that others failed to include her in important projects and to utilize her expertise when appropriate. She was hurt and could not understand their lack of caring and respect.

Doubts about whether this company was the right place for her began to surface.

Meanwhile, Yvonne's husband began to indicate he wanted a child, despite the fact that they had agreed to wait until her career was well established. Wanting to please him, she became increasingly attracted to the idea of having a baby.

I was not surprised to hear, two years after she began work, that she was pregnant.

"I'll only take a short maternity leave," she assured me. I suspected she was trying to assure herself. "Besides," she added, "my leaving for a while will show them all how much they need me."

Yvonne had her baby, and when the time came to return to work, she asked for a longer leave. She turned her attention totally to her child and home. Every room in the house came under her scrutiny, and she began to redecorate them, one by one.

At first Yvonne missed the excitement of work. But she liked the comfort and security of home and decided to be a full-time homemaker. "It's a relief not to worry about earning a living and career advancement," she confided, despite my expressions of concern about relinquishing what she had worked so hard for. "It feels good getting back to basics."

Yvonne formally quit her job at the end of her leave. I found it interesting that she waited until the last moment to do so.

I ran into Yvonne a year ago. No, she had not gone back to work. "I'm worried I'll never go back to my career," she said with great sadness.

As we talked, much became clear. Yvonne was no longer the upbeat, back-to-basics person I'd known a few years before. Her skills and confidence had faded. Staying home bored her; she wasn't challenged. She felt "out of it." What's more, her marriage was coming unglued. Her husband had stayed involved in exciting projects and they had little to talk about or share anymore.

Despite her talents, hard work, and career aspirations, Yvonne found her life, years later, sinking into a black hole of emptiness and disappointment.

What went wrong?

Self-Understanding: The Best Hope

The only factor that could have helped Yvonne save herself is self-understanding. The Socratic motto, "know thyself" carries as much wisdom today as it did for the ancients. Coupled with an understanding of the world around us, self-knowledge can empower us to make enlightened choices that promote our well-being.

To begin with, Yvonne carried a set of false expectations into the workplace: the myth of meritocracy (I'll be judged strictly on the merits of my work); the myth of reward (I'll be rewarded for my hard work); the myth of the corporation as family (everyone cares for everyone else, just like a real family); the myth of indispensability (I'm so special they can't get along without me).

Because of these myths, coupled with naiveté about the politics of workplace relationships, Yvonne isolated herself in her work. She shut others out of her projects, wanting to prove her independence and competence, but resented not being included in the projects of others. She shunned workplace politics in a mistaken belief that building links with others compromised her in some way.

These unrealistic expectations led to her disillusionment with her company and work. They made learning from her own mistakes difficult and paved the way for her to "escape" from the realities of the workplace.

The Cinderella complex, so common in women, allowed her to fall easily into a state of dependency on her husband and abdicate responsibility for her life. Her husband became her "savior" from a work situation that was no longer to her liking.

How did Yvonne sabotage herself?

Yvonne failed to build working relationships with her colleagues. Although disappointed in not getting a raise, she would not communicate that to her boss. She chose, instead, to complain to friends behind the scenes.

When disillusioned, Yvonne easily took the first "out" that presented itself, pregnancy, rather than trying to rebuild her position at work. By succumbing to her husband's desire for a child before she was ready, Yvonne violated her own long-term strategy for a balanced life. By quitting work, she undermined her skills and connection with her field.

Slowly, Yvonne eroded her self-confidence by lapsing into a state of dependency and passivity. She abdicated responsibility for her own life and economic independence. Ironically, she also threatened her long-term relationship with her husband as an equal by ending her professional and personal growth.

What could have made a difference for Yvonne? Certainly, knowing about the enemies within herself would have been a start. After her first troubling experience with the world of work, Yvonne should have analyzed what was happening and reassessed her unrealistic beliefs. Either staying with her company or moving to another firm to rebuild her career would have been preferable to a false escape from the difficult realities of life.

Understanding how we are conditioned as women is necessary for any real control over our lives and work. But understanding this is only a first step. Action must follow.

The process can start with an analysis of the childhood influences that shaped our thinking. From there, we need to examine the other messages that planted the enemies within us over the years.

Once we've examined the forces shaping each of our lives, we need to take responsibility for banishing the enemy within. From there, only acting on this knowledge can save us. This does not mean acting out of habit or conditioning, but out of a genuine freedom to choose based on our well-being in the real context of each of our lives.

In fairy tales, the Nice Girl kisses a frog to transform him into a prince. In real life, we need to transform ourselves. We alone have the power to change our false expectations, to conquer the enemy within, and to stop the self-sabotage. Only by realizing our power and using it to transform ourselves from victims to authentic human beings, can we ensure real control over our lives.

Prince kissing is out.

CHAPTER 3

The Communications
Gender Gap

Different Backgrounds, Different Languages

As a small child growing up in an immigrant Italian ghetto, most of the words I heard every day didn't sound anything like the words on the radio. The adults around me all spoke Italian and that seemed more normal to me than the English sounds on the radio. *They* sounded alien and we'd turn the button, watching the dial sweep across the numbers on the lighted panel until it rested at the Italian station.

The Italian language was part of who I was. But going to school changed all that; it made me feel Italian should be part of who I didn't want to be. I had a lot of growing up to do.

Speaking a language different from the majority, or dominant culture, made me feel like an outsider, like I didn't belong. In those days, people still used the phrase *melting pot*. I learned America was a melting pot all right—if you melted in *their* pot.

My older sister, as usual, bore the brunt of the difficulties. She spoke only Italian when my mother took her to school the first day. Later in life, we often heard the story of that frightening first day in an alien world, where nobody could communicate with her. And the next few weeks didn't get any better. Whenever Mary Antoinette tried to speak, the teacher snapped at her, "Speak English!"

My father had it a little easier growing up. Having come to America as a youngster, he knew English and could speak it well, although he usually didn't. Mom, on the other hand, came to America as a bride of twenty-eight. English came hard for her.

My mother often spoke of her struggles to learn the new language. Determined to become a citizen, she enrolled in language classes. Classes consisted of small groups of adults who met in someone's home with a tutor appointed by the Immigration and Naturalization Service.

My mother's group consisted of women, who, with children in tow, met in Mom's flat. The children were a source of contention for Mom because she had to watch that they didn't destroy anything. Their mothers apparently turned them loose and concentrated on class while my mother fetched refreshments (as any good Italian hostess would), scrambled after the kids, and tried to learn what she could in between.

The memory of taking the written test for citizenship remains vivid to my mother. She painstakingly struggled with each question, getting occasional help from her teacher who circulated around the huge room in the courthouse.

"Who was the first president of the United States?"

"Who would succeed the president if the president died?" My mother passed and swore allegiance to her strange new home.

So, armed with a rudimentary grasp of the language, little relevant knowledge of American history, and her citizenship papers, my mother was ready to melt into the foreign pot. But gaining access through naturalization proved very different from having citizenship by birth; the barriers were too profound.

Much later in life, I came to understand the analogy between a foreigner gaining access to citizenship and women gaining access to male prerogatives. When a country *gives* citizenship to someone, it's not the same as *having* it inherently.

They know they gave it to you; they don't think you have it by right. In a real sense, the receiver always remains something of an outsider.

Life is rooted in language in very profound ways. Language is the inner and outer expression of an individual's, or a people's, orientation. Because men and women have different orientations due to profoundly different conditioning, they have different languages.

Hearing versus Understanding

Like most women growing up, I was always told to be a Nice Girl. My mother said it. The neighbors said it. Visitors to our house would turn to me before leaving and say, "Be a nice girl, Rosie." Relatives would pat me on the head or give me a quarter and say, "Now be a nice girl." It sounded so positive and people presented it as a wonderful model to strive for.

At the same time, I heard adult women referred to as *girls* constantly, but I didn't understand the affront in the word. I also heard women referred to as *chicks* and *broads* but didn't understand or react to the insult. People called me *doll* or *honey* or *sweetie*, but I thought they were compliments.

Slowly, thanks to the women's movement, my consciousness evolved in the early 1970s. I began to hear the meanings behind words and to recognize the outside status I occupied even when I was on the "inside."

Among my earliest perceptions of the slights accorded women were those in academia, a male bastion only recently penetrated by women. I remember speaking at meetings and receiving no response, as if nobody heard what I said. I would assume my point sounded irrelevant or off the mark to others in the room. Then a few minutes later, some man would make essentially the same point I'd made. Suddenly, people would begin to discuss the point as though profundity itself flowed from this man's lips.

Then there were all those *man* words and phrases: the

philosophy of man, the *history of man*, the *brotherhood of man*, the *mailman*, the *policeman*, the *founding fathers*, etc. No women could be found anywhere outside the home, it seemed.

When I went to college, I became a *freshman*, and when I married, I became *Mrs. Joseph Agonito*. When I ran meetings I became a *chairman*. When someone wrote to me, I became a *sir*, and when I started my own business, I became a *businessman*. So, either I didn't exist, or I was an appendage of a male, or I periodically changed my sex.

At other times, people were at pains to focus on my sex, and therefore on my differences. People variously referred to me as a *woman philosopher*, a *career girl*, a *woman worker*, or a *housewife*.

If I was the only woman in a room with men, I'd be singled out for apologies when a man swore: "Sorry, Rosemary. I forgot there's a lady present." If I ate lunch with "the guys" and the conversation turned to technical matters, invariably one of them would lean over and say, "We must be boring you." If I entered an important meeting, frequently some man would trivialize my presence by publicly calling attention to my appearance: "Great outfit, Rosemary. You look terrific!"

Never would they say any of these things to a man. But as women, we are constantly reminded in a hundred seemingly innocent ways that we are different. When a group of women speak, they *chatter*, while a group of men *discuss*. When women argue, they *bicker*; when men argue, they *disagree*. When a woman manager does her job, she's *pushy* and a *bitch*; when a male manager does his job, he is *authoritative* or *strong*.

Beyond the generalized irritations that all women endure, specific incidents stand out in my mind. When I left university teaching to start my own business, I explored various insurance programs—business, disability, and the like. One insurance representative started by asking for my name and address. I gave him my address on Broad Road.

"Broad Road," he repeated as he wrote. "B-R-O-A-D? As in *woman*?" Needless to say, he didn't get my business.

Another time I attended a program for women business owners. The lecturer closed her presentation by telling the audience, "I know you're anxious to go powder your noses, so I'll close." Sadly, this trivializing comment came from a woman. But, after all, women aren't immune to the sexism in the language (or any other form of sexism, for that matter).

I couldn't help but notice, a few weeks later, a different comment at a meeting I attended with an overwhelmingly male audience. There the speaker closed his remarks with an appropriate statement: "I'll wrap this up because I know you're all extremely busy people."

Behavior messages, too, emphasize the differences, sometimes in seemingly innocuous ways. I remember one time when I tried to hold a door open for a man. I'd gotten to the door first; he was walking right behind me. But the man wouldn't let me hold the door open for him. Instead, he tried to nudge me back, away from the door.

I persisted. For me to move backward seemed silly; I had arrived at the doorway first. On the other hand, to go ahead meant letting the door close in his face. I only intended to extend a courtesy by holding the door for the person behind me. The man simply would not let me do it. What might almost be called hostility began to creep into his face and behavior. No way would he allow a woman to hold a door open for him.

No words were spoken. Instead, a flow of gestures, back and forth, set the tone for what can only be called an emerging confrontation. Finally, I chose to walk on, and the door closed on his extended hand. Clearly some assault on his manhood had occurred, at least in his perception.

When I shared the incident with a friend, she thought he was only trying to be chivalrous. Just chivalry? Maybe. But what does chivalry mean when only men practice it on women, when there is no reciprocity? Predicated on the weakness, helplessness, and fragility of women, chivalry has always affirmed the strength and dominance of men over women. It's hardly a compliment or a privilege.

Even when I became aware of the sexism in the words and behaviors of the people around me (and in myself), I still failed to grasp the deeper differences in male-female communications and what they meant for my ability to choose and function well.

The way we look at the world, the way we interpret events and the value and meaning we attach to these events are all dramatically different for men and women.[10] And mostly, we aren't aware of it. Why would we be? Although we're programmed from childhood to interpret, value, and feel differently from men, the male perspective is everywhere presented as the norm.

We're convinced men and women are all on the same wavelength because there's only one acceptable wavelength. Hence, we don't value or assert our own perspectives. We feel "out of it" or think something must be wrong with us if we see things differently. Too often, as a consequence, we act like Nice Girls, buying into whatever is presented to us in the guise of "truth and justice for all."

I certainly behaved like an accepting Nice Girl during my twenty-three years in the educational system earning diplomas and degrees. My disappointment in school over the absence of women who made any real historical contributions was never raised to a critical level. I never thought to ask a perfectly sensible question, "Were there *really* no contributions made by women historically, or were their contributions ignored or not recognized?"

When I studied art but never a single woman artist, I never thought to ask a perfectly sensible question, "Were there *really* no women artists, or has art created by women gone unrecognized?"

When I studied the "great" figures of the past, like Napoleon and Caesar, I never thought to question the concept of greatness, nor did I recognize the male bias in the judgments about who is "great." I didn't think to ask a perfectly sensible question, "Was Napoleon, who disrupted the peace of Europe for fifteen years, caused the maiming and death of hundreds of thousands, and brought pillage, rape, and destruction on countless civilians, *really* great?"

Napoleon is judged to be great because he was a winner and because he sat at the top of a hierarchy, according to a male competitive standard. Using that standard, the results of his actions are of no consequence.

When I studied the "father of modern science," Francis Bacon, I unthinkingly accepted his philosophy of science. That he sought to bring about man's mastery over the natural world, that he believed it was up to man to perfect nature and set it right, that he thought nature existed for man's use—none of this struck me as odd. I never thought to ask a perfectly sensible question, "If man's mastery over the natural world has resulted in destruction, harm, and threats to our very existence, why would anyone think that such 'mastery' has any merit?"

I didn't understand that a male perspective, valuing competition, winning, and dominance, lay at the very essence of the approach. That perspective continues today, not only in science (much of which serves the military) but in government and industry as well.

When I studied history, it never occurred to me that the way we divide history into periods—prehistoric, ancient, medieval, renaissance, enlightenment—is arbitrary and based on a particular perspective and set of values that has little objective validity.

The Renaissance (literally, "a period of rebirth") offered not a rebirth or flowering, but a closing down of options, a closing out of opportunities for at least half the population— women. During this period occurred the forgotten holocaust— the mass murder of women thought to be witches—sending women a powerful message about staying "in their place." The time was only a renaissance from a male point of view. The term "*renaissance man*" should have tipped me off.

If history accurately reflected the story of all people, including women, who have always been half the world's population, it would concern itself less with diplomacy, law, and war, and more with the social fabric of people's lives.

Democracy is another concept that reflects a male bias. Ancient Greece, the "cradle of democracy," hardly offered anybody freedom. Only a small minority of men enjoyed the rights and privileges of democracy. The overwhelming majority of people in ancient Athens, women and slaves, could not be citizens, had virtually no rights or privileges, and lived horrendously restricted lives. Of course, no teacher of mine ever mentioned women at all when discussing ancient Greece. And I never thought to ask a perfectly sensible question, "How can Athens be called a democracy—a government by the people and free of hereditary privilege—when at least half of its people had no role in the government by virtue of their anatomy?"

The "historians," whose trademark has been "objectivity," by a great feat of collective selection, never troubled themselves to notice such discrepancies. Or maybe they accepted them. The law is what the judge says it is.

When I studied the founding of the great American "democracy," it didn't occur to me that this country has never been a democracy in the accepted sense—a government of the people, by the people, for the people. My teachers never pointed out what seems obvious to me now. From its inception, the United States has been an oligarchy—a government of the privileged few, by the privileged few, for the privileged few. Women certainly were not allowed to play a role in it and could not claim to be its beneficiaries in any significant manner.

When "ordinary" people (including women) prospered, they did so in spite of the oligarchy, not because of it. Despite some hard-fought gains and the beginnings of change, it's still more true than not that white male anatomy and access to wealth are required for political power. But most Americans still believe we live in a democracy.

When I read Matthew Arnold's claim that we ought to study "the best that has been thought and said in the world," I should have asked some perfectly sensible questions: "Why is it assumed that only men of a certain race and class think and say the best?" "Why have we seldom valued what women think and say?"

There I was, all those twenty-three years in school, acting like my brain slept twenty-four hours a day. Being co-opted is a terrible thing.

Of course, the importance of recognizing the perspective, meaning, and value of all kinds of words and concepts goes far beyond the failures of the educational system. Much of it is inherent in how we conduct our lives. The word *beauty* presents a case in point. What the word has come to mean, as related to women, glares from the pages of magazines, reflects from the television screen, parades across Hollywood movies, and markets itself in a vast array of products.

The concept of feminine beauty bears no relationship to real women. The meaning is so narrowly defined and so artificial that it fits only a handful of women, relatively speaking, and even *they* don't really look like that—they are dressed and made up like Barbie dolls. Yet the conventional notion of beauty continues to tyrannize most women, who, for reasons of age, race, physiology, health, or preference, cannot, or will not, conform.

That this false image reflects nothing more than a male fantasy seems irrelevant. It is considered natural, normal, and objective. It certainly seemed so to me when I sat on the fashion board and entered the Young Miss America contest.

Then there's the "f" word: *feminism*. Feminists have long been maligned, trivialized, attacked, and dismissed, but mostly we are denied. The history and political science books reduce us to a handful of zealots who won women the right to vote.

The media assert that we are finished in this "post-feminist" era. Women themselves are fond of saying, "I'm not a feminist, but . . . " and proceed to recite a litany of examples that prove they *are* feminists.

It seems to boil down to the fact that feminists aren't Nice Girls. They fight back instead of passively waiting to be saved. They have the audacity to think they're equal as human beings and have a right to equal opportunities, free of oppression and discrimination. All in all, they don't behave the way women are supposed to behave. And many people, men and women, don't like that.

What is a feminist, really? A feminist is a person who understands the nature of women's oppression and discrimination and works to change it. Feminists come in all types: female and male, young and old, African-American, Asian-American, Italian-American, Native-American, and others.

Feminism is a proud and honorable heritage. As a woman, I have come to understand that what we have, we have because of feminists: the right to own property, the right to keep our wages, the right to vote, the right to our children, the right to speak in public, the right to be considered people under the constitution, the right to sit on juries, the right to divorce an abusive spouse, and the right to control our reproductive processes through contraception and abortion.

I also know that all of these rights could vanish without the vigilance of feminists. And I know that all those rights I *don't* yet have will only be won by feminists: the right to pay equity, the right to be seriously considered for the top offices in politics, church, and business, the right to equality under the law, and the right to move freely in society without the threat of rape or violence.

Closing the Communications Gender Gap

Oddly, it's often the day-to-day messages, rather than the larger issue of rights, that weigh us down as women. In the workplace, especially, it's the little messages that drive women crazy. That's because the little messages pile up in the words, body language, and behavior of men, threatening, like the proverbial straw, to break our backs.

The stories from the workplace frontlines are always the same.

- What woman doesn't find herself routinely interrupted by some man who thinks what he has to say is more important than what she has to say?

- What woman hasn't heard herself trivialized as a diminutive something or other, like a "terrific little . . . "?

- What woman hasn't had someone imply that she accomplished some important feat by using her sexuality?

- What woman hasn't had a man invade her private space by slapping his arm over her shoulder or hugging her, without waiting for her to indicate that it's OK?

- What woman hasn't been leered at, had her body checked up and down, or had men stare at her breasts?

- What woman hasn't been patronized, talked down to, treated in a condescending way, endured trivializing comments, or been "put in her place"?

- What woman doesn't know that when a man speaks, he's listened to more carefully than when she speaks?

- What mother hasn't been berated or frowned at for leaving work to care for a sick child ("See? Women aren't committed!"), while she must endure the widespread acceptance of men routinely leaving work to play golf?

- What woman hasn't been referred to as a toy, an animal, or a food rather than a person, in terms such as *doll, chick, fox, bunny, sugar,* or *honey*?

- What woman hasn't been singled out and treated differently in a group dominated by men?

- What woman hasn't been caught in the verbal one-upmanship so typical of the male competitive approach to conversation? "You did that? Well, let me tell you what *I've* done!"

The cumulative effect of all this falls heavily on the self-esteem of women while it puffs up the male ego. A steady stream of verbal messages, body language, and behaviors, predominantly from men, tell women that they are *different*—and *different* is unmistakably understood in a negative way.

Not only are we told we're different in the messages we receive, but the patterns of female/male communication are markedly different.[11] Male communication typically reflects a need to compete and win, a need to be superior, and a task orientation that expresses itself as dominant, controlling, and active. Female communication, on the other hand, reflects a need for acceptance and approval, a need to connect with people, and it may be interpreted as being accommodating, submissive, and reactive.

None of this is surprising in light of sex-role conditioning. Psychologists have long known that females are conditioned in such a way that their basic motivation revolves around the need for acceptance and approval, especially by men. Men, on the other hand, are conditioned such that their motivation stems from competition and a desire to win, to be "number one."

Accommodating, submissive, and reactive behavior (being a Nice Girl) flows from women's need to be accepted or connected, while dominant, controlling, and active behavior (being "king of the hill" or "macho,") flows from men's need to compete and win.

As a consequence, women care too much about what other people think and feel; men care too little. For men, the consequences of their behavior on others is usually irrelevant—

winning matters most. The relative ease with which men make war is a classic example of this mindset.

How do people generally look at the differences in male and female communication styles? People tend to see women's communication style as weak, mindless, trivial, and peripheral. They tend to see men's style as strong, rational, important, and central.

Actually, both communication patterns are extremes—passive on the one hand, aggressive on the other. Both are destructive in some sense. Female passivity tends to be self-destructive; male aggression tends to be destructive of others. For these reasons, we certainly don't want women behaving like men. Nor do we want men behaving like women.

The answer lies in a healthy, self-respecting, other-respecting middle ground. Both women *and* men should concern themselves with communicating effectively.

Passive behavior and communication say, "I value you more than me. What you think, feel, or want is more important than what I think, feel, or want." It sets the stage for victimization and dependency.

On the other hand, aggressive behavior and communication proclaim, "I am more important than you. What I think, feel, and want matters more than what you think, feel, and want." Aggression makes it easy to exploit, abuse, or control others.

The middle ground, assertive behavior and communication, says, "All parties involved are important. What I think, feel, and want *and* what you think, feel, and want matter."

Assertiveness is the only stance that involves mutual respect, reciprocity, self-control, and equal rights. It is incompatible with domination by others and, in turn, precludes me from abusing them. It fosters my power in the best sense of the word while encouraging the empowerment of others.

As open and honest dialogue, assertive communication says firmly and unapologetically, "I expect you to respect me, just as I respect you. You don't have to agree with me or even like me, but you do have to respect me."

Purging the Nice Girl

Although the concept of assertive behavior has been around for some time, we have a very long way to go before it even approaches the norm. Everywhere I go, I meet women who share their stories, ranging from daily annoyances to truly horrible experiences.

When I ask what they did in response, I almost never hear about an assertive response. Normally the responses described are passive Nice Girl reactions. These range from nonresponses ("I didn't want to hurt his feelings" or "I didn't know what to do") to indirect attempts to send clues (which are usually misread or ignored). Sometimes a woman will describe a bitter, aggressive reaction. It's a rare treat when I'm told about an effective, assertive response.

Yet for women, assertiveness is a necessary element in the struggle for change. It's the key to refusing victimization without buying into an aggressive male model. If I've learned anything over the years, it's that being a Nice Girl amounts to cooperation in my own oppression. Passive responses to the countless dominance gestures, words, and behavior of men reinforce the dominant-submissive pattern of male-female interaction. They send a message that such behavior is acceptable, and that I don't mind it.

In the beginning, the transition from passive to assertive behavior will feel uncomfortable and awkward. That's not surprising, since most women are accustomed to a passive mode. And others don't make it easy for us; people equate assertive behavior in women with aggression. That's because people *expect* us to be Nice Girls; when we behave like adult women in control of ourselves, it's *perceived* as extreme. Well it's not, and we shouldn't allow our confidence to be shaken by negative responses to positive behavior.

Once we move beyond that initial discomfort, purging the Nice Girl feels terrific. And, although men (and sometimes women) may react negatively at first, in the long run, they will respect us much more.

Breaking free of the Nice Girl in each of us, not only changes our behavior, but it transforms our mindset as well. We see ourselves in control, not controlled; powerful, not powerless. It does wonders for our self-esteem.

Will an assertive response always have the desired effect on the offender? No, not always. But I've found that it greatly increases the possibility of change for the better, since it's hard to exercise dominance over an assertive woman. Certainly, Nice Girl behavior will get me nowhere.

How can assertiveness be applied to particular on-the-job situations? I call my strategy "Purging the Nice Girl."

1. I need to be clear in my own mind about the verbal messages, body language, and behavior messages I object to.

2. I remind myself that much of this language and behavior is habitual, so I give the other person the benefit of the doubt and the opportunity to grow.

3. I instruct myself to stop being the accommodating Nice Girl by saying, to myself, "No more Nice Girl!"

4. Then I engage in open, honest dialogue, keeping in mind that the objective is to be treated with respect as an equal, not to crush the other person.

My "Purging the Nice Girl" technique can be expressed in many ways. The following are a few examples:

When an assertive woman is interrupted, she doesn't fall silent. She holds her ground and keeps talking until she finishes her point, or she firmly says to the intruder, "I haven't finished," and continues on.

When someone refers to an assertive woman in diminutive

terms, she tells him, "I assume you didn't mean anything by it, but speaking about adults in diminutive terms like *girl* and *little lady* trivializes them."

When a man implies she accomplished something by using her sexuality, the assertive woman calls him on it by replying, "I trust you're not implying I used my sexuality to land this contract. You're certainly aware of my training, experience, and awards in sales."

When a man hugs a woman or puts his arm around her and she doesn't like it, the assertive woman tells him, "Being hugged by my colleagues makes me uncomfortable. I trust you understand." She doesn't just smile and fume inside.

When an assertive woman sees a man staring at her breasts, she doesn't squirm in silence; she exposes the behavior by calling attention to it, "Do I have a spot on my blouse, Tom?" (He gets the message fast.) Or, she can say, straight out, "It makes me uncomfortable to have people stare at me."

When a woman who's determined to be heard gets no response, she persists, being sure that her tone of voice is firm and strong, "Perhaps my point isn't fully clear. What I'm suggesting relative to this issue is . . . Barry, what do you think about my suggestion?"

When an assertive mother is berated for leaving work early to care for a sick child, she "educates" her boss, "I have to leave work two hours early this afternoon because Suzie got sick at the daycare. At first I felt uncomfortable asking, but since it's acceptable for people to leave work to play golf, I knew you'd think this was at least as important."

When a woman is referred to as a toy, animal, or food, she expresses her preference, "I prefer to be called by my name."

Body language is especially important in the communications gender gap, since most communication is nonverbal. But the accommodating, submissive behavior of the Nice Girl we've been conditioned to adopt affects our body language as well as our speech, often without our awareness.

For instance, women take up less space, and not because we're smaller. This seems to happen especially in the workplace and less so in the home where, presumably, we feel more comfortable. It's almost as though we unconsciously try to shrink in place—by sitting with our legs or ankles crossed and eyes looking down (Nice Girls always sit with their legs crossed); by standing with our feet together, arms at our sides or folded defensively across the chest, head slightly down; or by leaning against something when we stand.

Seldom do we spread out in space like men. They stand with legs and feet apart, hands on their hips, gesturing or jingling change in their pockets. Or they sit, legs open, arms spread out, eyes looking straight ahead or staring. Or they use furniture in unconventional ways, putting their feet on desks, sitting on tables, turning chairs around and sitting on them backwards.

The differing messages behind these body language patterns are clear. A woman shrinking in space projects the message: I am insecure, powerless, defensive, and weak. I'm not sure I belong here (which may account for the prevalence of this body language in the workplace). A man spread out in space projects the message: I am in control, powerful, secure, and free to move as I please. I belong here.

There is no good reason for these body language differences except sex-role conditioning. It's one more vehicle, traditionally, for eliciting Nice Girl behavior, for keeping women in their place, for restraining women's movement, for ensuring women's subordinate position.

Women who work outside the home need to be especially aware of how we project ourselves through our body language, as well as our words. Equality in the workplace, or anywhere else, will hardly be forthcoming as long as we continue to play the accommodating, submissive, powerless role of the Nice Girl. The effect is the same, whether or not we know we're doing it.

It's important that we educate ourselves and other women, as well as men, about sexist language and behavior. We can't hang onto our own destructive sex-role conditioning and expect men to change theirs. Changing ourselves, when appropriate, is the first step to changing the world.

Accentuating the Positive

At the same time, there are plenty of things about being a woman that shouldn't be changed at all, that we should build on. Our values and perspectives as women have much to offer corporate America and society. If we look closely, the so-called "new" management style is loaded with approaches and values that women have used for a long time. Yet it's not taught as a female management style, and historically women have been labeled weak and ineffective when they did things this way.

Incidentally, there's no suggestion here that the differences in women's values and approaches are genetic. Rather, my own view is that our people-oriented conditioning and our experiences as women (including the oppression and discrimination we encounter) have resulted in some real differences between women's and men's values and approaches.

Regardless of their source, we need to stop assuming that male perspectives and approaches are the norm we should fit into. Trying to act like a man or behaving like an accommodating Nice Girl *both* constitute fitting into the male norm. To the extent that positive differences exist, we need to recognize, applaud, and use them. This is especially true in the workplace, where the dramatic shifts occurring in the economy demand fresh ideas and new approaches.

Male-female differences, as discussed earlier, seem to be rooted in the basic motivations conditioned in women and men—the need to connect with other people and the need to compete and win, respectively. Generally speaking, women engage in what Deborah Tannen[12] refers to as "rapport talk"—that is, communication that seeks to build connections and consensus between people. Men typically use "report talk," in which the speaker gains status in the group by telling others, in effect, "I have something to say; here it is." Furthermore, women tend to see people as interdependent, whereas men value individuality and independence. As a consequence, women work at keeping the group or community strong, while a man works at keeping himself strong.

Less comfortable with hierarchy and status differences between people, women tend to minimize or break down the demarcations that rank people "above" and "below" each other. Hence women's orientation leans toward egalitarianism. Men, on the other hand, are more accepting of hierarchy and status differences and, indeed, seek them as measures of winning.

Consequences, typically, are very important to women, who tend to engage in contextual or holistic thinking—considering individual judgments and actions in the context of the whole situation. Men, on the other hand, are more concerned about the immediate outcome ("who's winning?") and short-term gain ("what's the bottom line now?").

In debate and argument, women have a higher tolerance for accepting points that seem to contradict one another, reflecting the real complexities of life. Men tend to engage in dichotomous thinking (it's either . . . or . . .). And while men lean toward using categorical or abstract statements (ideas have validity in themselves), women use personal experience and examples to reach conclusions (ideas must be "tested" against actual experience, against reality).

All of these "female" approaches, in the workplace at least, contribute greatly to teamwork, cooperation, effective management, and high morale by creating the sense that everyone is valuable. They encourage creative thinking by looking at things in a different light and promote consideration of context and consequences for long-term stability and success. They constitute a positive force for moving organizations into the twenty-first century.

I read the wonderful story recently of a woman who had risen to plant manager in a male-dominated, multinational corporation. She accomplished this rare feat by bringing new ideas, people-oriented approaches, a holistic perspective, and concern for long-term goals to each level.

So unique and powerful was her management style that she stood out and so did her accomplishments. She was not afraid to take risks, to try new concepts, to establish different procedures. She rejected the traditional male authoritarian style that delivered edicts from above; instead, she stayed close to her people, treated them with dignity, and valued their input. It paid off—for her and her company.

Women have long been told that the male approach is the correct approach, the norm. Well, it's time to proudly proclaim that other approaches have value and usefulness—and they're ours. As women, we don't have to shy away from bringing our alternative perspectives into the workplace; we can make the case that they contribute a great deal.

In this way, we can enhance our value in an economic climate crying out for change. Instead of trying to fit into a male model in the belief that there's something wrong with us, we can contribute to our organizations by utilizing our strengths—and do ourselves a world of good in the process.

While I often think about the analogy between my childhood as an Italian in an American world and being a woman in a man's world, I know the latter is much more complicated. As a woman, I speak the same words as the men around me. I understand the dictionary meanings of those words as men do. I have access to most places men do. I conduct business in the same business world men do. I am married to a man. But it's not the same, any more than being a naturalized citizen is the same as being a birth citizen.

Nobody tells me to speak "male" the way the teacher told us Italians to speak English. Nobody actually says, "This is *the* correct perspective and it's male." People *do* tell me, "This is *the* way it's done." And I know what they mean.

Being "inside" can be the same as being "outside." That has to change.

CHAPTER 4

Changing Behavior—
Theirs and Mine

Finding a Model That Works

One of the most amazing personal changes I've contemplated relates to my mother and the circumstances of her coming to the United States. As a young woman, she left a tiny, isolated medieval village on a mountaintop in southern Italy to cross an ocean to a new life in the twentieth century with a strange man.

My father's first wife died and, like most Italian men of the period, he returned to Italy to find a new wife. Only an old-country Italian woman would do. Though he was fifty at the time, he set his eyes on the young Filomena Albanese.

For her part, Filomena had reached an age—twenty-eight—when the prospects of marriage had begun to dim. Not that she had had no prospects of her own. Talk of a boyfriend in Guardiarregia surfaced occasionally while I was growing up, although mystery always surrounded him. I found out recently that my mother's parents had squashed the romance between Filomena and her boyfriend. It seems two obstacles stood in their way—his illegitimate birth and his poverty. A single woman bearing and raising a child, as his mother had, presented too great a scandal—a wedding with that family was not to be. As for his poverty, it must have been extreme by village standards since virtually everyone there was poor.

Life was very hard in Filomena's village. The stone houses built into the top of the mountain sweltered in the summer and froze in the winter. The fireplace used for cooking provided the only heat, and wood had to be gathered and hauled great distances.

Women here had an especially difficult life. They rose before dawn, hauled water from the public fountain, cooked their meager food over a fire, washed clothes in the public square, worked in the fields, cared for their children and elders, preserved all their own food, tended the animals, and made their own clothing. Often they did all this while pregnant with the next child.

Filomena's life was hard, too. Her family of eight lived in a small, three-room stone house with the mountain as its floor. Every morning at dawn, she rose to tend the sheep in the fields and gather wood for the fire. Bread, cheese, and potatoes provided the staples of their diet; meat appeared on the table only on special occasions.

But what Filomena regretted most about her childhood was that she had to drop out of school in the third grade. She loved school. However, the circumstances of her life in the village, coupled with an unbending teacher, conspired to drive her out. Each morning, about an hour after my mother arrived for class at the beginning of third grade, her grandmother came to call her home to chores. The family reasoned it better for Filomena to get a little learning than none, so the comings and goings went on for a few days.

Filomena's teacher saw it differently and put her foot down: "Either you come to school or you watch the sheep!"

Filomena was out.

It's not hard to understand why my mother married Pop. Here came this tall figure from America, the land of wealth and opportunity in the European peasant's mind. Mom frankly admits to marrying him for a new life. He married her for a new wife.

It's staggering for me to think about the changes that entered my mother's life. She had never ventured further than the next town on a donkey. Her whole life had been spent in an isolated mountaintop village, whose recorded history dates back to at least the thirteenth century—a village whose physical structures and way of life had changed little through the centuries. In twenty-eight years, she had never been away from her family. She had only a second-grade education, and she married my father less than a month after meeting him.

My mother knew before she left Guardiareggia that one of Pop's daughters from his first marriage bitterly resented the union. Partly because of the subterfuge of his daughter and partly because he had to secure Mom's immigration papers, my father left Italy shortly after the marriage. So my mother, bedded in steerage and seasick the whole way, made the long, difficult voyage across the ocean alone, six months after her marriage to a man she hardly knew.

In May of 1933, Filomena Albanese Giambattista set foot on American soil. She had literally left one life behind and started a second life in an alien world surrounded by strangers. The behavioral changes required of her were enormous.

I often think about how my mother did it. She certainly didn't just fit in. There's no question that she embraced her new American life and changed her ways, yet she hung onto who she was: a generous, earthy, religious, hard-working, determined, family-oriented Italian woman. Along the way she influenced many people because she expected certain things of them.

That seems to be the key to successful behavior change. We learn to function in new situations (or old situations we see in a new way) by selective adaptation. That means adapting in such a way that we change our behavior while retaining the integrity of who we are; but *at the same time*, we influence others to change their behavior as well.

Put simply: I'll meet you halfway, but I expect you to

meet me halfway. Ideally, new behavior patterns emerge in both parties because the old ones don't work anymore—for anybody.

Adaptation is always best when it's mutual, although the burden falls heaviest on the newcomer and resistance to change is found on all sides. My mother had to change because she moved to the United States; the United States had to change because immigrants swelled the land. Neither could stay the same; new ways had to be found that respected both. To the extent that one or the other refused to adapt, misery, pain, or injustice resulted.

I think this simple model of selective adaptation has much to contribute to both the women's movement and to the social structures resisting that movement. Since neither side can, or will, give totally to the other, both must adapt. Out of these attempts to adapt, new structures, approaches, and behaviors emerge.

The problem, of course, with the traditional Nice Girl model lies in its one-sidedness; mutuality and reciprocity don't exist. Being a Nice Girl requires that the accommodating is always done by the woman. So the misery, pain, and injustice fall on her.

The interesting thing about my mother's case was her capacity to keep adapting her behavior throughout her life. When my father died many years later, Mom changed her life again, in dramatic ways, because at that point she found herself interacting with yet a different world.

This second transformation in my mother's behavior startled all of us. Her behavior shifted from subservience to independence; the patriarch was gone. First, my mother sold the old, three-family house where she'd lived since coming to America thirty-five years before. She bought a smaller house, and she managed her own finances. She began to spend a great deal of time with her widowed friends and went on tours with her church group. She drove her car everywhere and started to travel.

Although she had always been terrified of airplanes, she boarded the mysterious and frightening flying machine. She flew to Boston to visit her daughter, the doctor. She journeyed to Toronto to visit her brother and sister. She traveled to Washington to spend time with her nephew. She flew to see her remaining sisters in Italy three times, traveling around the country she had never seen as a child.

And each time she gets on a plane, she still asks, "But *what* holds it up?"

Making the Right Choices

Clearly, choice plays a big role in change—or lack of change. My mother chose freedom in widowhood over the slow death of perpetual mourning so common among the black-clad Italian widows of her day.

Choice is the essence of life. There's no moment in life when we're not choosing—not choosing is itself a choice. Together, the sum of all our choices make up who we are. This means the burden of choosing well is a heavy one. Along the way, we all make poor or self-destructive choices. Sometimes they can be redeemed; mostly they plague us to the end.

My strong-willed younger sister made her share of bad choices, like many of us. Two critical choices, in particular, shaped her life—one destroyed her. To escape a tyrannical father, and maybe two overachieving sisters, she dropped out of school and ran away from home. From that choice followed a series of events that shaped a harsh and difficult life for a dozen years—marriage at age seventeen, three children, and a mentally-ill husband unable to work.

Because at some point she determined to change her circumstances, she chose divorce and set about rebuilding her life under the most difficult of conditions. After a happy second marriage and another child, she learned to respect herself and grow in self-esteem. Everyone liked kind and gentle Mary Angela. In a strange way, she became the anchor of our family, the center that held us all together.

Mary's second choice, also made during the mindless adolescent years, ultimately proved to be her downfall: she began to smoke. That choice, and the lack of a choice to stop, led to lung cancer at age forty, with all its attendant horrors: removal of half of a lung, hospitalization on a respirator, damaging radiation, and a painful recovery.

This experience has helped me see smoking as a woman's issue; it hovers over a woman's life like a fog that won't go away and threatens to obliterate everything else. The tobacco industry targets young adolescent girls, especially the less educated. It concocts a sexy, glamorous image that appeals to girls already brainwashed to believe that sexy and glamorous is *the* way to look. It sells girls, who are dependent in most other ways, on the notion that smoking is a choice they can make, a way to be independent, to do what they want—to be free. Smoking is women's liberation itself, one particular brand of cigarettes implies in its ads. Then, when women are hooked, they have a much harder time breaking the habit than men.

Whatever else a woman works for or accomplishes, smoking introduces a ghostly specter that threatens to strike her in some deadly form, sooner or later. Girls and women need to hear the stories from the front, stories of the countless smokers destroyed by the most lethal drug of all—tobacco.

I remember well the agony of my sister's ordeal. A few days after surgery for lung cancer, Mary's heart stopped beating and she was resuscitated. The doctors said she'd be dead in a matter of hours. But by some colossal act of will, she refused to die. And she stopped smoking—but tragically it was too late.

Although she beat overwhelming odds and survived, her life was forever changed. A sword hung over her and her family during the following years spent in and out of labs and doctors' offices. Five years after her operation, she underwent heart surgery as a result of damage from radiation. During that episode, she died again, was resuscitated, and ended up on a respirator once more.

Still Mary survived and returned to her family, only to have lung cancer recur eight years later at age forty-nine. There's never a good time for such horrors, but Mary had put her life together, was entering the exciting world of computers, and had plans to venture out into the world of work.

Instead, she landed in the hospital again, on the dreaded respirator. The terror of her family was almost as bad as her own. She lay there, unable to speak, contemplating her death and writing instructions about cremation and the rest, while my sister, the doctor, insured that everything had been done that could be done. Her husband and children suffered her pain with her—we all did.

During those weeks in the hospital, Mary died again while holding my hand and again was resuscitated. I teased her about being like a cat with nine lives, but we both knew that she wouldn't make it to nine. She signed a "Do Not Resuscitate" order, and the lung cancer killed her after months of suffering and five painful, horrible weeks on a respirator.

Choices have consequences, although we cannot always foresee them. Maybe we don't think enough about long-term consequences because we're hobbled by the "happily ever after" myth. Or maybe it's our naive arrogance in thinking that bad things will never happen to *us* (like death—it always happens to somebody else). But living happily ever after *is* a myth, and bad things *can* happen to us.

Like my mother and my sister, my own life and work have been filled with choices and change. Through it all, the hardest part has been to change in such a way that I remain true to myself. But discovering my "real" self remains a challenge because it never stays the same. It, too, is in constant flux and growth.

It's also difficult to distinguish the Nice Girl caricature from my "real" self, which is hidden under layers of conditioned behavior. But the "real" me (at any given moment) is actually the sum of all the possibilities I choose to act on—like a seed that, in the right conditions, can grow into something truly wonderful and unique.

The most profound changes in my life came when I discovered feminism; I have never been the same since. It seemed like a veil fell from my eyes, and I saw the world in a totally different way.

A wave of insights swept over me during my involvement with women's studies, which began in the early seventies. The work of women scholars uncovered our "herstory"—both the contributions long hidden and the oppressions long glossed over. It analyzed everything from the fairy tales of our youth to the misogynist popular culture of the day, from the dysfunctional life of women in the home to the discrimination suffered by women in the work force.

What an incredible revelation for me! It's a revelation that relatively few women or men are exposed to, even today, since women's studies have yet to be fully welcomed into the curriculum at any level. Where they do exist, mainly at the college level, they remain ghettoized and optional.

Worse, some women's studies programs have already been co-opted. In an effort to gain acceptance into mainstream academia, they have been stripped of their original political mission. Legitimacy trades on the absurd notion that education is apolitical.

Education either reinforces the status quo or it questions the status quo. Both approaches are political and pretenses about some sort of pure objectivity are silly. The value of education lies in its many diverse points of view.

Many changes occurred in my consciousness. I began to understand my own unease over what my life should be about. Now I saw it as an externally and internally imposed repression of my talents and ambitions. I began to look at my marriage in a different way. I saw for the first time the script I unconsciously followed—one that culture had written for me. I saw the repressions and limitations for women built into the structure of the traditional family. I began to examine my Italian heritage, to see its strengths and weaknesses. I looked at my mother and father in a different way.

I questioned religion, especially Catholicism, which had been such a big part of my childhood. I had trouble reconciling my second class, inferior status within the church. I reread the New Testament, searching for clues about Jesus' thinking on women. His progressive viewpoint was revolutionary for his day, so much so that his attitudes and behavior toward women often shocked his own apostles. Jesus' liberal stance didn't seem to compute with the church's views of women. Something had gone badly astray.

I found myself examining everything: television, movies, advertisements, music, magazines, newspapers. . . . I began to understand how women are conditioned, how they are shaped into compliant, passive, sexy Nice Girls who adapt to the male agenda. I didn't like what I saw.

The changes in my consciousness, of course, could not stop there. They slowly began to affect my choices and behavior. For one thing, Joe and I had to come to terms with the patriarchal scripts we both played out in our marriage. Either we would rewrite those scripts and adapt to something new happening in our lives, or our partnership would die. It proved difficult, but we were fortunate. We learned together, struggled together, and grew together.

We tried to raise our two children as feminists. We seemed to succeed for a while, but ultimately popular culture and peer pressure won out. Parental influence, it seems, is a small part of what molds children, conventional wisdom to the contrary.

I had to come to grips with my membership in a church that seemed mired in its own dark ages, treating women as second-class citizens. In its eyes, our sole purpose as women appeared to be the propagation of the race. It refused to abandon its universal prohibition against divorce, birth control, and abortion. Furthermore, papal directives persisted in defining a woman's place as in the home. The church continued to associate the image of its spiritual god with the male anatomy and denied the priesthood to women. I walked.

At the college where I taught, a group of us began to agitate and seek funding for a women's studies program. When the program was finally established, I directed it and taught some of the courses, while speaking and writing on women's issues. I joined and helped form women's groups, and worked with young women. Finally, I determined to work full-time at my feminism and earn a living doing it. I felt it was important work (as important as anything else people were paid to do) and knew that the volunteer approach doomed the impact of the women's movement in the long run.

The "Get It Right, Guys" Strategy

During it all, I stumbled through the difficult process of interacting in a world that largely continued to operate in patriarchal terms. Advocacy for ending discrimination at all levels sprouted around the country. Collective protest shook the establishment, and consensus models began to challenge male authoritarian approaches.

But few, if any, models existed for individual day-to-day interaction in a sexist world, especially for at-work situations. There was little to help me answer such questions as: "What can I say or do when . . . ?" "How can I purge the self-destructive Nice Girl persona in my day-to-day behavior in a myriad of concrete situations?" So I struggled to make my own way, as other women did, and made a host of mistakes in the process.

Because my mother, with her second-grade education in a totally alien environment, learned about change, I figured I could too. Over the years, I developed some techniques using Mom's model of selective adaptation. That, coupled with the assertive communication skills I learned, formed the basis of my day-to-day dealings with a sexist world.

In time, I figured out a strategy that has worked well for me over the years in banishing my Nice Girl persona, especially in the workplace. The women I've shared it with usually find it helps them too. I call it my "Get It Right, Guys" technique because it gives the offending person a chance to change his behavior, to make things right without a knock-down confrontation that's probably going to hurt me more than him.

Of course, I don't always try to completely avoid knock-down confrontations. But I save them for those situations when all else fails or for particularly vicious behavior.

My "Get It Right, Guys" strategy works like this:

1. Unless necessary, I try not to treat the problem as a women's issue. (That's tantamount to telling people they're sexist, which will probably put them on the defensive. Defensive people focus on themselves, not on the issue in question. It's better to show them *how* they're being sexist without saying, "You're sexist.") Rather, I treat the problem as a professional concern.

2. I allow the person to save face. This means giving him or her the benefit of the doubt with the understanding that sex-role conditioning and stereotyping often work nonconsciously. (I'd certainly want to be given the benefit of the doubt and shown my offense if I did or said something racist, for example. I try to remember nobody's perfect, least of all me.)

3. I stress the benefits of my position for the person or organization. (People are usually more open and accepting when there's a positive outcome for them.)

4. Finally, I take control and turn the situation around. (Leaving the situation dangling may work against me because it allows the other person to make the next move.)

This technique has helped me deal with most situations in recent years, from the merely irritating to the really difficult. For example, like many women, I've been through the experience of making a suggestion or sharing a thought at a meeting, only to be met by no response, as if I never said a word. Then, later, I'd hear the same suggestion repeated by a man who would immediately be affirmed for "his" terrific idea.

Mostly, people seem unaware they're doing this; the mental filter is probably at work. Nonetheless, it's a serious problem, since it renders women "invisible" and prevents our ideas from being taken seriously.

In any case, as a young woman, I routinely fell silent in situations like this. These days I insist they "Get It Right, Guys."

Immediately after my idea is repackaged at a meeting, I say something like, "I'm so pleased to hear my suggestion reinforced by John. (face saving) He's certainly in an excellent position to know how helpful this will be to the company since it will bring in new clients and save money. (benefits) To pick up on a point I made earlier, let me suggest we start by . . . " (takes control)

This accomplishes my goal without crushing anybody in the process. Crushing somebody else in order to win is, after all, the type of behavior we often object to in men. Imitating poor behavior is not part of our agenda; changing it is. More important, I've stood up for myself.

A woman in one of my seminars tried the "Get It Right, Guys" strategy in a pay dispute. Martha accidentally discovered that a male colleague she had trained, with the same current job description, earned $5,500 per year more than she did. (It's a fairly common occurrence; there are many cases in which the gap runs from three to six figures.) They both have masters degrees from reputable schools, and she had several more years of experience than he did.

So Martha made an appointment with her boss and presented the problem. Her discussion went something like this:

"It's come to my attention that George makes $5,500 per year more than I do, despite the fact that we're on the same management level and have the same job description. I'm puzzled since we both have an MBA and I have several years more experience."

"I suspect George has been more aggressive than I have in asking for pay raises. (face saving) But I know you're aware of my many contributions to this company, the most recent being . . . I've put together a memo listing my contributions, and I'll leave it with you. (benefits) When pay raises are considered next month, I expect you'll want to correct this discrepancy." (takes control)

Martha got a hefty raise. No doubt her boss considered the alternatives, not the least being a lawsuit. She had given him a face-saving way out because she, too, understood the alternatives. Fuming in silence would have changed nothing; an attack would have made her boss hostile, defensive, and rigid; a lawsuit would have been a painful and costly last resort. Martha also recognized that she had, indeed, been lax in asking for raises and had operated on the myth that hard work would automatically be rewarded. But the point is that Martha didn't settle for the discrepancy in pay like a Nice Girl.

One of my friends, a professional woman in sales, told me how she worked for weeks preparing her first important presentation before upper management and colleagues. During the session, one man needled her, asking a series of questions, often irrelevant, that seemed designed to unsettle her. Monica had seen him do this to other women, and they all suspected he had problems dealing with women. Hence, she was ready with the "Get It Right, Guys" strategy:

"Tony, your questions raise some interesting issues and I'll certainly want to consider them. (face saving) However, I want to stress again the benefits of my approach. First, there's . . . Second, . . . Last, . . . " (benefits)

Then she added, firmly, "Now, I'd like to have input from those who have not yet spoken. Brian, what do you see as the benefits of my suggestions?" (takes control)

Tony's questions were aimed at rattling her. By refusing to

be rattled and handling him in a firm, professional manner, Monica no doubt won the respect of those watching the exchange. Growing flustered or angry would have probably reinforced the stereotype about how emotional women are and how they can't handle the tough situations.

The "Get It Right, Guys" strategy has worked for other women, too. A worker in a secretarial pool, Anita was responsible for providing secretarial support services for three sales reps. When a new replacement rep joined the team, Anita found him difficult to work for since he repeatedly gave her last-minute work that he needed "right away."

When she told him she already had other deadlines to meet, Mike would say, "This is really important. It can't wait."

Once she tried to send Mike an indirect message by continuing with her scheduled work. He was furious when he came for his papers.

"Maybe you're not up to this job!" he accused.

As time passed, Mike's work habits began to affect her ability to deliver services on time to the other two reps, not to mention her state of mind. Anita began to understand that her passivity contributed to the problem and invited Mike to take advantage of her. Finding the situation intolerable, she sought my advice.

The next time it happened, Anita said the following:

"Mike, we need to talk. I enjoy my job, but having to deal repeatedly with last-minute work when I already have deadlines is not good for any of us. I realize how busy you, Ruth, and Fred are, and I'm sure you're concerned about getting your clients' needs met." (face saving) "I see this as a scheduling problem that can be easily resolved so that all three of you can do your jobs with ease. I'll be less likely to make mistakes and more likely to have your work ready when you need it, if I get it on time. That way, an occasional rush job can be dealt with." (benefits) "I'm asking you, Ruth, and Fred to meet with me so we can work out a schedule that's fair to everyone. Both Ruth and Fred have agreed. What's a good time for you to meet?" (takes control)

Unfortunately, secretaries and other office workers, retail sales clerks, waitresses, nurses—for the most part, women—routinely suffer the brunt of controlling behavior such as this at work. Silently tolerating such behavior like Nice Girls sends a message that it's OK, that we don't mind. Complaining to friends, instead of taking action, raises everybody's level of frustration to no good end.

Another fairly common complaint of women is they don't receive the training men do or the important, visible assignments. One manager I know expressed disappointment at not being selected to attend a training session in Atlanta that would have benefited her and her department. Barbara felt overlooked in this way on a number of occasions. She realized that if this continued, her professional development would suffer. We talked and she resolved to speak up:

"Fred, I know money is tight and you probably couldn't send everyone to Atlanta you wanted to." (face saving) "But the training would be directly relevant to our department's work on the large X account, as well as others. The department and the company would benefit by . . . " (benefits) "I'd like you to reconsider sending me." (takes control)

As it turned out, Fred said that sending her wasn't possible.

"Then I'll look forward to being included in the next round of training," she replied firmly.

Chances are, her boss won't easily forget Barbara in the future, as he did during the period when she remained silent, waiting for something to happen. She's determined now to keep speaking up.

One woman, a construction worker, once told me about a really tough situation she encountered on the job. When refused a supervisory promotion she felt more than qualified for, Happy approached her boss.

"They're a tough bunch of guys down there, and they

don't want to work for a woman," he told her. "Construction is really no job for a woman. If you don't like it, you can quit."

Happy came away not so happy. She found his candor shocking.

"Doesn't he know he's admitting to sex discrimination?" she asked me.

I was not surprised. There seems to be a widespread feeling of invulnerability among men out there. After all, how many women do or even say anything in situations like these? Typically men expect us to be Nice Girls and put up with their abuse.

There's also a considerable amount of latent hostility toward women in the workplace that periodically rears its ugly head. Lots of men aren't very good at holding back their anger, especially when they feel threatened.

Since Happy's problem emerged in one of my seminars, the group discussed what she could have done or said. We suggested that she approach her boss again since she had not responded to his blatantly discriminatory statement. Doing nothing would have sealed her chances of ever receiving a promotion.

Happy's reaction—or lack of reaction—is a common one. Sometimes we are rendered speechless by an unexpected or outrageous remark, but later regret our silence. Or we respond ineffectively and later think of a hundred things we could have said. In any case, it's OK—indeed, desirable—to return to the person afterward and share our reactions to the incident by saying something like: "I've had a chance to think about what you said yesterday, and I'd like to respond."

One suggestion for Happy's second conversation with her boss went something like this:

"I can certainly understand how hard it is to adjust to change. I know it's not easy for the crew to accept a woman boss." (face saving) "But the demographics are clear—women make up two-thirds of all new workers, so they will increasingly fill these positions. Besides, discrimination is illegal. Since the company is in fact hiring women in construction, we're all going to have to adjust to each other so the company benefits." (Benefits. Note that by citing the illegality of his actions, she is indirectly naming a benefit, i.e., prevention of a lawsuit against the company. It also serves to put him on notice.)

"I'm willing to do my part, and I expect the men to do theirs. Let's get a representative group together to discuss these difficulties and what can be done about them. I expect to be promoted next time, since my qualifications are not in question." (takes control)

When I discuss these examples with women, some claim they could never do it. They give a litany of reasons: My boss wouldn't like it; I'd hurt his feelings; I'm afraid; I don't have the guts; I could never think of the right words; etc. Whatever the excuse, being a Nice Girl lies at the heart of the problem.

Then I ask for the reasons why they should do it. Invariably the list grows much longer: I feel terrible when I don't stand up for myself; my self-esteem suffers; I'm hostile to a colleague or boss who treats me badly; my work suffers; I'm constantly frustrated; I bring my frustrations home; I know they don't respect me when I'm passive; I'm powerless when I tolerate behavior I don't like; I'm not taken seriously; I'm used like a doormat; I'm reinforcing the stereotype of women as weak, passive, and unable to make tough decisions . . . .

Generally, if we try to resolve problems in the workplace on a one-to-one basis, we'll be perceived as more effective and in control. This gives the offender an opportunity to change his or her behavior, which is, after all, our main goal. We'll be less likely to suffer the resentment, retaliation, and even blackballing from our colleagues that often accompany grievances and lawsuits. And we'll refute the stereotype of the passive Nice Girl.

On the other hand, each of us has every right to expect appropriate officials to handle our grievances when we choose not to deal with them one-on-one. Certainly, there are some behaviors, especially habitual or vicious ones (sexual harassment, for instance), for which we need to seek help. But we should be realistic about what we're up against when we do.

Will using the "Get It Right, Guys" technique (or any other) always bring results? Of course not. But doing nothing will certainly not change anything.

When assertive strategies don't work, there's always the next step: raising the level of muscle. This means, very simply, increasing the strength of the "dialogue" with the offenders, letting them know what consequences we're prepared to visit on them. Sure, it's a threat at this point ("I'm prepared to file a complaint." "I'm meeting with a lawyer.") However, we should *never* make a threat we're not prepared to follow through with.

Happy, for example, can file a formal grievance, involve her company's human resources or personnel department, complain to the state Human Rights Commission, or bring a lawsuit, among other things. Incidentally, keeping a log with dates and names, and sharing what happened with two or more confidants (as corroborating witnesses) will facilitate these processes.

Dealing with Criticism

Criticism often presents another difficulty for women in the workplace.

Recently, I spoke with a woman who felt devastated by criticism. A competent, efficient office manager, Isabel found herself with a new boss one day after her own manager left the agency. Shortly after John arrived, he began to find fault with office procedures that had worked well for years. It didn't take long for the situation to escalate.

One day, while Isabel sat working with two of the secretaries on her staff, her boss burst into the office and literally screamed at her, "What the hell do you think you're doing?" followed by a harangue about some incident Isabel knew nothing about. Before she could respond, he stormed out, leaving her stunned and embarrassed before her staff.

Two days later, Isabel's boss referred to a procedure she had instituted as "stupid and appropriate only for mental pygmies." Devastated, Isabel began to cry. That made her boss angrier and he stomped out saying, "You have no business being in a position of authority."

As her boss's criticisms continued, Isabel felt increasingly powerless and paralyzed. Yet she played out the classic Nice Girl response—she just tolerated his abuse. Her stress and tension mounted and she began to cry often at home.

Isabel confided to her friends that her boss would never talk to another man like that. They agreed. He frequently snapped at the women on his staff while treating the men with respect.

Less than four months after her new boss's arrival, Isabel quit the job she had held successfully for over five years. Her boss had called her a "slut" while criticizing how she had greeted a client. In her exit interview, Isabel stated she was leaving for "personal reasons"; she didn't want to jeopardize her next job.

The onslaught of criticism Isabel endured had devastated her. Handling it poorly, or not at all, made her the classic victim Nice Girls often are.

Criticism is usually very hard to take, for anybody. But women, who place a high priority on the approval of others, especially feel the sting of criticism and tend to take it personally. Nice Girls want to be liked.

If not handled properly, criticism can undermine our self-confidence, negatively affect the quality of our work, and hurt our productivity. Even the fear of criticism can be debilitating since it often blocks our actions and words. We may not say or do something for fear of being criticized.

Conditioned as we are to seek the approval of others, especially men, women often fail to grasp a fundamental truth of life: it is *impossible* for everyone to like everything we do, just as we don't like everything others do. Therefore, accepting and giving criticism is a normal part of life. However, there are limits to what sorts of criticism we ought to tolerate since criticism can range from constructive to untrue to destructive. In dealing effectively with criticism, we need to first assess whether the criticism is valid or invalid.

When it's realistic and we see at least some truth in it, criticism is valid. Invalid criticism, on the other hand, is unrealistic and we don't see any truth in it. Basically there are four ways to deal effectively with criticism, all of them depending on its validity and on how it is delivered. I call this approach to criticism the "I Can Take It" strategy:

1. I accept it, if it's valid. In accepting criticism, I don't get defensive, make excuses, or put myself down. I focus on the specific criticism and address only that.

2. I disagree with it, if it's invalid. In disagreeing, I state the truth as I see it.

3. I set limits if the person is speaking or behaving aggressively. I make it clear that I'm willing to listen to valid criticism, but I will not allow myself to be abused.

4. I delay my response if I need time to consider it. I feel free to address a point later, after I've thought about it.

We've all seen people handle criticism poorly. Doing nothing at all, reacting defensively, lashing out aggressively at the person making the criticism, internalizing inappropriate criticism, failing to learn from valid criticism—all constitute a poor reaction to criticism and all undermine our self-esteem.

Jane, for example, did not handle her boss's criticism well, even though she knew it was valid and accepted it. Jane's male friend walked out on her suddenly one day, leaving her very upset and preoccupied. As a result, she did not put enough work into an important report due that week. Jane's manager called her in after reviewing the report and said, "Jane, this report is deficient. You didn't research the Dobbs account very well. I can't use it as is."

Flustered, Jane replied, "I'm really sorry. I've had such awful personal problems lately. It's hard for me to concentrate on my work. My boyfriend left me without a word, and I'm just devastated. We'd been together for two years and I'm having trouble dealing with this. The report's a mess. I know it. What do you think I should do about the report?"

By the time she had finished, Jane had managed to make herself seem not OK, when the issue before her was only that the report was not OK. What's more, she surely came away from that exchange feeling worse about herself.

A better response from Jane would have been, "You're right. This is not an example of my best work. I'll redo the report right away and have it on your desk by Friday." Here she would have accepted the criticism, reminded him of the usual quality of her work, and offered to correct the problem right away.

Too often we get hurt by criticisms, whether valid or invalid. Then we either fail to respond at all or we respond angrily and defensively.

This happened recently when I attended a meeting of an organization using my consulting services. A young woman, Ava, was put on the spot when the chair asked her to report informally on some figures. Although the request was unexpected, the figures were from a project Ava was supposed to have completed.

Visibly uncomfortable, Ava indicated she didn't have any idea what the figures would look like because she hadn't done the work yet.

The chair replied, "Ava, that work should have been done. We need this information now, not at your convenience."

Ava fell silent, unable or unwilling to respond.

"What could I have said?" she asked me later.

How about something like, "I understand, Matt. It's not like me to fall behind in my work. You'll have those figures by morning."

That response would have gracefully accepted the legitimate criticism, provided an opportunity to affirm Ava and her excellent record, and offered a solution to the problem. Remaining silent let the worse impression stand.

Not all criticisms are valid. Criticisms we disagree with hit us especially hard because they seem so unfair and uncalled for. The best way to stand up for ourselves in cases like this is to simply disagree with the criticism and state the truth as we see it. Handling invalid criticism well need not be difficult.

Drucia, a dedicated entry-level supervisor, was taken aback by her manager's reaction during an exchange they had. Harold asked her to work late a couple of hours before quitting time, as he often did. Normally, Drucia complies because she loves her work. However, on this particular night, she had special plans with her family, so she refused her boss's request, saying, "Tonight is really impossible for me."

Harold became irritated and charged, "You're not very committed to the company!"

Although stunned by the charge, Drucia kept her cool and replied, "I disagree, Harold. In fact I've worked late nine times this month alone. That indicates a serious commitment to the company on my part."

Drucia's response was effective since it clearly expressed disagreement with an invalid criticism and told the truth as she saw it. Drucia did not react defensively or lash out, nor did she try to explain her family reasons for not being available. Her reasons were her own business and beside the point. In addition, citing her family would have reinforced, wrongly, the common perception that women always put their families before their work.

The worst sort of criticism involves aggressive or abusive language or behavior, like Isabel endured. Although anyone can be a victim of such treatment, women seem to face the affront more than men. Perhaps it's a function of women being perceived as powerless and vulnerable, or maybe men tolerate it less. Certainly, putting up with all kinds of unacceptable behavior is part of being the accommodating Nice Girl.

Whatever the reason, criticism delivered in an abusive way should never be tolerated. It's important to let people know that, while we're willing to listen to criticism, there are limits as to what they can say or do. Our dignity itself is at stake here, and much more. Setting limits should be done assertively, not aggressively.

I've seen some women devastated and reduced to tears when criticized abusively, and I've seen others tear into the person doing the criticizing. Neither is effective and both leave us feeling rotten. But dealing with abusive criticism assertively will help us regain some control over the situation.

Mabel, a reentry woman who had been out of the job market for some time, shared with me how good she felt after handling abusive criticism well. Mabel was being trained to use a complicated computer software system by a co-worker with a short fuse. Naturally, Mabel made some mistakes as she struggled to master the system.

At one point, her co-worker became very critical, pointing to Mabel's errors and ending with, "You're stupid!"

Although upset, Mabel stood up for herself and handled the abusive criticism well. "I resent being labeled stupid. I lack experience, not intelligence." With a firm tone of voice and eye contact, she finished by telling him, "I expect you won't talk to me like that again." Chances are good he won't. Abuse gets heaped more readily on those who tolerate it.

Annie also handled criticism well. On finding a typo in an important letter, Annie's boss threw the letter on her desk. Although Annie seldom makes a mistake, he tore into her.

"This letter is shit! What the hell do you do with your time? I don't pay you to be careless and sloppy and waste my time."

Annie took a deep breath and replied, "Like everyone else, I occasionally make a mistake, and I'll certainly correct it. However, I can't allow you to talk to me like that. If there's a problem in the future, don't hesitate to call it to my attention, but not like that."

A few minutes later, Annie's boss apologized to her for his outburst.

Sometimes we're subjected to petty or inappropriate criticism. While not exactly crossing the line into abusive criticism, it's clearly insensitive. One of my friends complained about a co-worker, Becky, from another department who often made critical comments about the appearance of others. These comments seemed more like putdowns than constructive criticism.

While wearing a new suit one day, Jean ran into Becky at work.

"I hate that color with a passion," Becky said. "I'd *never* wear it. It reminds me of mashed bananas."

Ever in control, Jean met the woman's eyes and replied evenly, "Tastes in color are certainly different. Actually, it's one of my favorite colors and I enjoy wearing it."

In a brief reply, Jean had rejected Becky's insensitive criticism and affirmed the legitimacy of her own tastes.

If criticism takes us by surprise, as it often does, or we can't think of a response on the spot, it's a good idea to delay our response. We can say something like, "I'm really surprised by your point. Let me think about it for awhile." Later, when we're prepared to share our reactions, we can return to the person and say, "Bob, I was surprised by your criticism yesterday. I've had time to think about it, and . . . "

Chipping Away at Oppression

Many elements make the difference in life between being in control and being out of control, between change and lack of change. These include meeting people halfway, communicating to others our expectations about their behavior in dealing with us, making self-affirming choices, handling difficult situations, and dealing effectively with criticism.

If I cannot deal with the day-to-day problems that beat me

down because I'm playing the Nice Girl role, I cannot feel good about myself. Nor am I likely to enjoy the respect of others, which, as a woman, I already have a problem gaining. And beyond the esteem/respect issues, I'll likely pay a tangible price if I cooperate in my own oppression—a price in the bread-and-butter discrimination so often visited on women.

Having some strategies that chip away at the affronts and the abuses will arm me to meet each day as it comes. Standing up for myself, refusing to be the Nice Girl who gets abused and exploited, will send an ongoing message to the perpetrator that I, for one, am not going to take it any more. Along the way, I've realized that my indignation at the inherent sexism and injustice of systems and institutions is irrelevant as far as change is concerned. It's what I *do* with that indignation that matters. The issue for me now is how I can work to change the system over time, while, for the sake of my sanity and survival, I must function in it.

I was, at one time, much harder on myself and other women because we weren't changing the world fast enough. A few feminists still are, criticizing women for wanting a "piece of the pie" that's corrupt in many ways. I agree that ultimately we should "bake a new pie." But asking women who are struggling to survive and gain simple equity to engage in revolutionary change is tantamount to asking women to be martyrs all over again. Systems that have existed for thousands of years won't change easily. Many have a vested interest in not changing—or so they think.

Like Filomena Giambattista, it's best to plunge in and do the best we can with the world as we find it. And like our feminist foremothers who focused on a particular set of problems, it's best for each of us to tackle the issues of our own choosing, since nobody can tackle all the problems that need addressing. We're much more likely to affect change in our own small pocket of life. Too often, however, women—and men—are primarily concerned with global issues. We're telescopic in our desire for change, seeing the distant big picture while ignoring the day-to-day issues in our own lives that badly need to be resolved. But in fact, for most of us, changing the day-to-day problems is possible whereas addressing the global issues is extremely difficult, if not impossible.

I see this pattern in many of my feminist friends, the married women in particular. We join women's organizations, contribute money to women's causes, fret about the lack of an equal rights amendment, and march in protest when our rights are threatened. All that is great and absolutely necessary. But in our personal lives, too often it's business as usual. We make few demands on the men or children in our lives, carry the burden of household chores on our shoulders, accept primary responsibility for raising children, settle for part-time jobs without benefits, put our husbands' careers first, make ourselves endlessly available for the needs of others, take on our shoulders the work of preserving our relationships, and generally carry on like our mothers did.

Meanwhile, we assure our daughters they can be whatever they want to be. But at home they, and their brothers, see a very different story.

One of my friends felt strongly about wanting no children and thought her husband agreed. Ruby worked at a satisfying career and actively participated in women's organizations. Then, her husband decided that he wanted children; she still didn't but wanted to please him. Eventually she gave in and produced a child. That meant a major adjustment, so Ruby settled into part-time work and caring for the baby.

Ruby's husband went on with his life as usual. Shortly thereafter, he determined that one child wasn't enough and he had to have another. She complied again and produced another baby, while her career disappeared.

After the birth of his second child and lots of strange behavior on his part, Ruby's husband split, leaving her with the two children he insisted they have. He had met another woman. Devastated, Ruby had to put her life back together.

Maybe it's a function of getting older, or maybe I'm settling for too little. But these days I operate on the chip-away theory of change: if all of us chip away in our own spheres, the big picture will change much faster. After all, the big picture is the sum of all its little parts. And we can't change the big picture if its parts are all messed up.

Change only comes from those who want it—and insist on it.

CHAPTER 5

Power

The Power of Money

I learned a few lessons about power growing up. The first was that Pop had it and Mom didn't. We three sisters didn't either.

Partly my mother's powerlessness was cultural, but mostly, I figured out later, money was the source. Pop made money, though not a lot, and Mom didn't. That meant she was reduced to relying on his good will for her very survival—her food, clothing, and shelter. It was some time before I came to understand that phenomenon as the biggest argument against traditional housewifery.

Not having money growing up meant we didn't have much. For some strange reason, I remember the half-moon cookies most of all. When my mother had a little money left over, which wasn't very often, she bought half-moons at the corner grocery store. They sat lusciously in a big box covered with waxed paper on the store counter, gleaming with chocolate and vanilla icing.

My mother never bought enough for each of us to have a whole half-moon; that would have been extravagant. So the cookies were cut in half. But eating half a cookie never seemed like enough; my fantasy in those days lay in whole half-moons.

Not having money growing up also meant we didn't do much. I remember vividly the summer days my best friend and

I sat on my front porch watching the cars go by.

"What should we do today, Rosie?"

"I don't know. What do you think we should do today, Jeanette?"

As though there were any real options! Mostly we sat around and talked. I vowed that when I grew up I'd travel everywhere.

When I was fifteen, I went to work in a large department store selling candy. I'll never forget the sense of power that came with that first paycheck. Part-time work at $57\frac{1}{2}$ cents per hour didn't exactly add up to a fat paycheck, but it was mine.

Money meant I could do things and buy things. But mostly I squirreled it away in a tiny savings account that I'd had since the first grade. In those days, children were encouraged to save. We opened the accounts through school and once a week, on bank day, we brought our money to class and deposited it. I loved watching the pennies add up in my little red passbook.

It's funny how schizophrenic I was about money, too. One part of me was very clear about money and what it meant— power, freedom, opportunity. I saved like crazy to get myself out of poverty. Even the year I saved only $21.30, I thought I was buying my ticket out. The other part of me hummed along, oblivious to the need to support myself and examine my career options. I never connected powerlessness with the economic dependency entailed in the Prince Charming myth—or in my mother's situation. I don't ever remember talking to my girlfriends about the future or careers or how we'd take care of ourselves. Even in high school and college, we talked about boys all the time. We were all under a kind of collective spell.

When I started my graduate studies, I still went along childishly thinking, "I don't know what I'll be when I grow up." In those days, I never seriously explored my career options; I just drifted. Today, I still meet women everywhere who say, "I don't know what I want to do with my life." These are not recent graduates but women in their thirties, forties, and fifties.

Not knowing what to *do* with one's life is one of the most visible signs of powerlessness.

In the late 1960s, with the advent of the women's movement, it seemed like all of this would change substantially. By the 1970s and 1980s, the refrain from young women became, "I can be anything I want to be." Some have actually managed to be "anything," but mostly that's proved fleeting, too. Witness the continuing cultural obsession with motherhood, the huge number of dependent teen mothers who keep their babies, and the number of women who choose or yearn to stay home with no income of their own. Many of us still seem hell-bent on keeping ourselves powerless and vulnerable.

But, then, women still seem almost frightened of the word *power*. At my seminars, with some notable exceptions, women react negatively to the word or try to avoid using it. Power isn't "nice," they think. I remember the day a colleague told me about her sexual fantasies and then asked me what I fantasize about.

"Power," I said, without a second thought.

She looked at me in stunned silence, as though I had said something unthinkable.

We seem to have a similarly distorted concept of money. Just as too many women think power is destructive, we also tend to think money is dirty. That's understandable given that we've never had a surplus of either, and both have been used against us in some horrendous ways. Besides, Nice Girls aren't supposed to want power and money.

But clearly lack of power is victimization and lack of money is poverty. Wouldn't anyone want to avoid such problems?

Since lack of money is the root of powerlessness, in part at least, I find it puzzling that we don't address the poverty mentality so common among women. Often, even women with money operate on this mindset.

But nowhere is the poverty mentality clearer than in women's organizations. I'm not referring to national women's organizations here, but to the thousands of groups of women involved day-to-day at the local level. We don't seem to realize that money is power and therefore necessary to these women's groups. Why is it that, historically, women have raised enormous amounts of money for every cause under the sky, but when it comes to women's causes we nickel and dime ourselves to death? Too often, I've heard:

"We don't have the money."

"It can't be done."

"Let's get so-and-so to do it for free." So-and-so is usually another woman we seem perfectly willing to exploit.

Often, the people most intolerant of my consulting fees (which are comparable to what men charge) are women. They frequently find it hard to accept another woman making serious money but expect it of men.

Even the entrepreneurial women I work with have trouble accepting the concept of profit, at least in the beginning. When asked why they're in business, invariably they'll name every reason but profit, as if it's a dirty word. Yet, by definition, they are starting for-profit ventures. One woman, when pressed, acknowledged her business as a for-profit venture. "But do we have to *say* it?" she protested.

Ultimately, women's apparent aversion for power and money is symptomatic of deeper problems. I suspect we don't think we're worthy. And why would we think we're worthy when the world around us says we're not?

The power-of-money lesson has been reinforced many times in my life. Money bought me a college education. I worked full-time summers and part-time during school at my department store job and joined the credit union to save money. My weekly take-home pay in the summers was $22.24, $20 of which I saved. The remaining $2.24 didn't stretch very far, so I bagged my lunch and walked the three miles each way to work to save the bus fare. I was just a kid, but I was putting power in the bank so I could go to college. Of course, this was when it was still possible for students to pay their own way through school; today it's usually not.

Another lesson in the power of money came many years later, during my teaching career. A handful of us on the faculty succeeded in obtaining a large grant from the National Endowment for the Humanities, which enabled us to start what was probably the first international women's studies program in the country. The money not only paid the bills, but it gave us legitimacy and a measure of power. We were able to pay faculty to teach in the program, bring renowned scholars to campus to speak, establish a minor for students, and host events. Since I directed the program, it firmly set me on my present course.

These and other lessons I've learned over the years have led me to conclude that we don't recognize power in ourselves and we don't use it. This is sometimes true of men, but mostly it's true of women. We all have power, whoever we are. But having power without *using* it is the same as not having any power at all.

My mother exerted her inner power with my father only once that I can remember. Mostly she did his bidding, however tyrannical or irrational. But having to ask Pop for every dime was always distasteful to her. My father never was very forthcoming—quite the opposite. Having grown up in poverty himself, Pop hung on to what little he earned, accumulating it against an unseen threat.

When my mother had enough of Pop's control over the money, she announced she would take a job. She was forty-seven at the time. Pop ranted and raved and said no. But Mom used a local connection to get a job anyway, as a cleaning woman in the city police department.

Pop didn't talk to my mother for a long time. She would come home from work each day, make supper, and we'd all eat around a silent table. But it didn't stop her; she kept on working.

If power is the ability to move people, it must start with moving ourselves. Mom moved herself. She had her own money and wasn't totally dependent on my father. She helped me pay for my first jalopy while I was working my way through college. She helped my sister, the student doctor, buy her microscope and books for medical school. Mom helped my younger sister, after she dropped out of school and married. And she had a few dollars here and there to give to her religious charities.

Along the way, my mother helped herself, too. Although she still did Pop's bidding in all other matters, financial independence meant a great deal to her. She made friends working at the police department and, later, city hall. Her world expanded beyond the confines of home. Because she worked, my mother was able to collect her own social security in her old age.

The Power of Determination
Despite her servility at home, my mother taught me other lessons in power. After I bought an old car, Pop decided he'd like one, too. Since he felt too old to drive (he was twenty-two years my mother's senior), Mom had to learn. Although she was in her early fifties herself, she set to the task quite happily.

But learning to drive and passing both the written and road tests proved not so easy for a peasant Italian woman who had picked up just enough English to get by. She passed the written test immediately, but failed her first road test. Undaunted, she took a second road test, and a third, and a fourth. Each time she refused to give up. Then came five, six, seven, eight, nine, ten, and eleven. Still she failed.

"It's OK," we told her.

"We'll drive you where you want to go," we said.

That was not the same, and my mother knew it. So off she went for road test number twelve. Finally, she passed. From this, I learned about the incredible power of sheer determination. Failure is giving up.

The old yellow Pontiac my mother drove around was itself a source of power for her. It gave Mom freedom to come and go. She could visit her sister in Amsterdam, New York, 125 miles away. She could visit friends, do her shopping, and occasionally get away from Pop. No wonder Italians like my mother call the automobile *la machina*—the machine.

After Pop died, Mom traded in the old Pontiac for a new car. She called one day, very excited, to announce the news.

"What kind of car did you buy?" I asked.

"A red car," she beamed.

"Yes, but what *kind* of car?"

"It's red, that's all I know." Of course! That she had bought a new, red car was all anybody needed to know.

When, at age 85, my mother had to give up driving, she was devastated. The day the tow truck pulled her red Ford Maverick out of the driveway, she cried all day. Mom had lost, it seemed to her, some of her power. I've come to understand that the male love affair with the automobile pales next to the freedom and independence it's brought to women.

Mom's lessons about the power of determination followed me throughout my life. It enabled me to work my way through college and graduate school. It gave me the courage to pick up and move halfway across the country after I married. With everything we owned stuffed into our rickety old Ford and only fifty dollars in our pockets, we spent three days driving across the country to the University of Kansas.

When I determined, two years into our marriage, that the time had come to start living out my travel fantasies, I set about making it happen. I decided to save enough that year so we could travel to Europe the next summer. Joe earned a small stipend teaching as a graduate assistant and I taught junior high school at the time, hardly a lucrative profession.

We ate mostly beans and baloney that year and generally exercised what is these days called an austerity budget. At the end of June, we moved out of our small apartment, took a train to New York City, and, on July 1, 1964 (our third anniversary), boarded a huge oceanliner bound for Naples, Italy. With *Europe on Five Dollars a Day* in our pocket, we rented a small car and spent two glorious months driving through Italy, Switzerland, and France.

Retracing my ancestry to Guardiagreggia moved me to tears. My grandmother, two aunts, and many cousins still lived in the tiny village on the mountaintop. Although I had heard stories about this place all my life, I was unprepared for the reality of it. Life went on there as it had in the Middle Ages. I saw firsthand what my mother's childhood had been like—the stone houses with dirt floors, the small fireplace for cooking, the lack of running water and heat, the feather beds, the sheep and pigs grazing nearby, the donkey waiting to carry us where we wanted to go. Almost nothing had changed for hundreds of years.

I also witnessed firsthand how hard and powerless a woman's life was. Thirty years after my mother left her village, women still hauled water on their heads, built fires, cooked in a huge pot suspended from a bar over the fire, beat their clothes with stones in the public fountain, tended the animals, planted vegetables, and preserved their own food. Needless to say, they worked incredibly hard from dawn to dusk. I remember seeing groups of men every day sitting around the plaza drinking coffee while the women moved about, endlessly doing their chores.

My Aunt Christina had given birth the day before we climbed down the rocky mountain path to her cottage. How surprised we were to find that she had spent the morning working in the fields and was in the process of preparing a meal for us!

One incident, in particular, reflected the powerlessness of women for me. We planned an outing to Piedemonte, a village at the foot of the mountain. Great excitement filled my Aunt Francescina's house and plans were made for a picnic. It was clearly not an everyday event to travel such a distance, and in *la machina*, our rented car, no less.

When the appointed morning arrived, it suddenly became

clear that Aunt Francescina would not come, only Uncle Carlo and Cousin Mario. No, someone had to stay home to tend the animals, do the work, prepare the evening meal; it was taken for granted that a woman's place dictated she stay behind. We proposed various plans and protested to no avail. I'll never forget how sad and angry I was for my aunt as the car pulled away.

The trip to Europe and especially Guardiagreggia was one I'll never forget. Ironically, I had used power of determination to get there—to witness how very powerless the women there were.

The lesson of the power of determination served me well on other occasions. When I started my own business as a gender equity consultant in 1983, everyone said it couldn't be done.

"No one will *pay* you to promote women's rights," they all said.

But I figured if somebody could sell a pet rock, a book with no words in it, or a Hula Hoop, I could learn to market women's rights. Without precedents or models to draw upon, it took two years of pain and sheer determination, but it happened.

Recently I read the inspirational story of a local woman whose power of determination shaped her life. In the early seventies, Ruth was on public assistance. Determined to get off welfare, she convinced the county to let her do clerical work in exchange for her welfare check.

Over the years, she struggled to work her way up, eventually becoming a supervisor and earning a good income. She knows that none of her success was handed to her, that had she been a Nice Girl, she wouldn't be where she is today. "The county has been good to me, but only because I fought for what I wanted," she says. "You can't be a ladies' lady and just act the way men want you to. You've got to make your own way, and if you're tough enough and you stand up, somebody's going to listen."

The Many Faces of Power

The sources of power are twofold, external and internal. Money is only one external source of power, determination only one internal source. Authority (derived from a particular position), connection (with influential or active people), and resources (needed by others) constitute other forms of external power.

Inner power, on the other hand, is more important because it can't be taken away. It can come from possessing or having access to information (perceived as valuable by others), expertise (based on competence and skill), or personality (the ability to interact effectively with others).

Virtually everyone has power by virtue of one or more of these sources. The problem is we don't always recognize the power we have—or the fact that we can acquire power sources we don't have. Certainly, the Nice Girl syndrome keeps us from acquiring and using power.

In addition to individual power of an external or internal nature, collective power plays an important part in our lives. Back from our European trip, Joe and I moved into an apartment in Syracuse. One year later, we, and all the other tenants, were hit with an exorbitant rent hike. Joe and I organized a tenants' meeting to discuss the increase.

Virtually all the tenants came and everyone expressed outrage at the unreasonable and unwarranted hike. Yes, they all agreed, something had to be done. We could not accept the increase. A strategy had to be plotted. The meeting disbanded with everyone fired up and ready to take the next step of approaching the landlord.

Within days, Joe and I received a notice of intent to evict if we did not vacate the premises within thirty days. Word of the notice spread through the apartment complex. Just as quickly, everyone disappeared into the woodwork. No support was to be found anywhere; all protests against the raise were silenced and we were abandoned. What is the lesson here? If people don't stick together in hard times, they relinquish their power to others. Moreover, fear paralyzes, so it's best avoided at all costs.

Other lessons in collective power came in my work. The women at a liberal arts college where I taught were badly outnumbered by male faculty—there were about eight females. So we decided to meet once a month over tea to discuss common issues and concerns. We called ourselves the Feminist Fortnightly.

Those were wonderful times. We'd sip Earl Grey tea, laugh, and eat cucumber sandwiches in Corinne's cottage on the lake. We talked about the women's movement, happenings at the college, and books we'd read, like *The Woman's Room*[13] and *The Managerial Woman*.[14] Often, we attended conferences and lectures on women's issues together. And we figured out ways to deal with problems at the college by speaking in a collective voice.

Our meetings were not without controversy. Several of the male faculty accused us of being lesbians and of discriminating against men. One frenzied male professor even showed up at one of our teas, demanding to be admitted.

Apparently they felt threatened by what they perceived to be a power bloc. They called us a *cabal*, which Webster defines as "a number of persons secretly united to bring about an overturn or usurpation." While we were hardly a cabal, we did seem to exercise power as a group. It surprised us, I think, just how much.

Women alone are perceived as powerless. But a group of women, however small, are apparently perceived—and feared—as powerful. It's a lesson most women have yet to learn.

Joining other groups also empowered me along the way. When I took my first job as a philosophy instructor after acquiring my doctorate (long before the Feminist Fortnightly), I felt isolated and alone. Only one other woman taught in the department and she was on her way out, having been denied tenure.

The newly formed Society for Women in Philosophy

(SWIP) helped me feel empowered and supported. I attended meetings, read the newsletters, and grew to know other women philosophers. SWIP helped me solidify my feminist consciousness and gave me a voice. I began to write again.

Several years later, I became involved with a group in Seneca Falls who were determined to save our feminist heritage.

There in Seneca Falls, the first women's rights convention in the world had taken place in 1848, thanks to Elizabeth Cady Stanton, Lucretia Mott, and others. Chaired by an African-American, Frederick Douglass, the meeting surpassed even its organizers' expectations. Hundreds of people attended from miles around. That convention, which met in the Weslyan Chapel on Fall Street, had seen Stanton rise during the meeting to propose the vote for women to a hushed and shocked audience. Out of that meeting and Stanton's unexpected proposal grew the mighty suffrage movement and a 72-year struggle for women's right to vote.

In a great irony of fate, the Weslyan Chapel had become a laundromat and only a marker at the corner gave any indication of what had happened there so long ago. The Stanton house also stood in disrepair. The Hunt house where Stanton and others met to plan the convention, the McClintock house, where the Declaration of Sentiments was penned ("All men *and women* are created equal . . ."), the streets where Amelia Bloomer strolled in her revolutionary attire, the now-destroyed building where the first feminist newspaper, *The Lily*, was published—that heritage we determined to save.

Thanks to the efforts of many, the Women's Rights National Historic Park was born. I often think back to our ragtag, contentious group that started it all. There *is* power in numbers.

The strongest lesson in collective power came when I was fired from my college teaching position. I was never given an explanation, just that my services were no longer needed. My position as an assistant professor of philosophy, it seemed, had mysteriously disappeared.

All of this seemed especially strange because a few months before I had received the prestigious Jefferson award, given at ten colleges and universities around the country. My evaluations were consistently excellent. ("Agonito is God," one anonymous student had scribbled on a form.) Also, my book had just been released from a major publishing house, not exactly a routine occurrence at the small college.

On the other hand, I had already acquired the label "radical feminist" for my various activities. (A feminist is usually considered radical, in any case, as is anyone who works on behalf of women.) Whatever the reasons, I got canned. When word spread around campus, the kettle boiled. Most of the faculty signed a petition urging reinstatement. That helped. But what helped most was a massive student effort.

Students met, protested, wrote articles for the school newspaper, hung signs, and generally raised hell. The most dramatic display came during parents' weekend, when, at the college president's reception for parents, students unfurled a huge banner from the balcony, visible in every direction. The banner read, "Save Rosemary."

In the end, I was saved. A faculty slot suddenly opened up because so-and-so had left. But so-and-so had left *before* I was fired and wasn't even in my department. I got my job back thanks to the collective action of many people whose power had countered the power the administration had over my life.

In addition to collective power, we can empower each other, on an individual basis. Numerous people made a difference in my life—people who encouraged this effort or that, who said a kind word here or there, who went out of their way now and then. Ginny, for instance, is a wonderful feminist who directs a college continuing education department. We teamed up to establish a sex equity center and to write grants designed to help school teachers and counselors overcome their gender biases, to help adolescent girls build self-esteem, to encourage young women to consider nontraditional careers, and much more.

Tom and Mary Ann, of the New York State Education Department, have also supported and empowered me. Tom's gone out of his way more than once to help me find funding for projects to help women business owners overcome the barriers they encounter. Mary Ann has always managed, even in hard times, to fund our various sex equity projects in education.

I've had some mentors, too, at different stages of my life. Mentors can be incredibly empowering for women. In high school and college, Kate "took me under her wing," so to speak. The candy buyer at the department store where I worked, Kate served as my peephole to the world outside my small neighborhood. She taught me about business, took me on buying trips, and told me stories of the strange world of buying and selling. When I couldn't afford clothes for special events, Kate loaned me hers. When I needed somebody to speak for me, and Mom couldn't with her broken English, Kate was there.

A strong woman who carried herself with supreme confidence, Kate was the first career woman I ever met. As a young woman with athletic skills, she wanted to attend college badly but had had to go to work to help her family. Condemned to the pink ghetto of retail sales, Kate worked her way up to manager, then buyer, in a world dominated by men.

Bright, successful, and respected, Kate traveled everywhere and met interesting people. But she never married. Because she, too, was the daughter of Italian immigrants, that always seemed strange to me. An unmarried woman was a contradiction in my tiny world. But I lacked the conceptual context to analyze this apparent aberration and it never occurred to me that remaining single might be a choice for a woman.

My second mentor appeared in graduate school during my doctoral studies. Though "everyone" taught linguistic analysis in philosophy then (and probably still do), Fred specialized in phenomenology and existentialism. For me, his classes were the proverbial "breath of fresh air."

Fred never seemed to notice or react to the fact that I was

female; he simply treated me like a human being. This strange and wholly unusual phenomenon endeared him to me. He operated on the assumption that I was a capable scholar and he didn't hold me to a lower standard. And he never assumed, because I was a woman, that my personal life took precedence over my work.

When I foolishly "disappeared" for months to deal with our newly adopted child (or maybe out of fear of success?), Fred never berated me. Instead, he welcomed me back and encouraged me as always.

Inspired by my maverick mentor, I wrote a maverick dissertation. I remember the day I defended the dissertation. After the inhuman experience of battling the questions of a group of senior professors, none of whom worked in my chosen specialty except Fred, I sat in the outer office to await the verdict. I felt an endless and dizzying terror at the thought that five years of incredibly hard work might not, after all, be over.

I was still waiting when the secretary left for the day, nervously trying to reassure me they'd be out soon, and everything would be OK. Eventually they walked out, grim faced, and congratulated me on passing. I never did find out what kind of battle Fred waged on my behalf, but I knew he had fought for me and my ideas in that dissertation. He did not let them send me off to write a second dissertation more to their liking, as countless others had had to do before me.

I met my last mentor a couple of years after I started my own business. Bob, who directs a Small Business Development Center, understood *the system* like nobody I'd ever met. But unlike many people who work it to their own personal advantage, Bob used the system to benefit the disadvantaged—people with disabilities, veterans, and people of color. When I approached him with a project to assist new women business owners, we immediately connected.

I've learned much from Bob. He was a good antidote for the female conditioning I still carried around: think big, not small; without risk, nothing happens; pay attention to the politics of situations if you want to get anything done; understand the meaning behind the cliché "one hand washes the other." Mostly, I learned from Bob how to use the system to work for women's rights, which is another way of saying I've learned how to make the system responsive, here and there, to the needs of those outside the system.

The best part about all this, as I watched Bob over the years, was that he didn't sacrifice principles in any of his pursuits. Yet women are raised to believe that thinking big, being political, and expecting something in return couldn't be compatible with principle (often mistakenly equated with being a Nice Girl).

These were three amazing people—and all of them empowered me in some fundamental way, helping me build and exercise power and overcome my Nice Girl persona. Women need more mentors like them.

Old Game, New Rules: Dealing with Power Plays

Building and exercising our own power, however, is only part of the story. Fending off the power plays of others is another part.

The exercise of dominance over others has traditionally turned women off to power because we wrongly equate how power is exercised with power itself. Yet power itself is the ability to influence others, to shape events, and to achieve personal goals. An aggressive, authoritarian, hierarchical approach (consistent with the male competitive mode) is *not* inherent in power. Power can be exercised in a cooperative, egalitarian, and assertive approach that respects all involved.

To diffuse the negative aspects of the traditional male approach, women first need to understand it. Only then can we address and undercut the destructive power plays so common in the workplace. Many women mistakenly believe they must play by the male rules of the game to get ahead. That's part of the Nice Girl routine. But playing by rules structured to keep women in their place will only lead women where men want them to be. So, I've taken the old game and made my own rules.

The essence of the old game rests on a series of ongoing power plays designed, according to the competitive model, to yield a winner and a loser. In those power plays, women are definitely not scheduled to win, ever. Although I am not interested in winning at somebody else's expense, I'm certainly not interested in losing either. My "Old Game, New Rules" strategy is designed to make sure I (and other women) don't lose when I'm the object of some guy's power play.

Rule 1 I don't ignore the power play or back down. Because women are perceived as powerless and men as powerful, we're already at a disadvantage. Ignoring a power play or backing down—typical of Nice Girls— is tantamount to handing Mr. X a win at my expense.

Rule 2 I don't react defensively or become upset. Squirming, defending myself, or "losing it" acknowledges he's had the desired effect on me and that I feel powerless to deal with his power play.

Rule 3 I respect the person, not the act. Attacking the offender and imitating his aggressive behavior reduces me to playing his game on his terms.

Rule 4 I take control by addressing the power play on my own terms. This undercuts his destructive power play and redefines the rules of the game to fit my agenda, which he's trying to sabotage.

One of my colleagues put my "Old Game, New Rules" strategy to work when she found herself caught in a co-worker's power play. His agenda—for her to do all the work while he took all the credit—is one women often complain about. Peggy worked essentially alone on an important and difficult project for weeks. Periodically, she met with a senior colleague who was supposed to be involved in the project, but basically turned the work over to her. When they met, she reviewed her progress with him.

Scheduled to make her presentation on the project at a meeting of senior executives, Peggy welcomed the chance to be visible and to show the quality of her work. When she arrived at the meeting, her colleague was waiting outside: "Peggy, you won't have to attend today's meeting. I've got the presentation covered."

Although stunned at his obvious power play, Peggy kept her wits: "I appreciate your willingness to do the presentation, but I've got everything prepared. Besides, it wouldn't be fair for you to have to deal with details you're not familiar with."

With that, she walked into the room and began greeting those present by saying, "I'm really looking forward to sharing Project X with you."

Peggy refused to play the Nice Girl and become a victim.

Over the years, I've seen many women break down or be crushed by male power plays, but I've seen other women handle them well. Once I met a group of colleagues while out of town and had dinner with them. During the course of the evening, the group began talking about graduate school. Jane shared her intention to start work on her MBA. Peter, who I later found out routinely exercises power over women by putting them down, cut in, "Ho! What will you do with the kids while you're working and going to school—give them a videotape of yourself?"

Without blinking an eye, Jane shot back, "What a great idea! Is that what you do when you're away from home?"

In one swift comment, without getting defensive or angry, Jane diffused Peter's remark, refusing to be "put in her place."

Another woman shared with me her concern at being excluded from important meetings and decisions she should have been involved in. Although Brenda earned good money working as a supervisor in a nontraditional trade, she felt powerless and unimportant. The scenario played itself out repeatedly:

when these crucial meetings took place, the men in her shop would find some way to keep her busy or away so she couldn't attend.

The "Old Game, New Rules" strategy set her on a different path. The next time an important decision had to be made that affected her and her department, Brenda was determined to attend the meeting. But her boss took her aside to assign her a minor chore that *had* to be done then.

Brenda stood her ground, saying, "I can do that work this afternoon. Right now it's more important that I be involved in the meeting on Z's new contract. I'll see you there."

Brenda took control by asserting her right to be at the meeting, rather than asking for permission.

Sometimes the power play is more subtle. Vera told me about her refusal to be manipulated. While making a presentation to her organization's board, Vera began to feel the undermining presence of her colleague, Bob.

Bob sat conspicuously in front, in view of everyone. While Vera spoke, he set a negative tone by talking to the person sitting next to him and using body language (frowning, eyes looking around, arms folded tightly across his chest). His behavior said to all present, "You have nothing valuable to say; I'm closing you out; I've got more important things to do."

At an appropriate point in the presentation, Vera said to him, "Bob, you look confused. Can I go over the point for you?"

Bob froze. By calling attention to his behavior, Vera diffused its power over her. People who use power plays want them to have the calculated effect, but they *don't* want to be exposed using them. Now Bob had to deal with his behavior, rather than having Vera endure it.

The old "power to the people" slogan seems wrong to me. It implies taking power from the few who have it and giving it to the masses who don't have any. But people already have power—*all* people. We just don't always know it, and we don't always use it. Our real enemies are fear and fatalism.

CHAPTER 6

Sexual Harassment

Stories from the Front

Friedrich Nietzsche once said that women are the playthings of men. Apparently many men still think so.

Although I'm familiar with the shocking statistics on sexual harassment in the workplace, I continue to be amazed at the stories women tell me:

- Stories of men cornering them.
- Stories of men grabbing their breasts.
- Stories of men leering at them.
- Stories of men commenting on their appearance and parts of their anatomy.
- Stories of men telling sexist and off-color jokes.
- Stories of offensive and demeaning pictures of females hung at work.
- Stories of men propositioning them.
- Stories of men threatening their jobs, their promotions, their raises, if they don't "put out."
- Stories of attempted rape.
- Stories of rape.

There was even a story about a man who pressured his girl-friend into being tied up while he disrobed her from the waist up on the job for the amusement of a few of his co-workers.

And there's the story of the woman who was standing in her colleague's office, trying to confer with him on a project. As she spoke, he gestured for her to move to the left. In puzzlement, she shifted. More, he gestured, "You're blocking my view." The view, it turned out, was of a raunchy calendar of a nude woman directly behind her.

Another woman was repeatedly harassed by her boss, who constantly insisted she loved his attention. She, in turn, kept telling him she preferred no such treatment and only wanted to do her job. The day after he ripped her dress, she quit.

Then there was the woman whose male colleague confronted her in earshot of other employees. "You know," he blurted out, "You're very good looking, but your breasts are too small. You should have them enlarged."

In another workplace, several women recounted a similar story. It seemed that the guys in this particular hospital needed to have some "fun." But rather than harassing a single woman, they targeted women indiscriminately. Sitting next to the cafeteria line, they rated the passing women on their physical attributes, using a scale from one to ten. It was hard not to know what was happening; the men loudly proclaimed their ratings as the women walked by.

I worked with a lawyer on one case involving a seventeen-year-old salesclerk for a national department store chain. Tina's mother had recently died, leaving her alone to care for her younger sister. Without resources or support systems, Tina struggled every day to support herself and her sister while taking business courses at night.

Into this already dark picture entered a lecherous, older married man, Tina's boss. As though sensing her vulnerability, he moved in for the kill. Her boss began cornering Tina in the stockroom, trying to kiss her, touch her, and grab her breasts.

Though desperately needing her job, Tina complained to the store manager.

The outcome, however, testifies to the business-as-usual attitude that too often prevails in the workplace. The store manager spoke to the man and promptly returned Tina to his department. After her boss cornered and grabbed her again, Tina quit.

When I spoke to her at the request of her lawyer, Tina was agitated, frightened, and confused about why her complaints had not been treated seriously. She had quit among recriminations that *she* was a troublemaker out to destroy a man's career. She worried about the impact of a lawsuit on the man's family and about finding another job. It's particularly horrific when young women, who still trust the adults around them, find themselves so badly used.

The stories from the world of education aren't any better. Although I also know the shocking statistics on sexual harassment in academia, I continue to be amazed at the accounts of women students, young and old:

- Stories of teachers coming on to them.

- Stories of suggestive comments made in class by instructors.

- Stories of professors inviting them on trips out of town.

- Stories of instructors setting up "private lessons" that were anything but tutorial.

- Stories of professors failing students who refused to give in to their sexual demands.

- Stories of graduate advisors sabotaging the degrees of sexually uncooperative women.

- Stories of rape.

One graduate student I knew a couple of years back told me about her graduate advisor, the person who made crucial decisions about her professional studies and degree. This professor began to ask her to do this or that with him. In the beginning, these things involved academic projects. Slowly, they began to lose their professional aspect and she found herself alone with him, at his request, for no apparent academic reason.

Increasingly uncomfortable, she made excuses, only to find him getting angry and hostile. One day he cornered her in his office and suggested she stop acting coy and go to bed with him. When she refused, he told her in no uncertain terms that she would never get a graduate degree from that university. Devastated, she dropped out of school and abandoned her studies.

Harassment in education isn't limited to the college and university level. Increasingly, the stories coming out of schools, especially junior and senior high schools, aren't much better. There girls are subjected to harassment by teachers, counselors, and coaches. Their male peers subject the girls to a barrage of sexual comments about their bodies, their sex lives (real and imagined), and their ability to measure up to male fantasies.

One girl told me that walking down the hall between classes, especially when the guys are hanging out in "packs," sometimes feels like a race through a gauntlet, only it's a verbal pounding. And it's all done in "fun," so the girls think they're poor sports if they don't go along with the obligatory giggles at their own expense.

Harassed women are all ages and all races. The work sites are everywhere—in offices, in factories, in retail stores, on construction jobs, in utility plants, in social service agencies, in government, everywhere. The offenders are managers, supervisors, co-workers, peers, and clients. Male-dominated work environments, in particular, are the setting for some of the worst abusers and the most difficult situations for women. But whatever the form, sexual harassment is the acting out of power and dominance over the victim. And the victim feels it to be precisely that.

The pain these encounters bring into women's lives is difficult to hear. They can't do their work well. They become frightened, angry, and feel ashamed. They feel trapped and take days off to avoid contact with the offender. They have bad dreams and become irritable. Their stress levels skyrocket and they become ill. They blame themselves. Their family life is affected and relations with their mates are hurt.

Usually the ending to these stories is predictable. The woman leaves her job because of the harassment or is fired. Mostly, a victim deals with these assaults on her person and dignity passively. She rarely complains because she fears losing her job, or because she doesn't want to seem like a poor sport, or because she doesn't believe anyone will do anything. And, of course, being a Nice Girl dictates a passive response because we're trained to put the other person's well-being before our own, no matter what.

I've certainly behaved like a passive Nice Girl when sexually harassed, at least in my prefeminist days, so I understand the silence. I was fortunate, however, that the harassment I experienced never progressed beyond the verbal sort. More often, silence and passivity cultivate an escalation of harassment.

The Clarence Thomas Hearings

Occasionally victims find the monumental courage to take action. Like the rest of the country, I sat riveted to the television watching the Senate hearings on the sexual harassment charges brought by Anita Hill against Supreme Court nominee, Clarence Thomas. I'd heard it all a hundred times before—different faces, different names—but it still shocked and angered me. I'll never grow accustomed to it.

Despite the polls immediately following the hearings showing that most women believed Clarence Thomas, in the days, weeks, and months that followed, a wave of anger grew in American women. Membership in women's organizations shot up, contributions to women's causes poured in at an unprecedented rate, and the number of women running for public office jumped dramatically, as did the public's willingness to vote for them.

Evidence that the polls missed something in women's re-actions became apparent to me almost immediately. After the hearings, I attended the groundbreaking ceremony in Seneca Falls for the Weslyan Chapel monument. Construction of the Women's Rights National Historical Park moved forward in Seneca Falls, even if the politics of women's rights moved back-wards in Washington.

Town folk, park visitors, women's rights advocates, and politicians—men and women—gathered under a gray drizzle that matched the mood of the week. However, the gloom was anything but paralyzing. Buttons sported on lapels read "I be-lieve Anita and I vote." Congresswoman Louise Slaughter, who had marched with other women in Congress to demand a hear-ing, received a standing ovation. Everyone talked of the travesty in Washington and what we should do in response. Altogether, it was an energizing, spontaneous display of anger and activ-ism, hardly what anyone listening to the press would expect.

That women identified so strongly with Anita Hill's charge of sexual harassment didn't surprise me. Sexual harassment per-meates every workplace and most (if not all) of us have wit-nessed or experienced firsthand its ugly sting. But I thought a great deal about what in those hearings had pushed so many women out of their complacency and into an activist stance. This was an important question for me. While I find very few women who don't know how badly women are treated, I find many in the grips of a profound fatalism, a nothing-will-ever-change attitude. It's as though they sense a permanency about female victimization.

When I encounter this fatalism, I urge women to look at history. Not so long ago women couldn't speak in public, couldn't vote, couldn't serve on juries or be doctors or lawyers, and they had no right to their own wages or their own children. "Do you know," I ask them, "that your roots are in slavery? Not just black women, but white women, too."

White women start at the suggestion. But in ancient western culture, the term *family*, literally meant "the sum total of all the slaves under a man" (the Latin word *familia* comes from the word *famulus* meaning "slave"). A woman was considered her husband's slave and property. What's more, a man in ancient Rome had the right to put his wife to death without having to answer to the law. Nor were conditions much better elsewhere in the world.

Conditions *do* change, although sometimes glacially. Fatalism is the luxury of the weak.

Now suddenly, the Senate hearings burst on the scene, thanks to a handful of women on Capitol Hill. I saw people all around me fired up about one woman's charge of sexual harassment. On one level, what disturbed women most about the whole scene seemed obvious:

- Neither Anita Hill nor sexual harassment was taken seriously.

- Men once again stood in judgment of women; the lone woman was the victim.

- The victim was blamed: Was she a tool of Thomas's opponents? Was she a woman scorned? Did fantasy dominate her life? Did she indulge in pornography?

- The senators treated Anita Hill badly.

- The president of the United States refused to give Anita Hill a fair hearing because he concluded *before* the hearing began and *before* the evidence was presented that she had lied.

- For the most part, the African-American community, many of whom had opposed Thomas, rushed to defend its brother, not its sister.

All that was obvious, but it didn't quite explain the rage and depression that spread over so many women. It took me days to shake the dark cloud that settled over me after the vote to confirm Clarence Thomas to the Supreme Court.

But one woman's charge of sexual harassment wasn't what triggered the rage and depression. It was the underlying message sent to women everywhere: a woman's place is to support men, no matter what men do. A woman, whatever her status in life, does not have the right to challenge a man, especially a powerful man or a man with friends in high places. If she does, she'll be dealt with severely.

At some conscious or nonconscious level, most women understood the message. The press was wrong when they declared that most women just couldn't identify with Anita Hill.

Certainly professional women identified with Anita Hill. We understood, as never before, that education, position, personal stature, and credibility don't matter when push comes to shove—not if you're a woman. But other women understood too, maybe in a more frightening way. If they can do it to a woman of education, position, stature, and impeccable credibility, then they can do it to any of us—much more easily and savagely.

I think that's what moved women to fight back.

Understanding the Cultural Connections

Not only do acts of harassment against individuals plague women in the workplace, but sexual harassment of a cultural nature is everywhere. No woman escapes this.

Most women know what it feels like to walk through any city's "combat zone." The sleazy shops hawk their misogynist exploitation through a glare of lights. The assault comes from all sides.

But pornography doesn't stay in the combat zone; it creeps its way into our daily lives. Whether its soft porn or hard porn, it's all pornography. It blurs the line between sex and violence. It portrays women as subjugated, either brutally dominated by men or existing solely for their entertainment and pleasure. It's a multibillion dollar business in this country. And it's everywhere.

Advertisers still sell products using women's bodies. Beer ads are particularly offensive. The female anatomy is displayed everywhere, spreading the message that women like making themselves available. This shouldn't surprise us so much since we still raise girls to believe that their appearance and their bodies are their most precious commodity on the open market.

Magazines line store shelves enticing customers with images of scantily clad, seemingly mindless women spewing the message: "I'm available! I'm available! I'm available!" In the greatest misnomer ever, the "adult" bookstores, "adult" video stores, and "adult" whatevers, sell their woman-hating wares to people, mostly men, suffering from arrested adolescence, among other things.

Auto repair garages have their own versions of cultural sexual harassment with their oversized nude posters of women glaring down from the walls. Once I bought tires in a large garage where such a poster hung. It made me feel degraded and angry and I complained to the manager. He told me most of his customers were men and *they* didn't mind one bit. I minded and never did business there again.

At another garage I patronized, a sign appeared one day: "Don't ask to borrow our tools and we won't ask to borrow your wife."

This is no rare occurrence. Women are often equated with "things" like tools and even meat. A fairly common image in pornography is a woman's body on a butcher shop meat hook. On the beach one day, I saw a beach towel with a naked woman's body blazoned across it. Her body was sectioned off like quarters of beef and named for the meat parts they represented—rump, breast meat, ribs. Sadly, the towel belonged to a woman.

Hollywood, with rare exception, seems incapable of producing a movie without gratuitous sex in the form of naked women and explicit sexual acts. (I'm referring to *gratuitous* sex, not sex that is an integral part of the content.) Rarely, if ever, are the private parts of men displayed as they are with women. Hollywood producers understand that nakedness is incompatible with power; that the emperor without clothes is vulnerable.

Each day, television also moves further and further from wasteland to sewerland. Gratuitous sex and violence, usually in some form of sexual violence against women, dominate the screen.

Rock videos, in particular, have perfected the art of sexual exploitation. Young people grow up on a steady diet of horrific images: women bound and gagged, women in chains, women in cages, women crawling at the feet of men, women enjoying violence against them, women in postures and moves suggesting animals from cats to snakes.

If women's bodies generally are publicly available as commodities with entertainment value, then it follows that individual women's bodies will be viewed in the same way in offices, in workplaces, in schools, everywhere. That's a connection we better make if we hope to really end sexual harassment in the workplace.

We traffic in women's bodies everywhere in the marketplace while expecting that in certain corners of society (the workplace) women will not be treated as commodities. We universally treat women as sex objects, but tell men that in the workplace they must not act on that view of women.

As long as the dominant cultural message presents women as sexual creatures to be used for various commercial and entertainment purposes, ending sexual harassment in the workplace will be an uphill struggle. Mixed messages seldom lead to the desired outcome.

Dealing with Sexual Harassment

What to do about sexual harassment on the job looms as a monumental problem for women. But clearly, doing nothing means more than nothing is done. Passive tolerance reinforces the objectionable behavior because the harasser can easily interpret it to mean that the victim doesn't object. Besides, powerlessness is precisely the reaction that the harasser desires.

So what's to be done? Understanding the definition of sexual harassment constitutes the first step. I learned a long time ago that not all harassment of women is sexual, and not all of it is illegal.

Gender harassment, generally, refers to any differential treatment based on sex that persistently annoys, troubles, or hurts an individual or group. But however annoying, troubling, or hurtful a behavior may be, it is not necessarily illegal.

Condescending, patronizing behavior toward women may annoy me terribly. Being repeatedly called *girl* may trivialize me in the eyes of others. Hearing sexist language that persistently excludes women, such as *chairman*, may trouble me and hurt women, but they are not specifically illegal.

Sexual harassment, on the other hand, is a precisely defined, illegal form of gender harassment. All women should commit the legal definition to memory:

Unwelcome sexual advances, requests for sexual favors, and other verbal or physical conduct of a sexual nature constitute sexual harassment when:

1. *Submission to such conduct is made either explicitly or implicitly a term or condition of an individual's employment.*

2. *Submission to or rejection of such conduct by an individual is used as the basis for employment decisions affecting such individuals.*

3. *Such conduct has the purpose or effect of unreasonably interfering with an individual's work performance or creating an intimidating, hostile, or offensive working environment.*

This legal definition can be summarized as any *unwelcome* sexual attention, usually of a persistent nature. The more severe behaviors, such as denial of a promotion for refusing sexual advances, need not be persistent to constitute sexual harassment.

The word *unwelcome* provides the key to the definition. Hence, sexual behavior between consenting adults is not sexual harassment, although it may be unprofessional and lead to sexual harassment if one party stops consenting. Unwelcome sexual behavior can range from off-color jokes and nude posters to pressure for sex and rape.

Who decides if behavior of a sexual nature is unwelcome? Each of us does. The courts have moved to a "reasonable woman" standard: what a reasonable woman would object to. So we need to stop telling ourselves we're being poor sports or overly sensitive. We know how the behavior makes us feel, and we can be as reasonable in our expectations about acceptable behavior as the next person.

Beyond trusting our responses, we need to be aware of the actions available to us. Whether we prefer to deal with the problem one-on-one or file a grievance, human rights complaint, or lawsuit, is entirely a judgment call based on our individual circumstances. One thing is certain: ignoring the problem is never enough.

I've gathered some suggestions over the years that tend to work well for women, the immediate object being to stop the offending behavior. I call these my "I Won't Take It" strategies. While they're not miracle cures for sexual harassment, these suggestions have helped women retain a measure of control over what's happening to them, even in those cases when the strategies don't work.

At the first sign of harassing behavior, communicate your feelings, firmly and unequivocally, by simply saying, "No." Or you can say, "That kind of language is inappropriate and makes me very uncomfortable. I trust you won't do it again." Or, "I prefer to keep my personal life and my work completely separate. I'm sure you understand."

Say this in a very somber and serious tone, making sure that your body language fits the firmness of your words. Otherwise, if you smile or try to be nice, you're sending a mixed message.

Often, however, men assume that a woman is being coy and means yes when she says no. In those instances, nothing you say will make a difference. In any case, from a legal standpoint, the fact that you said no may be important later on.

It's also a good idea to keep a record of every act of harassment, however minor each may seem in itself. Showing patterns of behavior over time is very important in these kinds of complaints.

Keeping a written record means writing down the following:

- Who did the harassing.
- What the harasser did.
- When the incident took place.
- Where the harassment occurred.
- Names of witnesses, if any.

Many women have found a written log to be the single most important element in their battle against the harasser.

It would also be helpful to tell someone you trust about the harassment, such as a co-worker, a friend, an advisor, or a doctor. Better yet, tell two or more people. If necessary, they can later serve as corroborating witnesses for you.

If the harassment is causing problems of a medical or psychological nature, telling a doctor or psychologist about the harassment would be beneficial. Her or his testimony may be valuable later if you decide to complain or sue.

Meanwhile, you should become familiar with your organization's grievance procedure for sexual harassment so you'll be prepared if you decide to file a complaint. It's also helpful to explore external channels for complaints, such as your state's Human Rights Department, and legal steps, should the behavior continue or the company act inappropriately.

If the harassment continues and you still don't want to file a formal complaint, you can write a letter to the harasser. This letter should be written in a formal, businesslike manner and contain a number of key points.

First, include a factual, *nonjudgmental* description of what he did with dates and times. For example, one woman who experienced escalating sexual harassment wrote: "On December 10 during our 11 a.m. meeting, you put your hand on my leg and tried to touch my crotch. At the office Christmas party on December 18, just before 10 p.m., you asked me to go to bed with you."

Next, describe how you felt about the behavior and its effect on you. The woman above continued, "I feel angry and hurt and your behavior makes it difficult for me to concentrate on my work. I'm uncomfortable coming to work because of this, and my stomach is often in knots."

Clearly let him know that this behavior is sexual harassment, while giving him the benefit of the doubt. "You may not have intended to harass me, but your behavior is sexual harassment according to the legal definition. As such, it's against the law."

Hard as it may be to believe, some men still think women are flattered by sexual attention and desire it.

Finally, tell him what you want to happen next (usually, that the behavior must stop in all its forms). There's no need at this point to threaten a lawsuit and, in any case, that's strongly implied as an option when you state the behavior is illegal.

The object of all this is to give the harasser one last chance to change his behavior. Once you've gone public (as you may well choose to do), it will be a no-holds-barred battle with him against you. He will defend himself at all cost *to you*. Count on it.

After the letter is written, it should be sent certified mail with a return receipt indicating he received it. Needless to say, you must keep a copy of the letter with proof of receipt. For his part, he knows you have proof that he received the letter and would have to be extremely foolish to persist in the behavior or retaliate.

But if all else fails, try using formal channels in or out of the organization. It won't be easy, but there's no virtue in powerlessness.

The things you should *not* do include the following:

- Do not blame yourself for what happened. The harasser is to blame, not the victim.

- Do not delay in acting. Not only is the harassment likely to continue and even escalate if you wait, there is a time limit on legal action.

- Do not keep the problem to yourself. It's likely that others have been victimized by this person. Although collective action can be very powerful, you shouldn't expect others to be eager to join in a complaint.

- Do not choose your course of action based on the harasser's needs and reputation. Presumably, you've given him the opportunity to stop by saying no. But, in any case, you'll find yourself paralyzed into inaction if you put his well-being before your own. Besides, many offenders are guilty of harassing numerous women.

Will you always be successful if you fight back? Of course not. While sexual harassment is definitely one of those problems that can't be ignored, it remains impossible to fight every battle. So pick the problems that matter most to you and tackle them as best you can, without regard for winning or losing.

Sure, winning is ideal. But losing in a struggle that matters to you is OK, because the struggle itself sends an important message and because you obviously can't win if you don't try. There's something worse than losing: it's being powerless, being just a victim.

Some years ago, I half jokingly, half seriously, expounded the "Politics of Spite" to my friends in the Feminist Fortnightly. Intended to be used against the perpetrators of oppression and discrimination, it's a version of the old maxim, "Evil triumphs when good people do nothing." According to the Politics of Spite, if you can find no good reason for standing up to assorted tyrants, you should stand up out of spite. That means holding perpetrators accountable for their unconscionable actions so that they don't commit these acts with impunity. Perpetrators of injustice, by definition, make others pay a price. The Politics of Spite says, "Perpetrators of injustice will pay a price too, however small."

Such perpetrators shrink from public exposure. Injustice thrives and grows in secret, like a toadstool hidden in a dark forest. When illuminated with a spotlight its growth is stunted, even if for a brief moment. That's a pretty good reason for fighting back, even if you know you can't win. Maybe it's the Italian vendetta in me, but when all else fails, the Politics of Spite has its virtues.

Unfinished Business
We're fortunate the law has progressed to the point of recognizing sexual harassment in the workplace as a violation of a person's civil rights. But we're not so fortunate that sexual harassment of a public, cultural nature is still protected according to an extreme interpretation of free speech. Whereas sexual harassment in business is illegal, making a business out of sexual harassment is legal.

It seems that the workplace is the only place where a hostile environment matters. A hostile environment in the streets, on television, in a movie theater is legally acceptable. Of course, I can walk down another street, or turn off my television, or not go to the movies. But why is the burden of avoidance and lack of free movement placed on the victim? Why should I walk a longer route so that porn kings can hawk their misogyny, or not see a program I enjoy because the advertisers exploit women, or have to avoid most movies because women are gratuitously presented as commodities.

At work, the burden of change is on the perpetrators; everywhere else it's on the victim. In the workplace, we don't contend that the right of free speech absolutely takes precedence over everything. Nor do we say to victims of harassment, "You don't *have* to work there; you're free to leave," even though it may be so. It's another example of the schizophrenic American approach to rights: only extremes prevail, repression or license. Freedom with responsibility got lost along the way.

Of course, freedom of speech is a very important right and there are potential problems associated with any manner of censorship. But to tolerate the actual violation of one group's right (half the population!) in the name of protecting human rights in the abstract seems preposterous. The fear of possible, unbridled censorship apparently takes precedence over the present, real violation of women's rights.

It's no accident that on our streets and in our homes, women seldom feel completely safe. Rape is on the increase, with conservative estimates indicating that one in three women can expect to be raped at least once in her life. Growing up, I always felt a sense of unease and danger when I had to be out alone at night or when I found myself in isolated settings. I still feel that way.

The Canadians, who lack our absolutist traditions with regard to rights, have evolved to a more sensible position, at least in the case of pornography, which melds sex with violence and subjugation. In a harms-based approach, the Canadian Supreme Court has accepted the large body of research revealing pornography's harm to the safety and self-esteem of women. There, obscenity is no longer a question of taste (which is always based on male tastes, in any case), but a question of the harm it does to women's pursuit of equality.

Working women need to understand these connections very clearly. Just as pornography entails the subjugation of women, so does sexual harassment. Since sexual harassment involves the exercise of power over women and a view of women as existing for male purposes, it precludes equality between men and women. Being subject to male power and purposes makes virtually every element of the struggle for equality more difficult, if not impossible. Under these conditions, how can women be treated as candidates for anything other than positions servicing the needs of men in the workplace (not to mention the home)? How can working women be viewed as leaders entitled to admission to the executive suite? How is pay equity possible? How can violence against women, in all its forms, be stopped? How can women's contributions and perspectives be taken as seriously as men's?

The answer, of course, is that it's impossible. So, if we don't like this, we have to stand up and stop being "nice." We must refuse to let the status quo be maintained at our expense.

We need to understand that, as hard as standing up for ourselves is in the short run, not standing up is much harder in the long run.

Change happens, glacial or not, despite the forces of reaction. Our daughters, our granddaughters, and our great-granddaughters will see some of it in their lifetimes—just as we've seen some in ours.

CHAPTER 7

Success and Career Development

Careers and Motherhood

As a youngster, I often wondered about the meaning of my life. In those days, I thought I could find the meaning of life by scanning the blue sky or the setting sun or by listening to my priest pontificate about abstractions.

Now I work every day to *make* my life meaningful and to define who I am. Creating myself is the most difficult challenge I've ever undertaken.

Parenting, which many consider the most difficult work in life, is really the second most difficult. Creating ourselves is the hardest work. After all, making a child is a physical process and the rest of parenting involves lending support and guidance. Just as with every human being, each child ultimately creates the person she or he becomes. We cannot do this for them, only for ourselves.

The tragedy of women's lives lies in a *false* sense of motherhood instilled in us from earliest childhood. Motherhood, as we know it, means self-denial, self-sacrifice, and self-effacement. This definition demands that a mother suppress her own needs in the interests of her child, that her self-fulfillment remain secondary in a way that it never does for the child's father.

153

Hence, from this traditional view, creating myself as an autonomous human being and establishing the meaning of my own life is incompatible with motherhood.

Consequently, we women who try to live up to this false view of motherhood suffer destructive self-doubt, guilt, and a crisis of identity when trying to affirm the importance of our own lives. Women are led to believe that motherhood defines our being, when in fact motherhood and parenting is a process— a very important process—but a process nonetheless, a set of tasks not unlike others we engage in during life.

Because, historically, motherhood is promulgated as defining the very essence of women, we see in women everywhere the disastrous consequences of universal motherhood—the idea that if a woman is not a mother, no matter what she does in life, it amounts to little and she cannot be fulfilled as a human being.

Women have internalized this concept of motherhood as the very essence of womanhood. So, regardless of what we've accomplished, the pressure of the biological clock ticks louder and louder, drowning out the sounds of the authentic self.

It's not that women shouldn't be mothers and men shouldn't be fathers. But the choice should be free and appropriate to the person (and the child and the environment), not imposed as a condition of being.

People need to understand that parenting is important, good work (like other important, good work). But it does not automatically define the whole of who I am like some magic cloak I put on. It cannot take the place of creating myself as a person whose life has meaning in its own right.

Buying into motherhood when it's not freely chosen and appropriate can be a calamity. For those women who have given their lives over totally to motherhood, middle age (when children leave) is characteristically a period of great emptiness. Time and again in my own work, I see the tragedy of middle-aged women realizing they have abandoned their lives in the interest of a false view of motherhood. Having opted out or dropped out of the workplace, they return, desperately wanting an education or a career.

But the calamity often doesn't wait till midlife. Regret, severe postpartum depression, and trapped feelings are not unusual in women since we still overwhelmingly bear the burden of raising those children.

I remember my own feelings of denial and regret when I became pregnant with my first child before I was ready to make that choice. It put the process of creating myself as a writer on hold for a long time. Fortunately, I found parenting rewarding enough in the early years and I began my career as a college professor shortly thereafter. So I did not lose myself in the parenting process as many of my friends had.

Adopting a second child appeared to be a free choice at the time. I now know it wasn't. At some subconscious level, my "mission" in life of propagating and building a family dictated the choice.

I often think back to that first day at Kennedy Airport. After a long wait of several hours, a flight attendant emerged from the airplane ramp carrying what appeared to be a baby. We looked past the flight attendant, searching for a glimpse of our three-year-old child in the crowd emptying the plane.

Then the flight attendant with the baby called our name, "Agonito. Agonito."

The "baby" in her arms turned out to be our child, three-and-one-half-year-old Mae Ki Lee, badly malnourished and weighing only eighteen pounds. Our names were written on a square white cloth stitched to the front of Mae's coarse, brown print dress. On her feet were cardboard-looking slippers. She appeared every bit like a refugee from the World War II pictures I remembered seeing as a small child.

Mae was very frightened and very confused. She had gotten sick on the endless flight from Seoul, Korea, to Honolulu to Seattle to New York City.

All the way home to Syracuse, Mae sat, tense and alert, in

the backseat of the car with her strange new brother, who kept talking to her and trying to give her things.

And I sat in the front seat with an unspoken sinking feeling in the pit of my stomach. Here she was, as irrevocably mine as if I had borne her for nine months. This feeling rose from my stomach and swept over me. There was no turning back. I was a mother again. A son or daughter is there not just for eighteen or twenty years, but for life.

Recently, a woman I know told me that she was pregnant again.

"How do you feel about it?" I asked her.

A long silence followed as she searched for the right words. "Well, it's not exactly where I want to be at this point in my life."

Another pause. I thought about her three children, two of them twins. I remembered how she had been left a single parent after her first child's birth when her husband met another woman and how the twins had been unplanned, a by-product of switching from one form of birth control to another.

To my surprise, she then added, "I'm going to start working full-time when the child is born. I'll hire live-in help."

Despite having worked part-time with three children, she planned to work full-time with four children and hire live-in help, a move that would surely net her less income.

"Being here at work is what I really enjoy—being around people, talking to them," she explained. "Being with the children is work; this is where I come to relax."

Recently, I learned that the doctor told her she was carrying twins again. "I cry a lot," she says simply.

Is having children never a joy then? Of course it is. But the problem is that we lead girls and young women to believe it's all a joy, like playing endlessly with a cuddly doll. We fail to share the pain, the burdens, and the disappointments. And we neglect to point out that motherhood is not a substitute for creating ourselves as unique, authentic individuals. *We need to start doing that.*

Once we start portraying motherhood realistically, women will have the possibility of real choice. Only then will motherhood stop being a categorical imperative for every woman and will mothers be able to acknowledge their negative feelings without guilt and without condemning themselves as terrible people.

The happiest women I know are those who made their own choices in life, not the women who thought they were choosing when, in fact, they were playing out some yellowed social script of someone else's making.

It took me a long time to figure out that work, as opposed to relationships, is the essence of my life and how I define myself as a unique individual. It's not trendy to say these days, but what we *do* defines our lives and our identities. Of course we're members of familial and social communities, but *what we do in community* is what we "amount" to. A very big part of that is what we normally refer to as work, job, or career.

This is not to be confused with what we do to survive. Every creature does that, human or animal. I mean productive, constructive work in community, familial *and* social, because we are inevitably part of both.

Certainly relationships are important for everyone. Life is infinitely richer when we have mates, companions, and dear friends. But another person cannot be a substitute for meaning in my life. Others may come and go, live and die, but I always have myself with me. And it better be a self I love and value.

When I grew up, the focus for girls was almost entirely on relationships. Nice Girls got married, had babies, and centered their lives around familial ties. Work only mattered in the context of family (as a contribution to family), and nobody told us about "amounting" to anything else. Today, the focus for girls is still relational and familial, despite appearances to the contrary.

Sure, many girls and young women now think seriously about having a career, but mostly that's still secondary to the man she believes will become the center of her life. Most young women, including college students, still major in boyfriends, whatever their transcripts show. They're love junkies, educated in romance. That's borne out by research and by simply opening our eyes and observing girls and young women.[15]

Young men expect it to be that way too, by and large. In one of my recent seminars with college students, a young man piped up, "*My* wife's not going to work! She belongs home raising my kids." The other guys in the class nodded in agreement. The young women didn't say a word.

An unusual outburst? Not at all. I encounter young men with these attitudes everywhere I go. Despite widespread belief that the younger generation is more enlightened about these issues, the evidence points to the contrary: young women are still imprisoned by the Cinderella Complex. Young men, on the other hand, feel very threatened by women and the strides they've made.

Typical of the research is Cheryl Bartholomew's studies of the ideal marriage partner as viewed by young women and men.[16] After studying college students for three consecutive years in the late 1980s, Bartholomew found that women look for a successful, career-oriented husband who will be a good provider, while men look for an attractive housewife.

The women's description of their ideal mate (in order of importance) is this: ambitious achiever, attractive, intelligent, father/nurturer of children, probability of being a success, career-minded, able to provide financial support (in short, a security blanket). The men's description of their ideal mate is this: attractive, good listener, good cook, minimal degree of independence, warm and soft, willing to stay home, able to manage children, home, family, and social affairs (in short, a Nice Girl). It's the fifties all over again!

Why do so many women seem to rely on men to achieve, succeed, and provide financial support? It's not because women don't want to succeed themselves. We do. But we have ambivalent feelings about success, or maybe about our ability to achieve success, given how it's defined.

Redefining Success and Setting Career Goals

Traditionally, the American dream has been pervaded by one definition of success, epitomized in the person chairing the board of directors of a large corporation (certainly not of a volunteer group). Not much has changed. Success still means the attainment of the top position in an organization with all the accouterments of wealth, power, fame, and favor.

This definition never fit women. We could hardly aspire to the top of any hierarchy for most of recorded history. Even today, the glass ceiling bars all but a handful of women from the top of all kinds of hierarchies: corporate, governmental, religious, educational, sports, and more.[17] And the sticky floor keeps countless women trapped in low-paying, dead-end jobs.

Indeed, the very definition of success is male-oriented, reflecting as it does the male competitive model. In that model, winning is everything and winning entails somebody losing.

This is not an orientation women feel comfortable with. It's also a model that says to most people that success is not something you can achieve. By definition, success applies to the few, since only a handful of people, relatively speaking, occupy top positions.

We need to redefine success, and lots of other concepts for that matter. A number of alternate definitions of success exist:

- The attainment of one's own goals.

- Any accomplishment that marks a step forward from where a person was yesterday.

- All ongoing, day-to-day accomplishments.

Success is not the same for everyone, nor is it static; it is relative and changing. What is success for an Eleanor Roosevelt or a Margaret Thatcher is not success for a poor immigrant woman or a displaced homemaker with five children.

Growing up, I always wanted to "be somebody," but that was a vague wish that I couldn't define. However, I clearly saw what I *didn't* want to be: a secretary, a school teacher, or a nurse, even though that's what women mostly did then.

I did have my share of fantasies about "being somebody." The earliest childhood fantasy I can remember goes back to World War II. I often thought about sitting down with Joe Stalin and talking him out of his wicked ways. (Those power fantasies started pretty early.)

For my first thirty-one years, I wandered through life, falling in and out of opportunities with the aimlessness of a feather in the wind. After high school, I enrolled in a math program because I had done well in it; what I would *do* with it, I hadn't the foggiest notion. I registered at a college that wasn't my first choice for financial reasons and because they didn't require gym, which I hated.

When I started college, I made friends with a young woman majoring in the humanities. Not knowing why I was studying math, I changed to humanities. In my junior year, I chose an English major because my favorite instructor taught literature, I enjoyed it, and I didn't know what else to do.

At the end of my junior year, my college romance went sour and with it my plans to marry. So, during my senior year, I had to choose between the other two alternatives: graduate school or work. One of my friends wanted me to head for New York City's publishing world with her to begin work as a copy editor, but I had been offered a full fellowship to pursue a Master's degree in English. I chose more schooling because I still didn't know what I wanted to do.

I saw this career aimlessness in most of the women around me. Almost never did I see it in the men. Mostly, they all knew exactly what they were training to do.

Occasionally, when I talk about this aimlessness, someone will protest, "That was long ago. Women aren't like that any more!" I wish they were right. My own experience working with women from management to unskilled levels these days strongly suggests otherwise. Fundamental change for women is going to take longer than two or three decades.

Women still don't, as a group, plan for a lifetime of work. Yet goal-setting is so important for both women and men. Without clearly defined goals that provide direction of our own choosing, we merely react to whatever happens in our lives. And that's nuts! Besides being a recipe for long-term emotional disaster, it's an economic calamity, since women swell the ranks of the underpaid and the poor. Poverty undermines everything.

Harvard University conducted a longitudinal study that reveals the dimensions of the economic consequences entailed in not having life plans.[18] The study tracked its graduates in three categories—those without goals, those with clear goals in mind, and those with written goals and action plans. Those with no goals did the worst economically. Those with clear goals in mind did three times better economically than those with no goals. But those with written goals and action plans did *ten* times better economically overall.

Maybe it's because we're conditioned to believe the most important thing in a woman's life is marriage and children, regardless of anything else we may accomplish. Maybe it's because we lack sufficient female role models to inspire us. Maybe it's because nobody tells girls "This is what you need to do," the way men guide boys. Whatever the reason, the future is a fog for most women.

A fog certainly clouded my brain when I headed for a small university to do graduate work in a field I still wasn't committed to and didn't know what to do with. I cringe looking back: furthering my studies was second choice to marriage!

At graduate school, I met Joe Agonito and thoughts of marriage slipped to the forefront again. While Joe planned for his doctoral work, I planned to follow him around. We received our Masters degrees, got married, and headed for a large university in the midwest where he was to pursue a doctorate. I would look for work once I got there—any work. I guess I thought it didn't matter; I had Joe. Even though it didn't feel right, I was playing the role in the script.

I started job hunting at the university as soon as I arrived, expecting secretarial work, though I couldn't type my name. I was greatly surprised when the Chair of the English Department offered me a teaching assistantship in the English doctoral program. Their undergraduate program overenrolled; they needed somebody on short notice; and there I was, qualified to do the job. So, through no effort of my own, I found myself a doctoral student in literature.

It was an exciting year, full of the cultural life of a large university. But we were both homesick and Joe's doctoral program proved limiting in its approach. So off we went again, back to Syracuse, home for me and Syracuse University for Joe.

To support our family twosome, I landed a job as a junior high school teacher, which I always knew I didn't want to do. Teaching adolescents in school easily ranked as the most awful work I ever did. After two years, I got out, taking with me a healthy respect for people who do that work.

One short-lived writing career and a baby later, I fell into another opportunity, which ended up giving me some direction. About five months after I assumed the role of housewife and mother, I received a call from a local college, asking if I'd be interested in a full-time position teaching philosophy (my minor in college and graduate school). In the 1960s, teacher shortages were the rule.

I'd never given much thought to teaching college. Teaching elementary and high school had been ruled out, but becoming a professor had never occurred to me. Why would it? I'd never had a woman professor when I was a student. But actually, teaching philosophy made a lot of sense to me.

Why not? I'd try it! So I toted baby off to my mother who, by this time, had been badgered out of city hall by Pop. Mindful even then of how women are exploited in these situations, I insisted on paying Mom for her services.

Life began to fall into place during those two years as a philosophy instructor. I loved the work, my teaching received consistently excellent evaluations, I began to expand my research in philosophy, and I determined to get my doctorate.

With another teaching assistantship under my arm, off I went to the university, but this time by choice. It was the turbulent, exciting era of the late 1960s and early 1970s, and being in academia broadened my mind and my reach. By the time I graduated, the job market in academia had collapsed and few jobs existed. I struggled, like everybody else, but for the first time my direction was clear. After that, I did whatever I had to do to make my goals a reality.

The Family–Work Conflict
Through it all, accommodations had to be made at home. If I didn't play the housewife role, who would do the housework?

The process basically involved me learning to take myself seriously, grow in self-esteem, and expect everyone to share the menial burdens of life. I had to stop being everyone's Nice Girl. Although the whole process was not without pain, struggle, and backsliding, I was fortunate enough to have married someone with the potential and willingness to grow with me. I did not find myself, as women overwhelmingly still do, working two full-time jobs while married to a man with one full-time job. Joe, also a college professor, shared the burdens of home and parenting. As it turned out, he probably cooked, cleaned, and parented more than I did while the children grew, because I commuted long distances to work.

One incident in particular revealed just how central Joe was to the housekeeping in our home. My sister Mary cooked a wonderful dish at one of her family gatherings. My young son, Gian Carlo, complimented her.

"Aunt Mary, this is great!" Then, with complete spontaneity, he added, "Would you please give the recipe to my dad?"

Although it became a family joke of sorts, it marked a serious realization for us. Without noticing it, Joe had become an active parent with real responsibilities in the eyes of our children.

Because most women don't have that kind of arrangement, they find themselves perpetually exhausted. Despite their entrance into the labor force in large numbers, the domestic scene continues, business as usual, with women expected to bear the menial burdens of life. And too many women tolerate the situation.

For most women with families, the dual burden of parenting and domestic responsibilities remains the single largest barrier to success. That burden discourages employers from viewing women as seriously as male candidates for jobs, leadership roles, and promotions. Too often, it hinders women's ability to pursue additional study, to seek employment outside her immediate geographical area, to take on work that keeps her away from home for extended periods of time, and to pursue job opportunities wherever they lead. The lack of available child care and its prohibitive cost also present huge barriers for many women. The emotional stresses and physical exhaustion of parenting cut into career energy, because, typically, mother ends up doing most, if not all, of the parenting chores.

Indeed, considerable research indicates that parenthood results in men and women assuming very gender-specific roles.[19] After childbirth, a woman's self-image changes: her sense of identity as a worker and a spouse decreases. She becomes primarily a mother, regardless of her age at childbirth. When a man becomes a father, however, he still sees himself primarily as a worker and a husband.

Playing roles in a preordained script in relationships is catastrophic for women. I see the human wreckage of those scripts at all ages: the single parent teenager forced onto public assistance; the struggling young mother; the devastated displaced homemaker, without skills or resources; the bitter older woman whose failed dreams of achievement will haunt her to her death.

Women need to understand and acknowledge the essential importance of meaningful work in every human life, female and male. Does this mean raising children is not meaningful work? Of course not; parenting is very important work. But an adult life cannot be spent with children in the confines of four walls. It's not even clear that anyone cut off from the world of life and ideas *can* raise children well.

The issue of financial independence is also an important one. If for no other reason, the most tedious job is worthwhile if it brings a woman financial independence. Anyone who depends on another person or institution for her very existence (food, shelter, clothing) *will not* be a free individual.

What a financially dependent woman *will* be is vulnerable. With the divorce rate over 50 percent (higher among young people), with the separation and divorce rate approaching two out of three,[20] with so many men working for poverty wages, the security a woman bargains for in marriage is elusive at best. With estimates of the number of women battered by the man she lives with at about 40 percent[21], the lack of financial means to escape can be deadly.

Vulnerability is not a virtue.

Career Development

Career development is the somewhat inadequate term we use to describe creating ourselves, developing our talents and skills, growing in our work, learning new things, expanding our intellect and sensibilities, and moving to ever more challenging heights.

It helps, I think, to liken the process of career development to the production of a work of art. At any given point in my life, I have certain tools at my disposal (particular talents, skills, knowledge, connections with others), just as the artist does (canvas, paint, brushes). With these tools, I must create a life, a person, a unique individual, just as the artist must create a unique painting with a special vision.

I always think about one woman named Marie and her meteoric rise when I reflect on what women can accomplish. I've known Marie for a number of years and I love her story because it holds a message for all of us.

Marie worked as a bank teller and trained many new employees. Over the years, she stood on the sidelines and watched as the parade of men she taught moved on and up.

Despite her efforts, no promotion came Marie's way. So she returned to school while working at the bank and began her studies in history at the local community college. As a mother, she juggled work and school and managing a home.

Meanwhile, an elderly customer at the bank, who insisted on dealing only with Marie, began to tell her about his plans to retire. He told her, in broken English, about his line striping machine. For years, he'd run a line striping business, marking parking lots with his push machine.

"It's a good business. It's a good machine," the old man said. "You tell your husband to buy my machine. It make him a good business."

Each time he came into the bank, he urged Marie again to tell her husband to buy his machine. Marie became intrigued with the descriptions of the odd-sounding contraption. When she told the man *she* would buy the machine, he protested.

"No, no. For your husband!"

But he sold it to her anyway, and Marie began to practice line striping in her driveway, pushing the heavy machine up and down until she thought she had it right.

Then, nervously, Marie approached her first prospective client: her doctor. She knew nothing about the business, not even what to charge, so she offered the doctor 10 percent off what he'd paid for his last line striping job. He agreed, she learned about price, and off she went to stripe his parking lot.

At first the line striping business provided Marie with her college tuition and enough income so she could quit her dead-end bank job. She continued to focus on her studies and to view line striping as a temporary job. But at some point, as her income increased, Marie began to look at the operation as a real business. An ad in the Yellow Pages brought in a steady stream of clients while she completed her bachelor's degree.

One day the phone rang. The man on the line had seen her ad and explained that he needed a line striper. A vendor he had hired to stripe a section of the New York State Thruway suddenly dropped out and he needed somebody to pick up the job immediately.

"Can you do the work?" he asked.

This was the big time. So without a moment's hesitation, Marie answered, "Yes, I can."

When she hung up the phone, she broke into a cold sweat and was seized with a momentary panic. Parking lots, not state thruways, were her thing. But she found some courage and rushed down the street to a neighbor who worked on highway construction to ask for his help.

Then off she went with her machine to the endless ribbon of highway. When the site manager saw her begin, he realized she lacked experience. But he was in a bind, so he gave her tips. He told her about a mixture that had to be applied over highway lines. Ever creative, Marie rushed to the paint store, bought the mixture, and, with a hole punched in a coffee can, began to sprinkle it by hand on the line.

Today, Marie laughs about the story of her first big job. But that was a turning point that led eventually to major government contracts and a $2.5 million operation. Now Marie has modern equipment and crews working for her. The business has grown enormously since she began striping parking lots with her push machine.

And Marie did it all. She learned, she grew professionally, she stretched herself, and she wasn't afraid to ask for help when she needed it. Most important, she made opportunities and took risks along the way because she believed in herself.

Every time I drive on a highway at night and see the bright

white line guiding me safely on my way, I think of Marie. And when the white line isn't there and I have trouble seeing the road, I think of Marie and wish for the safety her line striping machine would bring.

Nor has Marie forgotten where she came from. A wonderful feminist, she generously gives her time to speak to women trying to reenter the work force or school.

Like Marie, Jan is another woman who didn't settle for too little in life. She woke up one morning to find a note from her husband saying he didn't want to be married anymore. Goodbye. That was it.

With two children, no job, no car (he took it), almost no money, and a rented house far from any city, Jan faced the toughest choices of her life. She could go on public assistance or go to work. But work meant she had to move out of her isolated home.

It was very clear to her that she had to act. Depression and fear paralyze, and paralysis was the last thing she needed.

Jan summoned up every bit of courage she had. She packed everything she could carry into large plastic bags and boarded a bus for the nearest large city with her children. Without money, she sought temporary shelter at the Salvation Army. Then, armed only with some secretarial skills from her high school years but no experience, she began to look for work.

Frightened but determined, she answered the want ads, one after another. Finally, she walked into city hall where the man interviewing her expressed doubts about her work. But Jan literally talked her way into the job, convincing him that no one would work harder than she would, because the job was the most important thing in the world to her. Something about her determination and enthusiasm touched him.

After getting the job, Jan rented a small apartment for her family. With only mattresses on the floors for a long time, they survived and did well. Today, Jan works for that same man and as his fortunes have risen in politics, so have hers. She has put her two children through college, serves on important community organizations, and leads an interesting life.

But not everyone is like Jan, who shook off her paralysis. I see many paralyzed women around me—women with intelligence, talent, and skills. Their paralysis has no physical basis; it's a paralysis of action and determination.

I find these women at all levels: homemakers who want to expand their lives beyond the domestic sphere, women on public assistance who want to support themselves, talented women stuck in dead-end jobs, management women locked into their positions but wanting to move up, women unable to act on their desire to start their own businesses, entrepreneurs who want to expand their businesses. Mostly they see themselves as stuck. And all of them are waiting for opportunities to happen *to* them.

In the recent movie, *Thelma and Louise*, an important point about personal responsibility and settling for too little emerges more than once.

When Thelma complains about all the years she's spent with her insensitive husband, Louise says, "We get what we settle for."

Later in the film, when Louise and her longtime boyfriend are commiserating about their lives, the message appears again. Her boyfriend, a musician, regrets that his life is a series of Saturday night gigs at some hotel. Louise has spent the years of her life waiting tables.

"We got what we settled for," she says simply.

Too often, unlike Jan and Marie, women settle for too little. Sure, I can rattle off the compelling reasons we settle for this or that. But there's always a price to pay, and *we* pay it, sooner or later.

Making Our Own Opportunities

Too many women don't understand that, mostly, we have to make our opportunities. Playing the waiting game (and becoming paralyzed in the process) is the old Prince Charming thing. The Nice Girl waits for salvation, for good things to come her way.

But opportunities are usually offered to men. Typically, that's not because of any overt conspiracy; it's worse than that. Women are invisible, that is, we simply don't come to mind when opportunities emerge. Those mental filters keep us from ever being considered, even when we're the best choice. And through it all, being the Nice Girl who stays in her place only perpetuates the problem.

This invisibility, coupled with the fact that women tend to wait to be recognized and promoted, spells *dead end* for women's careers. Becoming visible, breaking through the filter, therefore, emerges as one of the first tasks facing the woman who's interested in career development, regardless of what kind of job she holds.

How can you stop being the invisible Nice Girl who waits to be rewarded and become visible? Typically, it requires a concerted effort on a day-to-day basis. The following suggestions, after being considered in light of your own circumstances, can be worked into an action plan for taking control of your career:

- Be politically savvy and open contacts wherever you go.

- Build reciprocal relationships with people (that is, you help them and they help you).

- Let your boss (and others in a position to make decisions) know that you *are* interested in success and *expect* to be promoted. And keep telling them.

- Involve your boss in your career development by asking for advice and help.

- Get to know people from other departments in your organization.

- Volunteer for key projects and tasks.

- Actively pursue visible, important assignments that allow you to be tested.

- Understand the priority tasks and projects in your department and your company, and be productive in those areas.

- Be a problem-solver who helps overcome crises in the workplace and who builds a reputation as the one to call in difficulty.

- Contribute new ideas and put them in writing.

- Serve on important committees and task forces.

- Take part in company-sponsored events.

- Develop a specific area of expertise in your field so that others come to you for information and help.

- Be creative in your work so that you stand out. Working by the same formula as everybody else will ensure your invisibility.

- Share relevant ideas and articles with people in and out of your department. For example, if you spot an interesting article that relates to what Jane or John is doing, send a copy with a note saying, "Thought you might like to see this, if you haven't already."

- Send relevant memos about your work to people who might be interested, being careful not to breach confidentiality.

- At meetings, don't be a mere spectator; take an active part. Be prepared so your comments stand out as informed. Write a brief outline to pass out based on what you will say. Sit in a visible place in meetings, never in the back.

- Take or make any opportunity to chair meetings.

- Don't be afraid to be tested publicly. Welcome opportunities that come along, but do your homework and be ready. It's better to risk failure trying than to remain secure and untested in a crowd.

- Actively promote yourself. It's a crucial part of the process. Nice Girls feel uncomfortable talking about or touting their accomplishments because we're conditioned to think it's unseemly and immodest. That conditioning is part of the self-effacement we suffer. Just as we're pleased to hear and share the accomplishments of others, we should be pleased to share our own triumphs, however small or great.

- Quantify your accomplishments whenever possible (for example, I instituted cost-saving procedure X, which reduced secretarial time by 20 percent).

- Let your accomplishments be known in and out of the organization through newsletters, self-evaluations, newspapers, memos to your boss, or simply comments such as, "I'm very excited about what happened yesterday."

- Always acknowledge the role of others in your success.

- Be sure to praise the accomplishments of others.

- When people praise your work in a substantial way, ask them to put it in writing.

- Tell people what you want. If they know, you might get it; if they don't, you won't get it.

- Ask your boss for regular feedback on your performance, making the point that you want to improve and grow professionally.

- Ask someone you respect in your organization to give you specific feedback about your performance, your interaction with others, and your presentation skills. Make it clear that you want both positive and negative feedback. Seeing ourselves as others see us can help us grow.

- Foster positive working relationships. If tension exists between you and a colleague or superior, meet with the person. Say that you feel a tension and want to resolve it. Ask what you both can do to improve the working relationship.

- Do periodic self-evaluations for your own benefit, including an assessment of your strengths and weaknesses, your concrete accomplishments, your failures, and strategies for addressing your weaknesses to minimize their impact.

- Keep a file on yourself. In this file, place all items relating to your work, your specific accomplishments (on and off the job), your awards and honors, letters praising your work, and the like. It will constitute a complete record over the years and ensure that nothing is forgotten. Such a file, for your personal use, will put you in a strong position to summarize the specific high points of your career when asking for a promotion or raise. When you apply for a new job, you'll be in a great position to tailor your resume to that job.

- Whenever you try to sell yourself (to direct an important project, attend a conference, or get a promotion or new job), remember the basic principle of marketing: people buy based on what you can do for them, based on *their* needs. The issue is not how wonderful you are as such, but what you have to offer X.

- Carry yourself in a confident, self-assured manner. If you don't believe in yourself, why should others?

- As much as possible within your financial constraints, dress the part you want to play, not the stereotype others expect of you. Impressions and image are important, whether we like it or not. How we present ourselves is the visible manifestation of who we are at any given moment. Dressing the part also helps provide access.

- Be visible at professional and trade conferences by taking an active part.

- Join together with other women to urge the human resources or affirmative action department to establish a data bank on women who are potential candidates for management and executive positions. Your local woman's group should play an active role in assembling names and resumes for the data bank. Such information should then be made available to executives and managers responsible for promotions. This undercuts the frequent assertions of executives that there are no qualified women candidates and helps make women visible. Also, it may help build your networking base.

- Support other women in their career development efforts.

- Be invisible when it comes to participating in office gossip, but listen for clues about behavior that might be relevant to you.

- Don't broadcast mistakes and failures (as women often feel compelled to do). If you must talk about a mistake, use it as an opportunity to affirm yourself (for example, it's not like me to miss such an important point). Learn from your mistakes, and move on.

- If you reach a point where it's clear you're not going to progress any further (and you want to do so), face it and *act*. This means looking at the hard possibility of changing jobs or careers.

- Review this list often, making sure that you're taking advantage of every opportunity.

New Women Networking

Many of the previous suggestions are designed to eliminate one of the major problems women face in the work place today: invisibility. Our exclusion from the old-boy network constitutes another big barrier. These male networks are both formal and informal and are the fertilizer that grows the careers of men everywhere. Exclusion from these networks is a disaster for women's career development because it's tantamount to exclusion from crucial information, contacts, support, and help—everything that goes into growth and success. Therefore, women need to compensate for that exclusion.

There's no mystery about networks (male or otherwise), although they often exude a mystique that seems impenetrable. A network involves ongoing communication and exchanges between individuals or groups that are mutually beneficial. The benefits of networks, of course, flow from the sharing of information, the development of contacts, emotional support, a sense of solidarity and camaraderie, and collective political clout. The degree of career benefit overall relates to the power and connections of network members.

What can women do about exclusion from networks that, directly or indirectly, may hold the key to our ability to learn, grow, and advance in our chosen fields?

We can form alternative networks, as many women have. These women's networks can offer a number of benefits, but unless the women in them are well connected, the information and contacts will be limited.

Perhaps the most important benefit a woman's network or caucus offers is collective political clout, although women have not always recognized it. A group of women, however small, will be seen as having the potential to rock the boat, even as a threat. And that's OK. Women need to see this as something positive and to use this power as leverage.

Rather than backing off from collective action because we don't want to threaten anybody, we need to play this card.

There's no virtue in playing the game by their rules because we can't win a game that's stacked against us. Most, if not all, reforms happen because people organize to make them happen (more promotions for women, pay equity, affirmative action, access to nontraditional jobs, training programs, etc.).

In addition to forming alternative networks, there are many things we can do:

- We can keep trying to become part of existing networks. Often exclusion, like stereotyping, is nonconscious. We can ask to be included: "Would you mind if I joined the group for lunch?" The worst that will happen is that we won't be included (but that's where we were before, so it's no loss).

- If we're so inclined, we can learn to play the dominant networking sport, golf or whatever.

- We can link with a sympathetic male who is a part of the old-boy network (there's almost always one or two around). He may be willing to share information we need and serve as our advocate on the inside.

- We can join trade associations, which provide a valuable opportunity to network with colleagues in the same field, as well as a rich source of information.

- We can attend professional and trade conferences and connect with key people in attendance.

- We can join community groups, which offer the chance to network, meet people, learn, and make a contribution in the process.

- We can establish formal information sharing systems such as a telephone tree, a newsletter, or a place where people can deposit items of interest. Of course, these activities require organization.

- We can look for opportunities to open mentoring relationships with a manager or executive. Again, we often think we have to wait for those things to happen, when, in fact, we can help make them happen. Research with executive women reveals that *all* of them had some form of help from above in achieving their success.[22]

- We can build linkages with people in and out of the organization by proposing joint projects, joint committees, joint efforts, and the like. Working with others is one of the best ways to build lasting relationships.

- We can obtain needed information without being a part of traditional networks by becoming "detectives": by paying attention to the paper trails everywhere around us, reading memos, noticing to whom copies of memos are distributed, and so on; by reading between the lines of official company publications like the annual report (perhaps to find out what the company is *not* doing that might be valuable to its growth); and by studying corporate culture to figure out the company's values, heroes, acceptable behavior, and so on.

Women in Management and Leadership

Aspiring to leadership positions in the private and public sectors, in the for-profit and nonprofit sectors, is something women have been doing for a long time with limited success. While women have made gains in the number of management positions we occupy overall, the well-documented glass ceiling has prevented access to powerful, top-level positions.

Occupying leadership positions in large numbers ultimately provides women the best hope for change, assuming that women bring a different vision to those positions (not the old competitive, greed-oriented, win-lose mentality). Women in leadership means, simply, women having the power to make policy.

The barrier here lies in the deeply embedded view that women don't make good leaders, while men do. It's hard for people to see women as powerful figures as long as they view us as Nice Girls. But being a leader and exhibiting leadership skills is the best response and antidote to this kind of thinking. Unfortunately, women have to prove their leadership qualities; men are assumed to possess them.

To be perceived as leaders, we can seek out leadership positions in every relevant forum, in and out of the organization:

- We can chair committees effectively.

- We can serve as an officer in our trade associations (the higher, the better).

- We can direct important, visible projects.

- We can assume visible leadership positions in the community.

- We can volunteer to serve on, or direct, crucial task forces in an organization or in the community.

- We can publish articles that contribute to our field.

- We can offer innovative suggestions for enhancing our company's work, and otherwise show leadership skills, at every opportunity.

- We can ask to be sent to management and leadership training courses and seminars. Failing that, we can take them on our own, being sure to communicate the accomplishment to the appropriate people.

- We can educate ourselves in management skills by reading some of the many helpful books and articles now available, including those written especially for women.

- We can observe successful leaders we admire in our organizations and fields and learn from them.

- We can read biographies of leaders, especially women, noting strategies that might be helpful and applying those to our work.

- We can ask for more challenges and more authority in our present job.

- We can actively seek an entry-level supervisory or management position if we've never had paid experience in a management position. These lower-level positions are often available to women in a way that higher-level positions are not, and they provide an important testing ground, as well as experience.

- We can consider lateral moves that would enhance the opportunity for promotion later. We can especially consider a lateral move from a staff position (which serves others), to a line position (which directly affects the bottom line and affords the best potential for promotion).

- We can periodically assess which of our activities have actually involved managing or leading some endeavor or reflect management or leadership skills. We don't always recognize or give ourselves credit for leading.

Overcoming Career Aimlessness
Another barrier we must tackle is our own aimlessness when it comes to the future. Having poorly defined or vague ideas about our futures, our work, and even ourselves is a blueprint for disaster. It will make leading a meaningful life of our own choosing less likely. What's more, it will increase our vulnerability to the vagaries of an economic system that could care less about what happens to the individual.

Just as we use our talents, knowledge, and skills in the home, all of us need to start using the full range of our talents, knowledge, and skills in society, where the need for new perspectives and approaches is profound. Doing that in a meaningful way involves planning.

If we don't want to go through life merely reacting to, or being buffeted by, circumstances, we need to set goals and determine a specific career direction. This is part of creating our identities in a deliberate and self-conscious way. The most successful goal-planning exercises are written down, involve priorities, and have detailed action plans for accomplishing goals.

It's a good idea for us to lay out both short-term goals (six months to two years) and long-term goals (up to five years or more). To work, they must be coordinated with family responsibilities, but only after those responsibilities are equitably distributed among *all* members of the family. If the menial burdens of life are not shared equitably by all who benefit, and we must bear the burden alone, our present work and career goals will be limited and our frustration will most likely boil over.

In setting goals we should try to banish the knee-jerk "I can't" reaction from our vocabulary and thinking. Certainly there are things we can't do, but chances are we're underestimating our capabilities. Remember, each of us has more power than we think.

We should also bear in mind that no amount of goal-setting will help in the process of creating a meaningful life if we don't follow our action plan. We may find it helpful to reassess the goals and plans periodically because our lives constantly change.

One of the key elements in any successful action plan is a commitment to a lifetime of learning. None of us ever reaches a point when we've learned enough. Ongoing education, whether through a formal program of study or informal self-education (reading, attending lectures, traveling, talking to people), must be part of any plan for success, however we define it.

Part of that education must be knowing the truth about what's happening to women—to ourselves. The mainstream media and press will seldom give us that. But we can read the women's press that tells the truth about women: the new *Ms.* Magazine,[23] *New Directions for Women*,[24] *On the Issues*[25]—and support them in the process.

This Is *My* Life

Life is short, as the cliché goes. And we don't have an infinite number of chances to get it right.

At one of my career development seminars recently, a 60-year-old woman named Gloria hung back after class. I could see she wanted to speak, so I asked her what she was thinking about.

"I'm sad," she said. "Incredibly sad."

I asked her why.

"Because I never realized these things before, when there was still time."

It was the darkest moment in all my years of teaching. Few tragedies are greater than when a person believes her life has been wasted. But as long as there's breath left, there's still time.

Gloria went off, got hold of herself, and decided to make some changes. She traveled to New York City to explore a program at Columbia University and is researching her options. She is figuring how to get around her lack of resources, and making plans to cram a lifetime into her twilight years.

I remember a line in a movie I used to play in a women's studies class years ago. In the movie (*I Love You, Goodbye*), a housewife in her late forties decides to go to college. Everyone discourages her.

"But you'll be 52 when you finish," someone says.

"So what?" she answers, "I'll be 52 anyway."

Fear is the other thing that kills women's prospects of authentic self-definition and success. If we're afraid to try this or that, to pursue opportunities, to risk the wrath of family or an unreasonable partner, chances are we won't act. Instead, we'll keep playing the impotent Nice Girl, while the task of creating our own identities, of building meaningful work, of fulfilling goals, becomes remote, if not impossible.

In one of my business ownership training seminars for women, a budding entrepreneur described how she was converting everything she owned into capital to start a business.

Another woman jumped in, "But you could lose *everything*!"

"If I don't risk everything, I'll never do it. And I'll never know if I could have done it," replied the entrepreneur. "Look, what's the worst that can happen? If my business fails, I'll get a job as a waitress. I'll survive."

Not many women think like that. The list of potential negatives usually outweighs the potential gains in our minds. We're not taught to risk, and often most of what we own isn't ours, so we're unwilling to "gamble" with it.

Everything in life is a risk. Putting our lives in the hands of another person is a risk. But risking for meaningful work and independence, for an authentic life, is much less of a gamble and puts *us* in control.

It isn't easy to be a human being. Life is hard in the best of times. For women, who have been raised to be Nice Girls, to perpetually deny themselves in the interests of others, to conform to everyone else's agenda, life is especially hard.

Too often our lives are not in our control because females are typically raised by a set formula. That formula dictates a certain kind of life—a life of passivity, acceptance, and accommodation to others. It entails a state of perpetual childhood, a mandated powerlessness, characterized by the phrase "Nice Girl."

In adulthood, the Nice Girl syndrome reduces us to silly children running around worrying about who likes us and who doesn't, and what we can do to make so-and-so accept us. Our lives are at risk of becoming a caricature, shaped by the needs and wants of others: "Gee whiz, if I do this, will X be pleased?" Or "Gosh, I'd better *not* do that because I'll make Y angry." Or "Careful, careful, Z won't approve." So anybody can do anything to us and we'll take it. We'll stay in our place, according to the formula.

This state of perpetual childhood easily converts to victimization. In the day-to-day little things and when it really matters, the Nice Girl persona requires us to cooperate in our own oppression. And all the while we know, deep inside, that it's not an adult life or an authentic life. Our self-esteem plummets along the way as we accommodate the values of others and suppress our own needs in order to do what everybody expects of us in our futile crusade to please.

As long as this mold encases our true identities, life cannot be of our own choosing. As long as we continue to wear the mold, the possibility of an authentic, adult life escapes us.

But life is also full of hope and opportunities. It's a series of possibilities that appear at every turn. Out of those possibilities, each of us chooses and acts, constantly creating a unique self unlike any other in the world. That's an incredibly exciting venture and a wide open one.

The challenge for each of us lies in controlling that venture: envisioning our own possibilities at any given moment and choosing well among those possibilities. This creation of the self is an ongoing process involving everything we do, day in and day out. It means taking control of our lives.

Along the way, it's easy to get weighed down, held back, or even stopped, by the many internal and external barriers. Those barriers are real enough, but they're *not* insurmountable if we stand up and fight back, if we refuse to cooperate in our own oppression, if we reject victimization and say, "No more Nice Girl!" and mean it. Only then can we embrace the possibilities of the future with real hope and dignity.

Notes

Chapter 1

1 Peter Singer, *Animal Liberation* (New York: Avon Books, 1975).

2 Betty Friedan, *The Feminine Mystique* (London: Penguin Books, 1982).

3 "Mental phenomena" includes a range of events that extend far beyond conscious experience. The term "nonconscious" is used throughout to refer to mental phenomena occurring as a function of neurological information processing. These include the nervous system's processing of stimuli, classification of "data," memory, and all other information processing functions of mind which we are not aware of at any given moment. This nonconscious neurological information processing should not be confused with the Freudian concept of the subconscious mind as a repository for suppressed memories, which exert a disturbing effect in consciousness.

Chapter 2

4 Colette Dowling, *The Cinderella Complex: Women's Hidden Fear of Independence* (New York: Pocket Books, 1990).

5 Melinda Bingham's work with teen girls through the 1980s (in conjunction with Girls Clubs of America, now Girls, Inc.).

6 Terry Denny and Karen D. Arnold, University of Illinois, 1991.

7 Matina Horner, "Toward an Understanding of Achievement-Related Conflicts in Women, " *Journal of Social Issues*, 28(2), (1972): 157–75. Matina Horner's extensive research on fear of success revealed that women are often afraid of succeeding because they believe success will undermine their personal relationships. As a result, women tend to do things that sabotage their success without realizing it.

8 Sarah Hardesty and Nehama Jacobs, *Success and Betrayal* (New York: Simon and Schuster, 1987).

9 Dorothy C. Holland and Margaret A. Eisenhart, *Educated in Romance* (Chicago: University of Chicago Press, 1990).

Chapter 3

10 See the works of Judy Rosener, Sally Helgasen, Deborah Tannen, Marilyn Loden, Carol Gilligan.

11 Deborah Tannen, *You Just Don't Understand: Women and Men in Conversation* (New York: Ballantine, 1991).

12 *Ibid.*

Chapter 5

13 Marilyn French, *The Women's Room* (New York: Jove Publications, 1977).

14 Margaret Hennig and Anne Jardim, *The Managerial Woman* (New York: Pocket Books, 1977).

Chapter 7

15 Holland and Eisenhart, *Educated in Romance.*

16 Cheryl G. Bartholomew, *What's Wrong with This Picture?* (New York: Carlton Press, 1989), 38–39.

17 U.S. Department of Labor, Office of Federal Contract Compliance Programs. "The Glass Ceiling Pilot Study." (August 1991).

18 Cited in Robert McGarvey, "Getting Your Goals," *USAir Magazine* (July, 1989): 26.

19 Two major longitudinal studies:

Carolyn Pape Cowan and Philip Cowan, "Transition to Parenthood Study, 1979–1985," University of California at Berkeley.

Jay Belsky, "Transition to Parenthood Study, 1981–1988," Pennsylvania State University.

20 Teresa C. Martin and Larry L. Bumpas, *Recent Trends in Marital Disruption* (University of Wisconsin, 1989).

21 Studies vary. Some researchers put the figure lower, some put it as high as 50%. The 40% figure is an average and is widely accepted. Most recently, the National Victim Center (1993) reports that four million women are beaten annually by the men they live with. Before that, the U.S. Surgeon General had estimated six million women a year are victims of domestic violence.

22 Ann Morrison, Randall White, and Ellen Van Velsor, *Breaking the Glass Ceiling* (Redding, Massachusetts: Addison-Wesley, 1992).

23 *Ms.* Magazine, P.O. Box 57132, Boulder, CO 80322-7132. Phone: 212-551-9595.

24 *New Directions for Women* (bimonthly newspaper), P.O. Box 3000, Denville, NJ 07834-3000. Phone: 800-562-1973.

25 *On the Issues* (quarterly magazine), 97-77 Queens Boulevard, Forest Hills, NY 11374. Phone: 718-275-6020.

Bibliography

Aburdene, Patricia and John Naisbitt. *Megatrends for Women*. New York: Random House, 1992.

Bartholomew, Cheryl G. *What's Wrong with This Picture?* New York: Carlton Press, 1989.

Brown, Lyn M. and Carol Gilligan. *Meeting at the Crossroads: Women's Psychology and Girls' Development*. Cambridge, Massachusetts: Harvard University Press, 1992.

Brownmiller, Susan. *Against Our Will: Men, Women, and Rape*. New York: Bantam Books, 1975.

Brownmiller, Susan. *Femininity*. New York: Simon and Schuster, 1984.

Calyx Editorial Collective. *Women and Aging: An Anthology by Women*. Corvallis, Oregon: Calyx Books, 1986.

Carr-Ruffino, Norma. *The Promotable Woman*. New York: Wadsworth, 1982.

de Beauvoir, Simone. *The Second Sex*. New York: Penguin, 1986.

DePauw, Linda Grant. *Founding Mothers: Women of America in the Revolutionary Era*. Boston: Houghton Mifflin, 1975.

Dowling, Colette. *The Cinderella Complex: Women's Hidden Fear of Independence*. New York: Pocket Books, 1990.

Elgin, Suzette H. *Success with the Gentle Art of Verbal Self-Defense: Communication Strategies Across the Power Gap*. New York: Prentice Hall, 1989.

Estes, Clarissa P. *Women Who Run with the Wolves: Myths and Stories of the Wild Woman Archetype*. New York: Ballantine Books, 1992.

Evans, Sara M. *Born for Liberty: A History of Women in America*. New York: Free Press, 1989.

Faludi, Susan. *Backlash: The Undeclared War Against American Women*. New York: Doubleday, 1991.

Firestone, Shulamith. *The Dialect of Sex*. New York: Bantam, 1971.

French, Marilyn. *The Women's Room*. New York: Jove Publications, 1977.

French, Marilyn. *The War Against Women*. New York: Summit books, 1992.

Friedan, Betty. *The Feminine Mystique*. Penguin Books: London, 1982.

Giddings, Paula. *When and Where I Enter: The Impact of Black Women on Race and Sex in America.* New York: Bantam, 1985.

Gilligan, Carol. *In a Different Voice: Psychological Theory and Women's Development.* Cambridge, Massachusetts: Harvard University Press, 1982.

Griffin, Lynne and Kelly McCann. *The Book of Women: 300 Notable Women History Passed By.* Holbrook, Massachusetts: Bob Adams, Inc., 1992.

Hardesty, Sarah and Nehama Jacobs. *Success and Betrayal.* New York: Simon and Schuster, 1987.

Harragan, Betty L. *Games Your Mother Never Taught You: Corporate Gamesmanship for Women.* New York: Warner Books, 1986.

Helgasen, Sally. *The Female Advantage: Women's Ways of Leadership.* New York: Doubleday, 1990.

Henley, Nancy. *Body Politics: Power, Sex and Nonverbal Communication.* Englewood Cliffs: Simon and Schuster, 1986.

Hennig, Margaret and Anne Jardim. *The Managerial Woman.* New York: Pocket Books, 1977.

Higginson, Margaret and Thomas Quick. *The Ambitious Woman's Guide to a Successful Career.* New York: Books on Demand, 1980.

Hite, Shere. *The Hite Report on Female Sexuality.* London: Pandora Press, 1989.

Holland, Dorothy C. and Margaret A. Eisenhart. *Educated in Romance.* Chicago: University of Chicago Press, 1990.

Hymowitz, Carol and Michaele Weissman. *A History of Women in America.* New York: Bantam, 1984.

Kennedy, Marilyn M. *Power Base: How to Build It, How to Keep It.* Chicago: Fawcett, 1985.

LaRouche, Janice. *Janice LaRouche's Strategies for Women at Work.* New York: Avon, 1984.

Lerner, Gerda. *Black Women in White America: A Documentary History.* New York: Random House, 1978.

Loden, Marilyn. *Feminine Leadership: How to Succeed in Business Without Becoming One of the Boys.* New York, 1985.

Martin, Teresa C. and Larry L. Bumpas. *Recent Trends in Marital Disruption.* University of Wisconsin, 1989.

Morrison, Ann, Randall White, and Ellen Van Velsor. *Breaking the Glass Ceiling: Can Women Reach the Top in America's Largest Corporations?* Redding, Massachusetts: Addison-Wesley, 1992.

Pearson, Judy C. and Lynn Turner. *Gender and Communication.* Carmel, Indiana: Brown and Benchmark, 1985.

Pringle, Rosemary. *Secretaries Talk: Sexuality, Power, and Work.* New York: Routledge, Chapman and Hall, 1989.

Rix, Sara E., ed. *The American Woman 1990–1991: A Status Report.* Washington, D.C.: Special Libraries Association , 1990.

Sanford, Linda T. and Mary E. Donovan. *Women and Self-Esteem: Understanding and Improving the Way We Think and Feel About Ourselves.* New York: Viking, 1985.

Scollard, Jeannette. *Risk to Win: A Woman's Guide to Success.* New York: Macmillan, 1989.

Scott, Kesho Y. *The Habit of Surviving: Black Women's Strategies for Life.* New Brunswick: Rutgers University Press, 1991.

Steinem, Gloria. *Revolution Within: A Book of Self-Esteem.* Boston: Little, Brown and Company, 1992.

Tannen, Deborah. *You Just Don't Understand: Men and Women in Conversation.* New York: Ballantine, 1991.

Wolf, Naomi. *The Beauty Myth: How Images of Beauty Are Used Against Women.* New York: William Morrow and Company, 1991.

Index